SACRED SECRETS

Also by Jerrold and Leona Schecter

An American Family in Moscow

Back in the USSR: An American Family Returns to Moscow

Special Tasks: The Memoirs of an Unwanted Witness—A Soviet Spymaster
(with Pavel and Anatoli Sudoplatov)

Also by Jerrold Schecter

*The New Face of Buddha: The Fusion of Religion and Politics in
Contemporary Buddhism*

*The Palace File: The Remarkable Story of the Secret Letters from Nixon
and Ford to the President of South Vietnam and the American Promises
That Were Never Kept*
(with Nguyen Tien Hung)

Khrushchev Remembers: The Glasnost Tapes
(Edited with Vyacheslav V. Luchkov)

*The Spy Who Saved the World: How a Soviet Colonel Changed the
Course of the Cold War*
(with Peter Deriabin)

Russian Negotiating Behavior: Continuity and Transition

SACRED SECRETS

How Soviet Intelligence Operations Changed American History

Jerrold and Leona Schecter
Foreword by Strobe Talbott

BRASSEY'S, INC.
Washington, D.C.

Library of Congress Cataloging-in-Publication Data

Schecter, Jerrold L.
    Sacred secrets : how Soviet intelligence operations changed American history / Jerrold and Leona Schecter ; foreword by Strobe Talbott.—1st ed.
        p. cm.
    Includes bibliographical references and index.
    ISBN 1-57488-327-5 (alk. paper)
    1. Espionage, Soviet—United States—History—Sources. 2. Soviet Union. Komitet gosudarstvennoæ bezopasnosti—History. 3. Soviet Union. Glavnoe razvedyvatel§'oe upravlenie—History. 4. United States. Signal Security Agency—History. 5. Cryptography—United States—History—20th century. 6. World War, 1939–1945—Cryptography. 7. Soviet Union—Foreign relations—United States—History—Sources. 8. United States—Foreign relations—Soviet Union—History—Sources. I. Schecter, Leona. II. Title.
    DK266.3 .S364 2002
    327.1247'009'04—dc21   2001052809

Printed in the United States of America on acid-free paper that meets the American National Standards Institute Z39-48 Standard.

Brassey's, Inc.
22841 Quicksilver Drive
Dulles, Virginia 20166
First Edition

10   9   8   7   6   5   4   3   2   1

To Miriam Goshen Schecter.

To our children, Evelind, Steven,
Kate, Doveen, and Barnet.

To their spouses, Michael, Karen, Ari, Grischa.

To our grandchildren, Belle, Beth, Jeong Hwan,
Isabel, Sophie, Ben, and Zev.

Contents

APPENDIXES:

Chronology

1895	Treaty of Shimonoseki signed following Japanese victory in war with China over Korea. China cedes Formosa, Pescadores Islands, and Liaotung Peninsula with Port Arthur to Japan.
1896	Russia, Germany, and France "advise" Japan, with threat of force, to return territories to China.
1897	Russian activity in Far East follows construction of Trans-Siberian Railroad in 1891. Russians eager to control good harbors in Manchuria and Korea. Triple alliance among France, Russia, and Germany takes advantage of Chinese weakness, leads to scramble for concessions. Great Britain allied with Japan.
1904	The clash of Russian and Japanese interests in northeast Asia ignites the Russo-Japanese War, in which Japan prevails militarily but not conclusively. The war's high cost in lives lost and financial instability is enormous to both sides. Losses foment popular revolt in Russia.
1905	In the Straits of Tsushima between Korea and Japan, the Japanese navy annihilates a Russian fleet in one of the greatest naval battles in history. The treaty signed at Portsmouth, New Hampshire, with mediation by President Theodore Roosevelt, forces Russia to acknowledge Japanese influence in Korea. It transfers the Liaotung Peninsula and Southern Manchurian railway to Japan. Treaty provides no reparations from Russia, which causes riots in Japan.
1914	World War I begins in the Balkans; because of interlocking secret treaties, the war quickly engulfs Europe. Germans attack Belgium, France, and Luxembourg; the British come to their aid. First use of airplane raids on cities, for reconnaissance and bombing. First use of submarines to attack shipping and blockade Britain; airplanes attack submarines. Introduction of poison gas and tanks.
1917	In March, Tsar Nicholas II abdicates. In April, U.S. enters WWI on Allied side. November 6, Bolsheviks seize power.

1917–1921	Under name of "War Communism," Bolsheviks nationalize banks, trade unions, factories, church properties, repudiate national debt, nationalize landholdings, requisition farm production to feed cities.
1918	Establishment of Czech, Yugoslav and Polish independent governments. In January, President Woodrow Wilson outlines peace program of 14 Points, declaring independence for smaller nations, freedom of navigation, lowering of armaments. The Brest-Litovsk treaty, signed in March 1918 between Soviet Russia and the Central Powers, negotiates a separate peace for Russia. An attempt on Lenin's life instigates a reign of terror against intellectuals and the bourgeoise. October 1918, after sustained joint Allied military operations the Germans sue for peace. November 11 hostilities cease.
1919	June 1919 Paris Peace Conference leads to Treaty of Versailles. Founding of Third Communist International (COMINTERN) for propagation of communist doctrine for world revolution, which Lenin believes would be accomplished.
1918-1921	Russian Civil War: Leon Trotsky commissar of war against Whites (counter-revolutionaries) and foreign armies attempting to overthrow Bolsheviks. British, French, Americans intervene in the Civil War on behalf of the anti-Bolshevik factions.
	The Japanese and Czechs enter Vladivostok, Siberia, and Eastern Russia. After heavy fighting, Bolsheviks retake territory and set up buffer state, the Far Eastern Republic.
1921–1928	Lenin's New Economic Policy (NEP) abolishes the food levy and implements a more moderate grain tax. New land statute allowed small individual farms, hired labor and lease of land. Private commercial trade resumed but only on small scale. Less repression, emphasis on erasing illiteracy.
1922	Soviet Russia and Germany conclude the Treaty of Rapallo, bringing closer political and economic cooperation.
1924	Lenin dies, after which Stalin and Trotsky struggle for power within the Communist Party.
1927	New Economic Policy ends. Stalin prevails in his fight with Trotsky, who is expelled from the political bureau of the party.
1928	Stalin implements the first Five-Year Plan, speeding industrialization.
1929	Trotsky is exiled from the country and takes refuge in Constantinople. Bukharin and the Rightists are also expelled, leaving Stalin in complete control.
1930	Forced collectivization replaces small farmers. The most successful farmers are destroyed. Unsuccessful attempt to build economy, followed by trials of technicians for inefficiency and sabotage.

1932   The start of a devastating famine that kills millions and results in an easing of the state's repression of farmers. Purge of a million Communist Party members.

1933   Hitler's National Socialist Party, which is ideologically hostile to communism and the Soviet Union, comes to power in Germany. Soviet rearmament takes place; large build up of armaments on land, at sea and in the air. Soviets join the League of Nations, which they had been against, makes non-aggression pacts with neighbors. The United States government provides diplomatic recognition of the Soviet government, which promises to abstain from propaganda in the United States.

1934   Leningrad party boss, Kirov, is murdered. Stalin exploits the event, creating a regime of terror in which the old guard of communist leaders are tried for treason and eventually executed.

1935   The Third International decides that communists in foreign countries should support rearmament, even by bourgeois governments, to counter resurgent Germany.

1936   Civil war erupts in Spain. Italy and Germany support Franco's fascists, while the Soviet Union supports the Loyalists. Hitler denounces Bolshevism, concludes an anticommunist pact with Japan, and drives Stalin toward the Western democratic states. The Soviet Union initiates a new constitution, which guarantees equal rights to all voters; however, the Communist Party remains the only political group permitted.

1939   In Europe, collective security fails. Maksim Litvinov dismissed as Foreign Minister. Molotov's appointment signals a change in Soviet foreign policy, one which results in the Nazi-Soviet Non-Aggression Pact in August. With the signing of the Molotov-von Ribbentrop Pact (also known as the Hitler-Stalin Pact), seemingly implacable enemies had joined in a diplomatic revolution that leaves the world open mouthed with disbelief and pain. The Soviets stand by in a neutral stance when Germany attacks Poland on September 1. After England and France demand Germany remove its troops from Polish soil and get no answer, they declare war on Germany, setting off World War II. In the meantime, the Soviet Union and Japan fight a small war on the border between Outer Mongolia and Manchuria at Khalkhin Gol (River). September 16 Soviet Union signs a truce with Japan, September 17 Stalin invades eastern Poland, a move sanctioned by Hitler in the Molotov-von Ribbentrop Pact. U.S. Army orders copying of all Soviet Union's cable messages to its American offices. Whittaker Chambers, a former courier for Soviet intelligence, warns of the underground activities of Alger Hiss, Donald Hiss, and others in the State and Treasury Departments.

1940   Trotsky assassinated in Mexico.

1941   Stalin backs Yugoslav coup against pro-German monarchy; Germans attack within two weeks and take over country. Soviet Union and Japan sign a neutrality pact, and with Operation Snow, Stalin attempts to avoid a potential two-front war from east and west. In June, Hitler's armies invade the Soviet Union. Japan occupies French Indochina, U.S. imposes economic sanctions on Japan and the two sides move closer to war. The Hull Note proves to be an unacceptable ultimatum and Japan attacks Pearl Harbor in December. Germany and Italy declare war on U.S. KGB makes contact with Oppenheimer in San Francisco. Vasili Zarubin, his wife Elizabeth and Kitty Harris arrive in U.S., begin atomic espionage.

1942   Battle of the Atlantic, Lend Lease to Soviet Union, joint British-American invasion of North Africa, then Sicily, then Italy. Promise to open second front in France delayed. Work begins at Los Alamos to build a uranium bomb. Enrico Fermi succeeds in setting off first nuclear chain reaction in Chicago.

1943   Allied conferences in Casablanca, Cairo, Teheran. Battles for Kursk and Stalingrad turn the war against Germany. Roosevelt sets date for invasion of France.

                   Katyn Massacre revealed in press, Anonymous Letter to FBI revealing Soviet espionage in U.S. kept secret.

                   At Arlington Hall, Virginia, U.S. Army Signals Intelligence opens Soviet cable traffic, later to be code named VENONA, and attempts to decipher its codes, using early room size computers.

1944   Most successful initiators of atomic espionage, the Zarubins, recalled to Moscow. Einstein's Russian lover, Margarita Konenkova, assists in atomic espionage.

                   On June 6, 1944, D-Day, the Western allies invade France and open the second front in Europe. In the Treasury Department, Harry Dexter White pushes through an order to give plates to Soviet Union to print occupation currency.

1945   During the Yalta Conference in February, Alger Hiss meets with his Soviet control officer at conference, giving leads on Western allies' negotiating positions. Germany surrenders, Hitler commits suicide. FDR dies in March, Truman becomes president and soon learns that U.S. Army is working on Soviet Union's cable traffic, later code named VENONA. Test first atomic bomb in July, then use second and third bombs on Japan in August. Soviets have stolen the technology but can't make it work. Send KGB officers to Copenhagen to meet Nils Bohr, learn how to deal with problem.

Igor Gouzenko defects from the Soviet embassy in Canada. Elizabeth Bentley informs the FBI that she has served as a courier for the Soviet underground. She also supplies a list of Soviet sources and agents active within the U.S. government to the FBI, which begins to compare information from Gouzenko and Bentley to information emerging from the VENONA decrypts.

1946   The wartime alliance falls to pieces. Stalin reiterates the goal of world communist revolution. George Kennan, U.S. diplomat in Moscow, sends "The Long Telegram" to the State Department, warning of Soviet aims against Western interests. Churchill delivers his famous "Iron Curtain" speech in Fulton, Missouri.

1947   Truman asks Congress to support Greece and Turkey against communist guerillas, establishes Truman Doctrine. Secretary of State George Marshall proposes Marshall Plan for rebuilding Europe, including Soviet Union, but Stalin refuses to join. Kennan becomes head of Policy Planning in State Department, beginning of covert operations against Soviet Union. New technology allows American intelligence to track internal cable traffic of Soviet Union in real time.

1948   Berlin Crisis leads to Berlin Airlift. Sets long term division of Germany between East and West. Soviet Union takes over Czechoslovakia in bloodless coup d'état. VENONA begins to yield names of Americans in Executive Branch working for Soviet Union. Begin investigations of Coplon, Fuchs, Rosenberg, Hiss cases. Bentley and Chambers testify publicly. Harry Dexter White accused, protests his innocence and patriotism, but dies of a heart attack before case against him is formulated. NSC 20/4, first statement of national security strategy. Congressman Richard Nixon comes to prominence. Pumpkin Papers revealed. Truman calls charges "a red herring." Early Warning Program drops agents into Soviet Union to watch for significant military mobilization.

1949   The Soviet Union explodes its first atomic bomb. Alger Hiss stands trial, but the jury is dismissed. Mao declares The People's Republic of China.

1950   As a result of a second trial, Hiss is convicted of perjury. Senator Joseph McCarthy asserts that more than 200 Soviet agents hold jobs in the U.S. government, which launches another "Red Scare." Klaus Fuchs and Harry Gold are both arrested.

North Korea invades South Korea in June. Truman commits U.S. military forces immediately and prevents the collapse of South Korea. When General MacArthur crosses the 38th parallel, the tide of battle turns significantly against North Korea, and China intervenes.

1951   Julius and Ethel Rosenberg are convicted of treason (they are executed in 1953).

1952   Dwight Eisenhower elected thirty-fourth president of the U.S. Beacon Hill report on possibilities for new reconnaissance capabilities. First hydrogen bomb test.

1953   Stalin dies in March. The Soviet government puts down riots in East Berlin. An armistice ends three years of fighting in Korea. Herbert Brownell publicly accuses Truman of ignoring warning from J. Edgar Hoover that Harry Dexter White under Moscow's control. Oppenheimer's access to secret material suspended. Eisenhower organizes leading scientists to devise new intelligence technology. Soviet Union explodes their own hydrogen bomb eight months after American test.

1954   Oppenheimer hearings held to appeal his top secret clearance suspension. Teller testifies against him, comes down to who was in favor of H-bomb. Oppenheimer loses his challenge, no longer can work for top secret government agencies. McCarthy accuses U.S. Army of including communists. Government and press fight back, bring him down in disgrace. Eisenhower authorizes development of U-2 overhead reconnaissance planes. General accords divide Vietnam, ending the first Indochina war.

1956   Khrushchev's secret speech denounces Stalin. Copy leaked to CIA and world press. Hungarian uprising repressed by Soviet troops.

1957   Soviet Union succeeds in launch and return of first orbiting spacecraft Sputnik. Rudolph Abel arrested in Brooklyn, New York, but counterintelligence does not learn his mission: The Special Period, World War III.

1959   Castro takes power in Cuba, Soviet Union rushes advisors there to help and share in revolution. First CORONA satellite test launch.

1960   U-2 reconnaissance airplane shot down over USSR, pilot Francis Gary Powers captured.

     Khruschev promises "to bury" the West, make it communist. Corona satellite succeeds in filming earth from space, makes it impossible to mount major war preparations without detection. John F. Kennedy elected thirty-fifth president. During the campaign Kennedy promotes the idea of a "missile gap," in which the U.S. is dangerously behind the Soviet Union, but which does not exist in fact. The U.S. actually leads the USSR in ballistic missiles. Sino-Soviet split deepens.

1961   The attempt to retake Cuba from Castro results in the Bay of Pigs fiasco. Kennedy steps up military support of the anticommunist regime in South Vietnam. Colonel Oleg Penkovsky begins to spy for the U.S. and Great Britain. He provides operations manuals for Soviet missiles; President Kennedy relied on these manuals during the Cuban Missile Crisis. Soviet Union and East Germans erect the Berlin Wall in order to stem flow of refugees to the west. Super secret National Reconnaissance Organization (NRO) established by U.S. government.

1962   U-2 reconnaissance flights over Cuba indicate Soviet Union is preparing to place missiles in camouflaged sites. Cuban Missile Crisis brings two sides close to war but negotiation ends with withdrawal of missiles from Cuba. Penkovsky detected and arrested just before crisis. An act of Congress creates the Communications Satellite Corporation.

1963   Ngo Dinh Diem, president of South Vietnam, and his brother assassinated in coup in Saigon. Two weeks later President Kennedy assassinated in Dallas, Texas. Lyndon B. Johnson becomes thirty-sixth president.

1964   Congress approves Tonkin Gulf resolution. Large commitment of U.S. troops and arms to Vietnam. Nikita Khrushchev ousted, replaced by Leonid Brezhnev. First Chinese nuclear explosion.

1965   Early Bird establishes first commercial wireless communication across the Atlantic.

1968   Soviet Union sends troops to crush new Czech regime attempting to be less dominated by Moscow. Nixon elected thirty-seventh president. Arpanet connects four universities, precursor to Internet.

1969   Intelsat's first live TV broadcast from space covers the Apollo XI moon landing.

1970   Publication of *Khrushchev Remembers* around the world.

1971   Launch of Big Bird, KH-9, advanced reconnaissance satellite, a major step forward from KH-4B that preceded it.

1972   Nixon begins withdrawal of U.S. troops from Vietnam. Nixon accepts Mao's invitation to visit China. Nixon and Brezhnev hold summit to sign SALT and Anti-Ballistic Missile Treaty.

1974   The Watergate Scandal forces Nixon to resign. Gerald R. Ford becomes the thirty-eighth president. Second volume published of Khrushchev's memoirs, *Khrushchev Remembers: The Last Testament*.

1975   North Vietnam reneges on the 1973 Paris Peace Accord, invades South Vietnam. The U.S. abandons the government of South Vietnam, which quickly falls to communist North Vietnam.

1976   Launch of KH-11, Kennan\ Crystal, more advanced satellite. James E. "Jimmy" Carter elected thirty-ninth president. Endorses satellite reconnaissance. Soviet economy begins severe downward trend. Mao dies.

1979   The Shah of Iran is toppled by revolutionaries, who hold fifty-six Americans as hostages until January 1981. The U.S. loses its Iranian listening posts. The Soviet Union invades Afghanistan, which forces postponement of the Strategic Arms Control Treaty.

1980   Carter places an embargo on sales of technology and grain to the Soviet Union and, reversing years of deep cuts to the defense budget, begins to rebuild the military; however, foreign crises and the worsening U.S. economy cripple his presidency. Ronald W. Reagan is elected fortieth president.

1981   Warsaw declares martial law and suppresses the free labor movement, reversing an earlier decision that permitted the independent trade union Solidarity. Moscow begins Operation Ryan, which is designed to prepare the USSR to defend itself against an expected nuclear attack by the U.S.

1982   After a prolonged period of ill health, Brezhnev dies in November. Yuri Andropov, chief of the KGB, succeeds Brezhnev.

1983   Reagan greatly expands upon Carter's defense buildup. West Germany agrees to deploy Pershing II medium-range nuclear missiles. Reagan announces the start of work on Strategic Defense Initiative, ridiculed as Star Wars. The U.S. tests SDI unsuccessfully, but manages to blow up target. Deception designed to get more money for research. Soviet Union believes announcement of test success, believes it must keep up in new arms race.

1984   Andropov in poor health and dies in early 1984. The infirm Konstantin Chernenko succeeds Andropov, but dies in early 1985.

1985   Gorbachev succeeds Chernenko as general secretary of the Communist Party of the Soviet Union and begins *perestroika* (restructuring) of the Soviet economy.

1986   The nuclear power plant at Chernobyl explodes. Gorbachev is slow to reveal the magnitude of the catastrophe. Reagan and Gorbachev meet at Reykjavik, Iceland. Gorbachev tries to persuade Reagan to discontinue SDI, but the president refuses to stop research and testing.

1988   Gorbachev proposes to withdraw all Soviet troops from Afghanistan. The withdrawal is completed in February 1989, several months ahead of schedule. Lacrosse spy satellite launched, first self supplier of energy from solar panels.

1989   Protesters killed in Tiananmen Square, Beijing. Opening of Berlin Wall, brings outpouring of refugees to the west. Poles hold first free election. Iron Curtain refugee exodus.

1990   Iraq invades Kuwait. U.S. led coalition, Operation Desert Storm, repels Iraq, enforces UN sanctions. East and West Germany reunited.

1991   Boris Yeltsin elected president of Russia. Hardline communists at-
        tempt to take over Soviet Union in anti-Gorbachev coup but are
        defeated. Soviet Union dissolves into Commonwealth of Independent
        States, and Gorbachev resigns, ending seventy-four year reign of
        CPSU. Publication of third volume of Khrushchev's memoirs,
        Khrushchev Remembers: The Glasnost Tapes.

1993   At the World Trade Center in New York City, a homemade urea
        nitrate truck-bomb explodes in underground parking garage, killing
        six, injuring more than 1,000. Six conspirators convicted and sen-
        tenced to life in prison.

1994   Pavel Sudoplatov's oral history, *Special Tasks: The Memoirs of an Un-
        wanted Witness—A Soviet Spymaster* is published in the U.S. and
        around the world.

1995   NSA and CIA hold a ceremony to present the first releases of
        VENONA.

1996   In Russia, Vitalii Pavlov publishes his book, *Operation Snow.* Khobar
        Towers, residence of American military in Dhahran, Saudi Arabia,
        destroyed by suicide truck-bomber, killing 19, wounding 200.

1998   American embassies in Nairobi, Kenya, and Dar es Salaam, Tanzania
        attacked by suicide bombers; 213 killed and more than 4,000 wounded
        in Nairobi, 11 killed and 85 wounded in Dar es Salaam.

1999   Boris Yeltsin resigns the presidency and ensures that Vladimir Putin,
        a former KGB officer, succeeds him. Putin affirms Sudoplatov's reve-
        lation that Western scientists cooperated with Soviet Union, giving
        atomic secrets to Soviet physicists to help them make their own A-
        bomb. A Russian TV documentary affirms that in 1945, Nils Bohr
        met in Copenhagen with an officer of the KGB, to whom he supplied
        vital information in support of the Soviet reactor program.

2000   USS Cole suicide-bombed in harbor of Aden, Yemen, killing 17
        Americans and wounding 35.

2001   September 11, coordinated Al Qaeda attacks on World Trade Center
        and Pentagon, and a fourth hijacked airplane that crashed in Pennsyl-
        vania, kill more than 3,000. President Bush forms international coali-
        tion against terrorism that includes Chinese and Russian backing.
        American forces attack Taliban in Afghanistan, rout Taliban and
        Al Qaeda.

2002   War against Terror accelerates in Europe, Middle East, Philippines,
        and Indonesia.

Foreword by Strobe Talbott

Presidents Bill Clinton and Vladimir Putin were coming to the end of a private dinner in the presidential quarters of the Kremlin on June 3, 2000. They had spent much of the meal debating the American program to develop and deploy an antimissile defense system. Putin argued that the plan would translate the U.S.'s economic and technological advantages over Russia into an unacceptable new military advantage. The conversation, which opened their first summit, had run longer than scheduled, and the two leaders were overdue at a jazz concert in honor of the visiting Americans. President Clinton was just about to get up from the table when Putin said he had a story he wanted to tell. It concerned Joseph Stalin's decision to put his secret police chief, Lavrenti Beria, in charge of ferreting out the secrets—the sacred secrets, as Jerrold and Leona Schecter would say—of the American crash program to develop the atomic bomb during World War II. Beria gathered all the scientists who had anything to contribute to the quest and assigned each of them a task and a deadline. Those who accomplished their goal on time were made Heroes of the Soviet Union; those who didn't were shot or sent to the concentration camps. Later, after de-Stalinization, many of those who were executed or had died in the gulag were posthumously added to the honor roles.

Putin had words of praise for the American scientists who willingly helped the USSR develop its own A-bomb. They were not traitors to their country, he said. Rather, they were serving the cause of international peace. They understood, in a way that the American political leadership did not, that the only way to keep the peace was to preserve a balance of terror between the two principal contestants in a global ideological and geopolitical rivalry. Putin believed that an American monopoly of nuclear weaponry—like an American high-tech antimissile system—would upset that balance and increase the danger of a cataclysm.

Even as he told the story, Putin must have known that, deep inside the FBI, Robert Hanssen was functioning as a mole, providing the Russians, just as he'd provided the Soviets, with the names of Russian intelligence officers recruited by the FBI and CIA.

As a former officer of the secret services himself, Putin was proud of the role Soviet intelligence had played in defending the country's interests—just as he felt he was doing by stonewalling President Clinton on missile defenses. Spies, he was saying, are sometimes an indispensable auxiliary to statesmen and diplomats.

Spying has often been, like war itself, the conduct of politics by other means. That was especially true in the cold war, when the U.S. and the Soviet Union did not dare unleash their nuclear weapons against each other and therefore had to find other means to prosecute their competition. Putin would have had President Clinton believe that Soviet agents and their American accomplices served as a safety mechanism that kept the cold war from turning hot. It would be more accurate to say that the Soviets regarded spying as an equalizer in their otherwise unequal struggle with their capitalist enemies. The political culture of the Soviet Union, rooted in that of czarist Russia and the Bolshevik underground, put a premium on discipline and obedience, and on the sacredness of secrecy itself. It was Putin's alma mater—under its various acronyms and initials, from the Cheka to the OGPU, the NKVD, and the KGB, as well as its military sibling the GRU—that most embodied that ethos.

The security services were, in the unintentionally comic euphemism that the Soviets often used, the "competent organs" of the state. Whenever I heard this phrase, I took it as a tacit acknowledgment that virtually all the other agencies of the Soviet state were incompetent. Certainly many Soviets felt that way. Yes, the intelligence services were the servants of the Communist Party, but they were also in a sense its masters, since knowledge of the kind they possessed gave them power over everyone, even party big shots.

The unique role of Soviet intelligence also derived from the nature of the USSR. That state institutionalized mistrust of everyone (including comrades); it made brute force the arbiter in all transactions, and it based its foreign policy on the principle that history is a zero-sum game ("who will prevail over whom," in Lenin's phrase), in which victory goes to the merciless. Those precepts were at the very core of the way Soviet intelligence saw its mission and went about its business. Its mindset, its tradecraft, and its interaction with its principal adversaries in the West were integral to the theory and practice of Soviet communism.

It was, as Russians like to say, no accident that the Soviet Union's last chance at survival probably came and went with the brief rule of Yuri Andropov, the KGB chief who rose to the top job in the Kremlin; and the fate of the system was sealed when, after his death, the politburo turned to Konstantin Chernenko, a decrepit agitprop hack.

★ ★ ★

There are many shelves of books about the intelligence front of the cold war, and the Schecters have drawn from the best and most authoritative of those for their own history of the struggle.

They have also done a good deal of ferreting out of their own—from hitherto inaccessible archives and documents, and from the memory of veterans of the covert battles recounted here. In addition, they have an intuitive grasp of what used to be called Soviet reality, based on their own experience living in Moscow from 1968 to 1970, and again during the Second Russian Revolution between 1990 and 1993.

I first got to know the Schecters and their five children, who were enrolled in Soviet schools, during their first stint in Moscow, immediately after the Soviet invasion of Czechoslovakia in 1968. They reminded me of the Swiss Family Robinson—self-reliant, curious, enthusiastic, big-hearted, open-minded, hard-headed; they were citizens of the world in a strange land. They were gimlet-eyed about the worst of that political system, but they also appreciated the suppressed best of the country, its people and its culture. As a result, they have been able to penetrate the stereotypes, bringing to life not just the world-class villains who stalk these pages but those other Soviets, neither knaves nor fools, who give this story its human texture and realism. For example, it was through Jerry that I first met Mikhail Abramovich Milshtein, a Jewish orphan who was adopted by a Red Army unit and grew up to be a general in the GRU—and Alger Hiss's control officer. Milshtein, then in his seventies, was an analyst of international security matters on the staff of the Institute for the Study of the USA and Canada, an official think tank that served as a kind of oasis for what passed as "new thinking" in the intellectual and bureaucratic wasteland of the Brezhnev era.

The Schecters' contribution goes well beyond synthesis and the skillful retelling of individual spy stories and real-life thrillers. What they offer in this book is one of the great sagas of modern history—the life-and-death story of a mega-state, born of conspiracy and terror, whose lifespan was approximately the biblical three-score-and-ten allotted to an individual mortal. They shed fresh light on why the Soviet Union ended as abruptly and ignominiously as it did: its most cherished (and competent) institution, precisely because it worshipped secrecy and trafficked in lies, was at odds with the forces of openness that were sweeping the world in the late twentieth century, and that eventually found their champions within the USSR itself.

If there is one word that a coroner might use to explain the death of the Soviet system, it is *glasnost*—the realization on the part of Chernenko's successor, Mikhail Gorbachev, that a state so obsessively secretive and dishonest, so closed to the outside world, so relentlessly paranoid and hostile was, quite simply, doomed. The irony was that in seeking to save the system by opening it up, relying less on force and more on consensus, by integrating the USSR into the international community, Gorbachev inadvertently accelerated the disintegration of the old system and the old state; he was setting the scene for the emergence of post-Soviet, postcommunist Russia and the rest of the Commonwealth of Independent States, as well as the liberation of the Baltic states.

Glasnost did not begin with Gorbachev. It began thirty years before with Nikita Khrushchev's revelation of some of the ugliest truths about the Soviet past. Starting with his "secret"—and almost instantly publicized—speech on the crimes of Stalin, Khrushchev established himself as a precursor of Gorbachev's. Then, in retirement, he dictated his memoirs. The Schecters are not just chroniclers of that part of the story—they were participants in it as well, primarily through their role in the acquisition and publication of the memoirs. The Schecters provide fresh insight (some of it new to me, as a junior partner in the venture), based on, among other things, an extraordinary bit of sleuthing that took them to Victor Louis's own KGB case officer.

Who is Victor Louis? Good question. And there's as good an answer as we're likely to get in chapter 11. As on many other matters, the Schecters are uniquely qualified to probe, to explain, and to place events into the broader context of history and politics.

They are also well positioned to tell the American side of the story of the secret wars. They've lived in Washington since coming home from their family adventure in Moscow in the early seventies. As *Time*'s diplomatic editor and subsequently as an official of the National Security Council in the Carter administration, Jerrold Schecter learned much about the inner workings of American intelligence, getting to know many of those who lived the stories of intrigue told here. He and Leona (and their intrepid children) had also lived in Hong Kong and Tokyo, so they had seen U.S. foreign policy, including, in its less advertised dimensions, in operations abroad at the height of the cold war.

As the Schecters show, the U.S. adapted to the challenge posed by aggressive, relentless Soviet spying. Overcoming early scruples about whether gentlemen should read each others' mail and, when necessary, playing the deadly game with considerable vigor, the CIA—a relative newcomer to the American national security establishment—learned and practiced the craft of both defensive and offensive intelligence.

But there was always, on the American side, a palpable sense that this was a dirty business and an unnatural act, even if a necessary one. It's hard to imagine an American president bragging to his Kremlin counterpart about the brilliance of recruiting and running Oleg Penkovsky, a Western "mole" in the GRU (whom Jerrold Schecter has called, in the title of an earlier book, "The Spy Who Saved the World").

Nonetheless, while the Soviets were far more predisposed to espionage than their American adversaries, Yankee technology ultimately gave the U.S. a decisive edge in the "overflight wars" described in chapter 12. Most dramatically when Khrushchev tried to sneak intermediate-range missiles into Cuba, but on many other occasions as well, U.S. high-altitude aircraft and satellites, combined with high-resolution photography, made it increasingly difficult for the Soviets to hide what they were up to. Increasingly, *glasnost* was not just a policy option for reformers of the late Soviet period but an inescapable, pervasive fact of modern life.

This book, while focused on an era that is now over, has considerable relevance to understanding Russia today. In many respects, the most competent of Soviet organs has also proved to be the most durable survivor into the post-Soviet era. The statue of Vladimir Lenin's chekist-in-chief, Felix Dzerzhinsky, no longer stands in front of the old KGB headquarters on Lyubyanka Square. The KGB itself has been divided and, for purposes of its external role, renamed the SVR (Foreign Intelligence Service of the Russian Federation). But the powers that be in that organization still tend to see the world as a battleground and the West as inherently hostile to Russian interests. The CIA plays cat and mouse today with the SVR. One of the few senior officials that Boris Yeltsin retained from the Gorbachev leadership was Yevgeny Primakov, the head of the SVR. Primakov went on to be prime minister of Russia and continues to play an active role in Russian politics. Vladimir Putin is only the most prominent example of KGB alumni who have done well since the end of the USSR.

In that same dinner meeting in the Kremlin in June 2000, Putin pressed Clinton to stop criticizing Russia for its scorched-earth policies in Chechnya and authorize more cooperation between the CIA and SVR to combat international terrorism, especially the challenge posed by Islamic fanaticism.

Even at the time, there were multiple ironies in Putin's position. He had risen to the presidency of Russia largely through his vigorous, ferocious, and highly popular conduct of the war in Chechnya. He identified Russia's principal enemies there as protégés and accomplices of Osama bin Laden, the renegade Saudi millionaire who had been behind numerous attacks on American targets in the Persian Gulf, Africa, and elsewhere.

In fact, the origin and nature of the war in Chechnya were more complex than Putin acknowledged, as the Schecters make clear in chapter 13 of *Sacred Secrets*. Chechnya was not just the bloodiest crisis for post-Soviet Russia—it was also, in crucial ways, a direct consequence of the war in Afghanistan, which was the last great crisis for the USSR. Many of the rebels who were seeking to tear Chechnya out of Russia had fought alongside the Afghan guerrillas a decade before, and they derived material support for their secessionist struggle from the Taliban, the militant fundamentalists who had come to power in Kabul after the defeat and withdrawal of the Soviet occupying force.

On the other side of the war in Chechnya, many of the Russian commanders were veterans of Afghanistan, still embittered by their experience there and bent on revenge. They saw these new enemies that were threatening Russia as direct descendants of the old ones who had contributed to the demise of the Soviet Union.

In his meetings with Clinton, Putin depicted both Afghanistan and the Taliban as Frankenstein monsters created by the U.S. in the twilight of the cold war. As with his version of the role of Soviet spymasters and American scientists at the dawn of the nuclear age, the truth was more complicated. The Soviet Union bore its own responsibility for the radicalization of Southwest Asia that made that region a breeding ground for terrorism and instability. Chapter 13 of *Sacred Secrets* establishes those connections lucidly and persuasively.

But the ultimate irony came in the aftermath of September 11, 2001, and the terrorist attacks on New York and Washington. The first telephone call President George W. Bush received from a foreign leader was from Vladimir Putin. The Russian president's message was, "We've got to work together to eradicate this common enemy." The subtext was, "We told you so! And now you see why we need a free hand in Chechnya." Bush agreed on both points—explicitly on the first, implicitly on the second. More dramatically than at any time in the decade since the Soviet Union had begun to come apart at the seams, the U.S. and Russia were now on the same side, bound by their presidents to work together in meeting one of the defining challenges of the post–cold war era and to do so, above all, by concerting the energies and resources of the U.S. and Russian intelligence services. It is with that irony that the Schecters bring this remarkable story to a close.

Preface

The last decade of the twentieth century revealed a string of "sacred secrets" that changed history as we know it. These were the secrets of nations that the participants had sworn to carry with them to their graves, and had now decided to bring into the open. Motives are always hard to pinpoint with certainty, but in the cases where we met and interviewed the secret keepers, the clear and present purpose was self-justification. There appeared to be a desire for purification at the end of the millennium, a raising of secrets up to an altar for the Almighty and history to see and judge.

The demise of the Soviet Union in 1991 briefly eased restraints on secrecy and permitted access to documents in former Soviet archives. From memoirs published in the 1990s, from the VENONA messages, secret U.S. government intercepts of Soviet cable traffic released after half a century, from interviews, articles in the Russian military press, and revelations on television, a new clarity emerges showing the effect of Soviet espionage on American foreign policy.

The next step was to match the newly revealed intelligence operations with memoirs long available but little understood and, for the most part, not believed. When Elizabeth Bentley, Whittaker Chambers, Hede Massing, and Boris Morros, four Americans who worked for the Soviet Union and later denounced their communist controllers, first told their stories, only anticommunists believed them. Within the Roosevelt and Truman administrations there was disbelief and, in some cases, a call to test the mental health of the former Soviet agents who named prominent Americans among their former communist colleagues. This denial by the liberal left and an excessive Red Panic on the right left little room for calmly seeking the truth of the extent of Soviet intelligence on American soil. President Truman was informed of revelations from VENONA but kept the information secret and left no paper trail of his knowledge. American domestic politics and cultural life remain riven and scarred by a sixty-year-old controversy over communists in government.

The secrets in KGB memoirs, Soviet archival records and translations, and

National Security Agency (NSA) decryptions of Soviet wartime cable traffic, code-named VENONA, reveal:

Soviet intelligence operations to draw Japan and America into war, leading to Pearl Harbor.

The cooperation of J. Robert Oppenheimer in atomic espionage from 1942 to 1944.

Albert Einstein's love affair with a Soviet agent.

Three separate lines of Soviet intelligence activity in the United States: political, scientific, and Operation Corridor, which utilized Soviet émigrés and members of the White Russian community.

A star-and-satellite system, to surround Presidents Roosevelt and Truman and top government officials with Soviet agents and willing sources.

Harry Dexter White, a willing asset, first of Soviet military intelligence (GRU) and later the NKVD, providing American printing plates to the Soviet Union for postwar German occupation currency, which led to the Berlin Crisis of 1948.

Alger Hiss, a longtime asset of Soviet military intelligence (GRU), supplying his control officer with the American negotiating positions at the Yalta Conference.

The origins of the Korean War.

Colonel Rudolf Abel's preparations for war with the United States, the Special Period.

How advances in American satellite technology kept the peace and helped end the cold war.

From the authors' personal trove of secrets comes the first public account of how Nikita Khrushchev's memoirs reached the West.

The coming chapters, 1 through 5, examine the successes of Soviet intelligence operations in fending off a Japanese attack on Siberia in 1941, in atomic espionage, and in securing Stalin's hold on Eastern Europe and East Germany at the end of World War II. Chapter 5 explores the opening of VENONA traffic. Chapter 6 traces the secrets exposed in VENONA. The next chapters, 7 through 9, probe the center of American politics and the split that was formed in the postwar period between denial and panic over the effect of Soviet intelligence operations on American government and culture. The chapters attempt to define which accusations were founded in truth, which were excessive. Chapters 10 and 11 describe the first breaks in the wall of secrecy that isolated the Soviet Union from the West and the story of Nikita Khrushchev's memoirs. The final chapters, 12 and 13, contrast America's early failures in covert operations against the Soviet Union with the successes achieved through overhead satellite technology. American "eyes in the sky" avoided a third world war and created an information revolution. The conclusion examines the challenges facing American intelligence in the war against catastrophic terrorism exemplified by Osama bin Laden and his Al Qaeda network.

Despite American fears of the Soviet Union during the cold war, its best experts remained unaware of the disintegration that was taking place in their enemy's economy, military might, and civic society. The final demise of the Soviet Union and its breakup into independent states came as a surprise. The instability that followed poses to former cold war enemies the problem of reconstructing a viable relationship to deal with a changed world.

★ ★ ★

This book follows from our work with Soviet spymaster Pavel Sudoplatov in writing his oral history, *Special Tasks*, which first appeared in English in 1994.[1] Sudoplatov's disclosure of the Manhattan Project officials involved in atomic espionage and the ensuing controversy contributed to the public release of the VENONA files in 1995. Using the VENONA messages as a starting point, we looked for the complete originals in the Russian Intelligence Archives. In some cases, such as Harry Dexter White's plan for postwar Germany, mentioned in VENONA, the entire document exists in the Russian archives. Messages from Russian intelligence archives also amplify and clarify VENONA messages and help place them in context. Russian intelligence documents are cited in the footnotes without specific details. Copies of these documents, in the authors' possession, have been presented to the Hoover Library where they will be available to scholars and researchers in ten years. The names of confidential sources listed in the footnotes have been withheld at the request of the sources.

We have used the Russian style for spelling of names such as Maksim, Kapitsa, Ioffe and Aleksandr except when they appear in book titles and quotations. We use NKVD, (*Narodny Kommissariat Vnutrennikh Del*, People's Commissariat for Internal Affairs) in reference to the Soviet secret police and foreign intelligence service from the period 1934 to 1954, when it became the KGB, (*Komitet Gosudarstvennoye Bezopasnosti*, Committee for State Security.)

The authors can be contacted through the website, www.sacred-secrets.com. The bibliography for *Sacred Secrets* is available on the website.

Jerrold L. Schecter and Leona P. Schecter, Washington, DC

Prologue

The onset of Soviet intelligence operations in the United States began in the 1930s. The years from Hitler's rise to power in 1933 until America's entry into World War II after Japan's attack on Pearl Harbor on December 7, 1941, were a period of worldwide economic suffering. The Great Depression brought factory production to a standstill; prices for farm products dropped below the cost of growing food. The ravages of nature—windstorms in the southwest—drove the Okies (Oklahoma farmers) off their land in search of work and food in California. Young men without prospect of work rode the railroads, jumping off in places they had never seen before to look for jobs. In rural areas of Japan, workers and farmers died of starvation. In Germany, National Socialists and communists, both advocates of government protection for workers, fought and killed each other in the streets to determine which form of socially engineered recovery would come to power.

All of this suffering had one theme: capitalism had failed. A new economic system had to be born. The preservation of capitalism in the United States during the Great Depression in the 1930s was achieved by introducing social welfare, exactly what Bismarck did for Germany in the nineteenth century to undercut socialism. The New Deal supported big government. President Franklin Delano Roosevelt's (FDR's) reforms made the government a massive employer of both laborers and artists, regulated industry, recognized unions, and provided a safety net. Through income taxes, the government paid for all of it. The New Deal brought academics and left wingers into the Washington establishment, many of them Jews. For the political right, Roosevelt's innovations were socialism at best, communism at worst. For noncommunist liberal Democrats, such Republican accusations were an attempt to erase the New Deal.

During World War II, this basic conflict between left and right in American politics was subsumed by the war effort. After the defeat of Germany and Japan, there was hardly a breathing space before Soviet expansionism in Eastern Europe and revolutionary communism were the new enemy. This fear reached a peak from

1950 to 1954, fueled by Senator Joseph McCarthy. Even after his personal fall, the central issues of the New Deal's social welfare programs remain, still being fought out on the political battlefield. Where the two parties meet at the center, the benefits of Social Security, labor relations, control over the securities markets, Medicare, and civil rights remain sacrosanct.

The Soviet Union told workers that the world communist revolution was the answer to their yearning for economic security. However, they first had to perfect communism in one country. To accomplish this goal, Stalin took all power to himself; the Soviet people would trade security for freedom. Farmers were forced onto collective farms; the state starved landowners into submission or to death. Stalin expanded the country's industrial base by relying on forced labor and the *gulag*, a vast chain of labor camps, whose prisoners built dams and canals or mined raw materials in Siberia or the Arctic Circle. The internal police rooted out enemies of the people among the populace; the Red Army kept the borders safe from attack. The border police made sure that no one left and no one entered the country without strict control. No business to bring about capitalist profit entered the system. Joseph Stalin, whose name meant "man of steel," ruled the Soviet Union with an iron fist.[1]

The February Revolution of 1917 had removed the Romanov dynasty from power and established the Soviet Union along lines that resembled a parliamentary system. A second, or counterrevolution, the October Revolution of 1917 led by Vladimir Ilyich Lenin, did away with all pretense of democratic governance. Lenin and his coterie of believers then fought a civil war from 1918 to 1920 that gave the Communist Party total control, placing all police and military power in their hands to eliminate private property and the practice of religion. After Lenin suffered a series of strokes in 1922 and died in 1924, a struggle ensued among his followers that placed Stalin in power. Leon Trotsky, who at the time of the 1917 and 1918 conflicts had been equal in stature to Lenin and was commander of the Red Army, was forced into exile; he fled first to Turkey, then to Norway and Paris, and eventually to Mexico. From there Trotsky carried on an ideological competition for leadership of the world communist revolution.

Trotsky advocated revolution of all working classes simultaneously, an internationalism that swept aside the problems of making the revolution successful in one country before communism took over the world. Trotsky's followers formed a significant segment of the American and European left.

Stalinists and Trotskyites competed to help the Republicans crush the rebellion of Franco's fascists in the 1936–1939 Spanish Civil War. The fight between the two communist factions became a parallel war in which Stalin's intelligence agents murdered as many followers of Trotsky as they could identify, eliminating the effectiveness of Trotsky's challenge to Stalin's leadership. Franco, backed by Hitler and Mussolini, won and plunged Spain into forty years of poverty and isolation.

Stalin continued to support a return to power of the Spanish Communist Party through clandestine operations in Mexico, South America, and Italy.

Fear of Trotsky's secret penetration immobilized Soviet intelligence operations in the late 1930s. The NKVD, Stalin's secret police, heightened vigilance to ensure loyalty to Stalin, not to Trotsky. Intelligence officers and agents were recalled to Moscow for vetting, where hundreds were executed or sent to labor camps. Those who survived were sent abroad again after long delays. In a few cases, experienced officers, sensing the danger, fled to England and the United States rather than obey the order to return to Moscow for "career review."

The confusion over divided loyalties made it more difficult for NKVD officers to manage their "agents of influence" and "assets," many of whom were high-level American government officials and business leaders with communist leanings. Soviet intelligence had to be certain of their agents' loyalty before imparting instructions of supreme sensitivity. Moscow Center, foreign intelligence headquarters, wanted their "friendly sources" to influence American foreign policy to make it favorable to the Soviet Union. To catch up with the West, Soviet intelligence stations, *rezidenturas*, were given an annual wish list for stealing foreign technology without respect for patents or intellectual property rights.

Stalin's concept was to consolidate the dictatorship of the proletariat in one country, the Soviet Union, building its military strength to expand Soviet territory by conquest and subversion, overthrowing anticommunist regimes in neighboring states. Stalin believed he was surrounded by enemies. Stalin never forgot that the United States sent expeditionary forces to Siberia during Russia's civil war in an attempt to overthrow the new communist regime. When the Bolsheviks brought down the czar, they inherited the long enmity between Japan and Russia. Stalin both feared Germany and wanted to become its partner in world dominance. Stalin also feared internal opposition.

Using the 1934 murder of Sergei Mironivich Kirov, the Leningrad party boss, as a pretext for launching the Great Purge, Stalin carried on a brutal cleansing operation within the leadership to eliminate all his real or imagined competitors. It was the same technique that Adolph Hitler used a year earlier when he grabbed onto the event of the Reichstag fire to launch a reign of terror in Germany.

Stalin, secretary general of the Communist Party, announced that "enemies of the people" used Leonid Nikolayev, the gunman who shot Kirov, as their tool to try to overthrow the Communist Party of the Soviet Union. Stalin ordered the secret police apparatus under his direct control to arrest the suspects. Loyal party members who had come up with him through the ranks of the revolution, who for twenty years or more had worked for the establishment of the new state, were brought forward in show trials where they were forced under torture to confess that they were indeed enemies of the people. They speedily received a bullet in the back of the head.

The purges degenerated into neighbor informing on neighbor to the secret police. Building a modern industrial state was proving difficult and slow, resulting in a shortage of basic consumer goods and defensive armaments. Unable to deliver the promises of communism, Stalin feared rivals, dissenters, and the effect on his people of a glimpse of the outside world's higher living standards.

High ranking military officers were brought to trial and executed, making way for the next rank to be inspected for their loyalty to Stalin. He had soon decimated the strength of the military: 35,000 experienced officers were either shot or sent to labor camps; those who could defected to foreign countries. By purging the Red Army of its leadership and the cream of the officer corps, Stalin seriously weakened the Soviet Union's defenses.[2]

Estimates of the Stalin period indicate that the combination of the forced starvation of farmers who opposed collectivization, the executions, and the labor camps resulted in the deaths of 20 million Soviet citizens.[3]

★ ★ ★

In the summer of 1939, war was in the air. In Germany, Hitler's Nazi Party, the Fascists, set out to cleanse their society of non-Aryan people, whom he led his people to believe were the cause of their poverty. In the 1930s, Hitler instigated mob violence against Jews and confiscated their property. His storm troopers killed or expelled gypsies and Christian religious leaders who opposed the goals of the Third Reich. Hitler then called for *lebensraum*, space for his people to expand their domain, and began the occupation of neighboring countries.

Stalin had long and unsuccessfully negotiated with Great Britain, France, and Poland to unite against Hitler. British Prime Minister Neville Chamberlain's attempt to put off hostilities by giving in to Hitler's demands at Munich in 1938 had failed to satisfy German expansionism. Perceiving Great Britain and France to be weak, Stalin decided to look instead for partnership with Germany. Stalin was equally suspicious of the Germans and the British. He believed the British were maneuvering to encourage war between Russia and Germany to avoid a German invasion of England.[4]

In spite of three years of ongoing Soviet negotiations with the Western allies on how to counter a German attack, Stalin secretly joined sides with Hitler. Europeans and Americans who since 1936 had supported the Soviet Union's Popular Front policy against Nazi Germany and looked to Stalin for leadership in building a communist utopia were astonished and ashamed when Vyacheslav Molotov and Joachim von Ribbentrop concluded the 1939 Nazi-Soviet Pact of Non-Aggression in Moscow on August 23, 1939. It became known as the Hitler-Stalin Pact.

In their infamous pact, Hitler and Stalin joined forces to divide the globe between them. Their allies were Mussolini in Italy, Franco in Spain, and Hirohito in Japan. Hitler began the takeover of the rest of Europe and North Africa. Stalin immediately annexed the Baltic states—Lithuania, Estonia, and Latvia—and parts of eastern Poland, which he believed would provide a buffer zone for the protection of the Soviet Union. The Nazi occupation of Europe and North Africa had begun. Japan fought its way through Manchuria and into China, promising a Greater East Asia Co-Prosperity Sphere that would rid Asia of British, Dutch, and French colonialists and their protector, the United States. Hitler, Stalin, and Hirohito had a problem: none of them trusted one another. Stalin knew he was vulnerable, caught geographically between his untrustworthy allies.

The immediate advantage for Stalin was the license from Hitler to move Soviet troops into eastern Poland and the Baltic states, historically disputed buffer areas. The moves, Stalin believed, increased his security against invasion from Hitler's Germany. For Stalin there were other benefits from his Faustian bargain with Hitler.[5] For the first time since the October Revolution of 1917, the Soviet Union was accepted as an equal at the high table of international diplomacy. They now had a seat at the chessboard of territorial manipulations. For Stalin and the Soviet Union, it was a coming of age; it meant the Soviet Union was joining the leaders of the twentieth century as a force to be dealt with, and were no longer the Bolshevik upstarts who had violently ended the rule of a weak czar in a military coup d'état.

So shocked was FDR by this alliance that, shortly after the signing, he gave the go-ahead to U.S. Army Signals Intelligence to order American telegraph companies to keep copies of all official cable traffic between the Soviet Union, Germany, Italy, and Japan and their diplomatic and trade offices in America. These messages, and those obtained by wartime censorship, would provide the raw material to be decoded, translated, and given the code name VENONA.[6]

Should the agreement of the two totalitarian powers to divide Eastern Europe between them really be surprising? It was Germany, after all, that had made possible Lenin's passage in a sealed train from Berlin to St. Petersburg in 1917, setting off the events that overthrew the Russian czar and established the Soviet state. The sympathetic relationship between Germany and the revolutionaries in Russia brought about close military ties; cavalry officers of the Red Army secretly trained under Prussian professional soldiers, led by army chief of staff Hans von Seeckt. The decade-long relationship between the military leaders of Germany and the Soviet Union, which had come to a halt when Hitler came to power in 1933, was revived in September 1939 when German and Soviet generals reviewed the joint parade of Red Army and Panzer units at Brest-Litovsk to mark the division of Poland.

Stalin used his intelligence apparatus to fend off attack from Japan, and he succeeded; the tactics with which he attempted to keep Germany at bay on his western flank failed and flared into a punishing war for survival. Hitler started a full-scale offensive against the Soviet Union on June 22, 1941. The Japanese attack on Pearl Harbor on December 7, 1941, eased Stalin's fears of a Japanese attack on Siberia. A few days later, Germany also declared war on the United States, a devastating mistake. Hitler had given Stalin a new ally, the United States. World War II had begun. By making the United States his adversary in Europe, Hitler brought relief to Stalin's western flank. Hitler's declaration brought the United States, Britain, and the Soviets together in an alliance that defeated German aspirations to rule the world and brought about the unconditional surrender of the Third Reich.

After four years of fighting, first of conquest by Germany and Japan, then their defeat, the two aggressor countries lay in ruins. Hitler was dead; Hirohito had surrendered unconditionally. Those four years had brought about destruction that was unimaginable in earlier wars. Hitler's ethnic cleansers had killed six million Jews and other unwanted Europeans in a Holocaust that destroyed a civilization. Stalin's Politburo had approved the execution of 26,000 Poles, a whole professional and leadership generation whom the Soviets considered "counterrevolutionaries." Stalin had swept up whole populations, including women and children in the Baltic countries and Poland, to be used as slave labor in underdeveloped areas of the Arctic Circle and Central Asia.

For the first and only time in history, the United States used two atomic bombs for the final defeat of Japan, changing the balance of power in the world.

Despite the wartime alliance of the Soviet Union and the United States, Stalin never gave up the Soviet ideology of world revolution. He never gave up on his goal of overthrowing American capitalist democracy and replacing it with a Moscow-dominated regime. At the lowest points of despair after Hitler's invasion of the Soviet Union and the near defeat of the Red Army, Stalin still had an intelligence system that first Lenin, then he, had built from the first days of the Russian civil war in 1918. The Soviet Union used its intelligence apparatus against foe and friend alike. Stalin used it to keep track of German armies and to send guerrillas into enemy territory. He also put his intelligence forces to work inside the governments of England and the United States, not only to listen in on policy discussions that might affect the balance of world power for or against the Soviet Union, but also to secretly inject his own interests into the internal dialogue of his allies. To do this he needed agents and sources loyal to communism; Stalin's intelligence officers set up communist underground operations and manned them with men and women who were disillusioned with capitalism and looked to Moscow to build utopia on earth. Beginning in the 1930s and all during the wartime alliance, Stalin's agents conducted a "scientific line" of espionage in Great Britain and the United States that performed like a vacuum cleaner, stealing industrial and military secrets such as the processes for producing artificial rubber, for refining sugar, and for proximity fuses used in aerial warfare, as well as designs for new airplanes.

During World War II the Soviets mounted an enormous propaganda campaign to ask for compassion for the suffering of the Soviet people in the war. No mention was made in Russian War Relief fundraising drives and in pro-Soviet Hollywood films of the Hitler-Stalin Pact or the suffering of the Soviet people under their own police apparatus. The plea to Stalin's American sources was to pity the ally who was not receiving enough war supplies, not receiving its share of technical secrets to build an atomic bomb, the ally for whom the Western alliance was not providing a fast enough attack on Germany from Western Europe—a second front—to relieve pressure on the Soviet Union from Hitler's armies.

Once the Great Patriotic War (Stalin's term for World War II) was won, Stalin assumed his next enemy would be an alliance of Great Britain and the United States. Using refugees from the Spanish Civil War and Soviet intelligence officers, Stalin's agents constructed a new secret underground throughout Latin and South America and within the United States. These were "illegals" with false identities who appeared to be ordinary citizens, set in place to be ready for the "Special Period," the onset of a third world war against the United States. Conflict between the superpowers arose over the same questions of hegemony in Europe and the Middle East that had destroyed the partnership between Hitler and Stalin. The long period of cold war never became the hot war that Stalin had anticipated. Before it was over, the Soviet Union had broken apart into the same nation-states that had been taken over by the Soviet empire. The implosion of the empire was caused by weaknesses inherent in the communist system. Not armies but technological progress, not spying but the spread of the idea of freedom—those were the weapons that ended the cold war.

The full extent of Stalin's effort to pervert American foreign policy into conforming to Soviet revolutionary ideology and national interest remained undiscovered during World War II. Soviet espionage operations were clouded over by the aura of wartime cooperation against a common enemy and the political need to maintain the Soviet Union in the fight against Hitler. Fears that Stalin might enter into a separate peace with Germany or that the Red Army would not be able to sustain an offensive against Hitler's armies when the second front opened in Western Europe led U.S. Army Signal Intelligence to begin reading encoded Soviet diplomatic traffic in 1943, but the VENONA secrets did not emerge within the government until 1948 and were only publicly released in 1995.

Even though Truman never acknowledged publicly or by any paper trail of documents that he knew about VENONA, his administration began a counterattack against Soviet intelligence and Soviet preparations for war. The first efforts to infiltrate the Soviet Union's borders, by parachuting agents onto Soviet territory, by collecting data from travelers to determine any sign of a military buildup, or by moving agents with the help of anti-Soviet separatist groups, all bore little useful information. The human infiltrators were soon captured. Soviet intelligence proved more adept than the West's in stopping enemy agent activities.

The area in which the Soviets could not match the United States and Great Britain was in technological advances that gathered more information than human intelligence could provide. By the end of the 1940s, the West could listen to real time telephone conversations between government officials in the Soviet Union. Technical infiltration recorded internal Soviet telegrams, revealing the manufacture of munitions, movement of troops, and the work of chemical factories preparing to build an atomic bomb.

By the end of the Truman administration, planning had begun on gathering intelligence by satellite reconnaissance: cameras in the sky. President Eisenhower backed the production and mission of the U-2, the first aircraft that could photograph ground activity from high altitudes. The U-2 overflights of the Soviet Union ended in May 1960 when the Soviets shot down one of the planes and captured its pilot, Francis Gary Powers, but by then a new era of unmanned satellite reconnaissance had begun. The Corona program, the K-8, and the K-11 followed, each advancing the concept of "eyes in the sky" that could maintain peace between the superpowers by perceiving any military massing of troops and deployment of nuclear weapons.

Intelligence technology kept the peace during the cold war. It also had unforeseen results: the Information Age revolution in computers and satellite communications and the Internet. At the start of the new millennium, technologies continue to change the nature of warfare and intelligence.

One element of information gathering has not changed: the need for HUMINT, human intelligence. No camera or digital eye can relay the motivations or future planning of a potential enemy. The process of recruiting spies continues.

1 Stalin's Intelligence Game

Playing the United States and Japan against Each Other

In the spring of 1941, Stalin feared the Soviet Union would become trapped in the vise of a two-front war, crushed between Germany and Japan. To escape the trap, three separate Soviet intelligence operations in Chungking, Tokyo, and Washington, without knowledge of each other, manipulated Japan to attack American forces in the Pacific and bring the United States into World War II. In concerted covert efforts directed from Moscow, Soviet intelligence worked to divert Japanese expansionism south against "colonialist imperialism," so that Japan would take over French Indochina, the Dutch East Indies (Indonesia), and American interests in the Philippines protected by the U.S. Navy, instead of pushing westward through Siberia. Stalin's desperate purpose was to fend off a unified, two-pronged attack by Germany and Japan that he feared would destroy the Soviet Union. Stalin's nightmare was a German-Japanese "handshake in the Urals."

Attacking Southeast Asia meant the Japanese navy would come into conflict with the American Pacific fleet, which had been moved from southern California to Pearl Harbor in October 1939 and in May 1940.[1] Stalin signed a nonaggression treaty with the Germans in 1939, then a neutrality pact with the Japanese in 1941, playing the pride and duplicity of Berlin and Tokyo off against each other. His goal was to deflect a Japanese attack away from the Soviet Union. War between the United States and Japan was the alternative Stalin favored.

Retracing the reasons for Stalin's frenzy to push the Japanese to attack the United States reveals the answer to one of the great mysteries of the twentieth century. Both communist devotees of Stalin and anticommunist commentators have long wondered why Stalin entered a pact with the devil named Hitler, knowing what a dangerous ally he might become. The 1939 Nazi-Soviet Pact of Non-Aggression, signed in August of that year, was a landmark on the path to World War II. The answer to the mystery: Stalin was already fighting the Japanese in the Far East and he feared a two-front war.

Until recently, we had only one piece of the skeleton in the closet of history, the confession of Richard Sorge, a dynamic, heavy-drinking officer of Soviet military intelligence, the GRU (*Glavnoe Razvedyovatelnoe Upravlenie*), under cover as a German foreign correspondent in Tokyo. A statue of Richard Sorge, clad in a foreign correspondent's trench coat, stands in homage to him on a Moscow back street near GRU headquarters. Sorge enjoyed access to the highest officials of the German embassy and to members of the Japanese prime minister's cabinet before he was arrested by the Japanese and hanged for spying in November 1944.

Now there are new pieces to clarify those events: officially released, deciphered intercepts of Russian intelligence traffic during 1939–1946, code-named VENONA; the memoirs of Vitali Pavlov, an NKVD (*Narodny Kommissariat Vnutrennikh Del*, predecessor to the KGB) intelligence officer; and secret messages from the Russian archives, which throw new light on the work of Vasili Zarubin, an experienced NKVD intelligence officer sent to China during the tense months before Pearl Harbor. This is a Soviet intelligence success story, which changes the conventional history of the year 1941 and our memory of Pearl Harbor. It is a story that until now none of the participants wanted known.

★ ★ ★

In June of 1997, Oleg Tsarev, a Foreign Intelligence Service (*Sluzhba Vneshni Razvedke (SVR)*, formerly KGB) officer turned historian, led a group of well-known Western writers and intelligence specialists on a "spy tour" of Moscow. The authors were among this group. Once everyone was seated on the bus, Tsarev began his presentation with the reassuring statement that in the late 1930s and the beginning of the 1940s, until the first efforts to develop the atomic bomb, "the United States was not a main target of Soviet intelligence except as a balance against Japan." That seemed an odd interpretation of events for any of his guests on the tour who had read the VENONA intercepts of Soviet cable traffic. They knew that the Soviet Union had more than 200 controlled agents in America at that time, many placed in the highest levels of the government. However, not one of the guests asked for further explanation of Tsarev's cryptic statement.

On that early summer day graced by mild sun, Tsarev led his troupe, most of whom were British and American writers on intelligence, filling in details for their new books, others who were enthusiastic readers of spy books who had discovered an unlisted tour, through the KGB museum of famous cases and heroes. In the museum he scoffed at the question of why two noted officers, Gregory Kheifetz and Elizabeth Zarubina, who played critical roles in atomic espionage, were absent from the display case: "He was sent home for inactivity . . . she was too nearsighted to be an intelligence officer." Thus did Tsarev attempt to denigrate their roles in establishing the spy ring that plundered the atomic secrets of the Manhattan Project. Both officers had been fired during a purge of Jews from the KGB after World War II.

Later the group stood in dappled light under the trees shading the Kuntsevo cemetery on the outskirts of Moscow, where gravestones identified agents and officers who served the Soviet Union by assassinating its enemies and stealing atomic secrets. A studied silence fell over the writers, a silence filled with the tension of not giving away what they already knew while waiting with wary restraint for scraps of information that might enliven their research. Nobody joked or openly asked significant questions that might reveal what they were writing. Within this uneasy silence, it was Tsarev's job to plant the KGB's latest interpretation of past events. As the group was leaving the cemetery, he offered, without being asked: "Operation Snow never happened." The tourists within earshot did not question him further, but it was clear to those who followed the memoirs of former KGB officers that a sensitive espionage operation had been exposed.

What was Operation Snow? It is the title of a book published in Russian in 1996, but not in English, in which a high ranking retired KGB officer, Vitali Pavlov, recalled his mission to Washington in April and May 1941.[2] Pavlov, then a junior officer on his first trip abroad, was sent to the United States seven months before the Japanese attacked Pearl Harbor to meet with Harry Dexter White, then director of Monetary Research for the Treasury. Did "Snow" mean "White"? Yes, Harry Dexter White had been a Soviet "asset" since the early 1930s, providing information to Whittaker Chambers, a courier for the communist underground. By 1941 White was a top aide and adviser to Henry Morgenthau, Jr., Secretary of the Treasury. Pavlov wrote that the Soviets feared a Japanese attack from the east, and his mission was to discuss with White what could be done to keep the Japanese from joining forces with the Germans. Tsarev's reference to Operation Snow brought back into focus his earlier statement that in the years leading up to World War II the United States was not a main intelligence target "except as a balance against Japan." What did "balance" mean to the Soviet Union?

Before the spy tour, we had already made plans to meet the author of *Operation Snow*. After listening to Tsarev, we had more questions to ask when we visited Pavlov in his luxurious apartment reserved for retired government elite. We brought a friend to interpret from Russian, but he had no work to do because Pavlov spoke English flawlessly. Pavlov greeted us at the door but warned with a smile to beware: when we crossed the threshold, we were entering the territory of the old Soviet Union.

We sat in Pavlov's minimally decorated living room against expansive chair-to-ceiling windows; the flood of daylight etched his story in our memory.

★ ★ ★

In the spring of 1941, Vitali Pavlov, an eager 27-year-old intelligence officer, sat nervously in his office on the sixth floor of Lubyanka, NKVD headquarters, torn by fear of invasion. The Soviet Union was facing a two-front war with the threat of attack from Japan in the east and Germany in the west. Pavlov and his colleagues devised a plan for him to go to Washington and help deflect a Japanese attack on the Soviet Union. His mission was to be a "sacred secret" (meaning they would carry it to their graves with no paper trail). The goal: exacerbate tensions between the United States and Japan to divert Japanese expansionism away from Siberia and toward Southeast Asia, where Japan would come into conflict with the United States and its Pacific fleet. Pavlov's plan did not begin and end with him, but was part of a larger Soviet design to worsen relations between Japan and the United States, even if their efforts led to war, to prevent a Japanese invasion of the Soviet Union.

Pushing the limits of discord between capitalist powers was a central tenet of Lenin's foreign policy. Stalin learned it well and used it in the 1939 Non-Aggression Pact. Stalin's contribution was to set up intelligence operations worldwide to capitalize on these rifts to further Soviet interests. In this light we must examine Sorge, Pavlov, and Zarubin in their activities on the eve of the war.

Pavlov's mission in April 1941, when he met with Harry Dexter White, U.S. Treasury Director of Monetary Research, at the Old Ebbitt Grill across the street from the Treasury Department in Washington, D.C., was to confirm that White's thinking toward Japan was in line with Soviet interests. Soviet intelligence knew that White formulated all of Morgenthau's recommendations bearing on foreign relations, especially monetary policy toward China, Japan, and the Soviet Union.[3] In the name of peace in Asia, Pavlov urged White to demand that Japan remove its troops from China, which the Soviet Union knew the Japanese would never accept.[4]

The impetus for Operation Snow began in the top leadership of Soviet intelligence. It followed a report from New York NKVD *rezident* Gaik Ovakimian in January 1941 to Moscow Center suggesting that Harry Dexter White be used to press Soviet aims for the Far East. Ovakimian's report was the seed from which Pavlov's mission grew.

On January 30, 1941, Foreign Intelligence Director Pavel Fitin compiled a *spravka* (summary), which reported that the NKVD New York *rezident*, Gaik Ovakimian (code name, GENNADI), had cabled from New York to raise the possibility of using agents and friendly sources in America to influence the formulation of American foreign policy toward Japan. The summary went to Lavrenti Beria, head of the NKVD, and his deputy, Vsevelod Merkulov. The text read:

GENNADI reported 28 January from New York about agent possibilities of influencing from outside the formulation of USA foreign policy toward Japan because (1) USA cannot accept unlimited Japanese expansion in the Pacific region which affects its vital interests, (2) Having at its disposal the necessary economic and military might, Washington is capable of preventing aggression, but it prefers to negotiate mutually acceptable solutions under the conditions that Japan (1) stops its aggression in China and areas adjacent to it, (2) recalls its military forces from the continent and halts its plans of expansion in this region.

Signed Fitin (Chief of the Fifth Department, Main Administration of State Security).[5]

On this summary report are handwritten notes:

VERNO [verified] Captain of State Security Grauer under instruction of Comrade Merkulov. In view of the upcoming negotiations with the Japanese by the People's Commissariat of Foreign Affairs, Comrades Kabulov and Grauer are directed to urgently prepare information for *instancia* [the leadership, in this case Vyacheslav Molotov and Joseph Stalin]. Also undertake verification of GENNADI's sources, ZVUK [Jacob Golos], RICHARD [Harry Dexter White], and ROBERT [Nathan Silvermaster] in line with data from the First Special Department, special investigation department, and NKVD Lithuanian SSR pending to the fact that they were known to Shpigelglas, Gutzeit, Sobel, now arrested by us.

Signed Merkulov[6]

Merkulov was giving instructions for operational research on the intentions of the Japanese, to identify hidden motives behind the Japanese desire in early 1941 to sign a neutrality pact with the USSR. He was instructing his staff to check on Harry Dexter White's relatives in Lithuania for anti-Soviet activities to make certain of White's political reliability. This was the period following the Great Purges of the 1930s in which Stalin arrested "enemies of the people" who he believed were competing with him for control of the Soviet Union and the world communist revolution. Soviet intelligence organizations were regrouping and vetting their ranks. Moscow Center wanted to make certain that the purge and execution of suspected senior officers such as Shpigelglas, Gutzeit, and Sobel had not affected the loyalty of their own New York–based espionage chief, Golos, or the continued services of two American sources, White and Silvermaster.

At our meeting in Moscow, Pavlov recalled that he was a young, untried officer, impatiently sitting at his desk, raring for an operational assignment. "I wondered what I could do to implement the idea of influencing the Americans to deal with the Japanese," said Pavlov. He mulled it over with his mentor, Iskhak Abdulovich Akhmerov, the chief of NKVD illegals in the United States, who had returned to Moscow. Akhmerov also used the pseudonyms Michael Adamec, Michael Green, William Greinke, and the "street name" BILL by which he identified himself to his assets without providing a second name. Together they drew up a plan that Pavlov, then deputy director of the American section, submitted to Pavel Fitin, chief of the Foreign Intelligence Department, who passed it up to Lavrenti Beria for approval. Beria gave the go-ahead with the admonition, "No paper. There must be no trace of this mission."[7]

Fitin's summary reveals that the impetus for Operation Snow came from the top, following Ovakimian's suggestion. Fitin's report demonstrates that there are traces of Operation Snow in the NKVD archives, that not every shred of the paper trail was destroyed.

When Pavlov broke his long silence and published *Operation Snow*, first as an article in 1995,[8] and the next year as a book, he described his mission to Washington, DC, under the cover of a diplomatic courier. His English needed work before taking such a trip alone, and Akhmerov's American wife, Helen Lowry, the niece of American Communist Party leader Earl Browder, was called upon to give Pavlov language lessons. She tutored him in American behavior and manners at their Moscow apartment before his departure.

Stalin's internal purges, during which he had his suspected rivals for absolute power executed, exiled, or sent to labor camps, occurred in the period 1934–1939. During these purges, Stalin had about 100 senior Soviet intelligence officers re-called, including Akhmerov. Only about twenty-five survived. This was the period of "cleansing" for the intelligence services, with ensuing executions and banishments, during which foreign intelligence operations came to a near standstill. Pavlov's rapid rise to deputy director of the American desk of NKVD intelligence was a result of the purges. When these upheavals began to quiet down and intelligence officers went back to supplying the leadership with intelligence on war preparations in 1941, they found their system in suspended animation. Akhmerov was still being kept on the shelf in Moscow. Moscow Center first had to reassess its most valued assets in Washington, to see who was still working for them. They had to indoctrinate their agents and sources to the Soviet viewpoint in matters of diplomacy affecting Soviet national interest. It made sense to dispatch a young officer untainted by association with the previous suspected generation and still unknown in the United States to make the necessary call.

It was under these circumstances that Pavlov left for an inspection tour of the Washington *rezidentura* (intelligence station). His real mission was to determine whether the NKVD's important U.S. Treasury assets were still in place and would cooperate with the USSR. In his memoir, Pavlov states that before going to America the NKVD assessment of the situation was: "USA cannot reconcile with uncontrolled Japanese expansion in the Pacific area which affects their vital interests. Having adequate economic and military might, Washington is capable of preventing Japanese aggression but it prefers to reach mutually beneficial decisions with Japan if it (1) stops its aggression in China and bordering areas, (2) recalls its military forces from the continent and halts its expansion plans in this region, (3) pulls out its forces from Manchuria."[9] Pavlov's explanation is a replay of Fitin's *spravka*, reporting Ovakimian's suggestion from New York.

White contacted AGENT X [Joseph Katz] looking for BILL [Akhmerov] because he wanted to thank him for one idea that had been realized with great success. Akhmerov worked out the detailed plan for a meeting in Washington. It was called Operation Snow to match the name White. We understood that only by strengthening the position of the group in Japanese ruling circles who advocated the extension of Japanese aggression in China southward could we postpone the Japanese plan to conquer the northern territories. We understood that the doubts of the Japanese militarists to immediately implement their northern plans to a great extent depended on the position of the U.S. From what we knew about White it was clear that we could influence through Morgenthau the strengthening of a line in the American administration that would counterbalance the Japanese expansion. I was to pass on to White the above-mentioned three principles. It was presumed that White would formulate them himself to be presented to the American administration.[10]

With these instructions firmly in his mind, Pavlov left for Washington. If he succeeded, he would change history. He had been entrusted with a "sacred secret" so awesome that he did not reveal it for more than half a century.

★ ★ ★

For the Soviet Union, Japan was a threatening and ambiguous enemy. European Russians—citizens of Moscow and those west of the Urals—imbibe fear of attack from the east with their mothers' milk. Deep in their national memory is conquest by cruel Mongol hordes who ruled Russia for more than 200 years, from the thirteenth to the fifteenth century. Russians believe that the followers of Genghis Khan left no improvements, only a more defined slant to the cheekbones of Russians acquired through the rape of their female ancestors.

A more recent memory was the Russo-Japanese War of 1904–1905, in which the Japanese pushed Russia out of the Pacific rim areas it had moved into since 1895. The British *National Review* for September 1904 noted: "The military power of the Island Empire has been revealed."[11]

In the 1920s and 1930s, the Kwantung Army of Japan set out to rid Manchuria of its Chinese warlord ruler and create an autonomous state in the vast, untamed territory. The Japanese military hoped Manchuria would be a buffer zone against the Soviet Union on its border; it would provide space and resources for Japan's merchants and impoverished proletariat. On September 18, 1931, the Kwantung Army took over Mukden, "to keep order." In 1933 the Japanese invaded northern China proper.

The Soviet Union sent military advisers to both nationalists and communists, the two groups competing to rule China. The Soviet Union's goal in China was to control Japanese expansionism.[12]

In the early 1930s, the Soviet Union began a propaganda campaign against Japanese aggression through the Comintern, the communist international organization that, under Moscow's aegis, controlled communist parties worldwide. Soviet intelligence distributed the "Tanaka Memorial," said to be a 1927 memorandum from Baron Giichi Tanaka[13] to the Emperor, outlining Japan's imperial ambitions to become a "continental nation": Japan's destiny was to establish a predominant position in China and Southeast Asia. Tanaka's design would develop a new plan against Siberia.

The Communist Party translated the Memorial into English and first published it in the United States in the Comintern theoretical magazine, *Communist International*, in December 1931, then later reprinted it as a book. Evidence points to Soviet intelligence and propaganda organs jointly rewriting the actual document.[14] Tanaka's ideas had been skillfully manipulated to make Japan an aggressor. All of the Memorial's prophecies were to become Japan's strategy for World War II.[15]

Within Japanese leadership circles, both aggressive militarists and thoughtful intellectuals agreed on the moral rationale for invading China and pushing southward to control all of Southeast Asia, including the Philippines, Australia, and New Zealand. They believed in the spiritual unity of East Asians, and in ridding the western Pacific rim nations of imperial domination by European powers. The Japanese included the United States in this group-enemy image because American power competed with Japan for trade, political influence, and control of the seaways. Most important in Japan's antagonism against the United States was American support for China and its struggle to repel Japanese aggression. Japan considered America to be an imperialist nation not only for its own overseas territories, but because American naval forces also protected the colonial domination of the French, British, and Dutch in China, Indochina, and the East Indies, controlling the flow of oil, rubber, tin, and other natural resources necessary to military and industrial strength. The Japanese called their vision "The Greater East Asia Co-Prosperity Sphere." They saw themselves to be the liberators of East Asia from European and American imperialists.

Stalin never doubted that the United States would in some way support Japan in its dream of attacking Siberia. Ever since 1919, when the United States intervened on the side of the Whites during the 1918–1920 civil war, for a short time landing troops in Siberia to fight the Red Army, Stalin had a deep distrust of offers of friendship from America. This continued even after President Roosevelt granted diplomatic recognition to the USSR in 1933. Stalin believed that eventually the "capitalist-fascist-imperialists" in Washington would be overthrown in favor of communism.

With Japan's occupation of Manchuria in 1931, Stalin became preoccupied with the new threat from the east and put his military on a "half-war, half-peace" footing. As early as 1931 and 1932, while the Japanese army was invading Manchuria on the Soviet border, Stalin's intelligence services were setting up networks in California to sabotage shipping in case of a new Russo-Japanese war.[15]

★ ★ ★

In 1937 a shooting incident between Chinese and Japanese troops at the Marco Polo Bridge near Peking escalated into open war. The Japanese declared a "new order" in China. The question remained whether Japan's expansionism would be directed north to Siberia and the entire Soviet Far East, or south to secure Japanese military and commercial domination of China and Southeast Asia. Through China, Japan would be on its way to the riches of Southeast Asia, while ridding the East of Western colonialists.[16]

In June 1938, Soviet Commissar of State Security in the Far East Genrich Samuelovich Lyushkov defected across the Manchurian border and revealed to the Japanese occupation army full details of the levels of Soviet military strength in the region. Lyushkov, who took his family with him, feared he would be a victim of the purges Stalin was carrying on against his own officers. After he surrendered, Lyushkov was transferred to Tokyo, where he was interrogated by Japanese military intelligence and military attachés at the German embassy. Lyushkov provided the Soviet order of battle both in Ukraine and the Far East. His debriefing was turned into a memorandum of approximately 100 pages, "Report on a Meeting Between Lyushkov and the German Special Envoy, and Related Information."

The secret pages were photographed by Richard Sorge, correspondent of the German newspaper *Frankfurter Zeitung*, who used his journalist's cover to head a Soviet espionage ring in Tokyo. Sorge was a German national secretly working for the Red Army's Fourth Bureau, the GRU, military intelligence. Sorge, the son of a German father and Russian mother, became a communist while recovering from wounds he received fighting on the German side in World War I. His legs had been shattered and he was left with a lifelong limp. From having been an avid volunteer in the German army, he went into deep disillusionment and depression and emerged a dedicated Marxist. Sorge had close friendships with high ranking diplomats and military officers in the German embassy; one of them, the military attaché Major Erwin Scholl, lent the Lyushkov document to Sorge, unaware of the use the newspaperman would make of its pages.[18]

Lyushkov's main thesis: because of widespread discontent caused by Stalin's purge in the Red Army and strong opposition to Stalin in Siberia, the Soviet military machine in the Far East would collapse under a Japanese offensive. Lyushkov is also believed to have provided the military wireless codes being used by the Red Army. He described the location, organization, and equipment of twenty-five Soviet divisions. It was clear to Lyushkov's German and Japanese interrogators that his defection resulted from Stalin's purges of the Red Army high command and re-flected the army's weakened strength. For the Germans and Japanese, this informa-tion created the temptation to strike the Soviet Union soon, while it was weak from internal strife. To his Japanese and German friends, Sorge played down the importance of Lyushkov's information; he compared it to anti-Nazi books written by German refugees suggesting that the Nazi regime faced imminent collapse.[19] But Moscow was getting another message. Sorge later confessed: "One consequence of Lyushkov's report was a danger of joint Japanese-German military action against the Soviet Union."[20]

Western leaders were less aware of Stalin's problem in the East, which figured as strongly into his calculations as his alliance with Hitler. At all cost Stalin needed to avoid a two-front war. In fact, he was already at war with Russia's historic rival, Japan. In 1938 the Soviets and Japanese had fought each other in a series of incidents on the Manchurian frontier, about seventy-five miles southwest of Vladi-vostok, without a clear victory on either side. What began as skirmishes in January 1939 gradually brought in larger Japanese units; by May, major Japanese forces were engaged against Soviet-Mongolian units near Khalkhin-Gol (the Khalkhin river on the Manchurian border with Mongolia) and the town of Nomonhan. The Japanese call it the Nomonhan Incident. By July it had become a war, to which the Japanese brought heavy pressure to bear against the Soviet troops. Even while Stalin's and Hitler's emissaries were negotiating their infamous 1939 Non-Aggression Pact, Soviet and Japanese troops were battering each other at Khalkhin-Gol. In a decisive Soviet tank offensive that took place in August, General (later Marshal) Georgi Zhukov, then a corps commander, exhibited his aggressive leader-ship. Zhukov's massive armored assault was a totally unexpected innovation that defeated the Japanese and led to his rise in the Soviet officer corps.

With Sorge's microfilm of Lyushkov's report in hand, the Soviet High Com-mand knew what the Japanese expected when they pushed across the Manchurian border at Khalkhin-Gol. As a result, Zhukov built up his forces to much greater strength and overwhelmed the Japanese. Sorge continued to advise Moscow during the fighting, warning that although sizable Japanese reinforcements might be trans-ferred to the battlefield from North China and Manchuria, there was no evidence that large-scale units were being sent from Japan. This was the evidence, reported Sorge, for his standing firm on the view that "Japan had no intention of waging war against the Soviet Union." He repeated variations of this radio message several times during the fighting.[21]

At this point Zhukov assumed command of the Soviet First Army Group. For weeks he maintained a defensive posture, methodically but stealthily building up his forces. He created a three-to-two superiority in manpower, two-to-one strength in artillery and airplanes, and a four-to-one advantage in armor. He gathered 35 infantry battalions to fight 25 Japanese infantry battalions; 20 cavalry squadrons against 17 Japanese cavalry squadrons. Zhukov had nearly 500 tanks, 346 armored cars, and 500 planes to go up against the Japanese Sixth Army, which had no tanks. Zhukov drew the Japanese in without revealing his strength, then counterattacked for the kill. The attack against the Japanese forces came at 5:45 a.m., August 20, 1939, only three days before the announcement of the Non-Aggression Pact. The battle raged for more than ten days, until the Japanese were driven back across the frontier in disorder.[22] The defeat of the Japanese at Khalkhin-Gol forced a reassessment in Tokyo of plans for the timing to attack the Soviet Union and discredited the army officers responsible for the defeat.[23]

Red Army intelligence has never released evidence of the connection between Lyushkov's information and the defeat of the Japanese at Khalkhin-Gol. In 1941, when Sorge was arrested by the Japanese for espionage activities, a leading Japanese procurator, Yoshikawa Mitsusada, made the connection between the failure of the Japanese military operation at Khalkhin-Gol and Sorge's transmission to Moscow of the Japanese evaluation of Soviet strength based on Lyushkov's information. In their study of Sorge, F. W. Deakin and G. R. Storry wrote, "Sorge's activity in connection with the Lyushkov affair was one of the greatest services he rendered to the Fourth Bureau (Soviet Military Intelligence) during his Japan mission."[24]

When the fighting ended, it had changed the course of history. Khalkhin-Gol was the decisive turning point that created fear and doubt for the Japanese in their plan to attack the Soviet Union through Siberia. Two years later the Japanese focused south into Indochina, but until they attacked Pearl Harbor, Stalin was uncertain whether or not the Japanese would attempt another invasion of the Soviet Far East.

★ ★ ★

The fighting at Khalkhin-Gol had been escalating since April 1939, when the Hitler-Stalin negotiations began, and ended in mid September, only weeks after the pact was signed and Poland had fallen. When it was pointed out to a knowledge-able scholar of this era that the Battle of Khalkhin-Gol was waged in the same time period as the negotiations for the 1939 Non-Aggression Pact, he caught his breath in wonder that he had never matched the dates before. "Of course," he said, exhaling slowly. "With the Japanese at his back, Stalin had no other choice but to sign."[25]

A week after signing the pact, on September 1, 1939, German forces invaded the western half of Poland. In early September, Hitler gave Stalin the go-ahead to invade eastern Poland, which had been agreed between them would become territory to be taken by the Soviets. Stalin hesitated before attacking Poland, to make sure the peace settlement with the Japanese over the Manchurian territory that had been their recent battlefield was signed and the immediate danger from the east was over.[26] On September 17 at 6 a.m., the Red Army attacked, and within two weeks took over the eastern half of Poland, then quickly annexed the Baltic states. Stalin appeared to be allied with Hitler against the capitalist West.

It was only after Hitler invaded the Soviet Union in June 1941 that Great Britain and the United States accepted the explanation that in signing the pact Stalin hoped to buy time to build Soviet military strength and prepare for war against Hitler.

In retrospect, the April-to-September 1939 battle at Khalkhin-Gol had a rhythmic connection to the Non-aggression Pact negotiations carried on in the same months between Molotov and Ribbentrop.[27] When the battle was over and the pact was signed, Japan's illusion that the Germans would join them in crushing the Soviet Union from east and west had evaporated. Japan's leadership was furious with Hitler for refusing to consult with Tokyo, his supposed ally, before signing with Stalin.[28]

★ ★ ★

Despite the Soviet defeat of the Kwantung Army in Manchuria, Stalin and his generals could not rest assured that there would be no further Japanese attempts to invade from the east. Red Army intelligence had been essential to the Soviet victory, and it would stay alert in watching for Japanese intentions to attack the Soviet Union again.

Sorge's principal and most influential agent was Ozaki Hotsumi, a Japanese journalist and later a spokesman for the South Manchurian Railroad, who had spent years in China. Ozaki was well connected and highly respected, a member of the elite government establishment, when he began gathering information for the Soviet Union and trying to influence Japanese government policy through his high level contacts. Ozaki hoped for a communist revolution in wartime Japan, after which he and his colleagues would lead his country into alliances with the Soviet Union and a communist China. Ozaki's expertise on China made him a favorite of cabinet ministers and a group of officials known as the Breakfast Society, where he argued that Siberia had few developed natural resources, which made it a less-appealing target for takeover by Japan than Southeast Asia, rich in rubber and oil. His compelling argument was for Japan to advance southward.[29]

★ ★ ★

Trotsky was convicted of treason in absentia in 1937. In the United States, intellectual leaders attempted to understand the fight between Stalin and Trotsky; the respected philosopher John Dewey of Columbia University headed a Commission of Inquiry in Coyoacan, Mexico, where Trotsky was living, to expose the falsehoods of the show trials and to exonerate Trotsky of the charges against him. Stalin feared the pronouncements of the Dewey Commission (an offshoot of the Commission of Inquiry) because John Dewey's stature added legitimacy to Trotsky among American and world intellectuals. In 1940 Dewey planned a public meeting at Columbia University with Trotsky as the featured speaker.[30]

Stalin made his decision: eliminate Trotsky, and his movement would die with him. None of his followers had Trotsky's prestige or name recognition. The NKVD called on Ramon Mercader, a young Spanish revolutionary who had fought the fascists and was now living in exile. Mercader infiltrated Trotsky's entourage by pretending to be the fiancé of Trotsky's secretary, Sylvia Ageloff. In August 20, 1940, when Trotsky agreed to review an article Mercader had written, his assassin withdrew a mountain climber's pickax and fatally impaled Trotsky's skull. Trotsky cried out and Mercader was quickly captured. He pleaded the jealous lover defense. Trotsky, Mercader said, was trying to lure his fiancée away from him. He calmly went to jail, keeping secret his instructions from the Kremlin. For the next six years, until a defector told the truth in 1946, the world had to accept Mercader's cover story.

With Trotsky out of the way, and a Soviet pact with Hitler, it seemed to the West that Stalin was aligned with the Axis.

★ ★ ★

The 1939 Nazi-Soviet Pact of Non-Aggression was only one piece of an elaborate pattern of Hitler's deceit. In November 1940, Hitler notified Japan that he was drawing up a new agreement among the Tripartite Pact nations—Germany, Italy, and Japan—to include the Soviet Union. Originally designed in 1936 by Hitler as an anti-Comintern measure, the pact was to change its nature to include the Soviet Union in Hitler's efforts to divide the world into spheres of influence that would replace the British, Dutch, and French empires protected by American naval power. Hitler dangled the apportionment of the British Empire as "a gigantic world-wide estate in bankruptcy before the impassive Molotov who appeared to be in agreement."[31] Assurances by Hitler to the Japanese that they were included in his plans to divide up domination of the globe among the pact members softened the Japanese attitude toward the Soviet Union after the shock of Hitler's signing a nonaggression pact with Stalin.[32]

Stalin sent Molotov, the People's Commissar for Foreign Affairs, to Berlin in November 1940 to discuss the addition of the Soviet Union to the Tripartite Pact nations. Molotov told Hitler and German Foreign Minister Joachim von Ribbentrop that Stalin would agree to joining, but only as a real partner. Until the relationship among them and their spheres of influence were spelled out, the Soviets would keep open their lines of communication with China, which by implication meant including Britain and the United States.[33] Using a Soviet intelligence report from the United States, Stalin instructed Molotov on the eve of his departure for Berlin, "Tell them we were informed about German peace proposals made through Roosevelt to Britain. Does this correspond to reality? And what was the answer?" Molotov got no answer in Berlin to Stalin's question.[34]

"In the opinion of the German government," Ribbentrop said in Berlin, "the time is coming when it will be necessary to take practical steps to divide the former British empire."[35] Ribbentrop said the draft treaty declared that the four states shared the desire to cooperate "in ensuring their natural spheres of interest in Europe, Asia and Africa." The ten-year treaty, subject to renewal, included two secret protocols. One defined the parties' spheres of influence: the Persian Gulf and Indian Ocean were set aside for the Soviet Union, the South Seas were to be under Japan, Central Africa went to Germany, and North Africa, to Italy. The second protocol took account of Soviet interests in the Bosporus Straits and the Dardanelles.

Stalin had instructed Molotov to drive a hard bargain. He demanded assurances that Russia would be given influence in the Dardanelles and the Bosporus Straits with the right to establish Soviet military and naval bases in the area, leading to a warm-water port for the Soviet Union. "The Soviet government therefore believes that the quadripartite treaty should be accompanied by five secret protocols and not two, as suggested by the Reich Minister. We are looking forward to an early reply from the German government," said Molotov to Ambassador Schulenberg.[36]

A reply never came. When Molotov departed from Berlin in November 1940, Hitler gave instructions to his high command to prepare for Operation Barbarossa, the invasion of the Soviet Union. Conventional historical wisdom asserts that Hitler tricked Stalin, using the invitation to Molotov to visit Berlin to plant the idea of sharing world domination as a smokescreen to conceal his intention to attack the Soviet Union. It wasn't that simple.

Molotov's personal archive demonstrates that both Hitler and Stalin realized that their conflict of interests and ideology would inevitably lead them into war with each other. Both sides were building up their tanks, aviation, naval forces, and artillery in preparation for war. Stalin would not be ready for battle until spring 1942. Hitler was at war with Great Britain and hoped to take over the British Isles or impose a peace settlement on his terms in 1940 or early 1941. Stalin would not sit idly by for the total defeat of Britain because he believed European Russia, up to the Urals, would be next on Hitler's menu.

Hitler's seeming détente with Stalin encouraged the Japanese to press for their own pact with the Soviet Union, which would secure Japan's holdings in China and open the path into Southeast Asia.

With no response to Molotov's questions, Stalin's paranoia intensified. Joining the Quadripartite Pact and responding to a Japanese offer to make a neutrality pact meant becoming a member of the Axis powers, a radical step. The Soviet leadership, both in Stalin's governing circle and throughout the intelligence services, suffered a system-wide anxiety attack that set a new agenda in January 1941. The leadership was seeking reassurance that the Japanese offer was not a trick to lower the Soviet guard before a dual invasion from east and west.

It was in this atmosphere that Stalin gave the nod for the NKVD to send Vasili Zarubin, a senior intelligence officer with previous experience in China, to visit Chiang Kai-shek's wartime capital, Chungking, the capital of Szechuan province in western China. Zarubin's assignment was to assess to what extent Chiang could be relied on to continue to engage the Japanese and draw their forces away from an attack into the Soviet Far East.

Zarubin was to contact Chiang Kai-shek's chief of security, Walther Stennes, a former German SA officer (*Sturmabteiling*, storm troops or Brownshirts). Stennes served as an officer in World War I, and from 1925 to 1930 worked in the intelligence service for the Foreign Office. Stennes first met Hitler in 1927 and was in charge of building up the SA in eastern Germany. Stennes broke with Hitler in April 1931 for abandoning the revolutionary anticapitalist and antiparliamentary goals of National Socialism when Hitler agreed to accept a constitutional government. Stennes led a brief revolt and tried to form his own organization, the National Socialist Military Front, but without success. When Hitler took power in 1933, Stennes was arrested and placed in "preventive detention." After interventions by the military and the Vatican, Stennes was released on condition he leave Europe. In a face-saving solution, he was assigned to China as military adviser on the staff of Chiang Kai-shek. Stennes's strong totalitarian personality and his military security and police expertise appealed to Chiang, who relied on Stennes as the head of his personal bodyguard and as an intelligence expert. Stennes, a Soviet agent, was in the inner circle of Chiang's foreign advisers.[37]

Chungking was an inland redoubt on the upper reaches of the Yangtze River to which Chiang was forced to retreat in 1937 after the fall of the downstream cities of Nanking and Hankow. Built on a long, high, narrow bluff at the convergence of the Yangtze and Chialing rivers, Chungking from a distance loomed like a medieval town. Journalist Joseph Alsop, describing his wartime experiences, wrote:

Dirty and bomb-scarred, it resembled at first blush a series of muddy anthills. The only roads that were fairly flat and usable were those running along the top of the long bluff. Traverses from place to place were, therefore, accomplished by climbing and descending countless staircases cut in the rock . . . rubble was the most prevalent architectural motif since a large portion of the city was . . . being built up again as the result of the bombing.[38]

Zarubin was no stranger to China. He spent the early years of his intelligence career there in the 1920s and was familiar with the treacherous political terrain within the Chinese Nationalist and Communist landscapes. Zarubin had returned on missions and was the logical choice to travel to Chungking to check long-time NKVD sources and orient them to serve Moscow's ends. Most important was his man Walther Stennes, code-named DRUGG or FRIEND, whom Zarubin had recruited in Germany when he was assigned there in the 1930s.[39] Zarubin visited China from January to May 1941, relying primarily on Stennes for insights and introductions. Stennes had contact with Richard Sorge, who visited from Tokyo and briefed Stennes on the worsening German-Soviet relations despite the Non-Aggression Pact. Before he set up operations in Japan, Sorge had for years operated under Soviet military intelligence control in China. He was a familiar figure in Shanghai and Chungking.

Stennes had a wide range of sources, and with access to the diplomatic community in Chungking through his role as a Chiang adviser, he was able to feed Zarubin the most current information on American support for China.[40] The Russian historian of foreign intelligence, Vladimir Peschersky, confirmed that when Pavel Sudoplatov was NKVD deputy director of foreign intelligence, he ordered Zarubin to use Stennes for a strategy that would divert Japanese military activity toward Southeast Asia and away from the Soviet Union.[41] Moscow believed that for Japan to attack Siberia, it would need a hands-off attitude from the Americans; Zarubin wanted the United States to maintain its support for Chiang, which would increase hostility between Tokyo and Washington.

Stennes had the direct ear of Chiang Kai-shek and met regularly with Zarubin in Shanghai and Chungking, enabling them to advise Moscow Center of top level Chinese nationalist intelligence. The Generalissimo's warning to Roosevelt on May 12, 1941, that Germany would attack the Soviet Union within a month found its way to Moscow Center shortly after being dispatched to Washington.[42]

★ ★ ★

Despite Chiang Kai-shek's deteriorating position and rising Japanese ambitions that threatened American interests in Asia, FDR faced strong isolationist sentiment at home. In February 1941, the President decided to send a personal emissary to

Chiang, just as he had sent Harry Hopkins to see Churchill in London in January 1940; Hopkins was his "personal representative on a special mission," to reassure the British that the United States would support them.[43]

Roosevelt's choice was Lauchlin Currie, his 38-year-old personal economic adviser and administrative assistant.[44] Currie had never before flown on an airplane when he took off for China to sort out economic measures that would bolster Chinese military strength and halt further Japanese expansion into Southeast Asia.

On the White House staff, Currie became personally responsible for Far Eastern affairs. Lauchlin Currie does not show up in the VENONA intercepts until 1943; they had not been decoded and translated in 1945 when Elizabeth Bentley, a defector from the American Communist Party underground, named him to be a Soviet asset. From these intercepted cables and Currie's work in 1941—supporting the American Volunteer Group (AVG) of airmen (the "Flying Tigers") to fly 100 P-40 fighters against the Japanese invaders in China—it is clear that his seemingly beneficent intentions to help China and to avoid war with Japan backfired and heightened the Japanese perception that war with America was inevitable.[45,46]

The American consul in Burma reported that Tokyo radio announced "America's Penetration into China" on June 30, 1941. The Tokyo broadcast said, "It is estimated that America intends to send 100 planes to train the Chinese and revive the Chinese Air Force. America, in keeping air bases in China to help the Chungking Government, intends to convert China into an American colony."[47]

The Japanese were wrong in believing the United States wanted to make China its colony; the correct interpretation would have been that Americans felt a "moral responsibility for the future security of China," the words of Stanley Hornbeck, adviser to the State Department on Far Eastern Affairs. American missionaries who had long worked deep in the interior of China building churches, hospitals, and schools had been driven out by Japanese armies. On their return to the United States, missionaries gave life to the image that Japan was an aggressor nation. Their stories contributed to the national sympathy for China under attack.[48]

Roosevelt had strong positive feelings toward China. He loved to tell stories of the Delano family's connection to the China trade from which the family's wealth was derived. His mother's father, Warren Delano, had been a partner in Russell & Company, founded in 1824, which soon became as affluent and influential as the British East India Company; it had branches in all the treaty ports where its partners acted as American consuls. Sara Delano, Roosevelt's mother, lived in Rose Hill, the family home in Hong Kong, when she was growing up. At Hyde Park, Roosevelt was brought up among Chinese furnishings and artifacts, including a large blue-and-white porcelain garden pot in the library which, according to family tradition, had been used at Rose Hill for bathing the children.[49]

Roosevelt had no such fondness for Japan. From his days at Harvard in 1902,

Roosevelt had been impressed by Japan's plans for expansion as recounted by a Japanese student from an aristocratic family studying with him. In his diary for May 17, 1934, Henry Stimson, later to become Roosevelt's Secretary of War, recalled details of Roosevelt's

> extraordinary but impressive tale of the ambitions of the Japanese. This young Japanese boy had told him the making in 1889 of the one-hundred-year Japanese plan for the Japanese dynasty, which involved the following steps in the following order:
>
> 1. An official war with China to show that they could fight and beat China.
> 2. The absorption of Korea.
> 3. A defensive war against Russia.
> 4. The taking of Manchuria.
> 5. Taking of Jehol. [now Chengde, near the Manchurian border]
> 6. The establishment of a virtual protectorate over northern China from the [Great] Wall to the Yangtze.
> 7. Encircling movement in Mongolia and the establishment of the Japanese influence through instructors as far as Tibet, thus establishing a precautionary threat against Russia on one side and India on the other.
> 8. The acquisition of all the islands of the Pacific including Hawaii.
> 9. Eventually the acquisition of Australia and New Zealand.
> 10. Establishment of Japanese (using a word indicating a rather fatherly control, which the President said he could not quite remember) over all the yellow race, including the Malays.
>
> When young Roosevelt asked him what they were going to do to the United States, he said that the United States need not have any fear; that all they would do in the new hemisphere would be to establish outposts, one probably in Mexico and another perhaps in Peru; otherwise they would leave us alone.[50]

The timing of Zarubin's mission in China, at the same time Lauchlin Currie was representing FDR on a special mission to Chiang Kai-shek, underscores the importance to Stalin of moving Washington to confront Japan. Soviet intelligence activities in Chungking were part of a three-pronged effort, by Pavlov, Sorge, and Zarubin, to aggravate American-Japanese relations and draw the Japanese to the conclusion that they must strike south to solidify their domination of East Asia.

By the end of 1941, Zarubin was posted to New York and then Washington, where he became the NKVD *rezident* for North and South America, and where Currie, serving in the White House, was Moscow's valuable intelligence asset.

★ ★ ★

The dances of deceit continued in Berlin, Tokyo, and Moscow. The fears that kept the lights burning late in Lubyanka, NKVD headquarters, were different from the concerns at the Japanese foreign ministry. Hitler's seeming détente with Stalin encouraged the Japanese to press their own pact with the Soviet Union.

The 1939 Nazi-Soviet Pact of Non-Aggression put an end to the Japanese illusion that the Germans would help them to defeat the Soviet Union's influence in China. Since conquering China would be the decisive factor in their strategy to become the dominant power in East Asia, the Japanese signed a five-year neutrality treaty with the Soviet Union on April 13, 1941, under which the two nations "pledged to maintain peaceful, friendly relations" and to respect their mutual territories. In the event of military action by a third state against one or both of them, the other party would "maintain neutrality throughout the entire period of the conflict." Hirohito ratified the treaty on April 25, and the next day, *Pravda* announced that the pact had gone into effect.[51]

The Japanese-Soviet Neutrality Pact provided Stalin breathing space when looking eastward and enabled him to move troops from the Far East to European Russia in late May. Stalin remained uncertain and wary of a renewed Japanese attack. Sorge was still warning Moscow that the Japanese attitude might change at any time and that a powerful faction in the Japanese army opposed the pact.[52]

The day before signing the Soviet-Japanese Neutrality Pact, Stalin received Foreign Minister Yosuke Matsuoka in the Kremlin. Accompanying Matsuoka was Prince Saionji, who was one of Sorge's primary sources in the cabinet through Sorge's agent Ozaki Hotsumi.

At the meeting, Matsuoka told Stalin that it was "expedient for Japan and the USSR to sign the Pact because of our common interests." Matsuoka said he was in favor of expanding the 1940 Tripartite Pact among Germany, Japan, and Italy to include the Soviet Union. According to an official Soviet report of the meeting, Matsuoka outlined Japan's interests:

1. Japan has a treaty of alliance with Germany, but in no way does this mean that Japan will constrain the forces of the USSR in case something happens between Germany and the USSR. Japan would prefer to act as intermediary between the two states.
2. It is natural for the USSR to seek access to warm water ports on the Indian Ocean; Japan would accept that the USSR should have at its disposal the port of Karachi in India, part of the British Empire.
3. To liberate Asia it is necessary to get rid of Anglo Saxon dominance there.
4. Japan is now involved in a struggle with China, but not in a war with the Chinese people. Japan wants to drive out the Anglo Saxons from China.

Chiang Kai-shek is simply an agent of British and American capital. In their interests he wages a war against Japan.

5. The issue is "moral communism," said Matsuoka. Matsuoka suggested that the USSR and Japan jointly defeat the influence of British and American capitalism in Asia. In Japan it is not apparent, but a vicious struggle is going on between capitalism and moral communism.

Comrade Stalin says that the USSR in principle believes that cooperation with Japan, Germany and Italy is acceptable on big issues. Matsuoka stated that he had no objections to the treaty, apart from the protocol on the liquidation of Japanese concessions in Siberia and Sakhalin, which will revert to the USSR.

Then, Matsuoka, pointing to the area of the South Seas and Indonesia, said that Japan could supply the USSR with rubber and other products.

Stalin stated that the USSR would not agree to sell Northern Sakhalin to Japan, but promised to supply Japan with 100,000 tons of oil annually.[53]

In late 1940 and early 1941, Hitler encouraged the Japanese in their rapprochement with the Soviet Union; he suggested they look southward and attack Singapore. Hitler believed the defeat of British naval power in Southeast Asia would help Germany to knock Great Britain out of the war in Europe and prevent a second front, a direct attack on Germany.

In the long view of history, Japan's decision to sign a neutrality pact with the Soviet Union in April 1941, made without the knowledge that Germany had already laid plans to break its pact with the Soviet Union and attack on June 22, saved the Soviet Union from a two-front war.[54]

In the spring of 1941, Stalin activated a long delayed Yugoslav coup d'état in Belgrade that installed a pro-Soviet, anti-German regime. Stalin thought the removal of the pro-German government would occupy German troops throughout the summer, causing Hitler a year's delay in attacking the Soviet Union, until after the daunting rain and snow of the Russian autumn and winter.[55] (The Soviet leadership had in mind that in World War I the Serbs had held out against an Austrian and German invasion for ten months before the army had to retreat into Greece.) Instead, Hitler wiped up the Yugoslav army in two weeks. Stalin hastily backpedaled to disassociate the Soviet Union from the anti-German coup.[56] After Hitler crushed Yugoslav opposition to his domination of the Balkans, he accelerated preparations for war against the Soviet Union. German troops began to mass across the Soviet border in Poland.

The half year from partnership in dividing the world to deadly wartime enemies passed swiftly and with purposeful intent for Hitler, who was driving events; it came too fast for Stalin and his military and diplomatic bureaucracy to grasp the changes and respond effectively. The Japanese neutrality pact signed in April soothed Stalin into wishful thinking that Hitler would not attack because Berlin was part of Matsuoka's itinerary on the trip to sign the reassuring agreement between Japan and the Soviet Union. Since Matsuoka was signing the pact with Hitler's apparent approval, Stalin believed he was successfully buying time. In an unprecedented move, Stalin came to the Yaroslavsky railroad station to bid farewell to Matsuoka and his delegation.[57]

The long planned coup in Yugoslavia had failed, and with it the ambiguity of Stalin's intentions toward Hitler was erased. Stalin's plan to buy time was in jeopardy if not in extremis. Reports of a German buildup in Poland were coming through while Stalin desperately tried to forestall Hitler's attack.

Despite the neutrality pact with Japan, Stalin's intelligence apparatus, looking eastward, remained on high alert. Every effort was needed. Beria approved the long-shot manipulation, Operation Snow, designed to divert Japanese aggression away from Siberia by aggravating the strained negotiations between the United States and Japan.

2 ★★★ Operation Snow

Vitali Pavlov arrived in Washington to carry out Operation Snow at the end of April 1941. As a pretext for their meeting, Pavlov telephoned Harry Dexter White and said he was on his way to China, where he would meet up with White's friend BILL (Iskhak Akhmerov), who was then stationed there. Pavlov said he had a message to pass from BILL to White. Actually, Akhmerov was still in Moscow waiting for word from Pavlov.

Two years earlier, Akhmerov had met White in Washington after being tipped off by a Communist Party source in the Treasury Department that White was "antifascist" and had a favorable attitude toward the Soviet Union. Akhmerov asked Agent X (Joseph Katz, an NKVD agent who knew White) to arrange a meeting. When he met with White, Akhmerov posed as a sinologist on his way to China and the Far East. White agreed to meet Akhmerov after he returned, for a report on his travels. On the basis of their discussion in 1939, Akhmerov decided not to try to recruit White because it was unnecessary, Pavlov explained. Akhmerov already had highly placed sources in Treasury, and White's views were focused in a direction that was agreeable to Moscow.[1]

White appeared in the Old Ebbitt Grill wearing metal-rimmed glasses, resembling a professor, not a government bureaucrat, recalled Pavlov.

> I emphasized that what I wanted to pass on to him in the message from BILL was too important to be delayed until a personal meeting between them could occur. I passed to White a small written message, which contained the results of the research work BILL was undertaking in the sphere of Japanese-American relations. I noted that BILL was deeply alarmed by Japanese expansion in Asia. I also said that the ideas summarized in the message, according to BILL, might be of interest to White. When White read the message, he said BILL's ideas coincided very much with his own thoughts.
>
> He mechanically wanted to push the note into his jacket pocket, but having seen my extended hand returned it to me. I told him that I was soon

on my way to China and I asked what I was to tell BILL because he was very concerned whether the American leadership recognized the reality of the Japanese threat. BILL wanted to know if the Americans had any plans to halt Asian aggression.[2]

The note listed the three demands the Soviets hoped the Americans would make of the Japanese: stop their aggression in China and on its borders; recall their military forces from the continent, putting an end to expansionism; and pull out their forces from Manchuria. These were the points in a potential negotiation that the Soviets knew the Japanese would not accept. Pavlov continued:

White thanked me for the above mentioned ideas which corresponded to his convictions and awareness of the state of things in the region. He already was thinking over what might be undertaken. He believed that after acquiring support from an expert with profound knowledge on the subject he would be able to undertake necessary efforts in the necessary direction. "I may do something on that," said White. He spoke slowly and when he concluded, asked whether I understood him correctly. To soothe him, I repeated his oral message to BILL, word by word. He was nodding in agreement and appreciated my good memory. Our lunch came to an end and at White's request I agreed that he would pay for the lunch because he ordered it.[3]

Vitali Pavlov's description of his meeting with Harry Dexter White is remarkable for what he says and what he does not explain. The meeting was carefully planned both in Moscow and Washington. It was a clandestine meeting with a highly appreciated, confidential, and friendly source. Pavlov's description of his showing a message from BILL and then asking for it back is classic spy tradecraft (the techniques and procedures of espionage). Pavlov had been instructed to leave no paper trail for American counterintelligence. Pavlov, a neophyte at spy operations, checked for possible surveillance the whole time he was eating lunch with White, fearing he was being tailed.

Pavlov does not reveal his true motives and the goals for the meeting, as outlined in Fitin's *spravka*. He does not explain that he and his superiors knew that the three principles he was offering White—that the Japanese cease their aggression, recall their forces from China, and pull out their armies from Manchuria—were provocative to the Japanese and could not possibly serve to bridge the tensions he pretended he was trying to assuage.

White might not have understood that the diplomatic points he would soon incorporate into his briefing for the Secretary of the Treasury and finally for the State Department were in contradiction to the peace-loving idealism for which he was known. Certainly he knew that there was a commonality in Soviet and

American interests in China. He was aware of Moscow's concerns that conquest of China threatened the Soviet Union; the United States shared the Soviet desire to curb Japanese expansionism. From Pavlov's description of his adventure in Washington on the eve of war, White was accepting Akhmerov's suggestions as real alternatives to war. White knew that his efforts over the previous years to defend and bolster China in its confrontation with Japan were in line with the interests of the Soviet Union. Those measures kept Japanese troops tied down in China and prevented Japanese armies from conquering the Soviet Far East and Siberia. Was White aware that Pavlov's suggestions were framed to lead America into war with Japan?

While in the United States, Pavlov sent a one-sentence, ciphered cable personally to Fitin, "Everything is OK, as was planned, KLIM" (Pavlov's code name). Pavlov departed by ship for the Soviet Union via the Pacific in May and did not arrive in Moscow until July 1941. On June 22, before he reached his destination, the Germans invaded the Soviet Union. Another invasion from the east, creating a two-front war, remained a frightening possibility. Pavlov wrote:

> In Moscow I first of all met with Akhmerov. We thoroughly analyzed, not omitting any details, the progress of the operation and the reaction of H. D. White. Akhmerov's conclusion was that White behaved as was expected from him. We could be sure that he accepted our piece of advice and by all means would use it. We were to await his actions. I fully agreed with the conclusions of Akhmerov and reported the case to the director of foreign intelligence. After I reported to him, Pavel Mikhailovich [Fitin] told me that he immediately reported my cable to Beria. Therefore there was no need for me to report to Beria in person. "Now there are other urgent matters. The war has broken out." With this episode, Fitin summarized for us that Operation Snow was over. Akhmerov and I should forget about it.[4]

Harry Dexter White did not forget about his lunch with Pavlov. White's agenda was to keep in mind Soviet interests and inject them into American policy, making it appear that peace was his only objective. White kept his promise to "do something on that." In May 1941, after Pavlov made contact with him, White promoted the idea of "all-out diplomacy" to develop new American policies toward Japan and the Soviet Union.[5] White believed that significant arrangements could be made between countries on an economic basis "irrespective of their political differences."[6] Twice he advanced sweeping proposals to reconcile Japanese and American interests in the Far East. White suggested that the United States do away with its "old diplomacy" and substitute a modern approach in which the United States would be dealing with all-embracing economic, political, and social problems. He proposed a diplomatic effort to engage Japan and Russia, with the objective of detaching them from their German connections so that the United States could concentrate on defeating Germany.

To enable the United States to concentrate its forces in the Atlantic against a possible war with Germany, White's initiative called for the U.S. Navy to be withdrawn from the Pacific. The United States would recognize Manchuria as part of the Japanese empire, sign a twenty-year nonaggression pact with Japan, and grant Japan a $3 billion loan. The American Immigration Act of 1917, limiting Japanese entry to the United States, would be repealed. America would abandon its extraterritorial rights in China as an example for Great Britain to do likewise; Britain would return Hong Kong to the Chinese. A joint $500 million stabilization fund would be set up. All of these provisions appeared to be generous offers to deter Japan from joining forces with Germany.[7]

White's initiative also called for the Japanese to lease to the American government for three years such naval vessels and aircraft as the United States would select, up to half the existing Japanese naval strength; grant the United States and China most-favored-nation treatment in the Japanese empire; and sign a ten-year nonaggression pact to include Britain, China, the Dutch East Indies, and the United States.

As for the Soviets, they would detach from their nonaggression pact with Germany. The Soviets would have the right to purchase $300 million worth of goods from the United States annually; the United States would admit 5,000 Soviet technicians and 50 military attachés, grant Moscow $500 million credit, conclude a five-year mutual economic assistance pact, and extend to the Soviet Union most-favored-nation treatment. The Soviets in turn would stop their external propaganda, embargo trade with Germany, admit 5,000 American technicians and 50 military attachés to the Soviet Union, and sell $200 million worth of commodities annually to the United States.[8]

However, it was the final quid pro quo that White suggested, which appeared to be a logical part of such a deal, that the Japanese could not swallow: White called upon the Japanese to withdraw their forces from China and Indochina while abandoning their extraterritorial rights in China.

White presented the memorandum to Secretary of the Treasury Henry Morgenthau, Jr. on June 6, 1941, little more than a month after he met with Pavlov.

White's proposals did not evoke an immediate bureaucratic response. Morgenthau was occupied with the preparedness program for war with Germany if the United States were drawn into the European conflict. The Treasury was not directly involved in negotiations with the Japanese. Two weeks later, the problem of detaching Japan from Germany took on new meaning with Hitler's invasion of the Soviet Union.[9]

Pavlov followed Fitin's instruction to forget Operation Snow, until, according to Pavlov, "my reminiscences were stirred by Americans, but this happened only recently" (meaning 1991).[10]

Pavlov said he was referring to the memoir of New York congressman Hamilton Fish, who claimed that Harry Dexter White was a communist and an agent of Soviet intelligence. "On my part, as the participant in Operation Snow, I categorically state that White was never enlisted as an agent by Soviet intelligence," said Pavlov.[11]

Pavlov asserted forcefully that it would have been a mistake to try to recruit White as a controlled agent of the Soviet Union. It was unnecessary, he added, since White was surrounded with agents: Nathan Silvermaster, Victor Perlo, and two others in the Treasury Department, who reported on White's thinking and provided copies to their communist underground control officers of White's memoranda to Morgenthau. White knew his activities were being reported to Moscow; he was a willing source for contents of the internal discussions and decisions that involved policymaking at the Treasury Department. White also reported on interdepartmental discussions with the State Department. Pavlov's reference to Akhmerov's friendship with White confirms that White was in direct contact with a senior Soviet intelligence officer. Pavlov's reference to White's contact with Joseph Katz, a KGB liaison agent (X), further identifies White as a Soviet intelligence asset.

★ ★ ★

When Pavlov returned to Moscow, he became caught up in the effort to repel the German blitzkrieg. The mixture of nationalities and races that had been forced into the new Union of Soviet Socialist Republics was not yet absorbed and loyal to Moscow. Stalin was still combating guerrilla operations for independence in the western Ukraine; he had an uneasy border with Finland. Stalin knew he could not count on the loyalty of minority nationalities in the Caucasus, and he forcibly relocated the Chechens and Volga Germans inland to keep them from abetting the German invasion.

The German invasion was a shock but it was not totally unexpected. The buildup of German forces on the Soviet border and German reconnaissance flights over Soviet territory in the last weeks of May and early June had generated new fears of war. Stalin was determined not to provide Hitler a pretext to invade. On June 14, a month after a conversation between German Ambassador Schulenberg and Soviet Ambassador Dekanozov assuring each other there would be no war between Germany and the Soviet Union, TASS, the Soviet news agency, signaled to Hitler with its celebrated statement that the Soviet government saw a steady balance in the relationship between Moscow and Berlin. In spite of the buildup, the Germans made no claims nor issued any ultimatums to the Soviet Union, thus seeming to Stalin to preclude an outbreak of hostilities. Little did the Soviet leadership understand that they were taking their cue from the wrong mentors: Schulenberg, supported by Ribbentrop, opposed a war, but they were in a minority.

On June 5, only weeks after the Japanese signed their neutrality pact with Stalin, General Hiroshi Oshima, the Japanese ambassador in Berlin, reported to the Emperor and the high command that Hitler was ready to invade the Soviet Union. The Japanese response was the immediate drafting by the Army General Staff of a plan for opening a war against the Soviet Union while simultaneously advancing south in French Indochina. At the same time, the Army Ministry's Military Affairs Bureau prepared its own plan, which proposed postponing the attack on the Soviet Union "until the time ripens."[12] The disagreements over how to assess and respond to a German-Soviet war led to a major strategic review.

On June 22, when Hitler trashed his agreement with Stalin and attacked the Soviet Union, a hypothetical question became an urgent reality. Within ten days, the Japanese focused their military aspirations southward. On June 23, at a meeting of its top leadership, the Japanese Navy Ministry and the Navy General Staff approved a plan to move into the military bases and airfields in the southern part of French Indochina even if it meant "risking war with Britain and the United States." The Japanese navy's thinking was that war with the United States was probably inevitable but might be prevented by taking "an extremely hard line" toward the United States and Great Britain. By acting tough against American threats, war might be avoided.[13] To complete the takeover of China and Southeast Asia, which was the source of increasing hostility between the United States and Japan, Japanese navy officers believed they must first neutralize the threat of intervention by the American Pacific fleet based at Pearl Harbor.[14]

The German invasion of the Soviet Union offered the Japanese the opportunity to strike north and destroy Soviet power throughout eastern Siberia as far as Lake Baikal. The argument whether to move north or south was not resolved between the army and navy ministries and general staffs until Prince Fumimaro Konoe, the prime minister, convened an imperial conference on July 2. The document that emerged, "Outline of the Empire's National Policies in View of the Changing Situation," approved by the emperor, laid the groundwork for war with the Soviet Union, Britain, and the United States. The overall framework called for establishing the Greater East Asia Co-Prosperity Sphere, expediting the stalemated China war, and advancing south "to establish a solid base for the nation's self-existence and self-defense." The attack on the Soviet Union would depend on changes in the situation, but "preparations for war with Great Britain and the United States will be made . . . our empire will not be deterred by the possibility of being involved in a war with Great Britain and the United States."[15]

For the moment, the decision to go to war with the Soviet Union was put on hold awaiting advantageous developments growing out of Hitler's attack. At the same time, the military leadership approved secret preparations for a future attack against the Soviet Union. They also ordered troop mobilizations; during July and the first week of August, 700,000 to 800,000 Japanese troops massed in northern Manchukuo to be ready by early September to attack if the Germans succeeded in quickly destroying Soviet resistance in the west. On July 30, Emperor Hirohito suggested to Army General Sugiyama that he halt the buildup in Manchukuo because it was probably preventing the Soviet Far Eastern Army from redeploying to fight in the west. By August 9, the emperor canceled for 1941 the "planned" invasion of the Soviet Union.

Historian Herbert Bix explained Hirohito's reasoning:

No thought was given to aiding his ally Hitler. At this time the emperor did not desire a full scale war with either the Soviet Union or the United States; but if war had to be, he was more inclined to risk it southward into the Anglo-American sphere of interest than fight the Russians; and if the Soviet Far Eastern Army departed westbound, in relative terms Japan's war-power in the North would immediately improve.[16]

NKVD documents reveal that the Soviets, through Stennes, obtained copies of cables from Chiang Kai-shek (code name, SEGAC) to Lauchlin Currie. On July 2, Chiang cabled Currie:

Generalissimo just received following reliable information. Japan has already decided in near future to abrogate Soviet neutrality pact. Afterwards she will declare war on Russia.

Stop. Japan now is only hoping that in this affair America will maintain neutral attitude in which case she would take immediate action to attack Russia. Please inform President.

SEGAC[17]

On July 5, after the imperial conference in Tokyo, Chiang again cabled Currie to advise that, since July 2, "Situation has again changed."[18] Chiang requested a meeting for his ambassador in Washington, T. V. Soong, to meet with President Roosevelt. Another message to Currie, dated July 8, 1941, reported:

The Government has secured definite information that the recent Japanese Imperial Conference made the decision to move southward against Singapore and the Dutch East Indies first before coping with the Siberian problem. In accordance with this information all departments of the Government have received instructions from the Generalissimo to take immediate measures to meet this action.[19]

Although Stalin had these cables, he still remained suspicious. He had been flooded with information on the date of the German invasion and chose to ignore the warnings, believing that they were inspired by the British. Stalin believed that his old enemy Churchill had set out to draw Russia into the war after the fall of France and the threat of a German invasion of England.[20]

In July 1941, Roosevelt and Morgenthau entrusted both Lauchlin Currie and White to work out measures to deal with the threat of Japanese expansion in Southeast Asia. They were the hands who proposed an economic blockade of Japan, aggravating Japanese-American relations and leading directly to war.[21] The date of the embargo, July 26, 1941, was a month plus a few days after Hitler's attack on the Soviet Union, in the midst of Stalin's frenzy to divert Japanese aggression away from the Soviet Union.

The clash that led to the embargo began with the imperial conference in Tokyo on July 2 in the presence of the emperor. It was the last debate over whether the Japanese would attack north or south. The secret decision was to mobilize southward. The Japanese cabled their ambassador to the French regime at Vichy that they would push into southern Indochina on July 24, but a day before the deadline the French allowed the Japanese to take over without a fight. The arrogance of the Japanese so angered Secretary of State Cordell Hull that he urged Roosevelt to take action, even though the U.S. Navy planning division warned that a new embargo would lead to war throughout Malaya and the Dutch East Indies, drawing the United States into its net. American ambassador to Tokyo Joseph Grew shared the same view as the Navy. With help from Treasury, and the agreement of Secretary of War Henry Stimson, Roosevelt went ahead with the fatal embargo on July 26, freezing Japanese overseas assets and its vital supply of oil.

Oil supply had been at the center of conflict between Japan and Soviet Russia, and between the United States and Japan, since the 1918 Russian Civil War. The Allied Expeditionary Force put Japanese and American troops into Siberia in 1918 but the Americans withdrew first, leaving Japanese troops on the mainland. Lenin first established the Far Eastern Siberian Republic, ending ambiguity to claims for the disputed territory, then granted oil rights in Japanese-held areas to American developers. He was following his policy of encouraging conflict between "imperialist powers," believing that Japan and the United States would come to blows over Siberian oil rights. When the Japanese had been pushed out, he incorporated the Siberian Republic into the Soviet Union. The United States had expressed its opposition to the Japanese invasion of China and Indochina in 1939 and 1940, first by abrogating the long-standing Treaty of Commerce and Navigation, then banning the export of iron ore, steel, and scrap metals to Japan. With the second Japanese attack on Indochina, the United States imposed the oil embargo of July 1941, to which the interested partners—America, Britain, China, and the Dutch East Indies (later Indonesia)—all agreed. The embargo was unofficially known as the "ABCD encirclement of Japan."[22]

The Japanese leadership was torn by the oil crisis that resulted from the embargo. Military and government leaders held an anguished meeting on November 1, 1941. Their choice was between pushing farther south to overtake the Dutch oil fields or to negotiate with the ABCD powers. The Japanese Foreign Minister, Shigenori Togo, wanted to sue for a peaceful solution, but the military remained hawkish. War Minister General Hideki Tojo argued before the Konoe cabinet for a "sink-or-swim plunge" to fight on. The Konoe cabinet was forced to resign, replaced by Tojo as prime minister.[23]

NKVD documents and Sorge's confession reveal that the Soviet leadership was closely monitoring the embargo and its effect on U.S.-Japanese relations. Moscow Center had a play-by-play of the worsening crisis from three agent networks: in the United States, in Japan, and in China. In addition, they were able to eavesdrop on and decode diplomatic cable traffic between Tokyo and Berlin by breaking the Japanese code.[24]

During this time period, Harry Dexter White's career was moving upward. Appreciation of White's initiatives, which looked upon the Soviet Union as America's partner in defense against Germany, gave him high standing with Morgenthau. Because of a lack of action from the War Department and the Department of State, much of the thinking that prepared for war with Germany or tried to avoid war with Japan fell to Morgenthau and his research department. On August 5, 1941, fewer than two weeks after the oil embargo, White was promoted to be an Assistant Secretary of the Treasury. He was also to continue as Director of Monetary Research.[25]

American sympathies were with the Chinese. Since April 1939, the idea of a triangular trade deal among the Soviet Union, China, and the United States had been presented to President Roosevelt as a means for supporting China's struggle against Japan. The deal called for the Soviet Union to sell strategic materials such as chromium ore, mercury, and asbestos to the United States while delivering their value in armaments to the Chinese through Central Asia. White, in a special study for Morgenthau, urged approval of the deal, which was valued at $200 million, but it never became a reality because of strained Soviet-American relations. When the Soviet Union had invaded the Baltic states in October 1939, the United States had frozen Soviet assets in American banks.[26]

During the 1930s and 1940s, the Treasury Department was active in supporting Chinese opposition to the Japanese invasion. The support took such forms as buying up China's excess supply of silver, which allowed the Chinese to use American currency to purchase arms. American economic interests in keeping China's Open Door policy in effect were the driving force for Treasury policy as Japan and the United States clashed over trade. With trade issues in the ascendancy, diplomacy coming from the State Department was often heavily influenced by economic policy formulated by Morgenthau and his intellectual brain trust headed by Harry Dexter White.

Because many of the elements of conflict between the United States and Japan were economically motivated, President Roosevelt and his top aides assigned to the Treasury preparation of position papers and shaping of policy. Here the Soviets were more powerful than in the Department of State because their trusted source, Harry Dexter White, was surrounded by Soviet-controlled agents. White, whose family name was originally Weiss, was of Lithuanian origin, and the NKVD in Moscow kept a dossier on family members in the Baltic states, which had been annexed by the Soviet Union in 1940. But the NKVD did not have to twist White's arm with threats to make him deliver actions that would favor the Soviet Union. White did not have to take the initiative in suggesting measures for American policy toward Japan.[27] He was instructed by Morgenthau to draw up ideas for dealing with the growing crisis. Formulating negotiating positions with which to approach Japan, he included recommendations that were in the Soviet interest.

The connection between Chinese aid, Treasury policy, and the Soviet impact on influencing this policy emerged clearly with the opening of VENONA. The intercepted cables expose Harry Dexter White as a long-time Soviet intelligence source who revealed American intentions on policy matters and served as an agent of influence for the Soviet Union. Support for Chinese opposition to Japanese aggression fit hand in glove with the Soviet policy of keeping Japanese troops under pressure in China and away from Soviet borders.

The new light shed by VENONA on White's actions and motives draws us back to his writings in the formative period of 1940–1941 when he was pointing out that, although Stalin had a pact with Hitler and was friendly to Japan, the Soviet Union was different from Germany in that it had no designs for expansion. Therefore White looked to creating a "parallel line of action with Russia," which meant arms and aid for China coupled with a stronger stand against Japanese aggression, including a trade embargo on crude oil and scrap metals. His recommendations became Morgenthau's policy initiatives forwarded to President Roosevelt.[28] These ideas did not spring from White unaided. The Soviet ambassador to Washington, Konstantin Umansky (code name, EDITOR) had promoted a pro-Soviet line of action in informal discussions with Under-Secretary of State Sumner Welles and Morgenthau in 1940.[29]

The VENONA releases corroborate accusations against Harry Dexter White made by former Soviet agents Whittaker Chambers and Elizabeth Bentley in 1945 and 1948. White's handwriting was matched in documents brought before the

House Un-American Activities Committee, which Chambers turned over to the Justice Department on November 17, 1948. However, there remained the question of whether White's handwritten papers were delivered by him or by a Soviet agent working next to him who volunteered the information on his behalf. Bentley made it clear that White and the Silvermaster group, a communist cell in the Department of the Treasury, were engaged in "ideological espionage" as early as the mid 1930s.

★ ★ ★

Since the 1930s, the United States was a target of Soviet propaganda and industrial espionage. The NKVD, forerunner of the KGB, was a secret police apparatus that had a threefold mission on American soil. The NKVD operated through three "lines" of spying, as discussed below.

However, the construct by which they operated appears to have been the same: to surround a star source, usually a top policy maker, scientist, or political insider, with a ring of satellite figures who did the actual spying and handing over of material to their Soviet handlers. There were two kinds of stars. The first group willingly allowed the rings of satellites around them—Communist Party members and recruited agents under Moscow control—to transmit the innermost delibera-tions of the American government to Moscow. The stars included Assistant Secre-tary of the Treasury Harry Dexter White, State Department Director of the Office of Special Political Affairs Alger Hiss, White House assistant to the President Lauchlin Currie, and top scientists in the Manhattan Project organized to build the first atomic bomb. Another group of stars were unaware they were being exploited by satellite agents. They included Eleanor Roosevelt and FDR himself.

From VENONA and interviews with Soviet intelligence officers, it is apparent that Soviet intelligence used the system of stars and satellites to organize their American assets. Their priority was to gain access to influential public servants, policy makers, and scientists to be sources of information; these were star personali-ties, famous in their spheres of expertise, whom they would not attempt to recruit as formal agents, but whom they would exploit to influence American policy. Around the stars was a ring of satellites, most often American Communist Party members, who were recruited agents and couriers under control of professional Soviet intelligence officers. The NKVD officers were in occasional contact with the stars, reaffirming their friendship and, when possible, providing gifts or money. From the satellites around the stars, they received a constant stream of information on policy initiatives and the thinking that supported presidential decisions.

Harry Dexter White, Assistant Secretary of the Treasury and later a founder of the International Monetary Fund, was a star source because he was the intellectual mainspring for Treasury Secretary Henry Morgenthau, Jr. Among New Deal technocrats, Morgenthau himself was considered to be "not too bright."[30]

With a star like White, Soviet intelligence worked to create an ambiance of mutual understanding and to develop common interests. Their purpose was to orient his thinking to the policies and needs of the Soviet Union. Under the guise of supporting peace and improving U.S.-Soviet relations, Soviet intelligence manipulated White to introduce Soviet goals into Treasury Department initiatives presented to President Roosevelt by his trusted friend, Morgenthau. On those occasions in which he did the most harm to American interests, White's policy initiatives appeared to reflect idealism and avoidance of war, but in fact he was being used by Soviet intelligence to support the Soviet policy of averting Japanese invasion of Siberia. His cooperation led to results that were the opposite of his best intentions. He did not foresee that providing covert support for Soviet intelligence, which resulted in the United States demanding a troop withdrawal from China and imposing an oil embargo against Japan, would translate into a taunt for the Japanese to attack American naval forces at Pearl Harbor and not the Red Army in Siberia. Further damage occurred in 1944 when White insisted on providing printing plates to the Soviet Union for unlimited quantities of Occupation currency. This favor to the Soviet Union contributed to the Berlin Crisis of 1948.

In her testimony, Elizabeth Bentley lumped together sources and agents, pointing her finger at Harry Dexter White with the same force as toward Silvermaster, a dedicated Communist who ran the group, but who had no influence on policy. In fact, his cell was not subject to normal party discipline and the names of its members were known to most of the group, thus violating a basic rule of tradecraft, or *konspiratsia*, that members should be known only to the leader, and not each other, to preserve security.

Regarding the Soviet's threefold spying mission in America, Aleksandr Feklisov in Moscow, who had been Julius Rosenberg's handler in the early 1940s, shed some light. He explained that there were two "lines" of intelligence: one for gathering technical research and one for influencing policy, which did not interact with each other (he did not speak of the third line because, as of this writing, it is still officially secret).[31]

First was the scientific line, mandated to gather industrial secrets. By the 1940s, through Julius Rosenberg and his connections to Joel Barr and Alfred Sarant, the Soviets stole the early designs for radar and the proximity fuse used in antiaircraft shells. The scientific line was the center of Soviet espionage from 1942 to 1946, while the Manhattan Project was developing the atomic bomb. The Soviet leadership was at first dubious that such an energy source could work. Once convinced, however, they knew that if they did not develop their own atomic bomb, they would be a second-rate power behind American world leadership after the war against Germany and Japan had been won.

The second line was political, to enlist ideologically sympathetic bureaucrats and high level public servants to work for Soviet interests. The political line worked to and from Moscow, reporting the innermost deliberations of the federal government, and giving instructions to attempt to influence American policy decisions. The NKVD and the GRU, the intelligence arm of the Red Army and Navy, had officers in Soviet diplomatic missions, in buying agencies such as Amtorg, and undercover "illegals" with false identities who pretended to be private citizens. Their job was to befriend high level sources and their deputies; they then became the conduits through which messages were passed back and forth from Moscow.

The third line, the one that is still officially secret, is listed in Russian intelligence files as "Operation Corridor."[32] Its task was to try to control émigrés who had left behind their homes in the Soviet Union, using both blackmail and persuasion to make them work for the country of their birth. For this line, the Soviets used cultural exchanges and sent their most accomplished artists abroad to spread the word that the Soviet Union was composed of educated and accomplished intellectuals, not wild-eyed revolutionaries. At first their purpose was to achieve diplomatic recognition for the new nation born of revolution; the United States officially recognized the USSR in 1933. Later the émigrés were enlisted or forced to help in technological espionage and to influence high level government decisions. Their propaganda mission was to convince educated Americans that communism was the vanguard of political and economic organization and that the Soviet Union should be the model for all idealists. The combination of Operation Corridor and the suffering brought about by the Great Depression was successful in influencing a large number of American intellectuals that the Soviet Union was the model society to which the United States should aspire. They were convinced that a world communist revolution would bring jobs for all workers and equal sharing of the fruit of their labors.

Washington was fertile ground for planting Soviet spies during the late 1930s and 1940s. The best young minds came to the nation's capital to take part in the New Deal. They hoped to contribute to lifting the country and the world out of its crippling economic depression with deficit spending and government work programs. It was a feverish time of introducing new ideas in economic management and developing technologies. Out of this turmoil came heavy spending on research for war and the development of radar, proximity fuse munitions, the atomic bomb, and the first computers. A significant number in the intellectual community were Marxists or socialists of various stripes. They believed that the experiments in government organization taking place in the Soviet Union would bring answers to the questions of how to restructure the future in a model of economic stability with protection for every citizen.

The Silvermaster group melted into this intellectual elite, a small group of communists and idealists who believed they were saving the working men and women of the world by serving the Soviet Union. The group operated in the inner circles of the executive branch, all under the control of a Soviet intelligence officer based in New York. In the 1930s, the GRU controlled Harry Dexter White through its illegal *rezident* in New York, Boris Bykov, a crude, redheaded GRU officer with fifteen years of underground operating experience in Europe. Bykov spoke little English and communicated in German with a Yiddish accent to his courier, Whittaker Chambers, the link to White in Washington.[33] The Treasury Department cell relied on White to provide information and to initiate policies that would accomplish Soviet goals. All were aimed at protecting the Soviet Union from a Japanese invasion, even if it meant Japan going to war with the United States. Bykov was recalled during the purges, and control of White shifted to the NKVD. In 1942 Iskhak Akhmerov, a.k.a. Bill Greinke, chief of the NKVD illegals in America, was in charge of the Washington agents and sources, aided by a younger assistant, Norman Borodin. Akhmerov had ten agents at the top levels of the executive branch, scattered through cabinet departments.[34]

Borodin's role was to handle this elite group of sources. It was no accident that he was picked for this job. Norman Borodin's father, Michael, was political adviser to Sun Yat-sen and Chiang Kai-shek in the 1920s, during the period of civil war when communists and nationalists were joining ranks and then destroying each other. Michael Borodin was nicknamed "The Father of Red China."[35] Norman Borodin, born in America but steeped in his father's experiences, had the sophistication and cunning to accompany the master of illegals, Akhmerov, in his American assignment. Young Borodin could add vital details to the questions posed to high American sources because he understood not only intelligence tradecraft, but the nuances of the competition between the United States and the Soviet Union in their embrace of China.

Feeding information and advice to White from the Soviets, and reporting back the recommendations White was giving Morgenthau to their Soviet handlers, was a ring of controlled agents who worked with White on a daily basis. Contact between White and Akhmerov's group was carried out by Nathan Gregory Silvermaster, who worked in the Treasury Department under White. Elizabeth Bentley was the courier between Silvermaster and Soviet intelligence in New York.

Silvermaster emigrated to America from Odessa in 1914 and was an active communist on the west coast. He served as a courier for Earl Browder, the head of the American Communist Party, during a general strike in 1934 in San Francisco. It was through Browder that Silvermaster was introduced to the east coast NKVD intelligence network.[36]

Another star in the Silvermaster group was Lauchlin Currie, an outstanding economist, whom Morgenthau persuaded to leave Harvard and come to Washington, first as senior analyst at Treasury and later assistant director of research and statistics for the Federal Reserve Board. A 1932 memorandum written jointly by White and Currie, with a third economist, indicates that the two men had worked together at Harvard.[37]

★ ★ ★

Sorge was arrested in Tokyo on October 18, 1941, after the Japanese had definitely decided to expand into Southeast Asia. For the Soviet Union, the decision meant that Japan had become more deeply committed to expansion southward, relieving Siberia of its being the chief target of Japanese expansion. Stalin, however, was not convinced.

Sorge's services to Soviet military intelligence might have remained an untold story if the policy of silence of both the Soviets and the Japanese had prevailed. In October 1945, when the American occupation authorities negated the Peace Preservation Law after the war, the release of 500 Japanese political prisoners included eight of Sorge's espionage ring who were still alive. An excited Japanese official brought attention to this group, which included foreigners held by the Japanese, especially Max Klausen, Sorge's radio operator. When Klausen realized he was under surveillance, he managed to disappear into Soviet hands. In the course of the investigation of the vanquished Japanese government, court records of Sorge's arrest gradually came together. Only the briefest mention had been released to the Japanese press in May 1942.[38] A top secret document published by the Japanese Ministry of Justice contained Sorge's slowly and thoughtfully written confession composed before he and Ozaki were hanged in Sugamo Prison on November 7, 1944. Major General Charles A. Willoughby, General Douglas MacArthur's chief of intelligence from 1941 to 1951, received the material and reported its contents to Washington. When Willoughby's report reached Washington, the story was released to the press and then retracted, because a confederate of Sorge who was implicated in the report, the journalist Agnes Smedley, threatened to sue for libel. Following the lead from the confession, Willoughby's military intelligence sleuths found the Japanese court records of Sorge's trial and traced his activities back through the records of the Shanghai Municipal Police.[39]

Whether Japan would join Germany against England and America or against the Soviet Union was the focus of Sorge's mission in Japan, especially after the outbreak of the Russo-German war in June 1941. The large scale Japanese mobilization in the summer following the German invasion of the Soviet Union "gave us some cause for anxiety, but it gradually became apparent that it was by no means directed primarily against the Soviet Union," Sorge wrote in his confession.[40] Now Sorge could focus on "the decisive crisis in American-Japanese relations. In December the crisis finally resulted in war," but by that time Sorge was in Sugamo Prison. Without spelling out the "particular mission" of his espionage group, he does assert "our intense desire to accomplish it." He was able to work on this mission until he was arrested in October, and he considered it unfortunate that he was deprived of the opportunity to complete it.[41]

Conventional historical wisdom credits Sorge with warning Stalin about Hitler's imminent invasion in June 1941. However, Sorge's most important activity, on which history should make its judgment, was how his mission tied in to White's influence on American policy toward China and Japan. The similarities between the Silvermaster group around White and Currie in Washington and the Sorge-Ozaki cell in Tokyo are striking. Both were working in mid-1941 to avert a Japanese invasion of the Soviet Union. Both groups originated in Comintern networks and perceived themselves to be working for the world communist revolution. The Comintern was regarded by communist sympathizers as the international bulwark against fascism in Germany, Japan, and Italy. Communists who worked for the Comintern often did not realize that they were actually being used as spies for the Soviet government.

Ozaki Hotsumi in Japan, a fully controlled agent of Richard Sorge, was never formally recruited as an agent by Soviet military intelligence (GRU), to whom Sorge reported. Ozaki was an idealist in the same mold as White and Currie, all believing they could influence events and transform their own countries. Ozaki sincerely believed that his historical mission was to overthrow Japanese fascism in the name of communism. His published articles often proved prescient in warning the Japanese leadership against future defeats on the mainland, which gave him a reputation for integrity and unusual insight. He hoped that social justice in Japan would follow from integrating the wealth of natural resources of Southeast Asia with Japan's leadership under the banner of communism. Ozaki did not include in this projection a war with the United States or Britain. Neither Ozaki nor White were aware of the implications of their recommendations, which from the viewpoint of the Japanese leadership, required the destruction of American naval power to achieve their higher goals. In the final diplomatic notes that led to war from both the American and Japanese sides were fragments of their recommendations, mixed with harsher demands.

Neither White, manipulated by Soviet handlers, nor Ozaki, controlled by Sorge, used his influence to provoke. On the contrary, their suggestions appear at first glance to be yearning for peace and compromise. However, a careful examination of what they were really asking Japan and the United States to cede for the sake of compromise reveals how their influence actually helped bring about the war. The "compromise proposals" that emerged sounded like—and were treated as—ultimatums.

The only side that achieved its goals in these Far Eastern deliberations was the Soviet Union, which clearly understood the implications of these unsophisticated proposals. The Soviets were successful because they had created the combined impact of two highly placed men, White and Ozaki, who were operating independently but simultaneously to exert their influence on policymaking decisions in the

United States and Japan. These men never realized that they were acting primarily in the interests of the Soviet Union. In retrospect, it is clear that neither White and Currie nor Sorge and Ozaki could have provoked the war acting alone; only this fatal combination could have brought about four years of bitter and deadly conflict, and turned the course of world history. Japan's attack on Pearl Harbor in the long run not only led to the unconditional surrender of the Axis powers, but also brought about the first and only use of the atomic bomb in the history of war.

Germany's attack on the Soviet Union and Japan's against the Americans at Pearl Harbor occurred six months apart and bore a resemblance to each other. In both cases, the previous months' prelude to war saw steadily growing tensions that came to a head when the Soviet Union and the United States misread signals about their enemies' intentions. In both cases, Stalin and Roosevelt appealed for reasonableness, for negotiations to overcome the problems that the attackers felt were putting them in danger, but in both cases, Roosevelt and Stalin and their bureaucrats were unable to stem the flood of events. What began as catastrophes creating indelible national memories of suffering for the Soviet Union and America ended in the defeat of the aggressors and a permanent realignment of world power. Both the Soviet Union, which before World War II had been a supplicant state seeking diplomatic recognition, and the United States, which had acted as a junior partner to Great Britain, became world powers.

The only crucial difference between Roosevelt and Stalin was that Stalin had agents influencing the highest levels of the Japanese and American governments. In this prewar period, the United States lacked a central intelligence capability. Americans had little in the way of covert operations to gather and reveal enemy secrets. The U.S. Army and Navy had intelligence from their overseas attachés, who had small budgets to pay recruited informers; the State Department provided analysis, but did not evaluate and present their reports in unison with an authoritative voice. They did not coordinate their efforts and therefore the reports did not reach the desk of the president or his assistants in usable form. "If intelligence had been available in that form before Pearl Harbor, it might have eliminated the disaster that occurred," said Admiral Sidney W. Souers, first director of the Central Intelligence Agency, in a postwar interview.[42]

The responsible officials whose actions led to military conflict in the Pacific— in the United States, Britain, and Japan—were unaware that the USSR knew in advance what was behind their diplomatic maneuvers. They didn't know that Moscow had highly placed, reliable sources in Tokyo, Washington, Chungking, and London.

If we look at 1941 in the light of Pavlov's visit to Harry Dexter White, Zarubin's trip to China, and Sorge's activities in Tokyo, a phenomenon unique to the history of intelligence operations emerges—the ability of Stalin's intelligence operatives to manipulate Japan's hunger for power away from the Soviet Union and against the United States. From diplomatic correspondence, materials obtained from confidential sources, and memoirs of intelligence officers who participated, a picture emerges of how Soviet espionage agents influenced the American approach to negotiations with Japan in the perilous summer that preceded Pearl Harbor.

★ ★ ★

In Washington, in the spring of 1941, there appeared to be clear evidence that Japan was planning to attack the Soviet Union from the east if and when the Red Army was heavily engaged from the west.

Events overtook expectations. Soon after Pavlov set out on his mission, all calculations were upset by Germany's surprise attack on the Soviet Union. Stalin's juggling efforts to avoid attack from Germany had ended in failure. After June 22, the survival of the Soviet Union depended on averting simultaneous war on two fronts. Both diplomatic and clandestine efforts to sharpen the Japanese-American confrontation in the Pacific acquired top-level priority.

After Hitler's attack, the United States became a vital supporter of the Soviet Union. Soviet Ambassador Umansky immediately appeared at the State Department asking the American government to halt possible Japanese aggression against the Soviet Union. In general terms, the Americans assured him that diplomatic efforts would work in this direction. Umansky reported to Moscow that the State Department was attempting to conceal the sharpening of American-Japanese relations and the intensification of the struggle between them for hegemony in the western Pacific. Umansky also noted that the American authorities wanted to know what the Soviet position would be in case of conflict between the United States and Japan.[43]

On July 3, the Soviet *rezident* in New York, LUKA (Pavel Pastelniak) reported to Moscow, and his message was forwarded to the NKVD leadership:

NKVD Top Secret
First Directorate
3 July 1941
#9/41-47-30 Special Report
Addresses:
Beria
Merkulov
Kabulov

According to the data from the *agentura* [foreign intelligence network], from the circles of the American government, Japan intends to annul its pact of neutrality with the USSR and undertake an attack on the Soviet Union. Sources 29 and RICHARD [Harry Dexter White] are confident in the reliability of this information.

LUKA [Pastelniak, *rezident* in New York] referring to the verification of these sources reports the following about the possible position of the U.S. government in case Japan attacks the Soviet Union.

If Japan undertakes a blockade or a direct attack the American government alongside with its policy of rendering assistance to the USSR by means of supplies would immediately sever all sorts of economic ties with Japan such as supplies of raw materials, equipment, petrochemical products and planned financial transactions.

Signed Deputy Director of First Directorate NKGB [Maksim] Melnikov [Fitin's deputy][44]

On July 30, LUKA reported that, from Chinese sources available to the White House, the attack on the USSR was highly likely in the coming two months. At the same time, LUKA reported that there was disagreement among Japanese leaders concerning a firm policy course against the Soviet Union. The Japanese, he reported, were waiting for the outcome of the battle for Moscow before they took sides.

In July, August, and September, NKVD reports from Tokyo to Moscow, coming from an alternative ring to Sorge's, indicated there would be no Japanese attack against Siberia. These reports included interceptions by the Soviet intelligence service of coded messages between the Italian embassy in Tokyo and Rome.[45] Thus, Moscow had conflicting reports. Diplomatic channels judged that an attack was hardly likely and the Japanese were heading southward. On August 5 and 13, the Soviet ambassador in Tokyo, Jacob Malik, and the Japanese foreign minister confirmed, on behalf of their governments, adherence to their neutrality pact. Both sides stated, however, that the pact did not contradict their obligations to their own allies.[46] This confusing statement left open a number of variants: nobody knew who would side with whom in the event of war in the Pacific, or if Japan would attack the Soviet Union in the event that Hitler decisively defeated the Soviets on Stalin's western flank. On August 1, 1941, the NKVD intercepted instructions from the British Ministry of Foreign Affairs to the British ambassador in Tokyo that, in the case of a Japanese attack on the Soviet Union, Britain "would not automatically sever relations with Japan because the current agreement with the U.S.S.R. is specifically limited by joint actions against Hitler Germany and we have no formal agreements to sever relations with Japan in case it invades the U.S.S.R."[47] Even though Hitler's attack on the Soviet Union had made clear that Britain, the United States, and the Soviet Union stood together against the German menace to world stability, they had not yet sorted out their relationship to Japan.

The American *rezidentura* continued to receive orders from Moscow to create pressure on their American contacts to threaten the Japanese with sanctions. In November, LUKA reported to Moscow that their instructions were being carried out; his agents ROBERT (Silvermaster) and RICHARD (White) were "actively participating" in recommendations to Roosevelt "to prevent and impede Japan acting against the Soviet Union."

White was intensively dedicated, as part of his official duties, to monitoring events in the Far East. His amended proposal for Japanese-American compromise, which he had put forth in May, was presented to Morgenthau; after November 5 the Japanese made up their mind to attack the U.S. if by November 25 there was no diplomatic solution to the imminent conflict of interests in the Pacific. White submitted his memorandum on Japanese-American relations on November 17, 1941. His proposal was titled, "An Approach to the Problem of Eliminating Tension With Japan and Insuring Defeat of Germany." White's biographer, David Rees, called White's memorandum "a recasting of the introduction to his memorandum on a Pacific settlement of May, 1941."[48] White had returned to his earlier "all-out" effort to use diplomacy and military compromise. These terms, which offered peace and economic benefits in return for withdrawal of military aggression, were later offered by Secretary of State Hull and sounded like an ultimatum. The main argument inherent in White's memorandum, which soon drew support from the State Department, was prevention of a sellout of China to Japan, like Czechoslovakia was sold out to Hitler at Munich in 1938.

On November 20, 1941, the Japanese presented their own plan for a peaceful settlement, which required acceptance of Japanese domination over China in exchange for Japanese withdrawal from Indochina and resumption of commercial relations across the Pacific. Secretary of State Cordell Hull found this offer unacceptable. On November 26 Hull presented the Japanese the famous ten-point proposal known as the Hull Note. It was a shortened version of White's memorandum and included a multilateral nonaggression pact in the Far East, encompassing Britain, China, the USSR, the United States, and Japan. The conditions were that Japan withdraw its military, naval, and police forces from China. The Japanese took the Hull Note to be an ultimatum, and rejected it.

On November 26, the same day that the Hull Note was presented to the Japanese, Foreign Minister Togo urgently summoned Boris Smetanin, the Soviet ambassador in Tokyo, to confirm Soviet adherence to the neutrality pact signed between Japan and the Soviet Union in April 1941. The audience lasted three hours and Smetanin assured Togo of the Soviet Union's intention to abide by the pact. The same day the Japanese task force received a combat order to be ready to move against Pearl Harbor.

The next day, November 27, 1941, the Japanese foreign ministry cabled their embassy in Berlin with a message for Hitler: "Japan is going ahead with the Japanese-American negotiations with a dauntless attitude knowing that there may be many difficulties in the future course of the negotiations. However, Japan is exercising every care to see that these negotiations do not in any way affect the validity of the Tripartite Pact." The Japanese had checked with both the Soviets and the Germans to make sure they had not changed their hands-off attitude toward an imminent Japanese military attack in the Pacific.

On November 30, another message went from Tokyo to Berlin:

> The conversations begun between Tokyo and Washington last April during the administration of the former cabinet, in spite of the sincere efforts of the Imperial Government, now stand ruptured—broken. In the face of this, our Empire faces a grave situation and must act with determination.[49]

Following this were instructions on exactly what to say when meeting with Hitler and Ribbentrop:

> Say to them that lately England and the United States have taken a provocative attitude; both of them say that they are planning to move military forces into various places in East Asia, and that we will inevitably have to counter by moving troops. Say very secretly to them that there is an extreme danger that war may suddenly break out between the Anglo-Saxon nations and Japan through some clash of arms and add that the time of the breaking out of this war may come quicker than anyone dreams.

Unfortunately, the intercept of this message was not translated until December 6, too late to be acted upon.

In the Russian Intelligence Archives is a similar cable intercepted by the Soviets, dated November 27 instead of November 30; it is unclear when they read it. Its coincidence with the Tokyo-Berlin message intercepted by the Americans is striking:

> The negotiations with the USA are deadlocked. The Japanese government faces the necessity of taking a serious decision—meet Hitler and Ribbentrop secretly and explain the situation to them. The shifts of military forces might lead to military conflict earlier than is expected ... in case of war with democratic states Japan will continue to contain the Russians in the Far East and if the Russians unite with the democratic states and attack us, Japan will resist these efforts in a decisive manner. Explain to Hitler, however, that the main Japanese efforts will be concentrated in the south and we plan not to be involved in any actions in the north.[50]

Even if the Soviets read the message in time to warn the United States, they had no intention of allowing the Americans such a breathing space.

On December 1 in Tokyo, Smetanin was once again summoned to the Ministry of Foreign Affairs where he affirmed the earlier Soviet stand expressed in August and two days before: that the Soviet government was abiding by the neutrality pact in the face of rising tensions in Southeast Asia, China, and the Pacific.[51] By that time, the Soviets had the decoded November 27 message from the Japanese Ministry of Foreign Affairs to the Japanese embassy in Berlin instructing the ambassador to assure the Germans that Japan would soon move against Britain and the United States in Asia and the Pacific.[52]

A recent Russian assessment of Pavlov's mission to Washington confirms that the wording of Pavlov's instructions from the NKVD was similar in content and wording to the memorandum White sent to Morgenthau in May of 1941, after his meeting with Pavlov.[53]

The Russian article, published in a professional military journal, answers the two central questions: First, did the Soviet Union help bring about war between Japan and the United States in 1941? And, second, is there any verification for Vitali Pavlov's story of "Operation Snow"?

On January 21, 2000, the *Independent Military Review*, published in Moscow, stated that "the war in the Pacific could have been avoided. Stalin managed to prevent an attack against the USSR from a second front in the Far East. . . . Stalin was the real initiator of the ultimatum to Japan" that provoked the Pacific War. The article was a commemoration of 120 years since Stalin's birth, published under the title "Notes from the Archive."[54]

The author of the startling article was Vladimir Karpov, former editor of *Novy Mir*, leading Soviet monthly journal of literary and political essays. Karpov is a retired colonel of the GRU, military intelligence, a "Hero of the Soviet Union," and a biographer of Marshal Zhukov. Karpov wrote with authority that, in October 1941,

Harry Dexter White was acting in accordance with a design initiated by Akhmerov and Pavlov. He prepared the *aide-memoire* for signature by Morgenthau and President Roosevelt. . . . [T]he essence of "Operation Snow" was to provoke the war between the Empire of the Rising Sun and the USA and to insure the security of the interests of the Soviet Union in the Far East. . . . If Japan was engaged in war against the USA it would have no resources to strike against the USSR. . . . Stalin made up his mind to provoke the war between the USA and Japan, but because he wanted to conceal the work of his agents in this immoral operation, he ordered the destruction of all the records. Harry D. White was not a recruited agent . . . he acted out of his convictions . . . like with other American citizens. . . . [H]e was never told . . . that he was implementing Stalin's and Beria's instructions . . . or that he was putting into practice . . . the strategic plan of the Soviet Commander in Chief [Stalin]. . . . The strategic genius of Stalin was manifested in . . . being aware of the bitter confrontation between the USA and Japan; he took advantage of this favorable situation . . . and got rid of the menace of war on two fronts, the war the Soviet Union could not sustain.[55]

Only when we look at Karpov's account, written from a Soviet point of view, does Stalin's fear of attack by Japan become rational. Only when we look at the whole picture of Stalin's geostrategic vulnerability do we understand that for him the signing of the 1939 Nazi-Soviet Pact of Non-Aggression with Hitler was a necessity. Only when we look at the dates during which the pact was being negotiated and see that during this very same period the future Marshal Zhukov was fighting off Japanese expansionists in Manchuria, do we come to the conclusion that to preserve his country from a two-front war, Stalin believed he had no choice but to sign the infamous document. Even while making these allowances for Stalin's actions, Karpov noted that Operation Snow was an "immoral operation."

★ ★ ★

In the spring and summer of 1941, the VENONA intercepts gathered dust and gave no insight into the machinations of diplomatic manipulators in Moscow who were directing their agents in Washington and Tokyo. It was only in 1995, when Vitali Pavlov published his first revelations on Operation Snow in the Russian monthly newspaper *News of Intelligence and Counterintelligence*, followed in 1996 by a book of the same name, did the code name "Operation Snow" come to have meaning for historians. Only with Pavlov's story of his inspection mission to Washington does the wily diplomacy that led Japan to Pearl Harbor come into focus. Only after reading his account did we go back to reread the already-known escapades of Richard Sorge and his confessions in a Japanese jail and put them together with Pavlov's lunch with White.

In our interview with Pavlov in October 1997, he was hesitant to give himself credit for having influenced any concrete events; he only recalled a pleasant meeting with White in which he conveyed the Soviet desire for peace in the Pacific. He recalled the list of proposals that the United States might offer Japan to wean it away from its alliance with Hitler. He convinced White that these proposals might draw Japan into constructive trade with the United States and the Soviet Union, disingenuously including the military pullback provisions that Japan would have to agree to in return, never indicating that he knew full well these proposals were provocative and impossible for the Japanese to accept. Certainly, the Japanese were not about to cede the territories they had already conquered in Manchuria and China. It had taken them a half century to get the land back they lost in the turn-of-the-century wars.

Only a few weeks after Pavlov's lunch with White, when the Germans attacked the Soviet Union on June 22, Pavlov's proposals became all the more critical. Japan's aggression had to be diverted south rather than northward toward Siberia. By this time Pavlov was back in Moscow, where the leadership working for Stalin waited with bated breath for the expected attack from the east. They could do no more. They had to wait out the diplomatic exchanges between Tokyo and Washington, wondering what the outcome would be. They knew which outcome was dangerous to them, which outcome would mean that Japanese aggression was moving southward and away from the Soviet Union. They fully understood that, for the Japanese leadership, the southward option meant war with the United States.

"And what did you feel back in Moscow when the Japanese attacked Pearl Harbor?" we asked now retired senior intelligence officer Lieutenant General Vitali Pavlov, who in the dreadful winter of 1941–1942 headed the American desk of the NKVD Intelligence Directorate.

"We sighed a deep sigh of relief," Pavlov answered.

3 The War Years

Four days after the Japanese attack on Pearl Harbor in the early morning hours of December 7, 1941, Hitler declared war on the United States. Hitler's colossal error brought the United States into the Anglo-Soviet alliance fighting Germany, ending Roosevelt's dilemma of how to join the fight against Hitler without declaring war. The world's balance of power changed and so did the role of Soviet intelligence in the United States.

Vasili Zarubin was a senior major of State Security, the equivalent of a Red Army major general, when he was called to the Kremlin to meet with Stalin early in October 1941 to discuss his new assignment as NKVD *rezident* for North and South America. Hitler's armies had reached the outskirts of Moscow, poised to attack the capital. Stalin feared that Japan would exploit the moment of Soviet weakness and attack from the east; his nightmare of a two-front war still haunted him. The United States was sending aid to Moscow to repel the German invasion, but was still not at war. America's commitment to fight Hitler would be decisive for the Soviet Union, Stalin told Zarubin. Stalin said he feared that Roosevelt was secretly preparing to sign a separate peace agreement with Hitler that would keep America out of the war; he told Zarubin that finding the truth of this rumor was now a top priority. Stalin ordered Zarubin to set up an effective intelligence network that could not only monitor what was being discussed inside the White House and government agencies, but also influence events through friends of the Soviet Union.

Zarubin and his wife Elizabeth, his senior assistant, sailed from Vladivostok for San Francisco on October 12, and arrived on December 6, 1941. There they were joined by the highly skilled spy, Katherine Harris (ADA in VENONA), whom they had requested to work with them. The Zarubin's first assignment was to reactivate an old network of "illegals," intelligence agents living quietly in California with assumed identities, without diplomatic immunity. Put in place in the early 1930s, these "sleepers" were to do nothing except go about their daily normal lives until called upon to sabotage shipping that carried war supplies from the United

States to Japan. The Soviet Union feared these cargoes would be used to support a Japanese invasion of Siberia.

Overnight, the surprise Japanese raid on Pearl Harbor put those fears to rest. Over the next year and a half, intelligence reports from Britain, Scandinavia, and Germany concerning the development of nuclear weapons drastically altered Zarubin's mission in America.[1]

★ ★ ★

On January 27, 1941, director of Foreign Intelligence Pavel Fitin (VICTOR in VENONA), in a special letter to Ovakimian, New York *rezident* (GENNADI in VENONA), instructed him to "look into the state of research on the problem of uranium in the United States, particularly at Columbia University and the University of Minnesota."[2] Fitin emphasized that the subject was of particular interest to Soviet scientists.

Having received the same instruction, the NKVD *rezident* in San Francisco, Gregory Kheifetz (KHARON in VENONA), had been cultivating atomic scientists at the Radiation Laboratory at the University of California. He warmly befriended Robert Oppenheimer, already known as a brilliant physicist at the University of California when they met on December 6, 1941, at a party to raise funds for Spanish Civil War refugees. The party was at the home of wealthy San Francisco hostess Louise Brantsen, an intimate friend of Kheifetz. The two men agreed to meet for lunch the next day. At this time, Oppenheimer was still a consultant to Arthur H. Compton, director of the Metallurgical Laboratory at the University of Chicago. He had not yet been recruited to direct the building of the first atomic bomb, nor was he yet subject to strict surveillance and the controls of military secrecy. Therefore, when Oppenheimer met Kheifetz,[3] he still had no formal obligation to reveal his communist connections to his employer or to keep secret what he learned about the atomic project from his scientific colleagues.

Kheifetz was under cover as the Soviet consul named Brown. He greeted the Zarubins when they arrived in San Francisco harbor and then enlisted them to lay the groundwork for atomic espionage. The extended spying apparatus they built in the United States succeeded in stealing the technology that built the first atomic bomb.

More than a year earlier, in 1940, Soviet scientists had heard rumors of a powerful new weapon being developed in the West; a state defense committee warned the government to instruct intelligence officers to be on the watch for news in scientific publications of an atomic bomb being created from uranium. Moscow Center's questions were based on information in the Shanghai newspaper *North China Daily News* published on June 26, 1940, summarizing the research being done at Columbia University. Stalin had ignored the scientists but responded to the alarm from intelligence operations through the NKVD to begin research on nuclear weapons. Moscow Center ordered Ovakimian to acquire information on the work under way at Columbia and the research being done at the University of Minnesota by Professor Alfred Otto Carl Nier.[4] The intelligence communication to Ovakimian stated that the problem was of interest to Soviet physicists, who had begun their own research into the nature of uranium. However, no Soviet government funds were allocated for research.

There was no sense of urgency until September 16, 1941, when Donald Maclean (code name LEAF), who was a member of the Cambridge ring of British spies working for the Soviet Union, sent a sixty-page report from London warning that the British government was supporting the development of a bomb with unbelievable destructive force using atomic energy. The project to build the bomb was called Tube Alloys, code-named TUBE, and would be carried out by Imperial Chemical Industries within two years.[5]

Three months later, Maclean's report was backed up by similar news from the United States after Kheifetz met Oppenheimer.

While Kheifetz and Oppenheimer talked over lunch, the wily *rezident* let Oppenheimer know that he had heard about an atomic weapons project but that Moscow was too slow in realizing its importance. Oppenheimer expressed a similar concern, that the Germans would succeed in building atomic weapons before the allies. Kheifetz reported to Moscow that Oppenheimer told him about a secret letter from Einstein to President Roosevelt in 1939 urging research on the possibility of creating nuclear weapons, and that the scientist's plea had not elicited an adequate answer. (The idea for the letter had come from Leo Szilard, a Hungarian-born émigré physicist, who drafted the text for Einstein to sign and support. The young scientist who acted as chauffeur to bring Szilard to the meeting to get Einstein to sign the letter was Edward Teller, who later led the development of the H-bomb.)[6]

Kheifetz also reported after their lunch that outstanding physicists gathered in Great Britain and the United States, including refugees in flight from Hitler's takeover of Europe, were working together on a secret project. Nobel Prize winners and scientific giants such as Albert Einstein would take part, Kheifetz reported. Kheifetz told Moscow Center that the American government would spend 20 percent of its defense budget on atomic research. Despite America's entry into the war[7] against Germany and Japan after Pearl Harbor, and Lend Lease support for the Soviet Union's defense against Hitler, Soviet scientists were not included in the secret plans.

In October 1941, Oppenheimer attended the Schenectady conference on the uranium problem as an unpaid ad hoc adviser. In December 1941, Oppenheimer submitted calculations to Compton on neutron fission efficiency; Compton's reply was to request his further calculations. Oppenheimer's involvement deepened in April 1942 when Compton offered him a position as a regular consultant, which required him to fill out a government personnel security questionnaire, dated April 28, 1942. That same year Moscow instructed him to stop paying dues to the American Communist Party.[8] His fame and elevation to head the Manhattan Project came rapidly after he joined Compton; before that, he was one of a number of consultants.

At their lunch and at another meeting between them, Kheifetz was able to sense the extent to which Oppenheimer was willing to trust him. Kheifetz learned that Katherine Oppenheimer, the physicist's wife, admired the Soviet Union and had been married to a communist who was killed fighting on the Republican side against Franco's forces in the Spanish Civil War. She still had numerous contacts among her first husband's communist friends. Oppenheimer's brother Frank was known to be a communist, and Robert Oppenheimer often contributed money to causes espoused by the American Communist Party.

In 1943 a world famous actor of the Moscow Yiddish State Art Theater, Solomon Mikhoels, and a well known Yiddish poet, Itzik Feffer, toured the United States. They represented the Soviet Jewish Anti-Fascist Committee, which was attempting to raise money for the Soviet Union and spreading the message that Stalin had ended anti-Semitism. Kheifetz made sure that Oppenheimer received the news brought by Mikhoels that Stalin was about to set up a Jewish autonomous republic in the Crimea. Kheifetz later reported that Oppenheimer, the son of German-Jewish immigrants, was deeply moved to know that Stalin had guaranteed a secure place for Jews in the Soviet Union when the war against Germany was won.[9]

From the first meeting between Kheifetz and Oppenheimer in December 1941, through the early months of 1942 while the Manhattan Project was being organized and Oppenheimer was preparing to move to Los Alamos, the American Communist Party underground and Soviet intelligence were enlisting Oppenheimer's cooperation to obtain atomic secrets. A letter from the Soviet Intelligence Archives documents Oppenheimer's "cooperation in access to research" from 1942 to 1944 and Moscow Center's concern over American Communist Party contacts with Oppenheimer:

2 October 4 [1944] Top Secret
1107/M Urgent
Copy # 2
People's Commissar For Internal Affairs of the USSR
General Commissar Of State Security
Comrade Beria, L.P.

In accordance with your instruction of 29 September 1944, NKGB USSR continues measures for obtaining more detailed information on the state of work on the problem of uranium and its development abroad.

In the period 1942–1943 important data on the start of work in the USA on this problem was received from our foreign agent network using the contacts of Comrade Zarubin and Kheifetz in their execution of important tasks in line with the executive committee of the Comintern.

In 1942 one of the leaders of scientific work on uranium in the USA, Professor R. Oppenheimer while being an unlisted [nglastny] member of the apparatus of Comrade Browder informed us about the beginning of work.

On the request of Comrade Kheifetz, confirmed by Comrade Browder, he provided cooperation in access to research for several of our tested sources including a relative of Comrade Browder.

Due to complications of the operational situation in the USA, dissolution of the Comintern and explanations of Comrades Zarubin and Kheifetz on the [Vasili Dimitrovich] Mironov affair it is expedient to immediately sever contacts of leaders and activists of the American Communist Party with scientists and specialists engaged in work on uranium.

NKGB requests the consent of the leadership [Instancia]

Peoples Commissar of State Security USSR

Commissar of State Security First Rank

Signed/[Vsevelod] Merkulov

Handwritten note by Beria Inform about the approval. 2 X 44 [October 2, 1944]

// signed Beria[10]

In May 1943, when the Comintern was disbanded, Communist underground activities did not stop. There was a direct relationship between the Communist Party of the United States and the CPUSSR (Communist Party-USSR) through the Soviet party's International Department. The same Georgi Dimitrov, who had been the head of the Comintern, directed the International Department.

Merkulov's letter indicates that information on atomic bomb research was at first received through an American Communist Party network that was in contact with sympathetic scientists. The rationale among scientists who cooperated with the Soviet Union was fear that the Germans would develop an atomic bomb before the Western allies. Therefore the United States and Great Britain should share the development process with the Soviet Union to ensure that Hitler did not get the bomb first. Others in the scientific community believed one country should not have the monopoly on such deadly knowledge.

Merkulov's letter also confirms the difficulties the NKVD faced because of FBI surveillance of Communist Party members. By asking Beria to have the American Communist underground sever contacts with their members engaged in the Manhattan Project, the NKVD was attempting to remove American Communist Party members from intelligence gathering and replace them with professional intelligence officers. In June 1943, one month after the Comintern was disbanded, Zarubin suggested severing contacts between Communist Party representatives and Oppenheimer.[11]

Another indication of the problems of gathering atomic secrets through the American Communist Party emerged from Allen Weinstein and Alexander Vassiliev's search of the KGB archives. A report to Merkulov in February 1944 lists Oppenheimer (code name, CHESTER) to be a secret member of the American Communist Party, and states that the Communist cell to which Oppenheimer had belonged prior to working on the Manhattan Project received instructions to cease relations with CHESTER to avoid compromising him. Contacts with Oppenheimer were to be maintained only through Soviet intelligence channels.[12] In 1944 American Communist Party networks remained sources of information for the NKVD and GRU military intelligence *rezidentura*. For example, Louise Brantsen traveled from San Francisco to New York to meet with MOLIERE, code name for Pavel Mikhailev, who was the GRU *rezident* in New York.

One result of Kheifetz's sounding the alarm about an American superweapon was that he received assistance from Zarubin as soon as he arrived in San Francisco. Zarubin put his wife, Elizabeth, a captain in the NKVD, and her protégée, Kitty Harris, to work on the newly initiated operation. After they settled in Washington, Zarubin dispatched Elizabeth on frequent trips to California, where Kheifetz introduced her to the Oppenheimer family. Elizabeth became friends with Katherine Oppenheimer, with whom she could actively espouse her communist ideals and discuss the need for Soviet American cooperation against Hitler. Through Katherine, Elizabeth Zarubin and Gregory Kheifetz convinced Oppenheimer to agree to hire "antifascists of German origin," a seemingly small success that paved the way for bringing the physicist Klaus Fuchs, a leading spy for the Soviet Union, from England to work at Los Alamos.[13] They also placed young communist scientists in each of the three major labs, in Tennessee, Los Alamos, and Chicago, who provided couriers with secret documents about the development of atomic weapons from uranium.[14]

Moscow entrusted atomic espionage to only the most experienced and sophisticated intelligence officers, because they had to operate at the highest level of the world scientific community. A recent memoir by Zarubin's daughter Zoya demonstrates that the top ranks of Soviet intelligence officers thought of themselves as the cream of Soviet society who were bringing about the downfall of capitalism and the triumph of the communist world revolution. These secret heroes of communism included the Zarubins and the Eitingons, whose relationship to each other overcame their marital histories (Eitingon convinced Zarubin's first wife to get a divorce and marry him), and they stayed close to the end. Sudoplatov was the mid-level boss in Lubyanka, giving orders to Vasili, Leonid, Elizabeth (Zoya's stepmother), and their brethren in the field.[15] Zoya bemoans the irony of history that it was Sudoplatov who lived to tell the story of Soviet atomic espionage to the world, not the "romantic adventurers" who risked their lives doing his bidding.

They "did the job for Stalin"; at the height of their activities, "they had 29 agents in the Manhattan Project," many of whom have still not been identified.[16] In total, Sudoplatov's Department S channeled 659 scientific reports to Beria, his deputies, and the scientists working to build a Soviet bomb. Sudoplatov included one of his cover letters—dated August 28, 1946, #22/s/289, handing over 33 scientific reports on American research in nuclear energy, with drawings, to the deputy chief administrator of the Soviet atomic project in charge of secrecy—in the Russian edition of his memoirs, published after his death in 1996.[17] For Stalin, the acquisition of atomic secrets was crucial to the Soviet Union maintaining the "correlation of forces" in the postwar balance of power with the United States, and allowing the Soviet Union to maintain its leadership of the world communist revolution.

Zarubin's ablest lieutenant was Elizabeth. Her code name, VARDO,[18] appears in VENONA on numerous occasions. At one time VARDO was called upon to meet with and become a friend of Eleanor Roosevelt.[19] There was no follow up to record the results of the effort. Elizabeth, formerly Lisa Gorskaya, began her intelligence career as a junior case officer working under Felix Dzerzhinsky, head of the CHEKA.[20] There she met and became close to Yakov Blumkin, who had assassinated the German ambassador to Moscow, Count Mirbach, in 1918. Blumkin first opposed Lenin, then joined him, working for Dzerzhinsky and Trotsky. In 1930 the romantically involved couple were assigned to Turkey, posing as rare book dealers with prized Hasidic manuscripts to sell from the Central Library in Moscow. The proceeds were supposed to be used for illegal intelligence operations in Turkey and the Middle East, but by this time Trotsky was exiled to Turkey and Blumkin secretly gave some of the money to his former mentor. Lisa knew about the funneled funds and was outraged. She was a loyal Bolshevik who came from a revolutionary family related to Anna Pauker, founder of the Romanian Communist Party, and had an older brother who was killed carrying out terrorist activities for the communists. Lisa contacted two senior intelligence officers, Leonid Eitingon and Peter Zubov, who were on a mission to Turkey, and they had Blumkin recalled to Moscow on a Soviet ship. He was immediately arrested and later executed by a firing squad.

Vasili Zarubin, whose first wife had earlier left him to marry Eitingon, was assigned to work with Elizabeth. Vasili and Elizabeth traveled together for seven years pretending to be a Czechoslovakian business couple. They became a legendary spying team, credited with recruiting the only high level Gestapo officer to work for the Soviets, Willy Lehmann (code names: BREITMANN and DIKE). They married and had a son. Vasili's daughter by his first marriage, Zoya, said that his relationship to Elizabeth, originally arranged by the NKVD, became a mutually caring union.

During the years of travel together in the 1930s, the Zarubins visited the United States a number of times, using forged American passports. They roamed the country unnoticed by the American authorities. Among other missions, they were part of Operation Corridor, efforts to recruit defectors and émigrés from republics of the Soviet Union for spying operations in the United States.

Vasili was stocky, with red hair and a gruff, self-assured manner. He was a heavy drinker who issued orders and demanded results. He contrasted sharply with his refined, elegant wife who spoke French, English, German, and Russian. She was a smooth, urbane operator, a familiar face in American communist underground circles under the cover name Helen. Agents referred to her as "a very intelligent, very responsible comrade," clearly of a high rank in the NKVD hierarchy. The 1930s were the time of the Great Purges when foreign intelligence officers and agents were ordered back to Moscow for vetting, to make sure they were loyal and were not in contact with Trotsky. Despite their willingness to travel to Moscow for discussions, most who returned were shot or disappeared without trace. Elizabeth Zarubin received orders to bring two wavering agents, a married couple, back to Moscow. The visit was to persuade them to keep their faith in communism despite the recent assassination in Switzerland of their close friend, Ignace Reiss; he had refused to come to Moscow, and Elizabeth described him as a traitor.

The wife of the pair, Hede Massing, described Elizabeth in her memoirs:

The first thing one noticed about Helen were her strange, beautiful eyes—large, and dark, heavy-browed, with long, curled eyelashes . . . [her] small, delicate features. She had an authoritative air about her without being annoying or aggressive. Her English was flawless as was her German. She carried herself like an emissary of a great country, but she was ready and willing to talk and understand the problems of smaller people. She was too clever to be patronizing.[21]

Hede described Helen's ability to make Hede angry with her unbendable Marxism, and her talent in bringing little gifts to make up.

The Massings were supposed to pay a brief visit to Moscow but they were detained there more than seven months. By refusing to use forged passports and making it known that Hede was an American citizen with connections to other Americans who knew she was in Moscow, the Massings avoided being sent to a prison camp or disappearing. Finally they were allowed to return to the United States, where Hede later became a volunteer source of information for the FBI.

One of the purposes of the Zarubins' visits to America was to battle the influence of Leon Trotsky after he settled near Mexico City. In his memoirs, the stage and movie producer Boris Morros tells the story of a small-time theatrical agent who offered him Trotsky as a stage attraction in 1933. At the time, Morros was booking vaudeville acts for two Paramount theaters, one in Brooklyn and one on Broadway.

Morros, who had listened to his communist friends argue the virtues of Trotsky versus Stalin, didn't think that audiences looking for family entertainment would take an interest in Trotsky "fulminating against Stalin and his other persecutors in the Kremlin," but he didn't give a clear-cut answer. A short time later, he received a visit from a commercial representative from Amtorg, the Soviet trading organization in New York, who wrote down the names of Morros's relatives in Russia. He mentioned, to Morros's amazement, that it was a pity his brothers were in such bad repute with the government. Gradually, the Amtorg man got around to saying he heard Morros was going to book Trotsky on stage.

Morros suddenly got the message. The stage could provide Trotsky a priceless forum, attended by ordinary Americans, to argue that he was the real leader of the world communist revolution, not the power-hungry Stalin.

Morros promised to keep Trotsky off the stage as long as he was in charge of bookings. The Amtorg representative said he and Morros could be very useful to each other. Thus began a relationship that would have repercussions for the next two decades. Paramount promoted him to become general music director of their Hollywood studio in October 1935, where he nurtured the careers of Frank Loesser, Hoagy Carmichael, Ginger Rogers, Bing Crosby, and a long list of other stars. He worked on the first color feature and about fifty movies a year.

In the midst of this busy schedule, he received a visit from a man calling himself Edward Herbert, who had been sent by the New York Soviet vice-consul. Herbert was a redhead, "a thick-set man with powerful shoulders," who had a heavy Russian accent but spoke English, French, and German. Herbert told Morros, "Keeping Trotsky off the stage of your Broadway theater is something we'll always be grateful for." The tone of the messages he received from his Soviet contacts turned from appreciative to abusive and controlling. Soon Herbert showed up again and declared that he was really Vasili Mikhailovich Zubilin, now with the Soviet embassy. He was now better dressed and more self-assured. Soon Zubilin (Zarubin) was aggressively running Morros like an agent, telling him with whom to be seen. He boasted to Morros that he was head of the NKVD in America and could do anything he pleased, like getting Morros's father out of the Soviet Union.

On one occasion, the two men met in Washington where Morros was introduced to Elizabeth, who, he concluded, was present to pass judgment on him. Later he heard her described as a communist Joan of Arc whose words and judgment were taken as law. Morros's communist colleague acknowledged her to be the brains behind Vasili.

Morros describes how, frightened by Zarubin, he went to the FBI and offered to become a double agent. The truth of the matter was that the FBI was listening in on a call between Zarubin and Steve Nelson, an American Communist Party organizer, when they realized Zarubin's importance. The next call from Zarubin was to his old friend in Los Angeles, Boris Morros, to tell him he would visit in the next few days. After their meeting, the FBI moved in on Morros, offering him the chance to cooperate with them or face investigation of his relationship with Zarubin. Thus began Morros's ten years as a counterspy.[22]

Elizabeth coordinated her atomic espionage efforts with Lev Vasilevsky in Mexico City and Kitty Harris in Santa Fe, New Mexico; she also worked with Semyon (Sam) Semyonov in New York and physicist Bruno Pontecorvo, Enrico Fermi's protégé.

Kheifetz first met Pontecorvo in Italy in the 1930s and recommended that Pontecorvo contact Frederic Joliot-Curie, the French physicist who was close to the leadership of the French Communist Party. Joliot-Curie arranged a fellowship in Paris for Pontecorvo in 1936 when Mussolini began to persecute Italian Jews. The handsome, gregarious Pontecorvo met his petite Swedish wife,[23] Marianne Nordblom, in Paris and their first son was born there. When the Nazi troops neared Paris in June 1940, Pontecorvo fled to the South of France by bicycle, sending his wife and 2-year-old son ahead by train. They crossed the border into Spain, then Portugal, and from there sailed to New York, arriving on August 20, 1940, two days before Pontecorvo's 27th birthday.

Pontecorvo's first job in the United States was as a scientific researcher for Wells Survey, Inc., in Tulsa, Oklahoma, which did radiographic oil well logging. In the fall of 1942, Pontecorvo received an offer, which he promptly accepted, to join the group of British nuclear physicists arriving in the United States to take part in the Anglo-American atomic team. He worked briefly in New York and moved to Montreal where he concentrated on experiments for setting up the Canadian heavy water atomic pile at the Chalk River plant new Petawawa, Ontario. The Pontecorvos moved to Chalk River in 1944, and he made important nuclear contributions there. Two more sons were born in Canada. From 1943 to 1949, Pontecorvo traveled regularly to scientific gatherings in Canada and the United States. He was a conduit for giving atomic information to the Soviets through Lev Vasilevsky, who used the cover name Tarasov when he traveled to meet Pontecorvo from his base in Mexico City.[24] Pontecorvo remained in Canada both as a nuclear scientist and Soviet agent until 1949 when he transferred to the nuclear physics division of the British atomic energy center at Harwell, a notch higher in rank and pay than his colleague, Klaus Fuchs. Although they became acquainted, they were not particularly close friends.[25] KGB officers acquainted with the case told KGB defector Oleg Gordievsky that they rated Pontecorvo's work as an atomic spy almost as highly as that of Fuchs.[26]

After Fuchs's confession in March 1950, suspicion turned to Pontecorvo, but no smoking gun emerged. Pontecorvo had been granted British citizenship in absentia in 1949 for his contributions to atomic research during the war. After

Fuchs's trial, Pontecorvo volunteered to British intelligence that one of his brothers was a communist. In the summer of 1950, he resigned his post at Harwell and appeared happy to start a new job at the University of Liverpool. On August 22 he met with his brother and sister-in-law, which changed his carefree mood, and nine days later he began his move to the Soviet Union. Moscow Center had decided to evacuate Pontecorvo and his family.[27]

At the end of August 1950, Pontecorvo took his wife and three sons on vacation in Europe and disappeared after arriving in Helsinki. They were met at the airport by a car from the Soviet Legation and driven to the harbor where the ship *Bellostov*, which had waited six hours past its scheduled time of departure, weighed anchor as soon as the Pontecorvo family was on board.[28]

British intelligence later reported that Pontecorvo's wife was a communist, and indicated that she played a role in his espionage activities. Fermi's wife, Laura, later wrote that they met Bruno's wife only once in the years they were friends of "The Cub" (their nickname for Pontecorvo). She was painfully shy, Mrs. Fermi wrote: "She thawed one moment only, when after dinner she watched me load my automatic dishwasher. . . . In Stockholm [during their flight behind the Iron Curtain] the Pontecorvos had not visited Marianne's parents, whose home was fifteen minutes by streetcar from the station; nor had the parents been called on the telephone."[29] They had faithfully followed espionage tradecraft. Their defection to the Soviet Union was not revealed until Pontecorvo appeared at a press conference in 1956 to announce that he preferred "the free air of the Soviet Union." He never admitted his espionage efforts. He received two Orders of Lenin and other honors for his scientific work.[30]

★ ★ ★

Following orders from Moscow in 1942, Elizabeth Zarubin and Kheifetz persuaded Oppenheimer to break all his open contacts with the Communist Party. He was not to pay dues, contribute money, or support left wing causes.

Elizabeth used a trusted source, a refugee from Poland, to establish contact with Leo Szilard, the famed émigré physicist who had been one of the first to suggest to President Roosevelt that the United States begin research on an atomic weapon. Elizabeth sent Szilard a message: his cousin Karl was working in a secret Soviet laboratory, from which he hoped to return to Hungary when it was liberated from the Germans. It was a veiled threat to his cousin's freedom. Once the contact with Szilard was made, Elizabeth used it to exploit the idea of sharing nuclear secrets with the international scientific community. Szilard strongly promoted this idea, for which he drew the ire of General Leslie Groves, director of the Manhattan Project. Groves kept Szilard from working at Los Alamos on the atomic bomb.[31]

Kheifetz's report activated another Soviet intelligence officer in the United

States, Sam Semyonov, who received instructions from Zarubin relaying a message from Moscow Center sent March 27, 1942: he was to enlist agents and friendly sources among the technicians and scientists who would soon work on the research that became known as the Manhattan Project. Semyonov had been sent to study at MIT, where he had developed friendly relationships with budding scientists. Semyonov, whose code name in VENONA was TWAIN (after Mark Twain), was able to establish close contact with the Metallurgical Laboratory in Chicago, run by Enrico Fermi.

Semyonov also became the case officer for Julius and Ethel Rosenberg, who provided the Soviets plans for the latest military technology and were couriers in atomic espionage. There had been a separate line for scientific intelligence gathering since the late 1930s run by Julius Rosenberg, which included Alfred Sarant, operating out of Fort Monmouth, New Jersey, and Joel Barr at General Electric in Schenectady, New York. These men supplied information on early radar technology, proximity fuses, and the latest signals communications equipment. Semyonov was also the case officer for Harry Gold, the courier who received atomic secrets from the most active spy at Los Alamos, Klaus Fuchs. In addition, one of Semyonov's paid agents passed him the design drawing of the B-25 bomber, which was adapted and renamed in the Soviet Union.[32]

In late December 1942, Semyonov transmitted a report on the world's first nuclear chain reaction; Fermi accomplished this on December 2, 1942, at the Metallurgical Laboratory at the University of Chicago. A few hours after the pile of graphite went critical, Semyonov received a call with the message, "The Italian sailor reached the new world." Historians know that the speaker of those words was Arthur Compton, who was running the Met Lab where the experiments were conducted. How could he have given that signal to a Soviet spy? The answer comes from Semyonov's son, in Moscow, who said his father had an ongoing friendship with the Comptons since his MIT days. Semyonov's mentor there was Arthur's brother, Karl T. Compton.[33] Arthur Compton had no idea his words would reach a Soviet intelligence officer.[34]

On January 13, 1943, Moscow Center reported to the Soviet government a general description of the uranium pile put into experimental operation by Fermi. The report went to Mikhail Pervukhin, deputy prime minister in charge of science and the chemical industry, and to Igor Kurchatov, head physicist of the Soviet atomic project.[35]

Couriers gathered atomic information from Los Alamos and transmitted it through the New York and Washington *rezidenturas* and through a drug store in Santa Fe, which had long been used as a safe house for illegals. The drugstore safe house, originally purchased as a support center for the Trotsky assassination in 1940, was run by Kitty Harris. She served as a courier for atomic secrets and coordinator for the drugstore's clandestine activities. Harris carried documents gathered at the drugstore to the *rezidentura* in Mexico City, from where they were sent to Moscow.

Harris was the daughter of impoverished Soviet émigrés who came first to London, where she was born, and then to Canada when she was 8 years old. Her father, a shoemaker, could not support the family on his earnings, so Kitty worked in a tobacco factory from the age of 13, where she became a trade union activist. There she experienced violent strikes and labor confrontations; the Soviet Union became the symbol of her aspirations. She moved to the United States and became a member of the American Communist Party, where she met Earl Browder. Because of her dark brown eyes she was thought to resemble the heroine in the opera *Carmen*, from which she acquired her first code name, GYPSY. A later code name for Kitty Harris, AIDA, also came from an opera.[36]

In 1928–1929 she traveled with Browder to Shanghai where they lived together as husband and wife. Kitty became a clandestine courier for the Pacific Trade Union Center. She was constantly in danger, transferring money, documents, and party literature to Hong Kong, Batavia (Indonesia), and Manila. In 1929 Kitty returned to New York and in 1931 Leonid Eitingon recruited her for intelligence work. From Germany she crossed the borders of European countries dozens of times on risky courier operations. In Prague she met with G-91 (identity unknown) who was under close surveillance. The same tails followed her in the street and on trolley cars. Kitty ducked into a German bakery and complained to the baker that she was being followed and blackmailed by criminals. The baker led her to the back door of the shop where she fled. Later in Strasbourg, crossing from Germany to the French border, a border guard examined her passport and saw her birthplace listed as Chicago, Indiana. "Madame, I wonder whether Chicago is in the state of Indiana. According to my knowledge, Chicago is in the state of Illinois." Kitty replied, "The big Chicago is in Illinois, but the small city of Chicago is in the state of Indiana." The officer pointed to her customs declaration where she correctly had filled in Chicago, Illinois, as her birthplace. The officer returned her passport and said, "Madame, take back your bogus passport and return it to those who sold it to you. Let them also return your money to you." Kitty flushed with embarrassment, grabbed her passport, and left the train. But her assignment to meet a courier in Strasbourg was urgent. The next day she crossed the border by bus. This time the customs inspector was poor in geography and she reached her contact on time.[37] She traveled to Denmark, Sweden, France, and Czechoslovakia, and was a courier for the Wollweber organization, which committed anti-Nazi sabotage.[38]

In 1933 she began to work closely with a source of scientific information, code-named INHERITANCE, the manager of the industrial firm BMAG. Kitty received from him the formulas to produce chemical fertilizers and for the hydrogenation of fats. INHERITANCE worked for money; she paid him 35,000 Deutsch marks, a considerable sum at the time. Following the NKVD wish list, Kitty obtained data on the production of gunpowder and drawings for machinery to make synthetic coal and gasoline. The take was highly regarded by the General Staff of the Red Army.

Elizabeth Zarubina trained Kitty Harris in the use of forged passports, ciphers, and how to hide papers and money in her underwear. In the spring of 1934, the two women met for coffee in a small Berlin cafe. They quietly spoke German and no one paid attention to them. If they had been overheard the listener would have been surprised. Elizabeth was instructing Kitty by recounting an episode from her own experience:

When we worked in Paris, the mail from Moscow Center addressed to us was sent through the legal *rezidentura* in Vienna since my illegal chief was busy at that time. I was instructed to pick up an important envelope in Austria. Naturally, I did not know the contents of the envelope. I arrived in Vienna and met with the courier in a cafe. He gave me a thick illustrated magazine and told me the envelope was wrapped inside a newspaper in the magazine. We parted quickly and I returned to my hotel, opened the magazine and unwrapped the newspaper. The envelope turned out to be very big and sealed with consular stamps. It was too bulky to be carried in my handbag. How to carry it? I couldn't fold it in half because it was too thick and I couldn't leave it in my suit case. I was afraid of customs inspection. My problem was to cross three frontiers before reaching Paris, where I was based. I decided to open the envelope and put its contents into my handbag and into my underwear. So I opened it and found it contained two forged passports, one with my photograph in another name and nationality. There was a large sum of money in dollars and British pounds. The most interesting thing was a cipher notebook with several pages for ciphering and deciphering in the Russian language. I could not return the envelope so I destroyed it with all the stamps and seals and divided the material between my hand bag and inside my underwear.[39]

In 1934 Moscow Center recalled Kitty for training in radio communications and photography; she was to be tutored by Willy Fisher, a.k.a. Rudolf Abel. However, although Kitty spoke four languages fluently, she found radio communications difficult. She weathered the purges of 1937 and 1938 in Moscow, despite the turmoil in the NKVD. The London illegal *rezidentura*, which handled the Cambridge Five, was destroyed when Theodor Maly was purged and Arnold Deutsch was recalled. For nearly six months, Donald Maclean, who had joined the Foreign Office in 1935, was without a controller to contact. In the spring of 1938, responsibility for the Cambridge Five was turned over to the new NKVD legal *rezident* in London, Grigori Grafpen.

In April 1938, Kitty moved to London to provide courier service for Maclean. To avoid suspicion and provide a cover for frequent meetings, Kitty rented a flat in Bayswater, north of Hyde Park. Thus Maclean's visits to the lonely, attractive woman did not arouse any suspicion. Donald carried Foreign Office documents to the flat where Kitty photographed them. Then she turned the film over to the *rezident*, Grafpen.

When Maclean could not obtain documents, he dictated summaries of messages and memoranda from his photographic memory. Kitty wrote out the texts and passed them on for transfer to Moscow via diplomatic pouch. Maclean was so prolific in providing high-quality material that the NKVD set up a separate operation for him. Donald (LYRIC) and Kitty (NORMA) were to pose as lovers, but they soon consummated their meetings in a long love affair, first frowned upon by Moscow Center and then reluctantly accepted.[40] Their birthdays were one day apart, and on May 25, 1938, Maclean brought her roses and a pendant on a gold chain. When Maclean received a Foreign Office assignment to France, Kitty received an NKVD order to follow him.

The intelligence capabilities of Maclean, who was the second secretary of the British embassy in Paris, were considerably less than when he was in the center of the Foreign Office in London. In Paris, a mistake by a case officer of the Soviet *rezidentura* caused Kitty to miss a planned contact with Maclean in early September 1939. At Moscow Center, Kitty's failure to appear at the prearranged meeting was interpreted as her opposition to the 1939 Hitler-Stalin Pact signed only a few weeks earlier in August. However, Kitty, on her own initiative, appeared at the embassy and met Lev Vasilevsky, under cover as consul general. She assured him that she missed the meeting because of misunderstandings with the case officer, who had poor knowledge of French, and that she was still on the job working with Maclean. By 1940 the materials received from Maclean totaled 44 boxes, each of which contained 300 pages of documents.

Kitty was shocked when, on June 10, 1940, Donald Maclean married Melinda Marley, an attractive American student at the Sorbonne with whom he was having an affair. Kitty was upset but covered for Maclean by describing his behavior to their superiors as "boyish lightmindedness" and explained that, although Maclean had confessed to Melinda that he was in the spy business, he had not revealed Kitty's code name and "as before still works with us sincerely and with enthusiasm."[41] Maclean's marriage coincided with the German invasion of northern France. He fled with Melinda to England on a British torpedo boat. Kitty had to flee Paris and settle in Bordeaux, where the Vichy government was in charge. From there Vasilevsky arranged for her return to Paris. She stayed in a secluded room in the embassy until she could travel to Moscow. In the autumn of 1940, using bogus documents that made her the wife of a Soviet diplomat, Kitty traveled with the Soviet writer Ilya Ehrenberg, who described her in his memoirs as the strange wife of a Soviet diplomat who preferred to practice her French with him, avoiding speaking Russian.

After the German invasion of the Soviet Union, the NKVD decided to send Kitty Harris to the United States. She was selected for the mission by Vasili and Elizabeth Zarubin, who preferred to rely on people who were known to them or had previously worked for them. She proceeded to San Francisco ahead of the Zarubins and registered at a hotel as Eleanor Drevs.[42]

Kitty remained in the United States using false documents for a year. Spending so much time in the United States was a high risk because she had been publicly named twice in 1939 as a Soviet intelligence agent, once before the House Un-American Activities Committee[43] and the second time by Walter Krivitsky in October 1939 in his book, *In Stalin's Secret Service*.[44]

One of the case officers that was recommended to me was the American woman named Kitty Harris. Previously she was Katherine Harrison. She was introduced to me as the former wife of Earl Browder, the leader of the American Communist Party, and therefore quite reliable. At that time I urgently needed a woman agent to work in Switzerland. It was very good that she had an American passport. . . . She was in her forties with black hair with a good appearance. She had been closely connected with our intelligence service for many years. Kitty Harris appreciated the work of Browder and especially his sister who was an officer in our intelligence service in Central Europe. I endorsed her appointment for a foreign mission and as far as I know she left Moscow on April 29 (1937).[45]

In early January 1943, she moved to Mexico City. Kitty Harris used seventeen different names and code names because of frequent national border crossings and because of defections during her service in Soviet intelligence. In VENONA she is ADA and AIDA; in another reference, in 1938 when she received a passport in Toronto with the help of Jacob Golos, she is NORMA.[46] Her code names had to be changed when her case officers were purged. So many changes of name confused even such a professional as Kitty: in her file she is blamed for revealing her real name in moments of intimacy with Maclean, who gave their affair away by using one of her code names he was not supposed to know in a message to Soviet intelligence.[47]

When Kitty arrived in San Francisco, her first mentor was Kheifetz. He received his instructions from Zarubin, chief *rezident* for all of North and South America, including Canada and Mexico. His deputies were Vitali Pavlov (of Operation Snow) for Canada, who frequently came to Washington during the war; Pavel Pastelniak for New York, Lev Vasilevsky in Mexico, and Iosif Grigulevich, code-named

ARTHUR, for South America. In Washington, Vasili Dimitrovich Mironov, whose code name was probably MARKOV, the second secretary of the embassy, was one of Zarubin's deputies. All of Zarubin's deputies were to play memorable roles in the coming drama.

Elizabeth went ahead with her mission to find and reactivate the illegals, now to be used for a new assignment: attaining atomic secrets. Kitty Harris was put in charge of finding the two old illegal assets in California, one a dentist, the other a retail businessman, who had been in place since the early 1930s. The contacts with them had been severed in 1938 following the purge and imprisonment of Yakov Serebryansky, code-named YACOB, who was chief of the administration that ran illegals from 1934 to 1938. Another case officer[48] failed to find the two illegals in 1939 or 1940 during trips to the west coast. However, in 1941 Moscow Center learned that these agents, Jewish immigrants from prewar Poland, were close to the procommunist Oppenheimer family. Now it was Kitty's assignment to find the two because of their access to Oppenheimer's personal circle. They could be useful in the coming efforts to learn the secrets of atomic research. In October 1941, Serebryansky was released from prison; the war with Hitler led to the rehabilitation of officers who survived the purges in jail.

Serebryansky was the institutional memory for the illegals. His operational diary, confiscated when he was arrested in 1938, contained his notes on who was placed where. Leonid Eitingon, who had worked on placing the California illegals, was stationed in Turkey in December 1941–1942, of no use to the problem in California. From Moscow Center, Serebryansky supervised the search. After he briefed Kitty by cable, she quickly found the shop owner but had problems reestablishing contact with the dentist. The San Francisco telephone directory listed three dentists, all with the same first and family names. She made an appointment with the first listing, and asked for three false gold teeth on the right side of her mouth. The dentist opened her mouth and looked at her quizzically, "Miss, you don't need any false teeth." The second dentist made a pass at her and invited her to dinner, which she declined. The third dentist at first looked at her in confusion and appeared frightened, then answered with the prearranged reply, "You need false teeth not on the right side but on the left side."[49] This agent, code-named CHESS PLAYER, had received funds from the NKVD while he earned his medical degree in France before he emigrated to America in the 1930s.

CHESS PLAYER and his wife were friends of the Oppenheimers and introduced Elizabeth to them. They were active assets in Elizabeth's assignment to set up a ring of satellite agents around Robert Oppenheimer. The ring transferred America's developing atomic secrets to Moscow. Neither Elizabeth nor Oppenheimer handled the secret documents; for them it was a "no dirty hands" operation that avoided evidence of spying and limited the risk of being caught, jailed, or expelled.

In early 1943, Kitty arrived in Mexico City where Vasilevsky was the *rezident*.

It was about the time Oppenheimer was moving to Los Alamos, in March 1943. Vasilevsky, who had arranged Kitty's escape from France, also knew her brother, who fought in the International Brigade in Spain. Kitty was to serve as the *rezident-ura's* chief courier, a job that grew in importance because Vasilevsky's task was to maintain access to scientists working in the Manhattan Project. The burden on Vasilevksy was heavy; Kitty became his intimate assistant.

Under cover as a diplomat, Vasilevsky gathered atomic secrets in the southwest and from illegals in California. On a trip to Washington, he found the Soviet code clerk in a drunken stupor, after which he avoided the east coast embassy and sent everything through Mexico City. This is a partial explanation for why so little atomic espionage information appears in VENONA: to protect the security of atomic bomb material, Soviet intelligence arranged for some of it to be handled by a separate courier channel that operated through Mexico City, Santa Fe, and the Soviet consulate in San Francisco. The Mexico-based courier line operated out of a drug store on the Plaza in Santa Fe and was run with illegals who do not appear in the decoded VENONA traffic from Mexico City. Manhattan Project atomic secrets passed to couriers such as Harry Gold and Lona Cohen were handled by the *rezidentura* in New York City.

★ ★ ★

The Battle of Stalingrad began to turn against the Germans in mid-October 1942. After encircling the Germans and taking 90,000 men prisoner, the Red Army began a massive counteroffensive from Leningrad to the Caucasus in February 1943. Occupied Europe began to sense the weakening of Nazi military power. It was just about this time that Russian prisoners of war working for the Germans found bones dug up by a wolf in the Katyn Forest, near a dacha that the Germans had commandeered to use as a regimental headquarters since late summer 1941. Without realizing it, the POWs had come upon the site of a horrendous massacre that had taken place a year earlier and were walking among the mass graves of the victims. Villagers knew that thousands of Polish officers had been unloaded from freight cars two years earlier, so there had long been rumors in the area.[50]

The Germans first reported the graves to headquarters on March 1, then there was total silence for six weeks. By April 10 exploratory digging began to reveal mass graves, and the German high command began preparations for a propaganda blitz. They saw a golden opportunity to split the Allies. They brought a delegation of Poles from Warsaw to view the evidence. Radio Berlin broke the story on April 13, 1943. For four days there was stunned silence, followed by stories in the *New York Times* and the *London Times*. For three years the Russians had pretended they knew nothing about the fate of thousands of missing Polish officers. On April 15 they hit back with an angry attack on the German account, blaming the deaths on the German conquerors. The Polish press in London began demanding an explanation from the Soviets. Both the Poles and the Germans requested the International Red Cross in Geneva to investigate, which put pressure on the Soviets to subject the graves to scientific scrutiny that would determine how long the bodies had been buried. This would verify who was in control of the area at the time of the executions.

On April 19 *Pravda* lashed out at "Hitlerite lackeys. . . . Those Poles who . . . take up and support Hitlerite falsehood . . . will go down in history as the helpmates of Cannibal Hitler. . . . " The next day the *New York Times* headline declared, "*Pravda* Sees Poles as Duped by Nazis."

The Polish government in exile now stood accused of joining the Germans in a propaganda campaign against a major ally. The result was a breakdown in relations between the London Poles and the Soviet Union. Stalin immediately set out to create an alternative group to represent free Poland, supporting a communist party within Poland who merged with Polish communists returning from the Soviet Union. They displaced the London Poles and completed the sovietization of Poland, ready to welcome the Red Army's takeover in the fall of 1944.[51]

For the next half century, the confusion over who had committed the massacre at Katyn remained. Then in 1992, Russian President Boris Yeltsin, in what appeared to be an act of good will toward the Poles but also intended to discredit Gorbachev for not publishing the truth sooner, released the official document in which Lavrenti Beria, then head of the NKVD, requested permission to eliminate the Polish "counter-revolutionaries" captured in the 1939 attack on eastern Poland. The document recorded signatures of approval from the Politburo of the Soviet Union. The best of Poland's professional and leadership elite were shot in the back of their heads and buried in mass graves.

The furor in the world press over German accusations that the Polish corpses were the work of the Soviets apparently had its effect on a Red Army officer, Lieutenant Colonel Mironov, who had been at Katyn and who had been subsequently sent to work in the Washington *rezidentura*. Mironov, under cover as chief of the consular section, remembered that Vasili Zarubin, now head of the American NKVD operation, had been an interrogator at Katyn. Zarubin's job was to recruit Poles who would work as agents for the Soviet Union, and the few that he enlisted were sent elsewhere, a bizarre stroke of fate, saving them from execution. Perhaps Mironov was suffering from posttraumatic stress when he wrote a letter to Stalin denouncing Zarubin as a double agent. Mironov specified dates and hours of clandestine meetings in which he said the Zarubins were cooperating with the FBI. Mironov claimed he had followed the Zarubins to their meetings with American agents.

Despite the priority of their exploits on behalf of Moscow Center, Colonel Mironov's letter marked the end of Elizabeth Zarubin's and her husband's careers.

They were recalled in August 1944 and investigated for six months, after which it was determined that they had been wrongfully accused: all of the clandestine meetings to which Mironov had followed them were deemed to be legitimate Soviet intelligence operations and valuable efforts on behalf of their spying activities. Mironov was tried for slander and conduct unbecoming an officer and sentenced to ten years in prison; he was also declared to be a schizophrenic. He was discharged from the service and hospitalized in a Special Security hospital in Leningrad (now St. Petersburg).

The Zarubins never served abroad again. In the fall of 1945, Elizabeth Bentley had begun giving information on Soviet agents in America to the FBI. The NKVD leadership was afraid that her contacts with the Zarubins would place them under suspicion and prevent them from operating. Until President Boris Yeltsin's revelations in 1992 of Soviet guilt in the Katyn massacres, the Soviets claimed that the mass graves discovered there were the work of the German SS. Better not to risk sending Zarubin abroad again, where his eyewitness knowledge that only the Soviets were responsible for the Katyn murders might emerge under unforeseen circumstances. In the anti-Semitic sweep of the KGB in 1947, Elizabeth was retired on pension, and Vasili later resigned. In official KGB histories of the 1940s, they are given no credit for their atomic espionage successes.

The most potent reason for not reassigning the Zarubins abroad, however, was the fear that Mironov had written a similar letter to the FBI. As recently as 1992 to early 1994, while retired KGB Lieutenant General Pavel Sudoplatov was telling his story, he was not sure whether or not Mironov had succeeded in revealing a picture of NKVD activities in America to its wartime ally. The publication of Sudoplatov's memoir, *Special Tasks*, in April 1994 was the first public record of Mironov's letter to Stalin.[52]

Away from the sight of the media, however, Mironov's accusations, described in print by Sudoplatov, had an altogether different explosive effect. Behind the bureaucratic facades of the National Security Administration, where secret codes are deciphered and signals intelligence listens in on the world's conversations, Robert Louis Benson, editor of the VENONA intercepts, exploded with a cry of joy and a wide grin. For him and other keepers of the U.S. government's sacred secrets, affirmation that Mironov had written to Stalin was "like the clasp of two hands fitting perfectly into each other" to reveal the answer to a half-century's secret. Benson had Mironov's letter to the FBI in hand, received in 1943 but until now still half believed and half unbelievable.[53]

Colonel Mironov did not sign his August 7, 1943, letter to J. Edgar Hoover, director of the FBI; in it he refers to himself in the third person. In this top secret memorandum, declassified only fifty-three years later, on July 10, 1996, Mironov warned the Americans that Vasili Zubilin, second secretary of the embassy of the USSR, was really Vasili Zarubin, deputy head of the Foreign Intelligence Directorate of the NKVD. Moreover, he stated, Zarubin was really an agent of the Japanese and his wife Elizabeth, really an agent of Germany; every secret about America that their Soviet apparatus gathered also went to their common enemies. These charges, made in the "Anonymous Letter," as it came to be known in the FBI, plus accusations in the letter to Stalin that the pair were actually working for the Americans, were eventually discredited secretly by the Soviets, but the import of the letter had other longer term effects.

In the Anonymous Letter, Colonel Mironov described a vast spying network run by Elizabeth Zarubin that reached into the top ministries of the U.S. government, including the State Department. He gave a list of top agents that included Boris Morros in Hollywood, vice-consuls in New York and San Francisco, and engineers employed by Amtorg, the Soviet buying agency in New York. According to Miro-nov, other purchasing agents in Buffalo (in upstate New York) and Philadelphia were part of a ring that was stealing naval, industrial, and military technological secrets for the Soviet Union, unaware that they were also supplying the Germans and Japanese through the Zarubins. The letter said they had agents in all the industrial towns of the United States, stealing the "whole of the war industry" and taking strategic materials from Americans ports, chemical and aviation factories, and technical institutes. Also under Zarubin's jurisdiction, Mironov stated, were the Soviet vice-counsul in San Francisco, Gregory Kheifetz; the secretary of the Soviet legation in Canada, Vitali Pavlov (the same diplomat who had earlier carried out Operation Snow visiting Harry Dexter White in Washington); and Tarasov (cover name for Vasilevsky), secretary of the USSR legation in Mexico City.

In the last paragraph of the Anonymous Letter, Mironov wrote that General Zarubin and Colonel Mironov hated each other, and that both took part in the occupation of Poland where they were the "butchers" responsible for the death of 10,000 Poles in camps in Kozelsk and Starobelsk. These Poles were sent to the Katyn Forest, 150 miles to the west, where they were executed. (In all, 26,000 Polish prisoners were executed by Soviet security personnel.) "If you prove to Mironov that Zarubin is working for the Germans and Japanese, he will immediately shoot him without a trial, as he too holds a very high post in the NKVD," Mironov wrote. In closing he refers without identification to a high level agent in the White House.[54] Mironov did not make up the charges that the Zarubins were working for the Germans. They came from "admissions" by their old comrade Shpigelglas when he was tortured before his execution in the last years of the purges. Mironov had read the record of Shpigelglas's interrogation.

The Anonymous Letter astounded Hoover and his assistants. They were not in a position to know how much of it was true, how much distorted, much less to take action on the basis of its accusations. The Anonymous Letter had a rippling force that reaches from that time to this. In a sense, the Anonymous Letter marks the beginning of the cold war, because the doubt it instilled of Soviet sincerity in their wartime alliance with the United States changed a sharing relationship into a wary partnership. Until the Anonymous Letter, the FBI had been focusing on German espionage and subversion. Soon after it was received, the FBI started a "Russian Squad" to keep track of the activities of Soviet diplomats and trade bureaucrats on American soil. The VENONA intercepts contain reports to Moscow Center that FBI surveillance increased in San Francisco and New York. They also record Zubilin's complaint to Moscow that his activities in Poland had become known.[55]

In 1945 Vladimir Eitingon, the son of Leonid Eitingon, who was the senior NKVD field officer in charge of assassinating Trotsky and who helped set up Soviet atomic espionage in North America, received a report from the psychiatric prison hospital in Leningrad that a prisoner there was constantly speaking out names of secret American and British assets in the Soviet Union and abroad. From 1945 to 1949, Vladimir headed the anti-American and anti-British section in the counterintelligence department of the Leningrad NKVD Directorate.

Immediately after this report reached him, Vladimir got his chief to request from the registry department the full file on the prisoner and his case. To his dismay Vladimir found in the file a rash of attacks on Vasili Zarubin, his mother's first husband, and Elizabeth. The same night he took the train to Moscow, ostensibly to report the case to his superior in Moscow, but in fact to consult his father, Leonid. The elder Eitingon gave his son shrewd advice: do not mark the file with anything in your own handwriting or leave traces that you have seen it; through other hands—not yours—send it back to the archive and registry department with a note signed by your superior that the subject is mentally ill and it is no use to follow up his accusations.[56] The principle is the same in any bureaucracy, Soviet or American: no matter how innocent you may be, speaking of or revealing the crimes of others taints your reputation. Put it back in the file and make believe you never heard of it.

In July 1945 "pending to the newly established circumstances indicating high treason and continuous talk about top secret matters among unauthorized persons," Mironov was condemned to death by firing squad. Records in the Communist Party archives indicate he was expelled from the party "due to the decision to indict him on criminal charges by competent law enforcement authorities." According to other sources, Mironov attempted to smuggle the story of the Katyn Massacre to the American embassy.[57]

The peak of the Zarubins' success was in 1943–1944, creating the atomic espionage network. Their momentum came to a standstill as a result of Mironov's letter to Stalin; they sailed from New York in early August, 1944. When the Zarubins were recalled to Moscow, the Soviet espionage apparatus had to find new talent to complete the work that Elizabeth had started.

4 Nuclear Furies

A Love Affair and a Storm of Controversy

The KGB decision not to send the Zarubins abroad again interrupted their large-scale conspiracy to transfer atomic secrets from the Manhattan Project to the Soviet Union. In an attempt to recover and continue operations, the Soviet intelligence *rezidentura* in New York City enlisted the help of Sergei Konenkov, the preeminent Russian sculptor, and his beautiful young wife, Margarita Konenkova; Margarita had long been deeply involved in a love affair with Albert Einstein. From the time of his arrival at Princeton in 1934, Einstein was a target of Soviet intelligence. His scientific stature and penchant for political causes that supported the Soviet Union made him seem, to Moscow, a likely tool for Soviet propaganda in America.

Konenkov and his wife arrived in New York in 1924 for an exhibition of his sculptures, part of a Soviet effort to soften the new communist regime's image by demonstrating its interest in art and culture. Except for a brief trip to Italy in 1927, where they visited Maxim Gorky and his family, the Konenkovs remained in the United States for more than two decades, never giving up their Soviet citizenship. On more than one occasion, Konenkov let his friends in the New York *rezidentura* know that he yearned to return to the Soviet motherland. Konenkov received commissions to sculpt the busts of dozens of famous Americans; the couple was socially accepted among New York intellectuals and wealthy art benefactors.

The Konenkovs were successful assets for Operation Corridor among the émigrés, and perfectly placed for making the introductions and connections needed for atomic espionage. They were neither intelligence officers nor recruited agents; they were considered assets, Soviet citizens who could be called upon to serve the state. A former KGB general called Margarita "a talented amateur."[1] Their social life was useful to Soviet intelligence. Margarita acted as a "spotter" for likely candidates who espoused communist ideals and might become useful for Soviet intelligence operations.

The love affair between Einstein and Konenkova began when Konenkov sculpted his first bust of Albert Einstein in 1935. Einstein was smitten with her golden braided hair, her cool allure and European sophistication. While Konenkov sculpted, Albert flirted with Margarita and explained the theory of relativity. She recalled understanding nothing about relativity, "but I was looking at him very attentively. Einstein took a sheet of paper and tried to explain his ideas to me, but Einstein soon realized that while explaining his theory to me he was in fact joking. So instead of writing down a formula he himself drew a sketchy portrait of us and called it Almar for Al-bert and Mar-garita." Her nickname for Einstein was Al and he called her Mar. They referred to themselves together as "AlMar."[2] Their affair was interrupted only by the death of Einstein's second wife, Elsa, of heart and kidney ailments in 1936, and by Konenkova's stay in a sanitarium after she contracted tuberculosis.

In late 1944, Konenkova began carrying on the work of Elizabeth Zarubin, using Einstein's contacts at Princeton to spot young communist scientists for the Manhattan Project and report on the scientific activity taking place around Einstein. Russian-born physicist George Gamow, who did not work on the Manhattan Project but had frequent contact with colleagues who shared atomic bomb research with him, met with Einstein every two weeks to work on nonatomic U.S. Navy projects. Gamow was vulnerable to threats from Soviet intelligence because his and his wife's families were still in the Soviet Union.[3]

Margarita Konenkova does not appear in any Einstein biography. Their affair was another sacred secret until an article with a photo that included Einstein, Konenkova, and Oppenheimer appeared in *Krasnaya Zvezda* (Red Star), the official Russian army newspaper, on June 4, 1991.

Einstein played a paradoxical role in initiating atomic research in America. A group of leading physicists, fearing Hitler would develop an atomic bomb first, succeeded in getting Einstein to write the letter to President Roosevelt urging the government to begin serious research to build a weapon using uranium. Yet even after the government followed his advice, he was excluded from work on the bomb as a security risk unacceptable to the U.S. Army.

The star-and-satellite system was at work in Princeton around Einstein. Often in Einstein's company was Leon Theremin (born Lev Sergeyevich Termon), a highly original Russian inventor and engineer, credited in Russia for inventing the first television set in 1927. Theremin was also part of Operation Corridor. He was sent by the People's Commissariat for Education to New York, where he demonstrated an unbelievable device in Central Park: the "coffin of Magomet," weighing several hundred pounds, flew in the air under the impact of magnetic fields. Theremin was best known in America for inventing the Theremin, an electronic musical instrument that was technically the first synthesizer. He also invented the Terpsistone, an ether-wave musical dance platform that translated dancers' movements into music.[4]

Theremin's company produced unique safety signal equipment for the American military and for private enterprises. At Einstein's initiative, Lev Theremin helped develop telephone communications between the United States and foreign countries including the USSR. He was well informed about strategic technological innovations in the United States.[5]

Theremin remained a citizen of the Soviet Union while in the United States, and at the end of 1938, believing he should help at home, returned to the Soviet Union. The NKVD arrested Theremin on March 11, 1939; on August 15 of the same year, he was sentenced to eight years' imprisonment in the *gulag* on trumped-up charges of cooperation in the murder of Leningrad party chief Sergei Kirov, which had occurred while Theremin was in the United States.

Theremin was sent to the Arctic labor camp Kolyma, and then transferred to a *sharashka* (secret laboratory) where he worked in the NKVD/KGB system for almost twenty years. Theremin turned his skills for creating electronic musical instruments into designing listening devices.

In 1947 he was awarded the Stalin prize, 1st grade, for the Snowstorm *(Buran)* system. These instruments were for bugging from a distance; counterintelligence agents installed the device in an official American eagle seal, which young Soviet Pioneers then presented to the American ambassador in Moscow on Independence Day as a gesture of friendship. Technicians installed the eagle over the ambassador's desk, from which agents across the street listened to every word spoken in his study until it was discovered years later. Another version of how the bugging device was installed: Soviet intelligence duplicated the American eagle seal with the listening device built in it, and replaced the hanging seal with their own copy in the dead of night.[6]

★ ★ ★

Konenkova had long served as a spotter for Soviet intelligence, reporting on Einstein's friends, identifying those who might be amenable to working for the Soviet Union. The Konenkovs' friendship with Einstein brought them in contact with leaders of the scientific community. They met Oppenheimer several times at Einstein's home in Princeton. Elizabeth Zarubin knew the Konenkovs and called Margarita by the nickname Rita. Margarita confessed to Elizabeth that she had a long running affair with Albert Einstein, and that he told her that her husband's sculptural masterpieces reflected a new era in which a superweapon would defeat Hitler and open the way for a perfect world order. All nations would be afraid of a nuclear attack if they disturbed the new international framework for peace; the new superweapon was one of the greatest discoveries of this century, Margarita reported. She also relayed to Moscow Center confirmation that Oppenheimer shared the political views of Bohr and Einstein for sharing scientific discoveries.[7] During the year between Mironov's letter to Stalin in the spring of 1943 and the Zarubins' departure in August 1944, Elizabeth instructed Margarita in the arcane arts of spotting "progressive" or "antifascist" scientists and furthering their careers by introducing them to Oppenheimer for jobs at Los Alamos.[8]

With the imminent departure of the Zarubins, Konenkova's relationship with Einstein took on new importance for Soviet intelligence. Even though Einstein was excluded from the Manhattan Project he was in contact with George Gamow, Niels Bohr, Leo Szilard, and Otto Stern, his old colleague from his Prague days who was a consultant to the Metallurgical Lab in Chicago. Einstein's definitive biographer, Ronald W. Clark, believes "the evidence is not that Einstein knew how, or even if, the new weapons were to be used to finish the war; but it implies beyond all reasonable doubt that by the end of 1944 he knew that they were nearing completion."[9]

Niels Bohr, the Danish Nobel prize–winning physicist who had fled from German-occupied Denmark to Sweden, was flown in a Mosquito bomber to London in 1943; he spent most of the summer of 1944 at Los Alamos.[10] There he "instigated some of the most important experiments on the velocity selector, . . . enlivened discussions on bomb assembly and . . . participated very actively in the design of the initiator."[11] Bohr, traveling with a British passport under the assumed name of John Baker for security reasons, also visited Einstein at Princeton that summer. By the winter of 1944, Einstein had talked on many occasions with Otto Stern who expressed deep concern about development of the new weapons after the end of the war. Einstein wrote to Bohr about his visit from Stern on December 11, 1944, in which they discussed the new weapons. Einstein urged Bohr to use his influence on political leaders "to bring about an internationalization of military power."

In his letter, Einstein said that the news of new weapons being developed greatly disturbed him:

> [W]hen the war is over then there will be in all countries a pursuit of secret war preparations with technological means which will lead inevitably to preventive wars and to destruction even more terrible than the present destruction of life. The politicians do not appreciate the possibilities and consequently do not know the extent of the menace. Every effort must be made to avert such a development. I share your view of the situation but I see no way of doing anything promising.[12]

Then Einstein referred to his visit from Stern the previous day:

> It seemed to us that there is one possibility, however slight it may be. There are in the principal countries scientists who are really influential and who know how to get a hearing with political leaders. There is you yourself with your international connections, Compton here in the U.S.A., Lindemann in

England, Kapitza [*sic*] and Joffe [*sic*] in Russia, etc. The idea is that these men should bring combined pressure on the political leaders in their countries in order to bring about an internationalization of military power—a method that has been rejected for too long as being too adventurous. But this radical step with all its far-reaching political assumptions regarding extra-national government seems the only alternative to a secret technical arms race.

We agreed that I should lay this before you. Don't say, at first sight, "Impossible" but wait a day or two until you have got used to the idea.[13]

Bohr received Einstein's letter through the Danish legation in Washington and quickly went to see him at Princeton, where he persuaded Einstein to remain silent.

Bohr arrived at Einstein's house on Mercer Street in Princeton on Friday, December 22, 1944, for his meeting with Einstein, whose letter "could hardly have been more fortuitously ill timed; the names it mentioned could hardly have been more fortuitously ill chosen."[14] In April Pyotr Kapitsa had written to Bohr in London inviting him and his family to settle in the Soviet Union. Bohr had shown the letter to British intelligence officials to reassure them of his loyalty and they had approved his warm but innocuous reply. Then Bohr had a disastrous meeting with Churchill in which he tried to impress on the British prime minister the need to bring the Russians into a scheme for postwar control of atomic energy. In August Bohr was sympathetically received by Roosevelt, who promised to raise the matter with Churchill when they met in Hyde Park in September.

At their meeting, however, not only did Roosevelt and Churchill rule out the possibility of sharing atomic secrets with Stalin, but they initialed an *aide-memoire*, the last clause of which said: "Enquiries should be made regarding the activities of Professor Bohr and steps taken to ensure that he is responsible for no leakage of information, particularly to the Russians."[15]

Bohr's ideas were rejected as politically unrealistic and not viable in wartime. Now he had Einstein to contend with. "Bohr was in an awkward situation," explained biographer Ronald Clark. "He knew his Einstein. He knew that to a man of such trusting idealism the niceties of diplomatic protocol meant little. Whether he feared that Einstein might himself try to write to Kapitza [*sic*] or [Abram I.] Ioffe is not certain, but if he did the fear—with all his knowledge of how 'the secret' of the bomb was being kept from the Russians—must have haunted him."

Bohr was deeply upset and feared his own role in the Manhattan Project might be jeopardized. In an official capacity working for the project, he reported on the meeting to Washington in a private note. Clark believes that note "must have done much to vindicate the attitude of the 'people . . . in Washington' who three years earlier decided to restrict Einstein's knowledge of the Manhattan Project."[16] The account of their meeting, dated "December, 1944," referred to himself as "B" and Einstein as "X." The report stated that he had visited Einstein and explained that "it would be quite illegitimate and might have the most deplorable consequences if anyone who was brought into confidence with the matter concerned, on his own hands should take steps of the kind suggested."

Bohr continued:

Confidentially B could, however, inform X that the responsible statesmen in America and England were fully aware of the scope of the technical development, and that their attention had been called to the dangers to world security as well as to the unique opportunity for furthering a harmonious relationship between nations, which the great scientific advance involves. In response X assured B that he quite realized the situation and would not only abstain from any action himself, but would also—without any reference to his confidential conversation with B—impress on the friends with whom he talked about the matter, the undesirability of all discussions which might complicate the delicate task of the statesmen.[17]

Soviet intelligence counted on access to men like Einstein to provide the context of American intentions. Having control over Einstein's paramour gave Soviet intelligence a window to the world's most famous scientist. How much, if any, of "AlMar's" pillow talk dealt with nuclear weapons we will never know, but Konenkova saw enough of Einstein and shared his confidence to the degree that she, like he, knew there were dangerous new atomic weapons being developed that would change the nature of warfare and the world balance of power.

After the Zarubins were recalled, Margarita was transformed from a spotter into an active asset. Her new authority as executive director of Russian War Relief increased her credibility and provided a cover for her travels. Her appeals for help to the social contacts she had made through Einstein and through Konenkov's art at the elite level of American society added to the impact of propaganda portraying the Soviet Union as the besieged ally of the United States.

According to the top secret intelligence file of the Konenkovs, Foreign Minister Molotov granted permission for their return on the July 20, 1944.[18] The short summary in the file of Margarita Ivanovna Konenkova states: "The First Directorate of the NKGB positively assesses the stay of Konenkova abroad" (*dayot polozhitelnoye zaklyucheniye o prebuyvanii Konenkovoi zarubezhom*). The First Directorate was in charge of all foreign intelligence at the time. Molotov gave his consent for the Konenkovs' return to the USSR "with due provisions for their life-style as creative artists." The case history involving the Konenkovs is in the file code-named Operation Corridor.

In 1944, Margarita's old friend Natalia Konchalovskaya, a writer and sometimes NKVD informer, provided a recommendation for the Konenkovs' right to return to the Soviet Union. Konchalovskaya was summoned by the NKVD and ordered to write a personal letter to Konenkov hinting that the government was favorably considering his request to return home. Konenkov immediately replied to her through the Soviet consulate in New York with a patriotic letter in which he expressed his admiration for the leadership of the country and his happiness that he would be given the possibility to return to the Motherland. Konchalovskaya recalled that negotiations with Konenkov on the terms of his return to the Soviet Union took several years.

Konenkova persuaded Einstein to attend a meeting at the New York *rezidentura* in the autumn of 1945. The dramatic confrontation between Einstein and the Soviet consul general is apparent in a letter between Margarita and Albert.[19] The Soviets wanted Einstein to support their campaign for sharing of nuclear secrets four years before the Soviet Union had its own atomic bomb. Einstein agreed to meet with the consul, but refused to follow the Soviet propaganda line. However, by Einstein agreeing to the meeting, Margarita and her husband achieved their long-held wish: they were permitted to return to Moscow as heroes. After Einstein left the meeting in New York, he sensed he was being set up to be used by the Soviet Union and had no further meetings with the consul.

Although Molotov granted the Konenkovs permission to return to the Soviet Union on July 20, 1944, it was not until August 15, 1945, when Konenkova visited Einstein while he was on vacation at the Strauss family's estate, Knollwood, on Upper Saranac Lake in upstate New York, that her plans to return to Moscow became firm. On August 20, 1945, two weeks after Hiroshima, Stalin established a Special Committee of the State Committee on Defense on the utilization of the internal energy of uranium and the organization of increased intelligence about the uranium industry and atomic bombs. (See appendixes 6 and 7.)

The farewell banquet in honor of the Konenkovs was held by the Russian community on September 25, 1945, in the Three Crowns restaurant in Manhattan. Attending were members of trade unions and émigré organizations. The chairman, D. I. Kazushchik, paid particular tribute to Margarita for her outstanding services to the Soviet people and her attentiveness to the demands of the workers' organizations; the hearts of the Russians in America were sincerely devoted to Margarita Konenkova, and she enjoyed great respect, he said.[20]

All the time he was in America, no contact was permitted between Konenkov and his son by an earlier marriage, an officer in the Red Army, who remained in the Soviet Union. Only when the official announcement that the Konenkovs would soon return was made did the son know of his father's fate. The Konenkovs departed from Seattle for Vladivostok on the steamship *Smolny*, which carried the full collection of his sculptures made in America. They would form the basis for Konenkov's studio and museum. The Konenkovs arrived back in Moscow on December 12, 1945, after having been abroad for twenty-two years.

The final letter requesting exit visas for the Konenkovs, dated September 17,

1945, provides confirmation of the Konenkovs' activities in the United States. The request is addressed to the Soviet embassy in Washington from Alexander Yakovlev in the consular office in New York. Yakovlev, also known as Anatoli Yatskov, was a key officer in atomic espionage efforts run through the Soviet consulate in New York on East 61st Street. Stepan Shudenko, a well-known intelligence officer working alongside Yatskov, physically handed over the passports to the Konenkovs.[21]

Yatskov also supplied the Konenkovs with an official certificate for their journey across Russia from Vladivostok to Moscow, which requested cooperation from the authorities. This was another token of appreciation given to the Konenkovs in return for the work they completed for the Soviet state.

The Konenkovs returned to Moscow at the end of 1945 and were rewarded with a studio off Pushkin Square in the heart of Moscow; Margarita went on the secret payroll of Soviet intelligence. In 1946, despite his love for Konenkova, Einstein refused to accept the invitation of his Russian physicist friend, Pyotr Kapitsa, to come to the Soviet Union and work in his laboratory. Einstein, sensitive to Stalin's anti-Semitism, remained in America, supporting peace efforts and international control of nuclear weapons, but chastened in his views of Stalin's intentions and the Soviet Union as the future socialist model for mankind.

Some years after Margarita Konenkova returned to the Soviet Union, she renewed connections with Lev Theremin, the engineer she had known through her relationship with Einstein in the 1930s. By this time he had risen to prominence in the NKVD-KGB for his work inventing and installing bugging devices in the American embassy in Moscow.[22]

After his return to Moscow in 1945, Sergei resumed his friendship with Maxim Gorky's family and made a bust of Gorky's granddaughter, Marfa, who was married to Sergo Beria, the son of Lavrenti Beria, the much-feared minister of state security. One of the first sculptures Konenkov did on his return to Moscow was of the founder of the Soviet secret police, Felix Dzerzhinsky. Also after their return, the Konenkovs met with Pyotr Kapitsa at his dacha in Nikolina Gora, outside Moscow. There they exchanged reminiscences of famous physicists, and Konenkova briefed Kapitsa on her correspondence with Einstein. Konenkov revealed to Kapitsa that, under the influence of Einstein in Princeton, he had created a series of pictures on the fate of the world, called "Cosmogonia" or "Space Fantasy."

According to an official KGB historian, an internal memorandum in February 1946 addressed to Vsevolod Merkulov, people's commissar for state security, from the Second Directorate, asked permission to establish regular payments in the amount of 800 rubles per month to Margarita Konenkova in Moscow. The request from the counterintelligence directorate was to pay Margarita as a consultant of VOKS (All-Union Society for Cultural Relations with Foreign Countries) from the fund for unlisted personnel. It states that the plan for the use of Konenkova was developed jointly with the First Directorate of the NKGB for foreign intelligence. The fact that Konenkova was mentioned by name implies that she was regarded not simply as an informer, but rather as an unlisted, but paid, staff member of the state security machinery (in Russian, *Sotrudnik neglasnovo shtata kontr-razvedki).*[23]

★ ★ ★

"Love Letters By Einstein At Auction," "Notes Reveal Affair with Possible Spy" were the headlines in the *New York Times*, on June 1, 1998, announcing the auction at Sotheby's of nine autographic letters from Albert Einstein written in Princeton, New Jersey, November 8, 1945, to July 25, 1946, to Margarita Konenkova in Moscow. There are also four letters from Margarita to her husband, Sergei, on August 1945 and other dates. The letters indicate that "AlMar" were lovers.

The notes for the catalog by Sotheby's consultant Paul Needham do not speculate on how long Einstein and Konenkova had been lovers, but say:

It is obvious that at the moment of their parting, in the late autumn of 1945, their relationship was a passionate one. It is equally apparent, both from the letters and from other material here, which has survived by descent to a member of the Konenkov family, that Margarita's role was a challenging one. She had to juggle the wishes and needs of Einstein, of her husband, and of her handler. Love, manipulation and deception were inextricably mingled in her affair with Einstein. The family tradition that she had many other affairs, including with Rachmaninov and with the émigré artist Boris Chaliapin, suggest that she was well trained for her relationship with Einstein.[24]

In August 1945, Konenkova had written to her husband from Saranac Lake stressing the importance of the Soviet vice-consul's imminent meeting with Einstein. She expressed considerable nervousness: "Please write me as quickly as possible; I'm worried about the Consul and I'm not sure that he will agree to meet with him. But I'll try, anyway." She closes with regrets that in the rush to catch the train, she had no time to say goodbye to her pet white rats. On the 19th of August 1945, she wrote to her husband again saying that Einstein would be happy to meet with the consul and had so informed the latter: "I waited for the best moment to bring this up with Einstein." She then expressed various fears: had Mikhailov been in touch? She had kept her promise. She had done what he had asked—what of the packing for their return? Mikhailov should wait until September and see Einstein in Princeton—how are the rats? Writing on August 26, she said: "Why do you write so seldom? I told you and Mikhailov that Einstein would be happy to meet with him here; I'm surprised Mikhailov hasn't called. It's embarrassing, because Einstein asked when Mikhailov is coming."[25] The letters make it clear that arranging for Einstein to meet with the Soviet vice-consul Mikhailov was one of the conditions for the Konenkovs' repatriation. Mikhailov's real name was Pavel Melkishev; he was the GRU *rezident* in New York (code name, MOLIERE). After the war, he was promoted to major general and headed the GRU Department for American Affairs.

The authors met Sergei Konenkov, nephew of the sculptor, in the Konenkov studio and museum dedicated to his uncle's work; it faces toward Pushkin Square. Sergei's memories and family tales poured forth while we looked at Konenkov's sculptures of Einstein and of Konenkova. Sergei recalled that immediately after Margarita's death, the KGB searched her apartment and confiscated her correspondence. In 1998 a family member who preferred to remain anonymous, presumably Sergei, attempted to sell the letters at Sotheby's but the bids did not reach the reserve price he set.

In mid-December 1945, when the Konenkovs were returning to Moscow, Secretary of State James Byrnes, accompanied by James B. Conant, president of Harvard University, and Averell Harriman, ambassador to Moscow, sat in the Kremlin with Stalin and Molotov discussing the postwar control of atomic energy. The Soviets had already agreed to a plan to set up within the United Nations an atomic energy commission that would limit the use of atomic weapons and provide for the exchange of fundamental scientific information. Stalin laid down the Soviet line: only the weak could be frightened by the bomb. Both Stalin and Molotov were aware that Soviet intelligence had already stolen American atomic bomb secrets. At a Kremlin banquet, Molotov joked that perhaps Conant had smuggled a piece of the bomb into the Soviet Union in his vest pocket. Stalin reacted with anger and got to his feet with a toast, "This is too serious a matter to joke about. I raise my glass to the American scientists and what they have accomplished. We must now work together to see that this great invention is used for peaceful ends."

Conant sent a memorandum to Byrnes in Moscow on December 17 suggesting the stages by which the United States should share information: first "the electromagnetic method of separating Uranium 235," six months later "full details of the gaseous diffusion process," and a year after that "the full method for producing plutonium." In the final stage, the Americans were to dismantle all their bombs if agreement could be reached that no other nation could construct atomic bombs.[26]

Despite the generosity of the offer, the Soviets did not allow Conant to meet Pyotr Kapitsa or Igor Kurchatov, top Soviet scientists involved in the atomic project. Meetings continued only in the offices of the Ministry of Foreign Affairs, hammering out issues about sharing the administration of postwar Europe and functions of the United Nations. Not another word was said about sharing atomic bomb technology.

Conant and other Americans did not understand the Soviets' concept of sharing. The Soviets by that time had already stolen the information they needed from the United States to build their own bomb. There was no need to share. Three months earlier, on August 24, 1945, Stalin had signed an enactment for setting up a new, special institution, their own Manhattan Project. He guaranteed all out support for building the Soviet bomb in the shortest possible period of time.[27]

For Stalin, partnership with the West meant pragmatic relations with an adversary; he did not see mutual advantages in long term cooperation between the West and the Soviet Union. His thinking shaped by geography and the czars, Stalin believed the Soviet Union was surrounded by irreconcilable enemies. The ideology of the Communist Revolution created new enemies: real cooperation with capitalism would be fatal to the triumph of the new Soviet order. Lenin had introduced the cynical concept of "Special Partnership" with the "Main Adversaries" for dealing with Germany in the 1920s. Stalin revived it to take advantage of cooperation, first with Hitler, and then with the Western allies.

★ ★ ★

In 1946 Kitty Harris was recalled to Moscow and given a job teaching English. To avoid arrest after he was identified as a Soviet agent, Donald Maclean fled to Moscow in 1951, but there is no record that he and Kitty encountered each other there. On October 29, 1951, during new purges in which Jews were ousted from the intelligence service, Kitty Harris was arrested as a "hostile element" while on assignment in Latvia. She was interrogated seven times in a month to expose her "anti-Soviet views," and to determine if she was still in contact with any agents and what secret codes she still knew.

In February 1952, she was sent for "medical treatment" to the psychiatric prison clinic in Gorky, where she was held without charges for two years. After Stalin's death, she was released in Gorky in January 1954 and provided with a KGB pension of 1,500 rubles a month. (The average pension was then 500 rubles per month.) She resumed teaching English in Gorky.

Elizabeth Zarubin visited her often and reported the "satisfactory conditions" of her life in Gorky. Although Kitty had been granted Soviet citizenship in 1937, no record of this could be traced when she returned in 1947 from Mexico. Only later, after she was arrested, was it confirmed that she was granted Soviet citizenship under the name Katherine Garrison, a typical Russian mistake in mixing up the pronunciation of G for H.

In her diary, Harris wrote: "My life is destroyed. The only thing that I know for sure is that I am completely alone. Who is responsible for my suffering? Who will answer for the fact that for thirty years I met with my relatives only three times? Why did I have to travel that road to heaven?"

She died on October 6, 1966, in Gorky and was buried with military honors. The official report of her death noted: "Taking into account that the diaries of ADA do not contain secret information that might be used in our future operations and do not contain any historical value I believe that it is expedient to destroy the diary. Operational officer, Lt. Klimov."

Kitty's only property was two shelves of books and a pendant on a gold chain with the inscription "to KH from DM 25 V38," her birthday gift from Donald Maclean in May 1938.[28]

A surprising question arose out of the research process for this book: why are there two official but conflicting versions of the same Soviet agent's life story in Soviet intelligence files? A number of times in visiting Moscow intelligence shrines and researching old documents, we have been drawn up short and forced to look from one hand to the other at established versions of facts that blatantly contradicted each other.

When Oleg Tsarev led a spy tour of Moscow in June 1997, he stated unblinkingly that Elizabeth Zarubina, one of the most successful operators in stealing atomic bomb secrets from the United States, was "too nearsighted to be an intelligence officer." Tsarev said scathingly that Gregory Kheifetz, the consul general in San Francisco, who met Robert Oppenheimer at a fund raiser for Spanish Civil War refugees in December 1941 and succeeded with Elizabeth Zarubina in setting up a ring of young communist physicists around Oppenheimer at Los Alamos to transmit the atomic bomb plans through couriers, was recalled for inactivity.

Both Kheifetz and Zarubina were once high in the pantheon of Soviet intelligence, yet both had twice been purged from the Soviet intelligence service. Official historians of Russian intelligence hold a special sympathy for victims of purges in the 1930s when the service was headed by Yezhov and Beria, two security chiefs remembered for their Stalinist ruthlessness. After the war, in 1946–1947 the new generation of officers swept the records clean of the old heroes and their successes. Therefore, in the historiography of Russian intelligence written in the 1970s, to be purged under the Yezhov regime was to carry a sad memory of injustice; to be purged under the 1940s and 1950s generation of KGB leadership was to be compromised with the label "unfit for intelligence work."[29] Only the survivors can testify that "unfit" is a purge label as destructive to history as a bullet to the heart.

Zarubina and Kheifetz, although declared "unfit" in the 1990s, emerge in official documents from Communist Party archives to have been outstanding operatives. Their registration cards unequivocally state their acts of treachery against the

United States in the 1940s. Elizabeth Zarubina was born Lisa Rozensweig on December 31, 1900, in Bukavina, Romania, and in 1924 obtained Soviet citizenship. She was recommended by Ivan Zaporozets, assistant chief of the OGPU foreign department, to become an officer. She was given the new name of Gorskaya to prevent her relatives abroad from tracing her movements. She was sent on a mission to Turkey.

In Istanbul Zarubina was the "operational wife" of the GPU *rezident*, Yacov Blumkin, who told her about his ties with Leon Trotsky and his preparations to escape abroad. Gorskaya reported Blumkin's plans to the head of the foreign department and actively participated in his arrest.

On November 1, 1928, the Politburo decided to shoot Blumkin and ordered an investigation. "Gorskaya helped to prevent the escape of Blumkin abroad and detain him," said the official assessment.[30]

From January 1930 until June 20, 1938, she served as a case officer in the special reserve of the foreign department of the OGPU-NKVD, now the "operational wife" of Vasili Zarubin, and her name changed to Elizabeth Zarubina, with the sometimes cover name of Helen Zubilin. We know from the memoirs of Hede Massing and Boris Morros, agents who turned against the Soviet Union, that Vasili and Elizabeth were frequently in the United States during the 1930s (see chapter 3). During that period, in 1934, Zaporozets, who had been the deputy head of the Leningrad NKVD, was accused by NKVD chief Yezhov of being the organizer of the plot to murder Kirov. Since Zaporozets, an "enemy of the people," had at one time been Zarubina's mentor, on March 1, 1939, she was discharged from the organs of state security.

The officer who got her fired was the young and ambitious intelligence officer, Vitali Pavlov, who later traveled to Washington for Operation Snow. Pavlov suggested that "with the aim of rejuvenating the staff of the department I consider it necessary to send Zarubina to the department of personnel of the NKVD USSR," a euphemism for firing her.[31] Pavlov reported that she was unreliable because of her connection with Zaporozets. In early 1940, Zarubina was reinstated as a case officer.

Kheifetz, who became consul general in San Francisco, and made contact with Robert Oppenheimer, and William Fisher (a.k.a. Rudolf Abel, who was arrested in New York in a celebrated case in 1957), also suffered discharge and rehabilitation in this period.

For a month starting in November 1940, Zarubina was sent to Berlin to restore contacts with valuable agents, including the wife of a prominent German diplomat, and on April 7, 1941, she was promoted to the post of senior case officer.

From November 4, 1941, until November 16, 1944, Zarubina was serving abroad; this date records when she left for the United States. Her arrival in San Francisco began her most active period: she was a prime organizer of atomic espionage. We also know that both Zarubins were recalled because of Mironov's letter sent to Stalin accusing them of being secret agents of the FBI and the Gestapo. The Zarubins were cleared of working for the Americans, but these and other charges, which appear to be the ravings of an insane man, came from the record of purge interrogations of their colleague, Shpigelglas. These were the answers he had given under torture in 1938 before he was executed; the irrational charges remained on file.

Back in Moscow on December 20, 1944, Zarubina was named deputy head of a section. After the defection of Igor Gouzenko in 1945, the Canadian government expelled Vitali Pavlov and he returned to Moscow. He became deputy to Elizabeth Zarubina and then took over her post when she was again discharged from the service on September 14, 1946. The personnel department ruling—"Impossible to use the officer any longer"—meant she had been purged in the sweeping out of Jewish officers that occurred in the 1946–1947 period. Again the accusations by Shpigelglas under torture came into play.

The official record of 25 years remains:

Member of the CPSU since March 1928. Party card # 1856551. Awarded the Order of Red Banner on October 22, 1944 and the Medal for Victory Over Germany on May 9, 1945. Awarded badge of Honorary Chekist #1093, on 20 December 1934. Awarded OGPU certificate for the fight against the enemies of the first world proletarian state, December 30, 1932. Given military rank Lieutenant of State Security, 31 December 1940; Captain of State Security, February 11, 1943; Major of State Security, 20 February 1944; Lieutenant Colonel State Security, December 22, 1945.[32]

In 1967, in retirement, she was awarded the Badge of Honor, 50 Years of Cheka-KGB. The record appears quite different from that of the useless officer shrugged off by Tsarev in 1997.

The case of Gregory Kheifetz, born on May 7, 1899, near Riga, Latvia, is similar. His father was a leader in the BUND, the Jewish Social Democratic Party. For a year he served as the secretary of Nadezhda Krupskaya, Lenin's wife. From 1922 to 1931, he acted as Comintern (literally, Department of International Connections) agent in Latvia, Turkey, China, Germany, France, and the United States, sometimes posing, with his blue eyes and dark skin, as a student refugee from India. On June 16, 1931, he was transferred to the Foreign Intelligence Department of OGPU, predecessor of NKVD. He lived as an illegal in France and the United States and in 1936 moved to Italy as illegal *rezident*. There he recruited Bruno Pontecorvo, who later became a conduit for atomic secrets.

In June 1938, Kheifetz was recalled to Moscow, discharged from the service, and sent to work as an officer in the labor camp in Vorkuta. Five months later, he was fired from state security because of "poor health," another euphemism of the purges. The real reason was his membership in the BUND and charges that his uncle was a Trotskyite. On October 9, 1939, Kheifetz was reinstated in NKVD and on September 4, 1941, sent to be the consul general in San Francisco; there he became the authority for the communist underground in California. Mironov's letter ending the American career of the Zarubins also implicated Kheifetz in "suspicious contacts." He returned to Moscow through Mexico on September 18, 1944.

Cleared of Mironov's charges, Kheifetz continued to serve in the foreign intelligence directorate. On December 1, 1944, General Fitin, director of Soviet intelligence, assessed Kheifetz's career:

Has substantial experience in operational intelligence work abroad, especially under conditions as an illegal. Has a very high general cultural level which helped him to maintain relations with sources from the circles of *intelligentsia*. Politically well educated. Constantly works to perfect his Chekist qualifications and reads literature on issues of foreign policy. Actively participates in the social political life of the collective. Modest in manner, knows German and English, limited knowledge of French and Italian.[33]

On May 2, 1946, Kheifetz was promoted to chief of section of Department S, atomic espionage. A year later his work was again praised by personnel managers of the security service. On April 15, 1947, Minister of State Security Abakumov revised the assessment and stamped Kheifetz's file "Discharge." Kheifetz was fired in the same sweep of Jews as was Elizabeth Zarubina. For a year he worked for the Jewish Anti-Fascist Committee; it was then disbanded for "ideological divergency" and its entire leadership purged. On November 13, 1951, Kheifetz was arrested in connection with the case against the Jewish Anti-Fascist Committee, and on August 8, 1952, sentenced as a Zionist spy to twenty-five years in prison. On October 10, 1952, his case was reopened and he was implicated in the Doctors' Plot, alleged terrorism against Stalin. On February 2, 1953, the interrogator announced to Kheifetz that he was condemned to be shot. Stalin died a month later and Kheifetz was released, formally cleared of all charges and reinstated in the CPSU.

Kheifetz's decorations were: Order of the Red Star for "Successful Fulfillment of Special Tasks of the Government Abroad," December 21, 1943; and Medal for Distinguished Military Service, January 2, 1945. The history of his military ranks follows: Junior Lieutenant, State Security, November 9, 1939; Major of State Security, February 11, 1943; Lieutenant Colonel, State Security, December 15, 1944.[34]

If Kheifetz received a promotion in military rank upon his return from the United States, he could not have been "recalled for inactivity."

The same treatment was given to Semyon Semyonov (TWAIN in VENONA), recruiter of the Rosenbergs, and NKVD *rezident* in New York, San Francisco, and Mexico during the war who headed successful operations for penetrating the Manhattan Project: Apresian (MAY in VENONA) and Pastelniak (LUKA), Vasilevsky (YURY), Pravdin (SERGEI).[35]

These double biographies, the result of purges in the 1930s and late 1940s under Stalin, and again in Khrushchev's ascent to power in 1953, have infiltrated their way into the American academic dialogue of the 1990s. After the publication of Sudoplatov's oral history, SVR disinformation officers leaked charges from his 1953 purge trial to selected American academics to discredit his revelations.[36]

★ ★ ★

In 1992, long-retired KGB spymaster Pavel Sudoplatov wanted to tell his story. Reaching the end of his 87 years, he needed to make sure that his career on behalf of his vanished country was not forgotten by history. Releasing his story would fly in the face of the KGB authorities; no one in Moscow would publish it before it appeared in the West. We agreed to help him write down his oral history.

Sudoplatov's purpose was to clear his official biography of false accusations made against him after the arrest and execution of Lavrenti Beria. Sudoplatov's motive was to exonerate himself of the trumped-up treason charges made at his military trial; for these he was convicted and served 15 years in Vladimir Prison. Sudoplatov was jailed in the months following Stalin's death when Khrushchev was amalgamating power to take over the Communist Party and the government. Sudoplatov insisted he was not guilty of attempting a separate peace with Hitler in 1941, nor had he been the head of the Poison Laboratory whose products were used to kill Stalin's enemies, (the charges on which he was arrested in 1953). He admitted to being in charge of four assassinations under orders. Sudoplatov's final crime was to be on the wrong side of the power struggle after Stalin's death: he had worked under Beria. Khrushchev wanted him kept alive in jail, to be a witness against Molotov.

An equally important motive for Sudoplatov to recount his past was to take credit for his successes on Stalin's behalf, including the murders he committed under orders. In the late 1930s, he had killed a Ukrainian nationalist supported by Hitler by handing him a candy box with a bomb in it. Sudoplatov also directed the assassination of Leon Trotsky in Mexico. During World War II, he headed guerrilla operations and fed disinformation to the Germans with false radio games. After the Great Patriotic War, he again defeated separatists trying to break Ukraine away from the Soviet Union. Khrushchev's Central Committee had taken away his medals, and he wanted them back.

Sudoplatov related that his sources were "the top people" in the United States, even though he never set foot on American soil. He worked with Oppenheimer,

Fermi, Szilard, Bohr, and many others. He had a copy of his letter to the Central Committee, recounting his services to the USSR, extracts of which were published in a Russian-language biography of Stalin by historian Dmitri Volkogonov.

Thus in the early spring of 1992 began two years of interviews in which we were able to ask and have answered questions about the Rosenbergs, about Raoul Wallenberg, about the purges of the 1930s, about the Doctors' Plot of the 1940s, and about how the Soviets stole the secrets of the atomic bomb. With the help of his son Anatoli, a professor at Moscow University, Sudoplatov recreated an underworld of espionage in which Stalin's intelligence officers lived their whole lives with false identities, trained in deception, theft, and assassination, with strange family values and no morality except that which served communism. His memoir was a bolt of lightning, not only for what it told about Stalin and his crimes, but for how Soviet intelligence enlisted the world's leading scientists to give up secrets in the belief they were keeping the Germans from succeeding in building the atomic bomb first.

After the publication of *Special Tasks* around the world, but not in Russia in 1994, the SVR, successor to the KGB, attempted to put the secrets Pavel Sudoplatov divulged back in the box. By naming Oppenheimer, Szilard, Fermi, Bohr, Pontecorvo, and Gamow as scientists who knowingly cooperated with Soviet intelligence, Sudoplatov had ignited a firestorm. The SVR fueled the uproar in America by feeding contradictory information from Sudoplatov's double biography to journalists, academics, and physicists. The attacks reflected the views of Soviet scientists who worked on the bomb, who, fifty years before, had not known that the guidance they were getting from their own senior physicists was coming from translated stolen documents received in Sudoplatov's office. Sudoplatov's description of Zoya Zarubina, then a young translator working with Igor Kurchatov (the head of the Soviet atomic bomb program) to find Russian equivalents for the English terminology of Western nuclear physics, tarnished the credit that history had given them for their efforts. Soviet physicists, who had succeeded in building their own bomb modeled on the American plans that Sudoplatov's agents had stolen, felt their medals were being taken away from them by his revelations, which deflated what they had argued were their own contributions. Sudoplatov's unauthorized account of Soviet atomic espionage cut into a raw nerve in Moscow, where internal jockeying for bureaucratic power, budgets, influence, and medals was still alive.

The similarity of fabricated charges against Pavel Sudoplatov disseminated in the United States formed a pattern that could have come only from the KGB, transmitted through the writer Amy Knight and others, who were fed falsified records used to convict Sudoplatov in 1953. A number of the assaults on Sudoplatov in America were signed by a Russian émigré scientist whose long-standing ties to the KGB were well known in Moscow. Since then, Sudoplatov's accounts of Soviet intelligence history and atomic espionage have been borne out by new documents and confirmations by Russian intelligence experts.

The most surprising affirmations were casual remarks by Russian President Vladimir Putin in September 2000. In a CNN interview with Larry King, Putin asked conversationally: why had America's leading scientists at Los Alamos cooperated with the Soviets, helping them build their first atomic bomb? When Putin visited the Millennium Summit at the United Nations in New York, he appeared on *Larry King Live*; during the far ranging television interview, Putin discussed antiballistic missile (ABM) systems and the role of Soviet espionage in America during World War II. Putin warned that abandoning limitations on ABM systems

would disrupt the balance of strategical interest and forces which in my opinion is extremely dangerous. . . .

When discussing this matter with our American colleagues, I've always been tempted to remind them of the beginning of the arms race—nuclear arms race. I always recall the fact that initially nuclear arms emerged—were created in the United States. And subsequently, some scientists who invented those arms, in part at least, the secret concerning the A-bomb, on their own will transferred those secrets to the Soviet Union. . . . "Why did they do that?" I always ask my American colleagues: "Can you invent something of the kind?"

" 'No we cannot come up with anything like this.' " Neither can I, but your scientists could do that. They were smarter than you and I. But voluntarily they transferred those secrets to the Soviet Union because they wanted to restore the balance. And thanks to that balance humankind has survived without major conflict, large-scale wars, since about 1945.

If we disrupt that balance, then we'll put the whole world in great danger. Which doesn't serve the interests of Russia or other countries. In my impression, that's the most important thing, and why we seek to retain that balance; why we object to the deployment of the national ABM system is because of that.[37]

This remarkable statement, serving Putin's political purpose of retaining the Anti-Ballistic Missile Treaty, corroborated Sudoplatov's revelations that key American scientists, inventors of nuclear weapons, were participants in nuclear espionage on behalf of the Soviet Union.

Two months later, Moscow's government Channel Two, Russian Radio and Television (RTR), presented a documentary, *Twenty Two Questions to Niels Bohr*, aired on November 27, 2000. Lieutenant General Pavel Sudoplatov, shown in his photograph from KGB files, emerged as the organizer of atomic espionage and of the operation to send an intelligence officer versed in physics to visit Bohr in Copenhagen in November 1945. The first Soviet nuclear reactor had been built, but their scientists couldn't get it to work; could Bohr help them? Was Sudoplatov telling the truth in his memoir, *Special Tasks*, when he said that Niels Bohr had revealed atomic bomb secrets when he answered twenty-two questions posed to him by a Soviet intelligence officer in Copenhagen in 1945, or were Sudoplatov's critics correct in saying Bohr gave nothing?[38]

The show was based on Sudoplatov's oral history. The pattern of espionage by which the Soviet Union stole the atomic bomb was a sacred secret until Sudoplatov described it. Sudoplatov proudly disclosed that the top Western scientists who worked on the American atomic bomb had willingly shared military secrets with Soviet intelligence officers under cover as diplomats. For most of the scientists who cooperated with the Soviet Union, the motivation was to help a wartime ally in the race against Hitler to build the first atomic bomb. Soviet intelligence skillfully suggested that the documents were going to Sweden where Lise Meitner, a pioneer in nuclear physics and chemistry, had fled from Germany in 1938. The implication was that Meitner and other refugee physicists, by sharing American research, could speed the process of developing a nuclear bomb. Meitner never received the materials and was opposed to building atomic weapons. Sudoplatov explained how Soviet intelligence used any means, including lies and blackmail, to steal the design for its first atomic bomb from the United States. With atom bomb technology, they became an equal in the balance of terror that was to become the cold war. Without providing the names of living agents, Sudoplatov laid out the structure of espionage used by Soviet intelligence officers on American soil and in contacting Niels Bohr in Denmark.

Andrei Kokoshin, deputy defense minister and secretary of the National Security Council under President Boris Yeltsin, asserted in the documentary that Bohr, although not a controlled agent, was a friendly source who gave secrets that betrayed the West to Soviet intelligence officers visiting Copenhagen in 1945. Kokoshin stated that he would never have acted as Bohr did, giving away secrets entrusted to him to a foreign power.

Sudoplatov's account of atomic espionage was affirmed in two officially approved publications released by the Foreign Intelligence Service (SVR), in the fall of 2000:

In the United States full scale atomic research started after Pearl Harbor, December 7, 1941. In this work young and progressive scientists such as Robert Oppenheimer, Enrico Fermi and Leo Szilard participated. They were not our agents but Soviet intelligence officers maintained contact with them directly and through third persons.

VARDO [code name for Elizabeth Zarubina] through her connections managed to become acquainted with the American father of the atomic bomb, Robert Oppenheimer, and with an outstanding physicist, Szilard, who worked in the same area.[39]

In 1996, two years after *Special Tasks* was published around the world, the Russian edition was issued in Moscow, and two years of official Foreign Intelligence Service of Russia (*Sluzhba Vneshei Razvedki*, SVR) denials ended. Sudoplatov's memoirs became a best-seller; Russian espionage experts call his memoirs "an encyclopedia of Soviet intelligence." However, he lost the battle to get his medals back in his lifetime; they were returned to his family in 1998, two years after his death, and his name has been officially rehabilitated.

Despite President Putin's seeming openness about atomic espionage, Russian intelligence services have yet to disclose their role in copying the American bomb. After the publication of *Special Tasks*, the Russian intelligence services attacked Sudoplatov's account because he had no documents to prove his notes and recollections. Search for the documents led to confusion because the secret reports were not where they were expected to be, in intelligence archives; they were instead in presidential archives.

After the KGB's participation in the failed 1991 coup attempt against Mikhail Gorbachev, the SVR attempted to restore a positive image of Soviet intelligence. In 1992 the SVR provided archival documents on the development of the first Soviet atomic bomb to the journal *Voprossi Istorii Estesvoznania i Tekniki (Questions of History of Natural Science and Technology)*.[40] After publication and distribution to libraries throughout Russia, the journal was withdrawn from circulation because of the secret technical data it contained. However, the leak was enough to promulgate a disinformation myth, the fabricated code name PERSEUS, an imagined American scientist who provided secrets from the Manhattan Project. The search for PERSEUS distracted researchers and confused the hunt for the real spies.[41]

In 1995 President Yeltsin authorized the Ministry of Atomic Energy to prepare, for internal use, histories of the Soviet atomic project and of the creation of the hydrogen bomb. The ministry was directed to cooperate with the archival services of the Presidential Administration, the Foreign Intelligence Service, the Federal Security Service, and the Academy of Sciences of the Russian Federation to survey classified documents from 1938 to 1954. By November 2000, the four agencies had reviewed, edited, and published, in two volumes in abridged form, documents covering only the period 1938 to 1943. The most significant atomic espionage activity occurred from 1943 to 1945. The researchers found most of the intelligence documents in the presidential archives, in the files of Beria, Stalin, and Molotov.[42] Work on declassifying the later period is still under way and no materials have been released. The work is expected to be completed in two or three years.

The published documents from the presidential archives corroborate Sudoplatov's revelations:

After Moscow Center first heard from Gregory Kheifetz in December 1941 that Robert Oppenheimer was involved in work on an American atomic bomb, Moscow responded on March 27, 1942, with instructions to Vasili Zarubin, the Soviet chief *rezident* in the United States and Canada, to obtain information on chemical and bacteriological weapons, radar and the problem of uranium. The message from Moscow Center named a list of people to be immediately contacted [all the names are deleted from the document for internal use only]. The instructions stress the importance of the problem of uranium and the construction of "bombs with enormous destructive power which are being actively developed in Britain, Germany and the US. This problem is close to resolution. You should take serious action. For this you have the following opportunities [all this information is deleted]." The message is signed by VICTOR, the code name for Pavel Fitin, head of the First Directorate for Foreign Intelligence.[43]

An unsigned summary of intelligence information gathered by the NKVD agent network in the United States, dated January 13, 1943, provides a detailed description of the method used by Enrico Fermi in building the uranium reactor at the University of Chicago Metallurgical Laboratory in December of 1942.[44]

On April 6, 1943, the NKVD in Moscow prepared another summary on atomic energy signed by G. Ovakimian, whom the FBI had arrested for spying and expelled from New York in 1941. In 1943 Ovakimian was in charge of the American and British desk in the Foreign Intelligence Directorate in Moscow. The document contains a footnote explaining that the data on American, British, and German scientists who participated in the research is deleted. Even for internal use, the Presidential Archive editors were directed to eliminate the names of the scientists the NKVD contacted or who might have cooperated with Soviet intelligence.

The April 6 summary contains a full description of Enrico Fermi's first reactor and emphasizes that the scale of research in the United States is "considerably larger than in other countries. Hundreds of highly qualified scientific workers are engaged in the project and their work produced substantial results. Due to this the results of British research work, summarized here, do not merit great attention."[45] This document addressed to M. Pervukhin was forwarded by Merkulov, then the deputy head of the NVKD.

Beria removed the intelligence files when he left the NKVD to take charge of "Problem Number One," the project to develop an atomic bomb. It is plausible that in August 1945, after being appointed chairman of the Special Committee of the Soviet Government on Problem Number One, Beria consolidated all the intelligence material in his own secretariat. He was entrusted by Stalin "to undertake measures for the organization of foreign intelligence work on obtaining more full technical and economic information on the uranium industry and the atomic bomb" and the leadership of all atomic intelligence work.[46] Beria's removal of the files explains why these materials are in the Presidential Archives, not those of the Foreign Intelligence Service or the Federal Security Archives.

5 Opening VENONA

In the spring of 1943, at about the same time the Katyn Massacre story broke in the world press, serious tension mounted in the Grand Alliance among Britain, the United States, and the USSR over the opening of a second front into German-occupied France. The growing distrust continued until D-Day, the cross-channel invasion of Normandy, on June 6, 1944. The distrust was replaced with new tensions between the Western allies and Stalin when the Army Signals Security Agency began its attempt to decode secret Soviet cable traffic passing back and forth from Moscow to Washington and New York.

The Soviet Union was desperate for the allies to open a second front in France. So often was this demand repeated by Soviet diplomats in Washington that even officials who knew not a word of Russian could repeat the mantra *vtoroi front*, second front.[1] The joke going around London was that Soviet Foreign Minister Vyacheslav Molotov knew only four words of English: "yes," "no," and "second front."[2]

The leaders of the Anglo-American alliance, Roosevelt and Churchill, agreed that they should begin a second front against Hitler. The grand question that historians still ponder a half century later was: Should the second front be across the English Channel into western France, then on to the German heartland (the path finally chosen), or should it cut through the Balkans into Eastern Europe, which would have stopped the Soviets from taking over the countries between the Baltic and the Adriatic Seas and prevented the Iron Curtain from falling?

The British, led by Winston Churchill, favored a second front in the Balkans. The British were maneuvering to hold onto their empire gained from a century of expansion. Roosevelt had little understanding of Stalin's motives and ambitions. FDR was little prepared for the double endeavor of defeating Germany and Japan while managing two allies whose world views clashed with each other.

Stalin continued to demand a second front that would draw away thirty to forty German divisions from Operation Barbarossa, Hitler's eastern war against the Red Army. Roosevelt agreed that a massive military buildup in Britain, followed by an attack across the English Channel aimed at the industrial Ruhr valley, would effectively destroy German troop strength and war-making capacity. The plan took into account Eisenhower's analysis that "the prize we seek is to keep eight million Russians in the war," lest Hitler's forces be unleashed for the conquest of Britain and eventually the United States.[3]

Churchill hesitated before committing Britain to participate in opening the second front across the English Channel. In Britain's historic memory were the horrendous losses suffered in World War I, the sad poetry that still echoed the decimation of a generation of the nation's youth. Churchill was not prepared to bury again the numbers who died at the battles for Verdun, Ypres, or the Somme, nor to have to bring home gassed and wounded soldiers. Churchill saw the Soviet Union not only as a wartime ally, but also as a competitor for spheres of influence in postwar Europe. Would these battles bring peace or a fight between communism and Western liberalism in European nations that had first suffered under Hitler, then would be caught in a struggle between their saviors?

Roosevelt and Churchill discussed their opposing strategies at Hyde Park on June 19, 1942. Churchill urged Roosevelt to join Britain against Germany in North Africa and the Middle East. Roosevelt agreed, but his military leadership objected vehemently. General George Marshall was livid and strode from the room. Roosevelt sent Marshall, Admiral King, and Harry Hopkins to London in a last attempt to salvage "Sledgehammer," the planned cross-channel invasion.

In 1942, under Churchill's influence, British and American forces joined together in Operation Torch to recapture North Africa and move north through Italy. The military chiefs could only pray that the Soviets were not defeated before the allies could help them.[4]

For the Soviets, invasion of Italy was no substitute for starting the promised second front in Europe. The invasion of Italy was another marker in the initial stage of the secret cold war—the Russians understood that the territories occupied by Britain and the United States would be out of their sphere of domination. The Balkans had been part of the Russian sphere of influence. They remembered that in 1918 the Balkans opened the road for allied troops to appear in Central Europe on the outskirts of Austria and Hungary, areas that Stalin wanted to dominate.

Marshall called the Mediterranean campaign an "inappropriate theater" suctioning off their best efforts in an "interminable" dissipation of fighting power to defeat Germany. Marshall said we should not waste forces on "periphery pecking" in the Mediterranean.

During the brutal winter of 1943, the Red Army defeated twenty German divisions at Stalingrad. The ground shift at Stalingrad made the Soviet Union a power to be reckoned with, especially if it succeeded in defeating Germany with a direct allied attack from the west.

The Battle of Stalingrad was the turning point in the war against Hitler, the last eastward point after which, if they had succeeded, the Germans would have taken over the Caspian oil supply. After the Soviet victory in February 1943, Nazi-occupied Europe began to hope for deliverance. Soviet survival no longer seemed to be in question. Stalin continued to demand that the British and Americans open the second front in Western Europe to force Hitler to divert German forces from the eastern front, which stretched from the Finnish border almost to the Caspian. Although the Soviets had destroyed twenty German divisions and killed 200,000 troops in the historic battle, the Red Army still faced more than 200 Axis divisions. The Soviets were now on the offensive, pushing the Wehrmacht back across the Russian steppes, back to Europe.

Still FDR and Churchill delayed the second front. Meanwhile the Germans deployed thirty-six fresh divisions to the eastern front. Stalin wrote to Roosevelt about the grave danger in further delay of the second front in France.

Marshall hoped to fulfill Roosevelt's promise to Stalin to start the second front. Marshall's admonition to Roosevelt to do more for Russia to keep Stalin in the war rippled out of Washington into a broad campaign to influence American public opinion in favor of the Soviet Union. The call for a second front was backed up by a Hollywood movie, *Mission to Moscow*, based on a best selling book by Joseph E. Davies, former ambassador to the Soviet Union (1936–1938); Davies was an apologist for Stalin who defended Stalin's purges as cleaning up nests of "internal aggression." Photographer Margaret Bourke-White in her 1942 book *Shooting the Russian War* and popular journalist Quentin Reynolds effectively created sympathy for the Soviet Union under German attack. *Time* magazine made Stalin the "Man of the Year" and *Life* ran a special issue devoted to the Soviet Union in 1943. Russian war relief organizations sprang to life collecting clothes and food to be sent to Moscow.[5]

However, habitual Soviet secrecy created a situation in which they were their own worst enemies. The Russians would not allow allied military observers near the eastern front, nor would they give any information about their troop strength or their order of battle. Attacking the French coast demanded accurate, up-to-date intelligence: how could the allies attack until they knew what forces they would face? American Army Intelligence gathered intercepts to figure out where they would face German gun emplacements on the French coast. They needed to know German strength along the English Channel and how many divisions were fighting the Soviets on the Germans' eastern front. They tried to determine how many troops the Nazis could move against an allied invasion.

Despite the campaign in America to build a positive image of the alliance, showing Stalin as Uncle Joe and the Red Army as a dedicated fighting force, the U.S. military mission in Moscow was frustrated at every turn in its efforts to obtain hard intelligence on Soviet intentions and the actual strength of the Red Army.[6]

In Moscow the American ambassador, William H. Standley, complained that the Soviet Union was getting American Lend Lease supplies in large quantities but was keeping that fact from its people, leading them to believe that the Soviets were fighting unaided. The allied military high command worried whether or not Stalin had the forces and firepower to continue to engage Hitler's forces, and if Stalin was secretly negotiating a separate peace with Germany. If Hitler shifted his forces to the West, he could repel the allied invasion.

★ ★ ★

According to William Crowell, deputy director of the National Security Agency from 1994 to September 1997:

> The Russians were a critical part of success in the war. At that time they were the key to victory in Europe. We had no idea from them how they were doing. They just weren't telling us. Based on what little intelligence was available . . . it looked like the Germans were whipping them pretty bad. Even when the tide started turning it was very slow in terms of the push back. The Germans maintained a very viable force on the Eastern front until Normandy.[7]

In this arena of uncertainty, a quiet suggestion came from Army intelligence. As they pondered the question of Soviet intentions in 1943, they had still not opened the canvas bags of encoded messages accumulated since they first ordered telegraph companies to turn over copies of Soviet diplomatic traffic in the fall of 1939, soon after the signing of the 1939 Nazi-Soviet Pact of Non-Aggression. Reading the Soviet messages might reveal Soviet military capabilities and provide answers to the enigma of Stalin's objectives. That was how the decision was made to begin deciphering the telegrams that were later code-named VENONA. General Marshall no doubt believed in 1943 that reading Soviet messages might at best provide the intelligence needed to facilitate the opening of the second front. At worst, they might reveal if Stalin was negotiating a separate peace with Hitler. Neither General Marshall nor Army intelligence at the time imagined the grim secrets that the code breakers would uncover: more than 200 Americans at the top of the Washington bureaucracy and in American industry were spying for Moscow. Army intelligence opened a Pandora's box of troubles. It took five more years to go beyond fragments and begin to read the first Soviet messages that were deciphered; only then could American leaders conceive of the full extent of Soviet intelligence operations in the United States. When the decoding ended in 1980, the treachery of some Americans working for Moscow remained hidden under code names that have never been identified.

★ ★ ★

Ironically, the Army had not attempted to read the Soviet intercepts during the two years that Germany and the Soviet Union were joined in a deadly pact to share domination of the world. Between 1939 and 1941, while Hitler and Stalin carved up Poland between themselves and the Soviet Union annexed the Baltic states and waged war against Finland, the message traffic between Moscow and its embassy in the United States remained unread.

Those were torturous years for left wing Americans torn between those who imagined that the Soviet experiment with communism was the promise of a future utopia and those who saw the pact between Hitler and Stalin to be a clarifying display of cynical Soviet *realpolitik*. Hundreds abandoned the Communist Party, but the diehards defended Stalin. Roosevelt knew America would be drawn into the war in Europe, but he reinforced a dominant mood of isolationism at home with his 1940 campaign pledge not to send American boys to die on foreign soil.

In 1939 and 1940, Roosevelt was being attacked by isolationists from the political right and left while war clouds darkened in Europe. Influential New York leftist intellectuals argued that capitalism, not Hitler, was the real enemy and urged the United States to remain neutral in the European war. "The masses in Britain and France are not satisfied enough with the status quo to die for it," wrote the critic Clement Greenberg in 1940. He insisted that if the capitalists delivered economic power into the hands of the proletariat, German workers would desert Hitler and the war would immediately end.[8] The American Communist Party attacked Roosevelt and the United States as the real class enemy. Communist-dominated unions carried out strikes to sabotage American war preparations, and the Communist Party protested FDR's efforts to save England from the German blitz.[9]

In the spring of 1941, a note from Harry Hopkins to New York City Mayor Fiorello La Guardia equated danger from the American Communist Party with the threat of Hitler: "It seems to me that we have got to find a way to beat these people. From my point of view they are just as much a potential enemy as the Germans."[10]

The United States stood by in anguish while France, Eastern Europe, and the Balkans fell under the Nazi *blitzkrieg* that eventually reached into North Africa. Roosevelt quietly supported Great Britain, under sustained German air attacks, with Lend Lease aid of food, fuel, aircraft, and armaments.

Everything changed on June 22, 1941, when Hitler attacked the Soviet Union. The United States gave Lend Lease aid to the Soviet Union but still remained out of the war. After the German invasion of the Soviet Union in June until the Japanese attack on Pearl Harbor December 7, it was unclear whether the Japanese membership in the Tripartite Pact with Germany and Italy would draw them into the war on the Axis side, or the continuing diplomacy between the United States and Japan would avoid a bloody conflict. After the Japanese attack on Pearl Harbor, Hitler declared war on the United States and became the primary enemy of both America and the Soviet Union. The United States shifted its unbounded energy and resources to defeating the Axis, and made the war in Europe its top priority. In a drastic about-face, the Soviet Union—center of world revolution and godless communism—became an ally against Hitler and fascism. Code breakers focused on German and Japanese messages; the Soviet traffic remained in a secure warehouse.

★ ★ ★

On February 1, 1943, Army intelligence commenced work on the unread telegrams. Colonel W. Preston Corderman, an experienced signals intelligence officer with background in cryptanalysis, was named head of the Signals Security Service (SSS). He joined Colonel Carter Clarke, the head of Army Intelligence (G-2) in upgrading the production and dissemination of Army Communications Intelligence (COMINT).[11] From their review came the decision to proceed with breaking the Russian coded traffic. Because of the sensitivity of the project, the two officers sought approval from Secretary of War Henry Stimson and James Byrnes, Director of the Office of War Mobilization.

The question of whether to try breaking the Soviet code was taken up the chain of command. Normal practice was not to attempt decoding an ally's traffic. Colonel Clarke, who was responsible for the processing and distribution of all decoded messages to the Army and the White House, discussed with General Marshall the importance of obtaining better information on Soviet intentions. Clarke suggested to Marshall that an effort be made to read the stored Soviet messages. Marshall no doubt believed in 1943 that tapping into Soviet messages would provide the intelligence needed to help America's ally by moving forward to the second front. Marshall agreed and the proposal was made to James Byrnes. Byrnes approved the decision to proceed, and President Roosevelt was informed.[12]

Byrnes was known in the press as FDR's "assistant President," on whom the President had conferred "greater authority than a President had ever previously delegated and a new range of duties." His mandate included military procurement and he worked closely with Secretary of War Stimson and the Joint Chiefs of Staff.[13] Byrnes later became Truman's Secretary of State on July 3, 1945.[14]

The U.S. Army Security Agency's Signals Security Service, forerunner of the National Security Agency, began to examine encrypted Soviet diplomatic communications. The painstaking task of converting coded groups of numbers into letters and figuring out the message texts fell to a group of young American code breakers at Arlington Hall, the Signals Security Service facility housed in a former girls' school across the Potomac River from Washington. Arlington Hall still stands today; during the war it was a code-breaking factory where young female college graduates, wearing hats and gloves to work, helped expose the hidden relationship between Soviet intelligence and American bureaucrats at the highest levels of the government. The team recruited by the Army included code specialists, linguists, an archaeologist, school teachers, and recent high school graduates who served at Arlington Hall instead of going to boot camp.

The Soviet message traffic consisted of diplomatic telegrams between Soviet missions in the United States and Moscow. The National Security Agency estimates that there were a total of two million coded Soviet messages, of which 2,900 were decoded in part or fully. During the first months of the project, Arlington Hall analysts sorted the traffic by diplomatic mission and by the cryptographic system of the subscriber. The next step was to sort the messages into groups indicating the addressees and the subject matter.

Five separate cryptographic systems emerged. The heaviest traffic was to and from Soviet trade representatives: Lend Lease; Amtorg, the Soviet trade mission; and the Soviet Government Purchasing Commission. The other groups included diplomatic traffic; NKVD, the Soviet intelligence and espionage agency; GRU-Army, the Soviet Army General Staff Intelligence Directorate; GRU-Naval, Soviet Naval Intelligence.

Analysis of the traffic proved slow and difficult. The telegrams consisted of groups of six numbers, indicating to the code breakers that an additional layer of numbers had been added to the normal four-digit book codes. The first weakness in the Soviet code was found in October 1943, eight months into the work, by Lieutenant Richard Hallock, in peacetime an archeologist at the University of Chicago. Hallock discovered lapses in the cryptographic system of the Soviet trade traffic, thus providing a tool for further analytic progress. Using primitive computers with giant vacuum tubes and punch cards, Hallock discovered repetitions of numbers, indicating reuse of coded words. In 1944, his colleague Cecil Phillips, a recent high school graduate who would not get to attend college until the war's end, cracked the fundamental Soviet cipher when he discovered that the Soviets were using one-time code pads more than once. Moreover, the serial numbers of the pads were being sent uncoded.

The decrypted messages, which came to be known as VENONA, had a variety of code names, including BRIDE, BOURBON, WHISKEY, and DRUG. For more than 50 years, VENONA was so secret that its very name could not be spoken in public or revealed in print on pain of prosecution under federal law. For the decoders in the Army Security Agency, the law enforcers in the FBI, and the few lawmakers who funded the project, it was a sacred secret. Knowledge of the intercepts was kept secret until the National Security Agency and the CIA released it to the public in stages, beginning in July 1995.

By 1944 Army Signals Intelligence had limited success with one Soviet system not strictly a diplomatic code.[15] When Clarke reported to General Marshall, he urged that the decoders accelerate the work. They began to read the first Soviet messages by 1945. Marshall urged Clarke to advise President Truman of the decoding project.[16]

Only when the messages were broken after the war ended did they reveal a more sinister portrait of the Soviet Union than the ally portrayed in the flush of wartime friendship.

★ ★ ★

The results of deciphering the messages did not come in time to settle doubts about Stalin's plans for a separate peace with Hitler or to reveal strengths and weaknesses along the 2,000-mile Soviet battlefront against German armies.

Only years later, after the Soviet traffic had been decoded, would the Americans and British know the full bitterness with which the Russians greeted the Mediterranean campaign. In June 1943 Soviet intelligence learned once again that there would not be a second front in Europe: "The attack this summer will be in the Mediterranean." The June 9 message to Moscow from the Soviet military intelligence (GRU) *resident* in New York warned Moscow that "the Americans and British do not want to incur large losses, they are waiting for the Germans to open a new and large offensive in the East and if the USSR seems to be in a critical situation, the plans can be changed and an attack in France and Holland [65 groups unrecoverable (Author note: this portion could not be clearly dedoded)]." The Russians were angry with American admirals and with "fascist circles," for supporting air bombardment but not the commencement of allied ground operations in France.[17]

Nineteen forty-three was the year of the allied invasion of Italy. In VENONA interceptions, Soviet displeasure with invasion of Italy, rather than a Normandy landing, is evident. Officially, the displeasure comes in the form of saying that the Italian operation was not having any effect on the military strength of Germany, which was still battering the USSR on the eastern front.

It was the British who accomplished the biggest breakthrough in code breaking. Joined by Americans, they were reading the German ULTRA codes, which contained detailed operations orders, supply inventories, and battle plans.

In July 1943, the Soviets fought the greatest tank battle in history near Kursk on the open steppes southwest of Moscow; this encounter turned out to be the decisive one in the defeat of German armored forces on Soviet territory. Because the Soviets had learned in the spring that the German offensive (code-named Citadel) would take place 300 miles southwest, not due west, of Moscow as they had thought earlier, they were able to prepare a massive defense. The Soviet *rezidentura* in London had passed on this crucial information.

In 1995 John Cairncross, the "Fifth Man" of the Cambridge spies, who had earlier worked at Bletchley Park, the British decoding center, said that he supplied the warning about Kursk to the Soviets.[18] Moscow Center had the same information, in modified form, from its Lucy network in Geneva; by comparing the two reports, the Soviets came to the conclusion that Lucy was getting its information from official British sources. From this the Soviets decided that the British had infiltrated their network and that the Western allies were giving them truncated data, even on such a crucial issue as where the Germans were planning to attack. In fact, the British had modified the reports in order to hide their ability to read the German ENIGMA messages.[19] By playing tit for tat, holding back information on German troop strength and deployment on the eastern flank, the Soviets were delaying the second front they wanted so badly.

★ ★ ★

On August 11, 1943, a month after the decisive battle at Kursk, John C. Wiley, an expert on the Soviet Union, wrote to President Roosevelt. Wiley was a longtime friend of the Roosevelts' private secretary, Grace Tully. Serving in the Office of Strategic Services (OSS) in Washington, Wiley "succumbed to the urge" to explain recent events in Moscow and begged FDR to "forgive" him for inflicting his memorandum on the President.[20]

Wiley laid out the motives behind Stalin's decision to establish a Free German Committee at meetings in Moscow on July 12 and 13, from which came a manifesto to the German people, in the Popular Front manner, using the Soviet press and radio. The committee was built around the German section of the Comintern, supposedly in "dissolution," whose members included former communist deputies of the Reichstag in exile in Moscow. The manifesto offered the German people the chance to choose their own fate if they eliminated Hitler. "Amnesty was promised for all Hitler adherents who renounced him in good time and joined the movement for Free Germany," Wiley reported. "On August 6, Pravda, the official Communist Party newspaper, reproved the U.S. and Great Britain for failure to observe their pledges to open a second front," he continued.[21]

Wiley warned the President that "official emanations from Moscow . . . insist on the importance of Russia's role in the political future of the continent" and laid out Stalin's plans:

To prepare for the future, Soviet policy is being directed toward Hungary; Poland . . . northern Iran; . . . support of the Yugoslav partisans . . . Germany. The Free German manifesto was no spontaneous gesture . . . Stalin's speeches and a number of inspired articles and developments over the last nine months give a pattern . . . the manifesto and the studied grumbling over the second front reflect this planning.[22]

Wily cautioned that although the Soviet Union suffered grievously from a war unparalleled in casualties and destruction, the Soviet military situation was at that moment peculiarly favorable. "Soviet complaints over the second front, therefore do not stem from the same dire need for military succor that existed a year ago." He saw the German manifesto "as the opening gambit for a peace move," with the American "failure" to open a second front providing the alibi for a new Moscow-Berlin axis. "Soviet planning," noted Wiley, "is both daring and prudent."[23]

Wiley warned Roosevelt that the coalition to win the war was turning political. He warned that while the Soviets had disbanded the Comintern during the war, they had never repudiated its goals of a proletarian revolution, led by Soviet intervention, in Europe.

The United States "did not go to war; war came to us," Wiley wrote. Americans desire "only a relatively decent world without constant recurrence of military conquest." These "simple concepts may go askew if . . . we are maneuvered into aiding and abetting the rape of a large part of Europe by another and singularly similar European power," the OSS officer warned.[24]

Wiley concludes that

the situation is still fluid. At present, we face the dangerous paradox of having our political authority on the Continent of Europe diminish while our military strength is notably ascendant. Attack from the air and the destruction of great German cities are wounding Germany. Now, only Russia has land armies to retrieve the fallen game.

We must be fully prepared against political surprises . . . . [I]f such a surprise should be a union of Russian imperialism with Comintern revolutionary technique, joined with German military and economic competence, the result would be difficult to handle. Russian German collaboration is not as fantastic as it sounds. . . .[25]

Wiley's most far-reaching recommendation was to

expedite the setting up of a second front . . .—but in the Balkans, where it could best influence the course of the war, diplomatic relations with the Kremlin, and the peace to come. True, a Balkan front is difficult . . . but if it is merely very difficult but not impossible, we must by all means set up the Balkan front. An invasion of France and the Lowlands would give us no political authority in central and eastern Europe. Only a successful Anglo-

American invasion of southeastern Europe can give us a real voice in the eventual peace settlement. To err on the side of supposed caution . . . might store up the gravest dangers in the future.[26]

★ ★ ★

The subsurface war to decide the eventual peace settlement once Germany was defeated, reflected in Wiley's letter, continued through 1943 and 1944. Hungary joined Germany in declaring war against the United States and the Soviet Union in 1941, but by early 1943 a group of Hungarian politicians could see the tide turning against Hitler's armies. Through an exile in Istanbul, their diplomats in Stockholm, and their minister stationed in Berne, Switzerland, who was in contact with Allen Dulles of the OSS, the Hungarians sued for a separate peace. The Hungarians feared that if their capitulation was announced before American and British troops reached Budapest, the Soviets would invade and subject them to communist rule.[27]

Instead, the Germans attacked and took over Hungary. An unresolved question remains: who told the Germans about the Hungarian initiative? Staff members in the office of the OSS chief, General William (Wild Bill) Donovan, believed that "leftist" members of the OSS leaked the plan to the Soviets, who then let the Germans know so they could take over and prevent an alliance with the West. One of Donovan's staff was convinced that Duncan Lee, an OSS officer named as a Soviet asset by Elizabeth Bentley, told her and she relayed the plan to Moscow.

★ ★ ★

William Friedman, a legendary code breaker and the world's greatest cryptologist, broke the Japanese PURPLE code.[28] The ability to read Japanese messages provided a windfall not only in the Pacific but also in Europe. In November 1943, the Army Security Agency decoded a message to Tokyo from the Japanese ambassador to Germany, Baron General Hiroshi Oshima, that reviewed the status of German troops and armaments. There are claims that the Russians broke the Japanese PURPLE code and had the same message, but if they did, it was never shared with the allies. According to William Crowell:

The truth of the matter is that we intercepted that message and gave it to Eisenhower in November 1943 and Normandy happened in June of 1944. General Oshima was a friend of Hitler's and Himmler's and they gave him a total guided tour of Normandy. He knew the . . . number of troops and where every gun was placed and it was all in the message. Normandy wouldn't have happened . . . it may have been some other beach and it wouldn't have been as successful if there hadn't been that intercept.[29]

Thus, the effort to read Soviet traffic began in an attempt to determine Soviet strategic intentions and abilities, but it was a Japanese intercept between Tokyo and Berlin that focused allied attention on Normandy beaches for the D-Day landing.

In November 1943, Churchill and Roosevelt flew to Teheran, where the President met Stalin for the first time. Churchill had met before with the leader of the "sullen, sinister Bolshevik State I had once tried so hard to strangle at its birth."[30] Although Roosevelt had read Wiley's OSS analysis with interest in August, he believed he could use his well-developed political charms to make Stalin his friend.

Both Western leaders were surprised by their encounter with Stalin. They found him inscrutable, his icy surface still and correct, without human warmth, without gesture or mannerisms. He was also remarkably intelligent, shrewd and to the point, with spare words that needed no inflection to get across his meaning. When Roosevelt spoke of starting a second front, Stalin said that would be "of great value."[31]

At Teheran, Stalin and Roosevelt discussed postwar European borders. By this time there was a subtle understanding on the president's part that territory occupied by the Red Army would remain under Soviet power, and there was nothing he could do about it short of fighting a new war, this time against the Soviet Union. Roosevelt's warning that the United States would probably return to its prewar isolationism when Germany and Japan were defeated heartened Stalin. He could envision Soviet hegemony west to the Atlantic Ocean.

Finally the three leaders had to discuss the timing for Operation Overlord, the code name for the invasion of France to begin the second front. Stalin waited, eyes downcast, chain smoking and doodling, while Roosevelt opened the subject. To the surprise of everyone present, Roosevelt asked Stalin what he thought of delaying the invasion of France across the English Channel until May 1944. Meanwhile American forces could push through Italy and make new forays into the Adriatic and Aegean Seas, strategies favored by Churchill but not by Roosevelt's own military chiefs.

There was a tense delay while Stalin controlled his anger and replied in barely audible Russian. Roosevelt, Churchill, and their aides had to wait for the interpreter. Stalin's brilliantly conceived reply was his commitment that once the war was won against Germany, the Soviet Union would enter the fight against Japan.[32] At the time of the meeting in Teheran, the allies still had to cross 4,000 miles of the Pacific Ocean to bring the war home to Japan. The Soviet Union's participation would shift the fight from the reluctant Chinese combatants who were more concerned with the competition between Nationalists and Communists than fighting Japan, to the Soviet Far East. It would give the allies a land base from which to attack the Japanese islands. The Western allies hoped that a Soviet effort in East Asia would deter the Soviet Union from pushing beyond agreed armistice lines in Europe.

Then Stalin returned to the question of when the second front would finally be launched. He explained that Italy was divided from the rest of Europe by the Alps; it was not a base from which to attack Germany. Nor would the Balkans be an effective place to begin a campaign against the German heartland. It had to be northern France. Churchill again pressed for a drive into the Balkans. Stalin repeated that scattering allied forces was unwise; Overlord must be the priority. Churchill still equivocated about Overlord. Stalin exploded in a burst directed to ending the argument. He said he was there to discuss military matters and the Soviet Union was only interested in Overlord. Roosevelt, by his decision to reject a second front through the Balkans, then set a firm date for Overlord, the D-Day invasion of Normandy. The President's suggestion that dinner would soon be ready adjourned the meeting.[33]

Churchill fell into black despair. He no longer had the power to deflect Roosevelt into Mediterranean adventures. Roosevelt now concentrated on the central issue of attacking Germany from the west, the south, and the east simultaneously. Roosevelt's war council—Stimson, Hopkins, Admiral King, and General Marshall—rejoiced at the change in strategy. In that fateful encounter, Britain lost its dominating power in the Anglo-American alliance. Soon afterward, bowing to British public opinion, Churchill agreed to support the invasion of western France. The encounter between Roosevelt and Stalin at Teheran may have been the moment in which Roosevelt stiffened his back to the isolationists in the United States and changed America's international power status. Roosevelt's new-found resolution transmuted the antiglobalism that characterized the period between the two world wars and made the United States a force for international responsibility and development.

Roosevelt and Stalin agreed on Overlord, which brought about the end of the war in Europe. Stalin could not have predicted that day that the change he brought about in Roosevelt would bring them to a new threshold of competition. While Roosevelt and Stalin met in Teheran, American signals intelligence was already at work decoding Soviet messages that would change the image of the Soviet Union as an ally of the United States.

Only later, when the Iron Curtain dropped, sealing off Eastern Europe, did it become clear what the Soviets were angry about when talking to each other in VENONA messages. Stalin feared that the war's end would be a replay of Soviet chagrin after World War I when, totally engaged in their own revolution, the Russians were unable to stem the influence of the Western allies who came as liberators to Central Europe and the Balkans. The allies took over the historical area of influence that the czars had enjoyed and the Soviet regime hoped to continue.

Stalin's determination to keep history from being repeated was a factor in sealing off Eastern Europe under Moscow's domination. Churchill, well aware of the past, feared the spread of communist control into Greece and Italy. Once the German stranglehold was broken, the war in Europe would become a political struggle between the Western democracies and Soviet communism.

Looking back with the advantage of hindsight, some historians, both British and East European, believe that Roosevelt and his generals made a mistake when they focused the second front in Western Europe. They argue that Churchill was right: the attack on Germany should have come through Trieste, then through the Ljubljana Gap, into the Balkans, and then to the heart of Germany. Their reasoning is (1) that the effort to defeat Germany would not have been more costly in casualties, perhaps less; (2) it would have accomplished even more rapid relief to the Soviet western front; and (3) the Western allies fighting their way through Central Europe would have given the Soviets less scope for the Red Army to become entrenched as a permanently occupying force. The ideological Soviet curtain would have dropped much farther eastward.[34]

Hindsight, however, cannot change the conditions under which the decision was made. By the end of 1943, when Roosevelt gave the go-ahead at Teheran for Operation Overlord, the Soviet outlook had just undergone an enormous change. Stalin's victory at Stalingrad expanded his aggressive appetites. He was already pushing the Nazi armies back; his caissons were rolling toward the Atlantic. A second front in the Balkans should have been well advanced before Stalingrad if it were to accomplish the goals historians ascribe to it fifty years later.

Stalin's horizons had expanded with the signing of the 1939 Nazi-Soviet Pact of Non-Aggression. Until August 1939, the Soviet Union was a new concept, only two decades in being, that flew in the face of historical governance. Born in violence, its self-identity as the center of the coming international workers' revolution challenged all established civic principles. In its first twenty years, the Soviet Union worked to stabilize the relationship among its republics and to gain diplomatic recognition from foreign nations. Before 1939 the Soviet Union was a supplicant rather than an aggressor. Only during the months of negotiations preceding the pact with Hitler did Stalin and the leadership of the Soviet Union begin to visualize themselves as one of the dominators dividing the globe into vast hegemonies that would replace the traditional imperialist powers. The distrust among the future hegemons—Japan, Germany, Italy, and the Soviet Union—and the war that followed, placed Stalin's ambitions on hold. All of the Soviet Union's energies focused on survival.

Then the struggle turned. At Kursk and at Stalingrad, the scale of battle was enormous; if the Soviet Union could be victorious commanding such an epic field of men and war materials, what could it not accomplish with the right concentration of effort? As soon as the Germans and the Japanese, Stalin's two nemeses, were defeated, they would no longer be present to argue with him over who got what. The future belonged to Stalin in the way it once belonged to Genghis Khan. The difference was that Stalin could control much more of the globe than the Great Khan ever reached. He had the benefits of modern transportation and weapons, and a tool never used before, an ideology that promised a workers' utopia.

In *The Glasnost Tapes*, Khrushchev recalled: "After the defeat of Hitler, Stalin believed he was in the same position as Alexander I after the defeat of Napoleon— that he could dictate the rules for all of Europe. Stalin even started believing that he could dictate new rules to the whole world."[35]

Stalin and his Western allies also had an elementary misunderstanding of what each side meant when they planned spheres of influence in postwar Europe. In England and America, the leading commentators, E. H. Carr and Walter Lippmann, wrote about peacetime condominiums in which the Soviets and the West would use their military power to ensure the security of Europe. Both the Western advocates, and Maksim Litvinov, the Deputy Commissar for Foreign Affairs, who chaired a committee on the preparation of peace treaties and postwar construction, visualized an era of good neighbors based on a delimitation of spheres of security interests. Their idea was similar to the Monroe Doctrine, in which the United States asserted the right to forcefully keep out foreign intervention into the internal affairs of the states in the western hemisphere, but for the most part left them to govern themselves.

Stalin's and foreign minister Molotov's concept of "spheres of influence" was markedly different: they defined the phrase to mean occupation and installation of the Soviet system, ruled by Moscow. It meant the expansion of communism at the point of a bayonet. Litvinov later said that an opportunity had been lost; mutual understanding would only have been possible when the Soviet Union was still in danger, before the hubris that came with the Soviet Union's victory at Stalingrad in 1943.[36]

★ ★ ★

In 1943 there were more reasons to break the Soviet code and read their messages than preparing for the second front. The FBI had been providing information on surveillance and wiretapping of domestic and foreign communists since 1939 and had a program to infiltrate the American Communist Party with paid informers.[37] In 1942, Soviet intelligence, fearful of a compromise of its operations, ordered an end to espionage through the American Communist Party. The FBI had been following Steve Nelson, a.k.a. Steve Masarosh, a known party organizer, who was receiving secret technical information from Joseph W. Weinberg, a researcher at the University of California Radiation Laboratory run by Robert Oppenheimer. The FBI had a hidden microphone in Nelson's house and was able to listen to his conversations. In April 1943, Phil Branigan, the FBI espionage section chief in San Francisco, was "sitting on the tap" when he listened to a conversation between Nelson and Vasili Zarubin.[38]

Zarubin had come to the west coast to inform Nelson of the Central Committee edict removing espionage from communist parties and placing these activities under his command and control. Nelson argued in favor of continuing to take part in secret operations in America. Zarubin rebuffed Nelson because he had orders to make a clean separation between the activities of covert professional intelligence operatives and Communist Party members. Nelson proposed a compromise: that "the Soviets choose in each important city or state where espionage activities might be necessary, a trustworthy contact and allow that person to handle direct contact with the communist members to be given special assignments."[39] The FBI wanted to know more about the instructions Soviet diplomats were receiving from Moscow Center.

★ ★ ★

Oliver Kirby's first encounter with code breaking was in 1939 when he took cryptanalysis courses in the ROTC program at the University of Illinois. Kirby grew up in Bloomington, the son of a high school physics teacher and a Scottish-born mother from whom he inherited a gift for languages. His father, a crack shot, taught Ollie to shoot a rifle when he was 9 years old. Shooting no less than 200 rounds at target practice every night, Kirby became captain of the University of Illinois rifle team and a national champion. Upon graduation in 1943, he was assigned to Arlington Hall in the Army's Signals Security Service.

Kirby was chosen to be part of a Special Team, 45-man code-breaking detachment headed by William (Bill) Bundy, assigned to England to help crack the German operational message traffic, including troop movements and submarine routings, code-named ULTRA. Bundy's mother, Kay, and his recent bride, Mary Acheson, both worked at Arlington Hall during the war.

Lieutenant Bundy had been teaching cryptology at Fort Monmouth, New Jersey, for the Signals Intelligence Corps when he was assigned to bring a small contingent to Bletchley Park outside London and join the British decryption effort. Bletchley Park was the headquarters for GCHQ, the British Government Communications Headquarters. The group comprised the best of his students, men from ordinary backgrounds whose quickness showed in class. They joined a British group of chess champions, mathematicians, and lawyers. Within this group of elite minds was a smaller elite who later became famous in their fields: Supreme Court Justice Lewis Powell, James Bond creator Ian Fleming, Nuremberg war crimes prosecutor Telford Taylor, computer genius Alan Turing, and journalists Malcolm Muggeridge and Alfred Friendly.[40]

In January 1943, Kirby sailed to Europe on the *Mauritania*, a luxury liner converted to a troop carrier, to become a member of Bundy's expanded staff. Kirby spent the voyage seasick in the hold, the weather so stormy "that even the German submarines quit at that point. We had what we called the 'PHD' detachment, everyone in it had a Ph.D. except me," recalled Kirby.[41] These chosen few fulfilled their promise by breaking German army and navy operational codes and turning the tide of the war.

Bundy's detachment was based in the manor house of Little Brickhill, a former girls' school situated on a ridge, overlooking ponds and a stream; it was once the site of a Roman brick factory. The manor was a few miles from Bletchley Park, a former Victorian estate on fifty-five acres of land forty-six miles north of London.[42] Kirby wanted to be a code breaker, a cryptanalyst, what the professionals called a "crypie." He worked in Hut 6, a long, low wartime building with heating that stopped at the floor level. Cold feet were a normal part of hut life. Kirby's team read German army, air force, and tank corps messages around a wooden table.

Each German service had its own ciphers and they were changed daily on the ENIGMA coding machines. In order to read the German messages, the Bletchley crypies had to look for what they called cribs—a string of letters that formed a familiar pattern, such as a known phrase, title, or geographic name. With a crib, they could break the cipher for the day by running the crib through a simple mechanical computer called a *bombe* that would test what settings on the ENIGMA machine would produce a message like that. The teams of twelve men and women rotated on three eight-hour shifts. "The great thrill of each cryptanalytic attack was the spine tingling anticipation awaiting the result of the machine run testing of the crib applied to daily messages, hoping to hear the magic words, 'Got a hit,' " recalled Kirby. "Several weeks before D-Day we read General Rommel's report after inspection of their coastal defenses in France. This was the final guide to allied planning for the invasion."[43]

The deciphering of German messages gave the allied military commanders real time intelligence of the German war machine's daily operations and was a vital but unseen weapon to defeat Hitler. The ENIGMA intelligence made possible the most direct, economical, and life saving strategies for landing in France.[44]

By the spring of 1945, American, British, and Soviet forces prepared to launch a final assault on German strongholds in Europe and to seize the spoils of war. The topmost priority was to capture German scientists who had developed the V-2 rockets, physicists who were working on an atomic bomb, and those who had perfected advanced communications systems. The British had learned where the key scientific personnel were being held as bargaining chips by high level SS officers and Hitler's special guard.[45] "For about five months at the end of the war the Americans were looking for rocket scientists, communications and submarine scientists, anybody on the German side who was a brilliant guy. So were the Russians," said Kirby.[46]

A group of American officers named the ALSOS team were tracking down German physicists to determine how far they had progressed in building an atomic bomb.[47]

The British were in the game too. The Royal Marine Commandos established an allied Target Intelligence Committee (TICOM) to capture the same German scientific elite. Their mission, so secret it was an undocumented operation, was to capture and bring back German experts who might be of use to the United States and Great Britain in the postwar period.

Kirby's German language skills and marksmanship qualified him to be the American member of TICOM team six. He began practicing parachute drops and learning how to use a "care package" of drugs for immobilizing captives; he trained in using incendiary materials to start fires, and explosives and chemicals to generate toxic gas for immobilizing a barracks full of soldiers. The TICOM mission was to seize the targeted experts and their advanced communications equipment before the Russians could get to them.

Kirby's team flew into allied-occupied territory in Schleswig-Holstein, a part of northern Germany near the Danish border, in May 1945, just after the German surrender. In nearby Flensburg prison, Kirby found the captured chief of a German unit that intercepted Soviet communications. The German officer was only too eager to give Kirby a quick course in reading NKVD messages.

Germany was in flames; chaos reigned. In the final days of the war, Kirby witnessed Russian troops shoot German civilians "just to see what would happen when they fired a captured Schmizer automatic pistol." He watched planks floating down the river with bodies nailed to them. "We found a manor house that was full of the Berlin Library's first editions and stamp books scattered on the floor," left behind by displaced persons freed from prison camps who looted the house looking for gold and silver to trade for freedom. These were Russian prisoners of war trying to flee to the West to escape repatriation to the Soviet Union. Under Stalin's rules, captured Red Army officers and men were considered to be traitors to the Soviet motherland and faced execution or imprisonment in slave labor camps. "Some of the POWs told me that under Stalin if you were an officer and were captured your family was sent to Siberia because you were supposed to die fighting," said Kirby.[48]

In July 1945 Kirby found part of the cryptanalysis records of Goering's *Forschungsamt* (research institute), his intelligence arm responsible for signals interception. The Goering research staff had tapped telephones, opened letters, and solved encoded telegrams. They had been reading Russian NKVD messages. Kirby wrote:

The *Forschungsamt* were 200 percent Nazis who considered it traitorous to be interrogated, but they took me to an inn in Flensburg where they had dumped their records and papers. Hidden under a tarpaulin in one of the boxes was a partially burned Soviet code book which the Germans had obtained at Petsamo, Finland, back in 1941 when they joined with the Finns after the Russo-Finnish war. I sent it back to Washington through a friend in Naval Intelligence.[49]

In all, according to Kirby, there were three copies of the Petsamo code book. One was a partially charred 1,500-page original that General William Donovan had purchased from the Finns in November 1944. On the order of President Roosevelt and Secretary of State Edward Stettinius, who held the view that gentlemen do not read their allies's mail, Donovan was ordered to return the code book to the Russians; he personally returned it to Andrei Gromyko, Soviet ambassador to Washington. Donovan, of course, had made a copy and the Russians suspected as much.[50]

Another military intelligence team, headed by Lieutenant Colonel Paul Neff, located the signals intelligence archive of the German Foreign Ministry in a castle in Saxony in southern Germany. There, during the closing days of the war, Neff discovered another copy of the Petsamo code book. Neff's team managed to leave with the code book only a day before Soviet forces occupied the castle.

It would be another year and a half before the Russian code book would prove useful in decoding VENONA.[51] Kirby returned to Arlington Hall in August 1945 and joined what was then known as the Russian Project. Kirby said that the decoders had a hard time until they discovered the first repetitions, meaning that a Soviet cipher clerk had made the mistake of using a one-time pad more than once. The decoders were continually startled when they read NKVD messages. There in front of them was all the classified correspondence between Churchill and Roosevelt, meaning that a spy either in the White House or the British embassy had been relaying the highest level of British and American secrets to Moscow.

★ ★ ★

The code name GNOME appears often in VENONA, disclosing an intelligence operation of great concern to Moscow Center. The messages are explicit enough to indicate that GNOME was the long term effort to free Ramon Mercader del Rio, Trotsky's assassin, from prison in Mexico City. Ramon Mercader was a revolutionary veteran of the fighting in Spain; his brother had been killed when he tied grenades to his body and threw himself under an advancing German tank, and his mother had fought with guerilla forces. In 1940, Mercader posed as a young businessman supporting Trotsky and succeeded in killing him.

The purpose of NKVD pressure on their agents to get Mercader out of jail was to avoid his changing his confession and revealing his real identity. He had presented himself as one Frank Jacson, a wealthy businessman who had supported Trotsky's revolutionary activities until they competed for the same woman. In the early 1920s, the Mexican authorities and the world still believed that Mercader had killed Trotsky because he had tried to steal away his girlfriend. Mercader was a fully recruited Soviet agent acting under orders from Stalin when he killed Trotsky. GNOME prepared various avenues of escape but none was successful.[52]

Ramon Mercader's mother, Caridad, anxiously waited out World War II first in Tashkent, then in Moscow. Caridad had been sent to Tashkent as part of the evacuation of Moscow in 1942; there she confided to her cousin, a high ranking Spanish Communist Party official in clandestine operations whom she thought she could trust, that her son was Trotsky's assassin. In 1946 Caridad's cousin defected to Western Europe while on a Communist Party mission and revealed Ramon's identity to the police. The authorities in Mexico then matched Ramon's fingerprints with police records in Spain from the time he was arrested in 1935 or 1936 for taking part in antifascist demonstrations in Catalonia. They confirmed his identity. Ramon never admitted being an agent of the Soviet government, only that he was the scion of a wealthy family. After he was identified, his jailors stopped beating him twice a day and took him out of solitary confinement, but he served out his term of twenty years. He was released on August 20, 1960, and he returned to Moscow. Only when he was photographed wearing a medal, Hero of the Soviet Union, did reports appear in the West that Trotsky's assassin had received the highest military award of the Soviet Union. His portrait is on display in an album of heroes in the Museum of Foreign Intelligence and the KGB Club at Lubyanka. In the 1970s, Mercader became an adviser to Castro, and died in Cuba. His body was returned to Moscow and buried there with honors.

6 Truman Wrestles an Ogre Named VENONA

Following Franklin D. Roosevelt's death on April 18, 1945, new President Harry S. Truman inherited all the secrets and challenges that came with the end of World War II. FDR had kept his vice president in the dark on many major issues. For example, Truman knew nothing about the atomic bomb, nor had he played a role in Roosevelt's carefully crafted alliance with Stalin to defeat Nazi Germany. He had yet to learn about the existence of VENONA.

On June 4, 1945, barely six weeks after he assumed the presidency, Truman was told for the first time that U.S. Army code breakers were reading secret Soviet messages. Meeting in the Oval Office of the White House with Brigadier General Carter C. Clarke and his aide, Colonel Ernest Gibson, Truman learned that on February 1, 1943, Army Signals Intelligence had begun trying to read Soviet cable traffic between Moscow and the United States, although the Soviet Union was then an ally in the fight against Hitler.

The new president also learned that the Army's Signals Security Agency (SSA), under which signals intelligence operated, had been intercepting Soviet cable traffic since August 1939 when the Hitler-Stalin Pact was signed. At that point, the U.S. government had ordered Western Union, RCA, and other American cable companies to retain copies of all messages to and from German, Japanese, and Soviet embassies, consulates, and trading organizations, even though the United States was not yet at war with any of these countries. In October 1940, the Army's Signals Intelligence Service (SIS) directed its monitoring stations to copy Russian diplomatic traffic, the first time since the early 1920s that Soviet communications were made an intercept priority for the Army.[1] Hitler's astounding alliance with Stalin had raised alarms about the Soviet leader's motives. Was Stalin buying time by making a pact with the devil or was he in a partnership with Hitler, Hirohito, and Mussolini to rule the world?

★ ★ ★

General Clarke, head of Army Intelligence (G-2), was tall and straight-backed, with steel-gray hair. His entire career had been in Signals Intelligence; he was stern and demanding. Clarke had only a quarter of an hour to initiate the new president into the shadow world of codes and encryption, by which both friends and enemies hide their strengths and weaknesses and try to keep their intentions secret.[2] Army Signals Intelligence had in hand two Soviet code books abandoned by retreating armies in wartime Europe. However, the intercepted messages copied by the cable companies did not match the code books because, after having been coded into numbers equivalent to words, the text had then been encrypted with additional numerals from a pad of randomly chosen numbers to be used only once, a "one-time pad" (OTP) held by the sender and the receiver. Each page of the pad was destroyed after a single use; in theory, that made the cipher impenetrable. Clarke told the president that, despite these obstacles, initial work on the Soviet traffic indicated large scale Soviet intelligence operations in the United States. However, it was still too early to match code names in the traffic with specific persons and operations.

Afterward, Clarke told a few close associates that the meeting had not gone well: "It was NDG" (no damn good). President Truman had told Clarke that his report sounded "like a fairy story." The president found Clarke's explanation of the methods being used for recovering the text hard to believe and wondered how the information could be verified. Clarke did not show any messages to the president; he could only report that the efforts were under way and initial results were promising after two years of work.[3]

Truman's skepticism focused on three concerns: First were the problems of prosecuting in courts of law those named in the messages from top secret decoded cables. Truman had a very clear view of the Constitution and equal justice under the law: "We must understand, of course, that as a matter of government necessity, in the investigation of crime and subversion, it is essential for the investigative authorities to have sources of information which they cannot reveal. But when it comes to an individual being charged with a crime, under our procedure he has a right to be confronted with his accusers. If the government cannot produce witnesses in court, then it cannot prosecute. And if a man cannot be prosecuted in the courts, then he should not be persecuted by a Senate or House committee."[4]

Second was the liability to President Roosevelt's place in history, and third, the political damage to the Democratic Party. Roosevelt's policy of wartime alliance with Stalin would be open to criticism if the messages exposed senior American officials who abetted Soviet intelligence operations in the United States. The good feeling of alliance in a common cause to defeat Nazism would turn sour and add to tensions with Stalin. For FDR and Stalin, defeating Hitler had been paramount. Stalin had even disbanded the Communist International (Comintern) and paid lip service to freedom of religion in the Soviet Union to win American public support against a common enemy. Roosevelt, although wary of Stalin, optimistically thought he could charm the Soviet dictator and reach binding agreements with him on the postwar world order.

Although Roosevelt supported diplomatic recognition of the Soviet Union in 1933, he had a realistic appraisal of Moscow's proxy, the American Communist Party, and its intentions. In 1935 FDR had sent Labor Secretary Frances Perkins a memorandum suggesting the Labor Department deport alien communists active in the American labor movement. Roosevelt was convinced that we could "prove propaganda directed at the destruction of the Government." But the Supreme Court ruled that Communist Party membership did not provide adequate grounds for deportation. By 1942, with the Soviet Union as an ally, FDR told Attorney General Francis Biddle that "we could not deport communists" when Biddle suggested that we could and would.[5] During the war Roosevelt's aim was to engage Stalin in creating a condominium—or joint sovereignty—of the world's four "policemen" (the U.S., Britain, the Soviet Union, and China). His postwar goal was to restrain both Soviet expansionism and British (European) imperialism.[6]

Truman feared that new revelations of Soviet espionage would be used to support congressional allegations of communists in government. Since its creation in 1938, the Special House Un-American Activities Committee (HUAC) was the club used by Roosevelt's enemies to attack the New Deal.[7]

Truman knew about the ambiguities of code breaking and their dangerous political sensitivity; he was chairman of the Senate Special Committee to Investigate the National Defense Program, known as the Truman Committee, during the war. How should the decoded messages be interpreted, and when should they be revealed? Was it more important to protect sources and methods used to break the codes and follow the espionage trail or to come forward and define the threat and tell the American public how it was being contained?

When he headed the Truman Committee, Truman criticized the FBI for the failure of its listening post in Hawaii to report the plan and date for the Japanese attack on Pearl Harbor in time to take action to prevent it.[8] An investigation absolved J. Edgar Hoover, who manipulated skillfully to avoid direct blame, but Truman's criticism of the FBI had angered Hoover and made an enemy.[9]

Nevertheless, when Truman took office, Hoover tried to develop a personal relationship with the new president in order to bypass Truman's attorney general. He selected Marion Chiles III, a special agent from Missouri, whose father had been a boyhood friend of the president, to carry his message. Truman had known Chiles since he was a child; he was the perfect person to present Hoover's message. After a few preliminary remarks, Truman asked the agent why he was there. "With a message from Mr. Hoover," Chiles said. "Mr. Hoover wants you to know that he and the FBI are at your personal disposal and will help you in any way you ask." Truman looked at his friend's son, smiled, and remarked on Mr. Hoover's thoughtfulness. "But any time I need the services of the FBI," Truman added, "I will ask for it through my attorney general." The agent took the message back to Hoover, and according to William C. Sullivan, Hoover's former assistant, "from that time on Hoover's hatred of Truman knew no bounds."[10]

Truman, unlike FDR, had no taste for the incriminating gossip that Hoover offered on Washington officials and members of Congress. On May 4, 1945, Truman expressed his concerns about Hoover to Budget Director Harold Smith. Truman said he was "very much against building up a Gestapo." He indicated strong disapproval of the FBI snooping on the sex lives of bureaucrats and certain members of Congress, and questioned whether the presence of the FBI in South America was good for inter-American relations. Truman said he intended to limit the jurisdiction of the FBI to the United States, a plan he implemented.[11]

Hoover had other critics. His high-handed style, which created in the public mind an image of the omnipotent law-enforcing kingdom of the FBI, contrasted sharply with Hoover's rush-to-judgment reputation inside the government. In 1942 six German agents came ashore in rubber boats on Long Island with instructions to contact sympathetic German Americans who would harbor them during a sabotage mission. Two of the German spies wanted to defect and called the FBI. Hoover rushed to round up the other four before they had a chance to make their local contacts. Secretary of War Henry Stimson was furious that the FBI had not waited until the FBI had pinpointed their Nazi sympathizers so that the entire ring could be arrested.[12] This distrust of Hoover as hot-headed and self-serving would later drive a wedge between him and the White House that discredited the VENONA revelations in President Truman's eyes.

By 1944 there were rumors that the United States had broken the Japanese code, and in September Army Chief of Staff General George C. Marshall received information that New York Governor Thomas E. Dewey, in his presidential campaign that autumn against President Franklin D. Roosevelt, was planning to reveal that the United States had been able to decipher Japanese signals intelligence before Pearl Harbor. Dewey was prepared to publicly charge that Roosevelt had known of the Japanese plans to attack in advance and was criminally negligent for not taking action. A growing conspiracy theory claimed that the president had ignored the signs because he wanted the United States drawn into the war.

Only a secret mission to Dewey by then-Colonel Clarke on behalf of General Marshall kept the Republican candidate from exposing the success of MAGIC, the system for breaking the Japanese code. The letter from General Marshall explained that reading Japanese messages also gave us the German order of battle in Europe: Baron General Hiroshi Oshima, the Japanese ambassador in Berlin, was reporting to Tokyo every detail and boast he heard in his conversations with Hitler. The secrecy surrounding code breaking was sacrosanct because reading Japanese and German operational messages directly affected the outcome of major battles in the

Pacific and on the Russian front. Dewey agreed not to divulge the government's code-breaking success in the campaign.[13] Roosevelt was elected for an unprecedented fourth term.

Reading the Soviets' internal messages had far different implications for President Truman. First and foremost, the Soviet Union was America's ally, and Truman could not know in June 1945 that the atomic bomb would end the war against Japan only two months later. The new president believed he still needed the Soviets to help defeat the Japanese. He did not want to weaken the wartime alliance with embarrassing revelations: that the United States was intercepting and reading the internal messages of an ally, or that the Soviets had made the United States a prime target for their espionage activities. Truman's unerring political instinct told him that knowing about Soviet espionage on American soil, especially with the cooperation of American agents, would be a huge liability for the Democrats in the coming year's congressional elections. The good and the bad results of embracing the Soviets, making them partners in the war to free Europe of German fascism, would be credited to or blamed on Roosevelt and the Democratic Party. He could not have been in a hurry for Army Intelligence to reveal the identities of American spies or secret "friendly sources" with *klichkas*, Russian code names.

Truman had yet to meet Joseph Stalin, whom he would liken to the Kansas City political boss Tom Pendergast and to William Marcy Tweed, the legendary nineteenth century Tammany Hall leader. Taking FDR's lead, he still viewed Stalin as a fellow politician with whom he could make deals that would be kept. For the previous four years, the Soviets had been America's major ally in the epic fight to save Great Britain from being overrun by Nazi Germany and eventually to free Europe from German occupation. Stalin's grab for power in Eastern Europe, Greece, Iran, and the Dardanelles was still to come.

In 1945, four major counterintelligence breakthroughs helped the FBI make sense of the fragments from the Russian decoding project:

1. In May of 1945, the FBI carefully questioned Whittaker Chambers, whose warning in 1939 of Soviet espionage at high levels of the State Department, Treasury, the White House, and other government agencies had gone unheeded.
2. In August 1945, Louis Budenz, former Communist Party USA leader, told his story to the FBI.
3. In September 1945, Igor Gouzenko, a GRU code clerk, defected in Ottawa.[14] His disclosures led to the arrest and conviction of British atomic bomb spy Allan Nunn May. Gouzenko offered code names and clues to finding spies in the U.S. and British governments, including Alger Hiss, and explained the methods and equipment used in Soviet cipher systems.

4. On November 7, 1945, Elizabeth Bentley, a member of the Communist Party underground since 1935, who had been a Soviet intelligence agent handler and courier, agreed to tell her story to the FBI and name the members of Soviet espionage rings within the American government.[15] Her testimony forced Moscow to halt most of its espionage activity in the United States for fear that she had endangered both Soviet intelligence officers and their American agents. Her revelations confirmed Chambers' story. She provided the real names and activities of agents to match VENONA code names and assignments from Moscow in the decoded traffic.

On November 8, 1945, J. Edgar Hoover sent a memorandum to President Truman's Military Aide, Brigadier General Harry Hawkins Vaughan, at the White House advising him that "information has been recently developed from a highly confidential source indicating that a number of persons employed by the Government of the United States have been furnishing data and information to persons outside the Federal Government, who are in turn transmitting this information to espionage agents of the Soviet Government."[16] The top secret memorandum named:

- Dr. [Nathan] Gregory Silvermaster, a long-time employee of the Department of Agriculture.
- Harry Dexter White, Assistant to the Secretary of the Treasury.
- George Silverman, formerly employed by the Railroad Retirement Board and now reportedly in the War Department.
- Lauchlin Currie, former Administrative Assistant to the late President Roosevelt.
- Victor Perlow [sic], formerly with the War Production Board and the Foreign Economic Administration.
- Donald Wheeler, formerly with the Office of Strategic Services.
- Julius Joseph, Office of Strategic Services.
- Helen Tenney, Office of Strategic Services.
- Maurice Halperin, Office of Strategic Services.
- Charles Kramer, formerly associated with Senator Kilgore.
- Captain William Ludwig Ullman, United States Army Air Corps.
- Lieutenant Colonel John H. Reynolds, United States Army.
- Mary Price, former secretary to the newspaper columnist Walter Lippmann.

Hoover's memo for President Truman was based on the testimony of Elizabeth Bentley, who offered firsthand knowledge of the contributions delivered to her by sources who had been her former agents and assets in Washington. She named Silvermaster the head of the group, or what Soviet intelligence called "the pole," around which the ring operated.[17]

When Elizabeth Bentley named Harry Dexter White among the NKVD's secret assets in Washington, she was treading on the reputation of one of the most admired public servants in the federal government. The assistant secretary of the Treasury was known as a brilliant theoretician and an expert on the economic problems China faced in its long war against Japanese invasion. White was an idealist who, together with his wife, Anne Terry, had taken orphans into their home and who, as foster parents, guided them through college.[18] The FBI had questioned White on March 30, 1942, after his name appeared on a list prepared by the House Un-American Activities Committee (HUAC) of alleged members of the Washington Committee for Democratic Action, an alleged subversive organization. White denied membership during his interview with the FBI and labeled HUAC Chairman Martin Dies' practices "damnable, underhanded and cheap," saying that "the charges were made publicly which, in many instances, left the person accused in a defenseless position."[19]

Whittaker Chambers described White's participation in the Silvermaster cell of Soviet agents and the regularity of White's reports to Moscow on the inner workings of the Treasury. The first probe of White's loyalty came to no conclusion because it was supported only by Chambers' word, with no proof, and White was able to convince the investigators that they had the wrong suspect.

When the FBI heard the same allegations from Bentley, they dug out their old files in which Chambers corroborated her charges. By this time, they had some cover names from VENONA that could possibly apply to the allegations by the two former communist agents, but no surety came until 1950 that RICHARD and JURIST were indeed White.

During the war, White's contributions as a senior policymaker and economic expert enhanced his reputation. In June 1945, when Morgenthau resigned as Secretary of the Treasury, there was press speculation that White would be asked to stay on because "he was one of the few men in the country who fully understood the proposed International Monetary Fund setup by the Bretton Woods plan."[20]

In early 1946, only a month after the FBI warned the White House that White was under suspicion, Truman put White's name before the Senate for confirmation as the first American representative to the newly created International Monetary Fund (IMF). Hoover sent an urgent message to the White House to withdraw White's name because he was probably a spy for the Soviet Union. When presidential assistant and political aide David Niles heard of the FBI report he sputtered, "What? You want us to withdraw his name and lose New York?" He referred to the hotly contested congressional election of 1946 in which Republican charges of communist agents in the American government was a leading issue.[21] Niles is named in VENONA as the White House aide who could expedite American visas for Soviet agents because he knew who would accept bribes from the NKVD.[22]

Niles was doing his job when he worried about Democratic votes in New York. Roosevelt had built the New Deal on "a true concert of interests," which meant something for everybody. Truman had carried on his policy of bridging the gap between left and right politics. He did this by paying close attention to the voice of the unions, even when they were dominated by the Communist Party, by maintaining "the solid South" Democratic voting bloc, and by making sure the Democrats won in New York where pro-Soviet admiration for a wartime ally was still a strong sentiment. White was known to be critical of the hidebound Department of State bureaucracy and the encrusted diplomatic service elite who had been late to take a stand against Fascist Germany and had prevented Jewish refugees from entering the United States.[23] New Yorkers had not forgotten the *St. Louis*, a ship full of German-Jewish émigrés who had been turned back to Europe and probable death in 1939 on orders of the State Department. Harry Dexter White was known for his anti-German, pro-Soviet, anti-Japanese positions.

Truman did not withdraw White's nomination to be the American executive director of the IMF.

By 1946 Truman was caught between the Republican Party and the communists. The American Communist Party (CPUSA) was avidly organizing working class whites and blacks to demand government action against high prices, unemployment, and a coming depression in capitalist economies. War sector jobs had disappeared, and industry had not yet achieved its postwar momentum. The CPUSA took an active stance against passage of the Taft-Hartley bill regulating labor unions. Within American labor unions, a battle raged to rid the leadership of communists. In early 1946, Truman faced a slowdown in the midwest steel, electricity, and machine tool industries. The American communists took credit for attempts by the National Association for the Advancement of Colored People to end segregation in the military and, later, for their position against establishing a new draft. Hoover warned Truman that the American Communist Party, in demanding the release of GIs from the Army, was preparing for World War III.[24] Communists were active in organizing Henry Wallace's third party ticket for the 1948 elections.

Two speeches in 1946 removed any doubt that the cold war had begun. The first was Winston Churchill's address on March 5 in Fulton, Missouri, proclaiming that "an iron curtain" had descended on Eastern Europe from the Baltic to the Adriatic, sealing off the West from countries that had come under domination of Soviet totalitarianism. The second speech was by Stalin to his own people on July 30: he stated that war between the Soviet Union and its satellites against the United States and England was inevitable. It awaited only the rebuilding of Soviet military strength and war industries until they were equal to those of the West. In the meantime, Stalin asserted, the West would see a weakening of capitalism and a sharpening of worker discontent that would obstruct production.

In the coming decade, the nation would pay heavily for Truman's failure to expose Soviet intelligence networks within the United States. By treating the successes of VENONA as a "fairy story," the president ceded control of the issue of communist influence in the U.S. government to the political enemies from whom he hoped to keep it secret. The result turned America inward against itself, creating a paroxysm of name calling, finger pointing, and informing on former party members or suspected communists.

Keeping the decoded messages secret made it more difficult to bring known cases to court and conviction. The unsubstantiated charges led to fear and distrust of the government, and opened the way for the aberration of Senator Joseph McCarthy and his Red witch hunt. During the next fifty years, the cold war between the United States and the Soviet Union was mirrored by the domestic battles between the left, embittered by the excesses of McCarthyism, and the right, angered by the government's failure to expose the full extent of Soviet espionage in America. Truman made the mistake of treating Soviet spying as a domestic political issue instead of a national security problem.

When President Truman ignored J. Edgar Hoover's warning in 1946 not to appoint Harry Dexter White as the American representative to the board of the IMF and refused to believe accusations in 1948 that Alger Hiss was guilty of spying for the Soviet Union, Truman stumbled and eroded his credibility. By going ahead with the appointment of White to the IMF and branding accusations against Hiss "a red herring," Truman let Hiss cast a shadow on Roosevelt's legacy and accelerated the Red Panic Truman had hoped to avoid. The espionage activities of Hiss and White helped bring about unforeseen consequences that Truman later had to deal with on a larger scale: the Berlin Airlift and the descent of the Iron Curtain.

On December 8, 1941, the day after the Japanese attack on Pearl Harbor, Harry Dexter White was given the authority to act as assistant secretary by Treasury Secretary Henry Morgenthau, Jr., and White exercised the power of that position throughout the war. On December 14, 1941, Morgenthau directed White to prepare a memorandum on a joint allied stabilization fund for conducting the war against the Axis powers. After 1941, he was officially entrusted to map out policy for economic cooperation with the USSR. In early 1942, White took the leading role in the formulation of American policy for the postwar international financial order. The White Plan became the historic basis for the structure of the IMF. At the Bretton Woods Conference of July 1944, White and Lord Keynes were the dominating figures who created the IMF and its twin institution, the International Bank for Reconstruction and Development (later called the World Bank).

At the end of 1943, the allies began to make plans anticipating the defeat of Germany. At the Teheran Conference, Roosevelt, Churchill, and Stalin planned the final drive to break the Nazis' hold on Europe. Following the Conference, Harry Dexter White met in Washington for the first time with Soviet Ambassador Andrei Gromyko to discuss the matter of a common German occupation currency, to be known as Allied Military, or AM, marks. White was following Morgenthau's order to "take supervision over and assume full responsibility for Treasury's participation in all economic and financial matters . . . in connection with the operations of the Army and Navy and the civilian affairs in the foreign areas in which our armed forces are operating or are likely to operate."[25]

Steeped in the aura of high hopes generated at Teheran, the United States and Great Britain believed a common occupation currency for Germany was both practical and a symbol of the desired harmony among the allies. Britain and the United States agreed that the notes should be printed in the United States.

The United States scheduled the first printing to start on February 14, 1944, but by February 9 the Soviet government had still not indicated agreement to the plan. Pending the answer from Moscow, Harry Dexter White sent photostatic copies of the designs of the AM marks to Gromyko at the Soviet embassy in Washington. White asked Gromyko to forward the details to Moscow so that the Soviet government could "be informed of our plans here." White explained that the United States had scheduled production of notes to the value of 10 billion marks. White told Gromyko that the Treasury preferred joint issue of the marks to separate printing by each of the allies.

On February 15, Averell Harriman, the American ambassador in Moscow, reported to Secretary of State Cordell Hull that the Russians had approved the currency design with the wording, "Allied Military Authorities." However, Foreign Minister Molotov had informed him that "the People's Commissariat for Finance of the USSR considers that it would be more correct if the printing of the military currency also took place in the Soviet Union in the interest of guaranteeing to the Command of the Soviet armies a constant supply of such currency." Molotov confidently assumed his request would be met and asked to be informed in the near future when the USSR Commissariat for Finance could expect to receive the plates, the list of serial numbers, and the models of paper and colors.[26]

Molotov's insistence that the Soviet Union print its own AM marks for the German occupation aroused strong resistance inside the Treasury. Director of Engraving and Printing Alvin W. Hall believed that duplicate printing would create serious complications. Hall warned in writing that duplicate printing of the same currency violated traditional security rules, which might lead to forging of the currency, followed by national or international scandal. Undersecretary Daniel Bell upheld Hall's objections, stressing that, with no control over the Russian printing, there could be no accountability for funds. White was troubled. He feared the Russians would construe the rejection as lack of Western confidence. White insisted on a review before turning down the Russian request. The Russians must be trusted "to the same degree and the same extent as the other allies," White argued.[27] Undersecretary Bell, who outranked White, drafted a cable turning down their request for the plates, but it was not sent. Morgenthau intervened and decided to talk to Gromyko in hopes of persuading the Soviet Union to agree to a single American source for the AM marks.

At first glance, the idea of separate printings of AM marks appeared to be an invocation of allied unity. Big Three mutual understanding, it seemed, had never been higher. In reality, delivery of the plates to Moscow would mean the United States' loss of control of the printing and issuance of the marks before arrangements had been made for the occupation of Germany. For the Soviet Union, the plates were, as White's biographer David Rees has noted, "a blank check drawn on the Bank of Inter-Allied Unity."[28] That unity was about to crumble.

On March 18, 1944, Morgenthau and White met with Gromyko at the Secretary's home in a further attempt to convince him that the best course was for the U.S. to print the AM marks and supply the Soviet Union any amount it wanted. The Soviet government knew the advantages of a common occupation currency, provided it could be produced without any control from the West. They knew the value of a joint currency that required no convertibility. Gromyko rejected all of Morgenthau's pleas; Morgenthau promised to review the matter and get back to Gromyko in two days.

White argued at a Treasury meeting that even if the Soviets printed their own currency, it would have to be recognized by the United States. "In any case, the United States has not been doing enough for the Soviet Union all along and if the Soviets profited as a result of this transaction we should be happy to give them this token of our appreciation of their efforts," White said.[29] In the face of continued Treasury opposition by the Director of Engraving Hall, Morgenthau held off a decision and asked Admiral William Leahy, the President's chief of staff, to make the decision, thus passing the buck to the Combined Chiefs of Staff.

Morgenthau explained to Leahy that if duplicate plates were given to the Soviets, there would be a delay in printing the AM marks, which would prevent delivery to Eisenhower of half the total order of 10 billion AM marks that he had requested by mid-April. "It would therefore be appreciated," Morgenthau wrote, "if you would place the matter before the Combined Chiefs of Staff and advise me promptly whether in their opinion the military situation would afford such delay." Morgenthau sent both a copy of his letter and Hall's memorandum against granting the plates to Secretary of State Hull. The State Department advised Ambassador Harriman in Moscow by cable, "It is not expected that the Combined Chiefs of Staff will favor delivery of plates to the Russians."

In a final effort to convince Gromyko, Morgenthau sent White to see the Soviet ambassador on March 21 and read him Hall's memorandum of objections. According to White's record of the meeting in the Treasury files, Gromyko "remained unimpressed" and "he was clearly disappointed and skeptical as to the reasoning contained in the memorandum." Gromyko hinted that the Soviet Union would be interested in the possibility of printing its own currency. For two weeks there was no Soviet response. Then on April 8, Harriman reported to the State Department that Molotov was adamant in his request for the duplicate plates. If the reply was negative, Molotov pointed out, "the Soviet government will be forced to proceed with independent preparation of military marks for Germany of its own pattern. . . ."[30]

For White, the military currency issue was part of a larger pattern of developing American-Soviet relations that he had devised. In response to a request from Morgenthau, White had forwarded a memorandum on March 7 suggesting a $5 billion credit to the Soviet Union. His plan called for the Soviets to purchase American industrial and agricultural products over thirty years, to be paid for by Soviet strategic materials, creating markets for both countries and providing "a sound basis for continued collaboration between the two governments in the postwar period." In January 1945, White suggested the credit amount be raised to $10 billion. It became part of a wider plan for postwar aid to the Soviet Union that never materialized.

White was a visionary who believed that trade would bring peace. His scheme for "all-out diplomacy" included dramatic economic initiatives that he believed would influence Soviet behavior. Providing the Soviets with plates to print occupation marks would be a small measure of reparation for what the Soviet Union had suffered and lost at the hands of Nazi Germany, White argued.

The Combined Chiefs of Staff declined to accept responsibility for providing the duplicate plates to the Soviets. In a reply to Morgenthau on April 3, General George C. Marshall explained that General Eisenhower, the Supreme Allied Commander, needed the AM marks by May 1. After that, "if the United States Treasury and the State Department, in conjunction with the Foreign Office and the British Treasury, decided to furnish duplicate plates to the Soviet Government, it appears that this action could be taken any time after May 1, 1944, without interference with General Eisenhower's requirements for Allied military mark currency." If the Soviet government needed AM marks urgently, about 2 billion marks could be made available immediately for their use. The Combined Chiefs had decided not to make the decision.

White moved decisively by calling a meeting at which he announced to his Treasury colleagues that "the Combined Chiefs of Staff had directed that the glass positives [of the AM plates] be turned over to the Russian government." According to Hall's account of the meeting, he was not shown Marshall's letter.[31] White had decided to interpret the letter as military approval for turning the plates over to the Russians.

The staff, led by White, hurried off to see Morgenthau, who formally agreed that the plates be given to the Soviets. Morgenthau then gained the carefully ambiguous agreement of the State Department, without mentioning Marshall's letter. The State Department then called in Gromyko and told him of the decision to make the plates available to the Soviets.

A clear indication that White was following Moscow Center's instructions comes from an NKVD memorandum dated April 15, 1944:

MAY [Stepan Apresian, NKVD *rezident* in New York] reported 14 April that LAWYER [code name for Harry Dexter White] following our instructions passed through ROBERT [Silvermaster] attained the positive decision of the Treasury Department to provide the Soviet side with the plates for engraving German occupation marks, namely the consent was given to produce for the Red Army two billion occupation marks.

Signed OVAKIMIAN

Note: Immediately inform t. [for *tovarich* Comrade] Mikoyan[32]

On April 21, 1944, a War Department automobile carried the plates to the Soviet embassy, from where they were dispatched to Moscow via Alaska and Siberia.

White wrote, "My decision was correct both politically and militarily. The Russians had been holding up the Germans while the United States and England prepared for the invasion. There was every reason to trust them." Rees adds, "But it also seems plain that the initiative throughout the episode for the decision on the duplicate plates came from Harry Dexter White."[33]

According to Vladimir Petrov's study of occupation currency, the three Western allies put into circulation in their zones, excluding Berlin, about 10.5 billion AM marks that the United States had printed. Based on "a very conservative calculation," the Soviet military issued 78 billion AM marks.[34]

The AM marks distributed by the Red Army to its soldiers flooded the Russian zone and spilled into the areas controlled by the Western allies. The Soviet-printed marks created a black market and inflation. The Russians used the AM marks for back pay and current wages for their troops without regard to the normal pay scale, overrunning the marketplace with AM marks. Soviet finance officers were not accountable for the flow of AM marks they distributed. For the Soviets, it was another form of reparations. Soviet soldiers used their AM marks to buy watches, cigarettes, chocolate, nylons, and PX items from American soldiers. The Soviets could not exchange the AM marks for rubles, nor could they send them home. But American soldiers could redeem the Russian-printed occupation marks for American dollars at face value and send the dollars back to the United States. GIs sold watches to the Soviets for AM marks equivalent to as much as $1,000 each. By 1947, the U.S. Army faced a $271 million overdraft caused by Soviet-printed AM marks that had been redeemed from GIs engaged in black market sales to the Russians.[35] The more AM marks that flooded the market, the more the currency was debased, adding to inflation.

At the first meeting of the Council of Foreign Ministers from September 11 to October 2, 1945, in London, half a year after the victory over fascism, it was apparent that the East-West split was deepening between the Soviet Union and the Western allies over spheres of influence and occupation policy in Germany.[36] American High Commissioner for Germany General Lucius Clay arrived on the scene prepared for conciliatory treatment of the Soviet Union. In 1945 and 1946, Clay got along well with his Soviet counterpart, Marshal Vasili Sokolovsky, a sophisticated strategist who had once been a school teacher and could quote the Bible. Clay believed in cooperating with the Soviet Union and working toward four-power control of Germany.

However, by 1947, growing tensions between the United States and the Soviet Union began to be played out at the Allied Control Council in Berlin. Foreshadowing the Foreign Ministers November meeting in London, Marshal Sokolovsky attacked the Western allies with vilification and abuse. "By late 1947 the creation of a vigorous Western Germany as a bulwark against communist aggression had captured Clay's imagination."[37] Clay was determined to improve the German economy, come to grips with black market abuses, and institute a currency reform.

The Treasury and the American military government had drafted a plan in 1946, but it had been stalled by differences between the Soviets and the Western allies. The Soviet Union insisted that any currency reform allow them to continue printing the new currency on the same basis as the AM marks. Clay refused to consider such a plan and insisted that the Soviet side would have to agree to a single currency. This was anathema to the Soviet Union, which was determined to maintain its control of East Germany and force the United States to withdraw. When the Western allies proceeded with plans to form a West German government accompanied by currency reform, the Soviet Union responded by harassing allied movement into and out of the zones.

The allies insisted that the Soviet Union agree to four-power control of the economic policy for Germany and an end to the unilateral Soviet control of the Eastern zone, which was still feeding reparations to Moscow. In June 1948, currency reform in the three Western zones became the catalyst for German economic recovery. The reform was also a prime irritant to the Soviets; they responded with a blockade of road and rail traffic to the city of Berlin. The blockade began in June 1948 and ended, after a heroic airlift throughout the winter of 1948–1949, in May 1949.[38]

Harry Dexter White's handling of postwar German policy was overtaken and shielded from view by his successful mission to the Bretton Woods meetings to establish a new international financial order. White's effort to provide unlimited occupation currency for the Red Army was another thread in the tapestry of service he wove on behalf of the Soviet Union from the 1930s through the end of World War II. White was never formally recruited by Soviet intelligence. He was an asset, an uncontrolled "friendly source" whose positions, first as the head of the Bureau of Research for Morgenthau and then as assistant secretary, gave his Soviet handlers and Stalin direct access to a broad range of information and high level thinking. In his Treasury role, White coordinated information from all major government departments and provided key documents to Soviet intelligence. His position as Morgenthau's brain trust and policy planner was unique. White's research papers became Morgenthau's policy initiatives for President Roosevelt. White was a central "star" in the Soviet intelligence system's star-and-satellite strategy.

From White's assignment to design the postwar financial structure of defeated Germany came the Morgenthau Plan, which was to reduce Germany from a manufacturing and scientific powerhouse to an agricultural state. We do not know what instructions White received from his Soviet handlers, but we can reveal that his plan was promptly relayed to the Soviets and remains in their archives.

In September and October 1944, according to Soviet documents, White, under the code name RICHARD, was the source for the USSR's knowledge of American high level plans for Germany's postwar economic order. On October 1, 1944, People's Commissar for State Security Vsevelod N. Merkulov submitted a top secret *spravka*, or summary, to Stalin, Molotov, and Beria on plans for postwar economic order in Germany based on the considerations suggested by White (see appendix 8).

White designed the Morgenthau Plan to transform Germany from an industrial giant into a powerless agricultural state that could produce only a basic standard of living. The plan would split up large holdings into small farms. It would annihilate heavy and light industry, shipbuilding, mining, aviation, and armament production. Industrial equipment would go to Hitler's victims as reparations. The plan called for the deportation of up to fifty million people to work on public repairs in the countries that had suffered from German aggression, or to become foreign workers assigned outside Germany, many of them to Africa. Industrial areas—the Ruhr and Saar districts and some eastern areas—would be given to France or Poland, or placed under international control.

According to the Soviets' American source of information on the plan, opponents of the plan in the State Department argued that dismemberment of Germany's industrial capacity would retard the rebuilding of Europe and make it difficult to control the influence of the Soviet Union in Western Europe.

Soviet comments on the plan remarked that opposition to Morgenthau's proposal came from large American corporations and banks, the Catholic Church, and the Republican Party. The report in the Russian archive stated that Churchill was strongly against the proposals and discussed his views with President Roosevelt in Quebec in September 1944.

VENONA indicates that White gave the Russians the documents for numerous deliberations both within the Treasury Department and between Treasury and the State Department.[39]

By 1944 White was the major intellectual policymaking force in Treasury. White's ideas were being fed directly to FDR by his old neighbor from Hyde Park, Morgenthau. White passed his memoranda and the content of key conversations to Moscow through the Silvermaster satellite group, of which White was the central star. The communist underground's courier—who was the link between the Treasury communist cell and the Soviet control officer in New York and who transmitted the information to Moscow—was Elizabeth Bentley. She offered her secret knowledge to the FBI in 1945 and publicly named White before the House Committee on Un-American Activities on July 31, 1948.

When Whittaker Chambers worked as a courier for Soviet intelligence in the 1930s, Harry Dexter White was the chief monetary expert of the Treasury. According to Chambers, White "had been in touch with the Communist Party for a long time, not only through his close friend George Silverman, but through other party members whom he had banked around him in the Treasury Department."[40]

In the 1930s, Soviet intelligence had first approached White about becoming a member of an underground ring operated by J. Peters and later Colonel Boris Bykov, for whom Whittaker Chambers was a courier. To Chambers, White was not only a star but a prima donna, much taken with his own economic theories and his high minded ideals, on which he pontificated to the point of boredom.[41] White was in the care of Communist Party member Abraham George Silverman, a member of the American Communist Party underground, who was research director of the Railroad Retirement Board. Silverman's "chief business, and a very exacting and unthankful one too," according to Chambers, "was to keep Harry Dexter White in a buoyant and co-operative frame of mind."[42] When White came to the Treasury in 1934 from Harvard, he became increasingly brash and overconfident. "He could be disagreeable, quick tempered, overly ambitious and power went to his head," recalled Morgenthau.[43] White worked closely with Lauchlin Currie, an assistant to President Roosevelt in the White House, whom he had known since their days together at Harvard, and who was a member of the same communist underground ring.

White took full advantage of his stardom. Chambers recalled that White was willing to meet him secretly, and left the impression

> that he enjoyed the secrecy for its own sake. But his sense of inconvenience was greater than his sense of precaution, and he usually insisted on meeting

me near his Connecticut Avenue apartment. Since White was not a party member, but a fellow traveler, I could only suggest or urge, not give orders. This distinction White understood very well, and he thoroughly enjoyed the sense of being in touch with the Party, but not in it, courted by it, but yielding only so much as he chose.[44]

Silverman managed White, receiving documents and reports of highly classified policy initiatives, which he then passed on to Chambers. "Their relationship," explained Chambers,

seemed to have hinged for years on Silverman's willingness to let himself be patronized by White, to whom his sympathy was indispensable whenever, for example, the Secretary [Morgenthau] was snappish and White had one of his crises of office nerves. Each, in fact, was a tower of weakness—a leaning tower. But, as they leaned together, they held each other upright.[45]

At Christmas 1936, White accepted a gift of an expensive oriental rug from the Soviet illegal *rezident* in the United States, Boris Bykov. Bykov at first wanted to offer money to White, Alger Hiss, Julian Wadleigh, a State Department official, and George Silverman. Chambers, at that time working as an agent for Bykov, was horrified:

Money! They would be outraged. You don't understand. They are Communists on principle. If you offer them money, they will never trust you again. They will do nothing for you.
    "All right, so they are Communists," Bykov countered, "but it is you, BOB [Chambers's code name], who do not understand." He spoke with a patient cynicism that pled with my stupidity, which baffled him . . . "who pays is boss, and who takes money must also give something." In those words, as he stood beside me, I can still hear clearly the ring of Bykov's voice. He is saying: communism has turned to corrupting itself.[46]

Later in 1944, Soviet intelligence offered to pay the college tuition for White's daughter. The coded message to Moscow Center from the New York *rezidentura* explains that Mrs. White, "who knows about her husband's participation with us," complained about financial matters. The message breaks off, but the sense is that Mrs. White wanted her husband to leave government and go into private business so he could earn money for his daughter's college education. Silvermaster, head of the ring, explained to Mrs. White that, while "we would have helped them in view of all the circumstances, we would not allow them to leave CARTHAGE [Washington]." Moscow Center was warned that Silvermaster thought "RICHARD

[White] would have refused regular payments, but might accept gifts as a mark of our gratitude for [seven coded words undecodable] daughter's expenses which may come up to two thousand a year."[47] The message reported further that the illegal *rezident* in New York, Iskhak Akhmerov, told Silvermaster, "in his opinion we would agree to provide for RICHARD's daughter's education" but advised Silvermaster and other members of his group "against attempting to offer RICHARD direct financial assistance."

White's doubts about being a controlled Soviet agent and his refusal to be manipulated by lesser party members for their own gain create a portrait of White with nuances and shadings. White's brother and his daughters have written about White, describing him as an American patriot. Chambers told White that the secret material he was contributing went to the American Communist Party to serve a worldwide communist movement, not the Soviet Union. However, the VENONA message to Moscow in 1944 reports that Silvermaster, who was awarded a Soviet medal, "is sincerely overjoyed and profoundly satisfied with the reward [given him] in accordance with your instructions. He says his work for us is the one good thing he has done in his life. He emphasized that he did not take this only as a [personal] honor, but also as an honor to his group."[48]

White operated in a permissive wartime atmosphere of alliance with the Soviet Union and played a role in other major policy decisions that fit Stalin's strategy during World War II. The long-time Soviet "agent of influence" Armand Hammer claims he presented FDR with the idea of using British bases in the Caribbean and paying for them with war materials to help Great Britain defend itself against German attack in November 1940.[49] Hopkins, who did not know that Hammer had earlier delivered Soviet funds from Moscow to the American Communist Party, sent him to discuss his ideas with Harry Dexter White at Treasury. Hammer's idea became Lend Lease. Despite the 1939 Nazi-Soviet Pact of Non-Aggression, Stalin did not want Great Britain to fall because it would free Hitler to attack the USSR.

With FDR's death in April 1945, Morgenthau's eleven-year career in the Treasury Department came to an end. Truman, who opposed the Morgenthau Plan for Germany, refused to take Morgenthau to Potsdam for his meeting with Stalin, and Morgenthau resigned. White stayed on, valued because of his expertise in developing the new postwar International Monetary Fund.

White resigned from the IMF in May 1947. In September he suffered his first heart attack, which forced him to remain in bed until December. In October, federal marshals summoned him to appear before a federal grand jury in New York investigating allegations of communist espionage in the United States, but he was not able to appear for two full days of testimony until March 24 and 25, 1948.[50] The federal grand jury failed to return any indictments against the people named by Elizabeth Bentley. White and Nathan Gregory Silvermaster were the prime targets of the inquiry; there was no mention of VENONA or use of VENONA messages as evidence by the government since confirming identification of code names was still under way.

White's activities for the Soviet underground were never publicly confirmed until the VENONA documents were released in 1995.

Another idealist who served the Soviets in this period was Alger Hiss. VENONA reveals that after his service to the State Department at the Yalta Conference in February 1945, he flew to Moscow. There he received a high medal from the Soviet government. Until his death, and long after the opening of VENONA, he and his son maintained that he was innocent of spying or serving the communist cause. Soviet records reveal he secretly met with a high ranking officer of the GRU, Soviet military intelligence, during the Yalta Conference, and laid out for the Soviets all the strengths and weaknesses of the Western allies' negotiating positions.[51] From the information he supplied, the Soviets knew in which areas they could maintain hegemony after the war was over without serious objections from Roosevelt or Churchill. This was the formative period in which the Soviets prepared themselves for their domination of Eastern Europe and the construction of the Iron Curtain.

The final leg of the journey to Yalta in the Soviet Crimea was a flight that began in the middle of the night from Malta over Yugoslavia, Bulgaria, and Rumania to the airfield of Saki on the Black Sea. President Roosevelt and the American delegation landed at noon and were greeted by Foreign Minister Vyacheslav Molotov. Molotov welcomed them with vodka, champagne, caviar, smoked sturgeon, and black bread before the eighty-mile drive over the mountains to Yalta under heavy clouds that dumped rain and gusts of wet snow.[52]

The road was lined with troops of at least two divisions, each soldier standing within sight of the next, for the entire eighty miles. As the president's car passed, the soldiers, many of them young women, snapped to the Russian salute—an abrupt move of the arm to put the rifle at a 30-degree angle from the body. "Repeated thousands of times the salute was impressive," recalled Charles E. (Chip) Bohlen, FDR's interpreter at Yalta. The drive took five hours through mostly uninhabited, rugged countryside that was marked by gutted buildings and burned-out Nazi tanks. Bohlen was convinced the devastation President Roosevelt had seen hardened his view on Germany. "I'm more bloodthirsty than a year ago," FDR told Stalin when they met.[53]

It was already dark when they arrived at about 6 p.m.; they were shown directly to the accommodations in the white granite Livadia (Meadow) Palace, whose sixty rooms, completed in 1911, had been the summer home of the czars. The palace design was in the early Italian Renaissance style; the main motifs were taken from Florence. After the revolution, the palace was turned into a sanatorium. The retreating German troops had sacked it and taken everything, including plumbing fixtures, doorknobs, and locks.[54]

The palace's White Hall served as the site for the Big Three meetings, and its rooms were the living quarters for the American delegation. To accommodate them, the Russians had brought personnel and equipment by train from three hotels in Moscow to restore the palace buildings. President Roosevelt's suite consisted of a living room, a dining room (formerly the czar's billiard room), a bedroom, and the only private bath in the palace. The rest of the president's team bunked on the second and third floors, many two to a room in the freshly whitewashed quarters.[55]

The elaborate effort to restore the palace was not all for the benefit of the guests. In preparation for the conference, Soviet intelligence planted listening devices in the rooms of the president and the American delegation. The conversations were taped, then reviewed and translated daily by a trusted team of English speakers including Sergo Beria, son of NKVD chief Lavrenti Beria, and Zoya Zarubina, daughter of NKGB General Vasili Zarubin. Beria was in charge of security at Yalta. He did not openly attend the conference meetings or social events; he lurked in the wings offering Stalin choice gossip and insight into American intentions.[56]

In contrast to the Teheran Conference in 1943, where the State Department had no voice in policy discussions except for Ambassador Averell Harriman, State had a team of a dozen officers at Yalta. Before the conference, the State Department prepared for the president a series of "black books" covering the subjects to be discussed at Yalta.

Among the major issues to be resolved at Yalta was the establishment of the United Nations. Alger Hiss, then deputy director of the Office of Special Political Affairs at the State Department, was deeply involved in drafting language for such issues as veto power for the members of the Security Council.[57] At Yalta, Hiss primarily worked on the United Nations; an added task was to take notes of plenary sessions.[58] He was fully briefed on American strategy and had access to the "black books" that presented the American positions and options for action.

Bohlen recalled Hiss as being remote:

At meetings at Yalta, his slightly cavernous face always wore a serious expression. He was not an outgoing person, but one who seemed to regard his associates from a superior distance.

At Yalta Stalin demanded that all sixteen Soviet republics be admitted to the United Nations as members but then reduced the demand to three or perhaps two, Ukraine, Byelorussia and Lithuania. Roosevelt initially objected to the Soviet proposal on the ground that it violated the principle of one vote for each member of the United Nations.[59]

On the following day, February 8, Alger Hiss circulated within the American delegation a memo on UN membership that provided "Arguments Against the

Inclusion of Any of the Soviet Republics Among the Initial Members." "It is interesting to note that the memo gave a closely reasoned argument against admitting the Soviet republics on the basis that they were not sovereign states under international practice and had not signed the United Nations declaration," recalled Bohlen.[60]

Bohlen did not know Hiss personally and downplays his importance; he believed Hiss had no direct influence on the president:

> I do not believe that Roosevelt had any prior acquaintance with Hiss. He may have seen Hiss among the group of State Department officials brought into the White House for one subject or another. I know that the first time Roosevelt saw him at Yalta was at a general meeting of the leading American advisers on the morning of the first day. The President certainly shook hands with Hiss at that time. But I can testify with certainty that Roosevelt never saw Hiss alone during the entire proceedings of the conference. I am confident of this statement because, as Roosevelt's interpreter, I had to stay close to him in anticipation of a possible suggestion from Stalin for a meeting. Hiss sat in on the big conference but never at any of the private meetings that the President had with Stalin or with Churchill. I was in general contact with Hiss almost every day in one form or another, and can say that Hiss had no special views to offer on any subjects except those affecting the United Nations, which was his responsibility on the delegation.[61]

Yet, while he was at Yalta as a member of the State Department, Hiss met every afternoon with Major General Mikhail Abramovitch Milshtein, the English-speaking deputy director of Soviet military intelligence. Milshtein worked for the GRU, or Main Intelligence Directorate. Milshtein dressed in civilian clothes, under cover as a military adviser to the Soviet delegation. His real role as a GRU trouble-shooter was unknown to the American delegation, but he was no stranger to Hiss. Milshtein had been one of Hiss' control officers in the United States when Milshtein served as Soviet vice-consul in New York from 1935 to 1938. He received the Order of the Red Star in 1937 for his successful effort to ship arms from the United States to Spain for the Spanish Republican Army in their struggle against Franco. Milshtein was one of the few Jews who survived Stalin's purges of the intelligence services, and some of his colleagues said he was "Stalin's token Jewish general."

Milshtein's career flourished when he was placed in charge of the Red Orchestra, the clandestine Soviet intelligence network that existed throughout World War II in Europe. (It derived its name from the German secret service term for the head of a spy network, *Kapellmeister*, or orchestra leader.) Under Milshtein's leadership, both the GRU and the NKVD had their own agent networks communicating by radio, tapping out coded messages.[62] Milshtein was the deputy head of the GRU directorate in charge of overseas espionage. For the Soviets, he was the right man to contact Hiss at Yalta.

Since Hiss was a trusted note taker at plenary sessions and had access to the "black books," he knew the American positions on such unresolved issues as the future of Poland, the Soviet Union's entry into the Pacific War against Japan, and the role of France in the occupation of Germany.

Soviet intelligence had prepared carefully for Yalta. Stalin placed a high premium on psychological profiles of the American delegation, and they were more important to him than facts. Having Hiss on hand, the GRU could advise Stalin on how strongly Roosevelt was likely to persist in his positions. Both sides had the words and music for the conference, but not how would it be played out. Hiss could provide insights into American intentions. How far would the United States go in its support of the anticommunist Polish government in exile in London? Who in the American delegation was responsive to the Soviets? How important was the United Nations to Roosevelt? In the warm atmosphere of victory, it would not be suspicious for Hiss to talk to a Soviet adviser to the delegation in civilian clothes. Through Hiss's contact with Milshtein, American priorities and goals were open to Soviet intelligence.

In *Special Tasks*, Lieutenant General Pavel Sudoplatov noted that Hiss, in conversations with Soviet Ambassadors Litvinov and Oumansky, "disclosed official attitudes and plans; he was also close to our sources who were cooperating with Soviet intelligence. Within this framework of exchange of confidential information were references to Hiss as the source who told us the Americans were prepared to make a deal in Europe."[63] Hiss made it clear that the United States was not prepared to argue over the occupation of the countries where the Soviets had troops on the ground in Eastern Europe. By giving away the American and British positions in advance of the negotiations, Hiss abetted the lowering of the Iron Curtain.

Milshtein's performance at Yalta was "the highest point of his career," recalled a GRU colleague.[64] Milshtein is credited with having worked with Hiss throughout the conference and later was his covert host in Moscow when Hiss came to visit after the Yalta Conference. According to a senior retired GRU officer, major awards for GRU officers and agents had been received under a decree of the Supreme Soviet dated November 3, 1944. Hiss was reported to have received the Order of the Red Star; Milshtein was awarded with the Order of the Great Patriotic War, first grade, on February 24, 1945, following the Yalta Conference.

After Yalta there was rivalry between the GRU and NKVD over who would run Hiss. The NKVD initiative to take over Hiss, who was supplying mostly political, not military, information led nowhere. The GRU reported to Stalin, commander in chief of the Armed Forces, about its accomplishments with Hiss at Yalta. Stalin agreed to the GRU request and the matter was closed.

In the summer of 1944, Milshtein, traveling with a Soviet passport under the name Milsky, visited Washington and Ottawa. Traveling with him was a GRU illegal named Vauman Litvin who was assigned to take over from Arthur Adams, a GRU officer who had been living in America as an illegal. Milshtein returned to Moscow from his trip and reported favorably on the work of the GRU *rezidenturas* in Washington, where he is said to have met with Hiss, and in Ottawa. His "high assessment" nearly caused his downfall when GRU code clerk Igor Gouzenko and his wife fled from their apartment in Ottawa in September 1945, defected to Canadian authorities, and pointed to Alger Hiss as a Soviet agent.

Milshtein was accused of being responsible for the defection, but his brilliant work with Hiss at Yalta saved his career. It also helped him that he had recommended the recall of Gouzenko in autumn 1944. Milshtein had suggested that Gouzenko live within the confines of the embassy compound rather than in an apartment, which provided the opportunity for the Gouzenkos' escape and defection. Milshtein's warnings were ignored by the Soviet military attaché in Ottawa.

In the 1980s, Milshtein became a top official in the Institute for the USA and Canada, which arranged for American opinion leaders to visit Moscow.

The full extent of Hiss' contributions to Soviet military intelligence remains concealed in GRU files, but it is apparent that by supplying plain language texts of documents that were then encoded, Hiss helped Soviet cryptanalysts solve American codes or ciphers. In this category fall the famous "Pumpkin Papers," which Whittaker Chambers accused Alger Hiss of giving to him for transmission to Soviet agents; Chambers said he had hidden them in a pumpkin field on his farm outside Baltimore. David Kahn, a leading expert on the history of cryptology, has noted that, although Chambers never gave the particular rolls of film that constituted the actual "Pumpkin Papers" to his Russian control officer, Colonel Boris Bykov,

> they were representative of many other similar photographed documents, allegedly from Hiss, that he did pass on. They included, for example, a cablegram from the American embassy in Paris of January 13, 1938, marked "Strictly Confidential, for the Secretary." Though parts of some of these messages were sent in the nonconfidential GRAY code, others, stated Sumner Welles, who was Under Secretary of State in 1938, "would presumably be sent in one of the most secret codes then in our possession." When he was asked, "Would the possession of the document as translated, along with the original document as it appeared in code, furnish an individual with the necessary information to break the code?" he replied: "In my opinion, decidedly yes." At least one Russian expert [Isaac Don Levine, the Russian-born journalist who specialized in Soviet affairs] became convinced by mid-1939 from numerous conversations he had with General Walter Krivitsky, the defected head of Soviet military intelligence for Western Europe, that the Soviet cryptanalysts were reading American codes.[65]

How Hiss was handled and what his contributions were to the Soviet Union are the subjects treated in detail in a contemporary secret GRU training manual devoted to managing a high level asset. The case study of "Mr. Bliss," as Hiss is called in the manual, is cited as an example of how to run a long-time, highly productive agent.

The testimonies of Whittaker Chambers and Isaac Don Levine before the House Committee on Un-American Activities in 1948 contributed to bringing Alger Hiss to trial on charges of perjury. Hiss was convicted and sentenced to five years in prison. He continued to maintain his innocence until his death in 1996 at age 92.[66]

★★★ 7 VENONA Hits Pay Dirt

Names and places began to emerge from the number filled Soviet messages. Then the cryptanalysts got their first glimpse of what appeared to be code names, or *klichkas*, in the traffic, the first clear indication they were working on significant Soviet intelligence traffic. In late 1944, James Byrnes gave the Army Security Agency (ASA) approval to attack the Soviet traffic on an expanded basis. Still answering concerns about the propriety of deciphering an ally's messages, Carter Clarke told a colleague, "Byrnes said to work on it." Oliver Kirby, the cryptanalyst who had helped retrieve German and Russian information during the war, said he, too, had raised the question of working on an ally's codes. In a conversation with Clarke's aide, Colonel Lester R. Forney, Chief of the G-2 Security Group, Forney told him, "This is different. We have a go ahead from Jimmy Byrnes."[1]

The enhanced efforts showed promise of revealing the names of agents and details of operations; more staff was needed to process the messages. By 1945 Clarke assured Byrnes that the Signals Intelligence Service had experienced personnel coming back from overseas "who are all top notch." At the end of the war, there was growing concern among the Signals Intelligence staff about what would happen to the work they had already accomplished when code breaking no longer seemed necessary. The bureaucratic impetus to protect the agency and its personnel by finding them work made the "Russian problem" a natural candidate for expansion. "The psychic income was high for those working on the project. They all wanted to do the job. It was necessary to raise funds to continue our work," said Kirby.[2]

The number of code breakers and workers on the team expanded from six to fifty-two; including equipment, the annual cost came to about $1,500,000.[3] The VENONA program took on momentum in 1945 when the code breakers set up links based on the repetition of salutations and addresses—call signs—at the beginning of messages and began to figure out categories into which the traffic fit: military, commercial, diplomatic, or intelligence.

After December 1945, recoveries of words from coded numbers began to move from scraps to more complex notions like cover names, where operations were taking place, and what government offices were involved. The Army Intelligence people under Clarke quickly recognized from the structure and hints of the military content of the fragments that they had come upon a mother lode of secret agent communications.

The VENONA messages would reveal that more than 200 Americans in government and war industries were secretly working for the Soviets, either as assets, sources of information who were serving the communist cause and who accepted gifts from Moscow, or as recruited agents who took orders and payment from the NKVD and GRU.

When the code breakers became aware of the scope of the Soviet intelligence penetration, ASA head General Preston Corderman grew concerned over how the revelations would be received within the government's bureaucracy. Corderman's reaction was "to be astute enough to get something on the table so others would know that he was not the sole possessor of the information," explained Kirby.[4] General Corderman wanted to share the responsibility for the politically sensitive material and avoid becoming a target of recriminations if anything leaked. "Once you handle this kind of material it is easy to become tainted with it," noted Kirby.[5]

In early 1946, Signals Intelligence took copies of the decoded fragments to the FBI and Army Intelligence for the first time and began formal cooperation in 1947. In preparation for the briefings, the Arlington Hall team compiled data on areas of penetration into the U.S. government and industry, current status of the decoders' work, a "bigot list" (a summary of those who had access to the system and materials), and how the FBI and Army Intelligence roles were being coordinated.

When the decoded material indicated Soviet infiltration of the State Department, Clarke directed Kirby to bring the material to their attention. His visit was not received in the spirit of a fire alarm; the Department of State rejected outright the idea of Soviet spies in their midst. Kirby recalled:

The State Department kicked me out. Nobody was interested in the information. I'd say, "Look what I've got" and they would say, "That doesn't happen to be anything my boss has a priority on. The Russians are our friends and you'd better stop talking that way young man or we are going to have your scalp tied to the flagpole. So you and your little known agency had better not come around here talking about that kind of thing." I was referred first to the director of the State Department Bureau of Intelligence and Research. I started talking about what we had recovered and was told, "None of that stuff around here. You pack yourself out of here."

When I reported to Carter Clarke he was not surprised, and even seemed to be pleased. Clarke told me: "You've done your duty. You don't need to talk to them again. We will forget them from here on out." That's just what we did with a clear conscience. Since nobody at the State Department was interested they were not brought in at all.[6]

When Kirby joined the Russian project in 1945, the word was out within the very small circle of those directing the work that early in 1945 the President's wife, Eleanor Roosevelt, had complained to Secretary of War Stimson about "the reading of a friend's traffic" and urged it be halted. Stimson passed the word to Clarke, who scoffed and told his team, "Just keep going."[7] Later Kirby asked Clarke if Mrs. Roosevelt had actually intervened. "Yes," replied Clarke, "That's the gist of it, but we put a stop to that." Putting a stop to it, Clarke said, meant not doing anything about Mrs. Roosevelt's complaint. Clarke said he had passed the word that if Mrs. Roosevelt persisted, he would tell newspaper publishers in confidence of her interference.[8]

The President's wife was not the only leak in the security of VENONA. Soviet intelligence learned in 1944 that the United States was working on breaking Soviet codes. As mentioned earlier, Lauchlin Currie, FDR's administrative assistant on economic affairs and China policy, was supplying information to the Silvermaster group; Elizabeth Bentley was the group's courier and liaison with the NKVD *rezidentura* in New York. In 1945 Bentley described to the FBI a scene a year earlier in which Currie had come to one of the members of the Silvermaster group, "sort of out of breath, and told him that the Americans were on the verge of breaking the Soviet code." Currie denied making such a statement and insisted he was not a Soviet spy.[9]

Bentley said she relayed Currie's report to BILL (Akhmerov), her NKVD superior, who asked her, "Well is it a trap or isn't it a trap?" BILL assigned her to find out which code was about to be broken, but she was not able to obtain specific details.

A follow-up investigation by the FBI found another witness, a senior government official who preferred to remain unnamed publicly, who said that in the spring of 1944, Currie said he knew of a hush-hush matter, too sensitive to talk about. Currie said that he had "tipped off" the Russians about the imminent breaking of the "Soviet diplomatic code" because breaking the code "indicated our lack of trust in the Russians." The official said he rebuked Currie, but Currie had argued that he had done right by telling the Soviets in order to prevent sowing the seeds of distrust between allies.[10]

Inside the Armed Forces, the NKVD had a spy named William Weisband who, because of his command of Russian, worked on and had unlimited access to the code-breaking program. Weisband, born in Egypt of Russian parents in 1908, emigrated to the United States in the 1920s and was recruited by the NKVD in 1934. He became an American citizen in 1938. During World War II, he served in the Army Signal Corps on signals security in North Africa and Italy. He joined the Russian program in 1945; coworkers recalled that in 1946 Weisband had been present at the jubilant moment when they extracted the names of Western atomic scientists from a December 1944 NKVD message.

When Weisband first advised Soviet intelligence of the code-breaking program is unclear. According to Allen Weinstein and Alexander Vassiliev, who had access to archival records provided by the KGB, Soviet intelligence's contact with Weisband was broken off during the war and was not resumed until 1948.[11] In Moscow in 1997, Aleksandr Feklisov, who ran the NKVD technical line in New York from 1944 to 1946, insisted he had never heard of Weisband. Feklisov said he had his own agent in the Army Signals Intelligence in 1944 "who gave me decoded Japanese materials." Feklisov said the agent, then an Army lieutenant, might still be alive and refused to name him, but National Security Agency historian Robert Louis Benson believes the agent was Weisband. The VENONA code name ZVENO is Weisband. He denied involvement in espionage and was never prosecuted for it.[12]

British MI-6 liaison officer Harold Adrian Russell (Kim) Philby had served as a Soviet agent since his recruitment in 1934.[13] He was briefed on the Russian program translations and analyses on a regular basis after he arrived for duty in Washington in October 1949.[14] Philby had access to the first results of the code-breaking program under the terms of a secret intelligence-sharing agreement with the British.[15]

From 1945, when Elizabeth Bentley first described Lauchlin Currie's excited report that the United States was breaking Soviet codes, to the defection of British diplomat Donald Maclean in 1951, it was apparent that Soviet intelligence knew of the cryptanalytic breakthrough in VENONA.

The Soviets did not know that Army Intelligence was able to identify specific spies, nor to what extent agent operations were compromised. There was hesitation and denial on both sides, American and Soviet, in believing that their most secret systems were known to the other. Deep in the midst of the decoding process, the Americans' natural inclination was not to reveal what had already been accomplished until they had broken the traffic, and its names and secret operations poured forth. The impetus for continued secrecy transcended logic: the code breakers insisted on keeping the results of their work hidden even when they knew their activities were no longer a secret to their target, Soviet intelligence.

The successful World War II secrecy of ENIGMA at Bletchley, maintained for more than thirty years, had conditioned the NSA decoders to keep the same strict standards. The difference, of course, was that ENIGMA was providing real time intelligence used in battle planning and execution; VENONA was unraveling the bitter truth of past actions by American officials recruited or exploited by the Soviet Union. Revelation would have potent domestic political consequences, but the operational value of the material was virtually useless. ENIGMA established the mores of the culture of secrecy, in which the participants knew that wartime secrets were sacred—revealing them would expose operations and allow the enemy to change codes as well as expose sources and methods. In both cases, secrecy was continued long after it had ceased being operational. When a secret has been buried a long time, it becomes inert but not useless; it requires a special courage to bring it into the light.

Under a June 26, 1939, memorandum signed by President Roosevelt, the investigation of all espionage, counterespionage, and sabotage was to be controlled by the FBI, the Military Intelligence Division of the War Department (Army G-2), and the Office of Naval Intelligence.[16] Clarke understood the political dangers inherent in discovering an ally's intelligence operations on American soil. That was the reason he brought in the FBI.

From the intercepts, it was unclear who were the targets of Soviet spying operations and who was under cover working for the Russians.[17] Being mentioned with a cover name in a top secret cable did not necessarily indicate cooperation with Soviet intelligence. President Roosevelt had the cover name KAPITAN (captain) and Winston Churchill was KABAN (boar) to conceal their identities as targets of Soviet intelligence. This type of cover name, the FBI noted, "merely obscures the sense and thereby affords indirect protection of the agent and at the same time is calculated to baffle foreign intelligence organizations as to just what intelligence is being transmitted."[18] The messages used cover names primarily to designate Soviet agents. The messages described men and women in the process of carrying out espionage, which meant supplying classified documents or verbally passing highly classified information to Soviet intelligence. Julius Rosenberg was given the cover name ANTENNA, which was later changed to LIBERAL; periodically code names were changed for security. Klaus Fuchs was REST and CHARLES. Alger Hiss was ALES.

In 1948, Robert Lamphere, an FBI special agent who had successfully tracked Soviet intelligence agents while stationed in the New York field office, was promoted to case supervisor and transferred to Washington. When Lamphere was shown the first primitive decrypted messages by his colleague Wesley Reynolds, the FBI liaison with the Army Security Agency, he quickly arranged to meet Meredith Gardner, the venerable linguist and cryptanalyst at Arlington Hall responsible for major breakthroughs in the Soviet traffic. They were an intellectual match, but, in style, an unlikely team: Lamphere, the burly, rough-and-ready special agent from the coal mines of Idaho, who had worked his way through law school; and Gardner, a slender, quiet problem solver who spoke and read a half-dozen languages and had taught himself Russian.

Lamphere met with Gardner every two weeks, usually stopping first to eat at a favorite spaghetti restaurant on the Virginia side of the Potomac. Lamphere brought Gardner guesses, clues, and plain language messages to match the Russian language decrypts that were slowly revealing layer upon layer of Soviet espionage operations. Matching names and places with people was like solving an endless crossword puzzle. One batch of messages mentioned a woman, code-named SIMA, working in the Department of Justice, who had transferred from New York to Washington. With these clues, it took Lamphere's supervisor only thirty minutes to identify Judith Coplon, still working with wartime secrets in the same building where the FBI had its offices.[19] Coplon was nicknamed "The Spy Next Door." Thirty FBI agents followed her through the New York subway system to arrest her the moment she was ready to hand over classified documents to her Soviet control officer.[20] Coplon was twice brought to trial and convicted, but twice won on appeal and walked away free. Judge Learned Hand's reversal on appeal made the FBI appear to be in violation of Coplon's rights; the Justice Department was not prepared to reveal that its "confidential source" was the VENONA messages.[21]

Other VENONA messages contained the code name HOMER for a British diplomat supplying high level information to the Soviets. A message dated June 28, 1944, indicated that HOMER had gone to New York to be with his wife when she gave birth to their child. There was only one British diplomat in Washington who matched that description. The FBI focused on elegant, well-respected Donald Maclean, who in 1944 had been first secretary and acting head of chancery, and who had access to all of the embassy traffic, including the ambassador's personal cables to the Foreign Office. Forcing his wife, Melinda, to remain in New York while he worked in Washington—so that he would have a cover for his frequent trips to feed material to his control officer—turned out to be the smoking gun by which the FBI identified HOMER in VENONA. By 1948, Maclean was back in London. Lamphere sent word of the discovery to his MI-5 counterpart in London. However, British intelligence hesitated to act, unable to accept that one of their own was capable of treachery.

Lamphere coordinated the search for HOMER with the British Secret Intelligence Service (MI-6), whose representative in Washington was Kim Philby, later dubbed "the spy of the century." Dressed in a shabby tweed jacket, Philby listened sullenly to Lamphere's description of HOMER, his fellow spy, while sitting across Lamphere's desk at the FBI. Philby was at the same time betraying the progress on VENONA to his Soviet control officer, Yuri Modin, in London. Philby also had access to Meredith Gardner, who discussed progress being made in reading the Soviet messages.[22] The fox was in the henhouse.

Among the Cambridge spies, Maclean was the most important provider of political intelligence to Stalin. Maclean was then head of the American desk in London. His assignment came after heavy drinking bouts and a nervous collapse in Cairo from which he took several months to recover. The handsome, elegantly dressed Maclean was the very model of a Foreign Office official, but his double life took a heavy physical and mental toll. From his early days in the Foreign Office when he had Kitty Harris as his courier and lover, until his flight to the Soviet Union with Guy Burgess in May 1951, Maclean was a valuable spy for Moscow Center.

With the highest level of contacts and access, Maclean was a keen analyst of Western intentions. His advance reporting on the Marshall Plan turned Stalin against the aid plan for the Soviet Union and the Eastern European Communist bloc. While in Washington, D.C., from 1944 to 1948, as first secretary and head of chancery, Maclean had atomic energy security clearances with which he provided the Soviet Union information on American nuclear weapons capabilities and strategy.

Burgess' assignment to Washington in August 1950 put him in close touch with Kim Philby, and Philby made the mistake of inviting Burgess to live with him in his house, 4100 Nebraska Avenue in Northwest Washington, only a few minutes from the British embassy.[23] Burgess' behavior was so abusive—he obtained three speeding tickets in one weekend and was frequently absent from the embassy on drinking binges—that he was sent back to London in disgrace. Before he left, Philby warned him that the VENONA decryptions were closing in on them and that Maclean might be identified by his code name, HOMER.

At the end of April 1951 when Burgess returned to London, he was still not suspected, but Maclean had already been identified as a wartime Soviet spy in the Washington British embassy. The British Foreign Office failed to pursue the case even after the FBI informed MI-5 of a suspected Soviet spy in their ranks. It took weeks to gather the necessary evidence to proceed against Maclean. On Friday, May 25, 1951, the British security officials decided to interview Maclean on Monday morning. Since mid-April, Maclean had received no top secret materials, which gave him reason to believe he was under surveillance. He could not contact Modin to set up an escape.

Soon after Burgess returned to London, he received an urgent air mail letter from Philby, ostensibly about the car Burgess had left in the embassy parking lot. The letter ended with the warning: "It's getting very hot here." Through Anthony Blunt, Burgess advised Modin of the situation. The KGB authorized Maclean to defect to Moscow and urged Burgess to accompany him. On Friday night, May 25, Maclean's 38th birthday, Burgess drove to Maclean's home in Tatsfeld outside London and told him they were leaving for Moscow. The two drove at top speed to Southampton where they boarded a weekend cruise ship for France; the following morning, they went ashore in St. Malo. A taxi took them to Rennes, forty miles away, where they boarded a train to Paris. In Paris they changed trains and headed for Zurich, from where they flew to Prague; there they picked up KGB escorts.[24] Their arrival in Moscow, although heavily speculated upon in the press, was not publicly disclosed until 1956.

When Philby was later implicated with Maclean, the U.S. government knew that the Soviets knew the Americans had broken their code and were reading Soviet secret traffic.[25] Nevertheless, the Americans and British let the opportunity go by to lift the veil of secrecy over their decoding efforts, which might have made it easier to use the decrypts in legal cases against Americans revealed to be Soviet agents.

Under American law, charges of espionage have to be proven by documentary evidence, witness testimony, arrest during the actual transfer of documents, or a confession. The FBI carefully weighed the advantages and disadvantages of using VENONA information for evidence. A top secret internal memorandum weighed the pros and cons. The advantages were obvious. Public disclosure of the messages would "vindicate the Bureau in the matter of the confidence we placed in Elizabeth Bentley's testimony" and enable the government to convict a number of traitors "whose continued freedom from prosecution is a sin against justice."[26]

However, the FBI concluded that "the disadvantages of using VENONA information publicly or in a prosecution appear overwhelming." The biggest question mark was whether the deciphered messages would be admitted into evidence. If they were not, it would "abruptly end hope for prosecution."[27]

The FBI believed that

the defense attorney would immediately move that the messages be excluded, based on the hearsay evidence rule. He would probably claim that neither the person who sent the message [Soviet official] nor the person who received it [Soviet official] was available to testify and thus the contents of the message were purely hearsay as it related to the defendants. Consequently, in order to overcome such a motion it would be necessary to rely upon their admission through the use of expert testimony of those who intercepted the messages and those cryptographers who deciphered the messages. A question of law is involved herein. It is believed that the messages probably could be introduced in evidence on the basis of exception to the hearsay evidence rule to the effect that the expert testimony was sufficient to establish the authenticity of the documents and they were the best evidence available.

Assuming that the messages could be introduced in evidence, we then have a question of identity. The fragmentary nature of the messages themselves, the assumptions made by the cryptographers in breaking the messages, and the questionable interpretations and translations involved, plus the extensive use of cover names for persons and places, make the problem of positive identification extremely difficult. Here, again, reliance would have to be placed on the expert testimony of the cryptographers and it appears that the case would be entirely circumstantial.

Assuming further that the testimony of the Government cryptographers were accepted as part of the Government case, defense probably would be granted authority by the court to have private cryptographers hired by the defense examine the messages as well as the work sheets of the Government cryptographers. And in view of the fragmentary nature of the majority of these messages the defense would make a request to have its cryptographers exclude those messages which [the Army Security Agency] has been unsuccessful in breaking and which are not in evidence on the premise that such messages, if decoded, could exonerate their clients. This would lead to the exposure of Government techniques and practices in the cryptography field to unauthorized persons and thus compromise the Government's efforts in the communications intelligence field. Also, this course of action would act to the Bureau's disadvantage since the additional messages would spotlight individuals on whom the Bureau had pending investigations.[28]

The decoded messages could provide leads to develop cases for prosecution, but since they couldn't be used in court, the counterintelligence law enforcers had to collect other hard evidence to prepare an indictment.

In early September 1949, days before President Truman's September 23 announcement to the world that the Soviets had an atomic device, Lamphere and Gardner pinpointed Klaus Fuchs, confirming that he was an atomic spy. In the freshly deciphered text of a 1944 message, there was extensive data on the gaseous diffusion process, one of the key techniques used to obtain the type of uranium needed in the manufacture of the atomic bomb. "When I read the message," recalled Lamphere, "it became immediately obvious to me that the Russians had indeed stolen crucial research from us and had undoubtedly used it to build their bomb."[29] Lamphere dropped everything to follow the trail of the deciphered message. Part of it summarized a detailed scientific paper. Another part referred to the agent or messenger who had provided the information, indicating clearly that in 1944 the NKVD had an agent inside the British Mission to the Manhattan Project.

Working closely with his FBI colleague Ernest (Ernie) Van Loon, Lamphere obtained from the Atomic Energy Commission (AEC) a copy of the paper summarized in the NKVD message and a list of those who had come to the United States on the British team: "In two short days we had learned that Klaus Fuchs was one of the top British scientists on the Manhattan Project." Fuchs, a German refugee to Great Britain, had been sent to Los Alamos from 1943 to 1945 and returned to England to work on the H-bomb. Lamphere and Gardner were able to track Fuchs' courier, Harry Gold, and from him the path led to Julius and Ethel Rosenberg.[30]

On July 30, 1948, when Elizabeth Bentley testified before a Senate subcommittee investigating loyalty in the Executive Branch, her story became public. In hyped news stories foreshadowing her testimony, she was portrayed as the "Blonde Queen" of a "Red Spy Ring." Bentley was never a blonde; she had short, brown, curly hair, a round face, and ruddy complexion. When she came to the FBI in 1945, she was

37 years old, five feet seven inches tall, and weighed 143 pounds. Blue-eyed, with an easy smile, she seemed outwardly cheerful, but her deliberately proletarian taste in clothes gave her a dowdy look.[31]

In the process of revealing her intelligence activities to the FBI, Bentley named "over 100 names." Some she claimed were actively engaged in Soviet espionage; others were connected to some degree with communist activities. Of the fifty-one people investigated by the FBI, twenty-seven were employed by the U.S. government on November 7, 1945. The VENONA traffic identified thirty-seven of the people Bentley named, twenty-four of them had code names. Bentley's information on Assistant Treasury Secretary Harry Dexter White, Presidential Assistant Lauchlin Currie, and the Silvermaster group is confirmed in the VENONA messages. The initial reaction within the government and press was to downplay Bentley's revelations and make her an object of ridicule.

On August 16, 1948, the President's Chief of Staff Clark Clifford received a memorandum from his aide, George M. Elsey, following a meeting with Attorney General Tom Clark. Elsey advised,

> The President should not at this time make a statement regarding "spies."
> . . . Rather than face the charges raised by Bentley and Whittaker Chambers, attention will be given by Justice to the possibility and desirability of referring the question of Soviet espionage in the Federal Government to a bi-partisan commission, such as the Hoover Commission.

Elsey recommended that "Justice should make every effort to ascertain if Whittaker Chambers is guilty of perjury" and that Chambers' "confinement in mental institution" be investigated. In an effort to disprove the charges of espionage and passing classified information to the Soviet Union, Elsey advised:

> The Attorney General will furnish the White House with a description of the data Miss Bentley claims to have obtained for Soviet agents during the war; the White House should endeavor to determine how much of this information was freely available to the Soviet government through routine official liaison between the U.S. and the U.S.S.R. The purpose of this would be to make it clear that Miss Bentley was not successful in transmitting secret material to the Russians that they did not already have.[32]

Included in Elizabeth Bentley's list of sources and agents were Americans working for the NKVD at the highest levels of the Office of Strategic Services (OSS), which was closed down in October of 1945. When the new Central Intelligence Agency was established in 1947, a number of OSS officers joined its ranks. General Carter Clarke was determined to keep the CIA out of the restricted secret circle within the government that shielded VENONA. On May 20, 1949, two years after the CIA came into being, the Army Security Agency, which for six productive years had kept a tight lid over VENONA, was swallowed up in a reorganization that made them part of the new Armed Forces Security Agency (AFSA). AFSA was a consolidation of Army and Navy Signals Intelligence (SIGINT), reporting to the Joint Chiefs of Staff. The resulting bureaucratic battles between the services led to a struggle for access to and control over VENONA.

The wartime procedure was for Signals Intelligence to produce translated texts after collecting, analyzing, and decrypting targeted communications. They turned the texts over to the intelligence staffs of the Army and Navy for dissemination. The jealously guarded function of the intelligence staffs was to convert the solved and translated texts into intelligence reports and summaries, which they provided to selected users.

Until Army Signals Intelligence became part of the new unified AFSA, the VENONA program successfully bypassed these standard procedures. Secretary Byrnes, and later the first secretary of defense, James Forrestal, approved a maximum security plan under which the FBI was the only authorized user of VENONA decryptions and their translated texts. The FBI's Robert Lamphere had direct access to Meredith Gardner at Arlington Hall. This small island of cooperation enabled Gardner to concentrate his efforts on messages of immediate interest to Lamphere.

Two other users had access to the VENONA output: the White House and British intelligence. Under the British-USA (BRUSA) Agreement of 1948, the Army Security Agency gave its translated texts to the British Government Communications Headquarters. These decrypted messages were passed to MI-6, where Kim Philby had access to them and advised his Soviet control officer of progress in the American code-breaking program. Even though the U.S. Navy did not know that VENONA existed, Philby was regularly briefed on its progress and alerted Moscow.

VENONA messages of political importance were hand carried to Byrnes and Forrestal. The White House recipients were shocked when they saw confidential messages between President Roosevelt and Winston Churchill that had reached Moscow through the hands of a still unidentified Soviet agent in the British embassy in Washington. The decoders had brought the high level memoranda full circle back to their starting point, the White House.

The control point for VENONA material for the White House was General Omar Bradley, Chief of Staff of the Army, who in February 1948 became the titular head of the VENONA project and called himself the "front man" for guarding its secrecy. Soon after Bradley took over this function, he held a meeting with General Clarke, Kirby, and Frank Rowlett, chief of the intelligence division of the Army Security Agency. They agreed to maintain the security procedures that had been approved by Byrnes and later Forrestal. General Bradley was to be the doorkeeper who would keep the president and his designated staff informed of new VENONA revelations.[33]

At this meeting, General Bradley brought up General Clarke's unsuccessful meeting with President Truman in June 1945. Bradley said it was no wonder that the president found it difficult to comprehend the complex nature of the cryptanalysis methods necessary to decode the Soviet messages. More to the point, Bradley explained that the president's negative attitude toward Clarke's report of a potential major success in discovering Soviet espionage was a result of the not-yet-confirmed or validated information Truman was receiving from J. Edgar Hoover. General Bradley hoped he would be able to separate VENONA from the unchecked accusations Hoover was presenting to the president.[34]

One important example came on May 29, 1946, when Hoover sent by messenger a personal and confidential letter to George E. Allen, Director of the Reconstruction Finance Corporation, a close friend of Truman. Hoover warned that "information has been furnished to this Bureau through a source believed to be reliable that there is an enormous Soviet espionage ring in Washington operating with the view of obtaining all information possible with reference to atomic energy, and the commercial aspects of energy in peacetime, and that a number of high Government officials whose identities will be set out hereinafter are involved." Hoover then listed fourteen names, including Undersecretary of State Dean Acheson, Assistant Secretary of War Howard C. Peterson, Secretary of Commerce Henry A. Wallace, and Alger Hiss. In his book on secrecy, former Senator Daniel Patrick Moynihan calls the memo "baseless corridor talk." There were "scraps of truth here, but in the main it was fantasy and dismissed as such. Both fantasies *and* truth."[35]

Truman considered Hoover to be politically motivated against the Democratic Party, in league with Truman's political enemies.[36] In the 1948 presidential election campaign, Hoover actively supported the Republican candidate, Thomas E. Dewey, by supplying derogatory material on Truman's relationship with Kansas City Democratic party boss Tom Pendergast and maintaining pressure on the issue of communists in government.[37]

The absorption of the Army Security Agency into the unified Armed Forces Security Agency threatened VENONA's exclusivity and precipitated a high level bureaucratic test of strength to determine whether or not the CIA would be included in the small circle with access to the program. To prepare for the changeover to AFSA, General Clarke directed Kirby to brief Admiral Joseph Wenger, head of the Naval Security Group, on what the VENONA program had uncovered. When the two met on May 20, 1949, Wenger was amazed both by VENONA's successes and by the fact that he had heard nothing about its existence.

Clarke took upon himself the task of briefing Admiral Earl E. Stone, Director of the newly formed AFSA, about the existence and nature of VENONA. At their meeting in early September 1949, Admiral Stone was enraged to learn that VENONA had existed since 1945 and that it had achieved notable successes without his knowledge. The irate Stone refused to accept the need-to-know criteria laid down for the dissemination of VENONA material, even though the rules had been approved at the White House level to maintain its security. Stone told Clarke he wanted to review and change the procedures to fall in line with AFSA policies.

The two senior officers had a heated argument when Admiral Stone insisted that VENONA data be forwarded under AFSA auspices and AFSA procedures to the president and to CIA Director Admiral Roscoe E. Hillenkoetter. General Clarke assured Admiral Stone that the president was receiving VENONA output. He was adamant, however, that the newly formed CIA should not receive the secret material. Clarke took seriously the charges by Elizabeth Bentley that a number of her agents worked for the OSS and that others might now be installed at the CIA. Clarke did not want to give the Soviets continuing access to VENONA's successes and failures through what he believed were their spies inside the CIA. He did not want the NKVD in Moscow on VENONA's distribution list.[38]

Admiral Stone contacted Mickey Ladd, assistant to Hoover at the FBI, to arrange discussions about how the FBI and AFSA would interact. In particular, Stone wanted to know if the FBI was working with the CIA on VENONA. His questions set off a prearranged alert system for requests from anyone not cleared under VENONA procedures. Ladd put Special Agent Howard B. Fletcher on the request and brought it to the attention of Wes Reynolds, the FBI's liaison with ASA and then AFSA. From declassified FBI files comes Fletcher's memorandum to Ladd on October 18, 1949; it reported on a meeting with General Clarke and laid out the argument between Clarke and Admiral Stone about dissemination of VENONA materials to the CIA. Clarke turned to General Bradley for support. The differences, said the memo, "culminated in a conference with General Bradley [who] would personally assume the responsibility of advising the President or anyone else in authority if the contents of the material so demanded. . . . [Clarke] wanted to be certain that the Bureau . . . does not handle the material in such a way that Admiral Hillenkoetter or any one else outside the Army Security Agency, [text deleted here],[39] and the Bureau are aware of the contents of these messages and the activity being conducted at Arlington Hall."[40]

Another angry exchange occurred between Clarke and Stone; Stone would not accept the information control procedures approved and in use during 1946, 1947, and 1948. General Bradley again intervened to support Clarke's position of excluding the CIA from the VENONA dissemination list. Bradley discussed the problem with Secretary of Defense Louis Johnson (who succeeded Forrestal) and then informed Admiral Stone what procedures were to be followed for the VENONA program. It was not until 1952 that the CIA was initiated into

VENONA. According to former Director Richard Helms, the VENONA materials played only a minor role in CIA counterintelligence efforts.[41] In 1956, VENONA became part of James Angleton's responsibility as head of CIA counterintelligence. Angleton, who had been a long-time friend of Philby's before Philby was exposed, continued to hunt for Soviet moles in the agency, but VENONA was history, no longer of value in Angleton's fruitless search, which caused disruptive and damaging turmoil in the CIA's Soviet operations. Angelton was gone when Aldrich Ames began his treasonous activities for Soviet intelligence, but the legacy of Angleton's excesses in digging out ideological moles created a backlash against mole hunting that allowed Ames to remain in place for ten years.

In his book *Secrecy*, Senator Daniel Patrick Moynihan interprets the FBI memo from Fletcher to Ladd to mean that General Bradley was the cutoff point for VENONA material to be brought to the president's attention and that it never reached him.[42] However, Kirby, who worked for General Clarke, and had long, thoughtful conversations with General Bradley and Secretary Forrestal on VENONA, is certain the president was informed and was part of the dialogue.

Bradley's methods for informing Truman and his staff about new material coming out of the VENONA program were totally out of normal channels. To keep the VENONA program totally secret, visits by ASA representatives and General Bradley took place at locations selected by the White House principals. The White House Annex (now called the Eisenhower Executive Office Building) was a frequent choice for off-the-record meetings. "There was no sign-in or sign-out, only clearance by alerted gate guards at the entrances," explained Kirby.[43]

Defense Secretary James Forrestal was concerned about the secrets emerging from VENONA and in October 1948 asked Clarke for a meeting with a knowledgeable expert on the scope and content of the materials. Clarke designated Kirby, who had been deputy director of the Russian code-breaking program from 1946 and would continue through 1949. Kirby received a call at home and was asked to meet Secretary Forrestal at the Pentagon Executive dining room. According to Kirby:

> From there we went to a vacant room in the Pentagon, not his office. I took no notes and the discussions were treated as private and off the record.
>
> The Secretary of Defense grasped the significance of the extensive penetrations achieved by Soviet espionage. The VENONA messages revealed that the Manhattan Project had been completely compromised by the Soviets. Information on each phase of building the first atomic bomb was sent through NKVD channels to Moscow. Most classified U.S. military armament projects had been penetrated. Also, indications of espionage success at the Head of State levels astounded Secretary Forrestal.[44]

Forrestal's deepest concern, however, was whether or not the messages indicated the Soviets had established an extensive sabotage capability that could be used to damage any American war effort against the USSR. Kirby reported no such evidence in the messages broken up to that time.[45]

Forrestal also brought up President Truman's distrust of VENONA data. Truman's qualms over stimulating a communist witch hunt were reinforced by his reservations about the partially decoded VENONA messages because, Truman told Forrestal, "there are too many unknowns." The initial fragmentary, incomplete VENONA messages were ambiguous; they provided clues, times, and places, yet often lacked confirming details. "Even if part of this is true it would open up this whole Red Panic again," Truman told Forrestal.[46]

In response to initial findings of communist infiltration in the White House and top government agencies, Truman told Forrestal that he could not believe Roosevelt had been so fooled in his judgment of people close to him, referring to Hiss and White. Truman also said he did not believe that the infiltration could be so widespread.[47]

The second time they met, in 1948, Kirby raised with Forrestal the idea of publicly releasing the news that American intelligence had broken the Soviet code. Kirby argued that breaking cover would force the Soviet Union to halt or limit its intelligence operations against the United States. They would know they had been compromised. Changes in Soviet codes and operational methods in 1945 indicated that they knew the American code breakers were reading them; announcing the fact would further inhibit them. Kirby believed that revealing the full extent of Soviet penetration would remove the issue from politics and limit any Red scare because the cases would be acted upon and resolved.

Forrestal reacted forcefully. "He told me not to do anything about blowing cover. 'Forget that. No. Hell, no. Don't ever think about that again!' " Kirby said, smiling ruefully.[48]

Kirby related his conversations with Forrestal to Clarke and Bradley. Clarke's response to Kirby's argument for openness mirrored Forrestal's. " 'There will never be any revealing of the program,' Clarke lectured me," said Kirby. " 'If it blows or becomes known a lot of us and even our agency will be in deep trouble. We were the eavesdroppers; we were the ones who had this information. Our agency will suffer. We'll be tainted by association with it.' " Kirby likened Clarke's words to what would later be called "Being tagged Big Brother."[49]

After Truman was elected in a stunning upset victory over Thomas Dewey, he tried to put the communists-in-government issue behind him, choosing to define the problem as primarily one of partisan politics. He believed this issue was being exploited to the detriment of law enforcement in its effort to prevent Soviet espionage. In a memorandum to Attorney General Tom Clark on December 16, 1948, Truman wrote:

I wonder if we could not get a statement of facts from the FBI about the meddling of the House Un-American Activities Committee and how they dried up sources of information which would have been accessible in the prosecution of spies and communists.

Their meddling efforts were in fact a "red herring" to detract attention not only from the shortcomings of the 80th Congress but also contributed to the escape of certain communists who should have been indicted.

I'll appreciate it if you will look into this a little bit and we will talk it over at the Cabinet meeting tomorrow.

Signed\ HST[50]

There is no record of follow-up on the memo by the Attorney General or by J. Edgar Hoover. Given Hoover's strained relations with the president, especially after Hoover's support of Dewey during the election campaign, cooperation from the FBI in criticizing the committee was highly unlikely and unrealistic, despite the president's request. The White House saw Hoover as an enemy of the president who had politicized the FBI. The White House team around Truman viewed Hoover's campaign against communism as politically motivated and they tended to discount the charges of Chambers and Bentley.[51]

Bradley suggested Kirby make notes on how the project was developing after March 1949. Again in 1950, when Harry Dexter White and Alger Hiss were "positively identified" in VENONA, Kirby called General Bradley to inform him "that we have made a positive identification on our 'mutual friends,' which between us we understood to mean Hiss and White. Bradley said he would inform the President. When Bradley called me back later he said, 'The President was most upset and agitated by this.' Bradley reported President Truman's words, 'That G—D—stuff. Every time it bumps into us it gets bigger and bigger. It's likely to take us down.' " Kirby said there was "no doubt the President understood."[52]

Bradley asked Kirby if he was still taking notes on the decoding program. "Bradley told me to move away from it, not to give it special attention and not get involved in giving briefings to administration officials. Bradley said he would take charge of keeping the President informed."[53]

By moving away from VENONA, not giving it attention, and keeping it secret, Truman delayed the Red Panic, but he could not avoid it. By not breaking open the deep cover over what he knew about Soviet infiltration, Truman allowed his political enemies to take control of the issue and magnify it for their own ends. Attempting to stem the panic, Truman ordered the establishment of loyalty boards in 1947. By that time, congressional committees had taken over the investigation of disloyalty and introduced a virus into the American legal system that proved to have more harmful and longer lasting effects than any act of espionage.

Naming names was the destructive force. The demand by the House Un-

American Activities Committee that witnesses become informers, compelling individuals to describe not only their past or present Communist Party affiliation but to report on and denounce the activities of their friends and colleagues, became a genre of evil. Agreeing to name names abetted the committees' unconstitutional demands that witnesses state their political beliefs and explain their acts of political assembly even though membership in the Communist Party was not against the law.

Naming names allowed every grudge against and jealousy of coworkers to become weapons that ruined careers and forced men and women from their jobs. School teachers were fired. Blacklists darkened the entertainment field. Of the estimated 100 Hollywood writers and actors who testified, 30 named names.[54] The HUAC threat of jail sentences for contempt for those who refused to name names turned the hearings into a travesty of due process. There were no legal safeguards for witnesses. The hearings became trials without juries.

★ ★ ★

Beginning in 1946, Signals Intelligence in the Army Security Agency (ASA) Arlington Hall Station (after 1952, it became the National Security Agency [NSA]) developed a new program to collect and exploit plain text (uncoded) civilian telegraph traffic within the Soviet Union. The Soviet system is the rough equivalent of Western Union in the United States. Most of the messages were between individuals, but there were also significant amounts of uncoded traffic among Soviet agencies, factories, and government ministries.

Early in the reading and analysis of plain text Soviet traffic, the Arlington Hall analysts found that the USSR was using the original U.S. assigned Lend Lease numbers to track and transfer Lend Lease shipments. Of particular interest to the U.S. intelligence community were entire chemical and petrochemical plants sent by Lend Lease to the Soviet Union, usually assigned to the First Directorate of the Ministry of Heavy Machine Building, which was responsible for the Soviet atomic energy program. Immediately after World War II, equipment identified by U.S. Lend Lease requisition numbers was shipped within the Soviet Union to sites where atomic energy plants were being built. The plants produced weapons grade plutonium for nuclear weapons.

During the collection and analysis of the traffic to the First Directorate of the Heavy Machine Building Industry, analysts were surprised that the Soviet Union was receiving materials banned for export. While the program to exploit plain language intercepts within the Soviet Union has not been discussed publicly nor it contents released, Kirby believes the mass of real time messages from the Soviet internal telegraphic system should be studied. From it he believes will emerge a fuller understanding of the extent to which wartime U.S. Lend Lease materials were used to build the Soviet atomic weapons stockpile.

★ ★ ★

In 1946 the Soviet Union shifted from ally to adversary. The Soviet Union persisted in pressing the threat that communism would overthrow Western democracy and establish a worldwide revolution. Instead, at the end of the 1940s, a rising middle class flourished in America, widening the gap between those who still admired the Soviet model and those who wanted to put the bitter angers of the Depression and class warfare behind them. Home ownership in the new suburbs created a vision of capitalism bringing prosperity to everybody.

By the end of the 1950s, the threat of a world communist revolution had lost its credibility. The internal threat of communists in the American government faded away. The urgency to bring convictions based on VENONA diminished, but still the program was maintained under tight secrecy. Soviet nuclear capability created a standoff until Mikhail Gorbachev turned from world revolution and class warfare to restructure the Soviet economy.[55] The Berlin Wall collapsed in 1989, and in 1991 the Soviet Union dissolved.

There was no longer any reason to keep VENONA secret. Mysteries of history remained to be solved. Were the Rosenbergs guilty of atomic espionage? Was Alger Hiss a Soviet spy? Was Elizabeth Bentley spinning a web of fantasy and exaggeration? The VENONA messages could answer these still emotional, politically charged questions, but it was not until 1995, four years after the Soviet Union no longer existed, that the National Security Agency and the CIA produced the intercepts that gave substance to distrust of the Soviet Union a half century before.

According to Kirby,

Only through VENONA do you get some idea of how thoroughly and how successfully Soviet intelligence infiltrated the United States. VENONA is the tip of the iceberg because we were only able to read a portion of the traffic. We found a couple of hundred names and we still do not know who all of them were.[56]

The code-breaking efforts lasted until 1980. The cover names of one hundred or more Americans who were in contact with Soviet intelligence and have not been identified remain a source of potential embarrassment or evidence of espionage during wartime. Until 1980, when the code-breaking efforts ended, these people faced exposure. Now, despite suggestions to subject the traffic to new computerized searches to match additional cover names with the people whom the *klichkas* protected, such a program is unlikely. The identities of most of these spies and friendly sources, whose motivation in working for the Soviets was either money or ideology, remain hidden.

On February 22, 1946, George Kennan, then chargé d'affaires at the American embassy in Moscow, sent a five-part, 8,000-word dispatch, to become known as "The Long Telegram," to the State Department in Washington. Kennan, the deputy to Ambassador Averell Harriman, was frustrated and disillusioned with the way President Roosevelt had handled the peace negotiations with Stalin at Yalta and even more discouraged by Washington's continuing policies.[57] In the Long Telegram, Kennan laid forth his assessment of Soviet aims and behavior and his suggestions for dealing with them: "We have here a political force committed fanatically to the belief that with US there can be no permanent modus vivendi, that it is desirable and necessary that the internal harmony of our society be disrupted, our traditional way of life destroyed, the international power of our state be broken if Soviet power is to be secure." However, while "Impervious to logic or reason," the Kremlin is "highly sensitive to logic of force . . . it can easily withdraw—and usually does—when resistance is encountered at any point."[58]

Kennan's telegram "hit Washington like a lightning flash that suddenly illuminates a darkened landscape for miles around" and was taken up by Secretary of the Navy James Forrestal, who ordered it sent to the president and the Cabinet, to newspapers publishers and columnists, to senators and congressmen, bankers and businessmen, and made it required reading for thousands of Navy officers. Forrestal became Kennan's patron and was instrumental in having him appointed deputy head of the National War College when Kennan returned from Moscow in May 1946. Such patronage assured Kennan an influential voice in Washington.[59]

After he became the first secretary of defense in September 1946, Forrestal frequently consulted Kennan, mostly through his personal counsel, John T. Conner. Forrestal encouraged Kennan to expand his views on the Soviet Union in a policy paper that would reflect Forrestal's own views on countering Soviet power. After a rewrite, Forrestal pronounced himself "most grateful for your paper. It is extremely well done." Forrestal became the godfather of "containment," the central theme of Kennan's approach to dealing with Moscow. Forrestal sent a copy of Kennan's paper to Secretary of State George Marshall with his endorsement.

Kennan asked Forrestal to allow him to get State Department clearance for the paper and have it published. Forrestal agreed and Kennan had it cleared with the promise it would be published under the pseudonym Mr. X. When "The Sources of Soviet Conduct" appeared in the July 1947 issue of *Foreign Affairs*, outlining a containment strategy to counter the Soviet Union, it created a sensation. Public attention intensified after the *New York Times* Washington Bureau Chief, Arthur Krock, identified Kennan as the author.

Kennan and Forrestal had divergent assessments of the Soviet threat and the level of military strength required for successful containment. Kennan, a political strategist, never was called on to recommend specific force levels and weapons. Kennan "consistently expressed the view that a modest level would suffice, given his conviction that Soviet leaders would not resort to war unless they foresaw an easy victory. Forrestal, in sharp contrast, saw the Red Army as the enforcing instrument of a group animated by a fanatical ideology and bent upon global conquest. He thought the Kremlin was ready to use force whenever the odds favored it even slightly, and in 1947–1948 he believed the balance of power was unfavorable to the West."[60]

On March 12, 1947, President Truman appeared before a joint session of Congress appealing for aid to support Greece in its efforts to defend itself against several thousand communist guerillas. Congress voted $300 million for Greece and $100 million for Turkey. The Truman Doctrine was laid down: "It must be the policy of the United States to support free peoples who are resisting attempted subjugation by armed minorities or by outside pressure."[61]

On May 5, 1947, Secretary George Marshall selected George Kennan to be the State Department's first head of the Policy Planning Staff (known within the government as S/P). Marshall had just returned from a Foreign Ministers meeting in Moscow, which convinced him that the idea of approaching the solution to Europe's problems in collaboration with the Russians was a pipe dream. The secretary asked Kennan to leave the War College as soon as possible. It was a time of high tension. Kennan now had a major platform to influence American foreign policy.[62] From his new position, Kennan took part in planning a new series of American covert operations to undermine the Soviet Union. Although Kennan would later try to distance himself from what he considered the "over-militarization" of the containment strategy, "he was a resolute advocate of secret measures designed to weaken the Kremlin's control inside Russia and Eastern Europe."[63]

In February 1948, the Communist Party took over Czechoslovakia in a bloodless coup.[64] The cold war threatened to burst into open conflict, and Truman was determined not to be overtaken by events. "We are faced with exactly the same situation with which Britain and France were faced from 1938–9 with Hitler," Truman wrote from Key West, Florida, to his daughter, Margaret, on March 3, 1948. "Things look black. A decision will have to be made. I am going to make it."[65]

On March 5, General Lucius Clay, the American military governor in Berlin, sent a message to Lieutenant General Stephen J. Chamberlin, the director of Army Intelligence (G-2), warning about his growing concern over Soviet military intentions. In a top secret message, Clay wrote: "For many months, based on logical analysis, I have felt and held that war was unlikely for at least ten years. Within the last few weeks, I have felt a subtle change in Soviet attitude which I cannot define but which now gives me a feeling that it may come with dramatic suddenness." Clay's message hit Washington "with the force of a blockbuster bomb," recalled Forrestal, while Bradley said that "it lifted me right out of my chair." Forrestal copied the cable verbatim in his diary and saw that it was widely circulated throughout Washington.[66]

On March 6, Truman talked with Secretary of State George Marshall. Afterward Truman's aide, George Elsey, noted, "The Secretary is nervous—world keg of dynamite—HST shouldn't start it."[67] On the same day, Army Secretary Kenneth Royall asked David Lilienthal, chairman of the Atomic Energy Commission, how long it would take to move "eggs" (atomic bombs) to the Mediterranean.[68] Truman's advisers urged a major foreign policy speech and, although Secretary Marshall counseled caution, nothing warlike or belligerent, Truman warned his staff that, if Congress did not act, "the country is sunk." Marshall warned that Truman "might pull the trigger" with his speech. But Truman was determined: "It was better to do that than be caught, as we were in the last war, without having warned the Congress and the people."[69]

On March 17, 1948, the president addressed a joint session of Congress and told the American people that the situation in the world was not due to natural difficulties following a great war but "to the fact that one nation has not only refused to cooperate in the establishment of a just and honorable peace, but—even worse—has actively sought to prevent it. . . . Since the close of hostilities, the Soviet Union and its agents have destroyed the independence and democratic character of a whole series of nations in Eastern and Central Europe." The president warned, "There are times in world history when it is far wiser to act than to hesitate. There is some risk involved in action—there always is. But there is far more risk in failure to act."[70]

Truman urged Congress to support a Western military alliance and asked for passage of the Marshall Plan, enactment of universal military training, and the return of selective service, the draft. The United States was engaging the Soviet Union in the new cold war. The American covert action response to Soviet takeover threats achieved its first victory in the April 1948 Italian elections, when a communist takeover was thwarted. The CIA demonstrated successfully that psychological warfare, backed by strong financial support, could be effective in countering the communist threat.[71]

A more elaborate American covert action response to Soviet subversion grew out of National Security Council study NSC 20/4, the first formal statement of national security strategy, prepared in August 1948, which outlined the objectives of American policy toward the Soviet Union. Primarily, it adopted the views defined by George Kennan and his State Department Policy Planning Staff. NSC 20/4 stressed that Eurasia must not fall into the hands of hostile powers and accepted Kennan's argument that the Soviet Union sought political rather than military aggrandizement. The document's focus was on the steps necessary to eliminate the Soviet threat. NSC 20/4 committed the United States to a struggle against the Soviet Union "using all methods short of war" to reduce "the power and influence of the USSR to limits which no longer constitute a threat to the peace, national independence and stability of the world family of nations." The secret policy statement called for compelling "a basic change in power in Russia, to conform with the purposes and principles set forth in the UN charter." Its goals included: aiming for the independence of Eastern Europe, reviving nationalist sentiments among the peoples of the USSR, and the Kremlin abandoning efforts to subdue the non-Soviet world. It called for developing "situations" that would "compel" the Soviet leadership to modify its national security policy. The United States was prepared to sustain a covert action program to achieve the goals laid forth in NSC 20/4. The Soviet Union had yet to test its first nuclear weapon.[72]

On August 14, 1948, Frank G. Wisner was confirmed by the NSC to head the Office of Policy Coordination, which lasted for four years. In 1951 it was taken over by the CIA, still led by Wisner, who became the CIA's deputy director in charge of clandestine operations. Wisner, a charming Southerner who served in the OSS in Bucharest at the end of World War II, hoped to continue his career gathering intelligence on the Soviet Union. When he returned to Washington, he found himself a man ahead of his time. President Truman had disbanded the OSS, and the intelligence services were in disarray and feuding. Wisner resigned and moved to New York to pursue a lucrative law career.

Over lunch early in 1947 at the Down Town Association with Allen Dulles, who had also returned to his law firm, the two commiserated about the fate of the OSS and the current lack of an effective clandestine American intelligence organization. Dulles told Wisner that if he really was concerned, he should return to Washington and take a position in the government where he could work to restore the clandestine services to their rightful role. Wisner followed Dulles' advice and joined the State Department as a deputy assistant secretary in the Office of Occupied Territories. Dulles had recommended Wisner to head the Office of Policy Coordination when Dulles turned the job down for himself.[73]

When he started at the State Department, Wisner was very much subordinate to Kennan. By October 1947, Wisner had proposed seventeen programs of clandestine political warfare in four categories:

Psychological Warfare: "Direct mail, poison pen, rumors, etc."

Political War: "Support of resistance [underground], support of DPs [displaced persons] and refugees, support of anticommunists in free countries, encouragement of defection."

Economic Warfare (thus justifying access to the Exchange Stabilization Fund): "Commodity operations (clandestine preclusive buying, market manipulation and black market operations)" and "fiscal operations (currency speculation, counterfeiting, etc.)."

Preventive Direct Action: "Support of guerilla, sabotage, counter-sabotage and demolition, evacuation and stay behinds."[74]

All attempts to roll back the Iron Curtain through covert operations in Albania, Latvia, and Ukraine ended in failure. The programs were betrayed by Kim Philby, MI-6 representative in Washington, whose early warnings by letter to Burgess, then in London, permitted the Soviets to intercept and eliminate teams of Albanian nationals living in exile in the West who had landed on the Adriatic coast or parachuted into the countryside.[75] In an effort to maintain secrecy, the infiltration teams used primitive communications, which were readily broken into by Soviet signals intelligence. The Soviets also infiltrated émigré organizations and learned of Western plans, despite elaborate security precautions.[76]

At the time of the Berlin Crisis in 1948, Harry Rositzke, one of the founding fathers of the CIA, recalled, "It was an axiom in Washington that Stalin was plotting war." The CIA developed a program for "Early Warning" with radio equipped agents dropped by air to determine on the ground if a Soviet attack was imminent. The agents' task was to observe key Soviet military air fields and military bases for extraordinary activity indicating mobilization.[77] The program was cumbersome, costly, and the results meager, but there were no better alternatives. American intelligence recruited agents mostly from the émigré community, indoctrinated each with a "legend" or life cover story, trained them, and supplied them with false papers. There was no underground support system for the agents inside the Soviet Union, and most were captured or killed within a few weeks. Despite the fear of war, no early warnings of Soviet troop movements for an offensive into Western Europe or a strategic air attack were ever reported. Air dispatch of radio equipped agents virtually ceased in 1954.

★ ★ ★

Those who knew what was in VENONA—Clarke, Bradley, Forrestal, and the FBI—agreed to keep it secret, fearing they would find themselves in the middle of a political war between Democrats and Republicans over communists in government. They believed that releasing VENONA would violate national security procedures and that the shocking evidence would fuel endless political recriminations.

Carter Clarke carefully built support for the VENONA program by having Kirby brief a small, select group that included House Republican leader Les Arens and *Washington Post* publisher Philip Graham. When the names of Harry Dexter White and Alger Hiss were discovered in the VENONA messages, Clarke sent Kirby to brief Graham at his home in Georgetown. Clarke had known Graham during World War II when Graham was assigned to the Special Branch of the U.S. Army Signal Corps, which handled top secret, decoded Japanese and German messages. Clarke maintained contact with Graham after he returned to Washington and took over the *Post* with his wife, Katharine.[78] Kirby recalls that Graham was

Red Army General Georgi Zhukov commanded the brilliant counteroffensive at the battle of Khalkin Gol, on the border between Outer Mongolia and Manchuria, 1939.

Clyde Tolson and J. Edgar Hoover at celebration for 20 years of service to the FBI, July 26, 1937. *NARA collection*

Albert Einstein in is office at Princeton when he did wartime work for the U.S. Navy.
U.S. Navy

Brigadier General Carter Clarke,
deputy head of military
intelligence (G-2), created the
program to decode intercepted
Soviet message traffic on
February 1, 1943, which in 1962
became known by the code
name VENONA.
National Security Agency.

Female codebreakers at Arlington Hall working on the Japanese code during World War II. Meredith Gardner, second row far left, was the linguist who played a key role in translating the first decrypted Russian intelligence traffic. Gardner worked closely with FBI Special Agent Robert Lamphere. *National Security Agency.*

The Big Three at the Teheran Conference in November 1943, Left to Right Stalin, Roosevelt and Churchill. *FDR Library*

Stalin and FDR at Teheran in 1943. *FDR Library*

Left to right FDR, Secretary of State Cordell Hull and Presidential Advisor James Byrnes in 1943. *FDR Library*

Left to Right Charles (Chip) Bohlen, Roosevelt's interpreter and adviser, FDR,
Winston Churchill and Stalin dine at the Yalta. Conference, February 1945.
FDR Library

Soviet Ambassador to
Washington, Maxim Litvinov
served from 1941–1943, one of
the few who spoke up to Stalin
and considered defecting to the
West, but in the end returned
home with wife Ivy. *Thomas
McAvoy/TimePix*

Roosevelt and Stalin at Yalta. *FDR Library*

Captain Oliver Kirby awarded a commendation for his service on the Target Intelligence Committee (TICOM) service in 1944-45 by Colonel Lincoln Hayes, commander of the U.S. Army Security Agency in 1945. *National Security Agency*

Ivy Litvinov, wife of Maksim Litvinov, in early 1930s. *Authors' Collection*

Ivy Litvinov in London, 1972. *Authors' Collection*

Oliver Kirby in 1963. Kirby headed the Russian program to decrypt Soviet intelligence traffic from November 1949 –1952. *National Security Agency*

Elizabeth Bentley before the House Committee on Un-American Activities, 1948. *Stock Montage*

Lauchlin Currie appearing before the House Committee on Un-American Activities, 1948. *Stock Montage*

Alger Hiss worked in the Far East Affairs of the State Department while secretly passing on valuable top secret documents to Whittaker Chambers, a courier for the Communist underground. *National Archives*

FBI Special Agent John J. Walsh, in 1943 photo, located Alger Hiss' Woodstock typewriter used to copy classified documents. *Collection of John Walsh*

As an FBI counterintelligence specialist and investigator, Robert Lamphere, pictured here in his later years, was a pivotal figure in most of the major spy cases of the Cold War era. *Authors' Collection*

Yuri Andropov, former head of the
KGB from 1967 until May 1982.
Andropov was Secretary General of the
Communist Party of the Soviet Union
from November, 1982 to February 9,
1984, when he died of kidney failure.
Andropov suceeded Leonid Brezhnev
who died on November 19, 1982.
KGB archives

Vladimir Kryuchkov, head of the
First Chief Directorate, KGB, 1974-
88, was the first foreign intelligence
chief to become Chairman of the
KGB from 1988-91, when he was
ousted after the abortive coup
against Mikhail Gorbachev.
KGB archives

Major General Mikhail Milshtein in Colonel's uniform during World War II. He was promoted to Major General after traveling to the United States, Canada and Mexico in 1944 on an inspection trip and then meeting with Hiss at the Yalta Conference in February 1945.

Victor Louis reading Izvestia at his home in Peredelkino, outside Moscow. *Collection of Jennifer Louis.*

Retired KGB General Vyacheslav Kevorkov worked closely with Victor Louis and played a leading role in developing Ostpolitik with Willy Brandt .

Katherine Harrison aka Kitty Harris, ADA, AIDA, GYPSY and NORMA in VENONA shown in a photograph from her KGB file. Kitty Harris was Donald Maclean's courier and lover, Earl Browder's common law wife and later ran the drug store safe house in Santa Fe New Mexico for atomic espionage during World War II. *KGB archives*

Ramon del Rio Mercader aka Frank Jacson, in 1940 murdered Leon Trotsky in a villa in Coyoacan outside Mexico City, loaned to Trotsky by painter Diego Rivera. *KGB archives*

Iosif (Joseph) Romvoldovich Grigulevich code named ARTHUR, ARTUR and MAKS in VENONA. He failed to assassinate Trotsky and Tito but played a key role in establishing the Soviet underground in Latin America during World War II and then served under cover as a Costa Rican diplomat in Rome before returning to Moscow after Stalin's death in 1953. *KGB archives*

Harry Dexter White, Assistant Secretary of the Treasury and the first American Director of the International Monetary Fund, was a long-time Soviet asset, VENONA code name RICHARD. *International Monetary Fund*

Elizabeth Zarubina in 1940 photo from her personal file. *KGB archives*

Vasili Zarubin, Soviet rezident,
station chief for north and South
America, 1941-1944.
KGB archives

Gregory Kheifitz, Soviet consul
general in San Francisco who met
Robert Oppenheimer and organized
atomic espionage on the west coast.
Picture shows Kheifitz in 1940
personal file photo. *KGB archives*

deeply concerned with the VENONA revelations of high level Soviet penetration in the government. In 1948 the *Post* did not endorse a candidate for the presidency, but in the summer of 1951, the paper endorsed Eisenhower over Robert Taft for the Republican nomination. Graham, to his wife's chagrin, campaigned for Eisenhower against Democrat Adlai Stevenson.[79] In her revealing memoir, Katharine Graham wrote of the deep divisions at the *Post* created by the Hiss case and the attacks on the paper by Senator McCarthy:

> Phil had to tread a fine line in this very difficult time. He had been an ardent liberal, but in this period when he was fighting for the life of the paper he was clearly becoming more conservative and more anticommunist—mostly no doubt in response to events in the real world, but also to some extent in response to the constant attacks on the paper and on him personally.[80]

Kirby recalled Graham's deep unease and concern with the news of White and Hiss being named in VENONA. Graham knew that the Democrats were in trouble. VENONA was a time bomb that could explode and destroy the party of the New Deal in the 1952 election. Graham was disappointed with Truman for his inability to curb Senator McCarthy's excesses and halt the Red Panic. He turned to Eisenhower.

Graham, like the senior personalities in government briefed on the program, treated VENONA as a national security matter beyond his control. He never let it be publicly known that he knew about VENONA.

Cases of the Century

A lasting effect of Soviet espionage on American politics was to rend the country into two camps, those who listened to testimonies of former communists and believed the evidence that some of America's institutional leaders were working for the Soviet Union, and those who constructed barriers to believing the unwelcome truth of espionage in Washington. The split went deepest in the two criminal cases that left their names most firmly attached to the cold war, the trials of Alger Hiss for perjury and of Julius and Ethel Rosenberg for atomic espionage.

The Hitler-Stalin Pact of August 1939 set off alarm bells for Whittaker Chambers, an American agent for the secret communist underground who had broken with the Communist Party. Chambers felt compelled to warn the American government of the Soviet espionage threat. As part of their new alliance, the Soviets could be feeding American government secrets to the Germans. Chambers first told his story to journalist Isaac Don Levine, who tried to arrange an appointment with President Roosevelt. Levine introduced Chambers only as "Mr. X, a former courier for Soviet intelligence." The President's appointments secretary avoided a direct meeting and recommended he see Roosevelt's trusted adviser on intelligence, Assistant Secretary of State Adolf A. Berle.

Before Levine took him to meet Berle, he tested Chambers' credibility. He introduced Chambers to Walter Krivitsky, a defector who fled the Moscow purges. Chambers and Krivitsky traded stories and named their contacts in the Soviet spy network, convincing Levine that they were both telling the truth. Krivitsky later died of a bullet to his head in a Washington hotel room. The police called it a suicide; his close friends called it an NKVD murder.

The meeting with Berle was on September 2, 1939, the day after the German invasion of Poland. After dinner the three men sat on the grand lawn of Woodley Oaks, the palatial home of Secretary of War Henry Stimson, which Berle was renting. Chambers was tense, but several scotch and sodas stiffened his resolve to describe the range of espionage of the communist underground and to provide a list of names that Berle jotted down under the heading "Underground Espionage

Agent." Among those Chambers named were Alger Hiss, a rising star in the State Department, and his younger brother, Donald Hiss, a legal advisor in the State Department. Berle was agitated and told Chambers, "We may be in this war in forty-eight hours, and we cannot go into it without clean services." Chambers left after midnight and Berle, in great excitement, was on the telephone even before Chambers and Levine departed. Chambers "supposed that he was calling the White House."[1]

Nothing happened. Months went by until Chambers met with Levine, who told him Berle had taken his information to the president at once. "The President had laughed," Chambers recounted, "when Berle was insistent he had been told in words which it is necessary to paraphrase, to 'go jump in the lake.' " At first Chambers thought the government was investigating his story and Berle's response had been put out to conceal the government's real purpose, to watch and check. "I tried to believe that was the fact, but I knew that it could not be, for if the government were checking, it could not fail also to check with me."[2]

After a wait in which no one contacted Chambers, Levine prevailed on his friend, influential columnist and staccato-voiced newscaster Walter Winchell, to warn President Roosevelt. Winchell was courted by FDR soon after his inauguration in March 1933 with an invitation to the White House for a ten-minute private meeting. FDR told the gossip columnist to personally tell him anything Winchell thought the president should know. "That's an order!" Roosevelt snapped.[3]

In 1939 Winchell told FDR about Alger Hiss' spying for Moscow. Winchell said Chambers had confessed to Levine that he had been a Soviet agent together with Alger Hiss. "Leaning closer and pointing a finger in my face, he [Roosevelt] angrily said, 'I don't want to hear another thing about it! It isn't true,' " recalled Winchell. For months afterward, the President did not invite him to the White House.[4]

It was not until 1941, while he was a writer at *Time* magazine, that the FBI approached Chambers. After checking by phone with Berle for approval, Chambers told the special agents his story. From time to time until 1945, the FBI checked with Chambers on names and identities of communist agents, some of which he recognized. The next time Chambers heard from the government was when the House Un-American Activities Committee (HUAC) sent investigators to speak with him in the spring of 1948 and when it issued a subpoena for him to appear before the committee on August 3, 1948. That was his first public statement accusing Hiss of being a communist and working for the Soviets. Chambers testified, "I served in the Communist underground, chiefly in Washington, DC. . . ."[5] He then identified Hiss, his brother Donald, and six other members of an apparatus whose orders were to infiltrate the government and carry out espionage tasks for the U.S. Communist Party. Chambers also named Harry Dexter White, who he said was a valuable communist underground source of policy information for the

Soviet Union. Chambers' testimony before the committee followed that of Elizabeth Bentley.

Bentley had taken no documents with her when she defected from communist underground control. Therefore she presented no material evidence implicating White, and acknowledged that she had never met him personally. When Whittaker Chambers appeared before the committee, he corroborated Bentley's charges, adding that he had met with White many times and knew him well enough to ask him to break from "the communist movement."[6]

Two former communist underground couriers had now publicly accused White; the press demanded that he respond to their questions. "This is the most fantastic thing I have ever heard of . . . I am shocked. I never dreamed my name would be dragged into this," said White, who wired the committee asking for an opportunity to appear and refute the charges.[7] On Friday, August 13, 1948, White appeared before the House committee and was permitted to read a statement in which he offered to answer any questions that any member of the committee wished to ask. White testified:

I should like to state at the start that I am not now and never have been a Communist, nor even close to becoming one; that I cannot recollect ever knowing either a Miss Bentley or a Mr. Whittaker Chambers, nor judging from the pictures I have seen in the press, have I ever met them.

The Press reported that the witnesses claim I helped to obtain key posts for persons I knew were engaged in espionage work to help them in that work. That allegation is unqualifiedly false. There is and can be no basis of fact whatsoever for such a charge.

The principles in which I believe, and for which I live, make it impossible for me ever to do a disloyal act or anything against the interest of our country, and I have jotted down what my belief is for the Committee's information.

My creed is the American creed. I believe in freedom of religion, freedom of speech, freedom of thought, freedom of the press, freedom of criticism and freedom of movement. I believe in the goal of equality of opportunity, and the right of each individual to an opportunity to develop his or her capacity to the fullest.

I believe in the right and duty of every citizen to work for, to expect and to obtain an increasing measure of political, economic and emotional security for all. I am opposed to discrimination in any form, whether on grounds of race, color, religions, political belief or economic status. I believe in the freedom of choice of one's representatives in Government, untrammeled by machine guns, secret police or a police state. I am opposed to arbitrary and unwarranted use of power or authority from whatever source or against any individual or group.

I believe in government of law, not of men, where law is above any man and not any man above law.

I consider these principles sacred. I regard them as the basic fabric of our American way of life, and I believe them as living realities and not as mere words on paper. That is my creed. Those are the principles I have worked for. Together those are the principles that I have been prepared in the past to fight for, and am prepared to defend at any time with my life if need be.[8]

White's statement drew applause from the audience in the hearing room, and he faced the committee with confidence. When pressed about his colleagues in the Division of Monetary Research in the Treasury whom Miss Bentley named, and who would later be identified in VENONA as Communist Party members, agents, or members of the communist underground, White acknowledged that they worked for him. Lauchlin Currie, George Silverman, and Nathan Silvermaster were old and good friends. He said he was convinced that Silvermaster was not a communist and said he intervened on Silvermaster's behalf against removal from the Board of Economic Warfare in 1942 because, "I believe he is innocent." Again the audience applauded.[9]

The VENONA intercepts identified Silvermaster as a Communist Party member of long standing. As mentioned in earlier chapters, he had headed an active and productive spy ring and received a Soviet medal, the order of the Red Banner, which he called "the greatest accomplishment of my life."[10]

White readily agreed with the committee against placing communists in positions of trust in the government. He emphasized, "I can well understand and thoroughly sympathize with the view that if there is the slightest question of a man's being a communist, he ought not to be in a position—ought not to hold a position where there was any confidential information being passed; that even though there was not evidence or proof, a mere suspicion was enough."[11]

Rather than ask open ended questions relating to communist sympathies, Congressman Richard Nixon pressed White on whether or not he knew Chambers. Nixon asked whether there had been any circumstances in which White could have met Chambers when he was in the communist underground using the name Carl. Nixon then followed up by asking: "In other words, the point I want to clear up is that you are stating for the record that at no time did this man by the name Carl discuss with you the fact that he was leaving the Communist Party, and discuss also the matter of your, shall we say ceasing to be a friend of the Communist Party—shall we put it that way?"

White replied: "The first, certainly not to my recollection. The second, I certainly would have remembered, and the answer is 'No.' "[12]

Nixon never had an opportunity to pursue the question of whether White had known Chambers in the way he elicited from Alger Hiss that he did, in fact, know

Chambers. White emerged from the hearing to a shower of praise by friends and associates. Later that afternoon, White returned home to New York; he saw his doctor on August 14 and then left by train for his summer home at Blueberry Hill, Fitzwilliam, New Hampshire. During the train ride, White suffered chest pains. When he arrived in New Hampshire, his local doctor diagnosed a recurrence of a heart attack. White's condition continued to worsen; on August 16, he died of a coronary attack.

White's death appeared to end the case against him, and, initially, it created a strong backlash against the House Un-American Activities Committee. A *New York Times* editorial, "Due Process for Harry White," said:

> Mr. White's death was due to a heart condition brought about by years of arduous government service and aggravated by the ordeal through which he had to pass during the Committee hearings. . . . The Committee denied him the due protection of laws . . . permitted witnesses to make unsubstantiated statements . . . ignoring the Bill of Rights. This is the un-American way. It places in jeopardy a fundamental concept of American life.[13]

Chambers had not come to the committee to ask to make a statement. It was only after Elizabeth Bentley appeared on July 31, and publicly named a list of prominent Washington bureaucrats for whom she had acted as liaison with her Soviet case officer in New York, that the committee's chief investigator remembered corroborative material in interviews with Chambers a few months earlier.

Chambers told the committee that the party classified Hiss in a separate group, "young stars with a bright future," who would be increasingly valuable to the party and whose communist affiliation had to be protected by the utmost secrecy. Chambers served as courier for the Washington group of federal bureaucrats, who gave him copies of classified and secret documents taken illegally from the offices where they worked. He then delivered the stolen materials to J. Peters, head of the underground section of the party, in New York.

Chambers asserted that he and Hiss had first begun their rendezvous in 1934 when Hiss worked for the Nye Munitions Investigating Committee, where he had access to State Department secret documents. Hiss took the classified papers out overnight so that Chambers could photocopy them; then Hiss returned them, Chambers testified. "I knew him as a dedicated and disciplined communist. I collected party dues from him over two or three years," Chambers stated. Later Hiss worked in the Department of Justice and in 1936 joined the Department of State. He was known as "a young man on the way up." Chambers said Hiss was never an open member of the Communist Party. "He came in as an underground communist," bringing a romantic ideology about sharing with comrades, Chambers testified. He described the party discipline he shared with Hiss, which precluded church going, drinking alcohol, and having Marxist literature in his home. Chambers said Alger and Priscilla Hiss' only hobby was bird watching.[14]

Chambers told the committee he had broken with the party in 1938 and tried to persuade Hiss to leave the underground with him. Hiss refused and remained a believer in the party line. "We were close friends, but we were caught in a tragedy of history," Chambers said ruefully. They did not meet again in the ten years between their parting and the testimony.[15]

The Bureau had questioned Hiss in the late 1930s to ask if he had ever been a member of the Washington Committee for Democratic Action, which he denied. The FBI had then questioned Hiss in 1946, at which time Chambers was not mentioned, and again in May 1947, during which he denied knowing Chambers.[16]

Chambers' accusation of Hiss made headlines across the country. Americans who refused to believe that Hiss could be a communist were convinced that Chambers had set out to destroy Hiss for personal reasons. American liberals had already condemned the committee for its investigation of Hollywood in 1947 that forced those subpoenaed to name people they believed to be communists or face contempt charges and loss of their jobs. When Bentley and Chambers testified, the names of the committee members were an anathema to liberals. Truman had no friends on the committee. The chairman was James Parnell Thomas, a Republican from New Jersey, later convicted and jailed for payroll kickbacks. Next in seniority was Republican Karl Mundt of South Dakota, whose name became synonymous with the hunt for communists in government. The reputation of the committee had suffered from its earlier head, Martin Dies, known for his anti-Semitism and rabid anticommunism. Still included in the roster was Democrat John Rankin of Mississippi, who had hurt the committee's image by assailing Jews and Negroes.

The member of the committee upon whose name the events of August 1948 would forever hang like an albatross was Richard Nixon, Republican congressman from California. The brand of being an extremist remained, even though the *New York Times* reported that he "is at pains to keep the Committee on a legally sound path and has considerable reputation for fairness to witnesses."[17]

When the morning newspapers appeared on August 4, Hiss countered with a telegram to the committee in Washington from his home in New York, demanding the right to testify in denial of Chambers' accusations. He appeared before the committee the next day. Hiss testified first in executive session and later in open hearings; initially, he denied knowing a man named Chambers, or Carl, his undercover name, and said he didn't recognize Chambers' pictures either from the 1934–1938 period or from 1948. Hiss said he might have met socially in a group with the other members of the cell of federal bureaucrats organized by Harold Ware, son of communist leader "Mother" Bloor, to which Chambers said Hiss belonged—Lee Pressman, Nathan Witt, John Abt, Charles Kramer, and Victor Perlo—but he did not know them personally.

Hiss denied all of Chambers' allegations. "Mr. Hiss is lying," Chambers said.[18]

Later Nixon pressed Hiss to affirm or deny that Chambers had stayed overnight in his house a number of times, and whether or not he had sublet to Chambers and his family the apartment out of which he was moving for which there was still two months rent paid. Hiss asked how a self-confessed former communist had the same credibility as he, head of the Carnegie Endowment for International Peace, formerly a high ranking diplomat and one of the founders of the United Nations. Perhaps, he suggested, his accuser was a deranged man who had studied the details of his life and was trying to destroy him. The accuser and accused had not yet faced each other.

When Nixon followed his questions with requests for more details, Hiss became testy. He snapped that "whether it strengthens my case or not, I would prefer not to mention any names [of men he had worked for] unless you insist." Nixon began to think that Hiss was evasive, and since Hiss was a lawyer, he could only be giving unresponsive answers by design. Hiss conditioned each answer with "As far as I know" or "to the best of my recollection."[19]

Nevertheless, Hiss dominated the hearing, and most of the audience and press believed him. The committee had put Hiss on the stand in public view without facts as a basis for cross-examining him; they had put Chambers on view as a witness without establishing the credibility of his amazing story. The members of the press who had been hostile to the committee before now gloated at the committee's embarrassment. Nixon later tracked down the rumor of Chambers' drunkenness and mental instability, and found that a representative of a pro-Hiss left wing publication had promoted the negative image.

The committee and the nation had to answer the question of who was lying. Either Chambers or Hiss was not telling the truth. By the end of the first open hearing, Mundt had uttered the word "perjury" as a possibility that would face one or the other of the two witnesses.

Chambers and Hiss met in a New York hotel room to confront each other before members of the committee. Hiss examined Chambers' teeth and then recalled that he knew him in the 1930s by the name George Crosley (which Chambers used as his cover name). Hiss said Crosley was a journalist with notably bad teeth who came to interview him and he had allowed Crosley to use the apartment from which he was moving. He had also lent him a car, which he later gave or sold to a local dealer. Chambers said the dealer, who was a communist, took the car with the promise to give it to a "poor" communist in another city. The committee went to lengths to trace the car without success.[20]

Hiss had now changed the story he had first given, that he absolutely did not know Chambers; however, he denied all of his accuser's allegations. Hiss refused to take a lie detector test. The committee remained puzzled; the public and press remained torn between admirers and haters of the committee. Nixon consulted his friend William P. Rogers, who was then a Senate committee counsel; Rogers examined the sworn testimony of both witnesses and told Nixon that, on the basis of what he had seen, one of them was lying and that Nixon had the information to establish which one was credible.[21]

Before Hiss identified Chambers as George Crosley, the White House attacked the record of the committee's tactics. On the day Hiss testified for the first time, when most observers believed him over Chambers, a reporter asked Truman at a press conference, "Mr. President, do you think the Capitol Hill spy hearings are a good thing or do you think they are a red herring to divert attention from the anti-inflation program of your administration?"[22] The president answered that he did regard the spy hearings as red herrings, attacking the Eightieth Congress more specifically than he did in his usual tirade in which he called it the "worst" or "second worst" in history. Asked if the American people were not entitled to the information coming out of the hearings, the president spoke the memorable words again: "You can quote me . . . these investigations are simply a red herring. . . ." and later said the herring had a bad smell. Truman had already placed a freeze on release of information from investigations into the loyalty of federal employees. Mundt taunted Truman: "If it is all a red herring, what is there in the confidential files about former government employees that you refuse to let us see? Are you sure there isn't another kind of herring in the files?" New York Governor Thomas E. Dewey, running for president against Truman, spoke up to ask if exposure of communism in the government was a red herring. Truman gloried in the uproar and used it to help win the presidency.[23]

Truman had made the two words a new American idiom. A half century later, the echo of "red herring" lingers and raises the question, now that we know Truman had made a sacred secret of VENONA, if the expression was one kind of smelly fish covering up another.

Chambers had not offered any proof of his charges. The case might have ended there if Hiss had not then challenged Chambers to make the same accusations in a public forum in which he could be sued for libel. Chambers agreed to appear on *Meet the Press*, the popular radio talk show, full knowing that he was forcing Hiss to sue or accept his allegations.

The *Washington Post* correspondent posed the question to Chambers: "Your remarks [before the committee] were privileged . . . you were protected from lawsuits. Hiss has now challenged you to make the same charge publicly. He says if you do he will test your veracity by filing a suit for slander or libel. Are you willing to say now that Alger Hiss is or ever was a communist?" Chambers responded: "Alger Hiss was a communist and may be now."[24]

Chambers still believed Hiss would be afraid to sue him for libel, but exactly a month after the broadcast, Hiss sued for damages of $50,000. The Associated Press reported Chambers' response: "I welcome Alger Hiss' daring suit. . . . But I do not believe that, ultimately, Alger Hiss or anybody else can use the means of justice to defeat the ends of justice."[25] Hiss raised the charges to $75,000.

Chambers appeared for a pretrial hearing at the U.S. District Court in Baltimore. Hiss' lawyer dared Chambers to present documentary evidence to support his fantastic story. Chambers pulled a sheaf of sixty-five sheets of paper from the inside pocket of his jacket and thrust them on the table before him. "Alger Hiss gave me these when we worked together in the communist conspiracy," Chambers said. These were typewritten copies of forty-four documents taken from State Department files between January 6 and March 29, 1938, with addenda in longhand. Chambers had saved the papers to be a "life preserver" against threats from the party after he broke with the communist underground.[26]

Chambers said he had forgotten he had the documents and had not wanted to "do more injury than necessary" to an old friend who was one of the country's brilliant young men. He had only a week earlier found the papers, and he had changed his mind about using them because of the abuse heaped on him by the pro-Hiss faction, which was spreading rumors of his being a drunkard, insane, and a homosexual. He was also angry with Hiss' lawyers for their "rough handling" of Mrs. Chambers. He added to his testimony: "An ex-Communist is one of the loneliest of creatures. . . . in constant apprehension . . . afraid to trust anyone."[27]

Lawyers for both antagonists were startled when they read the evidence. The Department of Justice rushed to Baltimore and impounded the papers. The hearings were secret, but a leak to the *Washington Post* resulted in an article saying, "Some very startling information on who's a liar is reported to have been uncovered." A counterleak, believed to have come from the Department of Justice, brought about a United Press dispatch saying the perjury aspect of the Hiss-Chambers case would soon dissolve for lack of evidence: "there would be little use in going to a grand jury with the information obtained so far."[28]

Bert Andrews was the Washington bureau chief of the *New York Herald Tribune*; the *Tribune* was a leading independent Republican newspaper that ranked in public respect with the *New York Times* and the *Washington Post*. Andrews told his story in a book completed by his son after Andrews' death. He revealed how he began covering the story of the Hiss case without preconceived notions, but became enmeshed in its history when he pursued it further.[29]

Andrews knew from the conflicting reports that there had to be more to the story. The veteran newsman and his assistant began a round of calls to the lawyers on both sides, to the judge in Baltimore, and to the Justice Department, where they were told that the government could not comment because ". . . this is too hot."[30]

On December 1, four months after Chambers made his first accusation against Hiss, Andrews called Richard Nixon and urged him to go to see Chambers at his farm outside Baltimore. "I think Chambers produced something important at the Baltimore hearing," he later recalled telling Nixon. The congressman was about to leave for a long-delayed vacation with his wife, but he and the committee investigator, Bob Stripling, drove to the farm. Chambers was reticent to speak; he was afraid he would be held in contempt of court for breaking secrecy. However, when Nixon asked him if he had dropped a "bombshell" at the Baltimore hearing, he affirmed that he had, and that he still had more information. That same night Andrews came to Nixon's office and heard about the lack of results visiting Chambers. "You were too nice to Chambers," Andrews told Nixon. The newspaperman wanted to know why Nixon had not asked him for whatever else he had to prove his accusations. Had Nixon slapped a subpoena on Chambers? Nixon said later he hadn't thought about a subpoena until then. Andrews kept at Nixon, "Before you leave town get hold of Bob Stripling. Tell him to serve a blanket subpoena on Chambers to produce *anything* and *everything* he still has in his possession." Chambers could not be held in contempt for giving documents that had not been subpoenaed by the Baltimore court hearing the libel case.[31]

Stripling summoned Chambers to his office the day Nixon left on vacation and served him the subpoena. Chambers arranged to travel to Baltimore with two committee investigators, where he picked up his parked car and the three proceeded to his farm. Chambers looked for something he had hidden in his pumpkin patch. After putting on the yard lights, he found a pumpkin in which the top had been cut out and replaced, as if it were being prepared for Halloween. In it were three small aluminum cylinders wrapped in adhesive tape and two more rolls wrapped in oil paper. Chambers verified that he had given all he had.[32]

The investigators delivered the rolls of film, soon to be known as "The Pumpkin Papers," to Stripling's office on the morning of December 3, 1948. When they unrolled a section in a dark room, the first image revealed was: "Department of State Strictly Confidential." The investigators rushed to enlarge and print the film. Mundt issued a statement from his home in South Dakota: "There is now in the possession of the Committee, under twenty four hour guard, microfilmed copies of documents . . . removed from the State Department and turned over to Chambers for . . . transmittal to Russian communist agents."[33]

The astounding documents revealed a communist network in the State Department more significant than anything brought before the committee in its ten-year history.

Andrews cabled Nixon aboard ship, asking if the committee was about to reopen its investigation. In a second cable he told Nixon:

Documents incredibly hot, link to Hiss seems certain . . . results should restore faith in need for committee if not some members. . . . My liberal friends don't love me no more. Nor you. But facts are facts and these are dynamite. Hiss' writing identified on three documents. Not proof . . . Stripling says can prove who gave them to Chambers. . . . (signed) Vacation-Spoiler Andrews.[34]

Nixon returned from the Caribbean by Coast Guard plane, whale boat, rescue plane, crash boat, and a Navy plane sent by Secretary of Defense James Forrestal. By the time he arrived in Washington on December 5, the Justice Department, the grand jury in New York, and the committee were in a three-way free-for-all to discredit each other by leaks to the press. The Justice Department noted the committee's anti-Semitic performances under Martin Dies and its smearing of witnesses against whom it could not prove a case. The committee in turn pointed to Justice's disdain for potential threats to national security posed by internal communism. The committee also attacked the State Department for its seeming lack of interest in the case. Contained in the fight was a suggestion that Chambers might be the defendant on trial since he was the one illegally in possession of the papers. Nixon warned the Justice Department that indicting Chambers for perjury, or for crimes to which he had already confessed, would make him a felon and therefore useless in testifying against the real culprits. At this point, Chambers attempted to commit suicide but failed.

After the New York grand jury and the committee questioned a string of witnesses, and Hiss after each testimony, Hiss continued to deny all of Chambers' accusations. Nixon made a statement: "For the first time we have something more than one man's word against another's. . . . It will have the effect of puncturing the myth of the 'red herring.' "[35]

The grand jury lacked physical evidence to back up Chambers' story or to prove the allegation that in 1938 Mrs. Hiss had typed the documents he provided. The FBI identified the typing to be on a 1928 Woodstock typewriter, the same kind that the Hisses had owned in 1938. The FBI showed two letters typed by Mrs. Hiss on the Woodstock, which matched the typing on Chambers' documents. Hiss then attacked: "Until the day I die I shall wonder how Whittaker Chambers got into my house to use my typewriter."[36]

With the grand jury's term about to run out on December 15, 1948, it came to a decision and indicted Hiss on two counts of perjury: denying that he gave documents to Chambers and stating that he did not see Chambers after January 1, 1937.

Hiss' first trial began on May 31, 1949, and ended on July 8 when the jury was dismissed after it voted eight to four to convict. One jury member had boasted before the trial began that he would never send Alger Hiss to jail. A major problem for the jury was that Chambers had repeatedly lied to the House Committee, attempting to protect Hiss from charges of espionage, which did not help to make him credible. The second trial, from November 17, 1949, to January 21, 1950, convicted Hiss of two counts of perjury.[37]

No court had to decide what crimes of espionage Hiss had committed because the statute of limitations had already elapsed on the period in the 1930s when he was in touch with Chambers. No one accusing Hiss knew about his services to the Soviet Union at Yalta in 1945.

The vexing aftermath of the Hiss case was the backlash among liberals against other liberals who believed that Hiss was guilty. Diana Trilling, an avowed liberal and opinion leader among intellectuals, wrote that seeing the validity of Hiss' conviction put her among political bedfellows whom she considered most opposite to her own world views: the House Committee, the right wing of the Republican Party, and the Hearst newspapers. Historian Arthur Schlesinger, Jr., described the atmosphere in academia, where he encountered "ugly and vicious stories invented and repeated by respectable lawyers and college professors. . . ." He added, "The anti-Chambers whispering campaign was one of the most repellent of modern history."[38]

When Whittaker Chambers named Hiss as a communist spy in testimony before the House Committee, he provided the brand name of the typewriter on which Mrs. Hiss copied the documents. In January of 2000, FBI veteran John Walsh gave a firsthand account of tracing the Woodstock typewriter. He brought a new openness to the case, which had long been obfuscated by partisan writers attempting to make it appear that Hiss was framed. Walsh, an FBI agent who testified in the Hiss trial, described the Hiss case in plain language, clearing the obscurities created to vilify Chambers and discredit the FBI.

Walsh was in charge of verifying that the secret documents Chambers said Hiss provided to the Soviets were typed on Hiss' old Woodstock typewriter; in other cases, the FBI had been able to check accusations against physical evidence and had been able to clear the accused. Hiss said he had sold the typewriter in question to a Georgetown secondhand shop, but it was no longer traceable through the dealer. Washington police had extensive files on stolen typewriters because there was a rash of thefts from government offices, but after weeks of checking, they found nothing.

Walsh, working with three other agents, got the idea of looking for other letters that would have been written on the same family typewriter. The first stop was Landon, a private school attended by Timothy Hobson, Priscilla Hiss' son by her first marriage. When the FBI men arrived, a school official said, "Yes, there are typed letters from Priscilla Hiss. Hiss' lawyers were here already. How do I know whether to give the letters to them or to you?" The FBI reply: "Did you ever hear of a subpoena?"[39]

With a letter in hand, the FBI lab identified the typewriter with certainty to be the one on which the secret documents had been typed. When magnified a thousand times, every typewriter key has its own unmistakable pattern, like a fingerprint. Even after many years, the wear marks will show, but they will not erase the identifying characteristics. The FBI backed up this research with another letter written to Bryn Mawr, and tried to get a third from the Potomac School, where another Hiss son was enrolled. At the last destination, the headmistress, "dressed in an upper class fashion and with mannerisms to match, seethed with venom dripping from her mouth. She refused to give any letters and said that if Alger Hiss told her himself that he was a Soviet spy she wouldn't believe it."[40]

Next the FBI asked Hiss if there were any women who had worked as maids in the Hiss household. Hiss gave a list but left off a woman named Claudia (Clytie) Catlett, about whom the FBI had heard. Clytie, the matriarch of a large clan, was living in Winchester, Virginia, and willingly came to Washington, where Chambers was sitting in the FBI office. Clytie greeted him warmly and said she had often met him at Hiss' home. On the way back to Winchester, one of the FBI agents in the car asked Clytie if Hiss had ever given her an old Woodstock typewriter. Yes, he had, and she had given it to the Catlett brothers, her relatives, from whom it was easy to get it back. When the FBI agents tried to retrieve the typewriter from the Catletts, they learned that Hiss' lawyers had bought it from them for $50. The FBI waited a few days. "Now obstruction of justice was involved. We waited to give Hiss' lawyers a chance to come in on their own, which they did," said Walsh.[41]

Thus Hiss' trial was reduced to the question of perjury.

The daily press was divided; the four leading liberal columnists, Walter Lippmann, James Reston, Joseph Alsop, and Marquis Childs, were all pro-Hiss, as were commentators in *The New Yorker* and *The New Republic*. The two syndicates, Hearst and Scripps Howard, were pro-prosecution.[42]

In his careful study, *The Committee*, Walter Goodman concluded, "Those who in 1948 associated themselves with the sad cause of Alger Hiss made an error for which the liberal cause would pay in the next half dozen years."[43] The price was McCarthyism. American political equilibrium suffered from the "Stalinist Left and the Yahoo Right."[44]

For liberals, Nixon's name became synonymous with perfidy throughout his career. Proof of Hiss' perjury, and the implications of treason in the facts of the case, did nothing to breach the divide in American political attitudes. Hiss continued to deny his guilt during nearly four years in prison and throughout his life until he died in 1996. Only with the release of VENONA, which pinpointed Hiss at Yalta and traveling to Moscow after the conference to receive a medal from the Soviet Union, did most American liberals believe the justice of the verdict against him. A few still argue that he was not the only American at Yalta to visit Moscow after the conference: perhaps the VENONA code word ALES was someone else, not Hiss. In his memoir defending his father, Tony Hiss describes Alger as a kind and caring man who could not have been a spy.[45]

Hiss appears in the memoirs of NKVD Agent Hede Massing, who described a meeting with Hiss. They argued over which underground organization, hers (the

NKVD) or his (military intelligence, GRU), should receive the services of an agent she was attempting to recruit.[46]

Hiss epitomized the establishment American; it was hard to believe he worked for the USSR. He represented qualities that liberal ethnic Americans yearned to have for acceptance into the mainstream. Mrs. Hiss, a Quaker, was part of a culture that built America. Chambers was physically unattractive and a converted Catholic, therefore considered an arcane, neurotic intellectual by liberals, but a hero to Irish Catholic longshoremen.[47] The Hiss case forever shadowed Nixon's reputation. In 1988 Hiss published a memoir maintaining his innocence.[48]

In 1992, in the heady days after the fall of the Soviet Union, Russia's President Yeltsin designated General Dmitri Volkogonov, his Defense Adviser, to deal with outstanding issues between the United States and Russia. Volkogonov had been mandated by Yeltsin to oversee all government archives except those of the GRU. One of the long-standing sore points was the fate of American prisoners of war from the Korean and Vietnam wars. Volkogonov testified before the Senate Select Committee Investigating POW/MIA Affairs. When former President Richard Nixon read of Yeltsin's initiative on June 12, 1992, he wrote a note to Dmitri Simes, a Soviet academic who had emigrated to America in 1970; Simes had become a respected analyst of Russian-American relations and an adviser to Nixon.[49]

Dear Dmitri—
A personal request:
    Since Yeltsin is giving out information about POWs to the Senate—wouldn't he consider putting out the Alger Hiss file?
    Your friends at Carnegie might not like it but they are supposed to be dedicated to seeking the truth!
Thanks,
RN
Personal[50]

In 1992, Hiss' lawyer and friend, John Lowenthal, journeyed to Moscow to ask Volkogonov to clear Hiss' name. Volkogonov consulted with Yevgeny Primakov, then head of the Russian Foreign Intelligence Service (SVR, the successor to the KGB), asking him to search the KGB archives for evidence of Hiss serving as a Soviet agent. Primakov found no documents referring to Hiss and Volkogonov so reported to Lowenthal. On October 29, 1992, the *New York Times* reported that there was no record of Hiss in the KGB or NKVD archives and that Hiss was innocent. The *Washington Post* followed with a major article reporting that there was no record of Hiss as a Soviet agent in the KGB archives. Nor should there be. Hiss was an agent controlled by Soviet military intelligence. His records are in secret GRU archives that were not open to Volkogonov and remain closed.

Upon his return to Moscow, Volkogonov issued an elegant public retraction in a letter to the Moscow newspaper *Nezavisamaya Gazeta* on November 24, 1992: ". . . as far as I know, the agency in which those documents from the 1950s were reviewed was not the only one which was involved in intelligence. Furthermore, there are no guarantees that they all survived."[51]

When Alger Hiss died in 1996, the VENONA documents released in November 1995 were a critical source for commentary on his career as a Soviet agent. The key message from Anatoli Gromov, the Soviet intelligence station chief in Washington, to Moscow, dated March 30, 1945, refers to Hiss by the code name ALES, and notes: "ALES has been working continuously with the NEIGHBORS (code name for the GRU) since 1935." The message also reports that "recently" ALES and his whole group were awarded Soviet decorations.[52] The VENONA identification of Hiss as ALES and the confirming circumstances in the message implicating his wife and brother as part of his group of Soviet agents closed the case for all but diehard defenders of Alger Hiss.[53]

VENONA was not the only tool by which the FBI identified Julius and Ethel Rosenberg's espionage. If the Soviet intercepts, in which Julius' identity is covered with a code name and Ethel is openly named as his wife, were the only evidence against them, it would not have held up in court and they might have gone free. A brilliant job of investigation by the FBI led from Klaus Fuchs to David Greenglass, then to the Rosenbergs.

Special Agents Robert Lamphere and Ernie Van Loon traced the report on the gaseous diffusion process, described at length in VENONA, to Klaus Fuchs, a member of the British team at Los Alamos. By 1948 Fuchs had left Los Alamos and gone to work at Harwell Research facility, the British atomic laboratory. When the British security officer at Harwell accused Fuchs of espionage, he twice denied that he had given away secrets entrusted to him at Los Alamos. William Skardon, the MI-5 officer in charge of the investigation, patiently questioned Fuchs beginning in December 1949, trying to gain his confidence and making it clear that he had evidence against him, without revealing the existence of VENONA. On January 22, 1945, Fuchs said he wanted to see Skardon again, and on January 24, began to confess his role in atomic espionage.[54]

According to FBI sources, Fuchs said he could no longer betray his coworkers and wanted to confess. Listening to Lamphere and Van Loon tell the story years later, the likelihood Fuchs was telling the truth about his motive for confessing was slim; it appeared that he had made up his mind to use his confession for damage control, to minimize the scope of the British and American investigation. The first thought that sprang to mind was that a Soviet contact had reached him after he was accused and given him instructions what to tell and what to hold back. We later interviewed Aleksandr Feklisov, his case officer during this period, and asked pointedly if the theory of the Soviet contact was correct. Feklisov assured us it wasn't so. He had not seen Fuchs for six months before he was arrested, and when they last met Feklisov had urged him, for his own safety, to leave the West. "No, there is still much work to be done," Feklisov quoted Fuchs. "I know there is a dangerous minefield out there, but I will deal with it when the time comes."[55]

Fuchs told the British that he had given his technical messages to a courier he knew only as Raymond. All he could say about Raymond, based on the courier's questions to Fuchs, was that Raymond was knowledgeable about chemistry and engineering. It took Lamphere and his FBI team a great deal of effort to connect Fuchs' description of Raymond to Harry Gold, who worked for a chemical firm in Philadelphia. The first vague tip came from Elizabeth Bentley, who had at one time acted as courier to a chemist named Abraham Brothman. When questioned, Brothman said he met Jacob Golos, Bentley's control officer and lover, through Harry Gold. When questioned, both Brothman and Gold said they thought Golos was a businessman. However, the description and movements that Lamphere had of Raymond from Fuchs and his sister, whom Raymond had once visited (he had lost contact with Fuchs and wanted to know how to reach him), matched those of Gold. Fuchs had met with Raymond nine times in 1944 and 1945, in New York, near Los Alamos, and in Cambridge, Massachusetts. The FBI showed Fuchs the photographs they had of Gold, but he said he didn't recognize him to be Raymond. Only after the FBI took surreptitious photographs and film footage of Gold and showed them to Fuchs was Fuchs finally satisfied that Gold was "very likely" Raymond.[56]

Meanwhile, FBI agents had received permission from Gold to search his apartment, with him present. Gold denied he had ever traveled to Boston, where Fuchs' sister lived, or ever traveled west of the Mississippi River. When faced with a railroad timetable to Boston and a street map of Santa Fe, New Mexico, pulled out of piles of paper in his apartment, Gold slumped in his chair and admitted, "I am the man to whom Fuchs gave the information."[57]

The arrests of Fuchs and Gold were only the beginning. Lamphere said that interrogation of Gold led to the opening of forty-nine cases.

Gold was born in Switzerland, the son of impoverished Russian immigrants who came to Philadelphia in the 1920s. Growing up there, he suffered from anti-Semitism and believed the Soviet Union was the only country that protected Jews. After Gold graduated from high school, he went to work for a sugar company, then on to college for three semesters before his money ran out and he returned to the same job. Then came the Depression and he was laid off. A friend got him a job with a soap manufacturing company; a chemist named Tom Black wanted to leave the job and was able to pass it on to Gold. Gaik Ovakimian, the New York *rezident*, had recruited Black to work for the Soviets. Black pushed Gold into joining the Communist Party and induced him to steal the technology for refining sugar, which Black then gave to the Soviet Union. When Gold returned to college to finish his degree, his Soviet handlers paid the tuition. Gold later served as courier for the theft of technology to make synthetic rubber, an industrial secret with military applications.[58]

In the early 1940s, Gold's new control officer was Semyon (Sam) Semyonov (TWAIN in VENONA), the MIT-trained engineer who had made friends while at the institute with a whole generation of future scientific leaders. Working for Semyonov on the "scientific line," Gold continued to gather industrial technology; before they parted for new assignments Semyonov presented Gold a Soviet award of the Red Star. Then in 1943, Gold was assigned a new controller, Anatoli Yakovlev (a.k.a. Anatoli Yatskov), who had the cover name "John." Gold's new control officer, who operated on a higher level than Semyonov, made him the courier for Klaus Fuchs.[59]

It was a mistake of spy tradecraft by Yakovlev—to have one courier serve two sources—that sealed the fate of Julius and Ethel Rosenberg. If a courier was captured or if he defected, he should be able to reveal only one source. When Fuchs confessed, he had no idea that Raymond, who he believed served him alone, had strayed from the mandated rules for couriers and picked up secret material from another source. The purpose of his confession, to limit exposure of the ring, was betrayed without his knowledge. Gold had been traveling to New Mexico for two years, picking up materials from Fuchs, when Yakovlev asked him to make a side trip to Albuquerque to receive papers from another contributor of secret technology. Gold objected that he might attract attention from security officers by staying in the area an extra day, and that Fuchs was too important for them to take such a risk. Yakovlev needed the materials, and the regular courier, a woman, was unavailable; he ordered Gold to visit an apartment in Albuquerque. He was to have a torn Jell-O boxtop in hand that would match another piece of the same package; this would be the signal that would ensure his identity and verify the *bona fides* of the person giving him the papers.

When Gold was under interrogation, he did not know the names of the contact in Albuquerque who had given him drawings and descriptions of implosion lenses being worked on at Los Alamos. He only knew that he had given the young soldier and his wife five hundred dollars and that they made arrangements for a later rendezvous for further exchanges. Gold thought maybe the wife's name was Ruth, and when confronted with an Albuquerque street map, was able to identify the area of town he had visited.

Using VENONA references and Army furlough records, the FBI traced Ruth and David Greenglass, who had been living in an apartment that matched the street map. When Gold identified their photographs, the hardest work was done. On June 15, 1950, Greenglass was brought in for questioning and soon admitted that he had given materials from Los Alamos to a courier who he knew would transmit them to the Soviets. Clearly, his wife had been part of the conspiracy; he also implicated his brother-in-law, Julius Rosenberg, who had recruited him to work for the Soviet Union. Greenglass didn't name his sister, Ethel Rosenberg.[60]

The FBI investigation demonstrated that both Ethel and Julius Rosenberg graduated from the same high school on the lower east side of Manhattan, she in 1931, he in 1934. They began seeing each other in about 1932, much against the wishes of her parents, who disliked Julius. However, Ethel and her brothers lived in an apartment a floor above their parents, where Julius could visit her frequently and where he had access to *The Daily Worker* and other communist publications that were strewn around the apartment. Together Ethel and Julius became fervent communists, disdainful of friends and classmates who disagreed with their views.[61]

Julius attended the College of the City of New York (CCNY) and graduated in 1939 with a degree in electrical engineering. While in college he was secretary of the Young Communist League. Julius and Ethel were married on June 18, 1939. He landed a job as junior radio engineer with the War Department Signal Supply office in Brooklyn. From there he moved with the Signal Corps to Philadelphia and later to Newark, New Jersey. By the time his employment with the government was officially ended in December 1945, the Security and Intelligence Division had warned the War Department that Julius had belonged to communist front organizations in college and that Ethel had signed a Communist Party petition.

Five years later, the FBI learned that Julius was the center of an espionage network that collected military technology all through the war from his former engineering classmates at CCNY, Max Elitcher, Morton Sobell, William Perl, Joel Barr, and Alfred Sarant. Julius rented an apartment in lower Manhattan where the group photographed the secret material and transferred the copies to the Soviet Union. While Sobell worked for the General Electric Company in Schenectady, New York, during and after the war, he had access to meteorological and fire control radar; at his next job, with the Reeve Instrument Company in New York City, he also worked on secret data. The day that the FBI arrested Greenglass, Sobell failed to show up for work; six days later Sobell fled to Mexico, where the authorities returned him to the Texas border at Laredo. Agents of the FBI were waiting at the bridge.[62]

Ethel's younger brother, David Greenglass, had studied mechanical engineering and design when he was inducted into the U.S. Army in 1943. After brief assignments in engineering units, the Army transferred Greenglass to the Manhattan Engineering District, first to an ordnance plant in Mississippi, then to Oak Ridge, Tennessee, and later to Santa Fe, New Mexico. He had no idea he was working on research to build the first atomic bomb until his wife brought him that information from Julius and Ethel Rosenberg, his brother-in-law and sister.

David later stated that he at first opposed Ethel and Julius' attempts to make him a communist when he was a teenager, but after Julius gave him a chemistry set, the two became friends. According to David's wife, Ruth, he looked up to

Julius and followed him into the Young Communist League. Ruth said her husband converted her to communism but that, after World War II, both became disillusioned with Moscow's desire for world conquest and the Soviets' expulsion of Tito from the Comintern. Tito was Yugoslavia's wartime guerrilla hero against the Germans.

At his trial for espionage conspiracy, Greenglass revealed that Julius Rosenberg and his network were constantly on the lookout for workers in defense plants and members of the Armed Forces who could be recruited to steal secrets for the Soviet Union. Greenglass admitted under oath that, at the request of his sister and brother-in-law, he had given Harry Gold sketches of secret lenses he was working on at Los Alamos. Greenglass was an apprentice in a shop that prepared lens molds made for Dr. Walter Koski from the scientist's sketches. Greenglass' group worked under the direction of Dr. George Kistiakowsky of Harvard University; while at Los Alamos, Greenglass learned the identities of Oppenheimer, Harold Urey, and Niels Bohr.[63]

Greenglass said that his wife, Ruth, visited him in Albuquerque in November 1944, when he was working on a "restricted" project at Los Alamos. She told him that Julius had invited her to dinner at his home, 10 Monroe Street in New York City, and pointed out that his wife, Ethel, was no longer participating in communist activities. Ethel explained that they were no longer buying *The Daily Worker* or going to club meetings because Julius was at last doing what he had always hoped to do, which was to give information to the Soviet Union. Ethel and Julius informed Ruth that David was working on the atomic bomb project and they wanted information from him. Ruth said she thought getting materials from David was not a good idea and would not tell David about it. Julius and Ethel argued that the Soviet Union was fighting Hitler and was not getting all the information that was due to an ally. At first, David said, he declined to take part in the scheme, but he relented the next day and answered the list of questions Ruth put to him about the layout of the Manhattan Project, who the scientists were and how many technical people worked at Los Alamos.[64]

Lamphere later explained that the argument at the Rosenbergs' apartment, in which Ethel pressured Ruth to get David to participate in espionage, was the moment for which Ethel paid with her life in the electric chair. Ethel had asserted her authority as David's older sister to overturn his wife's refusal. Whatever doubt the prosecution had about the extent of Ethel's involvement in treason was negated with Ethel's one sentence of insistence: "Let Davy decide!"[65]

In January 1945, David came to New York on furlough. Julius was able to tell David what an atom bomb looked like, and his description matched the weapon that was later dropped on Hiroshima. Greenglass put down on paper what he knew about the experiments and drew sketches of the lens mold. He also gave Julius a list of possible recruits who might work for the communists. Ruth Greenglass was concerned that Julius would not be able to read David's handwriting, but he assured her that Ethel would type everything David had written by hand. Another woman whose husband was a long time acquaintance of David came to dinner; after she left, Julius decided that Ruth should move to Albuquerque, where the dinner guest would visit to be a courier for David's future secret information. In the event that she could not come and another person handled the pickup, Julius and Ethel gave David and Ruth half of a torn Jell-O boxtop; it would match the other half to be presented by the messenger.[66]

The messenger who arrived with half a Jell-O boxtop was Harry Gold.

Before Greenglass returned to Los Alamos, Julius arranged a meeting between him and a Soviet intelligence officer on a dark New York street. Greenglass rode around in a car with the unknown man, answering questions about high-explosive lenses, the curve of the lens and the means of detonation.[67]

In September 1945, Greenglass again visited New York on furlough, together with Ruth. After his suspension from the War Department in March, Julius returned to New York and took a job as assistant engineer with the Emerson Radio and Phonograph Corporation. From Julius' description of the bomb during their last meeting, David had known what to look for. He now had a clearer account to offer of how the fissionable material at both ends of a tube came together by way of a barometric pressure device to cause a "nuclear explosion." When he delivered these secrets to Julius, both wives were present. While Ethel typed the report Julius told David that he had stolen a proximity fuse while working at the Emerson Radio Corporation and turned it over to the Soviets.[68]

Julius wanted David to stay on at Los Alamos after he was discharged from the Army but David refused. Julius suggested that David go to college on the GI Bill, supplemented with Soviet funds. He urged David to become a student of nuclear physics at MIT or the University of Chicago where he could gather information for the Soviet Union.

After less than a year as an employee at Emerson, Julius began operating a series of machine shop businesses; he included David upon his return from the Army. The two remained in business together for three years, but they did not do well financially and parted with some resentments, Lamphere said. During the time they worked together, Julius told David that he had people in upstate New York and in Ohio giving him information for the Soviets. From "one of the boys," Julius learned about a sky platform that could orbit the earth like a satellite. He had information on atomic energy for airplanes. The Soviets had given Julius a citation, a watch, and a console table.[69]

When Fuchs was arrested in February 1950, Julius told David to leave the country. He would get money to travel from the Soviets. He warned him again in April and then on May 23 when the story of Gold's arrest appeared in the *New York Herald Tribune*. Julius gave David money and a complicated plan for getting passports that would eventually land him in the Soviet Union. Julius said he would also have to leave the country because he believed Elizabeth Bentley knew him. David took $4,000 and gave it to his brother-in-law Louis Abel (Ruth's sister's husband) for safekeeping. David later gave the money to his lawyer, O. John Rogge, to represent him.[70]

On March 29, 1951, the jury found the Rosenbergs and Morton Sobell guilty on all counts. Judge Kaufman postponed sentencing for one week until April 5. The Rosenbergs had shown no signs of contrition or confessing their guilt. Hoover consulted with his key aides and those who had handled the case. None of them favored a death penalty for Ethel, the mother of two small children. In his report to the attorney general, Hoover recommended that both Julius Rosenberg and Morton Sobell be sentenced to death; Ethel Rosenberg should be sentenced to thirty years and David Greenglass to fifteen years in prison.

Hoover's strategy was to threaten Julius with a death sentence and Ethel with a long prison term to get them to reveal their espionage activities and name the members of their ring. The FBI strategy remained the same from the time that Julius Rosenberg was arrested on July 17, 1950. Assistant Director Alan Belmont wrote a memo to D. M. (Mickey) Ladd, Director of Domestic Intelligence, suggesting the Bureau "consider every possible means to bring pressure on Rosenberg to make him talk . . . including a careful study of the involvement of Ethel Rosenberg, in order that charges may be placed against her, if possible."

The question of Ethel's complicity hinged on whether she had typed the data David Greenglass provided to Julius from Los Alamos in handwritten notes. In his initial interrogation on August 4, 1950, Greenglass insisted that Ethel was not present and had never spoken to him when he passed the materials. On February 23 and 24, 1951, Ruth and David Greenglass changed their testimony and told the FBI that Ethel had been present and had typed up the materials David gave Julius. Ruth's and David's testimony implicating Ethel was the government's major evidence against her. Ruth Greenglass, named as a co-conspirator, was not indicted and escaped jail sentence. David had chosen between his wife's freedom and his sister's death sentence.[71]

On April 4, 1951, the day before sentencing, Judge Kaufman had an *ex parte*—private contact between a judge and one side of a legal proceeding—conversation with the chief prosecutor, Irving Saypol. Such a private meeting was unethical under the rules of the bar.[72] The judge asked Saypol not to make any recommendations in court the next day. The decision would be solely his.[73]

Judge Kaufman sentenced both Ethel and Julius to death on April 5, 1951. Kaufman told the couple, "Your crime is worse than murder. Plain deliberate, contemplated murder is dwarfed in magnitude by comparison with the crime you have committed—but in your case, I believe your conduct in putting in the hands of the Russians the A-Bomb years before our best scientists predicted Russia would perfect the bomb has already caused the Communist aggression in Korea with the resultant casualties exceeding 50,000—and who knows but that millions more of innocent people may pay the price of your treason."[74]

By his testimony David Greenglass avoided having his wife indicted and he was sentenced to fifteen years in prison. William Perl was sentenced to five years in prison. Morton Sobell received a thirty-year prison term. Joel Barr and Alfred Sarant succeeded in fleeing the country. They later turned up under assumed names in Leningrad (St. Petersburg), where they established electronic factories under Khrushchev's patronage.

The Rosenbergs never admitted their guilt. Their execution was scheduled for the week of May 31, 1951. The sentence and the appeals that followed it again tore a divide in American public opinion.

Beginning in 1947, the National Security Agency, with the cooperation of the FBI, had decoded the VENONA messages naming Julius and Ethel and by 1950 had established that the code name LIBERAL was used for Julius. The VENONA messages named Ethel and Julius and members of his ring, including Alfred Sarant and David and Ruth Greenglass.[75] From NSA records, it is clear that the first mention of the Rosenbergs in the messages was deciphered in 1947, and by 1950, there was positive identification of both Ethel and Julius.[76] The incriminating messages had been decoded by the time of the trial but were not entered as evidence because using them would have meant revealing "sources and methods" of how they had been acquired. John L. Martin, a former Justice Department official with a long career in handling espionage cases, heard from his colleagues and believes that the Justice Department provided the top secret VENONA telegrams for Judge Kaufman to read in an *ex parte* communication. The purpose was to reassure the judge of the Rosenbergs' guilt and make it easier for him to pronounce death sentences on both Julius and Ethel, without having to publicly reveal the source of the information.[77]

Although the Rosenbergs' execution was initially set for the week of May 21, 1951, their appeals dragged on for two years. A year after their arrest in 1950 and four months after they had been found guilty in 1951, the campaign to "Save the Rosenbergs" from "legal murder" got under way, directed from Moscow. The Rosenbergs continued to plead their innocence, providing a venue for the propaganda mounting in Europe, and then around the world, to distract attention from the impact of "Stalinist consolidation." The new round of purges targeted the Communist bloc in the early 1950s and was carried out against the anti-Zionist "Doctors' Plot" in Moscow from 1952 to 1953. In Eastern Europe, Stalin purged communist leaders whom he perceived to have "nationalist" leanings in favor of those more subservient to the Soviet Union.

In Czechoslovakia, the Soviet conquerors ousted the party general secretary, Rudolf Slansky, and thirteen other party leaders, most of whom, like Slansky, were

Jewish. The Soviet authorities arrested them on fabricated charges of being Zionist agents and tried the group before a Communist Party kangaroo court in November 1952. The court sentenced to death eleven Communist Party leaders, including Slansky, and executed them.[78]

The Rosenberg case became a useful diversion to attack the United States for anti-Semitism and thereby mute criticism of Stalin's anti-Zionist purges. The initial articles in *The Daily Worker* in 1951 made no mention of a "frame-up," but the headline charged that the Rosenbergs had been "Made Scapegoats for [the] Korean War." On August 15, 1951, the *National Guardian* began a series of eight weekly articles by William A. Reuben, which compared the Rosenberg case with the Dreyfus Affair in France at the end of the nineteenth century and to the Sacco-Vanzetti case in America in the 1920s. Reuben charged the court with legal anti-Semitism. On October 10, a week after the series ended, the *Guardian* announced the formation of a National Committee to Secure Justice for the Rosenbergs.

On February 28, 1952, *The Daily Worker* attacked: "The Rosenberg case is a ghastly political fraud. It was arranged to provide blood victims to the witch hunters, open the door to new violence, anti-Semitism, and court lynching of peace advocates and Marxists as 'spies.' " Communist front organizations mobilized to demand clemency for the Rosenbergs in America. In forty countries around the world, the Communist Party organized demonstrations to free the Rosenbergs.

Albert Einstein, an advocate of most peace movements, had growing doubt about the motives of the Rosenberg defense committee. Einstein was the poster boy of the campaign; he had written to the *New York Times* urging clemency for the Rosenbergs and his name appeared prominently in the committee literature. However, when committee activists asked Einstein to sign a Friend of the Court petition to be sent to the Supreme Court, he balked. He confided to a colleague at Princeton that, while he still favored clemency, he did not want to become more deeply involved in a cause he now felt was "Communist inspired."[79]

In February 1953, President Eisenhower made public his decision not to grant pardon to the Rosenbergs. The execution was finally scheduled to take place at 11 p.m. on Friday, June 19, 1953.

There were 24-hour-a-day picket lines around the White House exhorting clemency for the Rosenbergs. The Soviet Union's campaign to free the Rosenbergs, "Victims of American Fascism," was in full swing throughout Europe. After a hurried final appeal arguing that the Rosenbergs were tried under the wrong law and should have been tried under the provisions of the Atomic Energy Act of 1946, Supreme Court Justice William O. Douglas considered a stay of execution only days before the scheduled execution.

On June 16, 1953, Attorney General Herbert Brownell, aware that Justice Douglas was considering a stay of execution, met with Chief Justice Fred Vinson to discuss contingency plans of what to do if Douglas intervened in the case. This second *ex parte* meeting was improper, yet another violation of the canons of judicial conduct that forbade lawyers from making such contact with judges while a case was pending. (Disclosure of the meeting was not revealed until July 14, 1975, as the result of a Freedom of Information suit initiated by Robert and Michael Meeropol, the Rosenbergs' sons, who had taken the names of their stepparents.) At the meeting, Vinson and Brownell agreed to reconvene the court from its summer vacation if Douglas held up the execution.[80]

Justice Douglas granted a stay of the Rosenbergs' execution at 11 a.m. on June 17, effective until October, accepting the argument that the case might have been tried under the wrong law. Douglas noted that if the Atomic Energy Act of 1946 was applicable to the Rosenbergs, Judge Kaufman's District Court had unlawfully imposed the death sentence.

The Rosenbergs had a new lease on life. The arguments that Justice Douglas said deserved more serious consideration could change the nature of the case. The Rosenbergs had been charged, tried, and convicted under the Espionage Act of 1947, which permitted a judge to pronounce a death sentence on his own determination without requiring any recommendation from the jury. But another law, the Atomic Energy Act of 1946, required that spies who passed atomic secrets could be executed only on the recommendation of the jury sitting in the case.

From the day they were indicted until three days before they were executed, the Atomic Energy Act, although applicable, was ignored by everyone with the power to restate the case.[81] The Atomic Energy Act stipulated that if the jury were to impose the death penalty, it could be done only when the jury found that the accused had the intent to injure the United States. The Rosenbergs' indictment under the Espionage Act charged them only with conspiring to commit espionage but did not charge them with conspiring with intent to injure the United States. If the brief presented to Justice Douglas by Tennessee lawyer Fyke Farmer were upheld, a new trial would be in order and the likelihood of execution diminished. Douglas agreed that a substantial part of the case had occurred after 1946, when the Atomic Energy Act was passed, and that the question was substantial enough to require full briefing and argument. He ordered the case sent back to Judge Kaufman for his decision on this point. Then it would go to the Second Circuit Court of Appeals and then back to the Supreme Court. At a minimum, it would give the Rosenbergs another year of life.[82]

Hope quickly turned to despair. On June 18, Chief Justice Vinson unexpectedly requested a special session of the Supreme Court and called the judges back from vacation. On Friday June 19, the day set for the execution before the stay, President Eisenhower and Brownell clashed at a Cabinet meeting. Present at the meeting was Emmet John Hughes, the President's speechwriter, who later recalled the scene in his memoirs. Brownell had reported that the Supreme Court would soon rule against the Rosenbergs and that the Justice Department was determined to proceed with the execution. The following exchange took place:

> *President:* I must say I'm impressed by all the honest doubt about this expressed in the letters I've been seeing. Now if the Supreme Court decides by, say, five to four or even six to three, as far as the average man's concerned, there *will* be doubt, not just a legal point in his mind.

> *Brownell:* Well, who's going to decide these points—pressure groups or the Supreme Court? Surely, our first concern is the strength of our courts. And in terms of national security, the communists are just out to prove that they can bring enough pressure, one way or another, to enable people to get away with espionage. . . . I've always wanted you to look at evidence that wasn't usable in court showing the Rosenbergs were the head and center of an espionage ring here in *direct* contact with the Russians—the *prime* espionage ring in the country.

> *President:* My only concern is in the area of statecraft—the *effect* of the action.[83]

The same day that Brownell met with President Eisenhower, the Supreme Court voted 6–3 to overrule Justice Douglas' stay of execution. Never before in the court's history had it vacated a stay by one of its members.[84] There is no direct evidence that Brownell showed the incriminating VENONA messages to Vinson to convince him of the Rosenbergs' guilt. As attorney general, Brownell knew the VENONA secret and, as Hoover's superior, he was in a position to ask for and receive any information he required. His comments to Eisenhower about intelligence information that could not be brought as evidence in court are a firm indication that Brownell was ready to use VENONA to see the Rosenbergs' sentence carried out.

Until the final moment, Hoover was still hopeful that the Rosenbergs would confess the details of their spy ring. On June 2, 1953, John V. Bennett, Director of the Bureau of Prisons, had visited Sing Sing and personally offered Julius and Ethel their lives if they would "fully cooperate." The Rosenbergs' lawyer, Emanuel Bloch, was strongly against them cooperating with the government to save themselves. The communist element that dominated the National Committee to Secure Justice in the Rosenberg Case could only be satisfied by the Rosenbergs' freedom or martyrdom. The Rosenbergs were more valuable to Moscow dead than alive in the cold war struggle. Radosh and Milton explain:

> For Bloch, any influence that might lead the Rosenbergs to consider confessing was unthinkable, and for reasons that went deeper than any abstract

demands of the Party line. Confession would have meant naming others—most likely many others, individuals who would then provide the fodder for a new round of atom spy trials—and perhaps, provide also the excuse for the wholesale roundup of leftists that so many in Bloch's circle believed was imminent. From this point of view, cooperation with the government could not possibly "save" Julius and Ethel Rosenberg. Rather, it would destroy them and everything they had suffered for, in a sense that not even the electric chair could.[85]

To the end, Hoover believed the Rosenbergs would break and turn state's evidence. The FBI set up an elaborate plan with the White House to halt the execution if the Rosenbergs agreed to cooperate in their final moments.

At 4:30 a.m. on June 19, 1953, six FBI special agents left the New York City field office for the thirty-mile trip north to Ossining, the site of Sing Sing prison on the Hudson River. Their schedule had been carefully planned so they would arrive while it was still dark and avoid attracting attention. The team included a young agent who could transcribe in shorthand at more than 170 words per minute; it had two offices on death row out of sight of the Rosenbergs. An open line to FBI headquarters had been established from Sing Sing. Hoover was linked with a direct connection to President Eisenhower in the White House. If the Rosenbergs agreed to talk, the President would commute their death sentence. The procedure was clearly defined. A rabbi would ask both Julius and Ethel, separately, if they were willing to confess. If they confessed, their lives would be spared; even if one was strapped into the electric chair, and suddenly indicated a willingness to talk, the execution would halt. A signal system had been set up for the FBI agents waiting at the end of death row. When an execution had been completed, the chief of the guards would step into the corridor and wave his arm. Twice the chief of the guards waved his arms: both Julius and Ethel Rosenberg died in the electric chair at Sing Sing Prison in Ossining, New York, during the night of June 19, within hours after the Supreme Court vote.

Hoover's gamble had failed, and the Rosenbergs, pleading innocence to the end, became martyrs. In Rome, crowds marched on the American embassy after the execution. The American critic Leslie Fiedler, who happened to be present in Rome, noted that the demonstration was less of a wake than a victory celebration.

After their deaths, the Rosenbergs were secretly awarded medals, Heroes of the Soviet Union. The Soviet Union could do no less—they had withstood all pressures to confess and had paid with their lives.[86]

Only with the publication in 1991 of *Khrushchev Remembers: The Glasnost Tapes*, the third volume of Khrushchev's memoirs, did the first authoritative confirmation emerge from Moscow of the Rosenbergs' role in atomic espionage. The tapes had been stored in a Zurich bank vault for twenty-one years awaiting the time when their revelations could no longer bring retribution upon the ousted leader or his family. The memoir delivered the openness—*glasnost*—promised in the title. Two generations of Americans who believed the Rosenbergs were innocent had to give up cherished certainties when Khrushchev praised the executed martyrs for their contributions to the Soviet Union. "I heard from both Stalin and Molotov that the Rosenbergs provided very significant help in accelerating the production of our atomic bomb," wrote Khrushchev.[87] Four decades of arguments for the Rosenbergs' innocence, from their children and their supporters worldwide, were negated in one sentence.

With the publication of *The Glasnost Tapes*, it became time for the Russian government to open other archives. Soon afterward, the spies Lona and Morris Cohen, living in Moscow since their release from jail in Britain, acknowledged in a television interview their work as couriers for Soviet agents stealing atomic secrets from the Manhattan Project during World War II.[88]

Khrushchev's revelation raised a strong objection from supporters of the Rosenbergs, who had long insisted that they had been framed by the U.S. government and were really innocent. Never before had a senior Soviet official, let alone a former leader of the Soviet Union, acknowledged the Rosenbergs' espionage contributions. Conspiracy theorists demanded that the publishers, Little, Brown and Company, withdraw the book, insisting that Khrushchev's comments on the Rosenbergs had been fabricated. To acknowledge that the Rosenbergs had been Soviet spies destroyed their martyrdom.

Pavel Sudoplatov's *Special Tasks* provides a fuller picture of the Rosenbergs' contributions to the Soviet Union. Sudoplatov defined the Rosenbergs as leaders of a major spy ring for military weapons secrets, which had played only a minor part in atomic espionage. Sudoplatov, who was in charge of atomic espionage from 1943 to 1947, summed up their contribution:

> The validity and usefulness of agent sources varied greatly. The involvement of the Rosenbergs in atomic spying was the outcome of our efforts to utilize any and all possible sources of information, but the Rosenbergs were never a significant source. They were a naive couple overeager to cooperate with us, who provided no valuable secrets. Their contributions to atomic espionage were minor. . . .
>
> It was clear from the very beginning that the case had acquired a political character far out of proportion to their actual role as spies. More important than their spying activities was that the Rosenbergs served as a symbol in support of communism and the Soviet Union. Their bravery to the end served our cause, because they became the center of a world wide Communist propaganda campaign.[89]

A year later Aleksandr Feklisov, the KGB case officer for the Rosenbergs, appeared on the Discovery Channel walking the same New York streets where he received top secret material from Julius Rosenberg. He called their execution for atomic espionage "Cold War repression," while confirming that Julius provided a sample proximity fuse and vital radar and radio communications information.[90]

★ ★ ★

The lingering question that emerges from the Hiss case, the Rosenberg case, and VENONA is: why did top-ranking Americans become communists and betray their own country to serve the Soviet Union? It is hard to imagine how so many smart people, misdirected idealists, believed the promises that communism would bring America a more just society. The Great Depression that began with the stock market crash of 1929 and created poverty across the globe was the formative experience of the generation serving in leadership positions from the early 1930s until the end of the war in 1945. The burden of widespread poverty made them prey to promises of financial security regulated by the state. Wartime propaganda, both Soviet and American, for sealing the alliance to fight Hitler in World War II, led these educated, generous, but misguided bureaucrats to give the Soviet Union the inside track on American policy planning and new discoveries in technology.

In Khrushchev's words: "The historical role of Marxist-Leninist teachings and the opportunities these teachings afford the working people of all countries are understood only by the most forward looking segment of society, the most advanced portion of the working class and intelligentsia."[91] Americans who looked to the Soviet Union for ideological leadership considered themselves "progressives."

To understand the attraction of the Soviet Union as the standard bearer for a future utopia, we must consider an analysis by Irving Kristol that takes us back more than two centuries to the Continental "radical" liberalism that gave rise to the French Revolution. Opposition to the oppression, corruption, and decadence of the *ancien régime*, indeed to all monarchies and aristocracies, led to an intellectual and spiritual belief that a new order could be constructed, an "enlightened" state that could embody the highest instincts and thoughts of mankind. By the early nineteenth century, this belief was coupled with a distrust and detestation of the market economy, considered the incarnation of self-interest. Enlightened government should be the master, not the servant of the economy. Powerful, intrusive government became the ideal of modern socialism, either social-democratic or Leninist.[92]

This ideology, for which Napoleon was the representative icon, liberated Europeans from their ghettos and eventually gave them suffrage. In countries of Eastern Europe, where these goals were not realized, devotion to this liberal ideal was even more intense. It was from this Continental seedbed of thought, a century of belief in a better future, that Jews and impoverished peasants emigrated to the United States in the four decades between 1880 and 1920. When the Bolshevik Revolution overthrew the Russian czar and all the patrimony he represented, bringing a new, strong-armed regime that promised to serve the interests of the people, some of the immigrants, and their children, felt a pang of disappointment that they had given up on the homeland too soon, that they had missed out on the revolution.

The first generation in America was caught in the middle between their parents' socialist yearnings and the American culture that surrounded them but did not wholly accept them. Antiforeign sentiment and unspoken quotas that limited their enrollment in prestigious universities or banned them from social clubs were constant reminders that they were not yet part of the establishment.

The dominating establishment, whose families had emigrated to America many generations earlier, held to an ideology that was a polar opposite to the liberalism of the French Revolution. Anglo-Scottish-American liberalism was the creed for which an earlier American generation had spilled its blood in the American Revolution, at about the same time that the Continent was undergoing its own change. This creed held that an enlightened civil society based on individual liberty was the utopia to die for. The off-Continent liberalism demanded an unlimited sphere of action in which to pursue one's own self-interest, without the threat of interfering government. This was the ideal of a "bourgeois" civil society. At the end of the twentieth century, its most extreme form was libertarianism. Its more moderate incarnation is the Republican Party.[93]

The East and Central European immigrants clustered in American urban centers where they were welcomed by the Democratic Party. The politicians in charge were often Irish, Americans of an earlier migration, who shared the newcomers' aspirations for economic equality and representative government. To the extent that the earlier immigrants were willing to share power within the Democratic Party, the newcomers provided a balance to the voting ticket and numbers to support them.[94]

The Republican Party, up until World War II, was identified in the minds of these immigrants as the social class that discriminated against the urban poor. They dominated large corporations and lived in affluent suburbs that kept out Jews and blacks. The excluded became the future leaders of the civil rights movement. They were the groups most attracted to socialist appeals when the country sank into the economically barren years of the Great Depression. It is no wonder, then, that these "excluded" embraced the ideals of the French Revolution and looked upon the American Revolution as irrelevant to their problems. The bourgeois ideal was for them a term of scorn. Their mentality and ideology, and their experience living through the Depression, left them vulnerable to communist appeals.

However, that would not explain why Alger Hiss, Whittaker Chambers, and

Elizabeth Bentley, whose origins were far from the city ghetto, became willing agents of the Soviet state. To understand their devotion to Moscow, we must look to the prophetic elements that were present in both Christianity and Judaism. Communists believed they had shed religion with the Enlightenment in the eighteenth century, but in fact religious impulses still gripped and shaped their deepest emotional predispositions. Their self-described high moralism, which entailed compassion for the poor and unfortunate, and assumed the goal of universal peace, was transmogrified from religion to communism. Christianity itself has been called an unchecked enthusiasm or outburst within the Jewish prophetic tradition. The French Revolution expanded and gave vitality to such a messianic sensibility in Europe, creating aspiration toward utopian structures that would solve all social evils. The combination of age-old messianic impulses and the ideal of progress in the eighteenth and nineteenth centuries provided atheistic idealists of the twentieth century with the mandate of regenerating mankind in a world communist revolution. In Priscilla Hiss's adherence to Quakerism and Chambers's conversion to Catholicism, we can see that religious sensibilities were present in their communist faith.

How did the activities of Soviet intelligence agents change American government policies? Did they really affect American political thinking and cultural life? Did they change American history? The answer is, "Yes, they did," but with one critical caveat: the success of Soviet intelligence depended on Americans being duped into hurting themselves.

Always, it was Americans recruited by Moscow, who believed they were helping humanity, who caused the most memorable harm:

The influence of American pro-Communist ideologues in the government heightened tensions that brought about war between Japan and the United States.

An idealistic American diplomat gave the Soviet Union the West's bargaining positions at Yalta, helping to bring down the Iron Curtain on Eastern Europe.

A high ranking American bureaucrat gave the Soviets the printing plates with which they issued so many occupation marks in postwar Germany that the Western allies had to change the currency to stop inflation; this led to the Berlin Crisis of 1948.

American scientists, who believed in sharing the fruits of scientific discovery, gave the Soviet Union atomic secrets, making them an equal in the balance of terror that followed the first explosion of a Soviet atomic bomb in August 1949.

Communism has receded into history, but a partisanship still exists in the United States splitting the country between two world views. At the extremes of the political spectrum are those who believed the cold war was America's fault versus those who believed the Soviet Union was an evil empire. With the aid of Irving Kristol's analysis, we see not liberals and conservatives, but two competing liberalisms, stemming from the French and American Revolutions, fighting each other to a draw in the presidential election of 2000. The two liberal philosophies are at the heart of capitalism. Few Americans look back to the vanished utopia of communism.

In the twenty-first century, modernization, the engine of capitalism, is again under attack. The frustrated sons of the Middle East and North Africa are disgusted with the customs and corruption of their parents' generation. Impatient for social change, they have perverted the peaceful religious teachings of Muhammad to spawn a terrorist coalition that portrays American military, economic, and cultural power as the enemy of the Muslim faith. Once more the United States is forced to lead a worldwide coalition to defeat the catastrophic violence that pits a false Islam, another imagined utopia, against the liberal philosophies of the Western world.

★★★
9 The Fifties

In the early 1950s, the editor of the University of Wisconsin student newspaper branded his contemporaries "a generation of jellyfish."[1] The editorial bemoaned the disappearance of the political fervor of the 1930s radicals, whose children now drank all night at their fraternity houses, wore uniforms of white buckskin shoes with cashmere sweaters, and thought not at all about politics. In the glow of prosperity, intellectuals ridiculed the growing postwar "consumer society" that emerged as a result of pent-up demand; jobs, new cars, and home ownership weakened the Depression appeal of the communist left. The hardening lines between wartime allies changed some American communists into cold warriors after the Soviet takeover of Czechoslovakia and the Berlin Blockade in 1948. At a communist cell meeting in New York in the late 1940s, prominent artists, including Adolf Gottlieb, who had long held the party line, got to their feet to protest orders to paint only in the style of "Socialist Realism."[2] The Korean War further eroded support for the American Communist Party.

On January 12, 1950, Secretary of State Dean Acheson appeared before the National Press Club in Washington to state that Korea and Taiwan were outside the defense perimeter of American concern in Asia. His high level policy statement was later widely interpreted as contributing to the decision of North Korean leader Kim Il Sung to invade South Korea. Backed by Moscow, Kim attacked across the 38th parallel at 6 a.m. on a rainy Sunday morning, June 25, 1950. With seven divisions, some 90,000 men, and 150 Soviet tanks, he took over Seoul, the capital of South Korea. President Truman responded with an order to the Seventh Fleet and American troops stationed in the Far East under the command of General Douglas MacArthur to defend the Republic of Korea (ROK) government of Syngman Rhee. A United Nations resolution supported the "police action" in Korea, and sixteen nations sent combat units to Korea. When American and United Nations forces threatened to destroy Kim's army in November 1950, the communist Chinese leader Mao Zedong sent troops and arms to help the northern invaders. A bloody war followed that ended in a stalemate and uneasy truce in 1953, back at the 38ᵗʰ parallel—right where the World War II allies had divided the Korean peninsula. The war cost the deaths of nearly 37,000 American military men. The Chinese Communists suffered 800,000 killed or wounded. North Korean military and civilian casualties were an estimated one million. The South Korean army lost 185,000 killed or missing in action, and suffered 500,000 civilian deaths.[3]

What did Stalin hope to gain by assenting to Kim Il Sung's invasion to conquer South Korea? Russian archives reveal that in 1950 Stalin was still haunted by a half century of fear that Japan would attack the Soviet Union from the east, the same motivation that impelled Operation Snow nine years earlier. The State Department's leading expert on Korea stated the case well in 1950: "Fear of a possible re-enactment of invasion from a resurgent Japan is at present an obsession of Koreans, both north and south. They see in the present U.S. policy of the creation of a strong Japan, a terrifying resemblance to the events of 1902–1904, which resulted in a Russian-Japanese war and their own loss of statehood."[4]

Recent scholarship into Russian archives demonstrates that the Soviets acted on the same fears that underlay their intelligence activities before the Japanese attack on Pearl Harbor in 1941. Their old enemy, Japan, was now a new threat because it was under the control of American Occupation troops. The victor and the vanquished together could create a joint attack on the Soviet Union, Stalin believed.

In June 1945, five years before the Korean War, Far East experts in the Soviet Foreign Ministry provided background for Soviet negotiators at the Potsdam Conference. The report recalled that, in the turn-of-the-century wars, Russia had struggled against Japanese expansion through Korea into Asia. Russia had been alone in the fight against Japan because England, the United States, and Germany had proven sympathetic to the Japanese. The policymaking message was: "Japan must be forever excluded from Korea, since a Korea under Japanese rule would be a constant threat to the Far East of the USSR."[5]

The Foreign Ministry report emphasized that

> the independence of Korea must be effective enough to prevent Korea from being turned into a staging ground for future aggressions against the USSR, not only from Japan, but also from any other power which would attempt to put pressure on the USSR from the East. The surest guarantee of the independence of Korea and the security of the USSR in the East would be the establishment of friendly and close relations between the USSR and Korea. This must be reflected in the formation of a Korean government in the future.[6]

Another briefing paper warned that "the character of the future government of Korea . . . will depend [on] whether Korea will in the future be turned into a breeding ground of new anxiety for us in the Far East or into one of the strong points of our security in the Far East."[7]

Mao had to make a choice between the Soviet-led "progressive" camp and the American-led "reactionary" camp, between the communist world revolution and old imperialist interests. Mao therefore issued his memorable statement on June 30, 1949, a year before the Korean War:

Externally, unite in a common struggle with those nations of the world which treat us as equal and unite with people of all countries. That is, ally ourselves with the Soviet Union, with the People's Democratic countries, and with the proletariat and the broad masses of the people in all other countries, and form an international united front. . . . We must lean to one side.[8]

By leaning to one side, Mao was erasing the years of tension between him and Stalin. Mao's "lean to one side" message demonstrated that he was no Tito; Mao was not creating an independent regime within the communist global camp.

In early 1950, Kim Il Sung went to Moscow to gain Stalin's support for reunification of Korea by military force. Stalin, concerned about American intervention, asked Mao's opinion, which was that the Americans would not enter the fray. Following this discussion, Stalin approved Kim's plan to attack South Korea. In his memoirs, Khrushchev is explicit: "For many years we insisted that the initiative for starting the Korean War came from South Korea . . . the truth . . . for the sake of history: it was the initiative of Kim Il-Sung, and it was supported by Stalin and many others—in fact, by everybody."[9]

Stalin had no desire to confront the United States in battle, even though he believed the war in Korea threatened Soviet control of Manchuria. Stalin preferred to use Kim as his proxy. In the early days of the Korean War, a Soviet worldwide propaganda campaign presented the United States' participation in the war to be an imperialist design in the Far East. The prominent radical journalist I. F. Stone accepted the general line of Soviet disinformation on the Korean War and proceeded to write a book, *The Hidden History of the Korean War*. The book falsely blamed South Korea, with American backing, for starting the war. Stone never retracted or modified this view. Stone appears in VENONA with the code name BLINY, or pancake.[10]

In November 1950, Soviet agents Donald Maclean, head of the American Department of the British Foreign Office in London, and Guy Burgess, a second secretary in the British embassy in Washington, had full access to American strategic planning and operational orders for the Korean War; these they passed to their Soviet intelligence control officers.[11]

Guy Burgess, "an extraordinary mixture of loathsomeness and charm," had arrived at the British embassy in Washington in August 1950 after nearly being dismissed from the British Foreign Service for drunken and brawling behavior.[12] It was to be his last chance. Before he departed London, Burgess produced for his KGB controller in London, Yuri Modin, a long, handwritten account taken from a report by British military intelligence describing the extent of Soviet aid to the Chinese armed forces. "In this way, a few weeks before the first hostilities broke out, we knew exactly what the West had managed to find out about our cooperation with the Chinese," wrote Modin.[13]

Maclean and Burgess forwarded the date for MacArthur's offensive north of the 38th parallel, November 26, 1950, to the Kremlin. What concerned the Chinese most was whether or not the United States would use atomic bombs against Chinese bases and power plants north of the Yalu River.

At the beginning of the war, President Truman had approved studies on how atomic weapons could be employed in battle, but the studies showed that high yield air burst weapons would not be effective against troops in the field. Using them across the Yalu River against bases and supply sanctuaries in China and Manchuria would enlarge the war and force Soviet retaliation.[14]

By the end of the fourth week of November, after a Thanksgiving dinner with all the trimmings for his troops, MacArthur was ready to launch his final offensive to end the war, bring the troops home for Christmas, and reunite North and South Korea. Under MacArthur's orders, the U.S./UN/ROK forces moved north on November 27, through mountain passes difficult to defend and far ahead of their supply lines. Their objective was to link up from east and west and close a giant trap to encircle North Korean forces at the Yalu River.

The Chinese let MacArthur's troops advance before springing their own trap on November 28 and 29. By then the Chinese People's Liberation Army (PLA) had an estimated 300,000 to 400,000 troops in Korea, most of them concealed in the central mountains; North Korea had regrouped and reequipped 65,000 of their troops.[15] Chinese troops attacked in screaming human waves to the sound of bugles and whistles calculated to terrify and unnerve the Americans. They overwhelmed the U.S. and ROK positions, forcing a full-scale retreat. The Chinese offensive retook Seoul on December 6, driving out the battered U.S./UN/ROK forces to regroup. Both sides suffered from the harsh winter. Hungry, exhausted Chinese troops paused in Seoul and along the 37th parallel to await the spring thaw.

"Even Genghis Khan wouldn't have tried North Korea in winter," wrote Major General Oliver P. Smith to the Marine commandant, referring to a case of severe frostbite that resulted when a soldier took off a glove in order to heave a grenade. The bitter cold claimed as many lives as the fighting. The troops brought back dead soldiers frozen stiff like "deer carcass tied to the top of a car."[16]

At a White House press conference on November 30, 1950, at the height of the overwhelming Chinese attack against the U.S. and UN forces in North Korea,

President Truman was asked if the United States was considering using atomic weapons.

The President replied: "There has always been active consideration of its use. I don't want to see it used. It is a terrible weapon and should not be used on innocent women and children who have nothing to do with this military aggression [from China]." Asked again in a follow up question by Merriman Smith, the veteran United Press reporter, "if use of the atomic bomb is under consideration," Truman replied, "It always has been, Smitty. It's one of our weapons."[17]

Truman's response brought headlines promising escalation in the Korean War and rattled the British, who were against extending the war north of the Yalu. Labor Prime Minister Clement Atlee feared a wider war against the People's Republic of China. The British were part of the UN Forces in Korea, and Truman had to hold together the UN coalition.

General MacArthur shared his plans with Sir Alvary D. Gascoigne, Britain's ranking political adviser in Japan, who became privy to proposed operations, bombing targets, and tactical decisions.[18] In the Foreign Office, Maclean received the secret messages between MacArthur and Gascoigne and passed their content on to Soviet intelligence in London through Anthony Blunt, Surveyor of the Queen's Pictures with access to the Royal Palace, another member of the Cambridge ring.[19]

Atlee hurriedly scheduled a visit to Washington to meet with Truman. In their private conversations, Truman assured Atlee that he had no intentions of using atomic weapons against the Chinese and would only consider their use if the Chinese and North Koreans forced American troops off the peninsula. Publicly Truman said only that "it was his hope that world conditions would never call for the use of the atomic bomb" and "it was his desire to keep the Prime Minister at all times informed of developments which might bring about a change in the situation."[20]

Both Burgess and Maclean had access to the secret transcript of the December 4–9 meetings between Truman and Atlee. Within days of the meeting, Moscow knew that UN forces would not use the atomic bomb in Korea or against Communist China.[21]

Although the British Foreign Office later tried to mask Maclean's access to classified materials during the Korean War, the evidence is overwhelming that he was deeply involved in espionage.[22] The information Maclean relayed to Moscow cost thousands of American and South Korean lives. Former Secretary of State Dean Rusk, who was assistant secretary of state for Far Eastern Affairs during the Korean War, wrote concerning Philby, Burgess, and Maclean: "It can be assumed that (1) anything we in our government knew about Korea would have been known at the British Embassy and (2) that officers in the Embassy of the rank of these three would have known what the British Embassy knew."[23]

In July 1953, half a year after Dwight Eisenhower's inauguration as president, he fulfilled his campaign promise to end the Korean War. The cease fire along a demilitarized zone at the 38th parallel still remains in place despite signs of rapprochement between North and South Korea.

★ ★ ★

The few voices who suggested that the enormous accomplishment of the Army's Signals Intelligence in decoding VENONA be made public were stilled by 1950. From their first encounter with the telegrams, the decoders had been under the restrictions of military secrecy never to speak the code name or reveal its contents. Now the president and his select circle who knew about VENONA had buried it below the level of public knowledge or discourse, meaning that everyone who knew the secrets would carry them to the grave.

However, every secret is "a heavy kind of chain" to carry, and comes to have a life of its own.[24] J. Edgar Hoover was frustrated by his inability to use VENONA messages as evidence in courts of law. He was irate that Judith Coplon was able to walk away free after she had been apprehended in the act of giving classified documents to her Soviet handler and had been convicted. She was the first undercover source to be recognized by a description of her activities in VENONA messages.

Hoover and his friend and frequent dinner companion, Senator Joseph McCarthy, were photographed together at horse race tracks in the years before the Wisconsin senator made his famous speech in West Virginia on February 9, 1950. Before a crowd in Wheeling, McCarthy waved a paper in the air that was purported to be a list of 209 known communist agents who had not been removed from their U.S. government jobs. The number he named was a fascinating one. On one hand, it could have been the exact figure from SIGINT decoders of VENONA. On the other hand, it could have been the number of State Department workers whom an internal loyalty board of review had listed as unreliable; that number was 283, minus the 74 who had voluntarily resigned.[25] However, McCarthy had only a number, without names.

Hoover's frustration, known within the FBI, plus the uncannily exact number and the lack of names lend credence to the theory that Hoover had vented his anger to his race track companion without divulging names or details.[26] This embodies two possibilities: either McCarthy absorbed the outline of what he heard from Hoover and turned it into a four-year scourge of American society to rid it of communists, or he was Hoover's pawn in a campaign to exert pressure on the White House to force action on the damaging information gathered in VENONA.

Wheeling was only the beginning. McCarthy repeated his accusations from college platforms, in the Senate, on radio, and on the new medium of television.

His attacks released a flood of long-repressed venom of neighbor against neighbor, of academic rivals, creating a chance to get enemies fired from jobs on the basis of their left wing beliefs or associations. Much of this history of anger at communist sympathies was left over from the bitterness of the Depression years. Hoover watched his old friend ranting without control, causing destruction to the stability of Americans' civic trust in each other, and he withdrew his support. McCarthy's excessive behavior had become a political liability.

Even the closest friends of Joseph McCarthy knew him as "an amiable pal without a deep sense of responsibility." The son of one of McCarthy's frequent companions related that his father arrived for lunch at the senator's office expecting a sandwich. McCarthy suggested that they go to a restaurant. He then called his friend to a back room in which constituents' mail was piled on a table. McCarthy opened a few letters until he found a $50 cash contribution. "Now we can go out for lunch," McCarthy said, pocketing the money.[27]

On November 6, 1953, Eisenhower's attorney general, Herbert Brownell, charged ex-President Truman with covering up a dangerous Soviet agent in his administration. In a speech to the Executives' Club of Chicago designed to defend the Eisenhower administration's record of vigilance in security matters, Brownell stated, "Harry Dexter White was a Russian spy." During the speech, he held up a document that J. Edgar Hoover had sent to Truman in 1946 just before Truman appointed White executive director of the International Monetary Fund; the document warned Truman that White was a controlled pawn of Moscow.[28] The White House had alerted two congressional investigatory committees to Brownell's speech only a few hours before he delivered it; Senator William Jenner issued a subpoena to General Harry Vaughn, Truman's military aide in the White House, to testify in executive session before the Senate Internal Security Committee. The chairman of the House Committee on Un-American Activities, Harold Velde (R.-Ill.), went so far as to subpoena Truman, who refused to appear, invoking executive privilege. Brownell's speech created a national furor, with congressional Democrats coming to Truman's defense.

Vaughn claimed that he and President Truman never saw the report. Later James Byrnes affirmed that they had received it but that President Truman had decided not to hold up White's appointment. At first Truman was stunned by the charge and said, "I don't know what they're talking about," then recalled that "as soon as we found out White was wrong we fired him." Ten days after Brownell's speech Truman defended his actions in a national radio and television address, explaining it would have been impossible to convict White with the evidence the government had in hand. Since White's appointment had already been approved by the Senate, Truman said he had decided to keep White in the government in a job where he could do little harm while the secret investigation was going forward. "He was separated from government service promptly, when the necessity for secrecy . . . by the FBI had come to an end," Truman said. To explain his initial lapse of memory about the circumstances of the FBI report, Truman pointed out that Eisenhower did not remember that he had met White in 1944 in a conference to discuss plans for postwar Europe.[29]

Hoover could let some of Truman's errors of fact go by, but he felt impelled to correct the impression that he had concurred in White's appointment to the IMF in order to continue surveillance on him. Hoover's testimony was the first time an FBI director appeared before a congressional investigating committee. Hoover stressed in his opening statement that the FBI does not express opinions or draw conclusions. He described seven communications sent to the Truman White House from November 8, 1945, to July 24, 1946, that should have convinced the president that White was a security risk. Then he stated the correction to Truman's speech that was the reason for his public testimony: "I did not enter into any agreement . . . to shift White from . . . the Treasury Department to the International Monetary Fund," refuting Truman's excuse that keeping White in the government was for further surveillance. Senator McClellan restated the question to allow Hoover to reiterate his denial that there had been any such conference between the White House and the FBI to form such a plan. Hoover added that, if it were up to him, he would have fired Harry Dexter White.[30]

Brownell later testified before the Senate Internal Security Subcommittee that much of the evidence against White was received by "wiretap" and was in secret FBI files, and therefore could not be used in court. He did not disclose that some of the wiretaps were carried out after White was no longer a government employee, which meant they were illegal and an invasion of privacy. No one made public reference to VENONA, even though clear evidence of White's work for the Soviets had been identified in the KGB intercepts by 1950. Brownell stated that he believed in disclosure of secrets, but the Eisenhower administration made no attempt to tell the public about VENONA. It remained secret.

Charge and countercharge continued for weeks. The Republicans' accusation that the Truman administration had been "soft on communism" was blunted by the distaste created by impugning Truman's loyalty. Brownell had made a national figure out of White, who had been dead for five years. He had also questioned the loyalty and patriotism of Truman. He had gone too far. The administration warned him to tone down his rhetoric, and J. Edgar Hoover reminded him that his statements that White was a spy did not come from any FBI report. Eisenhower held a press conference in which he held out the hope that "communists in government" would not be an issue in the 1954 congressional election.[31] Such bipartisan peace was not to be; Brownell's attack on Truman over the White case was one more stroke of the ax that sundered the American voting public into two bitterly antagonistic blocs for the rest of the century.

On December 14, 1953, at the urging of Admiral Lewis Strauss, chairman of the Atomic Energy Commission (AEC), President Eisenhower demonstrated his security consciousness when he ordered a "blank wall between Oppenheimer and any secret data," ending the Los Alamos director's access to the secrets of atomic science that he had led in creating. This action was based on Oppenheimer's past communist affiliations and his lies to Army security in the early 1940s when he was hired to head the Manhattan Project.

McCarthy continued to attack the Republican administration, instilling a sense of crisis to the task of bringing about the end of his irresponsible accusations. McCarthy went too far when he decided to begin investigating what he called communist activities in the U.S. Army. By attacking the U.S. Army as another hotbed of communists, based on the automatic promotion of an Army dentist who was a communist, McCarthy was drawing attention to the institution identified with the president. Would Eisenhower be next on his list? Supporters of Eisenhower were afraid that past criticisms of the president, at the end of the war when he was directing the occupation of Germany, would find their way into McCarthy's list of hidden treasons. In 1946 Eisenhower, as Supreme Allied Commander, had appointed a number of American occupation staff members in Berlin who turned out to be communists.

The vitriolic senator placed himself so far to the right of the moderate Republican administration of President Eisenhower that the government set out to destroy his position on the center stage of national politics. Eisenhower and his advisers feared that McCarthy would hurt the party in the 1954 midterm elections. On March 9, 1954, the popular commentator Edward R. Murrow attacked McCarthy in a broadcast that enumerated his misstatements and unwarranted attempts to attach a communist tag on innocent citizens. A fellow Republican, Senator Ralph Flanders, criticized McCarthy in the Senate, and two days later the Army accused him of attempting to get preferential treatment for his aide, David Schine, who had recently been drafted. McCarthy knew he was in trouble.[32] Before the secretary of the Army could confront him in a scheduled hearing, McCarthy latched onto a new, unrelated issue to draw attention away from the criticisms coming at him.

On April 6, McCarthy addressed the nation on television, charging that communists in the American government delayed American research on the hydrogen bomb for eighteen months. He asked rhetorically why had we delayed even while intelligence agencies were reporting that the Soviets were "feverishly pushing their development of the H-Bomb?" With the histrionic oratorical rhythm that was his trademark, McCarthy continued, "And may I say to America tonight that our nation may well die, our nation may well die because of that eighteen month deliberate delay. And I ask you, who caused it? Was it loyal Americans or was it traitors in our government?"[33]

McCarthy's initiative had picked up the echoes of a long-standing argument going on behind the closed doors of the Atomic Energy Commission. The debate had ended with President Truman's decision to build the hydrogen bomb in early 1950. The debate lasted less than four months, not eighteen months. However, what McCarthy had let loose would not end with his demise from the political scene. The arguments over building an H-bomb arose again in the removal of J. Robert Oppenheimer's security clearance.

On December 21, when Oppenheimer was notified of the "blank wall" separating him from government secrets, he received a long letter with the details of the accusations against him from General Kenneth D. Nichols, General Manager of the AEC, with the advice from Strauss that he could resign or defend himself at a hearing in which he could challenge the charges against him. Oppenheimer decided on the hearing in an effort to clear his name. By the time the hearing commenced on April 12, 1954, James Reston of the *New York Times* had gotten wind of the charges and urged Oppenheimer to go public with a defense in the press, disclosing the contents of Nichols' letter and rebutting them. Thus, on April 13, the news of Oppenheimer's suspension from his position as a consultant to the AEC and Nichols' letter appeared in the *New York Times* and the *New York Herald Tribune*. The AEC responded with a statement explaining that a Presidential Executive Order of April 1953, requiring a review of dossiers of employees and consultants about whom there was "derogatory information," had led to Oppenheimer's suspension after scrutiny by the commission and the Justice Department.

The charges against Oppenheimer stated that he had hired known communists to work at Los Alamos, and had attended meetings with Communist Party members but had declined to identify them when questioned by the FBI in 1946. Most damning was an incident in 1943. George Charles Eltenton, an English chemical engineer working at the nearby Shell Development Company plant in California, had approached a friend of Oppenheimer's to ask an unnamed person for scientific information on secret work being done at the Radiation Laboratory in Berkeley; there, one of two main efforts, the electromagnetic process, was being carried out to produce Uranium 235.

When Oppenheimer became director of the Los Alamos Atomic Laboratory and had to reveal all his affiliations, he told this story to the security officers who approved his clearance. Oppenheimer said that the secretary of the Soviet consulate in San Francisco had requested Eltenton to make the approach. Oppenheimer later described Eltenton's appeal for compassion for the Russians who were then "battling for their lives,"•but were not given radar and the products of American research because of difficulties in the "relations between these two allies." Oppenheimer reported that he and his friend, whom he later identified to be Haakon Chevalier, a leftist French professor at the University of California, believed it was treason to give the Soviets this information. (The Soviets managed to get the radar and other information through Julius Rosenberg and his spy ring.) The incident, and especially the manner in which Oppenheimer reported it when questioned by Army counterintelligence officers, had made him an object of investigations and later came to plague him in 1954 in his security hearing. Oppenheimer had first told the story in a way that would not implicate him or Chevalier, and then changed it to admit that Eltenton had approached his friend Chevalier to approach Oppenheimer. Changing the story, and saying that he was the object of the approach, caused his report to be suspect.

At the time that Oppenheimer first reported the incident, when he went to work at Los Alamos in 1943, Army counterintelligence held a suspicious view of him. "J. R. Oppenheimer is playing a key part in the attempts of the Soviet Union to secure, by espionage, highly secret information which is vital to the security of the United States," reported Army Captain Peer DeSilva, a member of the security staff. He said that Oppenheimer had "allowed a tight clique of known communists or communist sympathizers to grow up about him within the project, until they comprise a large proportion of the key personnel in whose hands the success and secrecy of the project is entrusted." DeSilva judged Oppenheimer to be either naive, or clever and disloyal.[34]

By this time the counterintelligence staff knew that since February 1943, the Soviets had been receiving secret material on the development of the atomic bomb. They believed that Soviet intelligence had penetrated the Uranium 235 separation plants in Tennessee, the weapons laboratory at Los Alamos, and the plutonium research center in Chicago. Soviet intelligence officers also had assets working on the electromagnetic process of separation at the Radiation Laboratory in Berkeley. In questioning Oppenheimer about the Eltenton approach, Lieutenant Colonel John Lansdale, chief security officer for the atomic bomb project, said that it was "an actual attempt at espionage against probably the most important thing we're doing," yet Oppenheimer had delayed reporting what he knew and refused to tell the real circumstances and names involved. Nevertheless, Oppenheimer's services were judged to be irreplaceable, and he was given clearance to continue working.[35]

After his success in developing the atomic bomb and sharing in the decision to use it against Japan in 1945, Oppenheimer had been an adviser to various government agencies. He attempted, with others, to establish international control of atomic energy, which did not succeed because of Soviet objections. In 1947, Oppenheimer became chairman of the General Advisory Commission (GAC) of the AEC. He also did work for the State Department and the Defense Department at the same time that he became director of the Institute for Advanced Study at Princeton; he stayed at Princeton for twenty years.

A second group of charges against Oppenheimer in the letter from General Nichols concerned the decision to develop an H-bomb. Nichols' letter said that in 1945 Oppenheimer's opinion was that an H-bomb was feasible, and then in 1949 he had opposed it, even after President Truman had decided to go ahead with developing "the super." Since Oppenheimer had become chairman of the

General Advisory Committee of the AEC, his powerful voice had "definitely slowed down its development."[36] This internal debate appeared to be the basis for McCarthy's accusation that treason was the cause of delay in developing the hydrogen bomb.

On the same day that the correspondence between Oppenheimer and the AEC was published, the *Christian Science Monitor* reported that McCarthy had been preparing a case against Oppenheimer. Soon after the presidential order that set the hearings in motion, *Fortune* magazine had published an anonymous attack on Oppenheimer, particularly relating to his attitude toward the H-bomb. McCarthy would have launched an immediate inquiry through the Permanent Investigations Subcommittee of the Senate but was dissuaded because of the security issues involved.

A cautious but favorable statement by "a high Administration official," soon publicly identified as Vice President Richard Nixon, backed Oppenheimer. "Dr. Oppenheimer, at least on the evidence I have seen, in my opinion is a loyal American. On the other hand the information in his file is voluminous and makes a prima facie case of security risk. . . . If the man is not a security risk, if he is not subject to blackmail he should have a right to work for the government." Nixon, noting Oppenheimer's left wing background, added that each case should be judged on its merits "particularly when dealing with an ideology which during the nineteen thirties had such an appeal among the intelligentsia and various other groups."[37]

Oppenheimer's friends argued that his flirtation with communism had sprung from a deep humanitarian concern and not from anything that could be classified as treason. In a 1948 interview in *Time* magazine, Oppenheimer defended his left wing past and communist associations when he said: "I'm not ashamed of it; I'm more ashamed of the lateness. Most of what I believed then now seems complete nonsense, but it was an essential part of becoming a whole man. If it hadn't been for this late but indispensable education, I couldn't have done the job at Los Alamos at all."[38]

Nixon knew Oppenheimer's background because Nixon had served on the House Committee on Un-American Activities, but he believed that left wing associations in Oppenheimer's past were not proof he was undependable. General Leslie Groves, with whom Oppenheimer worked at Los Alamos, offered a statement of confidence, as did the head of the AEC and the special assistant to the secretary of defense for research and development. The fact that Oppenheimer's clearance had been reaffirmed in a full-scale internal review of his record in February 1947, and in later routine reviews, had no influence when Eisenhower decided to suspend him.

At the time of his third clearance in 1950, Oppenheimer stood accused by two former communists, Paul and Sylvia Crouch, of lending his house for a special, secret section Communist Party meeting in 1941, which he attended. They said

Oppenheimer socialized with the same group of communists at later gatherings. Oppenheimer denied that he had been a Communist Party member or had offered his home for such a meeting, and his clearance went through.[39]

There was a clear differentiation between Oppenheimer's communist friendships and attendance at party meetings before he became the director of Los Alamos, and his postwar anticommunism.[40] Should the father of the atomic bomb have his access to classified materials taken away, or were his left wing views and communist associations prior to government service irrelevant? Thirty-eight witnesses testified in his favor; one, his Los Alamos colleague and H-bomb advocate, Edward Teller, spoke against him.

The top figures who had hired Oppenheimer and worked with him, including James Conant, General Groves, and Vannevar Bush testified that they had always known about his communist associates and left wing connections. They unanimously agreed that his service to the atomic energy program was so valuable that his dismissal would be a "very serious blow to our progress in this field."[41]

Oppenheimer's defense did not make sufficient use of his postwar criticisms of Soviet policy and contrast them to his beliefs and his friends from an earlier period. Instead, the prosecution exploited its advantage by describing at length his earlier associations and communist connections. His lawyer's failure to defend Oppenheimer's judgment and eliminate doubts about his loyalty, based on his character and associations that were well known to the security authorities from the beginning of his employment in the government, lost the battle.[42] When Oppenheimer was asked why he had not told the truth in the first place about the Eltenton approach and Chevalier's role as a go-between to get to Oppenheimer, his answer was, "Because I was an idiot."[43] Oppenheimer's voice of authority had been reduced to a whimper.

The second part of the charges against him, that he had a negative effect on efforts to build the H-bomb, was as bewildering then as it appears now. His defenders asked why he should be attacked for sincere opinions given in a losing argument.

In the fall of 1944, Oppenheimer is on record as a supporter of research on a thermonuclear bomb, but Teller testified that after the explosions of the atomic bomb in July and August 1945, Oppenheimer worked against its development. Oppenheimer's recollection was sharply different; he recalled that General Groves was in charge of further work at Los Alamos, and he did not want to start new projects before the Atomic Energy Commission was formed and could make the decision, which would not be until January 1, 1947. Teller continued to press for the H-bomb: he appeared before Senator Brien McMahon's Special Committee on Atomic Energy and convened a conference at Los Alamos to present the arguments.[44]

Oppenheimer's early inclination after the war was for international control of atomic weapons. In 1946 Oppenheimer was a principal member of the group under Deputy Secretary of State Dean Acheson that drafted the American plan for international control of atomic energy. The American proposal was popularly known as the Baruch Plan, after financier Bernard Baruch, whom Truman had appointed to present it to the United Nations; it failed to win Soviet approval.[45] When the Soviets rejected the plan, and proceeded with the takeover of Czechoslovakia and the Berlin Blockade, Oppenheimer began to think in terms of strategic capability. Oppenheimer hardly sounded like he was following the communist line in 1946 when he urged the United States to break off negotiations with the Soviet Union over international control of atomic energy. To continue negotiating, he said, would "give the Soviets chances . . . to dilute the strength of the plan . . . and to win propaganda victories." The Soviets would never accept international control because it would mean lifting the Iron Curtain, the breakdown of their closed society, he said. He further asserted that "the United States should never accept a prohibition of atomic weapons, giving up its nuclear advantage, without a comparable concession from the Soviets, such as opening their closed borders for the free movement of people and ideas."[46]

However, he drew the line at the idea of total war to destroy Soviet power; he believed it would destroy international relationships and our own way of life.[47]

After the AEC took over in January 1947, nuclear policy decisions went to the General Advisory Committee, to which Oppenheimer was elected chairman. He later testified that "we concluded that the principal job of the Commission was to provide atomic weapons and good atomic weapons and many atomic weapons."[48] Oppenheimer was interested in how they could be used in air defense of the continental United States. Research continued on fusion, to produce an H-bomb, but there was no military demand for an unknown, unproven weapon. In the face of financial and moral indecision, and the lack of priority given to the project, it continued but without official enthusiasm for it. Therefore the research group at Los Alamos working on the H-bomb dwindled to a dedicated few. All members of the AEC who were eligible to testify supported Oppenheimer in the hearings.

Oppenheimer became identified with the use of tactical atomic weapons for air defense of the United States when he participated in two study groups, Project Vista at the California Institute of Technology in Pasadena in 1951 and the MIT Lincoln Summer Study in 1952. These studies were related to an ongoing debate over the development of strategic air power, whose enthusiasts argued that swift penetration by a bombing force that flew deep into enemy territory could annihilate industrial capacity, opposing air forces on the ground, and civilian morale in a blast of armed might. Such a large, fast, and surprising force would reduce future wars to a few short weeks. The origin of this concept was a 1921 book, *The Command of the Air*, by the Italian strategist Giulio Douhet. It grew out of the long stalemates and heavy casualties of World War I and was still in play in the NATO attack on Serb forces in Kosovo in 1999. This approach required an air force that received the major share of the defense budget.

The strategic, big-air-force proponents interpreted the experience of the second world war as a rationale for their argument. They pointed to Dresden, Tokyo, Hiroshima, and Nagasaki. The opposing view was that Army and Navy forces had broken the defense lines of the Germans and Japanese and left them vulnerable to the air strikes that had such devastating effect.[49] The Strategic Air Command (SAC) became for its admirers the foundation of American military and defense policies, and they asked for seventy combat groups to provide national security. Although the Air Force share of the defense budget rose to 30 percent in 1949, that branch of the military believed they were the keystone of defense and wanted two-thirds of the budget.

Oppenheimer believed that the punishing effects of strategic air raids would create global instability and darken the name of democracy. He wanted instead to develop a wide range of battlefield nuclear weapons. New, fifty-kiloton atomic bombs—twice as powerful as the bomb used against Nagasaki—were tested and became the focus of the Defense Department. Oppenheimer's plan had backers in the Navy and Army, but it was a dissent from Air Force orthodoxy. His analysis that the atomic bomb would in the future be a deterrent instead of a weapon was an anathema to the Air Force.

Oppenheimer argued that atomic weapons opened a new era in which the use of strategic air power had to be rethought.[50] In the spring of 1948, the Sandstone series of tests in the Pacific proved the viability of new, more powerful, and more agile nuclear weapons for battlefield tactical use, and also the potential of nuclear power for submarine and aircraft propulsion. Oppenheimer chaired a group at the Pentagon in 1948 to examine these advances, which demonstrated that small amounts of fissionable material could develop large yields, thus permitting the miniaturization of atomic bombs into battlefield and tactical weapons.[51] Oppenheimer's enthusiasm for the new weapons did not endear him to the Air Force, which was to become his nemesis in the hearings.

By 1950 the United States was fighting communist armies in Korea, and the Chinese had entered the war. The Air Force was frustrated by not being allowed to drop atomic bombs on the industrial cities of Manchuria; it had the most powerful weapons yet invented but could not use them. At the same time, new tactical atomic weapons were developed and tested for ground warfare, taking away the Air Force's monopoly on delivering nuclear bombs.

Oppenheimer contributed to a report on the way tactical nuclear weapons could be used to support ground operations. Teller argued for a tactical H-bomb, which was spurned as unwieldy and unfeasible. One of the results of the report was the call for a vow of "no first use" of an atomic weapon, which negated the Air Force's concept of swift surprise and a first strike. The Air Force was displeased by the report and even though Oppenheimer was not associated with the no-first-strike vow, he became the target of the Air Forces's ire and objections.

Oppenheimer again became the target of SAC for his part in a study at MIT's Lincoln Laboratory in 1952, which proposed four concentric defense rings: ground-to-air missiles and antiaircraft guns, short-range interceptor aircraft, a distant early warning system with more interceptors, and finally a SAC force to attack and destroy Soviet air power at its home bases. The Air Force believed the plan was designed to curtail and eliminate strategic air power by increasing funds for air defense at the expense of SAC, and they blamed Oppenheimer.

Meanwhile, a team had formed around Teller to lobby for development of the hydrogen bomb. They included Wendell M. Latimer, professor of chemistry at the University of California, who believed the American response to the future challenge from the Soviets was "twiddling our thumbs and doing nothing," due to Oppenheimer's influence. Another was Admiral Lewis Strauss, a member of the Atomic Energy Commission, who had been a member of the review board that affirmed Oppenheimer's security clearance in 1947; he now wanted it taken away. Strauss' perseverance in attacking Oppenheimer created the impression, at the time, that he knew McCarthy was about to denounce him for approving Oppenheimer's clearance in 1947 and that he was sacrificing Oppenheimer to save himself.[52]

Senators Bourke Hickenlooper and Brien McMahon criticized the AEC. General Hoyt Vandenberg, Air Force chief of staff, was a foe of Oppenheimer and of the air defense system he had proposed in 1947. Vandenberg was in favor of a long-range bomber program that would carry H-bombs. The bomber program would bring large new allocations of funds to the Air Force. Strauss was also a big-bomber, big-bomb advocate.[53] Also in Teller's camp were Ernest Lawrence and Luis Alvarez, who had worked on the fusion bomb since their early days together at Berkeley. Other scientists, such as Karl Compton and John Von Neumann, believed that the United States had to build the most advanced weapon possible. Teller had the support of Thomas Finletter, secretary of the Air Force. The Soviet Union exploded its first atomic bomb on August 29, 1949, three years before it was predicted, which strengthened the case of those in favor of the H-bomb.

In January and March 1951, President Truman approved continued work on the superbomb, and later "all out development of hydrogen bombs." Both the failure of negotiations for international control of atomic energy and the explosion of the first Soviet atomic bomb had created an atmosphere of inevitability regarding development of the H-bomb. There were few voices of dissent in Congress or the nation.

Teller joined a group at the Livermore Laboratory in California to develop thermonuclear weapons.[54] Most important to Teller, then and to the present, was his sense of scientific mission; he believed that scientists should pursue the possibilities of understanding the physical universe as far as their abilities could take them. Scientists should reach out for knowledge without regard to what would become of their creations, the weapons that emerged from their discoveries. "We would be unfaithful to the tradition of Western civilization if we were to shy away from exploring the limits of human achievement. It is our specific duty as scientists to explore and explain," he wrote after the hearing.[55] He reiterated the same credo at Stanford University in 1998.[56]

Oppenheimer suffered the brunt of Teller's wrath and the venom of his associates who wanted the H-bomb to become a reality. Anger at its delay centered against Oppenheimer even though he had been one among many who opposed the "super." The advocates of the H-bomb, in league with the Air Force, were able to bring together a host of destructive forces to question Oppenheimer's credibility and take away his security clearance. The H-bomb would justify the bombers, which had taken a decade to develop and were now ready to use and duplicate. They would make the Air Force a new power center.

Senator McMahon called Teller into his office and showed him the charges enumerated against Oppenheimer. Teller said in 1998, "I listened and nodded."[57] The union of Teller, thirsting for support to crown his work on the H-bomb, and the Air Force, in a tug of war with the Army for funds to build an intercontinental bomber fleet, was the winning side at the Oppenheimer hearing.

The hearings that ended the government career of the father of the atomic bomb were a landmark in the partisan split between American political parties. However, the emotional turmoil surrounding the event in the press obscured the truth and layers of meaning behind the hearings.

Throughout the hearings, the charges against Oppenheimer centered around (1) his early communist connections and the lies he told to make them appear innocent of subversion; and (2) his sincere belief in and championing of the superiority of small nuclear weapons over the H-bomb. Only once, in the report by Captain DeSilva of Los Alamos security, was there a hint that Oppenheimer was employing known communists in the Manhattan Project and entrusting the nation's secrets to them. His conversations with the Soviet consul general in San Francisco, Gregory Kheifetz, which resulted in his becoming a willing source for the Soviet Union of classified military secrets, and his obedience to Soviet intelligence in separating himself as an open member of the American Communist Party to become an unlisted member from 1942 to 1944, were unknown to the Atomic Energy Commission and his prosecutors.

Nevertheless, for good reasons or for bad, his assailants were able to remove Oppenheimer's security clearance and, aided by his own testimony, stain his reputation. In the final verdict of the hearings, Oppenheimer's contract renewal and the restitution of his clearance were denied because of character flaws and poor judgment, not disloyalty to his country. The ironies inherent in this historical struggle for funds and power remained a secret for forty years. Then Pavel Sudoplatov told his story, and Moscow researchers dug up the memorandum reporting that Oppenheimer had agreed to cooperate in a subtle form of espionage: he never handed documents to any Soviet courier but knowingly facilitated the "sharing" of atomic secrets. The postman always rings twice.

The arguments over defense against a missile attack on the continental United States and over the value of rapid surprise attack by strategic air power are still with us.[58] The political divisiveness of McCarthy's accusations and of the Oppenheimer hearings still resounds between American conservatives and liberals. On both sides, most Americans have forgotten that it was a struggle for funds between strategic air power and battlefield nuclear weapons, between the U.S. Air Force and the U.S. Army, that brought Oppenheimer down; they remember only questions of disloyalty, which were not germane to the final verdict that removed from government defense deliberations its most active, brilliant, and devoted scientific servant. History will judge the balance between his contributions and his betrayal of confidence and trust in wartime.

★ ★ ★
10 The Beginning of the End
of the Soviet Empire

In November 1948, William Fisher, later known in the West as Rudoph Abel,[1] became the chief illegal *rezident* in the United States. Fisher crossed into the United States from Canada on November 17 and met Iosef Romvoldovich Grigulevich (ARTHUR or ARTUR in VENONA) in New York City on November 26. Grigulevich gave him $1,000 and three documents in the name of Robert Goldfus: a genuine birth certificate, a forged draft card, and a forged tax return.[2] By 1952 Abel had a forged American passport with a "legend" or "cover life" to protect him.

Fisher/Abel lived unobtrusively in Brooklyn, New York, from where he directed preparations to take over the Western Hemisphere in case the rising tensions between the United States and the Soviet Union turned into a new world war.

In secret Soviet archives, the future war was called the Special Period. Fisher created a network in California and the east coast of the United States, Mexico, Brazil, and Argentina. Their targets were military installations around Long Beach, California, on the west coast, and port facilities in Norfolk and Philadelphia on the east coast. He had permanent radio communication with combat troops in Latin America ready to move north through Mexico disguised as seasonal workers.

When FBI counterintelligence officers arrested "Rudolph Abel" in 1957, his captors did not know that his mission was to operate an underground insurgency network ready to go to war against the United States. Among his possessions, the FBI found connections to Helen Sobell, wife of Morton, who belonged to Julius Rosenberg's ring. Abel also had a connection to Morris and Lona Cohen, couriers for atomic espionage.[3] The first indication of his espionage goals came in Sudoplatov's memoir, nearly forty years later. His arrest was a celebrated case, in which he was later freed in return for the release of Francis Gary Powers, an exchange that took place on the Glienicke bridge dividing East and West Germany.

Grigulevich, the man who greeted Fisher, had from 1941 to 1944 been NKVD illegal *rezident* or *grupovod* (group leader) in Argentina and Latin America, subordinated to the *rezidentura* of NKVD in the United States.

The Spanish Civil War of 1936–1939 was two wars on the same soil: Franco against the Republicans and Stalinists versus Trotskyites. When it was over, it had spilled a river of blood. A flood of refugees fled to Moscow and to Mexico City, then on to the rest of South America. For the Soviets, it was a multiple opportunity: first, to eliminate Trotsky, who had settled outside Mexico City, by using Spanish revolutionaries who could operate unnoticed in Mexico; second, to organize a Spanish Communist Party in Latin and South America, directed by Moscow, that would return to Spain and take back the government from Franco's fascists; and third, to establish revolutionary communist parties in every country from the Texas border to the Antarctic Circle to be a military beachhead for the Soviet Union in a coming war with the United States.

The assassination of Trotsky in Mexico, directed from Moscow, was the Soviets' only success in this list of goals until Fidel Castro took over Cuba. It was Castro's own revolution, without Soviet help, but Moscow latched on to his coattails.

In Mexico, Grigulevich led a troop of inexperienced assassins in the first attempt to kill Trotsky, who escaped by hiding under a bed.

One of Grigulevich's assignments was to organize the Spanish Communist Party that would retake Spain from Franco. This meant trying to soothe the differences between Spanish émigré factions competing for leadership of the resistance movement. Eventually Delores Ibarruri won out over Jesús Hernandez, who attempted to displace her dominance.[4] Their argument takes up pages of VENONA. The Soviets supplied arms and radio equipment, and helped root out Franco infiltrators.

Another of Grigulevich's assignments in Mexico, and later in other countries of Latin and South America, was to organize a parallel illegal network separate from the Spanish émigrés. Moscow's two main goals were: (1) to set up a base for diversion operations (sabotage and guerrilla warfare) against the United States in case of war, a war named the "Special Period" in Soviet documents; and (2) to infiltrate governments and political associations to promote local communist parties and Soviet interests.[5]

Grigulevich frequently traveled to the United States, undetected by the FBI. To provide a safe station for his illegals, he bought a drugstore in Santa Fe, New Mexico, which, as described in earlier chapters, was later the gathering point for atomic espionage materials from Los Alamos. Lawrence Duggan supplied confidential information from U.S. government files to ARTHUR's group while the Soviets were normalizing relations with Colombia, Chile, and other countries.[6] Under the banner of hunting Nazis who escaped from Germany, Grigulevich was to keep tabs on American and British policy in South American countries. Grigulevich had an Argentinian passport; he was the son of a pharmacist who owned a drugstore in Argentina. His family, émigrés from Lithuania, was part of the Karayim community, a non-Israelite tribe that adopted Judaism.

After the war, Grigulevich turned from guerrilla warfare to diplomacy. Again his code name changed, now to MAKS, and he was inducted into the Communist Party of the Soviet Union, considered an honor for an agent living abroad. In 1945–1946, he moved to Italy, where he continued to help Spanish guerrillas prepare for retaking Spain from Franco. The guerrilla war in Spain ended in failure in 1950.

Using a Costa Rican passport, he befriended businessmen and officials visiting Italy from his newly adopted country. He followed instructions from Moscow to pay the ministry of foreign affairs to have himself appointed ambassador extraordinary and plenipotentiary of Costa Rica, in Italy and in Yugoslavia simultaneously.

Grigulevich was more successful in playing diplomat than in carrying out assassinations. He worked with Moscow's *rezidents* in Rome between 1944 and 1952. He helped them assess the anticommunist drive in 1948 when Primiro Togliatti, secretary general of the Italian Communist Party, was wounded in an assassination attempt and the communists were ousted from the government. From Vatican sources, MAKS (ARTHUR) learned that the anticommunist drive was limited and the party would not be barred. Therefore the communists should not provoke civil war but wait for another chance. MAKS informed the Soviets that the Italian government knew about communist arms caches kept since the war; he warned that an armed rebellion would fail. Instead he recommended exploiting anti-American sentiments in Italy.

MAKS reported to Moscow Center that Yugoslavia had not joined NATO, but had signed a secret military agreement with Italy and Greece to coordinate efforts in case of attack by the USSR via Hungary and Bulgaria. In 1952 Grigulevich visited Yugoslavia, which under Tito was attempting to remain communist but independent of Moscow. Stalin viewed Tito as another Trotsky, a competitor for leadership of the world communist revolution. MAKS made himself part of a social group close to Tito, and hoped to move quickly to a personal audience with the heroic guerrilla leader who had fought the Germans.

Stalin assigned MAKS to kill Tito and the others present at this meeting by spraying a dose of lung plague bacteria on them, against which MAKS would be inoculated in advance. In MAKS' file is a letter addressed to his wife, Laura, explaining his motives in assassinating Tito; he had written it under orders but never delivered it to her because the operation was aborted. The letter said Tito was one of gravest traitors of the cause of the world communist revolution, and his death was essential for eliminating discord within the world communist community. Tito's death would be a decisive blow to attempts by the United States and Britain to undermine formation of socialist states.[7]

Stalin's death was the event that canceled the order. Beria then wanted MAKS to investigate what the reaction of the Yugoslav government might be to restoring relations with Tito after Stalin's death. Beria summoned MAKS to Moscow,[8] but before he could be dispatched to Belgrade to meet Tito, Beria was deposed. When Khrushchev's faction arrested and executed Beria in 1953, MAKS' connection to Beria forced his retirement from the KGB.

Grigulevich spent the next thirty-five years until his death in 1988 in Moscow. He first worked in the Committee for Cultural Relations with Foreign Countries, later editing the *Journal of Social Sciences* in the Academy of Sciences and socializing with a group of other retired assassins.

Among those working for Fisher were Maria de la Sierra (code name, AFRICA), who had been Trotsky's secretary. Mikhail Filonenko and Vladimir Grinchinko, experts in sabotage who had learned their skills in the war against the Germans, posed as businessmen and offered jobs to seasonal workers who regularly went north to harvest crops. Field workers would be the unsuspected milieu in which the battle groups could move into California.

Another Fisher/Abel network in the United States used German immigrants on the west coast. Fisher recruited Kurt Wissel, a veteran expert in sabotage in prewar Europe, who emigrated to America and rose to the position of senior engineer in a major shipbuilding company on the east coast. Through his connections in the German communities on both coasts, Wissel lined up dockers and military personnel looking for additional income; he set up an infrastructure for sabotage operations and a network of safe apartments strategically located close to port facilities.[9]

The network Grigulevich had set up in Argentina during World War II was taken over and run by Grinchinko and his wife, Simona Krimka. Both were experienced and decorated KGB officers; Simona joined the NKVD in 1936 and served in the clandestine war in Spain.[10] She married Grinchinko in 1945; he had been a counterintelligence and intelligence officer on Soviet and American ships supplying Lend Lease equipment. On the British and American end of the Lend Lease trips, he picked up Western mannerisms and learned how to drive an American car.

Vladimir and Simona arrived in Argentina in 1947 posing as Jewish Holocaust survivors from Czechoslovakia. They were to work primarily on the Special Period. Simona had a married sister in Buenos Aires, and on this basis Simona got Argentinian citizenship; this would allow her husband, a Czech citizen, to remain with her in Buenos Aires.

Grinchinko became the illegal *resident* in Argentina; his wife was his assistant and radio operator. The orders to these decorated heroes were to lie low and to buy up passports and ID cards for support of illegal operations. They had a son and daughter in Argentina.

Mikhail Filonenko was the chief illegal *resident* of the KGB for Latin America in 1954–1960. He supervised the establishment of illegal networks in Brazil, Uruguay, Paraguay, Chile, and Argentina. Filonenko and his wife pretended to be Czechs who escaped from Chinese communists in Shanghai. They made contact with

American Chinese dockworkers who could load explosives on American ships bound for the Korean War, if and when the order came from Moscow. The order never came.

Fisher, operating from New York, ordered Filonenko to report on the Drop-Shot Plan, the proposed U.S. nuclear war attack plan against the Soviet Union. Fisher hoped that Filonenko's source in the Organization of American States (OAS) would help him penetrate the U.S. government's top secrets. The best the OAS spy could supply were documents on the position of the Latin American countries for the coming UN General Assembly session in New York.[11]

Fisher's mission was to learn the extent of military installations and supplies of ammunition available to support rapid American reinforcements if war started in Europe. He was to report shipments of military hardware and ammunition from California to the Chinese Nationalists during the Chinese civil war.

When Fisher was arrested in New York in 1957, Filonenko's network was warned that Fisher knew some covert addresses and meeting points in Latin America. Moscow Center froze use of the network. No one imagined that "Mister Kudna" (Filonenko), the prosperous Czechoslovakian businessman in wholesale trade, import-export operations—who had escaped communists in both Prague in 1947 and Shanghai in 1948, who hobnobbed with prominent Brazilian writers and artists, and who had three children, one born in Rio—was in fact the Soviet illegal *rezident*. On Filonenko's return to the Soviet Union with his family in 1960, he feigned an automobile accident crossing the Czech border into communist-controlled territory so that their deaths could be reported worldwide.

The war anticipated in the Special Period never happened. The plan to build up powerful communist parties after diplomatic relations with each state were established in the 1950s never came to pass. However, from Filonenko's reports, the Soviets had a window on the nuances and turmoil in South American and Latin American politics that became their entry card to Castro's successful revolution in Cuba.

When Castro took over in 1959 without any help from the Soviet Union, the Soviets rushed a team of advisers to help him. The Soviets offered oil, an endless market for agricultural products, ideology, and arms, and, for a brief period in 1962, mid-range missiles that could destroy the eastern half of the United States.

Moscow presented Castro a panoply of revolutionary opportunities based on their knowledge of country-by-country, inner circle, high level tensions throughout Latin America. For the next thirty years, Che Guevara's guerrillas and their successors followed these leads but they were no more successful than the Soviets in turning South America into a launching ground for the communist takeover of the United States. Guevara was killed fighting in Bolivia in 1967.

The net effect of these guerrilla uprisings in Latin America, and eventually in Africa, was to broaden the cold war to the Third World. The United States fought back in the Western Hemisphere by supporting the leadership in countries suppressing communist rebellions.

Often the military governments receiving arms and backup from the United States were brutal and excessive in their methods of preventing a communist overthrow of their regimes. The communists succeeded in spreading the judgment among European intellectuals and American academics that American support for rightist governments in Latin America made the United States and the Soviet Union immorally equal. It is called "moral equivalence."

The American half of the equation has flourished; the Soviet half has disappeared into history. At the start of the twenty-first century, the task remains of restoring relations between impoverished Cuba, still communist, and its wealthy neighbor to the north.

★ ★ ★

Maksim Litvinov's death in 1951, followed two years later by the death of Joseph Stalin in 1953, marked the end of the era of the founding Bolshevik revolutionaries. Unlike most of his contemporaries, who started out with Lenin and lived through Stalin's rule, Litvinov was not arrested or tried as an enemy of the people. Instead he argued and disagreed with the totalitarian leader on the most essential issues of their time: the wisdom of the 1939 Nazi-Soviet Pact of Non-Aggression and the postwar division of spheres of influence in Europe. Until he died, Litvinov talked back to Stalin in a stream of memoranda; he stood his ground alone, not part of a faction opposing Stalin.

Litvinov's world view was influenced by ten years' experience in Washington, first visiting as the Soviet foreign minister and later as the Soviet ambassador to the United States. He came armed with a revolutionary craftiness not unlike Stalin's. In 1933, when the United States gave formal recognition to the Soviet Union, Litvinov set two parts of the U.S. executive branch against each other and delayed for a decade the buildup of expertise that Americans needed to deal with the newly established Bolsheviks.

In the exchange of letters between President Roosevelt and Soviet Foreign Minister Litvinov officially establishing recognition of the Soviet Union by the United States are promises not to interfere in the internal affairs of either country, either overtly or covertly. Within days of the signing, Litvinov interfered in a subtle manner that made the White House the source of damage against the State Department. It is a story rarely told. It begins with the official exchange of letters:

The White House, Washington
November 16, 1933
My dear Mr. Litvinov: I am happy to inform you that as a result of our

conversations the Government of the United States has decided to establish normal diplomatic relations with the Government of the Union of Soviet Socialist Republics and to exchange ambassadors. I trust that the relations now established between our peoples may forever remain normal and friendly, and that our Nations henceforth may cooperate for their mutual benefit and for the preservation of the peace of the world.

I am, my dear Mr. Litvinov,
Very sincerely yours,
Franklin D. Roosevelt

Washington
November 16, 1933
My dear Mr. President:

I have the honor to inform you that coincident with the establishment of diplomatic relations between our two Governments it will be the fixed policy of the Government of the Union of Soviet Socialist Republics:

1. To respect scrupulously the indisputable right of the United States to order its own life within its own jurisdiction in its own way and to refrain from interfering in any manner in the internal affairs of the United States, its territories or possessions.

2. To refrain, and to restrain all persons in Government service and all organizations of the Government or under its direct or indirect control, including organizations in receipt of any financial assistance from it, from any act overt or covert liable in any way whatsoever to injure the tranquility, prosperity, order, or security of the whole or any part of the United States, its territories or possessions, and, in particular, from any act tending to incite or encourage armed intervention, or any agitation or propaganda having as an aim, the violation of the territorial integrity of the United States, its territories or possessions, or the bringing about by force of a change in the political or social order of the whole or any part of the United States, its territories or possessions.

I am, my dear Mr. President
Very sincerely yours,
Maksim Litvinov
People's Commissar for Foreign Affairs
Union of Soviet Socialist Republics

During the negotiations over recognition, Litvinov toured the State Department where he was taken to the Division of Eastern European Affairs. There he found an in-depth collection of books and documents on the czarist period, the Bolshevik revolution, and the Communist International, amassed by Robert Francis Kelley, a Russian scholar and diplomat who headed the division. Kelley was training future ambassadors to the Soviet Union such as Charles Bohlen, George Kennan, and Jacob Beam through a system of language and area studies, which included overseas Russian language immersion.[12] Litvinov paid Kelley the bitter compliment of saying that the division had better records on the history of Soviet diplomacy than did the Soviet Foreign Office itself. Then Litvinov complained loudly, "Is this non intervention?"[13] In 1937, an order came from the White House (those affected believed it was initiated by Eleanor Roosevelt) to dismantle the library and disperse it in the Library of Congress; the East European Department was eliminated and moved to the Western European desk. Kelley was sent to a minor post abroad. It took years to regain expertise in the politics and culture of the Soviet Union. By then Stalin, a wartime ally, had become a cold war adversary.

In his memoirs George Kennan pondered,

> I never learned the real background of this curious purge. . . . There is strong evidence that pressure was brought to bear from the White House. I was surprised, in later years, that the McCarthyites and the other right wingers of the early Fifties never got hold of the incident and made capital of it; for here, if ever, was a point at which there was indeed the smell of Soviet influence, or strongly pro-Soviet influence, somewhere in the higher reaches of the government.[14]

Even more curious was the fate of Litvinov, who served as foreign minister of the Soviet Union from 1930 until 1939. Before the signing of the 1939 Nazi-Soviet Pact of Non-Aggression, Stalin found it awkward to keep a Jew as foreign minister, and eased Litvinov out of the job. He lingered in the background until the German invasion of the Soviet Union, when Stalin called on him to serve as ambassador to the United States; Litvinov held this post from December 7, 1941, until mid-1943.

Litvinov met Lenin in 1903 at the second congress of the Russian Socialist Party in London, where he took the Bolshevik side. In the early revolutionary years that followed, Litvinov carried illegal literature into Russia and bought guns in Europe for the Bolsheviks with money from a bank robbery in Tblisi, the capital of Georgia. While buying guns in England, he met his British wife-to-be, Ivy Low, who accompanied him to Moscow and on his travels abroad. Ivy later published fiction and memoirs, and outlived him to tell his story.

Near the end of her life, Ivy described Litvinov's horror in 1939 when he learned that Stalin had signed a pact with Hitler. Litvinov was now out of job, living in isolation in their dacha outside Moscow. "Maksim went almost crazy, you know; never seeing anybody, or being seen . . . he started a diary . . . he said 'What do they mean? What do they mean? Do they really intend to link up with the Germans?'

... Then he wrote to Stalin: 'The *Rodina* [motherland] is in danger. All differences to be forgotten' if he was wanted in any way. He was. And they did take him on in some ... capacity. ... It humiliated him terribly. ... Then some time after that we went to Washington."[15]

In the American capital, the Soviet ambassador, who spoke fluent English, and his artistic, literary, avant-garde, British-born wife were sought after both by the American left and Washington socialites. Litvinov had a close relationship with FDR's confidant, Harry Hopkins; Litvinov visited Hopkins' home and sat on his bed to discuss problems when Hopkins was ill.[16]

Ivy continued in her oral history interview:

He wanted to stay ... [when he was recalled for consultations in 1943] I wouldn't. He went nearly mad ... he wanted to stay ... such an awful time ... what he longed for more than anything else ... he did not want to go back to Russia. It was not because he was afraid of his own fate but he was so longing to put down his ideas about it all. He thought he knew what went wrong with the Revolution ... he longed to tell the world from America. ... Of course he could not do that without staying behind—he was longing to—it is a great tragedy that he did not. So he started dictating to me his autobiography but he could not. ... He did quite a lot but did not get very far ... there were these pages which he typed out himself with two fingers in the dacha after the German pact ... no, after war was declared. ...

We had what they call angels ... we had boys [guarding them at the dacha]. We typed and typed ... [Maksim] carefully left it out on his desk. He wanted Stalin to see it ... hoping that while he was asleep they would come and copy it.

They could have photographed it ... they were such a low set ... this manuscript, which *was* dynamite, he took with him to Washington, left with me and said don't bring it back with you. Take care of it. ...

I stayed on when he ... was called back ... for consultations. Of course we knew he would never come [to America] again. He did nothing but quarrel with Stalin—unappeaseably [sic] quarrel with Stalin ... with Molotov ... with everybody. ... He was very bitter, he was terribly bitter. ... He wanted a second front ... he felt awfully stultified and frustrated because he couldn't do a thing in Washington.[17]

By 1943 Stalin had developed a personal relationship with Roosevelt and no longer wanted or needed to rely on Litvinov in Washington. He recalled Litvinov and replaced him. From then on, Stalin would deal directly with Roosevelt.

On January 20, 1943, Ivy wrote to an "intimate" friend in New York, Joseph

Freeman, "the only love of my life." Freeman was one of the editors of the communist journal *New Masses*:

> From the very first we both said we felt we should never go back, should die in the new world . . . if it weren't for the children he'd simply write and break off with them, and calculating, calculating what we'd have to live on . . . the chief reason he wants to stay is to write his memoir and show the world. . . .[18]

Litvinov departed for Moscow on May 7, 1943, leaving Ivy to follow later with their household goods. He told her not to bring his typed memoir back to the Soviet Union. "Well, he left me with his papers. . . . He left me, on flimsy cigarette paper, in Russian, this thing that he had typed." Ivy did not know what to do with the manuscript so she consulted Freeman. Together they placed the papers in a bank vault because "he couldn't bear it that this document . . . should die . . . should be lost. . . . It had to be paid for every month. I hadn't any money—Joe hadn't any money. . . . "[19]

In August Litvinov was demoted from the rank of ambassador. He sent Ivy a letter by courier instructing her to send his warm clothes and to clear his writing desk. Ivy left for Moscow via Vladivostok in November and arrived at the end of the year. In Moscow they felt "occasional moments of panic," fearing arrest. She kept a suitcase packed; he kept a loaded pistol at his side. In December 1945, two and a half years after she had given Freeman her husband's manuscript, Ivy wrote to Freeman appealing to him to destroy it. She made sure Freeman carried out her wishes by having another friend, Edward Carter of the Institute for Pacific Relations, witness the destruction of the papers. She said in her letter that her life had been poisoned by anxiety over the fate of the memoirs, referring to her husband's reproaches during this period of "struggle and anxiety."[20]

Litvinov died on December 31, 1951. Some of his memoranda to Stalin remained intact, and he had published an account of his youth in 1946. Within a year of his death, a manuscript purporting to be the journal notes of Maksim Litvinov, entrusted to Aleksandra Kollontai, the Soviet ambassador to Sweden and a close friend of Litvinov's, appeared in Europe. In the mid-1950s, the KGB called Ivy to the Lyubyanka Headquarters and questioned her about Maksim's memoirs. Ivy did not know what to say, but her hesitation ended and she told what she knew when she was shown yellowed papers that looked like those left behind in New York. The KGB did not allow her to read them. In 1955, *Notes for a Journal* was published in London by André Deutsch under a cloud of controversy.[21] The introduction by E. H. Carr acknowledged quarrelsome sections of the book, and critics suggested it might have been written by the émigré writer George Bessedovsky who defected in Paris from the Soviet diplomatic corps in 1929. The notes

Litvinov would have expanded into a book if he had defected were lost to the world. "Might have been some book, might have been some book," Ivy wrote.[22] In fact, the notes may still be in the SVR's possession.

When I (Leona) was having tea with Ivy about twice a week during 1969–1970 in Moscow, she did not discuss Maksim's memoirs. She was careful about conversations in her apartment, which might have been bugged. Instead we talked about Jane Austen and the Palliser Series by Anthony Trollope. Ivy said that early in their marriage she had given Maksim Trollope's nineteenth-century works with the promise, "If you read these you will know everything you need to know about British politics." Her social life included dinners at the apartments of Donald Maclean and Kim Philby, who had fled to Moscow in 1950 and 1953. She laughed while she described Melissa Maclean's desire to put up curtains and make their living quarters more comfortable. Her husband and his friends warned Melissa that these were bourgeois attitudes.

In 1987, after Ivy's death, the Litvinovs' daughter Tatiana donated her mother's papers to the Hoover Institution Archives at Stanford University.

Included in the bequest are six hastily typed pages, a chronology of Maksim's career dictated to Ivy in English: "Dates That Might Come Handy." The notes are a capsule history, a rare insider's view of the Soviet Union from its outlaw beginnings. The six pages cover the creation of the Soviet state, its fight for international recognition, the post-Kirov internal destruction of dissent in the Soviet Union, and the small events that in retrospect were a sure prelude to world war.

The first pages cover the prerevolutionary period from 1900: Litvinov escaping from jail in Kiev, buying arms, being arrested in Paris with stolen banknotes but being saved from the czarist police by French Minister Aristide Briand, then fighting for the Bolshevik cause among factions at the International Socialist Bureau in London.[23]

On January 3, 1918, the new Bolshevik government appointed Litvinov its first Soviet representative to London, but the British Foreign Office returned his official papers unopened. In June, Lenin appointed him ambassador to the United States; again his application was refused. In August 1918, the Allied Intervention began in Archangel, a port in the northwest USSR; this attack was a futile attempt to overthrow the new Bolshevik government with an expeditionary force. In September 1918, Bruce Lockhart, a British intelligence officer under cover as a diplomat, was arrested in Moscow. The British promptly put Litvinov in Brixton Gaol, a "Guest of His Majesty." In September 1918, the two prisoners were exchanged. Litvinov then wrote to President Wilson, asking him to stop the allied invasion of Russia.

Litvinov's notes for the 1920s record the new Soviet Union's struggle for acceptance at international meetings in Europe and at the League of Nations and their participation in disarmament conferences. In the early years, Litvinov's call for total disarmament was rejected as a communist trick.[24] The notes continue as summarized here (Litvinov's words are in quotation marks).

1920. "Wrangel driven out of the Caucasus" [the White defeat meant the civil war was ending].

1921. Litvinov becomes chief of all Soviet legations abroad.

1922. Litvinov calls disarmament conference in Moscow.

1922. Rapallo Conference. Resuming diplomatic relations with Germany "on the sly."

1923. Ivy and the children move to Moscow, but "Lenin worse (after his stroke)."

1925. Litvinov marks the Locarno Pact of nonaggression among Germany, France, England, Belgium, Italy as the "Beginning of Isolation of Soviet Russia."

June 1926. Churchill gave "virulent anti-Soviet speech."

1927. "Chamberlain in Geneva tries to create anti Soviet front. Briand presiding disagreed."

July 1928. Bought *Mein Kampf.*

1931. "Japan attacks China, Hitler waxing stronger."

1932. French Foreign Minister Herriot and Pierre Cot visit Russia, followed by a nonaggression pact with France. [It is likely that Cot was recruited as a Soviet agent on this visit. He appears in VENONA working for the Soviet Union.]

February 1933. After the Reichstag fire, Litvinov protests the arrest of Soviet citizens in Germany. He notes a series of political assassinations: Voikov [the Soviet ambassador in Warsaw], King Alexander II of Yugoslavia, Barthou of France, Vorovsky [Soviet delegate to Lausanne conference].

November 16, 1933. Litvinov, after establishing U.S. diplomatic recognition of the Soviet Union, gave a speech in New York on the Nazi threat to world peace. The next day he marveled at a "Trans USA Atlantic telephone conversation from the Oval Office to the Spiridonovka Wing." On his way home through Berlin, he refused to meet Hitler.

December 4, 1934. Kirov assassinated. Kamenev and Zinoviev arrested.

January 17, 1935. Litvinov elected to Central Committee at Party Congress.

1935. Eden traveled to Moscow and said that he and Churchill wanted to work with "Anyone who is for Peace and Against Aggression." A pact with Czechoslovakia; Benes visits Moscow. [Litvinov's tone is one of appreciation for Benes' visit, in contrast to the strong-arm tactics the Soviet Union used to depose Benes thirteen years later—in 1948—in order to impose a communist government directed from Moscow.]

1936. "Bad times really began." Civil War in Spain began in August. Litvinov agreed Soviet Union not to intervene if Portugal, Italy, and Germany abstained. In November, arrest of German citizens in Leningrad and Moscow; the Anti-Comintern Pact signed by Germany, Italy, and Japan followed. "Post Kirov trials."

1937. Rising tensions with Japan, two years after Soviet Union sold Japan the East China Railway. German intervention on Franco's behalf. The Soviet Union gave open help to Spanish Loyalists.

August 1937. Ambassador to Spain, Rosenberg, arrested.

1938. "Chamberlain rebuffs Roosevelt offer to cooperate against dictators" but "Churchill for collective security." Hitler announces plans to invade Czechoslovakia. Litvinov tells French representative in Moscow that the USSR is ready to fulfill its obligations under treaty to defend Czechoslovakia with French help. Growing problems between USSR and Japan over fishing rights, over sale of arms to China. Raid on Soviet consulates in Japan; closing two Japanese consulates in USSR. Purges "in full swing" in Moscow: Babel, Mandelshtam [avant-garde writers], Meyerhold [leading theater director] arrested. "Yezhov's career ending. Beria on the make." Each month brings more arrests.

December 1938. "Fall of Yezhov [Head of the NKVD]. Beria in full charge."[25]

The "Handy Dates" of the 1930s end before the 1939 Nazi-Soviet Pact of Non-Aggression, which for the Soviet Union was the dividing line between begging for acceptance of the Bolshevik regime and sitting as an equal at the table of international diplomacy. The pact was a tragedy for Maksim Litvinov. He had spent the last twenty-five years speaking at every international forum that would let him rise to his feet, building recognition for the Soviet Union with small increments. Stalin thought he had achieved it by teaming up with Hitler. For Litvinov, the pact meant giving away international respect for the Soviet Union he had worked for so many years to achieve. No wonder that Ivy said it had nearly driven Maksim mad.

The relationship between Litvinov and Stalin offers a rarely seen aspect of Stalin's character. According to both Ivy's and Maksim's testimony in their oral history and notes, Litvinov continually argued with Stalin. After Litvinov served as ambassador to the United States during 1941–1943, the two revolutionary compatriots continued to argue. After Stalin demoted him from ambassadorial rank, and was dealing with Roosevelt himself, Litvinov became a vice commissar (deputy foreign minister); he was still useful for his long years of experience and respect as a diplomat among Western leaders. One of the reasons that Stalin was dissatisfied with Litvinov in Washington was Litvinov's willingness to talk to Americans about his schemes for collective security. He "was unreceptive to thoughts of territorial security for the Soviets in terms of a belt of dependent states, which charmed the imagination of Stalin and Molotov." A British Foreign Office friend in Moscow confided to Litvinov's daughter Tanya, "The old man seems to have gone absolutely mad. He seems to be ignoring his instructions."[26]

The last entry in the Handy Dates was a handwritten notation for "November or December; Litvinov eased out of the Central Committee" (1945). In February 1946, a few months before Litvinov left office, Stalin gave his first postwar speech declaring that World War II had been a result of the inner contradictions of capitalism. The CBS correspondent in Moscow, Richard Hottelet, visited Litvinov in his office unannounced, and found the ex-ambassador cleaning out his desk to leave the Central Committee. Litvinov agreed to what became a famous interview, in which he scoffed at the "return in Russia to the outmoded concept of security in terms of territory—the more you've got the safer you are." He explained to Hottelet that the Soviets believed conflict between the communist and capitalist worlds was inevitable.[27]

By 1949, the postwar Jewish purges had begun; Molotov's wife, Zhemchuzhina (a Jew, like Maksim), was arrested and put on trial for being a member of the Jewish Anti-Fascist Committee. Litvinov challenged Stalin: "Do you consider me an enemy of the people?" Stalin responded: "We do not." Litvinov wrote, "Ivy came flying back from Sverdlovsk." Molotov's wife was sent into exile and released by Beria the day after Stalin's funeral.[28]

Despite Litvinov's differences with Stalin and his inner circle, he remained in Moscow, on reserve in case his diplomatic vision of peaceful coexistence was needed to deal with the United States and Great Britain. Litvinov died a natural death in 1951 surrounded by his family, not in the *gulag* or by execution.

★ ★ ★

In 1956 Nikita Khrushchev delivered a secret speech to a closed session of the Twentieth Congress of the Communist Party of the USSR in which he laid bare the crimes and brutalities against the Soviet people perpetrated by Joseph Stalin during his thirty years in power. His purpose was to initiate the first *perestroika*, restructuring of the Soviet system. This action lessened the weight of the government's hand but did not bring about changes in the structure of communism or improve the Soviet way of life. The speech did not remain secret; it was leaked to the West and became the first opening in the tight secrecy that kept Soviet citizens in and the rest of the world out of the Soviet Union.

On that day—February 25, 1956, a week short of three years after Stalin's death—the Twentieth Party Congress of the Communist Party of the Soviet Union was drawing to a close. Soviet government functionaries cleared the meeting hall of the Kremlin of all foreign comrades to prepare for a secret speech. First Secretary Nikita Khrushchev had a message to present to the Soviet Union's party faithful, for their ears only. "The delegates listened in absolute silence. It was so quiet in the huge hall you could hear a fly buzzing. You must try to imagine how shocked people were by the revelations of the atrocities to which Party members . . . had been subjected. This was the first that most of them had heard of the tragedy which our Party had undergone—a tragedy stemming from the sickness in Stalin's character," Khrushchev later said.[29]

The purpose of his three hours of revelations was to cleanse the Soviet Revolution of Stalin's crimes and make way for a new era. Khrushchev's purpose was also to assert his leadership of the ruling Communist Party of the Soviet Union. "After Stalin's death no single man was acknowledged as our leader. There were aspirants, but no clear-cut, recognized leader," he wrote in his memoirs.[30]

Khrushchev's historic speech described with shocking detail the crimes of the Bolshevik government from the time Stalin took over from Lenin in 1924 to Stalin's death in 1953. In 1954, shortly after the execution of Lavrenti Beria, who had been the last director of the secret intelligence service under Stalin, the Party Presidium had set up an investigatory committee under P. N. Pospelov, a dogmatic ideologist, to assess the cases of Soviet citizens arrested by the Stalin regime who were still in prison. It was the surprising report of this commission that formed the basis of the secret speech, which the Presidium demanded Khrushchev give because he was first secretary of the Communist Party of the Soviet Union (CPSU). As a result of the the commission's findings, Khrushchev announced that the reputations of 7,379 loyal communists whom Stalin's security chiefs had eliminated had now been rehabilitated. He recalled Stalin's repeated purges over the years in which his intelligence apparatus had created false evidence to destroy any up-and-coming leader or potential power center that might compete with his thirty-year dictatorship.[31]

In Khrushchev's secret speech, which takes up sixty pages of his memoir, he bemoaned the cult of personality that Stalin enjoyed, in violation of the Communist Party's principle of collective direction. He presented Stalin's repression as a battle between a leader who had usurped power and the collective will of the party.

Khrushchev claimed that Lenin had always tried to explain, to convince, never using the brutal fist of the state to establish communism. He told the story of Stalin's rudeness to Nadezhda Krupskaya, Lenin's wife, and the deep split that came about between Lenin and Stalin. He described the tactics of the Great Purges of 1936–1937, in which prosecutors wrote the confessions of high ranking officials to counterrevolutionary crimes and forced the defendants to sign them. Often they were sentenced after 20 minutes of a fabricated hearing and shot immediately. The listeners in the hall reacted with murmurs of indignation.[32]

Khrushchev's unprecedented outpouring of hidden crimes staked his claim to unchallenged leadership of the Soviet Union. He hoped to end the post-Stalin wrangling within the party and emerge with the voice of authority, without bloodshed. His intention was to sweep away the Bolshevik Revolution's evils and begin again with a clean slate. The excesses and brutality he described would justify the summary execution of Beria and about forty others of Stalin's hierarchy, plus the arrest with long prison terms for fifty more officials. These were the measures Khrushchev's junta had carried out in order to take over the government in the months after Stalin's death. De-Stalinization was to become the new party line. Instead it was the beginning of the end of the Soviet empire.

Khrushchev was attempting to create *glasnost*, "openness," an understanding of the Soviet past, and from that to bring about *perestroika*, a restructuring that would deliver the promises of communism. These were the concepts that Gorbachev drew upon thirty years later to rebuild the Soviet economy. Khrushchev's goal was the completion of the world communist revolution; he attempted to convince the regimes emerging from colonialism and attempting to overthrow past repression to come under the banner of Soviet leadership. Gorbachev attempted to withdraw the Soviet Union from its dominating and expensive role as ruler of Eastern Europe. He hoped the rebuilding of the economy would make it possible to keep up its competitive role in the arms race with the United States and hold the union together. Both Khrushchev and Gorbachev failed in these endeavors.

When Khrushchev gave his secret speech in 1956, the cold war was growing more dangerous with each advance in military technology. The West believed, wrongly, that the Soviet Union had more missiles, more advanced space vehicles, and more capability to destroy its competitors with air power. Fear of Soviet technical superiority was enhanced a year later with the launching of *Sputnik*, the first vehicle to orbit the earth.

Therefore the West received the news that soon leaked of Khrushchev's secret speech with satisfaction. The Kremlin's intention was to distribute the speech to the "fraternal" communist parties of Eastern Europe to assure them that the heavy hand of Stalinism was about to be lifted and that they would thrive under the new, reformist, purer Marxism now in power in Moscow. As soon as it was disseminated in Iron Curtain countries, intelligence agents working secretly for the United States and Britain put copies of the speech into channels to reach Western leaders.

The CIA knew about the speech within two weeks after Khrushchev delivered it to the party Congress. They could have gotten the speech from GRU Lieutenant Colonel Pyotr Popov, a Soviet "defector-in-place," a term indicating that he had come over to the West but stayed in Soviet government posts to spy for his new employers. Allen Dulles, director of the CIA, decided that transfer of the document by Popov was too great a risk. He was too valuable an asset in reporting technical information to risk involving him in political tasks. The CIA believed it could get the speech from Yugoslav sources who, although they were communists, kept Moscow at a safe distance so that the Soviets could not rule them within the Iron Curtain. At the last moment, the Yugoslavs decided it was against their own communist interests for them to be the conduit for the secret speech.

In Moscow, word of the speech was all over the city in the foreign diplomatic community. It appeared that Khrushchev's people were leaking word of the revelations, which might mean that it was a ruse to trick Washington into a dangerous complacency. There were copies of the speech in Poland, where victims of Stalin were beginning to return from the *gulag*, relieving the atmosphere of the hard-fisted repression that Poles had endured under Soviet rule. The CIA had no contacts in Warsaw who could get them a copy of the hottest new document.

The CIA's best asset in Eastern Europe was the intelligence service of Israel. Shin Bet, the Israeli counterintelligence service, had more than twenty agents within the Iron Curtain posing as diplomats; they in turn had agents loyal to them who were successors of former Zionist networks. Within the CIA, the liaison for Israeli intelligence was James Angleton, later famous as an overly suspicious counterespionage officer. In response to Dulles' order to get the speech, Angleton queried both Shin Bet and Mossad, the Israeli agency for foreign intelligence. They were already busily on the path of the secret document that was stirring up excitement in every capital.

In Warsaw of 1956, Wladyslaw Gomulka, later head of the communist party of Poland, was one of the recently returned political prisoners who had been purged and jailed by Stalin in 1948. Around him were a circle of Polish intellectuals, heady with the new freedom to talk with each other and with foreigners in the unrepressed period between Stalin's death and Khrushchev's ascendancy to power. Gomulka's wife, who was Jewish, was a friend of a Shin Bet officer code-named Victor.

According to Dulles biographer Peter Grose, less than two months after the party Congress, a man close to the Gomulka circle handed Victor a bulky package. The moment he realized what he had in his hands, Victor drove to the airport and took the first plane out. He landed in Vienna, called ahead to Tel Aviv, and then boarded the next flight to Israel. He arrived on Friday afternoon, just before the weekly shut-down for the Sabbath. When Victor delivered the package, the head of Shin Bet, Amos Manor, opened it and found it was in Polish, one of the few European languages he didn't know. He kept his secretary, who knew Polish, after sundown to type a translation. After three paragraphs, Manor was sure enough of what he had in hand to call David Ben-Gurion, the prime minister of Israel, who knew Polish and who would know the import of what he was reading. Manor drove two hours to Ben-Gurion's weekend *kibbutz* in the Negev desert to give him the speech to read. Manor arrived at seven in the evening after the Sabbath had begun. Ben Gurion, who was annoyed at having his Sabbath broken, agreed there was work that had to be done. The next morning he authorized Manor to transmit the speech to Angleton. Manor later remembered Ben Gurion's words: "If this document is authentic, Russia is on her way to democracy—only twenty-five or thirty years away."[33]

A courier flew to Washington as soon as the Sabbath was over and gave the speech to Angleton, who declared to Allen Dulles that he had "brought home the bacon." Analysts at the CIA convinced their colleagues that the speech was authentic by comparing it with other versions they were receiving and by believing that it could have been spoken only by Khrushchev, known for his own brand of Russian slang and manner of expression.[34]

Then came the hard decision—whether or not to let it out to the press and public. The CIA had to answer for themselves the question of all government secrecy: is a secret more useful hidden for future use or published for all to read and discuss? The CIA pondered whether Khrushchev's promise of de-Stalinization, published for all to read, would support the Soviet or American position in the cold war. There were top CIA analysts on both sides of the argument. Finally Allen Dulles made the policy decision to release it. The CIA gave the speech to the State Department, who gave it to the *New York Times* and the *Washington Post*.[35] The speech took up four solid pages in the *Times* of June 4, 1956.[36]

The Soviets did not deny the speech or call it a fake. The State Department said it had received the speech through "diplomatic channels," and it was many years later that the CIA took credit for obtaining it. Former CIA official Ray Cline stated that the CIA had acquired the speech "at a very handsome price."[37]

About the same time that the CIA admitted its involvement, Israeli journalists in Washington spread the word that getting the document was an Israeli intelligence coup. They said informally that Angleton's long relationship with Shin Bet and Mossad was the path by which the CIA had the text so promptly. The Israelis denied that their intelligence services had taken any money for supplying the speech to the CIA. The Israelis added a touch of charm to the story by saying that a Shin Bet agent often visited a certain Polish government office in Warsaw where he flirted with the receptionist. He saw a suspicious document on her desk and asked her to get him a cup of tea. While her back was turned to him, he slipped the document under his coat, copied it, and returned it to her desk the next day without its absence being noted. Every intelligence service builds its own mythology, which can either cover up what really happened or provide an indirect way to tell the truth. Let's call it "the James Bond syndrome."

The true story is that the document came from Victor, not the code name of the courier but the real name of Victor Grajewski, who was then a member of the Polish Press Agency and a Polish citizen. He acknowledged that a woman friend, who was secretary to the first secretary of the Polish Unified Workers' Party (the Polish Communist Party), Edward Ochab, had handed him the speech to read for a few hours. Without telling her the use to which he was putting the pages, he delivered it to the Israeli embassy in Warsaw, waited while a copy was made, then returned the speech to her with only his comments. A year later, Grajewski emigrated to Israel.[38]

After the speech appeared in print, Radio Free Europe, the CIA supported radio station, broadcast the terrifying details. Release of the speech created a whirlwind in the ranks of Soviet intelligence: " . . . for months, information about Communist Party desertions, arrests and bloody uprisings poured in" to the CIA. The Hungarian Revolution followed a few months later.[39] The brutal military liquidation of the uprising demonstrated that de-Stalinization did not mean the Soviet Union was loosening its grip on countries it counted within its own bloc. A repercussion of the speech was the breaking away of the French and Italian communist parties to become Euro-communists, independent of the Soviet Union.

The leaking of Khrushchev's speech removed the first stone from the foundation of world communism. The structure was drastically weakened.

In 1957, after reading Khrushchev's secret speech denouncing Stalin, Steve Nelson, a leading Party organizer who had argued with Zarubin for the right to participate in atomic espionage, quit the American Communist Party.

11 The Secrets of Khrushchev's Memoirs

How did Nikita Khrushchev dare to tell the innermost secrets of the Soviet Union in his memoirs and how were they brought to the West for publication by Little, Brown, a wholly owned subsidiary of Time Inc.? Who was the intermediary between the Khrushchev family and Time Inc? When the first volume appeared in December 1970, Khrushchev was still alive. To protect him and his family, the editors of Time Inc. agreed that they would not reveal how the memoirs were produced or who carried them out of the Soviet Union.

Getting *Khrushchev Remembers* into print was a carefully hidden operation with perilous moments threatening premature exposure. It began with Khrushchev's representative approaching me (Jerrold) at a British journalist's cocktail party in Moscow in the fall of 1969, when I was *Time* magazine bureau chief in Moscow. The path for approval of the project was through Murray Gart, Time-Life news service chief of correspondents in New York, and on up to Hedley Donovan, editor-in-chief of all Time Inc. publications. Khrushchev's go-between insisted that neither he nor Khrushchev be publicly identified as the source of the memoirs. By avoiding a direct connection between Khrushchev's circle and Time Inc., the originators of the memoir believed they were creating an ambiguity that would prevent the Soviet government from punishing or prosecuting them for sending state secrets abroad for publication in the West. The initial idea of how to avoid the consequences of revealing government secrets and intimate details of Kremlin rivalries was to use Khrushchev's tape-recorded memoirs as raw material for an "unauthorized" biography.

★ ★ ★

I met Victor Louis for the first time on August 24, 1968, when I was invited to a party at his home in Peredelkino, the writers' and artists' colony fifteen miles west of Moscow off the main highway to Minsk. The approach to Victor's house was on a back road through a grove of towering pines. High, green wooden gates lined the right side of the road, shielding the dachas of the Communist Party elite. His neighbors included retired Red Army marshals, generals, ministers, and their children.

It was a warm summer evening, four days after the Soviet invasion of Czechoslovakia. I had arrived in Moscow on August 22, the day after our family finished the ten-week Russian language course at the Monterey Institute of Foreign Studies in Monterey, California. Leona and our five children were to join me when school started in September.

A heavy gate hid the house from view until a handyman swung it open. Flower beds created by Victor's English wife, Jennifer, graced the cobblestoned courtyard leading to the house. On my right was an impressive garage for Victor's collection of cars, which included a Mercedes convertible and a Bentley. The three-story house with a sauna overlooked some five acres, which included a swimming pool ("the only private pool in the Soviet Union," he claimed) and a tennis court. It was hardly the Moscow I had been told to expect.

I had been invited by Victor's friend Vadim Biryukov, a journalist for *Novosti*, a state-controlled news agency which the leadership used to spread Soviet propaganda. Vadim was my *mamka*, or babysitter, a KGB officer from the Second Chief Directorate, responsible for internal security and counterintelligence and assigned to deal with foreign journalists. His job was to pass along and spin information when it suited Soviet policy and to keep watch over what I was working on.

The Ministry of Foreign Affairs Press Department, the Central Committee of the Communist Party, and the KGB carefully studied each of the more than twenty American foreign correspondents in Moscow. They maintained files on each of us and tapped our office phones and apartments. To interview Soviet officials, we had to request appointments and get approval in advance from the Press Department. Soviet journalists and bureaucrats had to report all personal contacts with foreign journalists to the Press Department.

On that balmy August evening, vodka and "reactionary Czech Pilsner" flowed at Victor Louis' house, which was designated neutral ground—the place to see and be seen, gather gossip, cultivate sources, and penetrate the domain of a carefully designated Soviet elite. Guests included high ranking translators, film directors, journalists, radio commentators, artists, and a few foreign correspondents. Officially, Victor, a Soviet citizen, was the Moscow correspondent for the *London Evening News*—the largest circulation evening paper in the world at the time. He and Jennifer were known for giving lavish parties with the best caviar, excellent food, fine wines, and Cuban cigars. That night the final accompaniment was a well-rehearsed rendering of Soviet goals and peaceful intentions in Czechoslovakia.

Victor greeted me with a half smile, "You don't look like a man who has just been rehabilitated." He was referring to the four-year banishment of *Time* magazine's Moscow Bureau because of a *Time* cover in 1964 with an unflattering portrait of Lenin. It gave an account of his *ménage à trois* with his wife, Nadezhda Krupskaya, and Inessa Armand.[1] The Press Department had relented and I was reopening the bureau. Talk of rehabilitation was also a subtle reminder that Victor had spent nine years of a twenty-five-year sentence in the *gulag*, from his arrest in 1947 until he was freed in 1956 after Stalin's death along with tens of thousands of political prisoners. Louis had been accused of espionage even though he worked with government permission in foreign embassies. He was arrested on a trumped up charge of spying for Brazil. Victor's smile suggested that he, too, was critical of the Soviet system. Later, when we grew to know each other, he would turn on me in anger if I suggested that the Soviet paradise was less than perfect; only he, who had suffered under the Stalinist system, had the right to criticize.

In the post-Stalin era, Victor had a remarkable rise. He was first an office assistant and translator working for Marguerite Higgins of the *New York Herald Tribune* and for Daniel Schorr of *CBS News*; then he signed on with Edmund Stevens, at that time the *Look* magazine correspondent in Moscow. In 1958 he married Jennifer Statham, who had been a governess for the family of the British naval attaché in Moscow. Victor became a correspondent in Moscow for the *London Evening News* and enjoyed a string of news scoops. He also dabbled in literary and theatrical deals.

Victor and his friends pirated the Lerner and Lowe stage musical *My Fair Lady*, and profitably produced it in Russian without ever paying the authors their royalties. Ironically, for many years to come Victor received the customary translator's royalties from the Soviet government. Victor accompanied the dissident writer Valery Tarsis to London in 1966 when he was permitted to emigrate. Tarsis had been incarcerated in an insane asylum and released. Victor's task was to cover the story of the writer's arrival and limit damage to the KGB, which had imprisoned Tarsis, when they arrived in England.[2] This was his formal coming out as a KGB disinformation agent. Jennifer flew direct from Moscow to Heathrow on their planned flight, while Victor and Valery arrived a few hours later via Warsaw, avoiding the waiting photographers. A press conference was organized a day later by the *Evening News*, providing Victor with one of his many scoops.

Later Victor carried a copy of Svetlana Alliluyeva's 1967 memoir, *Twenty Letters to a Friend*, to the West, where he made arrangements for publishing an unauthorized translation before her own appeared, thereby blunting the impact of revelations by Stalin's daughter.[3] He was first with the news of Khrushchev's ouster in October 1964, and with the 1968 death of Cosmonaut Yuri Gagarin, the first man in space. Victor Louis was also the first to report the Soviet invasion of Czechoslovakia.

The day we met, Victor took me aside for a tour of his house. He wanted to show off his collection of heavy, dark, wooden antique furniture and his office on the second floor studded with a collection of short wave radios purchased on trips abroad. He had the latest electronic gadget, a device for automatic phone dialing, unavailable in Moscow. Unfortunately it was incompatible with the dated Soviet phone system. Victor was tall, with a full head of wavy hair. His eyes appeared veiled and distant behind his heavy glasses. His ready smile was cynical, not joyous; it accented his constant awareness and assessment of conspiracy. Victor could take no remark at face value. He believed there were always hidden forces at play. He was on guard for betrayal, dishonesty, or duplicity. He created a palpable tension that demanded thoughtful, calculated responses.

His mood shifted from a host's graciousness to taunting America's weaknesses in Vietnam. He defended the Soviet Union's invasion to "discipline the ungrateful Czechs," what the Moscow newspapers were calling "the events in Czechoslovakia" and "German revanchism," the return of Nazism: "Can you imagine, after we saved them from Hitler," Victor remarked. Victor put on a bravura performance, complemented with scrap books of clippings to document his exploits in the fifty countries he had visited. Victor suggested that, since I was new in Moscow, I should hire him to be a "confidential adviser" with a monthly retainer. I was appalled at the idea, but smiled and turned him down. In my notes, I wrote: "He is tough and cynical in his approach to any relationship; he claims to have the best contacts in town, but he readily admits that even he does not have a line into the Kremlin. He wants a lot of money for not much work, such as providing tips."

I met Victor Louis in the following months only to exchange professional gossip at social occasions in the apartments of foreign correspondents. In the fall of 1969, Victor and I found ourselves alone with drinks in hand at a journalist's party. He said he had access to important memoirs of a high ranking deposed Soviet official; would I be interested for *Time* magazine? "Of course," I responded. "Who is he?"

"Molotov is writing his memoirs and I have been in touch with his daughter," replied Victor. "But this cannot leak or it will not happen."

"Fine," I said, "I'll check with my editors. Get back to me when you can show me a sample and are ready to proceed." Two weeks later, Victor called and picked me up in his pale-blue Mercedes, with the radio playing loudly, ostensibly to avoid being bugged, also, I supposed, to heighten the moment. With a curl of his lip and a sardonic smile, Victor looked at me and said, "You've passed the test."

"What test?" I asked.

"I wanted to see if you could keep a secret. I've heard nothing about Molotov's memoirs around town," Victor explained. "Now I have an even better idea. Can you handle Khrushchev's memoirs?"

"We could do both," I offered.

He quickly dropped the Molotov idea to concentrate on Khrushchev.[4] I explained that Time Inc. would offer the best opportunity to present the memoirs. They would appear in a book, published by Little, Brown and Company, a subsidiary of Time Inc., and be excerpted in *Life* magazine. Victor agreed to let me listen to

Khrushchev on tape and compare the recordings to Russian language transcripts. That would convince me, he insisted, that the memoirs were authentic.

In early November 1969, Victor drove me to Peredelkino to listen to the tapes in his office. Again, he insisted on playing the radio to avoid detection of our conversation in case he was being bugged. The recordings had been edited to make Khrushchev's story telling intelligible. References to politically controversial figures such as the writer Aleksandr Solzhenitsyn and fraternal Communist Party leaders had been omitted. The reminiscences were transcribed and typed in manuscript form with a rough table of contents.

"The 'family and friends' are doing more work," said Victor, who established that he was to be the sole source of the material. There would be no direct contact with the family and friends. Louis had ingratiated himself with the Khrushchev family over the years by providing gifts acquired on his trips abroad. He became more valuable when Khrushchev became a "nonperson" in 1964, following the Politburo's abandonment of him; his family members had also lost their official positions.

In 1967 Victor "test-marketed" the idea of allowing Khrushchev to surface in the West: he arranged for NBC producer Lucy Jarvis to film "Khrushchev In Exile" on the grounds of the deposed leader's dacha. Khrushchev's voice-over in Russian accompanied footage showing him walking in his garden. Although there was no on-camera interview, the show was a sensation, the first time Nikita Sergeyevich had appeared in the media since he was ousted. Both the *New York Times* and the *Los Angeles Times* named Victor Louis as the intermediary between the Khrushchev family and NBC. Stuart Loory, the *L.A. Times* correspondent in Moscow, described Louis as "a Soviet newsman-showman who has won the confidence of the Kremlin."[5] Victor worked on the project for more than a year with Jarvis and *Parade* magazine editor Jess Gorkin, who ran an article with pictures based on the show. Now Victor wanted to take a further, more daring step.

When there were no official complaints against the NBC show from the Kremlin, Victor decided to proceed with the memoirs. He collaborated closely with Khrushchev's son Sergei and grandson-in-law Lev Petrov, a journalist who worked for *Novosti* and had a KGB connection. Petrov was married to Yulia Leonidovna Khrushcheva, the daughter of Khrushchev's son Leonid, who had been killed during World War II. She was raised by the Khrushchev family.

Khrushchev was lonely, angry, and bored. He readily took to the idea of reliving his career: from his hardscrabble boyhood in the Donbas coal mining region, through his rise under Stalin, and, after the dictator's death in March 1953, upward to the high table of world power politics.[6] Dictating into a tape recorder restored his self-esteem and gave him a reason for being. To provide a measure of coherence to the project, Khrushchev had a list of questions to answer. Invariably he told stories, often repeating the same tale with slight variations two or three times, while he sat outside on a bench. His KGB guards knew he was working on his memoirs but did not attempt to stop him.

The concept of a Soviet leader writing his memoirs was so new, so contrary to the practices of the censored society, that Louis required an elaborate cover story to deflect Politburo attention from himself, the author, and his immediate family. Louis feared that, if the material were directly attributed to Nikita Sergeyevich, his former colleagues would punish him and the family members who created the project. Louis and I argued over the format for hours and during several meetings. Taking Khrushchev's unique first-person account and transforming it into a biography with material from other sources was unacceptable, I told Victor. Such a design would raise more questions about the authenticity of the material than it solved. He kept insisting that we invent "a new art form of some kind" to allow Khrushchev to tell his story.

"And don't think anyone is going to thank you. Don't think you're going to be a hero. You will do a great service but no one on this side will know your name," Victor cautioned me.

I flew to Helsinki to call Murray Gart and tell him that a major project was under way but it needed his approval. It was a given that my Moscow office and home phones were tapped 24 hours a day. (On holidays, one of the two office lines was always busy, but normal service resumed when the holiday ended.) I reported cryptically that there was a real possibility to obtain Khrushchev's memoirs for publication. Following our phone conversation, I sent an express air mail memorandum explaining the negotiating conditions:

The subject is not to be directly identified as the source of the material, nor is his agent in the Soviet Union to be identified in any manner. The agent suggests that the best way to deal with the material would be to include it in a major biography of the subject along with other material on him gathered from around the world.

The agent warned that the subject will in no way approve or acknowledge the authenticity of the material. In extremis, after publication, we might consider the prospect of him even denouncing his own memoirs.

Gart presented the proposal to Hedley Donovan who sent him to Moscow to approve the project. Gart's cover for the visit was the October Revolution anniversary celebrations in November. After watching the parade on Red Square, Victor drove us to Peredelkino for a late lunch with caviar, vodka, and borscht. The dessert treat came when he gave Gart a verbal summary of the material, and showed him the Russian language transcripts while we listened to Khrushchev's tape-recorded tales.

★ ★ ★

Victor Louis was a Stalin era *gulag* survivor. His manipulative skills and ability never to allow himself a moral judgment on his compromises of conscience and personal betrayals ensured his success as a unique KGB asset. Victor cast himself as the producer and the leading actor in a shadow play between two worlds, in which KGB Chairman Yuri Andropov remained the director. Victor stepped back and forth, playing a Soviet journalist who used his contacts to provide major scoops to the West, then serving as the KGB's point man to discredit intellectual dissidents such as Aleksandr Solzhenitsyn and Andrei Sakharov. Victor was an instrument of Yuri Andropov, yet separately pursued his personal agenda to gain wealth and force the Soviet Union to face the truth about itself with Khrushchev's memoirs.[7] He was a transition figure taking advantage of both the reforms and the failed *glasnost* of Nikita Khrushchev, and the stagnation of Leonid Brezhnev.

Vitali Louis was born in Moscow in 1928, the son of a Prussian engineer whose family had settled in Moscow, and a Russian mother, a brilliant musician from a noble family. He was baptized in the Smolenskaya church before his mother died, which was soon after his birth.[8] His father left him to be raised by his grandmother, godmother, and his nanny, but times were hard and they sent Victor to orphanages; he ran away from them to return to his grandmother's apartment. During World War II, at age 15, he wangled a place as a chef's helper at the posh Savoy Hotel in Moscow and then as a pastry maker at the National Hotel; he then began a round of jobs in foreign embassies as a messenger and fixer to support himself while studying at Moscow's Institute of Law. In 1947, two years into the course, he was arrested and sentenced to twenty-five years in the *gulag*. He managed to survive, it was said in Moscow, by becoming a *stukach*, or stool pigeon, a camp informer who was paid in extra rations. Louis's own version is that he had a festering tubercular bone in his leg, which permitted him to enter the camp hospital. At one stage it got so bad that he was told his leg would have to be amputated. Two friendly prisoner doctors saved his leg and rescued him from return to outdoor hard labor in the Siberian winter. Louis's disability permitted him to be transferred to a Karaganda prison camp in Kazakhstan. The most famous prisoner there was Aleksei Kapler, the Jewish film director whom Stalin had banished after his daughter, Svetlana, fell in love with Kapler and wanted to marry him. In Kazakhstan, Louis was assigned to run the camp store until he was freed after Stalin's death.

After his rehabilitation, Louis returned to Moscow and became a translator again, working for foreign journalists rather than embassies. While in prison camp, one of Louis' fellow prisoners was a Russian journalist who later introduced him to the *London Times* correspondent in Moscow, Ralph Parker, who provided access for him to the foreign press corps. Louis completed his university law degree at night school, teasing his young English wife about her reading the Bible at bedtime while he had to prepare coursework on Marxism-Leninism.

Louis cooperated closely with the KGB to carry out assignments but he was not a full-time staff officer with rank and salary. He was a unique, provocative, and protected freelancer, permitted to keep his earnings as a foreign correspondent and deal maker so long as he fulfilled his KGB assignments. Louis' news scoops and free-spending lifestyle offered a contrast to the puritan image of communist frugality. It was a perfect, calculated cover: how could a journalist with a Bentley and a Mercedes be an agent of the Soviet government?

Louis was known for his escapades in off-the-books diplomacy to countries with which the Soviet Union had no relations, such as Taiwan. He was an unofficial but authorized provocateur who left his back channel messages through nondiplomatic means. When Louis traveled to Taipei in October 1968, Radio Beijing branded his visit a "despicable provocation against the Chinese people by 'a so called journalist' who went to Taiwan to plot a criminal deal." Later in the autumn of 1969, when Sino-Soviet relations worsened, Louis traveled to Beijing where he wrote a story about the possibility of a Soviet preemptive strike against Chinese nuclear facilities at Lop Nor in a remote area of Xinxiang (Sinkiang) province.[9] His articles in the *London Evening News* signaled Soviet concerns and intentions, resulting in a swift, if temporary, scaling back of tensions between Beijing and Moscow.

Knowing of Victor's reputation as a Soviet disinformation expert, I was wary. Why deal with him? For good reasons. Khrushchev, sitting in his garden, recalling his glory days and the intricacies of the Kremlin power struggle, exposed the inviolate secrets of Stalin and his successors. For the first time, the world outside the Soviet Union learned from a key participant the motivations, aspirations, and brutality of the leadership of the world communist revolution. Khrushchev lifted the facade from utopia and told in pithy, first person prose the poverty, moral and physical, of life in the Soviet Union. It was a historic opportunity from which I could not walk away.

When I pressed Victor to tell me who had access to the manuscript and how it was being edited, Louis promised that "no outsiders" would edit the tapes or the manuscripts. It was his way of saying that the KGB would not be directly involved with the text. I warned him that unless the tapes and typescript contained undoctored, authentic material and a full narrative of events, there would be no book. The publisher required consultations with the author for clarifications and amplifications. Victor laughed heartily at the request. Direct contact with Khrushchev and his family was out of the question, Victor insisted. They needed complete deniability. The "special pensioner," or "the old man," as Victor sometimes called him when we were alone, could not be consulted about details of the publication. However, Victor would try to present my questions to Khrushchev during dictation sessions.

We agreed to find a way to protect Khrushchev from humiliation or jail, and at the same time to preserve the full complexity of his story. After listening to the tapes, we had no doubt whatsoever that Khrushchev's voice, "characterized by a curious and often intentional alteration between cautious insinuation and bold revelation, apparent indiscretion and deft evasion, earthy vulgarism and stilted euphemism," had to be retained.[10] Victor wondered if the book could be attributed to a Western biographer or known Kremlin expert. I assured him that only a first-person account, in Khrushchev's own voice, could pass the tough scrutiny of Western Soviet experts.

One thing was certain, I told Victor: Time Inc. was not going to print anything in the text that could not be verified in Khrushchev's own words. When the *Penkovsky Papers* were published in 1965 by Doubleday, they were purported to be based on the personal papers and diary of GRU Colonel Oleg Penkovsky that were smuggled out of the Soviet Union. The *Papers* were actually tape recordings of Penkovsky's debriefing sessions by a combined British MI-6 and American CIA team in London and Paris. The CIA, overanxious to protect "sources and methods," allowed that the material was a compilation of "hastily written notes, sketches and comments." Soviet experts who reviewed the book questioned how an experienced spy like Penkovsky could keep a diary in his desk. Although the contents of the book were genuine, based on recordings of his debriefings and the secret documents Penkovsky had passed to his handlers, the "diary" cast a cloud of doubt because it did not exist.

Negotiating with Victor Louis was exhilarating and exasperating. There was never a healthy give and take toward our agreed-upon goal. Victor assumed he was being cheated, that the project would be leaked, and that he, Khrushchev, and the family members involved in the project would be punished. Victor sulked, made outrageous demands, then in a flash changed from thunderstorm to bright sunlight while he tested new ideas. His goal was to gain acceptance for the memoir without directly exposing Khrushchev to be the knowing source of the book. Victor Louis had survived eight years in labor camps by making compromises and manipulating the anomalies of the Soviet system. Once again he was ready to make the system work to his advantage. Producing the memoirs was to be his crowning achievement.

We began a prolonged joust over what would be included in the material. Victor explained that for Khrushchev to reveal the content of Politburo meetings was to violate Soviet law. He said that Khrushchev could not admit that the Soviet Union had signed a secret protocol to the August 1939 Nazi-Soviet Pact of Non-Aggression by which Hitler gave Stalin the go-ahead to invade eastern Poland and take over the Baltic states. For Khrushchev, the protocol was still a matter of state security, not to be violated, even though the fact had long since been made public. In that case, I argued, Khrushchev did not have to say anything about a secret protocol, but it was essential that he discuss the prelude to World War II and why Stalin agreed to a pact with Hitler.

In the historic, groundbreaking memoir that emerged from his tapes, Khrushchev, in an effort to preserve his place in history, dared to reveal the secrets of life under Stalin. In his unique style, speaking as the ultimate Soviet insider, Khrushchev told tales from Stalin's dinner table immediately after the signing of the Non-Aggression Pact. Khrushchev said, "We knew perfectly well that Hitler was trying to trick us with the treaty. I heard with my own ears how Stalin said, 'Of course it's all a game to see who can fool whom. I know what Hitler's up to. He thinks he's outsmarted me, but actually it's I who have tricked him!' "[11]

Victor demanded a substantial advance on royalties from Time Inc. He intended to use his share of the advance money to travel freely in the West and to maintain his extraordinary lifestyle in the Soviet Union. He was planning to build a small ski lift on a hill near his home, he told me. Victor never had a thought of moving to England, where his mother-in-law would have welcomed him to her comfortable home and garden outside Dorking, an hour's drive from London. Victor knew his ties to the KGB would make it difficult to live abroad, his English wife knew it would be difficult for him to leave the Soviet Union permanently, and he had no reasons for defecting. He was invigorated by his life on the edge of two conflicting worlds, the KGB and the foreign press corps.

Victor asked for an advance of $1 million against royalties. He wanted to be paid in hard currency in a European bank so he would not be subject to American taxes. In a memo to Murray Gart, I wrote, "Members of the subject's family are involved in the project, and they appear to be motivated by financial reasons, or so the agent claims. He notes, for example, that while the subject lives comfortably, he did not leave office as a rich man." Money, however, was secondary. According to Victor, the driving reason behind Khrushchev allowing his memoirs to leave the country was because he "wanted to justify his place in history as well as his own vanity."

Khrushchev needed an alibi. His defense was that he did not know what was in the memoirs Time Inc. would publish. Therefore, Victor insisted, we could not have the tapes to publicly prove their origin and satisfy a demand for third-party authentication. He insisted on keeping the tapes and laid down as a condition that Time Inc. not publicize their existence. If, under pressure, Time Inc. were to play the tapes to certify the provenance of the memoirs, Khrushchev could not defend himself before the Communist Party Central Committee. Under no circumstances, he insisted, could Khrushchev's tapes be played publicly. Victor promised he would keep the tapes secure in the West, to be delivered to Time Inc. at a "safe time" in the future. He agreed to provide a sample reel of tape with excerpts that could be voice-printed while the final transcription was under way.

I asked Victor to get the manuscript ready for a showing to Time Inc. editors, who wanted to meet him in London as soon as possible. If the material was as revealing as the samples I had read and listened to in his study at Peredelkino, Little, Brown and *Life* would present the book in the first person voice of Nikita Sergeyevich. However, we would need to prove that it was truly Khrushchev speaking on the tapes. The sample reel he prepared contained selected passages I had chosen from the most controversial and personal episodes. They included the origins of the Korean War, Stalin's relationship with his daughter Svetlana Alliluyeva, Khrushchev's own account of the Cuban missile crisis, and his and Stalin's dislike for Mao Zedong. An independent firm of voice print experts, Voice Identification Services of Sommerville, New Jersey, conducted an exhaustive spectrographic analysis by comparing the sample tape with Khrushchev's recorded address to the United Nations General Assembly on September 18, 1959. The two voice samples matched.[12]

Victor wanted to maintain an ambiguity about how the material had been amassed for the book, while at the same time asserting that it was Khrushchev who had created the contents. Yet without producing a manuscript or tapes, the editors could not prove that all the material was Khrushchev's. At the end of February 1970, Victor came to London with a 510-page Russian language transcript of the tapes. We met at the Connaught Hotel, the epitome of discreet elegance with its polished wood, heavily carpeted staircases, and impeccable service. Victor irreverently called it the Coconut Hotel, pretending to have difficulty in pronouncing the name.

With Murray Gart's agreement, I called Strobe Talbott, my summer vacation replacement in Moscow in 1969, who was studying at Oxford University; I invited him to meet me at the Connaught with his best Russian-English dictionary. Talbott was then a 22-year-old Rhodes scholar. He was also a *Time* stringer (part-time correspondent) with excellent skills in Russian, which he had studied at Hotchkiss and at Yale. A few weeks earlier, Strobe had returned to Moscow to do research on his thesis at the Mayakovsky Museum. While he was in town, I asked him to turn a long article by the historian Aleksandr M. Nekrich from Russian into English to test his translating ability. I thanked him for a quick and excellent job before we flew to London together, he to return to Oxford, I to meet Victor and introduce him to Murray and a group coming from the United States. I still had not told Strobe about the memoirs.

At the Connaught, the team assembled that would be responsible for bringing the memoirs to press as a book and in a series of articles: Larned (Ned) Bradford, senior editor of Little, Brown and Company; David Maness, text editor of *Life*; and Murray Gart of Time Inc. We discussed at length who would be the best Soviet expert to translate and edit the book without breaking secrecy or attracting attention. If word of the project leaked before the book was ready for publication, the "competent authorities"—the KGB—could force Khrushchev to stop publication.

Names of prominent Kremlinologists and translators rose and fell: they might not be available, they might take too long, or they might have their own agenda. To get the job done quickly, I suggested we turn to a fresh face, someone skilled in Russian, with the stamina to complete the translation within six months. Why not try Strobe? I had seen his translation skills at work in Moscow. He had energy, discipline, and ambition. The team agreed to try him on the transcript.

I carried an attaché case with the bulky transcript to Strobe's small room on the upper floor of the Connaught. Strobe spent ten straight hours reading and making notes, breaking only for eggs Benedict and sweet tea from room service. By 10 p.m. that evening, he had completed a *précis* and we gathered in the drawing room of Gart's suite for Strobe's appraisal of the memoirs. Strobe had done a remarkable job of sorting through the manuscript and had produced a stunning summary. The richness and the range of Khrushchev's life leapt forth with emotion: the death of his first wife during the famine of 1921; his days at the Industrial Academy in Moscow in the early 1930s where Nadezhda Sergeyevna Alliluyeva, Stalin's modest wife and Khrushchev's fellow student, who came and went to the Kremlin by streetcar, befriended him and boosted his career by praising his work as district party secretary to her husband; the intrigues at dinner with Stalin, when a Politburo member could "come as a guest and leave as a prisoner"; his pithy, cutting reminiscences of Adenauer, Eisenhower, Kennedy, and Mao.

In the morning, I knocked on Strobe's door to wake him up and report that the editors had agreed to purchase the memoirs for publication and that Strobe was the first choice to do the translation. They had also decided to ask Edward Crankshaw, the highly respected biographer and critic of Khrushchev's life and career, to write the introduction, commentary, and notes to the memoir. The next step was for Strobe to do a rough translation of the transcript to determine the best format for publication. At first he hesitated, but quickly grew excited when I conjured the importance of the memoirs and his career as a foreign correspondent following the translation.

The next day we walked to Locke, the famous London hatter on St. James Street, and bought two hats for Victor to take as a gift to Nikita Sergeyevich. During the early negotiations, Victor had mentioned Khrushchev's fondness for fine hats and we purchased an oversized derby and a Tyrolean hat for him, asking Victor to send us a photo in return. Victor soon sent me a letter with a picture of Khrushchev sitting on a bench near the dacha wearing the Tyrolean hat, a confirmation that the special pensioner was part of the project.

Before leaving London, I also spent a day with Strobe at Oxford and met his long-haired, amiable housemate, Bill Clinton, who prepared omelets for our breakfast. I never asked Strobe how he told Bill about his new assignment.

Strobe agreed to do the translation on the condition that he could enlist the help of a Russian friend from Oxford, Yasha Zaguskin, then 70 years old. Zaguskin had fled with the White armies and taught Russian in the United States for thirty years before retiring to Oxford, where he rented a room from Boris Pasternak's sister, Lydia. A few days later, he and Strobe departed for Boston to work with Ned Bradford and begin translating what we code-named the "Jones Project." Strobe had not been told that Victor Louis was the intermediary, but on the flight from London to Boston, he put the pieces together and soon expressed his concerns to Bradford in person and to me by letter.

Larned Bradford was the last of a dying breed of talented and exacting book editors. His authors included Norman Mailer and John Fowles, author of *The French Lieutenant's Woman*. At one point in our conversations in London, he straightened his back and told Victor Louis that Little, Brown and Company had been publishing books for 200 years and he did not need to be told how to handle the transcript. By then the memoirs were already in the West and Time Inc. had agreed to buy them. Time Inc. paid a $750,000 advance against royalties to Victor Louis as the agent for the book. Little, Brown and Company would publish the book in December, and *Life* would feature excerpts in four issues: November 27, December 4, 11, and 18, 1970.

Bradford did not directly confirm Victor's role in answer to Strobe's question when they met in Boston, but told him that as publisher it was his responsibility to verify the authenticity and the historical value of the material. On both counts, Bradford said, the book was eminently worthy of publication. By July 1970, Strobe had finished the translation and gone off to Crankshaw's home in Kent to integrate his comments and footnotes into the text. My tour in Moscow was coming to an end. Leona flew ahead and bought a house in Washington to which we moved the family in late summer.

We did not know that two KGB officers had visited Sergei Khrushchev, Khrushchev's son, and demanded that he turn over the tapes and transcripts of the memoirs to the Central Committee of the Communist Party for safekeeping. "We've received information that foreign intelligence agents want to steal the materials," they told Sergei. The two officers promised that when Nikita Sergeyevich was released from the hospital for his heart condition, the Central Committee would provide help for him to complete the memoirs. Sergei tried to meet with KGB head Yuri Andropov to plead his case, but to no avail. Sergei insisted on a signed receipt and turned over twenty-eight tapes and sixteen folders with 2,810 pages of typewritten materials.[13] By then it was too late for the KGB to stop publication. The book was in its final stages of editing.

In August Strobe flew to Copenhagen to join Gart and me for a meeting with Victor Louis. Strobe had requested the tape recordings for several sections of the manuscript in order to clarify the translation. Louis wanted to see how the manuscript for the book was proceeding. We had still not agreed upon a title and Victor was still searching for a new art form that would allow Khrushchev's memoirs to appear without his by-line or any acknowledgment of the former leader's direct participation. Gart had scheduled a meeting of *Time*'s European bureau chiefs in Copenhagen to provide a cover story. He would fit in Victor between sessions and after the bureau chiefs left town.

Victor, Murray, and I had rooms at the Hotel d'Angleterre. Strobe stayed at the less palatial Hotel Royal. At that point, Murray did not want Strobe distracted by Victor Louis and had been reluctant for Strobe to come to Copenhagen. "We're dealing with a slippery bastard here," he told me, "and there's no need for Strobe to get involved with him." When I insisted that Strobe had to listen to the tapes with Victor, who would not relinquish control of them, Gart relented and agreed. We met in Gart's room and Victor carefully played the sections of tape for which Strobe had asked. We listened to Khrushchev's voice, matched his words to the transcript, and discussed the nuances of the tale he was telling. Strobe then urged Victor to lend us the tapes long enough for them to be voice-printed. Victor was noncommittal.

In his journal, Strobe recorded:

I persisted. He became testy and accused me of trying to take advantage of him. Didn't I realize how vulnerable he was? How vulnerable "the family" was? Didn't I realize that the tapes were their only "insurance policy"? The logic of his position escaped me, but the tactic was clear: to make him appear farther out on a limb than he had ever intended to go—lured there by the wealthy, powerful manipulators with whom he was dealing. From this first taste of an adversary proceeding with Victor Louis, I began to appreciate that for him a business negotiation was an exercise in histrionics. He would cast himself into the role of the naive but proud amateur entrepreneur who is only just learning how unfair and exploitative the big time can be. His petulance was fine-tuned to transmit just a hint of threat that he might walk out at any moment, shocked and disgusted at the bullying greed he had encountered. He bluffed not from a position of fake strength, but from one of fake weakness; he played his game as though he were down to his last chip, mostly because the rest of the table cheated, and besides, he had never meant to get into a game of such high stakes and low sportsmanship anyway. For me—a genuine novice—it was all fascinating and disorienting. I did not know it at the time, but it was a fleeting preview of similar, though more elaborate, scenes of high drama in the years to come.[14]

Victor was still sulking when he, Strobe, Murray, and I arrived for dinner at the Tivoli Gardens. His mood lightened when I encouraged his idea to produce a movie based on the book. Victor had still not agreed to Khrushchev telling his story in the first person singular. Following the heady talk about making a film, I again raised the question of the book's format, and now Victor readily agreed to our plan to use Khrushchev's voice in the text.

He listed his conditions. The book must not be called or advertised as a memoir. The cover and title page should not list Khrushchev as the author. To make it appear that the book was a compilation of Khrushchev's speeches and statements, given at all kinds of places and with different groups of people, there should be no reference to specific times and places when and where the statements were made. All references to the present on the tapes must be removed. No evidence of the tapes could appear in the text.

Victor had an inspiration. " 'Various sources at various times.' That is the formulation we must use," he insisted.

To satisfy Victor's fears, we agreed to include a few of Nikita Sergeyevich's public speeches as part of his reminiscences.

Then, with a threatening smile and hooded eyes, the dark Victor reemerged. He mentioned the problem that, since the Soviet Union was yet not a member of the international copyright convention, "you should be prepared for a leak or even piracy." Victor raised the possibility that Khrushchev himself might leak the transcript of the tapes if the book came under fire as an anti-Soviet document. He could not guarantee that some émigré organization would not produce a Russian version of the book based on the syndicated English excerpts. We could feel Victor conjuring new and more apocalyptic possibilities. He concluded his gloomy scenario with a Russian proverb: "We must do the best but be ready for the worst."

To deal with the primary problem for Khrushchev, we drafted and negotiated, word by word, a "publisher's note" that later appeared in the book:

This book is made up of material emanating from various sources at various times and in various circumstances. The publisher is convinced beyond any doubt, and has taken pains to confirm, that this is an authentic record of Nikita Khrushchev's words. Whether the author intended or expected his words ever to find their way into print, either in his own country or in the West, is a matter of speculation. The publisher takes full responsibility for the manner in which Nikita Khrushchev is represented here. Moreover, he does so with the confidence that the genuineness as well as the significance of these reminiscences speak for themselves.

"Reminiscences" was a painfully negotiated substitute for "Memoirs." There was no mention of tapes or voice prints, nor would there be in Khrushchev's lifetime. The compromise created the problem of a title page without an author, missing the traditional "By . . ." that normally gives a book its identity. At the end of our session, however, Victor again promised that, after Khrushchev died, he would turn all the tapes over to Time Inc.

The next day Louis received a phone call in his room at the d'Angleterre from a Danish reporter who asked him why he was in Copenhagen and what he was discussing with representatives of Time-Life. Victor hung up and marched in a fury to my room down the hotel corridor. Victor accused me of "a double cross" and "stupidity." Together we returned to his room. While I tried to make sense of what had happened and why he had been called, Victor shouted angrily that "nobody will get these tapes." He unrolled two reels of tape, cut them into small pieces with scissors and carefully flushed them all down the toilet.

"Mysterious Russian Journalist Meets American Colleagues," shouted a five-column headline in the next day's edition of Copenhagen's *Berlingske Aftenavis*. The story, written by Mogens Auning, a former Danish military intelligence officer, reported that "news of international interest is being made in Copenhagen, and important international newsmen are in Denmark." Further, it said that Louis, Schecter, and Gart were occupying rooms on the same floor of the d'Angleterre, where they were holding meetings and making calls to New York. The article made no mention of Strobe or Khrushchev, but speculated wildly that the outcome of our talks might "affect Sino-Soviet relations." The public exposure of our meeting brought it to an immediate end.

Despite Victor's fears and threats, the memoirs were still on track. We had agreed on the final specifics to protect Khrushchev from reprisals. On the flight home, Murray Gart surmised that *Time*'s Copenhagen stringer Knud Meister, a respected Danish journalist, might have been the leak. Annoyed at being cut out of the secret meeting with Louis, Meister must have checked with his own contacts at the hotel and leaked the story, Gart said. After the book appeared, and the debate over who and how it was produced waxed heavy, the Copenhagen meeting and Victor Louis' role were cited as the connecting link, but never confirmed by any of those who took part in the meetings.

By early November, Gideon de Margitay, *Life*'s specialist in handling major memoirs, sold foreign syndication rights to Europe's major magazines and newspapers. To preserve security, de Margitay provided a summary of the excerpts, which he allowed to be read in his presence and handed back to him. Nevertheless, there was soon a rash of newspaper reports that Time-Life was about to bring out Khrushchev's memoirs. When Harrison Salisbury, the *New York Times*' Soviet expert, heard the rumor, he rushed to congratulate Murray Gart on obtaining the memoirs. Salisbury said he was anxious for *Life* to share the syndication with the *New York Times*. In the negotiations, the *Times* insisted that it be given the excerpts to print a day before *Life* magazine appeared on the newsstands. The *Times*, which had obtained Svetlana Alliluyeva's book, *Twenty Letters to a Friend*, and shared syndication with *Life*, had insisted the *Times* appear first with the excerpts. The *Times*' demand was a deal breaker. Donovan was primarily concerned with an exclusive to boost the prestige of *Life*, which was facing serious financial difficulties.

When the first excerpt appeared, Salisbury and the *Times* openly turned against the memoir, casting doubt on its authenticity.

On November 6, Time Inc. announced that it was in possession of Khrushchev's reminiscences. A firestorm arose. The next day the *New York Times* ran an article by Lawrence Van Gelder quoting *Life*'s de Margitay telling buyers of the memoirs that it was based on notes from an unidentified interviewer in conversations with Khrushchev, notes that had been smuggled out of the USSR and rewritten in the West. The article identified Victor Louis, a suspected KGB agent, as the provider of the memoirs, whose motive was to bring in foreign exchange.

Further complicating the picture was the visit to New York of Leonid Zamyatin, who had moved from head of the Foreign Ministry Press Department to director general of TASS, the official Soviet news agency. He was accompanied by Mikhail Zimyanin, chief editor of *Pravda*, the newspaper of the Communist Party of the Soviet Union. They had been invited to the United Nations, and Vadim Biryukov, who accompanied them, suggested that an invitation to the Time-Life Building would be well received and improve relations. Donovan invited the two officials for dinner at 8 p.m., but they arrived nearly two hours late. Donovan ordered us not to discuss the Khrushchev project. The Russians never raised it, and we steered clear of it throughout the elaborate dinner, which ended near midnight. I had hoped to signal Biryukov that we would work out a way to inform Moscow of the book's contents before publication, but he was forced to leave the next day when he received word that his father had died.

Publication day loomed and I received an overseas call at home. Biryukov and Felix Rosenthal, *Life*'s interpreter and office manager, who had not been informed of the project, had flown from Moscow to Paris to request an advance copy of the book. Murray Gart agreed to telex them the *Life* excerpts forty-eight hours before the magazine was published. There would be no surprises in Moscow, nor would there be time for an organized preemptive strike against the memoirs. Zamyatin and Zimyanin were furious.

On November 23, Harrison Salisbury wrote that Soviet specialists suggested the material for the memoirs may have originated in a Western European center for the production of Soviet forgeries. He quoted Svetlana Peters denying Khrushchev's recollections (by then, Stalin's daughter was married to the American architect Wesley Peters and was living in Arizona). In an editorial the same day, the *New York Times* called upon *Life* to state more convincingly how and from where it received the manuscript and why it was so confident its author was Khrushchev.

The Communist Party's Central Control Committee, its disciplinary arm, summoned Khrushchev to its headquarters. The chairman of the Control Commission, Arvid Pelshe, ordered the former Communist first secretary and prime minister of the Soviet Union to sign a prepared statement categorically repudiating the memoirs. Khrushchev refused. Banging his fist on the table, Khrushchev warned Pelshe that any effort to curb him would put him in the position of Czar Alexander I who, according to legend, rose from his coffin and trudged across Russia dressed as a peasant, staff in hand, to tell the people his tale. Khrushchev argued with Pelshe over his right to dictate and write his memoirs: "As for what I dictated, I regard it as the right of every citizen and Party member," adding that "moral torture is the worst kind." Pelshe told Khruschev: "We would like you to define your attitude . . . by saying you are indignant and gave nothing to anyone."

To break the impasse, Khrushchev dictated a statement that was reported by TASS:

It is seen from reports of the press in the United States and some other capitalist countries that the so-called memoirs or reminiscences of N. S. Khrushchev are now being prepared for publication. This is a fabrication and I am indignant at this. I have never passed on material of a memoir nature either to Time or other publishing houses. I did not turn over such material to the Soviet publishing houses either. Therefore I declare this a fabrication. The venal bourgeois press has many times been exposed in such lies.

Per Egil Hegge, a Norwegian correspondent in Moscow and a respected Soviet expert, noted that Khrushchev's statement "must be one of the most confirming denials the world has ever seen, because it said between the lines that memoir material did exist. What Khrushchev denied was that he, personally, delivered such material to somebody—and nobody claimed that." The details of the criticism session with the Party Control Commission were unknown, but the TASS statement of Khrushchev's "denial" was encouraging. Khrushchev cleverly protected himself without branding the memoirs "anti-Soviet" or a forgery. But he paid a price and was hospitalized until the end of the year with recurring heart problems.

Criticism mounted that there were factual errors, perhaps innocently the failure of an old man's memory, but not so innocently, if the memoir was a forgery. Khrushchev's skillful denial made it clear that he had, indeed, exercised his right as a Soviet citizen and Communist Party member to dictate his memoirs. Demands continued for Time Inc. to reveal its source for the memoirs.

At a hastily called meeting in Hedley Donovan's office on the thirty-second floor of the Time-Life Building, the Jones Project team reviewed the situation. Donovan was Henry Luce's hand-picked successor, tall, raw-boned, and handsome, a newsman's Gary Cooper with the same ambling charm, integrity, and severity when necessary. From the beginning, Donovan knew about the conditions of the project and the identity of its intermediary. Once convinced that Time Inc. had a genuine memoir, he approved the purchase and the arrangements to protect Khrushchev.

Under the hail of criticism, the *Times of London*, which had signed a contract to pay $500,000 for first serial rights to excerpts from the memoirs, asked for a reduction in price. The controversy that surrounded the initial publication had reduced the expected boost in circulation, they argued. When Donovan heard about the request to rewrite the contract, he rose to his full height of 6 feet 3 inches and sent word to de Margitay not to budge. Remind the *Times* of its eagerness to share in the historic scoop, Donovan said, adding that the contract would remain in force, and it did. He further promised, "The memoirs will be vindicated, but we will not break our word not to discuss their provenance." For Time Inc. there was no question of the authenticity of the taped excerpts. They had been voice-printed. A positive signal had come from Khrushchev's carefully worded denial, which acknowledged he had been working on his memoirs.

We reviewed how the *New York Times* had turned against the Khrushchev memoirs after *Life*, with Donovan's approval, had decided not to let itself be scooped again by their demands to come out first. Donovan was a wall of calm and strength under the challenge to the credibility of the memoirs. Richard Helms, the CIA director, called Donovan and asked for an explanation of how the memoirs were acquired. Donovan and Helms had been in naval intelligence together during World War II and were old friends. Donovan sent Gart to Langley to brief Helms privately on the authenticity of the memoirs. The CIA was not informed in advance of the project and was not shown the memoirs in advance of their publication.

When the respected Kremlinologist Victor Zorza wrote in the *Manchester Guardian* that both the KGB and the CIA might be involved in *Khrushchev Remembers*, we all smiled in relief. "I see the Khrushchev book," wrote Zorza, "as the culmination of a bitter struggle between the KGB's 'disinformation department' and the CIA's own 'department of dirty tricks,' each of which has been manufacturing forgeries directed against the other side for more than a dozen years." Zorza was groping for an explanation. He posited that the KGB may have planted additional material in the memoirs in order to promote Soviet interests. Zorza found difficulty with some passages because they were surprisingly critical of the Soviet system or could be interpreted as serving the interests of anti-Stalinist factions in the Politburo. He suggested that the CIA had inserted them before the memoirs reached Time Inc.

Izvestia, the official Soviet government newspaper, took Khrushchev's oblique denial a step further and produced a story headlined, "In the Kitchen of Forgers." It identified Strobe Talbott as "a young sapling of the CIA" and raised Crankshaw's alleged ties to the British Secret Intelligence Service (MI-6), but there was no follow up. Obviously, the Soviets had made a decision not to pursue Khrushchev. The first excerpt in *Life*, while unprecedented and highly embarrassing to the

Central Committee of the CPSU, was well received in the West. The series unfolded in three more issues of *Life* and, when *Khrushchev Remembers* appeared in mid-December, the controversy over its authenticity stimulated interest and sales. Khrushchev's thrust was anti-Stalin but it was not openly anti-Soviet.

The reminiscences of the "special pensioner," not listed as the author, jumped onto the best-seller list and eventually sold 80,000 copies. The Jones Project was a success.

Doubts lingered over who was behind the memoirs, but a consensus quickly developed among diplomats and Soviet experts who had known Khrushchev that he was the author, speaking very much in character. The U.S. State Department convened a meeting of thirty government and academic experts at Airlie House in the Virginia countryside to analyze the memoirs' authenticity and origins; George Kennan was a participant. The tentative conclusion was that the material was real but that the KGB, once it realized it could not stop publication in the West, had tried to discredit the memoirs by saying they were a KGB plant and a forgery. The experts rejected rumors of Victor Louis' involvement as the intermediary between Khrushchev and Time Inc. because Louis was presumed to be a KGB agent. Khrushchev had somehow circumvented the KGB. The possibility that Louis might have become Khrushchev's instrument to deliver the memoirs to the West for precisely that circumvention did not gain much currency at the time. Nor did a theory that Aleksandr Shelepin, the former head of the KGB and a rival of Brezhnev, had sponsored the memoirs in an attempt to revive the reputation of Stalin.

I sent Victor a copy of the book by air mail to his Moscow office and he passed it along to the family. Khrushchev liked the chronological format of his career and that it was interspersed with twenty pages of pictures and appendixes, including a picture of his Politburo members. His secret speech at the Twentieth Party Congress was reprinted in full. His wife, Nina Petrovna, who initially had opposed the project, could read English. She changed her attitude about the memoirs after she read segments of the text and translated it, with the help of her son Sergei, to Nikita Sergeyevich in Russian. He was delighted, Victor reported.

In early spring of 1971, Khrushchev was again forced to return to the hospital to treat his heart condition. In the exclusive Kremlin hospital, his old friends and fellow patients congratulated him on the publication of his memoirs. They had listened to excerpts on short wave radio and urged him to continue. As soon as he was able to leave the hospital, Khrushchev resumed recording the highlights of his career. His voice was weaker than on the earlier tapes, but his criticisms were stronger and the range of events he covered more controversial, including the Cuban missile crisis and the internal politics of Soviet atomic scientists. Khrushchev continued dictating through the summer until shortly before he died in September

1971. It was evident from his comments on "the need to complete my work" that the dictation sustained his will to live during the final months. Victor Louis announced Khrushchev's death with an exclusive in the *London Evening News*.

Time Inc. had enough samples of the voice-printed tapes to prove the book was genuine. Victor Louis had promised us that after Khrushchev's death all the tapes for the book would be made available. In November 1971, Leonid Brezhnev was in Paris for a state visit and since I would be covering the story for *Time*, Victor suggested we meet for dinner. At a small bistro on the left bank near Boulevard St. Germain, we ordered pheasant cooked in sauerkraut and chestnuts, perfect with a pitcher of nouveau Beaujolais. We relaxed over the excellent meal and Victor told me how Khrushchev had produced enough tapes for a second volume. As soon as we had a chance to evaluate the new material, Victor was prepared to negotiate the contract for a sequel.

Toward the end of the meal, Louis complained about a splinter in his hand, and started to touch it, wondering how to extract the sliver of wood in the heel of his palm. Unexpectedly, a middle-aged woman leaned over from a neighboring table and, speaking in English, offered him the use of a mini first aid kit she carried in her purse. Victor gratefully accepted and tried to carry off the moment with aplomb, thanking her profusely. We looked at each other in silence while the woman and her companion paid their bill and left the restaurant. Foolishly, we assumed everyone spoke only French; we hoped the details of our conversation about a second volume had not been overheard. I tried to reassure Victor that it was only when the woman saw him trying to remove the splinter that he had attracted her attention, but Victor brooded. I paid the check and we left, chastened by thoughts of our exposure in Copenhagen. We would be in touch, I assured Victor.

Early in 1972, Murray Gart flew to Moscow to discuss the status of the *Time* Bureau. John Shaw, an experienced and fearless Australian foreign correspondent, replaced me as bureau chief after a gap of two years. The Soviet Press Department agreed to Shaw only on the condition that he come on a journalist-tourist visa, which would allow the visa to be revoked at a moment's notice and not be subject to reciprocity under the informal quota in effect between Washington and Moscow. Gart used the visit to Moscow to meet alone with Victor Louis, who promised to make "the full batch" of new tapes available for examination. Gart stressed that Time Inc. would have to receive all the outstanding tapes for the first volume as well. In order for there to be a second volume, Time Inc. would have to be in a position to publicly establish the authenticity of both volumes with the tapes. The second volume would verify the authenticity of the published memoir. Victor asked for a list of the passages that needed tapes. Gart promised to provide "an inventory of the necessary confirming tapes."

Victor provided a letter of authorization for use of the key to his safe deposit box at the Swiss Bank in Zurich, to be given to Gideon de Margitay. In April, de Margitay flew to Zurich, picked up the tapes for the new volume, and left a detailed list of the original tapes that we required. Strobe Talbott, who was then *Time*'s East European correspondent based in Belgrade, was called back, instructed to come to New York to attend a VIP screening of a television documentary based on *Khrushchev Remembers*, produced for Time-Life Films by Harold Mayer Productions. The next day Strobe flew to Washington to work on the tapes.

There were between 60 and 100 hours of new tapes to be evaluated and summarized. Strobe set up shop in the second floor sitting room in our house in Washington; the room was quickly converted into a studio of tape decks and Uher recorders, sophisticated machines that could be played at various speeds. Slowing the tapes was useful in listening to rapid, slurred, or otherwise difficult speech. Our son Steven, then 15, served as technical assistant to copy the tapes, which had originally been recorded at the slowest speed of $^{15}/_{16}$ of an inch per second, onto new reels to play at the more convenient speed of $3\frac{3}{4}$ inches per second. Strobe listened to the tapes with headphones and called me over to catch choice descriptions by the old man. Victor had provided an outline of the material Khrushchev dictated in the last year of his life. As he progressed with his evaluation, comparing the tapes to the outline, Strobe discovered they didn't match: a great many of the subjects covered in the outline for volume 2 were missing from the tapes. Victor had sent all the tapes for the first volume but he had withheld nearly half, some 50 hours of tape, for the second volume.

I was furious and called Victor in England where he was awaiting our response. He readily acknowledged that he had delivered only half the tapes. Surely we could decide from that large sample whether "part two" of the memoirs was worth "lots more money." He would provide the remaining tapes when we offered him an acceptable contract. By stressing that "the new book contains material as good as the first," Victor made it clear that he was looking for a hefty advance. Victor said he was in no hurry to come to terms; he would return to Moscow in two weeks. We could also get in touch with him through "Granny," Mrs. Statham, his mother-in-law.

Strobe and I met with Murray Gart on how to resolve the impasse. We argued that it would be best not to let Victor return to Moscow without the terms of a new contract. One could never predict conditions in Moscow. Since the tapes were in the West, we should acquire them as soon as possible. We planned a face-to-face meeting in Dorking, where Victor felt on safe ground. Victor seemed unconcerned by British counterintelligence monitoring his phone calls. He said he felt flattered by the additional security in the shape of two gentlemen in plain clothes whenever they arrived unannounced at the front door to check on his whereabouts. His mother-in-law's house was his sanctuary and he preferred it over a hotel suite in Paris or Zurich.

The overnight Pan American flight from Dulles to Heathrow arrived at 7:30

a.m. on May 1, 1972. We rented a car, then checked into an airport motel for a shower and breakfast before driving to Dorking. Strobe drove on the left side while I navigated with a map through green forests on two-lane roads, twisting and turning our way to Westhumble Place, Mrs. Statham's home. Victor was waiting and came straight to the point: "Well, since you've come all this way to talk to me, I assume you've brought a contract."

"No, we haven't," I replied.

"Well that's fine, because I haven't brought the new tapes. I've only got the confirming tapes from volume 1 here. If you want the new tapes, they are in a safe deposit box in my name in Zurich." He waved a letter granting power of attorney for access to the vault and said he would fill in the name of any person we stipulated. All we had to do was to get authorization from New York for a contract acceptable to him. For the new volume, he asked for a $400,000 advance.

We were off on a steeplechase of negotiation. I insisted that he was obligated to turn over the new tapes as part of our original agreement. He and the family would make a sizable amount of money since, with no advance up front, there would be a higher royalty percentage. We just did not understand, Louis countered; he and his associates needed an advance not only to compensate for the risks they were taking but to cover the bribes necessary to bring the tapes out of the Soviet Union. "I had to pay off plenty of people to get the first book out, and I'll have to do it again this time," he grumbled at Strobe and me.

"What sort of people?" I asked, hoping to gain an insight into exactly how he had engineered the transfer of tapes to Europe.

"Border and customs types, and others, too," Louis replied, but he refused to elaborate. Nor would he name his associates other than to refer to family and friends, with whom he would share in the proceeds. To strengthen his position, Louis added that he and his team were in no hurry to conclude a deal, perhaps not until Brezhnev retired. Only a sizable advance would make it worth taking the risks for a new volume. No contract, no tapes. Or so it seemed for openers.

It was my turn. There was only one Marxist-Leninist cliche I liked to quote: "Life itself shows us that the situation has changed," I said, reminding Victor that the bottom had fallen out of the market for memoirs in America. Clifford Irving's hoax of Howard Hughes' life story, foisted off on *Life*, raised doubts about all new sensational memoir projects. Victor listened carefully while I explained that, by withholding half of the tapes, he had weakened, not strengthened, his negotiating position. He had created distrust and anxiety in New York. Nothing could proceed until he fulfilled his original pledge to provide all the tapes, old and new.

Victor feigned anger and hurt. Why should he be penalized because *Life* had been duped with the Hughes memoirs? Besides, from his standpoint the American market for memoirs was not so bad after all. Harrison Salisbury of the *New York Times*, he claimed, had offered him $1 million for the new Khrushchev tapes. "Why don't we forget about Time Inc. and Little, Brown and sell the second volume ourselves. You and Strobe can work with me," said Victor, taking out his checkbook. He then wrote out two checks for ten thousand pounds each to Strobe and me. We refused to take the bait. We said his idea was unacceptable. Clearly, Victor did not want to pursue this line and suggested perhaps Strobe and I needed a break to "talk things over." (When we arrived back in Washington, the checks were waiting for us. We had the Time Inc. lawyer return them with a formal rejection.)

Strobe, whose role was "good cop" and technical expert, to my "bad cop" negotiator, revived the discussion by reminding Victor of the immense historical value of the memoirs and the achievement he had already accomplished. A second volume would remove all doubts about the genuine nature of the tapes, and once that hurdle was crossed fewer questions would focus on how the tapes got to the West. This was the kind of proposition that made Victor's juices flow. He loved to conspire; Victor served many masters, but always his own survival and success were paramount.

After our next break, Victor returned to the drawing room, opened a briefcase, and, with no further explanation, laid the "confirming tapes" we had requested for *Khrushchev Remembers* on the table. Victor had tested us. He realized we could not proceed until he provided the tapes he had promised. Only when it appeared that all was lost and we would have to withdraw had Victor yielded. We tried to act nonchalant, as if we'd always expected Victor to come around.

No longer could we say that Victor was not a man of his word. Strobe held onto the package of tapes until he found the opportunity to slip out to the car and lock them in the trunk. We were back on track. Victor realized that it would be folly to switch to another publisher, but he delighted in threats that created uncertainty. Despite his delaying tactic, it was readily apparent that he, too, was concerned that *Khrushchev Remembers* be accepted as genuine. Legitimacy was primary. The price for the second volume was secondary.

Victor pressed as hard as he could for an advance to pay himself, the family, and his overhead. The first-volume receipts had more than repaid Time Inc. the $750,000 advance, and foreign sales were still being credited to his account. Time-Life Films had made a documentary movie of the book. When he was in Moscow, Louis' main concern was that the memoirs not be judged to be part of an anti-Soviet campaign to undermine Brezhnev.

I assured Victor I would work on getting him a contract and would raise all his demands for a substantial advance and higher royalties. He again agreed to provide us with the rest of the tapes, and we parted with his promise to be in touch when they were ready. During the summer of 1972, word came that the tapes were ready to be picked up in Dorking. Victor was not there when I arrived and Mrs. Statham handed me the package. The only thing missing was the full tapes of Khrushchev's reminiscences of the Twentieth Party Congress.

While sorting the additional tapes at home in Washington, I received a telephone call from Gregory (Grisha) Freidin, a 26-year-old Russian émigré and friend from our two years in Moscow; he had married the American scholar Victoria Bonnell. Grisha was on his way to begin graduate work in Slavic languages and literature at the University of California in Berkeley. "I think I have a job for you," I told Grisha, and invited him to Washington.

As soon as he arrived, I handed Grisha the earphones. After twenty minutes, he tore them from his head and smiled: "It's either Zoshchenko or Khrushchev."[15] Grisha began transcribing the tapes and, by the summer of 1973, they were ready for translation. Strobe returned from Belgrade and invited Grisha to his family's home in Chagrin Falls, Ohio, where they worked on the translation of *Khrushchev Remembers: The Last Testament.*

Early in planning the second volume, we decided to undertake a systematic, scientific authentication of the tapes. Time Inc. again contracted with Voice Identification Services, this time to analyze all 180 hours of the new and old tapes and certify that they contained only Khrushchev's voice. We wanted to make sure nothing had been inserted or changed. Spectrographic analysis of voice printing is an electronic process based on the fact that every individual's voice is unique, just like the whorls of skin on a fingerprint. The sound of an unknown person's voice is broken down electronically into a visually identifiable wave pattern, or spectrogram, which when printed out can then be compared against a sample of a known voice. If the known and unknown prints "match" in at least ten different "points of identification," the known and unknown samples can be defined as having been spoken by one and the same person. The known sample used to test the Khrushchev tapes was again a recording provided by the United Nations of his address to the General Assembly. Because of Khrushchev's frequent stops, starts, and interruptions in the tapes, Voice Identification Services had to make nearly 6,000 separate spectrograms. Each was examined for the ten points of coincidence that are required for a conclusive "match" in voice printing. In their final report the experts wrote:

> Identification must be absolute; there is no such thing as partial identification. We have positively identified 175.5 of the 180 hours of tape recording or 97.5 percent. We are able to state that these 175.5 hours of tape were recorded by Nikita S. Khrushchev. Further, in no instance throughout the entire 180 hours of tape was there any evidence that there was anyone other than Nikita S. Khrushchev speaking. In those portions of the recordings when we were unable to make an identification, it was not necessarily because it was a different person speaking, but rather because the frequency response of the recordings was inadequate or the recordings were too badly distorted for voice print identification.

Strobe reviewed the 4.5 hours that could not be authenticated because of the poor technical quality. He found the episodes were inconsequential, dealing with World War II, Khrushchev's 1956 trip to Europe, and agricultural policy.[16]

By October 1973, the voice printing and translation were advanced far enough to prepare for publication of the book. We could then donate the tapes and transcripts to the Russian Research Center and the Oral History Library at Columbia University. Marshall Shulman, who headed the Russian Research Center, was an early believer in the authenticity of the memoirs; he had broached with Murrary Gart the possibility of Time Inc. donating the raw materials for use by scholars and bona fide researchers. There was no problem in Time Inc. making the gift because the copyright for the English language translations was registered by Little, Brown and Company. The Soviet Union had joined the International Copyright Convention only in 1972, which meant it had no claims to the 1970 publication.

In my initial conversations with Victor Louis, we had discussed the goal of preserving the tapes for posterity and eventually preparing a Russian language edition to which the family would retain the rights. In the neo-Stalinist reality of Leonid Brezhnev's Soviet Union, such far-out wishful thinking seemed, Aleksandr Solzhenitsyn was fond of saying, like throwing peas against a stone wall to make it crumble.

We agreed there was to be no authorized Russian language edition until Khrushchev's heirs decided to print one. Shulman accepted this condition and drew up a deed for transfer of the materials. Hedley Donovan called for a meeting with Gart, Talbott, and me to discuss the handover of the materials to Columbia. Donovan said he wanted "maximum revelation up to and perhaps including the naming of the intermediary"—whom he did not name. All that was fine, but Victor Louis was still insisting on a contract. He wanted what he hoped would be a final face-to-face meeting to "seal the deal."

Catching up with Victor was no easy matter. He had to obtain a new visa every time he traveled to England. I had been promoted from White House correspondent to diplomatic editor and was now covering Henry Kissinger, who had himself been promoted from national security adviser to secretary of state after Nixon's reelection in 1972. Kissinger planned a quick tour of the Middle East in mid-December which would end in a multilateral conference on the Arab-Israeli conflict in Geneva on the 18th, 19th, or 20th of December. Victor agreed to meet me there at the Davidoff cigar store. In the best tradition of spy tradecraft, whoever arrived in Geneva first would go the cigar store each day at noon until the other arrived. The Israelis and Arabs, who had no regard for Khrushchev's new memoirs, allowed their differences to force a postponement of the conference and our meeting was delayed. Later in December, we crossed paths in Paris and I showed Victor the working title for the new volume, *Khrushchev Remembers: The Last Testament*, and a table of contents. He was pleased and made no new financial demands. He agreed that the Khrushchev family might be named as the source of the material in the introduction I would write for the new volume; "family and friends" was the formulation we agreed upon. We shared a cab to Orly airport and Victor stared out the window. Without looking at me, he murmured, "Well, maybe they'll punish the others." Victor realized that the memoirs were no longer under his control, yet he hoped that we would come up with a way to shed his responsibility for transferring the tapes and transcript from Moscow to the West. To preserve his credibility in Moscow, it was essential to his defense that Time not identify him as the intermediary, no matter what speculation floated around him.

There had been no time or place to discuss the contract, and Victor asked for a final meeting in January in Dorking.

Talbott was in England again working with Edward Crankshaw, who had agreed to write the preface for the new book. By January 21, 1974, all the pieces fell into place. Victor was in Dorking when I arrived in London. First I met with Strobe and than called Victor from the Connaught Hotel the following day.

"Where are you? What's going on here? I've been waiting for you to call since yesterday. Do you think it's easier for me to get here than for you?" Victor shouted on the phone. Strobe was standing nearby, and I told him Victor was grumpy.

"He's back to his old self," Strobe said.

Strobe rented a scarlet MGB sports car and we drove to Dorking in the rain, arriving at 5 p.m. I hoped to set us off on the right foot with small gifts of perfume for Jennifer and Mrs. Statham, a bottle of champagne and a fine claret for Victor. Not to be topped, he produced a box of La Coronas from "Gavana," using the Russian pronunciation. Mrs. Statham served tea, crumpets, and rum cake. Strobe complimented Jennifer on her healthy appearance. Her tearose white porcelain skin glowed in the fireplace light when she drew the heavy red velvet curtains. She laughed, "I've been taking yoga lessons and I've gotten our cook to cut down on fat."

It hardly seemed the moment to bring up the memorandum of understanding I had brought for Victor to sign. Before I could decide, Victor said: "Let's see this so-called memorandum of misunderstanding. I know you'll have good news and bad news for me." I handed the memorandum to him and he flipped through it quickly, returned it to the envelope, and said, "All right, now what is the bad news?" Through a light supper and afterward over cigars and coffee, Victor did not try to discuss the memorandum except to crack little jokes complaining that according to the terms he would be "hereinafter known as the Agent." "Now everyone will know I am an agent," he said mockingly. When he came to the clause referring to an edition for the physically handicapped, he quipped, "I guess this means my own share has been cut down so that all I have left is the rights to the braille version." Strobe noted wryly that Khrushchev's tales would lend themselves very well to a book-on-tape.

Victor stopped and gave Strobe a long, disturbed look. He sensed a problem that was not covered in any memorandum of understanding: "I want it understood that the tapes are not to be used commercially. I don't want them being played over Radio Liberty and broadcast back into the USSR. It's very important that this project not become anti-Soviet propaganda."

Then, making it clear we would not pursue the memorandum any further, he asked: Why did the American satellite crash in the Soviet Union? Answer: Because our standard of living is so high. We laughed appropriately, then moved on to Watergate and détente. Louis predicted that Brezhnev would not suffer politically if Nixon were impeached, especially if Kissinger remained in office: "Nixon is a personality Brezhnev can deal with—they hugged each other in the U.S.—but Kissinger is such a personality, too." By 10 p.m. we had exhausted the small talk and Victor indicated by his distracted manner that he was ready to call it a night.

On the drive back to our hotel in London, we reviewed the evening. On the surface it appeared that Victor had accepted the memorandum, which offered no cash advance, low royalties, and was basically a continuation of the original contract. The bad news was that he had not signed it.

The following morning we returned to Dorking. No sooner had Victor closed the wooden front gate behind us than he attacked in true Stalin negotiating style. "I hope you two guys are prepared to negotiate a serious contract today. That thing you brought yesterday was a disgrace. I listened politely, but now let's be serious." Louis insisted that the royalty schedule be improved and he demanded a bigger share of the foreign and syndication rights. Victor enjoyed the give and take of bargaining and concocting new ways to do business. Victor first asked for what he called "a guaranteed minimum yield" for him and his partners. In fact, publishers base their advances on an estimate of how many copies a book will sell and Victor had done his own quick figuring to come up with a minimum figure of $150,000. That sounds like an advance, we said. "No, it's an after-the-fact guarantee," he offered with a smile.

"After what fact?" we asked.

"After your people in New York and Boston overcome their fears and realize that the book will do well," Victor insisted.

I explained risk and reward in book publishing and other businesses in the West. "You know, in our country," Victor explained, "we must live for today. Long term rewards are a luxury we cannot always afford." I promised to raise the question of an advance in New York. Victor toyed with his ballpoint pen as if ready to sign but then reconsidered and launched yet another round of dickering over the terms. By tea time in the late afternoon, Strobe became impatient, reminding me that we had to be back in London by 8 p.m. for a telephone conference with Larned Bradford of Little, Brown. We pointed out again to Victor that launching the second volume was not easy. We had our own "Kremlin politics" to deal with in New York. Not everybody at Time Inc. was as committed to the project as we were. I urged him to sign and he did.

There were still vital loose ends to confront, such as Hedley Donovan's demand for "maximum disclosure." Victor agreed that we could say that "family and friends" had provided the tapes but asked us not to describe the chain of events leading to the delivery of the material. That could lead to formal legal sanctions or loss of Communist Party privileges for the family. In the Soviet Union, Victor would perpetuate the story that Khrushchev's grandson-in-law Lev Petrov, who had been ill and died after the taping, was involved in the transfer of the tapes to the West. Victor urged us to provide an advance copy of the new book to Soviet Ambassador Anatoli Dobrynin in Washington. Victor's arcane reasoning was that if the book were presented as a complex, sophisticated view of the pressures and realities of Soviet politics, not an anti-Soviet revelation like Solzhenitsyn's *Gulag Archipelago*, it might serve, for internal Soviet consumption, as an antidote to the brutal picture of the Soviet Union as a labor camp. "It would make perfect logical sense for it to appear in the way I'm suggesting. In Russia, you know, they like things which are countermeasures against other things," said Victor.

He still needed protection, he insisted. Public confirmation of his role would force the Soviet authorities to act against him. It was essential that the book not be used as propaganda.

"Remember," he said, announcing a critical new element, "the authorities have copies of some of the tapes—not all of them, but enough to compare what they have against the published version and judge whether the edited material has been twisted into a more offensive document than the original."

Victor refused to respond to our question of how the "authorities" had obtained "some tapes" but he said they did not know the full extent of the material or that another volume was in preparation. We could present the tapes to scholars and experts, but we still had to protect the individuals involved and avoid an official scandal in Moscow. Victor Louis' own motives were to enhance his image as a journalist-entrepreneur and someday, when all the tapes had been published, to take credit for masterminding and executing the Jones Project. He hoped to change his image from a disinformation character assassin to a world class historical preservationist.

At the end of March, I had accompanied Kissinger to Moscow for a meeting on arms control with Leonid Brezhnev. I met briefly with Victor, who, as I was leaving, hinted in a throwaway line that "there might still be some missing pieces to be revealed but only when the timing is right." Victor was deliberately vague about the contents and refused to be drawn out.

Publication of *Khrushchev Remembers: The Last Testament* was scheduled for mid-

April 1974. Time Inc. announced that Khrushchev's tapes would be made available to scholars and Soviet experts. The collection of materials would be turned over to the Oral History Library at Columbia University, dispelling doubts of their provenance. Who was behind the memoirs and why they were released in the West became less of an issue once the essential question of authenticity was resolved. Theodore Shabad, a *New York Times* Soviet affairs expert, had written skeptically when the first book appeared in 1970. Now he hailed the impending release of the tapes for resolving doubts about the memoirs. "There had been earlier speculation," wrote Shabad, "that the Khrushchev memoirs had been taken abroad by Victor Louis, a Soviet journalist who has often been described as a middleman for the KGB, the secret police. Some Soviet affairs experts had even questioned the authenticity of the memoirs."

On April 11, 1974, Time Inc. and the Columbia University Oral History Library invited a group of American and European specialists for a presentation of the tapes, transcripts, and voice-print reports.[17] Marshall Shulman provided a home for the archive and presided over the meeting. The evening went well. Tape recorders with reels of Khrushchev's tapes and Russian language transcripts stood next to copies of the book for comparison. Shulman explained how the materials would be catalogued and opened to scholars and bona fide researchers. We were feeling vindicated and proud of the project, now in its fifth year. Strobe and I described our work with the memoirs. I was asked if this was the final volume. "I hope so," I joked.

Victor was out of sight and mind until Michel Tatu, the highly respected Soviet affairs editor for *Le Monde* and an authority on Kremlin politics, asked about Victor Louis' role in the memoirs during the question and answer session at Columbia University.

"His involvement or noninvolvement bears directly on the extent to which the memoirs are officially sanctioned; so please tell us about Louis," Tatu asked.

We had prepared for the question, and the answer, while unsatisfactory, was firm: "Many names and theories behind the memoirs had been speculated upon," but we were not going to comment on any of them specifically. We hoped the material and its contribution to history would speak for itself. There was no follow up from the experts, even the early skeptics. When Tatu returned to Paris, he analyzed *Khrushchev Remembers: The Last Testament*, for *Le Monde*, focusing on the *"mode de transmission."* Tatu concluded that, as long as Victor Louis was presumed to be "an official Soviet journalist," the memoirs were to be judged as "authentic but censored."

The second volume received favorable reviews; controversy shifted from who had made it available to analyzing and challenging Khrushchev's claims and his version of events. As we were finishing the second volume, Victor again hinted that there was still more to come in the distant future when Brezhnev was gone and a new politics of openness was triumphant.[18] It would be a time with no fear of retribution for publishing what had been edited from the first two volumes. The distant hope of a Russian language edition published in Moscow could become a reality.

Despite the Nixon-Brezhnev efforts toward détente in 1974, Khrushchev's *Last Testament* rankled the Kremlin Politburo. By then Strobe was the State Department correspondent for *Time*; he was aboard Secretary of State Henry Kissinger's plane en route to Moscow when word came that he would not be granted a Soviet visa. Kissinger did nothing to protest and Strobe was forced to leave the press party when Kissinger's plane refueled in Copenhagen.

After Mikhail Gorbachev took power, Sergei Khrushchev wrote to him in 1986 requesting return of his father's tapes, seized in 1970, which were held at the offices of the Central Committee. Sergei received a favorable reply and a runaround; the tapes could not be found. For nearly two years, he waited. Finally in 1988 he received 400 pages of text but no tapes.[19] Sergei gave an interview to the Yugoslav newspaper *Vjesnik*, in which he said he believed his father's memoirs would eventually be published in the Soviet Union, and "I am working on that." Strobe read the interview, contacted him, and arranged for Time Inc. to provide copies of all the transcripts in Columbia's Oral History Library, as well as copies of missing tapes. In 1989 and 1990, the first excerpts appeared in Russian in a number of Soviet academic and popular journals. Sergei embarked on a mission to publish a comprehensive version of all his father's memoirs in Russian and in English, on which he is working as of this writing.

In the summer of 1989, Victor called to say that the final batch of tapes was ready for transcribing and for English language translation. In the summer of Gorbachev's *glasnost*, Victor decided to release the final batch of tapes that had been stored in a vault in Zurich. These were the tapes containing the sections that we were certain, from maddening gaps that occurred in key points of the narrative, had been edited out of the tapes we received in 1970 and 1973. Nikita Khrushchev had approved the deletions because "they might constitute military secrets and incidental references to people then in power in the USSR."[20]

Leona and I picked up the tapes in Zurich from Victor's banker. Back in Washington, we joined forces with Vyacheslav (Slava) Luchkov, a visiting scholar and translator, whom we had first met in Moscow in 1968. Slava and his wife, Rita, transcribed the tapes. Unexpectedly, there were more than 300 hours of Khrushchev reviewing his career, often repeating the same story with slight but significant variations. Over the next year I edited and organized the remaining memoirs, probing Slava's native Russian understanding for shades of meaning. After twenty years, the deletions for political reasons emerged. The state secrets appeared in *Khrushchev Remembers: The Glasnost Tapes*, published by Little, Brown in 1991, completing the memoirs. No other Soviet leader, before or after, has told his tale with such candor.

★ ★ ★

Victor Louis never told me that KGB General Vyacheslav Kevorkov was his contact and control officer. Nor did he explain that he told Kevorkov that Nikita Khrushchev was taping his memoirs. Kevorkov reported to KGB chairman Yuri Andropov that the project was under way. On March 25, 1970, Andropov advised the Central Committee in a top secret report:

N. S. Khrushchev has recently started work on memoirs of the period of his life when he occupied senior Party and state posts. These dictated memoirs contain detailed information constituting exclusive Party and state secrets on such specific questions as the defense capability of the Soviet state, the development of industry, agriculture, the economy in general, scientific and technical achievements, the security organs, foreign policy, relations between the CPSU and the fraternal parties of socialist and capitalist countries, and so on. He reveals discussions at closed meetings of the Politburo. . . . Under these circumstances, it is imperative that urgent operational measures be taken to permit the monitoring of Khrushchev's work on his memoirs, and to prevent the entirely likely leak of Party and state secrets abroad. With this aim in view, it seems sensible to establish operational secret surveillance of Khrushchev and his son, Sergei. . . . We also think it would be desirable to summon N. S. Khrushchev to the Central Committee again and to warn him of his responsibility for the publication and leak of Party and state secrets and to demand that he draw the necessary conclusions.[21]

On March 27, 1970, Andropov, accompanied by another Politburo member, I. V. Kapitonov, informed Khrushchev about "the exchange of opinions at the Politburo." Their intervention had little effect "except to make Khrushchev and his son Sergei act with greater caution."[22] On July 11, 1970, the KGB seized the tapes and transcripts from Sergei Khrushchev for "safekeeping" and to "prevent theft by foreign intelligence agencies."[23] By that time, the transcript was in the West and it was too late to stop the project.

In September 1999, the authors attended a CIA-sponsored conference in Berlin to discuss intelligence issues marking the end of the cold war. After two intriguing days of listening to the opening of secrets by intelligence officers who had taken part in covert operations forty years earlier, we slipped away from the conference and flew to Cologne. There we met retired General Kevorkov. Through his KGB duties, Kevorkov had intersected the lives of a number of our Moscow contacts, who had told us the necessity of our meeting him. In between a whisper and a deep throaty voice, they told us of his primary role in establishing *Ostpolitik*, the back channel between Soviet leaders and the West German government of Willy Brandt and Egon Bahr.

Kevorkov had been at the right hand of Yuri Andropov, the KGB chairman. Among the Soviet intelligence elite, Andropov was hailed as a modernizer who instituted selective repression instead of mass repression, and could have reformed the system if he had not died from kidney disease in 1984. Andropov, still described as an innovative idealist by Kevorkov, was infamous in the West for arresting dissidents on the grounds of mental illness and throwing them into lunatic asylums where they were drugged into submission. Among his earlier duties, Kevorkov had been in charge of the *mamkas*, KGB officers assigned to develop contacts with foreign journalists to determine what they were reporting from Moscow; the *mamkas* would also feed them disinformation at critical moments. The friend who had told us to be sure to meet Kevorkov was Vadim Biryukov, who had left the KGB to become editor of the successful magazine *Business in Russia*.[24]

We had no trouble spotting Kevorkov when he met us at the airport. His slim waist and jutting chest, combined with a watchful impatience, marked his military bearing even in jeans and a light blue denim shirt. We made small talk during the ride into downtown Cologne, where he parked and we walked to the sunny side of the city's great Gothic cathedral. At an outdoor cafe that occupied the plaza in front of the cathedral, we found a table where we could face each other. Kevorkov listened carefully while we spoke of Biryukov and other mutual friends.

There were a few words about Khrushchev's memoirs, but Kevorkov still did not seem to know who we were. Was he playing for effect or had Victor Louis compartmentalized my role so that Kevorkov did not know the details of how Victor had worked with me and Time Inc.? Then Victor's words of more than thirty years before came back: "You will do a great service but no one on this side will know your name."

There was no need for us to negotiate the next step; both sides would tell their story of how the Khrushchev memoirs were initiated and brought out of the Soviet Union. It was clear from the concentrated intensity and depth of breathing on both sides that each was listening to a story that overturned the internal myths creating our self-identity over a lifetime, the memories of milestone events.

Kevorkov said that he and Andropov had known and approved of Khrushchev's interviews with television producer Lucy Jarvis when she visited his dacha and later put together the show for NBC early in 1967. Soon afterward, Khrushchev's son Sergei, his grandson-in-law, Lev Petrov, and Victor Louis, who arranged the meetings, got the idea of translating the full interviews. From there the idea of an unauthorized biography emerged. They would publish the book in the West and attract worldwide attention, restoring Khrushchev's place in history. Kevorkov said he liked the idea of building up the credibility of his agent, Victor Louis, who was instrumental in the original NBC project. This would help make Victor an authoritative figure with his own channel by which other contacts and projects could be accomplished. Victor could be used as an unofficial envoy, not a spy. Before Andropov became ill with his kidney disease, Kevorkov said, he brought Victor to Andropov's apartment where the three sat around and planned new overseas escapades for Victor to further Soviet foreign policy goals.

Kevorkov said he had only one concern for the cabal around Khrushchev. He wanted to be sure he could tell Andropov there would be no remarks criticizing or assessing the regime then in power, Brezhnev and his Politburo. Khrushchev's "family and friends" quickly replied that there would be no references to or discussion of the current government. Andropov could rely on their promise, because they would decide what tapes left the dacha, what was deleted, and what was stored for a future generation to interpret.

Kevorkov told us he gave the nod to the project and never looked at it again until it was in print in sixteen languages, a worldwide phenomenon. He said he had not expected much to come out of the interviews because he knew Khrushchev's fragmented way of speaking, his colorful but incomprehensible provincial expressions. Kevorkov said he could not imagine, until he saw the book in print, how a translator could make sense out of Khrushchev's excessive and often disconnected ramblings. The KGB had copies of the tapes and transcripts, he explained, but did not think them a problem. How could a serious book emerge from such a jumble of stories, he asked? "We were amazed with how Strobe Talbott's translation made a book out of such material." True to their word, the interviewers had not asked any questions about how Khrushchev had been ousted and what Khrushchev thought of Brezhnev.

The timing in Kevorkov's rendition of the story of how *Khrushchev Remembers* was recorded and transmitted was somewhat puzzling. According to him, Victor had looked for a magazine publisher to bring out the interviews before the secretive arrangements in Moscow. Kevorkov said the first publisher Victor approached, Jess Gorkin of *Parade* magazine, turned him down because he believed the project was too expensive for them to undertake. Kevorkov said Gorkin suggested Victor go to *Time* magazine, which in 1968 was the leader in the magazine field. Sitting next to Gorkin was Lloyd (Skip) Shearer, chief editor of *Parade*, who said, "Go to *Time* and ask for Strobe Talbott as the translator. One of these days he will be my son-in-law."[25] However, Victor Louis felt that to go to *Time* in New York was to risk confidentiality; he decided to make the approach through the Moscow Bureau. Kevorkov said he did not know that the first approach to *Time* went through the Moscow Bureau. Nor had he heard of me or the details of the transfer of the tapes to the West.

"That's right. I was told no one in Moscow would know my name," I said.

Leona and I sat in bemused silence for a long time. Then we asked why, if Kevorkov and Andropov knew the memoirs were going to the West, they allowed the most astounding revelations in Soviet history, barring only the 1956 speech to the Twentieth Party Congress, which got to the West by theft, to be taken out without KGB control over its content?

Kevorkov did not have to think for long. "You know, Khrushchev was sitting in his dacha outside Moscow, out of power. What could he do to us? This was the first time we had passed power from one leader to another without bloodshed. We wanted the whole world to know that we are a normal country."

The Overflight Wars

By August 29, 1949, when the first Soviet atomic bomb was detonated, Stalin had effectively isolated the Soviet Union and Eastern Europe from the outside world. The CIA, which had only been in existence for two years, did not yet have a station in Moscow. The Soviet military could carry out its planning, production, and deployment activities with the utmost secrecy. In the late 1940s and early 1950s, the CIA and Air Force began efforts to identify military and industrial targets in the Soviet Union. Breaking the VENONA messages was valuable for understanding espionage in the past, but their content lacked current operational value.

The search for targets began with sifting through German aerial reconnaissance photographs dating from the 1940s. In December 1946, the joint service Far East Command had organized Project Wringer, the interrogation of German and Japanese prisoners of war returning from forced labor in the Soviet Union. Wringer employed 1,300 specially trained military and civilian personnel in Germany, Austria, and Japan to question thousands of prisoners repatriated from the USSR. Until 1951 most of the strategic intelligence for targets in the Soviet Union came from Project Wringer.[1]

The Strategic Air Command began flying aerial reconnaissance, ELINT (electronic intelligence), and COMINT (communications intelligence) flights near the Soviet Union from which came vital information about border defense installations and radar sites. Early efforts with conventional aircraft such as the RB-47 and RB-45C probed Soviet radar, but failed to penetrate the heartland, the sites of missile manufacturing and deployment.

Limited penetration overflights of Soviet territory began in 1950 and continued during the Korean War. In 1952 President Truman authorized a photography overflight to determine whether or not the Soviet Union was massing TU-4 bombers (copied directly from the American B-29) near Alaska, which would have put them within range for a one way, suicide mission to drop nuclear weapons on the United States. After aerial refueling, a single B-47 flew into Siberia west of Wrangel

Island and turned eastward, exiting Soviet territory through the Chukotskiy Peninsula over the Bering Strait. The photographs taken by the B-47 established that there were no TU-4 bomber squadrons near Alaska.[2]

Intelligence on bases within the Soviet Union, the state of the economy, and military preparations remained hidden. The Air Force was "desperate for intelligence from the inside of Russia."[3]

After Stalin's death in 1953, the CIA began an intelligence gathering program using nonofficial travelers from the United States and friendly foreign nations. The program, code named REDSKIN, focused on major metropolitan areas and the primary transportation routes. Travelers were asked simple questions; their answers were then correlated to estimate the size and quality of Soviet aircraft, atomic energy capacity, and missile production. A traveler might be asked to identify the color of smoke coming from a specific factory or the color of a sand pile. Serial numbers on Soviet boxcars and aircraft and products photographed at Soviet trade fairs helped analysts to deduce annual production figures. The numbers indicated what materials were being used in production and the availability of machine tools. This crazy-quilt mosaic required skillful triangulation of sources, some verified with amateur photographs taken on the sly from civilian aircraft. Early discovery of SA-2 antiaircraft missile sites in the late 1950s came from REDSKIN photographs.[4]

Most Soviet strategic capabilities—bomber forces, ballistic missiles, submarine forces, and nuclear weapons plants—were concealed from outside observation. The U.S. Air Force, in search of targets for strategic bombing, turned to the American scientific community for new methods of acquiring intelligence through aerial reconnaissance.

By the end of the 1940s and into the early 1950s, American listening posts could monitor Soviet radio voice and data traffic in the air and produce real time signals intelligence. The National Security Agency found a way to tap into Soviet internal teletype communications. These teletyped messages were uncoded, clear transmissions on a multichannel communications network similar to Western Union that carried operational data on Soviet industrial and military production. These intercepts were a major source of data for analyzing Soviet military strength and strategic intentions.[5]

When the cold war intensified, demand for detailed military intelligence of the Soviet Union multiplied. In March 1950, the U.S. Air Force was assigned the responsibility for long-range strategic missiles, including ICBMs, and jurisdiction for military satellites. The RAND Corporation, supported by the Air Force, was directed to complete a study for a military Earth satellite. RAND's report in April 1951 projected a fully stabilized spacecraft that employed a television camera to scan the earth and transmit the images to receiving stations. The RAND report encouraged Air Force leaders to believe that periodic, directed observation of the Soviet Union might soon be conducted from extremely high altitudes.[6] To confirm these findings the Air Force called upon American scientists and space experts for advice.

Carl Overhage of Eastman Kodak chaired the team of fifteen professors and experts, which included Dr. Edwin (Din) Land, founder of Polaroid; Richard S. Perkin of the Perkin-Elmer Corporation, a high-technology innovator; and Air Force optics specialist Lieutenant Colonel Richard Leghorn (later the founder of Itek). This elite group gathered in Boston in an office over a secretarial school on Beacon Hill and produced the seminal, classified report that was to become the catalyst for a new era of satellite reconnaissance. The Beacon Hill Report of June 1952 recommended imaginative but still unproved approaches to obtain information for national intelligence estimates. Its fourteen chapters covered radar, radio, and photographic surveillance and examined the use of passive infrared and microwave reconnaissance. One of the report's predictive recommendations called for the development of advanced reconnaissance vehicles, specifically high altitude reconnaissance aircraft. The report stated:

We have reached a period in history when our peacetime knowledge of the capabilities, activities and dispositions of a potentially hostile nation is such as to demand that we supplement it with the maximum amount of information available through aerial reconnaissance. To avoid political involvements, such aerial reconnaissance must be conducted either from vehicles flying in friendly airspace, or—a decision on this point permitting—from vehicles whose performance is such that they can operate in Soviet airspace with greatly reduced chances of detection or interception.[7]

Soon after President Eisenhower took office in January 1953, he reviewed the nation's intelligence capabilities and found them lacking. He deplored the quality of America's intelligence estimates of Soviet strategic weapons and the paucity of reconnaissance of the Soviet bloc.[8] Eisenhower feared a surprise nuclear attack and was determined to develop the technical means to assess Soviet intentions. He was familiar with aerial photography and made frequent references to the postwar findings of the U.S. Strategic Bombing Surveys (USSBS), which showed that wartime analysis of aerial photography was "amazingly accurate and that some 80–90 percent of U.S. military intelligence came from it."[9]

Eisenhower expressed his concerns for good intelligence to Brigadier General George Goddard, the U.S. Air Force's top expert in aerial photography. "Without it you would have only your fears on which to plan your own defense arrangements and your whole military establishment. Now, if you're going to use nothing but fear and that's all you have, you are going to make us an armed camp. So this kind of knowledge is vital to us," Eisenhower told Goddard. The president had expressed a revolutionary philosophy of defense.[10]

Fears were growing. In the spring of 1953, a top secret RAND Corporation study pointed to the vulnerability of the Strategic Air Command's U.S. bases to a surprise attack by Soviet long-range bombers. In August 1953, the Soviet Union detonated its first hydrogen bomb, manufactured from lithium deuteride, a technology more advanced than the heavy water method used by the United States.

At the May Day air show in 1954, the Russians displayed a new long-range jet bomber of their own design, the Myasishchev-4, given the NATO designation Bison. The bomber was first spotted on April 18, 1954, apparently rehearsing for the May Day flyover of the Kremlin. Two bombers were flown one day, two the next, and three the following day. The new bomber generated a crash effort to determine the total number of Bison bombers. Military attachés with telephoto lenses photographed the bombers from the roof of the U.S. embassy. They rushed the exposed film to Washington. Enlargements revealed two-digit numbers in the teens on the nose of the bombers, indicating series production of at least twenty bombers.[11]

Dino A. Brugioni, a senior officer at the National Photographic Interpretive Center, recalled, "A number of intelligence analysts raised the possibility that different numbers were being painted on relatively small numbers of bombers, but the U.S. Air Force, which at the time had prime responsibility for estimating Soviet bomber strength, would not agree with this evaluation."[12] Allen Dulles later acknowledged in his memoirs that the Soviets had deceived the CIA. They had flown the Bison bombers in circles around the Kremlin day after day to create the impression that they had built a large number of bombers.[13] When the Air Force told Eisenhower that the Russians would have more than 30 Bison bombers by the end of 1955 and about 500 by mid-1959, the president immediately ordered an increase in production of B-52 bombers. In testimony before Congress in 1956, the Defense Department estimated the Soviets would have 600 to 700 Bison bombers in operational units by 1969. Actually, the bomber suffered from technical problems, and only about 100 were ever produced.[14] The Russians had shifted their emphasis from bombers to ICBMs. By then the Air Force had promoted a "bomber gap" to encourage more spending on B-52 intercontinental bombers.

On March 27, 1954, President Eisenhower told a group of his science advisers, "[T]o anyone bearing the responsibility for the security of the United States, the situation was highly unsatisfactory." Science adviser James R. Killian noted that the Pearl Harbor syndrome, fear of a surprise attack, "haunted Eisenhower throughout his presidency."[15] In August, Killian established a special panel of experts, again including Dr. Edwin H. Land, who headed Project 3, the so-called Land Panel, to work on technological capabilities for aerial reconnaissance. Land was a hard-driving activist, "My motto is to select things that are manifestly important and nearly impossible." Land's view was that "every known reconnaissance technique should be used."

Brugioni defined the unique properties of aerial photography: (1) it captures and freezes an instant in time; (2) it can be studied at length and in detail by people from a wide variety of backgrounds and disciplines; (3) it constitutes a precise geometric record that can be measured, scaled, and quantified; (4) it becomes a record of the earth's surface—a catalog of things, activities, and relationships; and (5) it is duplicable and manipulable—it can be enlarged, enhanced, and reproduced, and it can provide near-synoptic coverage of large areas.[16]

On November 24, 1954, Eisenhower authorized a top secret CIA program to develop the U-2, a high altitude reconnaissance aircraft that would be able to conduct deep-penetration reconnaissance missions over the Soviet Union. The multifaceted collection system that was to become the hallmark of American strategic intelligence was so secret that its code word designation was never referred to publicly. According to National Reconnaissance Organization historian R. Cargill Hall, fewer than 350 people in the United States knew of the U-2 and its mission. They included four at the White House, about four in Congress, and all Lockheed, Air Force, and CIA people involved, including pilots and mechanics.

The overhead satellite program was treated with equally stringent security; there were no public references to code word designations or descriptions of satellites until 1978, and then only with the euphemism "national technical means of verification." The systems, photographic satellites for overhead reconnaissance and signals intelligence listening posts, kept track of the Soviet Union's nuclear arsenal, its intercontinental ballistic missiles (ICBMs), submarines, and heavy bombers.

The CIA utilized electronic intercepts of missile telemetry to determine the characteristics of Soviet ICBMs. The data that an ICBM radios to its ground stations allow its engineers to monitor the missile's performance in flight; however, an adversary's listening posts can also intercept the data. One of the key issues in the SALT II strategic arms negotiations was forbidding the encoding of telemetry signals; without encoding, it would be possible for both sides to monitor the characteristics and capabilities of each other's missiles. Uncoded telemetry signals provided the essential building blocks for arms control verification. Thus it was possible to verify the total carrying capacity of a missile or its "throw weight," a good indicator of the number of nuclear warheads it might be carrying.

In June of 1957, while the first Soviet SS-6 stood on its launch pad at Tyuratam in Kazakhstan, U.S. Signals Intelligence (SIGINT) specialists at listening posts in Turkey were monitoring signals from the site. A U-2 overflying the site took a series of paired stereoscopic photos of the Soviet missile. The missile's first test flight took place in August, and a second, three weeks later. Both times, when the missile radioed its telemetry, or performance data—fuel consumption, engine thrust, burn time, heading, speed, warhead separation point, altitude, range—to Soviet tracking stations on the ground, a U.S. listening post at Karamursel, thirty-seven miles southeast of Istanbul, also picked it up and taped it.[17]

The space race began in earnest and partly in the open after the Soviet Union launched *Sputnik*, the first spacecraft to orbit the earth, on October 17, 1957. The American public's reaction, a frenzy of self-doubt, motivated President Eisenhower and the nation to catch up to and surpass the Soviet Union. From the time the Soviet Union launched *Sputnik*, the debate raged over whether the Soviet Union was ahead of the United States in science and technology. *Sputnik* was a warning that the Soviet Union might be ahead of the United States in the production of intercontinental ballistic missiles. The resulting competition to dominate outer space brought about new means to monitor missile developments. Human intelligence, while still important in confirming technical intelligence, could not compete with the hard factual reality of photography from space.

A few months later, in February 1956, President Eisenhower approved the development of Corona reconnaissance satellites, which revolutionized the collection of intelligence in the 1960s.[18] After the Soviets shot down a U-2 on May 1, 1960, and captured its pilot, Francis Gary Powers, the United States terminated all aerial overflights over the Soviet Union and concentrated on Corona. President Eisenhower justified canceling U-2 flights over the Soviet Union in 1960 by citing two developments: the capability of the new Soviet SA-2 surface-to-air missiles to shoot down the high-flying reconnaissance planes and the progress being made to photograph the earth from space, out of reach of Soviet missiles.

The Corona satellite program took fourteen launchings to succeed in bringing back acceptable (40+-meters resolution) film coverage of the Soviet Union. The first reconnaissance satellite to return to earth with film landed on August 19, 1960. At 8:30 a.m. on August 24, before a National Security Council meeting to discuss the future organization of overhead satellite photography, Presidential Adviser Edwin Land spread a roll of developed film across the carpet to President Eisenhower, who was standing beside his desk in the Oval Office. President Eisenhower, Director of Central Intelligence Allen Dulles, and his team of advisers inspected the photographs. The film from the first successful Corona mission provided more photographic coverage of the Soviet Union than all previous U-2 missions. The satellite's camera had photographed 1.5 million square miles of the Soviet Union and East European countries. This imagery identified sixty-four Soviet airfields and twenty-six new surface-to-air missile (SAM) sites. The results were stunning.[19] These piercing "eyes in the sky" made it possible to detect any military buildup that could lead to a major war.

The Soviets were aware of the satellite surveillance, but unlike the U-2, they could not stop it. Corona opened a new era of strategic transparency, reducing the possibility of significant strategic surprise, the fear factor President Eisenhower had defined. This new transparency reassured both sides and helped prevent a full scale hot war or a preemptive first strike. During the cold war, both sides relied on the doctrine of mutual vulnerability to deter nuclear attack, what became known as "mutually assured destruction," or MAD. The ability of the United States to monitor Soviet missile sites made arms control agreements realistic.

At the NSC meeting on August 25, 1960, after viewing the Corona film, Eisenhower approved the formation of a new office to coordinate and supervise satellite reconnaissance. In September 1961, under President Kennedy, it became the super-secret National Reconnaissance Organization (NRO) headed by Air Force Under Secretary Joseph Charyk. A colleague of Robert S. McNamara at the Ford Motor Company after World War II, Charyk had come to Washington with McNamara during the Kennedy administration. The NRO was established to place a civilian at the head of an organization to balance the competing interests between the CIA and the Department of Defense (DOD).[20] When first formed, the NRO was hidden under the cover of the Office of Missile and Satellite Systems within the Office of the Secretary of the Air Force. So deep was the secrecy surrounding the NRO that not until 1992 was its existence publicly acknowledged.

Advances in overhead reconnaissance created a new art and science of photographic analysis. National Intelligence Estimates by the CIA took on growing sophistication and influenced decision making. The new precision made it possible to count weapons. Estimates were now verifiable and erased doubts about the accuracy of human intelligence.

To avoid informing or provoking Soviet leaders, Eisenhower ordered that no American reconnaissance photographs ever be released publicly. The policy was adhered to until the Reagan administration, when the Department of Defense's annual review of Soviet military power included photographs of Soviet military bases and missiles.

The downside of secrecy surrounding the reconnaissance programs was that it led to domestic political controversy over Soviet capabilities. The space photographs defined the real number of Soviet heavy bombers and eliminated the "gap," but the figures used in interservice rivalry for budget allocations among the Air Force, Army, and the Navy continued to contradict National Intelligence Estimates of Soviet ICBM strength. Eisenhower refused, for national security reasons, to discuss sources and methods used to gather the information upon which the estimates were based.

Eisenhower distrusted intelligence estimates of the Soviet Union in the 1957–1960 period. He asked his science adviser, Dr. George B. Kistiakowsky, to lead a panel of experts in evaluating Soviet strategic capabilities versus those of the United States. After a month's work, the blue ribbon panel reported: The United States was far ahead of the Soviet Union both in weapons research and in the deployment of strategic weapons. Soviet weaponry in missiles and bombers was not nearly comparable with what the United States possessed during the Eisenhower administration—yet U.S. military and defense industry testimony in yearly congressional budget battles continued to describe the United States lagging behind the Soviet Union. Kistiakowsky summed up the situation when he said, "We went looking for a body but only found a skeleton."

Brugioni was one of the experts who evaluated the photographs. He believes the report stimulated considerable reflection by President Eisenhower, and was one of the sources for his expression of "serious concern about the danger of an unbridled military industrial complex."[21]

In 1954 the Bisons created the "bomber-gap" controversy in strategic intelligence, followed by the so-called "missile-gap," which began in August 1957 when the United States detected that the Soviets had carried out the first successful test firing of an ICBM. Khrushchev bragged in November 1959 that the Soviet Union had "such a stock of rockets, such an amount of atomic and hydrogen warheads, that if they attack us we could wipe our potential enemies off the face of the earth."[22] Khrushchev claimed a single plant produced 250 missiles a year and that the Soviet Union was turning out missiles "like sausages coming from an automatic machine, rocket after rocket comes off the assembly line."[23]

Even though President Eisenhower knew Khrushchev was bluffing, he declined to discuss classified estimates of Soviet missile strength publicly. He feared compromising the security of the new top secret reconnaissance programs.

On February 16, 1959, General Nathan B. Twining, the Air Force chief of staff, told the Senate Foreign Relations Committee, with Senator John F. Kennedy present, that Soviet missile tests had not been proceeding "as rapidly or regularly" as had previously been suspected. In addition, Twining pointed out that the rapidly developing U.S. strategic nuclear force of long-range bombers, Polaris submarines, and intermediate-range missiles, based in Britain and Italy, more than made up for any potential and theoretical Soviet advantage in intercontinental ballistic missiles.

"In other words, General, you don't accept the theory that there is a missile gap and this is a period of maximum peril," Kennedy said.

"No, I don't," Twining replied. He reminded Kennedy, "Congress was convinced there was going to be a gap in bombers and instead we are way ahead of them." Eisenhower knew that many of his Democratic critics understood the true state of affairs but, to preserve sources and methods (the U-2 and signals intelligence), he refused to publicly break the secret. National security prevailed over domestic political expediency.[24]

During the 1960 presidential campaign, Senator Kennedy, influenced by his friend and former secretary of the Air Force, Senator Stuart Symington, charged that the Eisenhower administration had permitted a missile gap to exist in the Soviet Union's favor. Kennedy charged that the Eisenhower administration had allowed the Soviet Union to exceed the United States in missile strength and had placed the nation at a strategic disadvantage. Kennedy knew that the charge was false, but persisted in using it as a campaign issue against Nixon and the Republicans.[25]

After Kennedy was elected, both the bomber gap and the missile gap disappeared. Eisenhower arranged a briefing for the president-elect of all photographic intelligence systems. After one of the briefings, Eisenhower told Kennedy: "The enemy has no aerial photographic systems like ours."[26] Defense Secretary Robert McNamara announced on February 6, 1961, that there was no missile or bomber gap in what he thought was an off-the-record meeting with Pentagon reporters. When the news appeared the following day, McNamara went to President Kennedy and offered to resign, but Kennedy refused to accept his resignation.

In June 1961, the CIA's Office of National Estimates (ONE) estimated that the Soviet Union had 50 to 100 ICBMs and would have 100 to 200 in 1962, 150 to 300 in 1963, and 200 to 400 in 1964. The analysts sensed something was missing. If the Soviet missile program was as far along as Khrushchev claimed, more sites should have appeared on satellite photos. Were they hidden, as the Air Force suggested? The analysts joked that the Air Force counted a Soviet missile site under every cloud or flyspeck that appeared on the satellite photos.

The estimate did not reflect the information provided by GRU Colonel Oleg Penkovsky, America's most valuable spy in the cold war. Titled "The Soviet ICBM Program" and distributed on May 16, 1961, through a top secret code-word channel, Penkovsky's message was unequivocal and to the point: Khrushchev was bluffing. The Soviet Union was trying to create the impression that it "already had a tremendous military potential when in reality it is only being developed." The Soviet Union only had the capability of firing one or two missiles. "There are not hundreds in testing sites. There may be only tens in that category." The Soviet Union did have medium-range missiles being produced in great quantities and they could be launched at any time, but ICBMs that could reach the United States were another story. They were not ready for war, "but in two or three years there will be a different picture."[27]

Penkovsky's information influenced Edward Proctor, former deputy director of intelligence, to suggest revising the estimate. If Penkovsky's information were correct, the Soviet Union would have only 25 or fewer ICBMs in 1961, 25 to 50 in 1962, 75 to 150 in 1963, 175 to 250 in 1964, and 300 to 400 in 1965.

There was no hiding from the Corona program cameras. By August 1961, photography supported Penkovsky's report and led to a revision of the National Intelligence Estimate in September. The missile gap had disappeared, but not without a struggle. The greater the Soviet missile threat, the bigger the Air Force budget; if the threat were real, it enlarged the role of the Strategic Air Command and the Air Force missile program. By 1961 the responsibility for missiles with a range under 1,000 miles was assigned to the Army, and those with a range over

1,000 miles went to the Air Force. The Navy had its Polaris program for submarine-launched missiles. On September 21, 1961, a new National Intelligence Estimate reduced the projection of Soviet strength from 50 to 100 operational ICBM launchers to fewer than 35 missiles.

Kennedy, previously a champion of Air Force estimates of Soviet superiority, now lost interest. Air Force claims were contradicted by the new intelligence community consensus. The Corona pictures and Penkovsky's reports from inside the Soviet system overwhelmed unsubstantiated Air Force conjecture. Shifting public perception from the idea of American strategic inferiority to one of American superiority was difficult. A drawn-out bureaucratic struggle for budget allocations ensued before the shift was made public.[28]

In his memoirs, Eisenhower stressed the importance of aerial reconnaissance:

> During the four years of its operations, the U-2 program produced intelligence of critical importance to the United States. Perhaps as important as the positive information—what the Soviets did have—was the negative information it produced—what the Soviets did not have. Intelligence gained from this source provided proof that the horrors of the alleged "bomber gap" and later the "missile gap" were nothing more than imaginative creations of irresponsibility. U-2 information deprived Khrushchev of the most powerful weapon of Communist conspiracy—international blackmail—usable only as long as the Soviets could exploit the ignorance and resulting fear of the free world.[29]

Eisenhower also bequeathed to Kennedy a plan to attack Cuba and overthrow Fidel Castro's revolution. Under the attack plan drawn up with full CIA backing during Eisenhower's last year in office, Cuban "freedom fighters" in exile formed a brigade of fifteen hundred men. Kennedy asked the Joint Chiefs of Staff to review the plans for the invasion and they reported back that "La Brigada" seemed capable of handling the operation. All of Kennedy's advisers, with the sole exception of Senator William Fulbright, agreed that the operation should proceed. Effective air cover was essential for success of the amphibious operation. La Brigada landed on Zapata Beach on the Bay of Pigs, April 17, 1961, three months after Kennedy took office. Kennedy, fearing the political consequences of the air raids, canceled American air support. That left the landing forces without air cover or strategic bombing, and Castro's air force easily attacked the invaders, destroying their ammunition. After three days of fighting with no air cover, the invasion force surrendered. The Cuban exiles suffered 300 men killed and hundreds more wounded. Fidel Castro emerged victorious, humiliating the new president and setting the scene for the most dangerous event in the history of the world—the 1962 Cuban Missile Crisis.[30]

Contrary to popular myth regarding the Cuban Missile Crisis, the real stars were not those who have been portrayed on movie screens or television. The only senior member of the Kennedy administration who suspected that Nikita Khrushchev was planning to place offensive surface-to-surface nuclear missiles in Cuba was CIA Director John McCone. On August 10, 1962, after examining U-2 photographs of Cuba and secret intelligence reports, McCone dictated a memorandum for President Kennedy "expressing the belief that installations for the launching of offensive missiles were being constructed on the island."[31] At a National Security Council meeting attended by President Kennedy on August 17, McCone argued that the Soviet Union must be placing surface-to-surface missiles in Cuba. Secretary of State Dean Rusk and Defense Secretary Robert McNamara expressed the view that the buildup was purely defensive. They argued that the Soviet Union had never placed offensive missiles outside its own territory.

McCone was the only Republican on President Kennedy's national security team, not an enviable position. Yet he persisted, basing his argument on what he called "a judgment factor." Although McCone had no hard information that offensive missiles were in place in Cuba, the U-2 flights over the island to monitor the Soviet buildup revealed a pattern of surface-to-air missile sites for defensive antiaircraft missiles. McCone asked himself what the SAMs were protecting since they were not defending airfields. He deduced that offensive strategic Soviet missiles would soon be introduced in Cuba:

The obvious purpose of the SAMs was to blind us so we could not see what was going on there. There they were with 16,000 men with all their ordnance equipment and then came the ships. There was nothing else to ship to Cuba but missiles. That was my argument. We didn't see the missiles. They were on the ships and we had no agents on the ships. We really didn't know what was on the ships, but some things you can deduce. That was one of them.[32]

On August 29, McCone married Theiline Piggot in Seattle, Washington; the couple planned to honeymoon in Saint Jean-Cap-Ferrat in the south of France. Before his departure, McCone left orders for reconnaissance planes to overfly Cuba every day, but Rusk and McNamara cancelled his order. Rusk feared a U-2 with a civilian pilot would be shot down and "create a hell of a mess."[33]

On September 4, Soviet Ambassador Anatoly Dobrynin called on Attorney General Robert Kennedy. The president used his younger brother Bobby to pass private messages and to handle delicate situations. Through Bobby, the president was able to make his views and concerns forcefully known while avoiding direct presidential involvement. Bobby Kennedy told Dobrynin "of President Kennedy's deep concern about what was happening in Cuba." Dobrynin said this was not a matter to be concerned about. Nikita Khrushchev had instructed him, Dobrynin said, to assure President Kennedy that there would be no ground-to-ground missiles or offensive weapons placed in Cuba. Dobrynin insisted the Soviet military buildup in Cuba was not of any significance and that Khrushchev would do nothing to disrupt the relationship between the United States and the USSR during the period prior to the November congressional elections.

That same day, after being briefed by Bobby Kennedy, the president issued a statement that there was no evidence of "offensive ground-to-ground missiles" or of "other significant offensive capability" in Cuba. "Were it to be otherwise," Kennedy warned, "the gravest issues would arise."[34]

During the same period, Robert Kennedy met with Georgi N. Bolshakov, a Soviet military intelligence officer operating under cover in the Soviet embassy as information counselor and editor of *Soviet Life* magazine. Bolshakov, who had established a back-channel relationship with the attorney general, told him that he had just returned from a meeting at Pitsunda on the Black Sea with Khrushchev and First Deputy Premier Anastas Mikoyan. Khrushchev instructed him to assure the president that "no missile capable of reaching the United States will be placed in Cuba." Mikoyan added that only defensive surface-to-air missiles (SAMs) were being installed in Cuba.[35]

When McCone returned to Langley and discovered that there had been no overflights of Cuba during his absence, he was furious. On October 14, after more than ten days of bureaucratic infighting and heavy cloud cover over Cuba, U.S. Air Force pilots resumed the U-2 flights. A team at the National Photographic Intelligence Center reviewed the photos taken during the U-2 flight and identified a pattern that conformed to SS-4 medium-range missile sites in the Soviet Union.

Thanks to Penkovsky, the CIA had received a treasure trove of Soviet military secrets, including manuals for the SA-2, a surface-to-air antiaircraft missile, and the SS-4 and SS-5, intermediate-range missiles and their ground equipment. Penkovsky had photographed the manuals with a Minox camera and slipped the tiny rolls of film, hidden in a candy box, to Janet Chisholm, the wife of the MI-6 station chief in Moscow (the candy was ostensibly a gift for her children, who were playing around their baby carriage while she waited for Penkovsky to appear in the park opposite the Central Market).

When experts checked the U-2 photographs of freshly dug Cuban missile sites against the manual for SS-4 missiles, the evidence was irrefutable. Later that morning, President Kennedy's advisers showed him photographs of the SS-4 medium-range missile-launching installations under construction in San Cristobal, Cuba. To the untrained, naked eye, the photographs looked like a football field being excavated. To the analysts, the patterns being carved in the earth were characteristic of the deployment markings or "signature" for the installation of SS-4 missiles. The missiles had a range of 1,100 miles; they could hit Washington, D.C.

Formal identification of the sites was based on the triangulation of three sources of evidence: the U-2 photos over Cuba, photo reconnaissance pictures of SS-4 sites in the Soviet Union, and the missile's manual (provided by Penkovsky). Art Lundahl, the head of the CIA's Photographic Interpretation Center, identified the missile sites by reading the U-2 photographs. Lundahl and his team could analyze changes in the status of the sites and operational details with fine tuned precision by referring to the extensive details of the missile in the classified manual.

The manual Penkovsky supplied allowed the CIA to estimate for President Kennedy how long it would take to complete the installation and make the missiles operational. Richard Helms recalled:

> We looked at the power and fuel lines, launching booms and all the other details which were in the manual. The assessment gave President Kennedy three extra days.
>
> The big issue at the moment was whether to send in the Air Force to take out the missile bases and the whole Cuban Air Force. With the aid of the material Penkovsky delivered we were able to tell the President "this is what we've got here and it will take them X days to be ready to fire." It gave President Kennedy time to maneuver. I don't know of any single instance where intelligence was more immediately valuable than at this time. Penkovsky's material had a direct application because it came right into the middle of the decision-making process.[36]

On October 22, 1962, President Kennedy announced to the American people and the world:

> Within the past week, unmistakable evidence has established the fact that a series of offensive sites is now in preparation on that imprisoned island. The purposes of these bases can be none other than to provide a nuclear strike capability against the Western Hemisphere . . . [and] constitutes an explicit threat to the peace and security of all the Americas. . . . This sudden, clandestine decision to station strategic weapons for the first time outside of Soviet soil, is a deliberately provocative and unjustified change in the status quo which cannot be accepted by this country, if our courage and our commitments are ever to be trusted again either by friend or foe.

President Kennedy's decision not to bomb the SS-4 missile sites and negotiate a withdrawal with Nikita Khrushchev probably avoided nuclear war. Without the

U-2 aerial reconnaissance, the missile sites would not have been discovered until they had become operational and the balance of power had changed in the Western Hemisphere. Khrushchev would have eliminated his own missile gap with the United States and threatened the entire east coast of the United States with SS-4 medium-range and SS-5 intermediate-range nuclear missiles.

"War over Cuba was avoided because every weapons system was correctly identified in time to give the President and his policy advisors time to think, to make a rational estimate of the situation and to devise means of dealing with it with a maximum chance of success and a minimum risk of global war," said McCone.[37]

The reasons Khrushchev placed the SS-4 missiles in Cuba remain a matter of contention.

In his memoir, *Khrushchev Remembers*, he said:

It was during my visit to Bulgaria that I had the idea of installing missiles with nuclear warheads in Cuba without letting the United States find out they were there until it was too late to do anything about them. I knew we'd have to talk to Castro and explain our strategy to him in order to get the agreement of the Cuban government. My thinking went like this: if we installed the missiles secretly and then if the United States discovered the missiles were there after they were already poised and ready to strike, the Americans would think twice to liquidate our installations by military means. I knew that the United States could knock out some of our installations, but not all of them. If a quarter or even a tenth of our missiles survived—even if only one or two big ones were left—we could still hit New York, and there wouldn't be much of New York left. . . . The main thing was that the installation of our missiles in Cuba would, I thought, restrain the United States from precipitous military action against Castro's government. In addition to protecting Cuba, our missiles would have protected what the West likes to call "the balance of power." The Americans had surrounded our country with military bases and threatened us with nuclear weapons, and now they would learn just what it feels like to have enemy missiles pointing at you; we'd be doing nothing more than giving them a little of their own medicine.[38]

Khrushchev failed to calculate the deep but controlled anger and resolve he would produce when President Kennedy discovered his deliberate and blatant deception.[39] If U-2 photographs and signals intelligence had not confirmed the presence of Soviet missiles in Cuba, Khrushchev could have succeeded in making the missiles operational. He would have created a new strategic reality, foreclosing removal of the missiles except by military action.

In their exhaustive study of the Cuban Missile Crisis, Aleksandr Fursenko and

Timothy Naftali explore the reasons for Khrushchev's solitary decision. Most obvious was Khrushchev's burning desire to bridge the missile gap between Soviet inferiority and American superiority by directly threatening the eastern seaboard from Miami and New Orleans to Washington, D.C. and west to Dallas and Houston, all within the 1,100-mile range of the SS-4 medium-range missiles. The SS-5 intermediate missiles with a 2,100-mile range could reach the entire country short of San Francisco and the Pacific Northwest.[40]

A forgiving version of Khrushchev's impulse, pressed in the 1980s and backed by former Defense Secretary Robert McNamara, was that Khrushchev was defending Cuba against an American invasion when he made his decision. Others cite Soviet anger at the American decision to station Jupiter missiles in Turkey. Another version points to Khrushchev's decision to preserve the status quo in Cuba and prevent Mao Zedong from replacing him as the leader of international communism. While each played a part in Khrushchev's decision, Fursenko and Naftali suggest that Khrushchev's perception of Kennedy's actions in Southeast Asia and the lack of progress over negotiations in Berlin "bespoke a new found American arrogance" that Khrushchev could not ignore. They argue: "Khrushchev felt he needed a bold move to remind Washington of Soviet power. . . . At the same time he wanted to demonstrate to Castro personally and dramatically that the Soviet Union would defend his revolution."[41]

Fidel Castro had seemed to be moving away from Moscow. Soviet efforts to advance the careers of communists in Castro's entourage had backfired. Castro defied Soviet domination of the Cuban political elite; he did not want his revolution to become a client state of Moscow. By this interpretation, Khrushchev transferred the offensive missiles to Cuba to solidify their comradely relationship.

The most convincing explanation came from Khrushchev himself when he spoke of "our missiles protecting what the West likes to call 'the balance of power,' " what the Soviets call "the correlation of forces."[42] Through deception, Khrushchev tried to change the military balance of power in the Soviet Union's favor by leapfrogging the expensive process of building enough ICBMs to threaten the United States. With medium- and intermediate-range missiles in place in Cuba, virtually all of the United States would be held hostage to a Soviet nuclear attack.

In the end, Khrushchev backed down. He had to recognize the reality of his own words: "Any fool can start a war, and once he's done so, even the wisest of men are helpless to stop it—especially if it is a nuclear war."[43] Khrushchev's plan was foiled by discovery of his duplicity in time for President Kennedy to alert the American people and world leaders. Kennedy was able to forge an agreement to withdraw the missiles by secretly promising to withdraw obsolete American medium-range missiles from Turkey. The written history of the Cuban Missile Crisis sublimates the role of intelligence to play up the brilliance of the president and his Executive Committee (EXCOM), which met for two weeks to resolve the crisis. McGeorge Bundy, President Kennedy's national security adviser, edited the records of the meetings, which are now housed in the Kennedy Library. In these records, there is neither direct reference to Penkovsky's contribution, nor praise for McCone: when President Kennedy told McCone, "You were right all along," McNamara, without any explanation, said, "But for the wrong reasons"; a nod of assent came from Secretary of State Rusk.[44]

Both American and Russian officials involved in the crisis created the myth that it was resolved because both sides realized the futility of nuclear war, not because of American nuclear superiority. In his analysis of the Cuban Missile Crisis, McGeorge Bundy noted: "Recognition that the level of nuclear danger reached in October 1962 was unacceptably high for all of mankind may be the most important single legacy of the Cuban missile crisis."[45]

In the abstract, Bundy is certainly correct, but the immediate reality concerned America's nuclear superiority and its military intelligence capabilities. President Kennedy prevented a nuclear war by calling Khrushchev's hand before he could establish operational missiles in Cuba, a threat that would have changed the strategic balance. "Intelligence, like knowledge, is power. Photographic intelligence, because of its currency, reliability, and relevancy, is an especially effective tool," wrote Dino A. Brugioni.[46]

Intelligence paid off: overhead reconnaissance and secret Soviet manuals allowed Kennedy to make informed and forceful decisions. Kennedy was willing to compromise with Khrushchev by agreeing privately to remove American Jupiter missiles from Turkey in exchange for Khrushchev publicly pledging to withdraw Soviet missiles from Cuba. This exchange of promises was a critical part of the agreement, which President Kennedy's court historians have obscured in their efforts to defend his reputation.[47]

In October 1964, Khrushchev was ousted in a bloodless coup and forced into retirement. The Soviet press referred to his "hare-brained schemes" but never directly mentioned the Cuban Missile Crisis he had instigated.

★ ★ ★

After the Cuban Missile Crisis, America's focus shifted from the threat of nuclear war with the Soviet Union to the "People's War of National Liberation" in Vietnam. In 1961 President Kennedy sent a team of military advisers to support President Ngo Dinh Diem, a Roman Catholic who had spent two years at the Maryknoll Seminary in Lakewood, New Jersey, in the 1950s. Diem had made a favorable impression when he met with then-Senator Kennedy and prominent American Catholic leaders, including Francis Cardinal Spellman of New York, Supreme Court Justice William O. Douglas, and Senator Mike Mansfield. Initially the

Kennedy administration portrayed Diem's South Vietnam as an anticommunist state fighting for its existence against communist domination by North Vietnam.

However, Diem's authoritarian methods for putting down dissent from Buddhists lost him the support of Kennedy's advisers and the American press covering Vietnam. There were rumors of a separate peace with North Vietnam negotiated by Diem's brother Ngo Dinh Nhu, excluding the Americans, which angered Washington. With the acquiescence of U.S. Ambassador Henry Cabot Lodge, a rival faction of South Vietnamese generals deposed both brothers in a coup d'état in November 1963. When they surrendered, they were brutally slain. The country was left without a clear leader until General Nguyen Van Thieu became chief of state in 1965.[48]

Three weeks after the death of Diem and Nhu, President Kennedy was assassinated in Dallas on November 22, 1963. After Kennedy's death, the American commitment escalated throughout the 1960s under President Lyndon B. Johnson. By the end of 1965, there were nearly 200,000 U.S. troops in South Vietnam; the number rose to 549,500 before the American withdrawal began in 1973. More than 50,000 American soldiers gave their lives in a failed attempt to save South Vietnam from communist takeover.

The United States Government did not understand the depth of animosity between North Vietnam's two communist supporters, the People's Republic of China (PRC) and the Soviet Union. In 1960, Communist leader Ho Chi Minh was receiving support from both the Soviet Union and China. The ideological rivalry between Mao Zedong and Nikita Khrushchev changed to open enmity when the Soviet Union failed to provide the Chinese with a promised atomic bomb during the Taiwan Strait crisis in 1958–1959. In April 1960, celebrating the ninetieth anniversary of Lenin's birth, the Chinese published a series of polemics accusing Khrushchev of "revising, emasculating and betraying" Lenin's heritage by endorsing such principles as peaceful coexistence, the noninevitability of war, and the possibility that communists could come to power by nonviolent means.[49]

Mao and Khrushchev disagreed on global strategy and challenged each other for leadership of the world communist revolution. The resolve that appeared to unify the two communist powers during the Korean War was now unraveled. In 1961, the Soviet Union halted all aid and withdrew its economic advisers from China. Signs of turmoil within the Sino-Soviet alliance deepened with the Chinese test of its first nuclear bomb in 1964. In his thrust for domestic power during the Great Proletarian Cultural Revolution, Mao accused Moscow of ideological heresy. The Soviet embassy in Bejing became a frequent target of Chinese demonstrators asserting their nationalism by throwing bottles of ink against the embassy walls and windows.

While American policy makers speculated on the consequences of a Sino-Soviet split, they made no serious effort to exploit the rift in Vietnam. American policy toward Vietnam focused on fear of Chinese expansion southward. The "domino theory" contended that if South Vietnam fell, then all of Southeast Asia would be swept into the Chinese Communist orbit.

The Vietnam War escalated rivalry between the two communist powers. There was bitter competition between the Soviet Union and the People's Republic of China for the leading role in aiding North Vietnam. Hanoi needed Soviet aid but resented any attempt to weaken its own sovereignty. There was heavy tension between Soviet military advisers in Hanoi and Vietnamese military and political officials. Soviet officers who served as advisers in Hanoi recalled a weekly briefing after their SAM battalions had shot down twelve American jets. The North Vietnamese briefer told the group that the Soviets had shot down two American planes after firing a large number of rockets, and that North Vietnamese army women had shot down ten enemy jets with their rifles. The Soviet general who suffered through the briefing commented that in the future, the Soviet Union might send more rifle bullets instead of rockets. Afterward, the North Vietnamese briefer took the Soviet general aside and explained the subtleties of politics in a "people's war."[50] Meanwhile, American pilots were dying, shot down by clandestine Soviet antiaircraft missile batteries.

A group of new North Vietnamese fighter pilots, fresh from training in the USSR, wanted to mount a suicide attack to destroy an American aircraft carrier, in the style of the Japanese kamikaze attacks of World War II. The Soviet commander, General Mikhail Kislitsin, warned the North Vietnamese that they would not get within twenty miles of the carrier in the Gulf of Tonkin, but the young jet pilots were hard to convince. The North Vietnamese insisted that Soviet intelligence supply evidence to back up the general's warning. They then prepared to mount the operation. As an initial step, they decided to move some of their SAMs to the coast to attack aircraft defending the carrier. The Soviet commander tried to convince the North Vietnamese of the futility of their placement of the SAMs, but another senior Soviet officer thought the attack might work. The North Vietnamese persisted. When the SAMs were moving, they were detected by American night reconnaissance. Early the next morning, a wave of American bombers destroyed the SAMs before they could fire a shot at the attacking aircraft.[51]

The Soviets and the North Vietnamese were deeply suspicious of each other even though they were allies. Soviet officers demanded to see the central military command center of North Vietnam but were continually refused. When Marshal Batitsky came to Hanoi, he walked at the head of the delegation up to the command post. A guard halted him at the door. The guard would not let the Soviet marshal enter because he did not see Prime Minister Pham Van Dong, behind Batitsky. The enraged marshal picked up the diminutive prime minister and carried him in front of him for the guards to see and open the entrance.

Despite the vast quantities of Soviet aid to North Vietnam, the North Vietnamese refused to give the Soviets any of the downed U.S. jets to study. Only once, on the anniversary of the October Revolution, did the North Vietnamese give the Soviets an American jet, with an inscription painted in red: "A gift to the Soviet Government." The North Vietnamese were so suspicious of the Soviets that they destroyed films of Soviet advisers shown with North Vietnamese by exposing them to the light. Before the major Tet offensive in 1968, the North Vietnamese told the Soviets that the plans had been betrayed and they were not going to attack after all. This was pure disinformation, aimed at preventing the Soviet Union from betraying the North Vietnamese battle plans.

When Premier Alexei Kosygin visited Hanoi, he asked Pham Van Dong for an American M-16 rifle; the prime minister equivocated. The Soviets ended up buying one from the Cambodians for $10,000. Later, when the Vietnamese asked the Soviets if they would drop an atomic bomb on the Americans if they invaded the north, the Soviet ambassador equivocated in a similar fashion.

A Soviet colonel recalled that when he arrived ten minutes early for a meeting in the Soviets' mess hall, the Chinese military advisers were just leaving. The North Vietnamese quickly changed a slogan in the mess hall that put down Soviet revisionism and replaced it with one supporting their Soviet brothers.

The Chinese communists were the primary aid givers to North Vietnam but there was a wary tension between Hanoi and Beijing. Hanoi's strong pride of independence grew out of Ho Chi Minh's fierce Vietnamese nationalism and the bitter fight against the French. North Vietnam, historically a vassal state of China, treaded a thin line between being a supplicant for aid from its more powerful communist allies and maintaining its own course in prosecuting the war against the south.

According to Soviet military intelligence, the Chinese had a secret agreement with the North Vietnamese to send troops in to help North Vietnam if the Americans invaded north of the 17th parallel. The Soviets knew this through Ho Chi Minh's two Soviet doctors, who reported to the GRU (Soviet military intelligence). Mao tried to test the agreement by telling Ho that the Americans were planning a major offensive. The Chinese offered to send People's Liberation Army (PLA) troops into North Vietnam. Ho refused, saying in effect, "thanks, but no thanks."

The Soviet participation in the Vietnam War was a secret. There were an estimated 10,000 Soviet antiaircraft artillerymen fighting in Vietnam during the course of the war. At the same time, President Nixon and Secretary of State Henry Kissinger were attempting to create détente with Moscow. The Soviets dressed in civilian clothes and tried to maintain a low profile. At first the Soviets operated their own SAM batteries with the North Vietnamese looking on and learning. One Soviet soldier wrote home to his mother, asking her to light a candle in church for him. That was their private code that he had shot down an American plane. Gradually, the Soviets shifted command and control of the SAMs to the North Vietnamese. One to two Russian advisers remained with each battery.[52]

The most famous SAM officer, Major Fyodor Ilyinikh, commanded one of the three SAM divisions that operated independently near the 17th parallel in 1965–1966. Ilyinikh became a living legend when his SAM battery shot down three American jets with one missile on July 24, 1965. The Soviet Defense Minister rewarded Ilyinikh with a case of cognac, and the Vietnamese honored him with the name "second to Ho Chi Minh."

Ilyinikh told his son Yuri that his unit captured two U.S. pilots on September 15, 1965. The pilots were interrogated by the GRU man in the division. Afterwards, with no explanation, Ilyinikh ordered the senior U.S. pilot shot. When the North Vietnamese found out what had happened, they insisted that Ilyinikh, despite his fame for downing the three jets, be sent home. Other Soviet units had up to four American prisoners. The North Vietnamese objected strongly to this practice. They did not want the Soviets taking American prisoners. The North Vietnamese insisted on their sovereignty and maintaining control of all prisoners.[53]

One of the still-unanswered and aggravating questions of the Vietnam War is whether or not American pilots shot down and captured by Soviet surface-to-air missile teams were sent to the Soviet Union as prisoners of war. The 1992 Joint Russian-American Commission was headed by former ambassador to Moscow Malcolm Toon and General Dmitri Volkogonov. The commission never substantiated reports of American prisoners of war sent to the Soviet Union from Vietnam. In his exhaustive study of American POWs in Vietnam, Malcolm McConnell concludes:

> common sense indicates that at least a few American POWs may have been transferred from Indochina to the Soviet Union for intelligence exploitation. Unfortunately, as with the equally tantalizing issue of American POWs held after the war in Laos, there has been widespread irresponsible speculation on the "Moscow bound" prisoner-transfer issue.
>
> The general pattern of this activity has been to incorporate scattered and inconclusive intelligence reports into plausible theories masquerading as definitive proof that American prisoners were transferred from Vietnam to the Soviet bloc.[54]

The Soviets were fighting against skilled pilots. As the war progressed, and American electronic countermeasures improved, the Soviet kill rate decreased. Soviet SAM technicians reported that they needed to fire a greater number of missiles to down a lesser number of American planes. Although they maintained high security and dressed in civilian clothes, the Russian technicians understood that the Americans knew of their presence in Vietnam. On one occasion, warned of an imminent raid by U.S. paratroopers, the Soviet SAM teams destroyed their secret documents and went on full alert, but the attack never came.

The Sino-Soviet split, which broke into open border warfare over the Damansky Islands in 1969 and 1970, led to the Chinese communist invitation for President Nixon to visit Beijing in 1972. Yet the signals from North Vietnam remained mixed; the North Vietnamese leadership avoided public displays of favoritism toward either of its two primary suppliers of weapons and commodities. The North Vietnamese refused secret Soviet entreaties to negotiate with the United States.[55]

So deep was the antagonism of Mao and his successor, Deng Xiaoping, toward the Soviet Union that when Deng visited the United States in January 1979, after the normalization of relations, he secretly agreed with the United States to establish intelligence and military cooperation. In discussions between Deng and National Security Adviser Zbigniew Brzezinski they reached agreement in principle to jointly establish new collection facilities in western China capable of monitoring Soviet missile tests. The listening posts aimed across the Chinese border into the Soviet Union replaced the U.S. Tacksman Signals Intelligence collection stations in northern Iran, closed by the Islamic government after the fall of the Shah that year.

Deng's 1979 discussions in Washington marked a dramatic change in U.S.-China political relations, but even more significantly in military and security cooperation. The Chinese were to play a secret role in supporting the Mujahedeen, the Afghanistan freedom fighters, in their war against the Soviet Union after Soviet troops invaded on Christmas Eve and Christmas Day, 1979.

Nine months earlier, on March 28, 1979, the CIA's National Intelligence Officer for the Soviet Union, Arnold Horelick, sent a warning to Turner. Horelick wrote that the Afghan regime of Soviet puppet Nur Mohammed Taraki was deteriorating so rapidly that it would demand Soviet assistance and intervention. This, he said, would "evoke overt political and barely disguised covert military assistance to the [anti-Taraki] insurgents from Pakistan, Iran, and perhaps even China." Such action, he presciently noted, "would lead to a sharp deterioration of Soviet relations with Pakistan and possibly a call from Islamabad for the United States to deter or oppose Soviet military intervention in Pakistan and provide military assistance to states aiding the insurgency."[56]

Horelick's memo spurred a White House decision to provide covert aid to the anti-Soviet Islamic rebels six months before the Soviet invasion. On December 30, 1979, Brzezinski appeared on the Sunday morning public affairs program *Issues and Answers* to reiterate, with President Carter's authorization, American support for Pakistan. Brzezinski repeated the wording of America's 1959 security assurances to Pakistan and reminded the world and the Soviet Union that they were still valid. He drew a parallel between the crisis in Afghanistan and the one President Truman faced in Greece and Turkey.

In February 1980, Brzezinski, accompanied by Deputy Secretary of State Warren Christopher, visited Pakistan to affirm America's commitment to deal seriously with the security dimensions of the Soviet challenge. Brzezinski negotiated "cooperative responses to the Soviet action in Afghanistan," which "yielded tangible results."[57] In the Khyber Pass, Brzezinski stopped to visit Pakistani fortifications. I (Jerrold) was accompanying Brzezinski as the spokeman for the National Security Council. When Brzezinski was handed an AK-47 Kalishnikov rifle to examine, he waved it in the air, a symbol of defiance against the Soviet invasion of Afghanistan. News cameras caught the moment and the next day his gesture of American opposition to the Soviet invasion appeared on the front pages of newspapers around the world.

On the way back to Washington, Brzezinski stopped in Saudi Arabia and obtained a commitment of Saudi financial support for the Afghan forces. The covert aid developed into a series of secret training camps for Mujahedeen freedom fighters in western China near the Afghan border. The Afghans had covert support from the Americans, British, Chinese, Saudis, Pakistanis, and Egyptians. They received American Stinger missiles to attack Soviet helicopters. Clandestine purchases of Soviet arms from Egypt, Czechoslovakia, and China, plus renegade Soviet army stocks in Afghanistan, supplied the Afghan fighters. In a memo to the president describing covert aid to the Afghan struggle against the Soviets, Brzezinski noted, "We now have the opportunity to give the Soviet Union its Vietnam."[58]

★ ★ ★

The negotiations for intelligence cooperation culminated in Beijing from December 27, 1980, to January 7, 1981, with a secret visit by Director of Central Intelligence Stansfield Turner and Robert Gates, then National Intelligence Officer for the USSR.[59]

Deng made it clear to Turner that the Chinese leadership's resolve to cooperate with the United States was "a major strategic decision" for them. For both China and the United States, the listening posts provided a warning of Soviet nuclear weapons developments and intentions.

When the Chinese offered listening posts facing the Soviet border, the United States already had "eyes and ears" in the sky. The best listening posts were beyond reach of earthlings in a system of satellites. The Corona program had compiled an impressive list of intelligence achievements by the late 1960s. Veteran CIA officer Miles Copeland reflected that "a satellite circling the world . . . will pick up more information in a day then the espionage service could pick up in a year."[60]

By the time Richard Nixon became president in January 1969, the Corona program was being phased out, but not before the satellites provided conclusive evidence during the late 1960s that the Soviets had newer and bigger ICBMs and were developing ABM systems to defend them. The Soviet Union was determined to match and exceed America's nuclear weaponry.

The Corona reconnaissance satellites had been a good start, but more effective arms control required higher resolution photographs than those provided by Corona's camera. The primary mission of reconnaissance satellites was to provide early indication and warning (I&W) of surprise Soviet attack against the United States or NATO forces in Europe. With Corona, it still took four or five days to retrieve the film—ejected in gold capsules with parachutes over the Pacific Ocean to avoid being affected by damaging radiation—for processing by Eastman Kodak and analysis by the National Photographic Interpretation Center (NPIC).

A new-generation satellite reconnaissance system, the KH-9, code-named Hexagon but unofficially called the Big Bird, was first launched on June 15, 1971. The KH-9 system could photograph an area of the earth 80 by 360 miles, twice that of its predecessor, the KH-4B. It carried four film buckets, allowing it to remain aloft longer, which increased its lifetime in space from about 50 days when first launched to 275 days by the early 1980s. The Big Bird monitored compliance of the 1972 Interim Agreement, which froze the deployment of additional ICBMs for five years, and the 1972 Anti-Ballistic Missile Treaty, which limited construction of ABMs to only one site, thus ensuring that neither superpower could prevent retaliation if it launched a first strike.

The Soviet Union, despite its early lead in the space race with *Sputnik* in 1957, did not acquire its first overhead intelligence photography until August 1962, nearly two years after the first Corona photos. The Soviet systems had shorter orbital lifetimes, which meant that the Soviets had to launch more photo reconnaissance satellites than the Americans during the 1960s and 1970s. The Soviets averaged thirty to thirty-five annual launches, while the United States was averaging six to ten.[61]

By mid-1974, imagery analysts had concluded that the Soviet large scale deployment of ICBMs had largely come to an end with just over 1,600 deployed, of which 1,400 were operational.[62] Even with greatly improved reconnaissance, there were still disputes and doubts over Soviet intentions. Were the Soviets placing multiple warheads on their missiles? What was the range of the new long-range TU-26 Backfire bomber? Could it carry nuclear weapons to the United States and return without refueling? Most experts believed it could not, but the Soviet Union wanted it excluded from the SALT agreement.

The United States needed a near-real-time system capable of providing high-resolution photography or imagery.[63] The goal was "a single satellite that could produce uniformly high quality area surveillance and close look imagery and get it down as the event being watched was happening."[64]

The answer to the need for early indication and warning of a Soviet attack was the KH-11, a new electro-optical system, not dependent on film, which was launched in December 1976. Code-named Kennan/Crystal, the system produced high-resolution imagery on a near-real time basis. The KH-11's system consisted of arrays of tiny charge-coupled devices (CCDs) that collect particles of radiated energy and capture them into tiny receptors called picture elements, or pixels, which automatically measure their intensity. The CCDs are capable of detecting even small amounts of electromagnetic radiation reflected from the earth's surface. The radiation is focused onto the arrays by a powerful telescope and a series of highly polished mirrors. Voltage readings are amplified, converted to a digital format, and downlinked to antennae located at Fort Belvoir, Virginia. The data values of the pixels are converted into gray tones and assembled into black-and-white pictures of the earth's surface, which appear in a continual stream of images.[65]

Since they did not rely on film, the KH-11s stayed in orbit longer and could cover 40,000 potential targets, double the number handled by the KH-8 and KH-9. Because it did not eject film capsules, for nearly a year the Soviets did not realize that the KH-11 was a reconnaissance satellite. The first KH-11 imagery became available on January 20, 1977, the inauguration day of President Jimmy Carter. He was shown the imagery the next day and was amazed at its quality. Carter immediately saw the importance of the KH-11 system to SALT negotiations, that it provided unassailable verification. He expressed his determination to press ahead with arms control.[66]

Then, at the end of 1978 a disgruntled CIA watch officer, William Kampiles, after only eight months on the job, quit and stole a copy of the KH-11 technical operating manual, which he sold to the Soviets at their embassy in Athens, Greece, for $3,000. The KGB officer who initially interviewed Kampiles at the Soviet compound was Serge Ivanovich Bokhan, who was also working for the CIA. Bokhan got word to his control officer and Kampiles was arrested when he returned to the United States. He was tried and sentenced to forty years in prison, but the damage was done. Tipped off by Kampiles' theft, the Soviets covered construction sites for submarines and missile silos when the KH-11 passed overhead.[67]

When Carter was inaugurated in 1977, the Soviets were counting on quick completion of the Vladivostok negotiations that Leonid Brezhnev had conducted with President Gerald Ford and Henry Kissinger. However, Carter wanted the Vladivostok Accord substantially revised to include reductions in the number of strategic bombers, MIRVs (Multiple Independent Reentry Vehicles), and heavy missiles the Soviets would be permitted to have. Brezhnev rejected Carter's suggested revisions and was not prepared to move to lower limits until the Vladivostok Accord had been digested by the Soviet military. It would take two more years of negotiations before SALT II satisfied both sides.

When the negotiating issues grew more complicated with the presence of smaller weapons, such as mobile missiles and cruise missiles, so did the problems of verification. The Soviets were behind the United States in the technological sophistication of their surveillance systems and still dependent on film-return systems. However, they were obtaining high-resolution photographs and, by 1982, had their first near-real-time electro-optical system.[68]

The fall of the Shah in early 1979 and his replacement by Ayatollah Khomeini ended American influence in Iran. It meant the closing of two key signals intelligence (SIGINT) stations in the mountains on the Iranian border used to monitor Soviet missile tests at Tyuratam in Kazakhstan. The Iranian stations at Behshahr and Kabkan could intercept telemetry signals from Soviet missiles, which revealed their operating characteristics and number of warheads.

In an effort to calm critics of SALT II, Carter reassured the American public of U.S. capabilities to effectively monitor any SALT agreement. Carter referred to "national technical means" of verification, the first time any government official spoke openly of U.S. surveillance satellites. Carter warned Soviet Foreign Minister Andrei Gromyko that Soviet encryption of missile tests would prevent verification and an agreement. Brezhnev agreed to halt encoding of telemetry transmissions, and Carter agreed to lower his demand for substantial cuts. Carter and Brezhnev signed SALT II in Vienna in June 1979.[69] At the Vienna Summit, President Carter extracted a promise from Leonid Brezhnev that the Soviet Union would not produce more than thirty Backfire bombers a year.[70]

Despite verification problems, the Carter administration considered America's methods "adequate" to the task of detecting any significant violation before it could affect the strategic balance. However, from June to December, the agreement signed at Vienna foundered. The Soviet invasion of Afghanistan in December 1979 derailed Senate ratification.

The KH-11's capabilities, however, satisfied the security demanded by SALT's critics. Both sides agreed informally to abide by the provisions of SALT II, which indicated confidence in the technical means of verifying compliance."[71]

In December 1988, the imaging capabilities of the intelligence community expanded dramatically with the deployment of Lacrosse, the first all-weather, synthetic aperture radar satellite that provides its own energy rather than depending upon reflected sunlight for illuminating targets. Lacrosse has the capability to penetrate darkness, clouds, and some natural camouflage. It relies on a very large radar antenna and a series of solar panels for providing electrical power to the radar transmitter. The satellite emits bursts of microwave radiation toward the earth's surface; the landscape features reflect this radiation back to the satellite where it is captured by the antenna, converted to a digital format, and relayed to a ground receiving station, all in a matter of seconds. The digital data can be analyzed either in a "soft-copy" or raw format, or in the form of black-and-white images that resemble satellite photographs. Resolution is estimated at between two and five feet, sufficient to identify weapons as small as tanks or armored personnel carriers.[72]

From the beginning of satellite overflights, the Soviets knew they were being watched by "eyes in the sky" and could do nothing about it. They could not mount a nuclear first strike or any major military buildup without being seen from space. The worldwide communist revolution that Stalin and his successors planned never happened, in large part because the Soviets could not hide their military preparations nor match American technological advances. In the silent overflight war to inspect "denied territory," satellite reconnaissance and communications interceptions created transparency, vital to keeping the peace between the United States and the USSR.

★ ★ ★

Joseph Charyk, head of the National Reconnaissance Office since it was established in 1961, left the government in 1963 to bring satellite communications to civilian use. That year Congress established the Communications Satellite Corporation, the entrance into the communications age. Charyk, one of the founders, said:

> Communications satellites were the key to opening the Information Age. It became more and more difficult to live in isolation. For a long time the Soviet Union was able to maintain secrecy by controlling communications, both internally and with the outside world. Now North Korea is the only country with secrecy, the only country not connected to global communications.[73]

Charyk traveled to all major countries, urging them to build satellite stations and join an international organization to be known as Intelsat. The first members were Canada, Great Britain, France, Germany, Italy, Japan, and Australia. In April 1965, Intelsat launched Early Bird, the first commercial satellite to provide wireless telecommunications with Europe across the Atlantic. No longer were international telephones dependent on undersea cables. Within four years, Intelsat established the first global communications system, using earth-to-spacecraft communications and back again, making every message reachable almost anywhere in the world. A formal treaty in 1969 broadened usage of the satellites, requiring payment on the basis of usage. The income paid for further development. New regional and private systems connecting smaller countries rapidly proliferated. What began as a government-sponsored project was superseded by private enterprise and the Information Revolution.

In 1969 Intelsat transmitted footage of the Apollo XI landing on the moon, the first live television broadcast from space. Transmitting images became possible as a result of the digital technology that had been developed for reconnaissance satellites.

The KH-11, originally a military successor to the Corona, was designed by Bell

Telephone Laboratories in New Jersey in 1970. Its digital technology later came to be used in hundreds of civilian applications. The charge-coupled device (CCD), the first digital photography in space, became the home video digital camera and the digital still camera. Most CCDs, smaller than a postage stamp, are used for medical imaging, plasma physics, and space telescopes for astronomy.[74]

The most permanent result of the catch-up program that followed the launching of *Sputnik* in 1957 was the increased funding of government-sponsored research in American universities. For major American universities to work together and communicate, it was necessary to connect major computing centers around the United States. The centers were to be set up so that messages could continue to flow even if one or more of the computers were destroyed by an enemy attack.

In the late 1960s, the Department of Defense and the Advanced Research Projects Agency (ARPA) created the Arpanet. It was the nation's first computer network, linking the supercomputing centers of four west coast universities: University of Utah, UCLA, UC Santa Barbara, and Stanford Research Institute. By 1971 Arpanet had grown to fifteen sites that could communicate with each other by the first electronic mail, or e-mail. By 1972 the four original universities had grown to about fifty participants. During the next ten years, other computer networks formed, unattached to Arpanet. How to communicate among all the networks was the next problem to solve. All users had to agree on a set of protocols that all computers could use to communicate with each other. The initial system, a Transmission Control Protocol/Internet Protocol (TCP/IP), told computers how to break down and reassemble packets of information called bytes. Two computers communicating with each other had to make identical settings to receive each other's packets. The Internet Protocol (IP) is an agreed-upon way for all Internet computers to label and route information packets.[75]

With the establishment of TCP/IP in 1982, the Internet was born. In 1986 the National Science Foundation funded the creation of a network that allowed universities across the United States to connect. This step provided the first explosive growth spurt in the history of the Internet. In two years, the number of computers on line jumped from about 2,000 to almost 30,000. In its first ten years, between 1982 and 1992, the number of computers joined by the Internet increased from 235 to 727,000. From 1992 to 1998, the number of computers on the Internet jumped to 29,670,000. A new lifestyle had overtaken the United States.

★ ★ ★
13 Deception and Revelation

Early in January 1980, less than a month after the Soviet Union invaded Afghanistan, recently retired Lieutenant General Edward L. Rowny was pleasantly surprised when he received a telephone call from presidential candidate Ronald Reagan. Rowny, the military arms controller on the U.S. delegation in Geneva, had resigned in protest against the SALT II agreement signed by President Jimmy Carter in June of 1979. Reagan told Rowny he liked his congressional testimony against the strategic arms limitations agreement and invited Rowny to meet and discuss arms control with him at the Hay Adams hotel in Washington, DC. Rowny recounted to the authors that they met alone for nearly four hours in Reagan's hotel suite with a view across Lafayette Park onto the White House. Reagan told Rowny he was dispirited with the prevailing strategy of mutually assured destruction (MAD) and asked if it were viable.

"We are playing Russian roulette. They are holding a pistol to our head and we are holding a pistol to their heads. That's very risky," Reagan said. "Why don't we put on a helmet?"

"We don't have one," replied Rowny.

"I have more faith in science than apparently you have," said Reagan, who asked Rowny to become a campaign adviser. Rowny hesitated. Reagan asked why.

"People say you are a wild cowboy."

Reagan laughed and remarked that Rowny had a similar reputation. "You don't look like Genghis Khan to me," Reagan said. Rowny agreed to join the Reagan campaign team.[1]

Also working on the Reagan campaign was Dr. Edward Teller, father of the H-bomb, who believes that science can build a shield against nuclear weapons. In 1966, Teller, then head of the Lawrence Livermore Laboratory, north of California's Silicon Valley, met Reagan for the first time. They were introduced to each other at Stanford University by W. Glenn Campbell, director of the Hoover Institution on War, Revolution and Peace. After Reagan was elected governor in

November, Teller invited him to become the first governor of California to visit the Livermore Laboratory.

On November 22, 1967, Reagan toured the laboratory and was briefed on a major current project to test ballistic missile defense system warheads capable of destroying incoming missiles. For two hours, Reagan carefully followed the scientists who explained the progress and deficiencies of the early antimissile system. Teller recalled, "The topic was quite new to the governor, and he understood the essence and importance of what we were discussing. When the briefing was finished, I knew that Reagan had listened; I believe that he understood, but I had no idea whether he approved of the work or not. . . . Fifteen years later, I discovered that he had been very interested in those ideas."[2]

Ronald Reagan became the fortieth president in January 1981. Reagan loathed the SALT process; he "did not content himself with fine tuning the balance of terror; he wished to end it."[3] Moscow believed Reagan's desire foreshadowed nuclear war.

In May 1981, Soviet leader Leonid Brezhnev, ill and aging, denounced Reagan's anti-Soviet policies in a secret address to a major KGB conference in Moscow. Brezhnev had expected that the harsh rhetoric of Reagan's 1980 campaign for president would give way to a willingness to meet and negotiate differences. Instead, Reagan made no overtures; he expanded programs to increase American military strength, which had begun under President Carter after the Soviet Union's invasion of Afghanistan in 1979.

KGB Chairman Yuri Andropov, who was to succeed Brezhnev after his death eighteen months later, stunned the audience at the conference when he declared the new Reagan administration was actively preparing for nuclear war. Andropov announced a Politburo decision ordering the KGB and GRU to cooperate in a worldwide intelligence operation to collect strategic information on the presumed plans by the United States and NATO to launch a surprise nuclear strike against the Soviet Union. Called Operation RYAN, the acronym for *Raketnoy-Yadernoye Napadenie* (Nuclear Missile Attack), the plan emerged from "a potentially lethal combination of Reaganite rhetoric and Soviet paranoia."[4]

According to Christopher Andrew and Oleg Gordievsky, who first revealed details of Operation Ryan in 1991, its leading advocate on the Politburo was Minister of Defense Marshal Dmitri Ustinov, an old-line Bolshevik who had been Stalin's armaments commissar in 1941. Ustinov, who died in 1984, believed to the end in the inevitability of war between capitalism and communism.

The announcement of Operation Ryan astonished the KGB's sophisticated American experts who, while not doubting Andropov's alarm at Reagan's policies, saw no signs of an impending war. Nevertheless, the KGB First Chief Directorate's Institute for Intelligence Problems, acting on the belief war was imminent, applied newly developed intelligence concepts to the problem. According to its theory, deviations from peacetime routines in a wide variety of areas—military, political, economic, health, administration, and civil defense—could provide preliminary warnings of Western preparations for a nuclear first strike. *Rezidenturas* in Western capitals received instructions to check on increased purchases of blood from donors. The acceleration of nighttime activity at key government offices such as the Pentagon, an indication of war planning, was to be measured by a count of lights on and the number of cars parked at night compared with daytime activity.[5]

On March 8, 1983, Reagan spoke to the National Association of Evangelicals in Orlando, Florida. In his speech he branded the Soviet Union "an Evil Empire." In response, the KGB was instructed to create a slogan: "Reagan Means War."[6]

On March 23, 1983, President Reagan gave a speech in support of the 1984 defense budget in which he inserted his radical and utopian proposal for a Strategic Defense Initiative (SDI). His goal was to build a space-based antimissile shield that would provide defense against nuclear-tipped ICBMs, rendering them "impotent and obsolete." His support came from Rowny, and scientists led by Teller.

For Teller, SDI, like the H-bomb, was another "technically interesting project" to stretch the boundaries of science as far as humans could take them. He did not shy away from the military implications of using x-ray laser beams in space to detonate small nuclear weapons to destroy incoming missiles, part of the initial concept, but Reagan insisted that no nuclear weapons be used in space.[7]

Teller recalled that when Hitler invaded Belgium and Holland in 1940, he was at a scientific conference in Washington at which the participants listened to President Roosevelt address the nation.

> The President said, "You scientists are accused of having made the weapons that made this invasion possible. If you won't go to work on weapons, Hitler will conquer the world." I have to tell you . . . I felt that Roosevelt was talking to me personally. In the audience [of one thousand scientists], I was the only one who knew that the President knew about atomic weapons and what we did would determine the outcome. It was a direct challenge to me. From that time on I wanted to do it.[8]

In his second inaugural address in January 1985, Reagan focused on SDI. He told the American people, "I have approved a research program to find, if we can, a security shield that will destroy nuclear missiles before they reach their target. It wouldn't kill people. It would destroy weapons. It wouldn't militarize space, it would help demilitarize the arsenals of the earth. It would render nuclear weapons obsolete."

Senior officials, led by Defense Secretary Casper Weinberger, took up the cry; by April, opinion polls showed that the American public favored a complete defense against nuclear attack, not a partial defense of missile silos or command centers. Senator Sam Nunn, the respected Democrat on the Senate Armed Services Committee, questioned SDI and argued that rhetoric calling for an impenetrable shield against nuclear weapons "is irresponsible." Nunn, and critics who called Reagan's plan Star Wars after the science fiction movie and television series, argued that it was destabilizing: a space-based antimissile shield would allow the United States a first-strike capability without retaliation by the USSR. Like the Soviet Union, the critics argued that Reagan's plan was a grand escalation of the cold war because it overturned the doctrine of mutual vulnerability, which had kept a tenuous peace. The Soviet general staff viewed space-based technology primarily as an offensive weapon to launch ballistic missiles, not to defend against them. However, the momentum of American public support for SDI encouraged Congress to approve $3 billion of the $4 billion requested for SDI research in 1985.[9]

After he took power in 1985, Gorbachev's "new thinking" advocated *glasnost* and *perestroika* (openness and rebuilding), but the Soviet economy continued to fall. Forced to cut back on the Soviet Union's international thrust, Gorbachev began the Soviet withdrawal from Afghanistan, abandoned the Sandinistas in Nicaragua, withdrew from Indochina, and reduced Soviet commitments in Africa.

Gorbachev publicly pressed for arms control negotiations, but imagery from above continued to produce evidence that the USSR's programs to modernize and diversify its strategic missile force was steadily moving ahead. Imagery analysts counted 1,400 silo-based and mobile ICBM launchers, more than 800 of which had been replaced since 1972; the fifth generation of Soviet missiles was moving into place. The Soviet Union possessed 62 ballistic-missile-carrying submarines, the world's largest force, with 944 nuclear missiles. The Soviet Air Force had 180 Bear and Bison heavy bombers and 125 Backfire bombers, which the U.S. Air Force insisted could be easily modified to reach targets in the United States The precision of the estimates underscored the importance of overhead surveillance.[10]

On April 26, 1986, one of the four operating reactors at the Chernobyl nuclear power plant near Kiev exploded, casting lethal radioactivity into the atmosphere. As the poisonous debris began to settle over Poland, Finland, Sweden, and Norway, the Soviet Union's affected neighbors escalated their demands for information. It took two days for a public announcement of the accident, nine days to contain the fire resulting from the explosion. On the tenth day, the Soviet government called a press conference, but provided little specific information about the accident. Gorbachev did not appear in public to discuss the disaster until the middle of May.[11]

Intercepted telephone and two-way radio messages, in combination with KH-11 imagery, enabled American intelligence analysts to make "detailed assessments of the catastrophe as it was unfolding."[12] Landsat, the U.S.-government-owned satellite system, published images of the Chernobyl site within three days of the accident; higher resolution images by France's SPOT satellite followed.[13]

The Chernobyl details focused world attention on the worst peacetime nuclear disaster in history and forced the Soviet government to act. Chernobyl was a classic example of surveillance systems helping to limit damage by mobilizing a rapid worldwide response and clarifying the extent of the catastrophe to lessen fear and quell distorted rumors. Gorbachev's failure to promptly inform the Soviet people, provide emergency aid, and accept responsibility for Chernobyl caused a critical loss of credibility for him and the Communist Party of the Soviet Union.

Despite his troubles at home, Gorbachev reached out to Reagan for another summit, with the precondition that Reagan abandon SDI. Gorbachev was under heavy military pressure to eliminate the program. The Soviets knew their failing economy was unable to match America in a new arms race for a space-based defense.[14]

Reagan would not give up SDI. Gorbachev dropped the demand, suggesting they meet for discussions with no agenda at Reykjavik, Iceland, on October 11 and 12, 1986. Unexpectedly, he offered major arms reduction proposals and convinced Reagan to agree both sides would end production of all ballistic missiles and nuclear weapons within ten years. Reagan said he would go along only if SDI research and development could continue. Gorbachev refused to budge on permitting SDI research outside of the laboratory. "It's 'laboratory' or nothing," Gorbachev said.

Reagan would not yield. Over and over he told Gorbachev that "SDI isn't a bargaining chip." "If you are willing to abolish nuclear weapons, why are you so anxious to get rid of a defense against nuclear weapons?" Reagan asked.

"Mr. President," Gorbachev said, "you have missed the unique chance of going down in history as a great president who paved the way for international disarmament."

"That applies to both of us," replied Reagan.[15]

In the summers of 1983 and 1984, the U.S. Defense Department had conducted a series of four tests to intercept nuclear missiles in space with another missile. The tests were known as the Homing Overlay Experiment (HOE). The first three attempts failed, but the fourth, in the summer of 1984, succeeded in destroying the targeted incoming missile. The results were made public and presented to Congress, which continued to fund further research and development for the $30 billion program.

The American success was the centerpiece of an elaborate deception program approved early in Secretary of Defense Weinberger's term of office (from 1981 to 1987). Weinberger would neither confirm nor deny that he had approved the deceptions, but ten years later he told *New York Times* reporter Tim Weiner, who broke the story in August 1993: "You always work on deception. You're always trying to practice deception. You are obviously trying to mislead your opponents and to make sure they don't know the actual facts."[16]

The deception plan called for destruction of the test missile by alternative means, whether or not the killer missile actually struck it. In the first tests, explosive devices were implanted in the missile to be attacked, setting off an explosion that simulated the effect of a strike by the interceptor missile in the event it flew by without hitting the target. The Pentagon expected the Soviet Union's sensors to monitor the test.

In the first two Homing Overlay test flights, the interceptor missed the target by too wide a margin to fool anyone. The third test also failed. In the fourth and final test flight, "steps were taken to make it easier for the interceptor's sensor to find the target," according to a report by the Government Accounting Office (GAO). First the target missile was heated, presenting a larger bull's eye for heat-seeking sensors on the interceptor missile. Then the target missile was turned sideways in flight so that it presented its broad side, a bigger target than a head-on encounter would provide. Together these measures made the target missile appear 2.1 times its normal size to the sensors on board the interceptor missile, more than doubling the chances of the interceptor missile striking the target. This time the test was successful.[17]

"The hit looked beautiful so the Congress didn't ask questions," said one of the scientists involved in the double-purpose deception plan, designed both to fool the Soviets and to assure continued appropriations for SDI development.[18] In 1984 project officials described the test as proof that the program could clear a crucial technological hurdle, the first time a missile had ever intercepted a long-range ballistic missile in flight. It was nearly seven years before project researchers again hit a missile with another missile after numerous failures.

The deception effort succeeded in misleading the Soviet military into believing that SDI worked. The Soviet military leadership believed in 1984 that an American first strike might be in the making. The first reported American success with an earth-based ABM heightened Soviet fears and accelerated military spending. Moscow spent tens of billions of dollars it could ill afford reacting to the SDI program, according to Raoul Z. Sagdayev, who headed the Soviet Space Research Institute in the 1980s. Soviet scientists believed that President Reagan's "peace shield" was a technological fantasy, but the Soviet high command insisted on measures to counter SDI, including an all out effort to upgrade Moscow's land-based ICBMs, explained Sagdayev.[19]

The Defense Department reported in January 1991 that a prototype ERIS test missile had successfully hit a mock warhead in space. The Strategic Defense Initiative Organization (SDIO) estimated that the first ABM site with 100 interceptors could be built without much technical risk for $10 billion by the target date of 1996. A network of sites to cover the entire United States could be completed for $25 billion. By the spring of 1992, the cost estimate for the first site had doubled to $20 billion and a second ERIS test failed.

Between January 1990 and March 1992, the Pentagon conducted seven test flights of SDI interceptors. The program appeared to be on track until a GAO report found that SDIO officials had exaggerated the success of four of the tests. The other three tests were correctly portrayed as either complete failures or only partly successful. None of the so-called Brilliant Pebbles, independent interceptors loaded with sensors and computers and designed to crash into missiles in flight and destroy them by collision, had tested successfully, despite SDIO claims that one had "accomplished all of its main objectives." After a report by David S. C. Chu, assistant secretary of defense for program analysis from 1991 to 1993, the Defense Department vetoed the idea of building the system without thorough tests required by law and regulations. Chu recommended that the system not be built until it was thoroughly tested and that the deployment target be moved to 2002 or 2003.[20]

In an interview, Chu explained that "it is not surprising that a system as ambitious in scope [as a strategic defense missile] was unsuccessful in its initial tests. The demand for immediate perfection is unrealistic." Chu expressed concern with expectations for weapons testing based on one or two pass-fail tests. Instead, he said, a constructive approach based on trial and error and analytical correction of the physics, the components, and the system must be repeated over and over to achieve success of any weapons system.[21]

Between 1983 and 1999, the United States spent $60 billion on antimissile research and conducted nineteen intercept tests. Five intercepts were successful, fourteen failed to hit the target. SDI called for earth and space-based antiballistic missile systems.

The Soviet Union had no idea that the SDIO tests included a not unusual form of deception. The promoters of SDI wanted to leave the impression, both with America's adversaries whose missiles were its potential targets, and with the U.S. Congress, the source of continued funding, that the tests were as successful as they could be at this stage. They wanted to convince both audiences that building the system, despite its staggering costs, was feasible.

A giant gap between successful testing and full-scale deployment of a reliable antimissile system remains to be filled. President George W. Bush still faces the problem both his father and President Clinton failed to solve. On December 13, 2001, President Bush announced that the United States would unilaterally withdraw from the Anti-Ballistic Missile Treaty in six months. The treaty, signed during the cold war in 1972, prohibits the development, testing, and deployment of strategic defense systems and components that are based in the air, at sea, or in space.

President Bush has tried to reassure Russian president Putin that U.S.–Russian relations will not suffer despite the U.S. withdrawal from the treaty.

★ ★ ★

Only after the breakup of the Soviet Union in 1991 did the final secret of the cold war emerge—that it had ended a decade earlier.

In 1994 we met Vladimir Kryuchkov, who headed the KGB's First Chief Directorate in charge of foreign intelligence from 1974 to 1988; he was deposed after he led the failed coup d'état in August 1991 against President Gorbachev. After his ouster from the KGB, Kryuchkov escaped a prison sentence and was freed. He settled into his luxury apartment with high security, located on a tree-lined street behind the Ministry of Foreign Affairs off the Arbat. The yellow-glazed brick apartment building had the look of privilege in a neighborhood of faded houses, heavily repainted embassies, and run-down government offices.

In 1994 Kryuchkov was advising communist members of the Duma, planning to write his memoirs, and plotting a new career as a kingmaker for the return of the Communist Party old guard. His gleaming apartment, which he shared with his wife, contained a suite of rooms with polished wooden parquet floors, contemporary crystal chandeliers, and oil paintings by Soviet artists. The usual cooking odors of Moscow apartments were missing, replaced by a sparkling clean but sterile modernity. After we crossed his doorstep and exchanged cautious greetings, Kryuchkov began to shout at us that the United States had tricked him and the Soviet leadership into believing that President Reagan's Strategic Defense Initiative was successful when the Pentagon announced favorable test results. White-haired and balding, Kryuchkov was intense, and forceful. "You fooled us, with Star Wars," he raged as we started to discuss the state of Russian-American relations. "You fooled us." He was still angry over the inability of the Soviet Union to detect that President Reagan's Strategic Defense Initiative (SDI) tests were not the success that the Pentagon had announced in 1984. Kryuchkov believed that the impact of SDI testing on Soviet military spending in the 1980s had helped to destroy the Soviet Union.[22]

America's experiment with missile defense was not the cause of the breakup of the Soviet empire. Rather, it was an awakening to Soviet leaders that their economy was going downhill and could not pay for an equivalent shield. It meant a shift in the "correlation of forces," a shift in the military balance. The threat of equivalent power with the United States, based on military strength and a nuclear arsenal, could no longer be sustained.

The Soviets' belief that American SDI tests of an earth-based antimissile system were successful proved more influential than the facts. After Gorbachev tried without success at Reykjavik to get Reagan to back off and stop development of

SDI, he returned to Moscow and attempted a new *perestroika*, but the forces of disintegration overcame his best efforts.

For a long time, American analysts in the CIA and economists in academia did not recognize the growing gap between the Soviet peoples' desires for more consumer goods and the failure of a state-planned economy to supply them. Western studies continued to believe in the "reasonableness of efficiency in central planned economies," without keeping an ear to the "outcasts" who criticized the system.

Evaluators at the CIA and the National Bureau of Economic Research looked at five measures of Soviet expenditure: agriculture, energy, manufacturing, defense, and foreign aid. They miscalculated the size of the military in relation to the overall economy, and how both compared with the American mix. They did not foresee that central planning had a corrosive effect on human capital, meaning that it degraded the work ethic and discouraged invention.

From 1950 to 1959, the Soviet economy, measured as gross national product (GNP), grew at a healthy rate of 6 percent a year. Khrushchev boasted, "We will bury you," meaning the Soviet Union would overtake and surpass U.S. production, defeating capitalism without war. In the first years of his leadership, the New Lands program expanded planted acreage and lifted agricultural output. Reduction of military spending added to economic growth. Foodstuffs and consumer goods were noticeably better than under Stalin.

After 1959 the government's investment in the civilian sector slowed and so did the rate of economic growth. Competition with the U.S. in military and space programs took resources away from civilian needs. The rate of economic growth dropped to 2 percent annually. The military took the best scientific and engineering talent; the chemical industry, automation and modernization of industry in general suffered the loss. The gains in agricultural output of the New Lands program proved to be temporary, followed by disastrous harvests after the natural moisture and fertility of the new acreage were used up and not replaced.[23]

Khrushchev was forced to buy grain from abroad. He needed chemicals and machinery to produce fertilizer. The Soviet government had to spend its gold reserves and seek foreign credit. At the same time, the Soviets tried not to decrease military spending. Their costs for economic aid to the Third World, part of their attempt to expand the world communist revolution, rose unabated. The Soviet economy slowed to 2 percent growth in the 1960s, then contracted further in the 1970s. The turning-point year, after which the economy did not recover, was 1976; the expensive invasion of Afghanistan in 1979 exacerbated the problems.

CIA estimators erred in assessing the size and growth rate of the Soviet economy. They believed until the 1980s that the overall GNP of the Soviet Union was 56 percent of the American gross product, when the truth was closer to 30 percent. Moreover, they underestimated the military burden, citing it as 11 to 15 percent of the Soviet economy, when the Soviets were spending 25 percent of their budget on military personnel and arms. In addition, the estimators gauged East Germany's economy as 80 percent as large as that of West Germany; the truer figure was that communist East Germany's total output was only about a third as large as capitalist West Germany.[24]

The problem was that U-2 imagery and satellite reconnaissance could not determine Soviet productivity. Watching trains and counting factories did not disclose output. For a time at the end of the 1960s and early 1970s, American and Soviet visionaries talked about "convergence" of the two economic systems: they would both change to meet at a common norm that would create compatibility. Even though they could see that capitalism had a higher growth rate than socialism, these academic analysts believed in the uniqueness of the Soviet economy, based on "special realities" of the Soviet political and economic system that couldn't be compared with standard Western measurements.

Even after Western economists realized that the Soviet economy was not the sturdy ark they had earlier conceived it to be, they lacked the courage to acknowledge what their own eyes were telling them: the extent of the Soviet weakness. During internal debates in the 1980s, analysts at the CIA accused proponents of the new, clear vision that they were motivated by political preconceptions that America was stronger. The "old thinkers" refused to believe the tales told by Soviet émigrés of how badly the Soviet economy functioned, arguing that "anecdote is not evidence."[25] These analysts found it difficult to determine how much was being spent for defense because dollars and rubles were not comparable, they said. The new, younger analysts said to take a look at the conversion tables, it was not so hard to compare the currencies if you were ready to believe the incomprehensible.[26]

The Communist Party of the Soviet Union established total control over individuals in work, play, and family affairs, a formula for permanent poverty. Self-identity as private property suffered from the revocation of land and home ownership. The result was that even the property of the self, each person's individual identity and will, was submerged into the demands of the collective. The mute acceptance of death or life at the hands of the state, evident in the confessions of purge victims, is testimony to the end of belief in individual freedom.

The loss of personal identity has left a startling legacy for the postcommunist era. Life expectancy for males has dropped to new lows; fewer children are being born. The unborn, orphans, and abandoned street children have been labeled "a lost generation." The population of Russia is shrinking.

Gorbachev believed he could rebuild the economy by allowing more freedom of speech while still maintaining state ownership of property. "Speculation" or seeking to make a profit, which had been considered immoral even from czarist times, remained a sin. Moscow police arrived with clubs to disperse housewives attempting to form a street market with home-grown herbs and radishes.

Sergo Beria, a rocket scientist, whose father, Lavrenti Beria, had been in charge of building the first Soviet atomic bomb, was working on his memoirs in 1993. In an interview, Beria recalled that in the 1930s and 1940s, Soviet intelligence was like a vacuum cleaner, sucking up whatever technology it could lay its hands on. The take included atomic bomb secrets, proximity fuses, the design for safety shaving razors, the process for refining sugar, and the formula for synthetic rubber. The Soviets stole the design for night vision devices, and on-board radio location and naval radio location finder systems. They produced the MIG-29 and the SU-27 with the help of stolen plans. They copied the TU-4 from the B-29.

Beria believed this pattern for developing technology led to the demise of the Soviet Union. No society can prosper, he said, if it always has to try to recreate the technology after it has already succeeded elsewhere, because the thief can never catch up with the arc of the arrow that leads invention and productivity. Every street thief runs out of the money he has stolen; he can never get ahead because he has not learned how to make money. Thus, said Beria, stealing technology leaves the thief permanently trailing behind those he has robbed.[27]

Conclusion
Looking Back, Looking Forward

The storm that raged over Sudoplatov's revelations in his oral history brought forth long preserved secrets from the American side. Two separate camps, those who did not want to believe his description of atomic espionage, and those who wanted the proof to back up his allegations, demanded the government issue the VENONA transcripts, which they already knew existed. At a press conference on May 3, 1995, called by the late Les Aspin, then chairman of the President's Foreign Intelligence Advisory Board (PFIAB), the two sides and the host panel had a shouting match.

The purpose of Aspin's panel was to deny that the FBI had any materials that would verify Sudoplatov's claims. Aspin read aloud a letter from FBI Director Louis J. Freeh, which asserted that the FBI "has classified information available that argues against the conclusions reached by the author of *Special Tasks*. The FBI, therefore, considers such allegations to be unfounded." Freeh did not make the information available to Aspin or members of the President's Foreign Intelligence Advisory Board. The letter created a rumble of dissent in the audience. To quiet the argument, Aspin threw his hands in the air and said the last word had not been spoken on the subject. Two months later, on July 10, the NSA and the CIA held a celebration ceremony to begin the release of VENONA.[1] The FBI declined to participate.

For fifty years, the NSA, the FBI, the CIA, and a succession of presidential administrations had dithered with the question of whether or not to release 2,900 decrypted intercepts of Soviet cable traffic between Moscow and its intelligence officers in America from 1939 to 1946. A significant number of code names still remain unidentified in the traffic.

Why did it take fifty years for the government to release the VENONA transcripts and why finally in 1995?

The answer depends on whom you believe: officials who contend that the National Security Agency had been working for years to prepare the material for release to the public and they were finally ready, or former CIA Director John

Deutsch, who approved the release. Deutsch acknowledged that the atmosphere that led to disclosure of VENONA was infected by the Aldrich H. Ames case. After Ames' 1994 arrest the agency's approval rating dropped to a deep negative. "Why only tell about failures? Why not successes?" Deutsch asked rhetorically. It was the same reason the CIA told the public about the overhead reconnaissance Corona program, which had also been a sacred secret. "CORONA was exciting, interesting. Let's do it," with VENONA, Deutsch said. He concluded that the old arguments against revealing sources and methods were no longer valid.[2]

Other NSA officials stated that the opening of the secret trove was in response to the furor created by Sudoplatov's revelations. Within the CIA, seasoned intelligence officers remarked that the patterns of espionage Sudoplatov had outlined rang true to their own knowledge.

The release of the VENONA messages confirmed espionage by the cast of Soviet intelligence officers Sudoplatov had described. The intercepted telegrams labeled Donald Maclean, Judith Coplon, Harry Dexter White, and Alger Hiss. The messages spotlighted atomic theft by Fuchs, the Rosenbergs, and Theodore Hall, but provided no evidence on the cooperation of Robert Oppenheimer, Leo Szilard, or Bruno Pontecorvo, who was in contact with Enrico Fermi. The cooperation of top Manhattan Project scientists with the Soviets was protected because those reports went through channels other than VENONA, for example the drugstore safe house in Santa Fe run by illegals, which transmitted information through Mexico City. Pontecorvo fled to the Soviet Union in 1950 and announced his defection in 1956. Only later, through documents in Russian presidential and intelligence archives, was Oppenheimer's cooperation unmasked. Still uncracked code names remain in VENONA. The full extent of and final word on Manhattan Project infiltration by Soviet espionage remains buried until the further opening of Russian archives.

Much of the apoplectic response to Sudoplatov reflected denial of the still-unacknowledged counterintelligence failure of the FBI and Army security to prevent Soviet atomic espionage during World War II. The FBI has refused to declassify and release documents relating to VENONA to independent scholars and researchers even though more than fifty years have passed since they were operational secrets.

Counterintelligence has been the weak link between the CIA and FBI; crippling counterintelligence disasters have shaken both agencies. They have failed to prevent the flow of American intelligence secrets to China, the Soviet Union, and its successor state, Russia, which resulted in the compromise of nuclear secrets and the death of Soviet agents working for the United States. From 1985 until he was arrested outside his home in Arlington, Virginia, on February 21, 1994, Aldrich Ames was Moscow's mole inside the CIA. Ames betrayed the identities of ten Soviet intelligence officers working for the United States, which led to their executions. By

1986 it was clear to the CIA that virtually its entire stable of Soviet assets had been imprisoned or executed, but it was another eight years before Ames was arrested. The CIA's security officers were unable to identify the mole, and hesitated to bring the FBI into a case that reflected its inability to detect a traitor in its own house. Ames sold compromising information to the KGB for $2.7 million; his treachery rivals the crimes of former Navy Warrant Officer John Walker in terms of who did the most damage to American national security. Over a period of eighteen years, Walker sold the Navy's top secret cryptographic systems, weapons system details, and wartime targets in hostile countries to the Soviet Union.[3]

The FBI lost two of its most important Soviet assets through Ames' June 1985 disclosures to Soviet intelligence. Robert Philip Hanssen, a senior FBI counterintelligence officer, also betrayed these two KGB officers and a third KGB officer; Hanssen was arrested on February 18, 2001. Hanssen volunteered his services to the KGB in 1985 and continued to provide information through 1991; after a pause, he resumed supplying information from 1999 through February 2001. Both cases have underscored the need for restructuring the nation's counterintelligence mechanisms.

On December 28, 2000, President Clinton signed a Presidential Decision Directive on "U.S. Counterintelligence Effectiveness—Counterintelligence for the 21st Century," CI-21. President Bush proceeded to implement the directive, designed to deal with emerging threats and adversaries, to eliminate "piecemeal and parochial" counterintelligence capabilities.[4] In the struggle against terrorism, counterintelligence is the most effective tool for preempting or aborting terrorist strikes.

Historically, counterintelligence required well planned investigations to establish proof that could raise espionage cases to the level of successful prosecution. As in the cases growing out of VENONA messages fifty years ago, it was not enough to have intelligence information if it could not be used in court. Only in the Rosenberg case could the FBI, using the leads from Klaus Fuchs' confession, follow through to find all the tentacles of that spy ring and develop evidence with which the government was able to successfully prosecute.

The problem still remains of propriety under the law when counterintelligence develops into criminal prosecution cases against American citizens. The FBI's failure in the case against Wen Ho Lee, an atomic scientist suspected of giving secrets from Los Alamos to China, underscores the need for better training of FBI street agents. During an ongoing foreign intelligence case, the Justice Department's Office of Intelligence Policy and Review (OIPR) carefully proscribes and monitors the contact between FBI agents and prosecutors.[5] Such barriers between criminal and national security investigations are likely to become less stringent in response to the overriding demand to prevent terrorism. Nevertheless, the civil rights of American citizens must be safeguarded against abuse.

Government insiders say that developing successful prosecutions presents new problems: when emphasis is placed on delivering cases to court, crime tracking and prevention are neglected. The enormous range of capability created by satellite intelligence—and its byproduct, information storage and retrieval—promises a new era of counterintelligence and crime detection. However, coordinating the pieces to perceive and stop terrorism before it wreaks havoc means taking manpower away from its accustomed tasks. Whose budget should pay for the time lost? A new bureaucratic management system is needed to cross over jurisdictions and integrate the terrorist leads that are available, but not acted upon, to halt acts of catastrophic destruction.

At the same time that the problem of failed counterintelligence was being discussed in the early days of the George W. Bush administration, the new Defense Secretary, Donald Rumsfeld, gathered a team of experts known for unconventional thinking to develop an American force posture consistent with a revised threat assessment. Led by senior strategist Andrew (Andy) Marshall, who has been producing net assessments of America's military force posture since 1973, the team is attempting a drastic rethinking and transformation of the military both in terms of personnel and weapons. The changes they are considering have been under study by academics and defense think tanks since the end of the cold war.[6]

Strategists must deal with the Revolution in Military Affairs (or RMA), which has brought power to small groups of irregular forces and transnational terrorist organizations with sufficient weapons to create civic and economic disruption.

The plan to counter this threat would reduce visible armaments such as aircraft carriers and tanks; instead, the military would rely more on space and undersea vehicles for weapons delivery systems. Drones with real time photographic reconnaissance capability, equipped to fire missiles at targets, are increasingly seeing battlefield use. The new priorities include developing information warfare to limit computer attacks on military and industrial infrastructure, and developing new forms of blockades. The mission requires defending against nuclear weapons of mass destruction, and developing the means to counter biological warfare and bioterrorism. New systems of urban warfare are in the making: vision equipment to allow soldiers to see at all times of the day and night through smoke and in basements and tunnels; bunker busters, recoilless hand-held projectiles capable of piercing walls and armor; thermal, electronic, and visual "badges" to mark all friendly soldiers, immunizing them from attack both by each other and future unmanned fighting vehicles; and nonlethal weapons for use in peacekeeping and police operations and in storming buildings that may contain civilians (an example is quick-drying and immobilizing plastic foam).[7] Special forces will play the predominant role.

The concept of fighting two wars at once (hypothetically, North Korea and Iraq) has been transformed to a global terrain. From traditional emphasis on the massive use of troops and strategic bombing, the military will change to new technology based on precision strike forces, space satellites, and electronically gathered intelligence. Battle casualties counted in the thousands and tens of thousands, a memory of the American Civil War, World Wars I and II, the Korean War, and Vietnam, promise to be relegated to the history of soldiers used as "cannon fodder." In the twenty-first century, military strength will be described in terms of stealth, speed, range, unprecedented accuracy, lethality, strategic mobility, superior intelligence, and the political will to prevail.[8]

On September 11, 2001, the future became the present. Americans watched in horror while three passenger airliners, hijacked by suicidal terrorists, destroyed the twin 110-story towers of the World Trade Center in New York and part of the Pentagon. A fourth hijacked airliner crashed in the Pennsylvania countryside. The attacks by one or a group of terrorist organizations, which did not claim public credit, killed more than 3,000 people. President Bush declared the attacks an act of war, naming as the prime suspect Osama bin Laden, leader of the Al Qaeda terrorist network, which executed the bombings of American embassies in Africa in 1998.[9] The premeditated crashes also closed down the financial sector housed in lower Manhattan for four days, grounded all air traffic for a week, and sent shock waves through the American and world economies.

The terrorists waged a war without armies, with no ground rules to protect innocent civilians. They shattered the industrial world's sense of security. The attacks in New York and Washington evoked intense anger at the failure of American intelligence and law enforcement agencies to prevent what was seen as preventable destruction of lives on an epic scale. Defeating an enemy without a defined front requires a combination of military, economic, political, and psychological warfare. Intelligence is the point of the spear. For centuries, sending ground troops into the forbidding terrain and tribal treachery of Afghanistan, where bin Laden was in hiding, proved futile for imperial powers such as Great Britain and the Soviet Union.[10] Russian officers who fought in Afghanistan warned American military leaders not to repeat their mistakes.

The American military campaign to oust the Taliban and bin Laden from Afghanistan was brief and successful. By providing American special forces advisers to Northern Alliance troops and combining air and logistic support for anti-Taliban forces, the U.S. Central Command routed the Taliban and Al Qaeda fighters, taking thousands of prisoners. Al Qaeda bases and training centers in Afghanistan were destroyed as the search for bin Laden and Taliban leader Mullah Omar continued in early 2002. The war utilized the new technology sooner than expected, and it worked. The remaining task was to fathom the structure, organization, and training bases of the the radical Muslim terrorist leadership left behind and to destroy them.

President Bush built a broad international coalition to fight terrorism; the process meant downplaying differences on human rights and antimissile defense with his Chinese and Russian partners. Russian President Vladimir Putin agreed to provide information about international terrorist infrastructure, whereabouts, and training bases.[11] Unlike the American view that the war in Chechnya is an excessive repression of a breakaway minority, Putin saw Chechnya as another case of Muslim terrorism backed by bin Laden's Al Qaeda. Putin told President Clinton that bin Laden visited Chechnya four times during the war to offer support, and a top bin Laden deputy, Colonel Khattab, helped escalate the war in 1992. Russian support for the broader antiterrorist war connects to the continuing conflict in Chechnya and the actions there of radical Muslim terrorists.[12]

Putin faces criticism from his own generals for allowing America's military presence in Central Asia. They fear the loss of traditional Russian influences in the former Soviet republics. Uzbekistan, Tadzhikistan, Kazakhstan, and Kirghistan agreed to cooperate with the United States by allowing both use of their air bases and overflights of their airspace against the Taliban, when the Taliban were the ruling government in Afghanistan and protective hosts of bin Laden. American petroleum experts warn that sharing power with Putin in Central Asia will give Russia control over the pipelines and the export flow of Central Asian oil. This, combined with Russian oil production, would give them a degree of control over about sixteen million barrels of oil per day, roughly double the production of Saudi Arabia.[13]

The United States and Russia must also face the existence of thirty-five sites where the Soviet Union established bacteriological warfare laboratories and storage facilities. The new coalition with Russia must agree on how to eradicate these cesspools of death.[14]

Equal to the shock of the attacks on the World Trade Center and the Pentagon was the realization that the terrorists had infiltrated the west's open society and lived freely, planning in secrecy from apartments in California, Florida, New York, and New Jersey, and in Great Britain, Italy, and Germany. The clandestine cells were small and autonomous, often remaining under cover for years. Their organization is reminiscent of Soviet intelligence officers who lived as "illegals" or "sleepers," operating under cover in the United States and South America in the 1930s, 1940s, and 1950s. The Soviet illegals lived like normal citizens, waiting for orders to spring into action in case of war with the United States, which never came.

The first response to the September 11 attack on the World Trade Center and the Pentagon was to compare it to Pearl Harbor. Ever since December 7, 1941, American presidents have struggled to counter the Pearl Harbor syndrome, fear of surprise attack. The appointment of the Beacon Hill Commission during the Truman administration and President Eisenhower's decision to implement its recommendations to develop the U-2 and "eyes in the sky" reconnaissance satellites led to America's technological superiority. Priorities change in wartime, and the role of intelligence multiplies. If the past is a measure, liaison relationships among intelligence agencies will smooth the way for new techniques in surveillance, code breaking, and coalition intelligence sharing.

In the middle of the twentieth century, the shift began from an emphasis on human intelligence (HUMINT) to technical collection, which can record real time information but rarely predict intentions. In the political and military war against terrorism, the need for human intelligence sources has grown geometrically.

Human intelligence can reveal the opposition's capability by exposing its personnel, their agents, and their assignments. HUMINT gathers the codes for classified communications and wartime contingency plans. The best agents are those who can reliably predict if an adversary intends to wage war, what its attack plan is, and when it will commence.

Thanks to Polish Colonel Ryzard Kuklinski, who escaped to the West, the United States knew in advance that the Soviet Union was preparing to invade Poland in 1980, under the guise of a "peaceful exercise," and crush the Solidarity workers' movement. With this foreknowledge, the U.S. government warned Leonid Brezhnev of the "far reaching consequences of East-West relations and that American policy toward the Soviet Union would be directly and very adversely affected." President Carter asked for and received support from Germany and Great Britain to threaten the Soviet Union with economic sanctions if the invasion went forward. Unlike the invasion of Czechoslovakia in August 1968, for which the United States adopted a passive stance, the Western allies were on record warning the Soviet Union of the consequences of military action in Poland.[15] Human intelligence paid off with information that avoided an invasion and maintained stability between the superpowers. In the late 1990s, intelligence experts called for an expansion of HUMINT.

Terrorism is political warfare. Technological tools, while essential, still have not replaced the critical factor of human intelligence. Assessing the enemy's intentions, then integrating the informed analysis into decision making, is the way to turn anger against terrorism into victory.

HUMINT, associated in the public mind with covert operations, came under attack in the 1970s. Vietnam, the death of Salvador Allende in Chile, Watergate, and covert assassination operations against Fidel Castro and African leader Patrice Lumumba generated increasing hostility toward the CIA. Investigative journalist Seymour Hersh published an exposé in the *New York Times* on December 22, 1974, that ran on page one under a three-column headline: "Huge CIA Operation Reported in U.S. Against Anti-War Forces, Other Dissidents in Nixon Years." Hersh's article charged: "The Central Intelligence Agency, directly violating its charter, conducted a massive illegal domestic intelligence operation during the Nixon administration against the antiwar movement and other dissident groups in the United States, according to well-placed government sources." Hersh's article resulted in two congressional committees and a presidential commission investigating the agency's domestic spying, opening mail of American citizens, and assassination operations.[16]

Senator Frank Church, who headed the Senate investigation, called the CIA a "rogue elephant on the rampage." The result was greater congressional scrutiny of the CIA and tighter requirements for approving covert operations. President Carter's CIA Director Stansfield Turner cut back on the hiring of new field officers to cultivate sources and gather human intelligence. New restrictions prohibited CIA officers from working under cover as journalists, clergy, or aid workers. In 1995, as a result of human rights abuses in Latin America, the CIA issued orders that forbade the hiring of paid agents with unsavory or potentially embarrassing backgrounds, unless approved by headquarters. These restrictions and the ban on assassinations issued in an executive order by President Ford in the mid 1970s will now be reviewed to permit broader action against terrorist cells.

Despite advancing technology, determining an adversary's intentions and advance warning of terrorist operations remain the critical element of intelligence gathering. The HUMINT task is for long term penetration of radical Muslim terrorist organizations such as Osama bin Ladin's Al Qaeda. The Middle East intelligence agencies who have dealt with bin Laden insist that Al Qaeda is not truly Islamic, but is a murderous, amoral organization that hides behind and perverts Koranic verses. In the Koran and the Sunnah, the spoken and acted examples of Mohammed, life is sacred, given and taken only by God. Suicide is outlawed. However, a widely dispersed minority believes that Islamic culture is in danger of being extinguished through Western influence. The solution, these revolutionaries believe, is to establish an Islamic state untainted by the infiltration of Western power. Terror is justified under the guise of protecting Islamic culture.[17]

The immediate threat is from terrorist cells with the potential for bacteriological warfare or for planting a nuclear weapon on a boat or truck to be detonated within the continental United States.[18]

The terrorist attack on September 11, 2001, overshadowed the debate on the need for a National Missile Defense (NMD) and made urgently credible calls for a comprehensive National Homeland Defense (NHD). Two years earlier, in September 1999, Defense Secretary William S. Cohen established the U.S. Commission on National Security/21st Century. He approved $10.4 million to review the early twenty-first century global security environment including potential "wild cards." In its first report, the commission warned that among new threats "is the prospect of an attack on U.S. cities by independent or state supported terrorists using weapons of mass destruction." In its final report of March 15, 2001, *Road Map for National Security: Imperative for Change*, the commission concluded that "attacks on American citizens possibly causing heavy casualties are likely over the next quarter century."[19]

The commission's March 2001 report urged the president to create a National

Homeland Security Agency (NHSA) responsible for integrating security efforts of various U.S. government agencies such as the Customs Service, Border Patrol, and Coast Guard. After September 11, President Bush acted quickly to enact the commission's recommendation. In his speech to Congress and the nation on September 23, he named Pennsylvania Governor Thomas Ridge to head the new NHSA cabinet position.[20] However, his appointment has not resolved the internal bureaucratic turf battles among government agencies that prevent and delay effective integration of antiterrorist efforts.

The history of intelligence gathering and ideological conflict shows that those who place themselves inside the adversary's mind to fathom his intentions are the most successful. In the Cuban Missile Crisis, it was CIA Director John McCone, whose unconventional thinking and managerial expertise, applied to the problem of Soviet shipments to Cuba, intuited the arrival of Soviet nuclear missiles capable of reaching the east coast of the United States. Out-of-the-box thinkers, the innovators, are the winners in intelligence wars.

The cold war demonstrated the power of political and psychological warfare. Programs such as Radio Free Europe and Radio Liberty, which succeeded against the Soviet Union in the cold war, are models for dealing with the terrorist ideology of radical Islam. Supplementing the Voice of America by creating a Radio Afghanistan could expose the falsity of bin Laden's messages, which pervert Islamic scripture. Radio, television, and the Internet, feared by Muslim extremists, can be weapons for spreading ideas to Muslims who want to choose integration into the world economy. Appealing to women in the Muslim world is another means to modernization. Bringing the message of a better life through economic development, thus ending their isolation, has a basic appeal to the disenfranchised and downtrodden.

The purpose of terrorism is to destroy. Bin Laden's terrorists want to destroy modernization—Western wealth, values, and power—and to destabilize the Middle East. His primary target is Saudi Arabia and its oil riches. Bin Laden's radical, apostate Islam distorts Mohammed's message of peace. Radical Islam provides no solution for the poverty of Central Asia and the Middle East. Its banner calls for ridding the region of American military bases and foreign business activity, a goal counterproductive to bringing the regions into the world economic community. Such a regression precludes the benefits of technology and advanced communications.

America and its coalition allies possess the will to prevail. Fighting the war against terrorism has redefined common interest. Pressing disagreements with Russia, China, and Europe have been put aside. Instead, former enemies pool their intelligence forces to identify, shut down financially, and root out a radical terrorism that breeds on poverty and resentment. The intelligence talents, human and technological, that grew out of World War II and the cold war can serve the war against terrorism. A top priority is the destruction of germ warfare capabilities and stockpiles. The longer term response, based on American political will and leadership, seeks ways to rectify the poverty, resentment, and cultural isolation of North Africa, the Middle East, Central Asia, the Philippines, and Indonesia.

America prevailed against expansionist regimes in Japan and Germany; against Soviet infiltration of the executive branch of the government; against agents ready to carry out sabotage on American military installations and ports. America fought back painfully in Korea and survived the humiliation of leaving Vietnam. Americans prevailed by will, by innovation, by productivity, by scientific leadership, which created the satellite reconnaissance transparency that kept the peace. The intelligence skills of the last fifty years, occupied by preventing nuclear war, neglected the incipient terrorism welling up from radical Islam. Coalition intelligence sharing—exposing terrorist cells, controlling the flow of money, outlawing and destroying bacteriological stockpiles—will be brought to bear against the new threats.

The Soviets stole the atomic bomb, the bin Laden terrorists have stolen the American sense of security. Thieves are left behind by history. Modernization, innovation, and the maximizing of human talents, all antithetical to the Islamic Jihad, have always created the future—and will again.

Acknowledgments

W e would like to thank the Smith Richardson Foundation for its support of our research.

The concept of *Sacred Secrets* is reflected in the life of Oliver Kirby, the National Security Agency official who began working on VENONA in 1945. His testimony and recollections provide a living memory and documentation of the untold history of VENONA.

We received significant contributions of material from John Walsh on the Hiss case, Michael Chapman on the details of J. Robert Oppenheimer's membership in the American Communist Party, and the late Vyacheslav (Slava) Luchkov, a dear friend from our first days in Moscow in 1968, who interviewed Sergo Beria.

In tracking the career and public downfall of J. Robert Oppenheimer, we are indebted to historian John Major for his skillfully balanced account, *The Oppenheimer Hearings*.[1] For the story of Operation Snow, we appreciate the historical detail offered by General Vitali Pavlov. David Rees, *Harry Dexter White: A Study in Paradox*, provides the historical context for Pavlov's revelation and an overview of White's career.[2] Peter Andrews did a great service in publishing his father's story, *A Tragedy of History: A Journalist's Confidential Role in the Hiss-Chambers Case*.[3]

We also want to thank Michael Abramowitz, Gerald Haines, William Taubman, Richard Schroeder, and Doug Schwarz for helping fill in vital details.

All along the way we have been assisted by our Russian friends, who were eager to set the record straight. Thanks to Christian Ostermann and his colleagues, Katherine Weathersby and Chen Jian, in the Cold War International History Project at the Woodrow Wilson Center for Scholars in Washington, DC. The ground-breaking Korean War studies of Weathersby and Chen affirmed our correlation between Moscow's fears before Pearl Harbor and Stalin's motivations for backing Kim Il Sung's attack on South Korea in 1950.

Special thanks to Richard Solomon, William Odom, Hayden Peake, R. Carter Hall, and Robert Louis Benson, who offered helpful critical comments on the manuscript. We remain responsible for any errors. The archivists at the Franklin

Delano Roosevelt Library, the Harry S. Truman Library, and the National Archives were gracious in steering us to documents and providing photographs. Elena Danielson, archivist at the Hoover Library, a continuing source of support, pointed us to the papers of Ivy Litvinov, a friend from our first stay in Moscow. Our neighbor, Martha Mautner, brought to attention the rarely told story of Maksim Litvinov's attack on Soviet expertise in the State Department. Robert Conquest led us to important secrets. Svetlana Bobrova was an informative guide to the Konenkov Museum in Moscow.

We thank Warren Strobel whose initial suggestion and encouragement was the genesis from which this book evolved. Roger Donald provided support and valuable insights.

Thanks to Cyril Muromcew for his precise translations. Our editor, Rick Russell, himself a military historian, guided us to enrich the historical background in which "sacred secrets" were born. Christina Davidson offered valuable help in preparing the manuscript. Deirdre T. Ruffino was a skilled and perceptive copy editor.

Appendixes

APPENDIX 1. FBI letter to David Lilienthal on Robert and Frank Oppenheimer's monthly contributions to the American Communist Party, April 21 and 23, 1947

APPENDIX 1. *(Continued)*

April 21, 1947

JULIUS ROBERT OPPENHEIMER

A highly confidential and reliable source of information having access to certain records of the Communist Party in San Francisco reported that the Financial Committee report available in November of 1946 contained notations as follows:

"X-1 (Berkeley Professor) started through the solicitation of Thomas Addis, monthly $150. Last record on my books April 1942. Tom should be consulted.

"X-2 (Professor's brother), monthly $150, also PW monthly $150. My record of last contribution October 1942. Leo may have additional information."

On another sheet of paper was noted:

"Check Harry re Frank be for intro."

On still another sheet of paper was noted the following:

"F.O., Berkeley. Get Harry after them."

On the basis of information available it appears that the initials "F.O.," the name "Frank" and the symbol "X-2" refer to Frank Oppenheimer, and the symbol "X-1" refers to his brother, Julius Robert Oppenheimer. It would appear, therefore, that Frank Oppenheimer some time prior to and up to October, 1942, contributed $150 monthly to the Communist Party and another $150 to the "People's World" and that his brother, Julius Robert Oppenheimer had contributed $150 monthly to the Party until April, 1942. It was also indicated that Frank Oppenheimer was to be recontacted for the purpose of renewing contributions.

It has been ascertained from a thoroughly reliable confidential source that Frank Oppenheimer was visited on February 19, 1947 by Al Richmond and Harry Kramer, members of the Communist Party and also members of the staff of the "Daily People's World," at his home in Berkeley, California. The interview lasted for a period of about two hours. It was later learned through a highly confidential and reliable source that Kramer had felt the interview to be unsatisfactory. He is reported to have said that he believed that had contact been made three or four weeks earlier there was a 50-50 chance that Oppenheimer might have been induced to make financial contributions as he had previously done. Kramer is said to have stated, "I think we lost about ten G's."

JNA/dme
100-237735
cc: J. Robert Oppenheimer file.

APPENDIX 2. Letter to L. Beria on Oppenheimer's cooperation with Soviet Intelligence, October 2, 1944

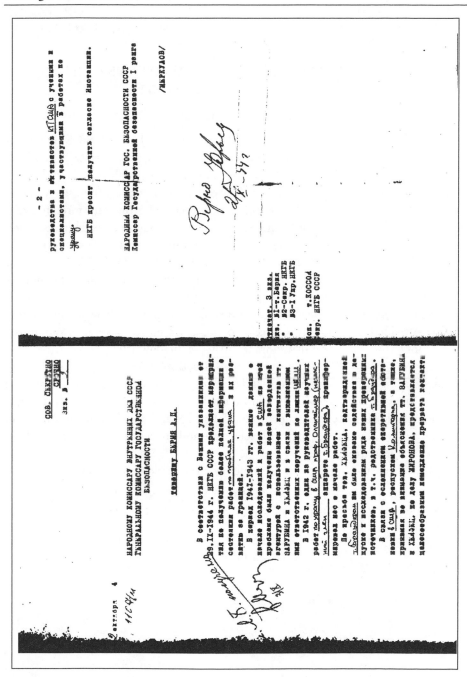

Appendix 2. *(Continued)*

---

2 October 4 [1944]   TOP SECRET
1107/M   URGENT
               Copy #2

TO: PEOPLE'S COMMISSAR FOR INTERNAL AFFAIRS OF THE USSR
     GENERAL COMMISSAR OF STATE SECURITY

Comrade BERIA, L.P.

In accordance with your instruction of 29 September 1944, NKGB USSR continues measures for obtaining more complete information on the state of work on the problem of uranium [handwritten] and its development abroad.

In the period 1941-1943 important data on the start of research and work in the USA [handwritten] on this problem was received from our foreign agent network using the contacts of Comrades Zarubin and Kheifetz in their execution of important tasks in line with the Executive Committee of the Comintern.

In 1942 one of the leaders of scientific work on uranium in the USA, professor Oppenheimer [handwritten] (unlisted [*nglastny*] member of the *apparat* of Comrade Browder) informed us about the beginning of work.

At the request of Comrade Kheifetz, confirmed by Comrade Browder, [handwritten] he provided cooperation in access to the research for several of our tested sources including a relative of Comrade Browder [handwritten].

Due to complications of the operational situation in the USA [handwritten], the dissolution of the Comintern (handwritten) and also taking into account the explanations of Comrades Zarubin and Kheifetz on the Mironov affair, it seems expedient to immediately sever contacts of leaders and activists of the American Communist [handwritten] Party with scientists and specialists engaged in work on uranium [handwritten].

NKGB requests to obtain the agreement of the leadership. [*Instancia*]

PEOPLES COMMISSAR OF STATE SECURITY
OF THE FIRST RANK Signed/MERKULOV

[Handwritten note by Beria] "CORRECT" [October 2, 1944]
                // signed Beria[1]

OFFICER IN CHARGE Kossoi
Chief of Staff of NKGB SECRETARIAT

---

[1] See previous page for document in Russian

APPENDIX 2. *(Continued)*

Printed—3 copies
No. 1 Comrade Beria
No. 2 Sec. NKGB
No. 3 Dep. NKGB

On Page One Signed Agreement of LB "Received." Signed Merkulov on 3 October 1944.

Author's note: The original document was typed with blank, underlined sections. The missing information was written in later by hand. This security measure made sensitive information available only to "need to know" officials.

APPENDIX 3. Letter to NKVD USSR M. G. Pervukhin on atomic espionage reports received from the USA, April 6, 1943

№ 160

Письмо НКВД СССР М.Г.Первухину
о направлении разведматериалов

№ 52/6234

6 апреля 1943 г.
Сов. секретно
Только лично [1]

В соответствии с перечнем вопросов, составленных проф[ессором] Курчатовым, полученным от Вас 23.III с.г. [2]), направляю для использования сообщение о ведущихся за рубежом работах над проблемой использования атомной энергии урана.

В материале даются сведения о лицах и организациях, ведущих разработки по этой проблеме в США, Англии и Германии, а также о намечающемся чрезвычайно интересном направлении — возможности получения урановой бомбы из изотопа урана U-238, считавшегося до сих пор балластом в урановой руде [3]). В связи с этим может отпасть необходимость в разделении изотопов урана.

При использовании направляемого материала, также как и всех наших материалов по данному вопросу, прошу учесть особую их секретность и важность, в связи с чем к ознакомлению с ними может быть допущен весьма ограниченный круг лиц.

Приложение: 4 стр. перевода с английского языка [4]).

Зам[еститель] народного комиссара
внутренних дел Союза ССР Меркулов

АП РФ. Ф.93, д.1(43), л.33. Подлинник.

---

[1]) Вписано В.М.Меркуловым от руки.
[2]) См. документ № 151.
[3]) Так в документе, возможно, имеется в виду, что уран-238 может быть использован в реакторе для наработки бомбового материала — см. документ № 171.
[4]) См. документ № 161.

№ 161

Из справки 1-го Управления НКВД СССР
«Использование атомной энергии», подготовленной
по агентурным данным [1])

Не позднее 6 апреля 1943 г. [2])
[Сов. секретно] [3])

[...] [4]) Масштабы работ, проводимых в Америке, значительно шире. В ней принимают участие сотни высококвалифицированных научных работников, и их работа дала более ощутимые результаты, в связи с чем результаты английских работ не заслуживают большого внимания в излагаемом ниже.

330

Appendix 3. *(Continued)*

Translation   No. 160   p. 330

LETTER TO NKVD USSR M.G. PERVUKHIN
ON THE DISTRIBUTION OF INTELLIGENCE MATERIAL

No. 52/6234   April 6, 1943
                                                                   Top Secret
                                                                   Eyes Only[1]

In accordance with the list of questions prepared by Prof. Kurchatov received from you on March 23 of this year[2] I am sending you for your use information about work carried out abroad related to the utilization of atomic energy in uranium.

The material contains information about persons and organizations working on that problem in the United States, England and Germany. It also deals with the emergence of a highly interesting trend, i.e., the possibility of making a uranium bomb using uranium isotope U-238, considered thus far to be a ballast in uranium ore[3]. In view of that one may avoid the necessity to split uranium isotopes.

When using the enclosed material, as well as all other of our material pertaining to the above question, please be aware of the high level of secrecy and importance and, in this regard, only a strictly limited circle of individuals may be allowed to familiarize themselves with [their content].

Attachment: 4 pages of translations from English[4].

Deputy People's Commissar
for Internal Affairs of USSR Merkulov

AP RF F.93d.1.(43) Original

---

1) Added in V. M. Merkulov's handwriting.

2) See document No. 151.

3) The document may possibly indicate that uranium-238 may be used in a reactor to prepare bomb material—see document no. 171.

4) See document No. 161.

* * *

APPENDIX 3. *(Continued)*

Translation   No. 161   p. 330

No. 161

FROM THE INVESTIGATION BY THE FIRST ADMINISTRATION OF
NKVD USSR
"Utilization of Atomic energy" prepared from agency's information 1)
No later than April 6, 1943 2)
[Top Secret] 3)

[. . .][4] The scale of work in America is much broader. Hundreds of highly qualified scientific workers take part and their efforts have resulted in more tangible achievements and, because of that, the results of English work do not deserve a great deal of attention as can be seen below.

End of page

Authors' note: Footnotes for Document 161 not available

APPENDIX 4. Excerpts from I. B. Kurchatov's reply concerning the content of intelligence materials received from the USA, April 1943

№ 163

Из отзыва И.В.Курчатова
о содержании разведматериалов, поступивших из США[1])

29 апреля 1943 г.
Сов. секретно

Материал освещает:
1) общую организацию работ по урану в Америке,
2) проблему «уранового котла», работающего на смеси «неразделенный уран — графит»,
3) ход исследований в Америке по трансурановым элементам эка-рению и эка-осмию.
Ниже дается   анализ каждого из указанных выше разделов материала.
[2]) [...]

§ 2. Проблема «уранового котла», работающего на смеси «неразделенный уран — графит»[3])

Изложенные в материале по этой проблеме данные представляют особо большой интерес.
Как у нас в Союзе, так и в Англии (если судить по материалу, анализ которого был представлен мной ранее на Ваше усмотрение[4]), *утвердилось мнение, что возможность осуществления котла*, работающего на смеси «неразделенный уран — графит», является крайне сомнительным. В противоположность этому в рассматриваемом материале содержится утверждение о возможности технической реализации этой системы.
Этот вывод имеет громадное значение, так как создание уранового котла, работающего на смеси «неразделенный уран — графит» не требует решения новой сложной технической задачи — выделения больших количеств изотопов. Поэтому в странах, располагающих большим количеством урана (Америка, Англия, Германия), такой котел может быть создан в очень короткий срок, его осуществление не потребует постройки новых заводов, так как может быть использована уже существующая техническая база.
Как уже отмечалось мной в записке на Ваше имя по поводу эка-осмиевой бомбы[5]), урановый котел не только даст возможность использовать внутриатомную энергию, но может также *явиться средством для получения ядерного взрывчатого вещества*. Кстати, как указывается в материале, собственно решение этой задачи является основным в американских работах по созданию котла «уран — графит».
Если выводы, которые изложены в материале, правильны, задача создания ядерной бомбы близка как никогда к своему разрешению. Решение задачи создания ядерной бомбы этим путем является особенно неприятным для СССР, потому что оно требует очень больших количеств урана для первоначального пуска котла.
По данным, изложенным в материале, котел должен состоять из *1000 тонн графита и 100 тонн урана. Америка, Англия и Германия уже сейчас имеют такие запасы урана*, а в нашем распоряжении только 0,1—0,2 тонны этого металла. Все разведанные к марту 1943 года запасы урана в нашей стране составляют около 100 тонн, причем к концу 1943 года намечено выработать из руд 2, а к концу 1944 года — 10 тонн урана и его солей. Может ока-

[1]) Авторский заголовок документа: «Отзыв об американском материале на 4 страницах» («материал» — см. документ № 161). В сопроводительном письме И.В.Курчатов пишет М.Г.Первухину: «Направляю Вам отзыв о материале на 4 страницах, переданном мне т. А.И.Васиным. Прошу Ваших указаний разведывательным органам СССР о получении дополнительных сведений по вопросам, подчеркнутым в отзыве синим карандашом» (АП РФ. Ф.93, д.1(43), л.47).

[2]) Далее опущен § 1 об организации работ в США и противоречиях в информации об этом между американскими и английскими материалами.

[3]) Здесь и далее курсивом выделены части текста, подчеркнутые автором синим карандашом.

[4]) См. документ № 151.

[5]) См. документ № 157.

APPENDIX 4. *(Continued)*

No. 163

FROM I.B. KURCHATOV'S REPLY
CONCERNING THE CONTENT OF INTELLIGENCE MATERIALS
RECEIVED FROM THE USA[1]

April 29, 1943
Top Secret

Materials deal with:
1. General organization of work on uranium in America.
2. Problems with "uranium pile" working with a mixture of "undivided uranium-graphite".
3. Development of research in America on trans-uranium elements eka-rhenium and eka-osmium.
   Also, there is an analysis of each of the above mentioned parts of the material.[2][. . .]

Paragraph 2. Problems with the "uranium pile" operating with a mixture of "undivided uranium-graphite"[3]

Problems contained in this material on this problem are of singularly great interest.

As in our Union, and also in America (judging by the material the analysis of which I presented to you earlier for your consideration)[4] *there exists a firm opinion that the possibility of realizing a pile* working on a mixture of "undivided uranium-graphite" appears to be highly doubtful. In contrast to that in the material under examination there is an assertion about the possibility of a technical realization of this system.

This conclusion is of tremendous significance since the building of a uranium pile operating with a mixture of "undivided uranium-graphite" does not require a new complex technical solution, i.e., the emanation of large amounts of isotopes. Therefore countries which have at their disposal large amounts of uranium (America, England, Germany) can easily build such a pile in a very short time, do not have to build new plants since this can be done on already existing technological base.

As already mentioned in my note addressed to you about the eka-osmium bomb,[5] a uranium pile not only will allow us to use internal atomic energy but may also be *the means of obtaining nuclear explosive material.* By the way, as shown in the material the solution of this problem is the basis of American endeavors to build a "uranium-graphite" pile.

If the conclusions, presented in the material, are correct, the task of building an atomic bomb has never been so close to its solution. The task of building an atomic bomb in this manner is especially awkward for the USSR because this requires very large amounts of uranium for the initial start-up of the pile.

According to data contained in the material, a pile must consist of *1000 tons of graphite and 100 tons of uranium. America, England and Germany already have such stockpiles of uranium,* while there are only 0.1-0.2 tons of this metal at our disposal. All located supplies of uranium in our country as of the end of 1943 amount to some 100 tons. By the end of 1943 it is projected 2 tons can be extracted from the ore and by the end of 1944 it is expected to obtain 10 tons of uranium and uranium salts.

(End of page 335).

---

1. Author's title of the document: "Reply concerning American material on four pages" (Material-see document No. 161). In the accompanying letter I. V. Kurchatov writes to M. G. Pervukhin: "I am sending you commentary on the material on four pages transmitted by comrade A. I. Vasinin. I ask you to instruct the intelligence organs of the USSR to obtain additional information on questions underlined with blue pencil. (APRF [Archive of the President of the Russian Federation] 93, d (43), 1.47.

2. The next paragraph concerning the organization in the USA and contradictions in information concerning the above between American and English materials have been omitted.

APPENDIX 5. Letter to NKGB USSR M. G. Pervukhin on the content of intelligence material from England and the USA, August 1943

документов, разведчики получили и передали физикам образцы урана, его окиси, тяжелой воды, графита, бериллия и др.
   ²) Далее текст дописан А.И.Васиным от руки. При выявлении приложение не обнаружено.
   ³) Подпись отсутствует.

№ 179

Письмо НКГБ СССР М.Г.Первухину о содержании разведматериалов, поступивших из Англии и США

№ 1583/м   12 августа 1943
                                                  Сов. секрет

Сообщаем следующие дополнительные сведения о ходе работ по ведущихся в США и Англии:

1. *Направление работ*

Как уже сообщалось нами ранее (в письмах от 6 апреля и 16 ию работы в США ведутся, главным образом, в направлении разработки а машин (т[ак] наз[ываемый] «урановый котел» или «пайл») по типу уже щенной в ход первой опытной машины на 200 ватт ²).

Работы же по разделению изотопов урана рассматриваются в связи с этим только как вспомогательные, ведущиеся параллельно с основной работой по строительству атомных машин. В настоящее время в США проектируется одновременно две разделительные установки: на 600 ступеней с выходом продукта удвоенной концентрации и на 2600 ступеней с выходом 90 % продукта. Производительность каждой из них — 1 кг/день урана-235 в пересчете на 100 % продукт.

По примеру американцев, англичане также решили построить в Канаде атомную машину, мощность которой — 200 кВ, т.е. в тысячу раз больше мощности первой американской машины. Место строительства нам пока неизвестно, по некоторым предположениям — в окрестностях Монреаля. Строительство уже начато и по плану должно быть закончено через 12–18 месяцев.

2. *О сотрудничестве англичан и американцев в работах по урану*

Сотрудничество научных работников США и Англии осуществлялось в форме взаимного обмена научными материалами и командировками отдельных ученых.

С начала текущего года англичане перенесли значительную часть своих работ по урану в Канаду. Туда было вывезено необходимое лабораторное оборудование, весь запас тяжелой воды, после чего, в феврале мес[яце] с.г. туда выехала бригада научных работников во главе с физиком Хальбаном. Предполагалось, что в ближайшее время в Канаду будет переведена остальная часть работ по урану, и коллектив научных работников должен был быть доведен до 100 чел[овек].

Такая переброска вызвана следующими причинами:

1) ведение работ по урану в условиях воздушных налетов, которым подвергается Англия, представляет большую опасность;

2) в Канаде находятся месторождения урановой руды;

APPENDIX 5. *(Continued)*

3) близость к американцам позволяла англичанам надеяться на укрепление сотрудничества с ними.

По полученным нами последним сведениям, несмотря на территориальное сближение, сотрудничество англичан и американцев со времени переезда англичан в Монреаль не только не укрепилось, но, якобы, почти прекратилось. В связи с этим, англичане оказались в довольно затруднительном положении, так как им отказывают даже в необходимом лабораторном оборудовании, и они вынуждены привозить его из Англии.

При переговорах по вопросу о дальнейшем сотрудничестве американцы выдвинули такие условия, принятие которых англичанами означает полную монополию американцев на работы по урану. Эти условия американцы обосновывают:

1) необходимостью сохранения тайны;

2) опасением, что иностранцы, находящиеся в британской территориальной армии, могут по окончании войны передать своим правительствам ставшие им известными сведения по урану;

3) опасением, что британское правительство может передать сведения об американских работах правительству Советского Союза по существующим между ними соглашениям;

4) неэквивалентностью обмена в связи со значительными успехами американцев в их работах по урану.

Предполагается, что наиболее непосредственной причиной расхождения между американцами и англичанами являются их успехи в разрешении проблемы утилизации энергии медленных нейтронов в результате работы их первого опытного уранового котла.

Народный комиссар государственной безопасности СССР В.Меркулов

АП РФ. Ф.93, д.1(43), л.71–72. Подлинник.

---

[1] См. документы № 160, 171.

[2] Речь идет о реакторе Э.Ферми.

APPENDIX 5. *(Continued)*

Translation   No. 179   p. 381

Letter to NKGB USSR M.G. Pervukhin
on the content of intelligence material from England & USA

No. 1583/M   August 12, 1943

Top Secret

Herewith the following additional information on the progress of work underway in USA and England:

1. Direction of work

As we mentioned earlier (letters of April 6 & June 16),[1] work in the USA is being done mainly towards the development of atomic machines, the so-called "uranium pot" or "pile" of the type as the already working experimental machine with a 200 Watt output[2].

Work on the separation of uranium isotopes, however, are viewed in this regard as auxiliary ones, conducted in parallel with main efforts to build atomic machines. At this time in the USA two separation installations are being designed simultaneously: one with 600 stages with a product output of double concentration and the other with 2600 stages with an output of 90% product. The output of each of them is 1 kg/day of 235 uranium, as recalculated to a 100% product.

Following the American example, the English also decided to build in Canada an atomic machine with an output of 200 kilowatts, i.e., one thousand times bigger than the first American machine. The building site is so far unknown to us but presumably in the vicinity of Montreal. The construction is underway and according to the plan should be completed in 12-18 months.

2. About the cooperation between the English and Americans on uranium

The cooperation of scientific workers of USA and England consisted of mutual exchanges of scientific material and assignments of individual scientists.

Early this year the English transferred a significant part of their uranium work to Canada. They moved the essential laboratory equipment, their whole supply of heavy water and later, in February of this year a team of scientific workers headed by Hallbine [?] also went there. It was assumed that in a short time the remaining work would be moved to Canada and the collective of scientific workers would be up to one hundred strong.

Such a transfer was due to the following reasons:

1. Work on uranium under conditions of air raids on England became very dangerous;
2. Canada has deposits of uranium ore;

3. Being close to Americans gave the English hope to strengthen their cooperation.

According to latest information available to us, in spite of territorial proximity, the cooperation between the English and Americans at the time of the English transfer to Montreal not only failed to become stronger but, allegedly, nearly stopped. Because of that the English found themselves in an awkward situation since they were refused the necessary laboratory equipment and they were forced to bring the equipment from England.

During negotiations about future cooperation the Americans presented conditions the acceptance of which would have meant total American monopoly over the work on uranium. These conditions were explained by the Americans as follows:

1. Need to preserve secrecy;
2. Concerns that foreigners serving in the British Territorial Army could, after the war, hand over to their governments their acquired knowledge about uranium;
3. Concerns that the British Government could inform the government of the Soviet Union about American work in accordance with existing agreement between them;
4. Non-equivalency of the exchange in view of significant American successes in their work on uranium.

It is presumed that the most direct reason for the differences between the Americans and the British are their [American] successes in solving problems of energy utilization of slow neutrons resulting from the work of their first experimental uranium pile.

People's Commissar for State Security USSR   v. Merkulov

AP RF F. 93, d. 1 (43), 1. 71-72. Original

---

1. See documents No. 160, 171.
2. Reference to E. Fermi reactor.

* * *

APPENDIX 6. Establishment of Special Committee of the [USSR] State Committee for Defense on the utilization of the internal energy of uranium, August 20, 1945, pages 80 and 84 (pages 81–83 missing).

кв-5.

80

Совершенно секретно

Особая папка.

ПОСТАНОВЛЕНИЕ

ГОСУДАРСТВЕННОГО КОМИТЕТА ОБОРОНЫ

N 9887сс/ов.

"20" августа 1945 года   Москва, Кремль.

"О Специальном Комитете при ГОКО"

Государственный Комитет Обороны ПОСТАНОВЛЯЕТ:

1. Образовать при ГОКО Специальный Комитет

т.т.

    1. БЕРИЯ Л.П. (председатель)
    2. МАЛЕНКОВ Г.М.
    3. ВОЗНЕСЕНСКИЙ Н.А.
    4. ВАННИКОВ Б.Л.
    5. ЗАВЕНЯГИН А.П.
    6. КУРЧАТОВ И.В.
    7. КАПИЦА П.Л.
    8. МАХНЕВ В.А.
    9. ПЕРВУХИН М.Г.

2. Возложить на Специальный Комитет при ГОКО руководство всеми работами по использованию внутриатомной энергии урана :

развитие научно-исследовательских работ в этой области,

л.

л. 84

справок о его работе или работах, выполняемых по заказам
Первого Главного Управления. Вся отчетность по указанным
работам направляется только Специальному Комитету при ГОКО.

12. Поручить Специальному Комитету в 10-дневный срок
внести на утверждение Председателю ГОКО предложения о передаче Первому Главному Управлению при СНК СССР необходимых для его работы научных, конструкторских, проектных, строительных организаций и промышленных предприятий, а также
утвердить структуру, штаты и оклады работников аппарата
Комитета и Первого Главного Управления при СНК СССР.

13. Поручить тов. БЕРИЯ принять меры к организации
закордонной разведывательной работы по получению более полной технической и экономической информации об
урановой промышленности и атомных бомбах
возложив на него руководство всей *разведывательной*
работой в этой области, проводимой органами *разведки*
(*НКГБ, РУ КА. и др.*).

ПРЕДСЕДАТЕЛЬ ГОСУДАРСТВЕННОГО
КОМИТЕТА ОБОРОНЫ

И. СТАЛИН

APPENDIX 6. *(Continued)*

No. 80

Top Secret
Special file
Stamp: declassified

DECREE
STATE COMMITTEE FOR DEFENSE
No. 9887
August 20, 1945   Moscow, Kremlin

"On the Special Committee at GOKO"

State Committee for Defense DECREES
1. To form a Special Committee at GOKO consisting of comrades
   1. BERIA, L.P. (Chairman)
   2. MALENKOV, G.M.
   3. VOZNESENSKI, N.A.
   4. VANNIKOV, B.L.
   5. ZAVENYAGIN, A.P.
   6. KURCHATOV, I.V.
   7. KAPITSA, P.L.
   8. MAKHNEV, V.A.
   9. PERVUKHIN, M.G.

2. To charge the Special Committee at GOKO with the management of all work [handwritten & underlined] on the utilization of the internal energy of uranium:
   to develop scientific-research work in this field.

APPENDIX 6. *(Continued)*

Translation

5.   84

. . . information about his work or work done on order of the First Main Administration. All accounts concerning aforementioned work shall be sent only to the Special Committee at GOKO.

12. To instruct the Special Committee to present within 10 days for approval by the Chairman of GOKO proposals for transmission to the First Main Administration at SNK USSR dealing with the essential to its work scientific, construction, design and building organizations as well as industrial enterprises. Also to confirm the structure, staffing and rates for workers of the apparat of the Committee and of the First Main Administration at SNK USSR.

13. To instruct comrade BERIA to take measures and organize [handwritten & underlined] external intelligence work in order to obtain more complete technical and economic information about [handwritten & underlined] uranium industry and about atom bombs. He is also tasked with the management of all [handwritten & underlined] intelligence work in this field to be carried out by the organs of intelligence service (NKVD, RUKA. and others) [Handwritten & underlined].

CHAIRMAN OF THE STATE COMMITTEE
FOR DEFENSE

(Signature)

I. STALIN

APPENDIX 7. Protocol no. 1 of the meeting of the Special Committee of the [USSR] State Defense Committee, pages 1 and 4 (pages 2 and 3 missing).

СОВ. СЕКРЕТНО
(ОСОБАЯ ПАПКА)

ПРОТОКОЛ № 1
ЗАСЕДАНИЯ
С П Е Ц И А Л Ь Н О Г О Комитета
при ГОКО

От 24 августа 1945 г.   г. Москва, Кремль

Члены Специального Комитета при ГОКО: тт.Берия Л.П.,
Маленков Г.М., Вознесенский Н.А., Ванников Б.Л.,
Завенягин А.П.,Курчатов И.В.,Капица П.Л.,Махнев В.А.,
Первухин М.Г.

Присутствовали:
(при рассмотрении
1 и 2 вопросов)

Члены Технического Совета при Специальном Комитете:
тт.Алиханов А.И., Вознесенский И.Н., Иоффе А.Ф.,
Кикоин И.К., Харитон Ю.Б.

24.2.⁻²1. Информация академика Курчатова И.В.

Поручить Техническому Совету рассмотреть детально состоя-
ние работ, проводимых лабораторией № 2, и свои предложения о
плане дальнейших научно-исследовательских и практических работ,
а также о привлечении к участию в этих работах других научных
учреждений и отдельных учёных, конструкторов и иных ценных спе-
циалистов внести на рассмотрение Специального Комитета.

24.2. 2. О штате и порядке работы Технического
Совета при Специальном Комитете

Поручить Техническому Совету рассмотреть вопрос о штате и
порядке работы Технического Совета предварительно на своём
заседании.

APPENDIX 7. *(Continued)*

4.

за 2 дня до заседания по телефону Секретарём Комитета.

3. Материалы (записки, проекты предложений и т.д.) не рассылаются. Члены Комитета в необходимых случаях могут лично знакомиться с материалами у Секретаря Комитета.

4. Список приглашаемых на заседание Комитета лиц утверждается в каждом отдельном случае Председателем Комитета.

Члены Технического Совета, работники Первого Главного Управления и аппарата Комитета принимают участие в заседаниях Комитета по тем вопросам, в разработке которых они участвуют.

Руководители наркоматов и ведомств принимают участие в обсуждении только того конкретного вопроса, который касается данного наркомата или ведомства (а не всего вопроса повестки дня).

34.8   10.   О Секретаре Специального Комитета
при ГОКО

Утвердить Секретарём Специального Комитета при ГОКО т.Махнева В.А.

Председатель Специального
Комитета при ГОКО

Л. Берия
(Л.Берия)

APPENDIX 7. *(Continued)*

Translation

Top Secret
(new file)
Stamp: Declassified

Seal of USSR

PROTOCOL No. 1
OF MEETING OF THE SPECIAL COMMITTEE AT GOKO
(State Defense Committee)

Dated: August 24, 1945   Moscow, Kremlin

Members of the Special Committee at
GOKO:
Comrades Beria, L.P.; Malenkov, G.N.;
Voznesenski, N.A.; Vannikov, B.L.;
Zavenyagin, A.P.; Kurchatov, I.V.; Kapi-
tsa, P.L.; Makhnev, V.A.; Pervukhin,
M.G.

Present
(at consideration
 of questions 1 & 2)

Members of the Technical Council at the
Special Committee: comrades Alikhanov,
A.I.; Voznesenski, I.N.; Ioffe, A.F.;
Kikomzhi, I.K.; Khariton, Yu.B.

1. Information presented by Academician Kurchatov, I.V.

To instruct the Technical Council to examine in detail the state of work carried out in laboratory No. 2 and present own proposals concerning plans for further scientific and research as well as practical work, and also plans for bringing
in other scientific institutions and individual scientists, designers and other valuable specialists. The above is to be presented for consideration to the Special
Committee.

2. Concerning staffing and work schedule of the Technical Council at the
   Special Committee

To instruct the Technical Council to examine the question of staffing and
work scheduling of the Technical Council at its session 2 days prior to the meeting by the Committee's Secretary by telephone.

Appendix 7. *(Continued)*

3. Documentation (notes, design proposals et cetera) is not for distribution. Members of the Committee may see the documents, when required, personally at the Committee's Secretary.

4. A list of persons invited to meetings of the Committee shall be confirmed on a case by case basis by the Chairman of the Committee.

Members of the Technical Council, members of the First Main Administration and of the Committee's Apparat participate in the the Committee's meetings on issues that they are involved in.

Heads of People's Commissariat and of departments are to participate in the deliberations of only such concrete issues that relate only to such Commissariat or department (but not to the whole question of the agenda).

10. Pertaining to the Secretary of the Special Committee at GOKO

To be confirmed by the Secretary of the Special Committee at GOKO, comrade Makhnev, V.A.

Chairman of the Special Committee at GOKO

(Signature)

L. Beria

APPENDIX 8. The Morgenthau Plan, from Russian Intelligence Archives

In accordance with a message received from the source close to Secretary of the Treasury Morgenthau, his plan for postwar order in Germany is as follows:

1. To annihilate all big industry of Germany, both heavy and light, including shipbuilding and merchant shipbuilding. To close all main mines on German territory.
2. All industrial equipment of Germany transferred to the countries that suffered from German aggression.
3. To leave in Germany only agricultural production.
4. The Ruhr district should be partitioned from Germany and placed under international control, enabling the countries that suffered from German aggression to take away from the industrial facilities in the Ruhr industrial equipment that would compensate for the damage they suffered.
5. The Saar district should be transferred to France and some eastern areas of Germany to Poland.
6. The workers who would be available after the liquidation of German industry should be utilized in public repair works in territories previously occupied by Germany.

In the future, Morgenthau believes it will be expedient for the German workers to remain abroad involved in industrial production. Morgenthau believes the implementation of this plan will mean a drastic cut in Germany's population of up to 50 million people.

The Source, who is one of the authors of the above mentioned plan, informed that both Morgenthau and his associates did not thoroughly study the issue of distribution of German workers at the present moment but they do believe that this measure might be quite feasible. At any rate, Morgenthau pointed out, there would be enough space in Africa to settle the Germans.

Morgenthau's recommendations do not include receiving reparations from Germany during a long period of time. He believes that industrial equipment as the compensation for the inflicted damage for the countries that suffered from German aggression might be disassembled and taken away from Germany in the course of six months. The Morgenthau project does not foresee any assistance to be rendered to Germany. The aim is to make it use its own resources to insure to its population a basic standard of living, with due account for the development of agriculture. In this connection it is suggested to split the holdings of large landlords into small farms to insure the possibility for 30-40 million people that previously worked in industry to be engaged in agriculture.

According to the Source, in the State Department and in the War Department there are alternative plans in accordance with which Germany should remain an economically strong state which would be in the position to counter Soviet influence in Western Europe.

This problem is under study in particular by the Interagency Committee on the Countries of Western Europe headed by deputy secretary of war McCloy. This committee submitted its own suggestions on postwar order in Germany for the endorsement by the War Department.

The above mentioned recommendations are as follows:

1. Joint occupation of Germany by allied powers.
2. Putting on trial prominent fascist leaders.
3. Repayment by Germany of reparations over a period of five years.
4. Disarmament of Germany.
5. Liquidation of German aviation industry and armament production industry.
6. Preservation of the rest of German industry and placing it under international control.
7. Installment in Germany of a control system that would insure total control over the country's economy.

As was reported earlier, Morgenthau did not agree to endorse the second plan because it meant that Germany would retain its status as a powerful industrial state.

The suggestions of Morgenthau are negatively assessed by Secretary of War Stimson and by the War Department in general. In the State Department there is no unified opinion on the future of postwar Germany. Hull has not made a final decision on this matter. According to the Source the Secretary of State sympathizes with the Morgenthau plan. The State Department prepared its own suggestions on the issue of postwar Germany. According to the information available some time ago these suggestions were sent to London to inform Wynant on the issue. These suggestions, however, are not endorsed by the president and should not be regarded as directives.

The leading policy makers on postwar Germany in the State Department, Dan, Pasvolsky, Berle and others, react very negatively towards all plans to diminish the strength of Germany and its agrarianization. They support preservation of Germany as a developed industrial country. They believe that without German industry some European countries cannot exist. This point of view was expressed in a talk between the Source and Special Advisor to Hull on postwar issues, Pasvolsky. The Morgenthau Plan received assessment from the chairman of the military-industrial committee Krug.

The head of the administration of the problems of foreign economy Crowly, on the contrary, supports Stimson's point of view.

APPENDIX 8. *(Continued)*

Besides government circles the negative attitude on diminishing the economic might of Germany is shared by the following influential groups:

- The largest corporations (Rockefeller, Ford, Dupont, General Motors, General Electric) and banks see in the restoration of German industry big prospects for investing their capital, to strengthen their influence in the German economy.
- Leaders of the Catholic Church and the Republican Party share reactionary views and believe that the only serious obstacle towards controlling the influence of the Soviet Union in western Europe may be an economically strong Germany.
- Liberal circles, including German emigrants, believe that democratic order in Germany will be positive not only for Germany but also for other European countries.
- Morgenthau called the arguments of his opponents, who claim that Europe cannot exist without German industry, unfounded. He also rejected claims that his plan contradicts human treatment of Germans. According to Morgenthau, he simply wants to rule out any possibility for Germany to unleash a war in the future.
- Although the president sympathizes with the Morgenthau plan, he is indecisive because of strong opposition and has not made a final decision. It is unlikely that he will make this decision before the elections.

The Morgenthau Plan was discussed between Roosevelt and Churchill in Quebec in September. According to our Source, Churchill called Morgenthau's suggestions unacceptable. Signed:

People's Commissar for State Security [Vsevlod] Merkulov [PETROV in VENONA]

Source: This is the full text of a summary that is partially recounted in VENONA, New York 1119-21 to Moscow, August 4\5, 1944; also New York 1271-4 to Moscow, September 7, 1944.

APPENDIX 9. VENONA message no. 1822, Washington to Moscow, March 30, 1945, identifying Alger Hiss as ALES

MGB

From: WASHINGTON

To: MOSCOW

No: 1822

30 March 1945

Further to our telegram No. 283[a]. As a result of "[D% A.'s]"[i] chat with "ALES"[ii] the following has been ascertained:

1.   ALES has been working with the NEIGHBORS[SOSEDI][iii] continuously since 1935.

2.   For some years past he has been the leader of a small group of the NEIGHBORS' probationers[STAZhERY], for the most part consisting of his relations.

3.   The group and ALES himself work on obtaining military information only. Materials on the "BANK"[iv] allegedly interest the NEIGHBORS very little and he does not produce them regularly.

4.   All the last few years ALES has been working with "POL'"[v] who also meets other members of the group occasionally.

5.   Recently ALES and his whole group were awarded Soviet decorations.

6.   After the YaLTA Conference, when he had gone on to MOSCOW, a Soviet personage in a very responsible position (ALES gave to understand that it was Comrade VYShINSKIJ) allegedly got in touch with ALES and at the behest of the Military NEIGHBORS passed on to him their gratitude and so on.

No. 431   VADIM[vi]

Notes: [a] Not available.
Comments:
       [i]   A.: "A." seems the most likely garble here although "A." has
             not been confirmed elsewhere in the WASHINGTON traffic.
       [ii] ALES: Probably Alger HISS.
       [iii] SOSEDI: Members of another Soviet Intelligence organization,
             here probably the GRU.
       [iv] BANK: The U.S. State Department.
       [v]   POL': i.e. "PAUL," unidentified cover-name.
       [vi] VADIM: Anatolij Borisovich GROMOV, MGB resident in WASHINGTON.

8 August 1969

Notes

Preface

1. Pavel Sudoplatov and Anatoli Sudoplatov, with Jerrold L. and Leona P. Schecter, *Special Tasks: The Memoirs of an Unwanted Witness—A Soviet Spymaster* (New York: Little, Brown, 1994).

Acknowledgments

1. John Major, *The Oppenheimer Hearings* (New York: Stein and Day, 1971).
2. David Rees, *Harry Dexter White: A Study in Paradox* (New York: Coward, McCann and Geoghegan, 1973).
3. Bert and Peter Andrews, *A Tragedy of History: A Journalist's Confidential Role in the Hiss-Chambers Case* (Washington, DC: Robert B. Luce, 1962).

Prologue

1. See Robert C. Tucker, *Stalin as Revolutionary, 1879–1929* (New York: W. W. Norton, 1973), pp. 130–133. Iosif Djugashvili was born December 21, 1879, and died March 3, 1953. He used the name Koba as a revolutionary and signed "I. Stalin" after the Bolsheviks took power.
2. Pavel Sudoplatov and Anatoli Sudoplatov, with Jerrold L. and Leona P. Schecter, *Special Tasks: The Memoirs of an Unwanted Witness—A Soviet Spymaster* (New York: Little, Brown, 1994), p. 87; and Robert Conquest, *The Great Terror: A Reassessment* (New York: Oxford University Press, 1990), pp. 182–213.
3. Conquest, *The Great Terror*, pp. 484–498.
4. Gabriel Gorodetsky, *Grand Delusion: Stalin and the German Invasion of Russia* (New Haven, CT: Yale University Press, 1999), pp. 318–321.
5. Sudoplatov et al., *Special Tasks*, pp. 96–102.
6. Robert Louis Benson and Cecil Phillips, *History of VENONA*, vol. 1 (Fort Meade, MD: National Security Agency, 1995), pp. 9–11. An effort by the Navy against Russian diplomatic traffic, begun in 1938 "and which perhaps continued into 1941, produced no results and did not influence later work on this target." The encrypted Russian diplomatic messages came from two principal sources:

intercepts of commercial circuits by Army Signals Station 3 at Fort Sam Houston and clandestine photography of Russian messages filed at the U.S. cable companies.

Chapter 1—Stalin's Intelligence Game: Playing the United States and Japan Against Each Other

1. John Costello, *Days of Infamy* (New York: Pocket Books, 1994), pp. 44–45.
2. Vitali Pavlov, *Operatsia Sneg* (Moscow: Gaia Iterum, 1996). Pavlov, code-named KLIM in VENONA, was NKVD *rezident* in Ottawa from 1944 to 1945, when he was forced to return to the Soviet Union because a Soviet embassy code clerk, Igor Gouzenko, defected and revealed the names of Soviet spies. Gouzenko's exposure of their intelligence apparatus was the first major postwar break in the Soviet intelligence network.
3. David Rees, *Harry Dexter White: A Study in Paradox* (New York: Coward, McCann, and Geoghegan, 1973), pp. 107–131.
4. Authors' interview with Vitali Pavlov, Moscow, 1997.
5. Russian Intelligence Archives.
6. Russian Intelligence Archives. Sergei Shpigelglas was head of the NKVD's illegal section until he was arrested, tortured, and executed in 1938; Gutzeit and Sobel were senior officers who were executed in the purge of 1938.
7. Authors' interview with Vitali Pavlov, Moscow, 1997.
8. Vitali Pavlov, "Operation Snow," *News of Intelligence and Counterintelligence*, (Moscow, August 1995).
9. Pavlov, *Operatsia Sneg*, p. 33.
10. Pavlov, *Operatsia Sneg*, p. 33. See also John Earl Haynes and Harvey Klehr, *VENONA: Decoding Soviet Espionage in America* (New Haven, CT: Yale University Press, 1999), pp. 267–268. Joseph Katz was one of the KGB's most active liaison agents. Born in Lithuania in 1912, he emigrated to the United States and went to work for the KGB in 1938. He left the United States for Europe after Elizabeth Bentley's defection, had a falling out with the KGB, and settled in Israel where he died in 1998. He is referred to in 33 deciphered VENONA messages. Retired FBI Agent Robert J. Lamphere describes his efforts to arrest Katz in Israel in his book written with Tom Shachtman, *The FBI-KGB War* (New York: Random House, 1986), pp. 279–282.
11. The Military Correspondent of the *Times*, *The War in the Far East, 1904–1905* (London: John Murray, 1905), p. 1.
12. Conrad Brandt, *Stalin's Failure in China, 1924–1927* (Cambridge, MA: Harvard University Press, 1958), p. viii. Again in 1946 and 1947, Stalin advised Mao Zedong to make peace with Chiang Kai-shek. See Vladimir Dedijer, *Tito Speaks* (New York: Simon and Schuster, 1953), p. 331.
13. General Baron Giichi Tanaka, former chief of the operations section of the Japanese army's General Staff, was prime minister of Japan from 1927 to 1929.
14. Herbert Romerstein and S. Levchenko, *The KGB against the Main Enemy*

(Lexington, MA: Lexington Books, 1989), pp. 53–59. See Romerstein and Eric Breindel, *The VENONA Secrets: Exposing Soviet Espionage and America's Traitors* (Washington, DC: Regnery, 2000), p. 41, and note 15, pp. 520–521.

15. Richard Storry, *The Double Patriots: A Study in Japanese Nationalism* (Boston: Houghton Mifflin, 1957); reprint, Westport, CT: Greenwood Press, 1973), p. 298. Storry warns against interpreting Japanese political history in the decade between the Manchurian Incident and Pearl Harbor "as the product of a single grand conspiracy." Yet he readily acknowledges that "those who knew Japan before the Pacific war can recall occasions when conviviality loosened tongues to release all manner of vaguely phrased predictions of Japan's march to her destiny as the mistress of Asia. But this was part of the climate of the day."

16. Miyagi Yotoku became a member of Sorge's ring in Tokyo in 1935. He was earlier recruited in California by Soviet intelligence officer Leonid Eitingon, who was attached to a sabotage unit that worked with the Comintern. Miyagi was to help form combat groups in California in the event that the United States supported Japan in a war against the Soviet Union. By 1935 he was reassigned to Tokyo and became a trusted agent for Sorge. Interrogated in prison after the arrest of the ring, Miyagi was unable to identify the intelligence officer who had recruited him to work for the Soviet Union; he could only recall that he had a foreign accent. Sudoplatov's memoirs reveal his connection with Eitingon and Soviet intelligence operations. Pavel Sudoplatov and Anatoli Sudoplatov, with Jerrold L. and Leona P. Schecter, *Special Tasks: The Memoirs of an Unwanted Witness—A Soviet Spymaster* (Boston: Little, Brown, 1994).

17. John Toland, *The Rising Sun* (New York: Random House, 1970), pp. 6–8.

18. Robert Whymant, *Stalin's Spy: Richard Sorge and the Tokyo Espionage Ring* (New York: St. Martin's Press, 1998), p. 105.

19. Whymant, *Stalin's Spy*, p. 105.

20. F. W. Deakin and G. R. Storry, *The Case of Richard Sorge* (New York: Harper and Row, 1966), p. 200.

21. The most extensive account of the battle is Alvin D. Coox, *Nomonhan: Japan against Russia, 1939* (Stanford, CA: Stanford University Press, 1985), which relies primarily on Japanese sources and interviews. See pp. 909–910.

22. Georgi K. Zhukov, *Marshal Zhukov's Greatest Battles*, ed. and introduction by Harrison E. Salisbury, trans. Theodore Shabad (New York: Harper and Row, 1969), pp. 7–8.

23. Herbert P. Bix, *Hirohito and the Making of Modern Japan* (New York: Harper-Collins, 2000), p. 351. The officers from the Kwantung Army responsible for the defeat were transferred in disgrace but quietly restored to positions of influence by the army high command.

24. Deakin and Storry, *The Case of Richard Sorge*, p. 201. Russian historians disagree. *Izvestia*, May 1998, argues that Khalkhin-Gol came as a surprise to the Soviet Far East Forces; only reinforcements by tanks and air units with experience in the Spanish Civil War and the genius of Zhukov ensured Russian victory.

Nikolai Yezhov (1900–1941), head of the NKVD from 1936 to 1938, was tarred with responsibility for both Lyushkov's betrayal and Alexander Orlov's defection in Spain. He was later executed.

25. Confidential source.

26. Albert Seaton, *Stalin as Military Commander* (London: Praeger, 1976), p. 89.

27. Marshal Brement, in the *Journal of Military History*, Spring 1993, explains the relationship between Khalkhin-Gol and the 1939 Nazi-Soviet Pact of Non-Aggression.

28. The battle of Khalkhin-Gol had been the largest tank battle in history until it was overshadowed by the Battle for Kursk in World War II and Operation Desert Storm by combined American and allied forces against Iraq in 1991.

29. Chalmers Johnson, *An Instance of Treason: Ozaki Hotsumi and the Sorge Spy Ring* (Tokyo: Charles E. Tuttle, 1977), pp. 154–155.

30. Albert Glotzer, *Trotsky: Memoir and Critique* (Buffalo, NY: Prometheus Books, 1989), pp. 255–274.

31. Rees, *Harry Dexter White*, p.109.

32. Gordon W. Prange, with Donald M. Goldstein and Katherine V. Dillon, *Target Tokyo: The Story of the Sorge Spy Ring* (New York: McGraw-Hill, 1984), p. 349. Sudoplatov et al., *Special Tasks*, p. 96, asserts, "The strategic goal of the Soviet leadership was to avert war on two fronts at any cost. ... The Kremlin leadership was ready for a compromise with any regime, provided it guaranteed stability for the Soviet Union. The first priority of Stalin and his aides was the fulfillment of their geopolitical aspirations to transform the Soviet Union into the largest superpower in the world."

33. Prange, *Target Tokyo*, p. 324.

34. Molotov's archives, handwritten notes in Russian. Copy in authors' possession.

35. Valentin Bereshkov, *At Stalin's Side* (New York: Birch Lane Press, 1994), p. 47.

36. Bereshkov, *At Stalin's Side*, pp. 50–52.

37. Barbara W. Tuchman, *Stilwell and the American Experience in China, 1911–1915* (New York: Macmillan, 1970), p. 320.

38. Joseph W. Alsop, with Adam Platt, *"I've Seen the Best of It": Memoirs* (New York: W. W. Norton, 1992), p. 158.

39. *Courier of Russian Intelligence*, May 1991. Stennes' earlier control had been the NKVD *rezident* in Tokyo, Vladimir Dolbin, who had come to Shanghai the previous autumn, November 1940.

40. Vladimir Peschersky, official historian of Russian Foreign Intelligence, in *Journal of Russian Military History*, no. 3 (1998).

41. Stennes escaped with Chiang to Taiwan in 1948. He returned to East Germany in 1950 and continued to work for Soviet intelligence until 1952.

42. SEGAC [Chiang Kai-shek] letter, Lauchlin Currie papers, Hoover Institution Library, Stanford University, Palo Alto, CA.

43. Robert E. Sherwood, *Roosevelt and Hopkins* (New York: Harper and Brothers, 1948), pp. 230–233.

44. Roger J. Sandilands, *The Life and Political Economy of Lauchlin Currie* (Durham, NC: Duke University Press, 1990), pp. 90–95.

45. Sandilands, *The Life and Political Economy of Lauchlin Currie*, p. 166. American mercenaries were shooting down Japanese Zero fighters with the tactics developed by General Claire Chennault, the raw-boned, leathery leader of the AVG. Chennault won his way into Chiang's favor by shooting down 40 Japanese aircraft for a bounty of $500 a kill in a modified American Hawk-75 monoplane.

46. These unofficial volunteers were illegally released from Air Corps duty to serve as the backbone of Chiang Kai-shek's air force. Originally conceived as an air arm to bomb the Japanese mainland with B-17 bombers, the Flying Tigers (their planes were painted to look like tiger sharks with open jaws ready for a kill) lost out to Great Britain in the Washington battle for aircraft allocation, and became primarily a fighter unit.

47. Secret Report, Toungoo, Burma, Oct. 19, 1941, by Austin C. Brady to State Department, American Embassy, Chungking, from American Consulate, Kunming, Lauchlin Currie file, Hoover Institution Library.

48. Staff of the Asahi, *The Pacific Rivals* (New York: John Weatherhill, 1972), pp. 86–87.

49. Tuchman, *Stilwell and the American Experience in China*, p. 174.

50. Henry L. Stimson and McGeorge Bundy, *On Active Service in Peace and War* (New York: Harper and Brothers, 1947), pp. 301–302.

51. Bix, *Hirohito*, p. 394.

52. Prange, *Target Tokyo*, p. 328.

53. Archives of the President of Russia, File 45, Op. 1., D.404, pp. 91–101 in typed version, sealed copy. Also see Bix, *Hirohito*, pp. 392–395.

54. A year later, in 1942, American naval victories in the Coral Sea and the Battle of Midway and the Marine's capture of Guadalcanal made Japanese ideas of attacking Siberia unthinkable.

55. Recent releases of records of Stalin's meetings with Yugoslav military leaders in Moscow in April 1941 confirm that this was his view.

56. Gabriel Gorodetsky, *Grand Illusion: Stalin and the German Invasion of Russia* (New Haven: Yale University Press, 1999), pp. 137–154.

57. Gorodetsky, *Grand Illusion*, pp. 198–199.

Chapter 2—Operation Snow

1. Vitali Pavlov, *Operatsia Sneg* (Moscow: Gaia Iterum, 1996), p. 31.

2. Pavlov, *Operatsia Sneg*, pp. 33–40.

3. Pavlov, *Operatsia Sneg*, pp. 33–40.

4. Interview with Vitali Pavlov, Moscow, June 1997.

5. David Rees, *Harry Dexter White: A Study in Paradox* (New York: Coward, McCann, and Geoghegan, 1973), p. 114. "An 'all-out' effort involves in diplomacy as in military strategy the fullest use of every economy and political advantage," declared White in May 1941.

6. Rees, *Harry Dexter White*, p. 102.
7. Rees, *Harry Dexter White*, pp. 117–118.
8. Rees, *Harry Dexter White*, p. 118.
9. Rees, *Harry Dexter White*, p. 118.
10. Hamilton Fish, *Memoirs of an American Patriot* (Washington, DC: Regnery Gateway, 1991), refers to historian Anthony Kubek, *How the Far East Was Lost, 1941–1949* (Chicago: Henry Regnery, 1963), based on testimonies of Whittaker Chambers, Alexander Barmin (Soviet defector in Greece in the 1930s), Bentley, and Guzenko naming White as a Soviet agent.
11. Interview with Vitali Pavlov, Moscow, June 1997.
12. Herbert P. Bix, *Hirohito and the Making of Modern Japan* (New York: Harper-Collins, 2000), pp. 394–395.
13. Bix, *Hirohito*, p. 395.
14. Gordon W. Prange, with Donald M. Goldstein and Katherine V. Dillon, *Target Tokyo: The Story of the Sorge Spy Ring* (New York: McGraw-Hill, 1984), pp. 324–325.
15. Bix, *Hirohito*, pp. 397–398.
16. Bix, *Hirohito*, p. 399.
17. Lauchlin Currie Archive, Hoover Institution Library, Box 1.
18. Lauchlin Currie Archive.
19. Lauchlin Currie Archive.
20. Gabriel Gorodetsky, "Churchill's Warning to Stalin," in *Grand Illusion: Stalin and the German Invasion of Russia* (New Haven: Yale University Press, 1999), pp. 155–178.
21. Rees, *Harry Dexter White*, pp. 116–123.
22. Staff of the Asahi, *The Pacific Rivals* (New York: John Weatherhill, 1972), p. 88.
23. Staff of the Asahi, *The Pacific Rivals*, pp. 88–89.
24. NKVD documents from 1941 in Russian Intelligence Archives.
25. Rees, *Harry Dexter White*, pp. 109–111.
26. Rees, *Harry Dexter White*, p. 109.
27. In early 1941, White asked Ernest Hemingway, who was about to make a trip to China, to brief him on his return. In August, Hemingway told White that the nationalist government had become a dictatorship. However, the communist evaluation of their own war effort against the Japanese should not be taken at face value, because the nationalists under Chiang Kai-shek were playing a far more effective role in repelling the invasion. Rees, *Harry Dexter White*, pp. 118–119.
28. Rees, *Harry Dexter White*, p. 109.
29. Russian Intelligence Archives.
30. Interview with Robert Nathan, Arlington, VA, June 1998.
31. Interview with Aleksandr Feklisov, Moscow, October 1997.
32. Russian Intelligence Archives.

33. Sam Tanenhaus, *Whittaker Chambers* (New York: Random House, 1997), p. 110.

34. Interview with Vitali Pavlov, Moscow, October 1997.

35. Borodin's real name was Grusenberg. He had become a Social Democrat in 1903; the Social Democrats split into Mensheviks and Bolsheviks. He became a Menshevik and was forced to flee Russia in 1905 for America where he became a school principal in Chicago. He returned to Moscow in 1917 and became a Comintern agent, turning up in Mexico, Spain, Turkey, and America. In September 1923, he arrived in Canton as personal adviser to Sun Yat-sen and chief of a large Soviet mission. Conrad Brandt, *Stalin's Failure in China, 1924–1927* (Cambridge, MA: Harvard University Press, 1958), pp. 41–42, 195–196, fn. 70.

36. Allen Weinstein and Alexander Vassiliev, *The Haunted Wood: Soviet Espionage in America—The Stalin Era* (New York: Random House, 1999), pp. 157–158.

37. Rees, *Harry Dexter White*, p. 37.

38. Maj. Gen. Charles A. Willoughby, *Shanghai Conspiracy: The Sorge Spy Ring— Moscow, Shanghai, Tokyo, San Francisco, New York* (New York: E. P. Dutton, 1952), pp. 122–125.

39. Chalmers Johnson, *An Instance of Treason: Ozaki Hotsumi and the Sorge Spy Ring* (Tokyo: Charles E. Tuttle, 1977), pp. 64–67.

40. Willoughby, *Shanghai Conspiracy*, p. 206.

41. Willoughby, *Shanghai Conspiracy*, p. 206.

42. "Post Presidential Memoirs," December 15, 1954, Papers of Harry S. Truman, Harry S. Truman Library, Kansas City, Missouri.

43. Russian Intelligence Archives.

44. Russian Intelligence Archives.

45. Russian Intelligence Archives.

46. Ministry of Foreign Affairs of Russia Archive.

47. Russian Intelligence Archives.

48. Rees, *Harry Dexter White*, p. 121.

49. Ministry of Foreign Affairs of Russia Archive.

50. Ministry of Foreign Affairs of Russia Archive.

51. Ministry of Foreign Affairs of Russia Archive.

52. Ministry of Foreign Affairs of Russia Archive.

53. Vladimir Vasilievich Karpov, "The War in the Pacific Could Have Been Avoided in 1941. Stalin Managed to Prevent the Attack against the USSR from the Second Front in the Far East," *Nezavisimaya Gazetta, Independent Military Review*, no. 2 (January 21–27, 2000): 5. See also Roberta Wohlstetter, *Pearl Harbor: Warning and Decision* (Stanford, CA: Stanford University Press, 1962), pp. 233–234.

54. Vladimir Karpov, "Notes from the Archive," *Independent Military Review*, Moscow (January 21, 2000): 1.

55. Karpov, "Notes from the Archive," p. 1.

Chapter 3—The War Years

1. Pavel Sudoplatov and Anatoli Sudoplatov, with Jerrold L. and Leona P. Schecter, *Special Tasks: The Memoirs of an Unwanted Witness—A Soviet Spymaster* (Boston: Little, Brown, 1994), p. 173.

2. Russian Intelligence Archives.

3. Sudoplatov et al., *Special Tasks*, pp. 174–176.

4. *History of Soviet Atomic Project*, 1938–1949, vol. 1 (Moscow: Ministry of Atomic Energy, 1999), p. 223. The document contradicts the official version that Soviet intelligence noticed a halt of public information on atomic research and deduced that secret research was under way.

5. Other versions cite John Cairncross, the "Fifth Man" of the Cambridge Five, as the source for the Tube Alloys report. Cairncross denied passing the report to Soviet intelligence in a telephone interview with the authors in 1993, confirmed by a signed fax from Cairncross in Italy.

6. Interview with Edward Teller, Palo Alto, CA, November 1998.

7. The United States never declared war on Japan. FDR asked Congress to acknowledge the existing state of war.

8. See appendix 1 for FBI letter on Oppenheimer paying Communist Party dues.

9. Sudoplatov et al., *Special Tasks*, p. 188.

10. See appendix 2 document citing Oppenheimer as an unlisted Communist Party member.

11. Russian Intelligence Archives.

12. Allen Weinstein and Alexander Vassiliev, *The Haunted Wood: Soviet Espionage in America—The Stalin Era* (New York: Random House, 1999), p. 184. The authors note that "it cannot be independently corroborated" that Oppenheimer was a "secret member" of the Communist Party. They cite the recall of Gregory Kheifitz to Moscow in 1944 for failing to recruit atomic scientists as evidence that Oppenheimer never agreed to be a source of information. This explanation was KGB disinformation sowed to discredit Pavel Sudoplatov's assertion that high ranking American scientists, including Oppenheimer, Fermi, and Szilard, knowingly cooperated with Soviet intelligence. In fact, Kheifitz was recalled in 1944 because he was named in the Mironov letter to Stalin (see pp. 64 and 82). Moscow Center feared Kheifitz was compromised and might be arrested.

13. Sudoplatov et al., *Special Tasks*, p. 193.

14. Sudoplatov et al., *Special Tasks*, p. 199.

15. Inez Cope Jeffery, *Inside Russia: The Life and Times of Zoya Zarubina* (Austin, TX: Eakin Press, 1999).

16. Interview with Yuri Modin, Moscow, 1997. Modin ran the Cambridge ring and, at times, the scientific line.

17. Pavel Sudoplatov, *Special Operations: Lubyanka and the Kremlin, 1930–1950* (Moscow: Gaia, 1996), pp. 357–360. See also appendixes 3, 4, and 5 at the end

of this book on the receipt and distribution of atomic espionage materials from the United States and Great Britain.

18. *Vardo* is the Georgian word for *rose*. It was the name of one of Beria's lovers (who were also his secretaries), Vardo Maximilashvili; she was a student of Elizabeth Zarubina in the Special Purpose Intelligence School in 1940.

19. Msg. no. 786-7, New York to Moscow, May 26, 1943, VENONA, p. 223, in Robert Louis Benson and Michael Warner, *VENONA: Soviet Espionage and the American Response, 1939–1957* (Washington, DC: National Security Agency, Central Intelligence Agency, 1996).

20. Abbreviation for Extraordinary Commission to Combat Counterrevolution and Sabotage, 1917–1922, the first Soviet security service.

21. Hede Massing, *This Deception* (New York: Duell, Sloan and Pearce, 1951), pp. 224–225.

22. Boris Morros, as told to Charles Samuels, *My Ten Years as a Counterspy* (New York: Viking Press, 1959), pp. 7–41. Interview with Robert Lamphere, 1998.

23. Sudoplatov et al., *Special Tasks*, p. 85.

24. Sudoplatov et al., *Special Tasks*, pp. 212–213, 217; also Christopher Andrew and Oleg Gordievsky, *KGB: The Inside Story* (New York: HarperCollins, 1990), p. 318.

25. Oliver Pilat, *The Atom Spies* (New York: Putnam's Sons, 1952), p. 193.

26. Andrew and Gordievsky, *KGB: The Inside Story*, p. 318.

27. Laura Fermi, *Atoms in the Family: My Life With Enrico Fermi* (Chicago: University of Chicago Press, 1954), pp. 253–257.

28. Fermi, *Atoms in the Family*, pp. 253–257.

29. Fermi, *Atoms in the Family*, pp. 253–257.

30. Andrew and Gordievsky, *KGB: The Inside Story*, p. 379.

31. Vladimir Antonov and Vladimir Karpov, *Secret Informers of the Kremlin* (Moscow: Gaia Iterum, 2000), p. 77. Richard Rhodes, *The Making of the Atomic Bomb* (New York: Simon and Schuster, 1986), pp. 502–510.

32. Interviews with Semyonov's widow, Glafira, Moscow, 1997 and 1998.

33. Interview with Semyonov's son Ilya, Moscow, 1998.

34. Sudoplatov's statement about the message received from Semyonov is confirmed in the secret KGB textbook, *The History of Soviet Intelligence Operations* (Moscow: KGB Publishing House, 1971); classified for internal use. According to the two confidential Russian sources we interviewed in Moscow in 1997, Semyonov's words are also in the KGB *Enormoz* (Enormous) file on atomic espionage.

35. Archive of the President of the Russian Federation.

36. Also ADA and NORMA in VENONA.

37. Igor Anatolievich Damaskin, *Seventeen Names of Kitty Harris* (Moscow: Gaia Iterum, 1999), p. 233. Damaskin is a retired colonel of the Russian Foreign Intelligence Service.

38. Sudoplatov et al. describe the operations of Ernest Wollweber, who later became minister of security in the German Democratic Republic, in *Special Tasks*, pp. 24–25, 364–365.

39. Damaskin, *Seventeen Names of Kitty Harris*, pp. 230–231

40. John Costello and Oleg Tsarev, *Deadly Illusions* (New York, Crown, 1993), pp. 207–209. See also Christopher Andrew and Vasili Mitrokhin, *The Sword and the Shield* (New York: Basic Books, 1999), pp. 82–83.

41. Damaskin, *Seventeen Names of Kitty Harris*, pp. 230–231.

42. Damaskin, *Seventeen Names of Kitty Harris*, p. 229.

43. Kitty Harris was exposed as an agent of Soviet intelligence by Benjamin Gitlow, who testified in September 1939 before the House Un–American Activities Committee headed by Martin Dies. Gitlow told the committee that Kitty Harris, the wife of Earl Browder, had received $10,000 for the Pacific Union Secretariat and left for China with Browder. "I believe that she is an agent of the OGPU and Margaret Browder, Earl Browder's sister, is a member of the Soviet intelligence center. As far as I understand Browder testified that he never knew Katherine Harris," testified Gitlow, who insisted that Kitty Harris was Browder's wife. He said Kitty Harris was probably forced to work outside the United States and speculated she was working in Europe or Asia.

44. W. G. (Walter) Krivitsky, *In Stalin's Secret Service: An Expose of Russia's Secret Police by the Former Chief of Soviet Intelligence in Western Europe* (Philadelphia, PA: Saturday Evening Post, 1939; reprint, with appendixes of FBI documents and Flora Lewis' 1966 *Washington Post* article "Who Killed Krivitsky?," *In Stalin's Secret Service: Memoirs of the First Soviet Spy Master to Defect*, introduction by Sam Tannehaus (New York: Enigma Books, 2000), p. 216.

45. Krivitsky, *In Stalin's Secret Service*, p. 216.

46. Weinstein and Vassiliev, *The Haunted Wood*, p. 86.

47. Costello and Tsarev, *Deadly Illusions*, pp. 210–211.

48. Konstantin Kukin, code-named IGOR in VENONA.

49. Damaskin, *Seventeen Names of Kitty Harris*, pp. 230–231.

50. Allen Paul, *Katyn: The Untold Story of Stalin's Polish Massacre* (New York: Scribner's, 1991), pp. 203–215.

51. Amos Perlmutter, *FDR and Stalin: A Not So Grand Alliance, 1943–1945* (Columbia, MO: University of Missouri Press, 1993), p. 163.

52. Sudoplatov et al., *Special Tasks*, p. 197.

53. Interview with Robert Louis Benson, Washington, DC, 1999.

54. Benson and Warner, *VENONA*, pp. 51–52.

55. Robert Louis Benson and Cecil Phillips, *History of VENONA*, vol. 1 (Fort Meade, MD: National Security Agency, 1995), p. 66.

56. Interview with confidential Russian source, Moscow, 1997.

57. Christopher Andrew and Vasili Mitrokhin, *The Sword and the Shield: The Mitrokhin Archive and the Secret History of the KGB* (New York: Basic Books, 1999), pp. 112–124.

Chapter 4—Nuclear Furies: A Love Affair and a Storm of Controversy

1. Conversation with Oleg Kalugin, Washington, DC, 1999.
2. Sergei T. Konenkov, *Moi Vek (My Century): Memoirs* (Moscow: Izdatelstvo Politicheskoi Literatury, 1972).
3. Pavel Sudoplatov and Anatoli Sudoplatov, with Jerrold L. Schecter and Leona P. Schecter, *Special Tasks: Updated Edition* (Boston: Little, Brown, 1995), p. 493.
4. The Theremin was used for the sound effect of *The Green Hornet*, the 1938–1952 radio serial, to create the loud buzzing of an amplified bee, representing the invasion of a giant insect hunting public enemies. Albert Glinsky, *Theremin: Ether Music and Espionage* (Urbana, IL: University of Illinois Press, 2000), pp. 193, 200.
5. *News of Intelligence and Counterintelligence*, article on Lev Theremin, vol. 5 (Moscow, August 1994).
6. Interview with Peter Masia, Moscow, June 1997. Masia was a KGB officer stationed in Washington during 1948–1950, working on scientific intelligence. From 1953 to 1970 Masia was in charge of counterintelligence operations against the American embassy in Moscow.
7. Igor Damaskin, *Women Intelligence Officers and Women Spies* (Moscow: Olma Press, 2000), pp. 157, 183.
8. Sudoplatov et al., *Special Tasks: Updated Edition*, p. 493
9. Ronald W. Clark, *Einstein: The Life and Times* (New York: World, 1971), pp. 573–575.
10. Richard Rhodes, *The Making of the Atomic Bomb* (New York: Simon and Schuster, 1986), pp. 482–485.
11. Clark, *Einstein*, p. 574.
12. Clark, *Einstein*, p. 575.
13. Clark, *Einstein*, p. 575.
14. Clark, *Einstein*, p. 576.
15. Clark, *Einstein*, p. 576.
16. Clark, *Einstein*, p. 577.
17. Clark, *Einstein*, p. 577.
18. In the section of registration of Soviet citizens living abroad, Sergei Konenkov's file number is 137994–42; Margarita's is 137993–42.
19. Sotheby's, Catalog for Sotheby's Sale 7151, *Fine Books and Manuscripts including Americana*, New York, June 26, 1998, p. 433.
20. Marie Turbow Lampard, "Sergei Konenkov and the Russian Art Exhibition, *Soviet Union/Union Sovietque*, 1980, 9.77.
21. Shudenko is listed as NAZAR in the VENONA materials and is identified as a colleague of Yatskov by former FBI Special Agent Robert J. Lamphere. See also Robert J. Lamphere and Tom Shachtman, *The FBI–KGB War* (New York: Random House, 1986), p. 28, where he spells the name Choudenko.

22. See *News of Intelligence and Counterintelligence*, 1996.

23. Confidential Russian source.

24. Sotheby's, Catalog for Sotheby's Sale 7151, p. 433.

25. Sotheby's, Catalog for Sotheby's Sale 7151, p. 433.

26. James B. Conant, *My Several Lives* (New York: Harper, 1970), p. 482.

27. See appendixes 6 and 7.

28. Igor Anatolievich Damaskin, *Seventeen Names of Kitty Harris* (Moscow: Gaia Iterum, 1999).

29. Russian Intelligence Archives.

30. Central Committee of the Communist Party of the Soviet Union (CPSU) Archives.

31. Summary, February 13, 1939. Top secret Summary on the Operational officer of the reserve of the fifth department of GUGB (Main Directorate State Security), Russian Intelligence Archives.

32. Central Committee CPSU Archives.

33. Central Committee CPSU Archives.

34. Central Committee CPSU Archives.

35. Russian Intelligence Archives.

36. See Amy Knight, *Spies Without Cloaks* (Princeton, NJ: Princeton University Press, 1996), and Amy Knight, *Who Killed Kirov? The Kremlin's Greatest Mystery* (New York: Hill and Wang, 1999). In a forum at the Woodrow Wilson Center in Washington, DC, Knight asserted that Sudoplatov did not hold the offices he claimed in his book, the same charge simultaneously released by Russian intelligence in Moscow.

37. CNN.com transcripts, September 8, 2000, *Larry King Live*, pp. 6–7.

38. Sudoplatov et al., *Special Tasks: Updated Edition*, pp. 205–207. An analysis by an American nuclear engineer in 1995 showed that the first 15 questions revealed little, but the final 7 questions evoked answers that were secrets Bohr was not free to give.

39. Vladimir Antonov and Vladimir Karpov, *Secret Informers of the Kremlin* (Moscow: Gaia Iterum, 2000), p. 77.

40. "*Voprossi Istorii Estesvoznania i Tekniki*" ["*Questions of History of Natural Science and Technology*"], Academy of Sciences, Moscow, no. 3 (1992): 107–134.

41. See Joseph Albright and Marcia Kunstel, *Bombshell: The Secret Story of America's Unknown Atomic Spy Conspiracy* (New York: Random House, Times Books, 1997), pp. 267–277.

42. Some documents are in the file of Mikhail Pervukhin, deputy prime minister 1941–1957, who was in charge of the Soviet chemical and machine building industries and the State Planning Commission during this time. He was a major figure in the development of Soviet heavy industry and the atomic program.

43. *History of the Soviet Atomic Project, 1938–1949*, vol. 1 (Moscow: Ministry of Atomic Energy, 1999), p. 223.

44. *History of the Soviet Atomic Project*, p. 331.

45. The summary contrasts with Nigel West's assessment of the British agent network, "which played a decisive role in obtaining atomic information until the end of 1944." Nigel West and Oleg Tsarev, *The Crown Jewels* (London: HarperCollins, 1998), p. 235.

46. Decree of State Committee of Defense #9887, August 20, 1945; see also appendix 6 and 7.

Chapter 5—Opening VENONA

1. Interview with Gertrude Lash, New York City, November 17, 1998.

2. Mark A. Stoler, *The Politics of the Second Front: American Military Planning and Diplomacy in Coalition Warfare, 1941–1943* (Westport, CT: Greenwood Press, 1977), p. 43.

3. David M. Kennedy, *Freedom from Fear: The American People in Depression and War, 1929–1945* (New York: Oxford University Press, 1999), p. 573, quotes from Alfred D. Chandler, Jr., et al., eds. *The Papers of Dwight David Eisenhower*, vol. 1 (Baltimore: Johns Hopkins Press, 1970), p. 391.

4. Kennedy, *Freedom from Fear*, p. 579.

5. Amos Perlmutter, *FDR and Stalin: A Not So Grand Alliance, 1943–1945* (Columbia, MO: University of Missouri Press, 1993), pp. 102–108.

6. See Bradley F. Smith, *Sharing Secrets with Stalin: How the Allies Traded Intelligence, 1941–1945* (Lawrence, KS: University of Kansas Press, 1996).

7. Interview with William Crowell, Maryland, September 23, 1997.

8. Florence Rubenfeld, *Clement Greenberg: A Life* (New York: Scribner's, 1997), pp. 60–62.

9. Richard Gid Powers, *Not Without Honor: The History of American Anticommunism* (New York: Free Press, 1995), p. 155.

10. Robert E. Sherwood, *Roosevelt and Hopkins: An Intimate History* (New York: Harper and Brothers, 1948), p. 283.

11. Robert Louis Benson and Cecil Phillips, *History of VENONA*, vol. 1 (Fort Meade, MD: National Security Agency, 1995), p. 12.

12. Benson and Phillips, *History of VENONA*, p. 12. Telephone interview with Oliver Kirby, March 12, 2001, based on his conversations with Carter Clarke on the history of VENONA.

13. James F. Byrnes, *All in One Lifetime* (New York: Harper and Brothers, 1958), pp. 186–187. Byrnes was a powerful political figure from South Carolina who became FDR's Director of Economic Stabilization in October 1942 and head of the Office of War Mobilization in 1943. Interview with Oliver Kirby, Washington, DC, September 26, 1997.

14. Robert Louis Benson, *Introductory History of VENONA and Guide to the Translations* (Fort Meade, MD: Center for Cryptologic History, National Security Agency, 1995), pp. 1–3. Interview with Oliver Kirby, Washington, DC, September 26, 1997.

15. Benson, *Introductory History of VENONA*, pp.1–3. Interview with Oliver Kirby, Washington, DC, September 26, 1997.

16. Benson and Phillips, *History of VENONA*, p. 38. General Ralph J. Canine, Director of NSA, told the FBI on December 9, 1953, that no Russian codes had been broken in 1942 and 1943, p. 38.

17. Msg. no. 885, New York to Moscow, June 9, 1943, VENONA, Fourth Release, vol. 1, p. 98.

18. John Cairncross, telephone interview with and signed confirming fax to the authors, August and September, 1995.

19. Pavel Sudoplatov and Anatoli Sudoplatov, with Jerrold L. and Leona P. Schecter, *Special Tasks: The Memoirs of an Unwanted Witness—A Soviet Spymaster* (New York: Little, Brown, 1994), p. 142.

20. John C. Wiley, Office of Strategic Services, Washington, DC, August 11, 1943, personal letter to the President of the United States, declassified by authority of the CIA #007622, September 10, 1974, reproduced from holdings at the Franklin D. Roosevelt Library, Hyde Park, New York.

21. Wiley, Office of Strategic Services.

22. Wiley, Office of Strategic Services.

23. Wiley, Office of Strategic Services.

24. Wiley, Office of Strategic Services.

25. Wiley, Office of Strategic Services.

26. Wiley, Office of Strategic Services.

27. R. Harris Smith, *OSS: The Secret History of America's First Central Intelligence Agency* (Berkeley and Los Angeles, CA: University of California Press, 1972), pp. 104–105.

28. David Kahn, *The Codebreakers; The Comprehensive History of Secret Communication from Ancient Times to the Internet* (New York: Scribner's, 1996), p. 21. The Americans had their own heroes: William Friedman, Colonel Abraham Sinkov, Solomon Kullbach, and Frank Rowlett, nicknamed The Four Horsemen.

29. Interview with William Crowell, Maryland, September 23, 1997.

30. Kennedy, *Freedom from Fear*, p. 675.

31. Kennedy, *Freedom from Fear*, pp. 676–679.

32. Kennedy, *Freedom from Fear*, pp. 681–682.

33. Kennedy, *Freedom from Fear*, p. 683.

34. Forrest C. Pogue, *George C. Marshall: Organizer of Victory* (New York: Viking Press, 1973), pp. 410–420.

35. Nikita Khrushchev, *Khrushchev Remembers: The Glasnost Tapes*, trans. and ed. Jerrold Schecter, with Vyacheslav V. Luchkov (Boston: Little, Brown, 1991), p. 144.

36. Jonathan Haslam, "Stalin's War of Peace: What If the Cold War Had Been Avoided?" in *Virtual History: Alternatives and Counterfactuals*, ed. Niall Ferguson (New York: Basic Books, 1999), pp. 362–366.

37. Richard Gid Powers, *The Life of J. Edgar Hoover: Secrecy and Power* (New York: Free Press, 1987), pp. 236–237. When World War II ended the FBI increased the number of paid informers in the CPUSA. As party membership declined FBI insiders joked that the only regular dues paying members of the CPUSA were FBI informers.

38. FBI source in interview with authors, 1997.

39. David J. Dallin, *Soviet Espionage* (New Haven, CT: Yale University Press, 1955), p. 469. In July 1952, Nelson was sentenced in Pittsburgh to a 20-year prison sentence that was overturned on appeal. He died in 1993. See Sudoplatov et al., *Special Tasks*, pp. 186–188. Also interview with Ernest (Ernie) Van Loon, Phoenix, Arizona, April 29, 1997.

40. William Bundy was the head of the team sent to Bletchley; he worked for the ASA during the war. He later became Assistant Secretary of State for Far Eastern Affairs and was long-time editor of *Foreign Affairs*.

41. Interview with Oliver Kirby, Washington, D.C., September 26, 1997.

42. Kirby got to know the Bundy brothers, Bill and McGeorge. "Later on when Alger Hiss was in trouble and both McGeorge and Bill were going to bat for him I did get in touch with Bill. I never told him anything specific about VENONA. I simply said, 'Hush, he is guilty as all get out.' He never asked any questions, but he did hush." Interview with Oliver Kirby, Washington, DC, 1999.

43. Interview with Oliver Kirby, Washington, DC, 1999.

44. Kai Bird, *The Color of Truth* (New York: Simon and Schuster, 1988), pp. 72–77. Oliver Kirby's notes are in authors' possession.

45. See Christopher Simpson, *Blowback* (New York: Weidenfeld and Nicolson, 1988); Linda Hunt, *Secret Agenda* (New York: St. Martin's Press, 1991); Joseph Loftus, *The Belarus Secret* (New York: Knopf, 1982); Tom Bower, *The Paperclip Conspiracy* (Boston: Little, Brown, 1987).

46. The Soviet teams under the command of General Ivan Serov were under orders to bring German scientists back to the Soviet Union and to locate the records of White Russian organizations in Eastern Europe and Germany. See Sudoplatov et al., *Special Tasks*, pp. 168–170.

47. The ALSOS (Greek, for *groves*) Mission, led by Colonel Boris Pash and Dr. Samuel A. Goudsmit, was sent to France in 1944 to search out and capture German scientists with knowledge of the German program to develop an atomic bomb. The U.S. needed to know how far the Germans had come to build their own weapon and whether they would succeed before the United States. By September 1944, it was clear that the Germans were still at the level the U.S. was at in 1940. See Samuel A. Goudsmit, *Alsos* (New York: Henry Schuman, 1947).

48. Interview with Oliver Kirby, Washington, DC, September 26, 1997.

49. Interview with Oliver Kirby, Washington, DC, September 26, 1997, and his notes.

50. Christopher Andrew and Oleg Gordievsky, *KGB: The Inside Story* (New York: HarperCollins, 1990), pp. 284–285.

51. Interview with Oliver Kirby, Washington, DC, October 1997.

52. John E. Haynes and Harvey Klehr, *VENONA: Decoding Soviet Espionage in America* (New Haven, CT: Yale University Press, 1999), pp. 276–283.

Chapter 6—Truman Wrestles an Ogre Named VENONA

1. David Alvarez, *Secret Messages, Code Breaking and American Diplomacy, 1930–1945* (Lawrence, KS: University Press of Kansas, 2000), p. 201.

2. Presidential Appointments List, 12:45 p.m. to 1:00 p.m., June 4, 1945, Truman Library, Kansas City, Missouri.

3. Interview with Oliver Kirby, Washington, DC, September 26, 1997.

4. Harry S. Truman, *Memoirs by Harry S. Truman*, vol. 2, *Years of Trial and Hope* (New York: Doubleday, 1956).

5. Kenneth O'Reilly, *Hoover and the Un-Americans: The FBI, HUAC and the Red Menace* (Philadelphia, PA: Temple University Press, 1983), pp. 51, 310–311.

6. Warren E. Kimball, *Forged in War: Roosevelt, Churchill and the Second World War* (New York: William Morrow, 1997), p. 242.

7. Ellen Schrecker, *Many Are the Crimes: McCarthyism in America* (Boston: Little, Brown, 1998), pp. 90–91.

8. Richard Gid Powers, *The Life of J. Edgar Hoover: Secrecy and Power* (New York: Free Press, 1987), p. 274. In the spring of 1941, Dusko Popov, the playboy son of a wealthy German family, was recruited by the *Abwehr*. He immediately reported the overture to British intelligence and became one of Britain's most successful double agents. The Germans gave him an assignment: to find out details on Pearl Harbor for the Japanese. Popov gave the questionnaire to the FBI upon his arrival in New York City, but Hoover disliked Popov's loose lifestyle and distrusted double agents. The director never passed the inquiries in the Japanese questionnaire regarding Pearl Harbor to President Roosevelt, nor did he warn the president that two German agents had been ordered to study the defenses at Pearl Harbor. See Curt Gentry, *J. Edgar Hoover: The Man and His Secrets* (New York: W. W. Norton, 1991), pp. 269–273.

9. Powers, *The Life of J. Edgar Hoover*, pp. 274–276.

10. William C. Sullivan, with Bill Brown, *The Bureau: My Thirty Years in Hoover's FBI* (New York: W. W. Norton, 1979), p. 38.

11. Robert J. Donovan, *Conflict and Crisis* (New York: W. W. Norton, 1997), p. 76.

12. Interview with Lloyd Cutler, Washington, DC, May 1997. Curt Gentry, *J. Edgar Hoover: The Man and His Secrets* (New York: Plume, The Penguin Group, 1992), pp. 287–293.

13. Ronald Lewin, *The American Magic: Codes, Ciphers and the Defeat of Japan* (New York: Farrar, Straus and Giroux, 1982), pp. 3–12.

14. "While Gouzenko's revelations were important to Allied counterintelligence efforts, they had no bearing on the VENONA breakthroughs," insists historian

Robert Louis Benson. In technical terms of code breaking, Benson is correct, but in practical terms of the identification of Soviet agents, and the addition of new names and code names, the Gouzenko revelations were significant.

15. See Hayden Peake's Afterword in the paperback edition of Elizabeth Bentley, *Out of Bondage* (New York: Ivy Books, 1988), pp. 226–229, for a skillful, meticulous study of Bentley's career as a Soviet agent.

16. Robert Louis Benson and Michael Warner, eds., *VENONA: Soviet Espionage and the American Response, 1939–1957* (Washington, DC: National Security Agency, Central Intelligence Agency, 1996), pp. xiii, 69.

17. Elizabeth Bentley described the "pole" method of establishing a ring of individuals to gather information. The term "pole" is the designation of the individual at the apex of the organization, which is a self-contained unit.

18. Maurice Bernstein, *"All Still!" Life Among a Thousand Siblings*, unpublished manuscript, 1998, pp. 167–169.

19. Memorandum for Mr. E. A. Tamm, Re: Harry Dexter White, Assistant to the Secretary of the Treasury, Internal Security, Hatch Act, March 30, 1942, p. 2.

20. David Rees, *Harry Dexter White: A Study in Paradox* (New York: Coward, McCann, and Geoghegan, 1973), p. 354, quoting a July 9, 1945, United Press story.

21. Interview with Robert Lamphere, Green Valley, Arizona, October 16, 1998.

22. Msg. no. 786, New York to Moscow, June 1, 1944, VENONA, in Benson and Warner, *VENONA*, p. 289.

23. Irwin F. Gellman, *Secret Affairs: Franklin Roosevelt, Cordell Hull and Sumner Welles* (Baltimore, MD: Johns Hopkins University Press, 1995), p. 153.

24. Letter from Hoover to Vaughan, October 18, 1945, Subject File FBI-C, Truman Library, Kansas City, Missouri.

25. Rees, *Harry Dexter White*, p. 177.

26. Molotov to Harriman, February 14, 1944, Harriman Papers, Library of Congress, box 171, chron. file February 6–14. See also Rees, *Harry Dexter White*, pp. 180–181.

27. Rees, *Harry Dexter White*, pp. 181–182.

28. Rees, *Harry Dexter White*, p. 184.

29. Vladimir Petrov, *Money and Conquest: Allied Currency in World War II* (Baltimore, MD: Johns Hopkins Press, 1967), pp. 122–123.

30. Rees, *Harry Dexter White*, p. 186; Harriman to Hull, April 8, 1944, Harriman Papers, Library of Congress, box 171, chron. file.

31. Rees, *Harry Dexter White*, p. 189.

32. Russian Intelligence Archives.

33. Rees, *Harry Dexter White*, p. 191.

34. Petrov, *Money and Conquest*, pp. 196–200.

35. In June 1947, the Senate Committee on Appropriations held two days of hearings on occupation currency transactions, and criticized both the Treasury

and War Departments. In 1953, with the Republican in control of the White House and both houses of Congress, Senator Karl Mundt initiated another hearings into the occupation currency scandal focused on the role of Harry Dexter White. For a defense of White, see Bruce Craig, *Treasonable Doubt: The Harry Dexter White Case, 1948–1953* (Ph.D. thesis, Washington, DC, American University, 1999), pp. 216–258.

36. W. R. Smyser, *From Yalta to Berlin: The Cold War Struggle over Germany* (New York: St. Martin's Press, 1999), pp. 27–49.

37. Jean Edward Smith, *Lucius D. Clay: An American Life* (New York: Henry Holt, 1990), p. 443.

38. Smith, *Lucius D. Clay*, pp. 480–481. Smith quotes Clay as attributing the Russian blockade of Berlin to the failure of the London Foreign Ministers meeting, the currency reform, and the establishment of Bizonia, the jointly controlled British and American zones, which the French were later to join. Smyser, *From Yalta to Berlin*, pp. 57–60, offers a skillful summary of Stalin's problems with East Germany and Molotov's failure at the Foreign Ministers conference.

39. Msg. no. 1119-21, New York to Moscow, August 4/5, 1944, VENONA, in Benson and Warner, *VENONA*, pp. 319–322; msg. no. 1271-4, New York to Moscow, September 7, 1944, VENONA, in Benson and Warner, *VENONA*, pp. 329–331.

40. Whittaker Chambers, *Witness* (New York: Random House, 1952), p. 383.

41. Chambers, *Witness*, pp. 383–384.

42. Chambers, *Witness*, p. 29.

43. Rees, *Harry Dexter White*, p. 384.

44. Chambers, *Witness*, p. 383.

45. Chambers, *Witness*, p. 384.

46. Chambers, *Witness*, p. 414.

47. "Financial Assistance for 'RICHARD' " discusses offer to pay White's daughter's college expenses; msg. no. 1634, New York to Moscow, November 20, 1944, VENONA, in Benson and Warner, *VENONA*, pp. 375–377.

48. Msg. no. 1657, New York to Moscow, November 27, 1944, VENONA, in Benson and Warner, *VENONA*, p. 381.

49. Bob Considine, *Larger Than Life: A Biography of the Remarkable Dr. Armand Hammer* (New York: Harper and Row, 1975), pp. 115–116. Armand Hammer, with Neil Lyndon, *Hammer* (New York: Putnam's Sons, 1987), pp. 266–268.

50. The 79-page transcript of White's often uncharacteristically vague testimony has been released and is available in the Truman Library, Kansas City, Missouri.

51. Confidential GRU source.

52. Charles E. Bohlen, *Witness to History* (New York: W. W. Norton, 1973), p. 173.

53. Bohlen, *Witness to History*, p. 173.

54. Bohlen, *Witness to History*, p. 174.

55. Bohlen, *Witness to History*, pp. 173–174.

56. Pavel Sudoplatov and Anatoli Sudoplatov, with Jerrold L. and Leona P. Schecter, *Special Tasks: The Memoirs of an Unwanted Witness—A Soviet Spymaster* (New York: Little, Brown, 1994), p. 230.

57. Alger Hiss, *In the Court of Public Opinion* (New York: Knopf, 1957), p. 148.

58. Bohlen, *Witness to History*, p. 179.

59. Bohlen, *Witness to History*, pp. 194–195.

60. Bohlen, *Witness to History*, p. 194.

61. Bohlen, *Witness to History*, p. 195.

62. The history of the Red Orchestra, and how German army intelligence and the Gestapo dismembered it, ranks with the greatest spy stories of World War II. The GRU's treatment of the Red Orchestra leaders as traitors at the end of the war instead of heroes remains a black page in GRU history. See Sudoplatov et al., *Special Tasks*, pp. 137–145.

63. Sudoplatov et al., *Special Tasks*, p. 227.

64. Confidential GRU sources.

65. David Kahn, *The Codebreakers* (New York: Scribner's, 1996), p. 638.

66. Hiss defenders are still trying to clear his name. See John Lowenthal, "VENONA and Alger Hiss," *Intelligence and National Security*, 15, no. 3. (Autumn 2000).

Chapter 7—VENONA Hits Pay Dirt

1. Interview with Oliver Kirby, Washington, DC, September 26, 1997.

2. Interview with Oliver Kirby, Washington, DC, October 28, 1996.

3. Interview with Oliver Kirby, Washington, DC, September 26, 1997.

4. Interview with Oliver Kirby, Washington, DC, September 26, 1997.

5. Interview with Oliver Kirby, Washington, DC, September 28, 1997.

6. Interview with Oliver Kirby, Washington, DC, September 28, 1997.

7. Interview with Robert Louis Benson, Washington, DC, February 22, 1999. Benson was told of the incident by Frank Rowlett, the head of intelligence at the ASA, who worked with Carter Clarke.

8. Interview with Oliver Kirby, Washington, DC, September 28, 1997.

9. Herbert Romerstein and Stanislav Levchenko, *The KGB Against the Main Enemy: How the Soviet Intelligence Service Operates Against the United States* (Lexington, MA: Lexington Books, 1989), p. 112. David Kahn, *The Codebreakers* (New York: Scribner's, 1997), p. 638.

10. Robert Louis Benson and Cecil Phillips, *History of VENONA*, vol. 1 (Fort Meade, MD: National Security Agency, 1995), p. 38.

11. Allen Weinstein and Alexander Vassiliev, *The Haunted Wood* (New York: Random House, 1999), pp. 291–293. Also see "Who Was Willliam Weisband?" in *VENONA: Soviet Espionage and the American Response, 1939–1957*, ed. Robert

Louis Benson and Michael Warner (Washington, DC: National Security Agency, Central Intelligence Agency, 1996), p. xxviii.

12. "Who Was William Weisband?" in Benson and Warner, *VENONA*, p. xxviii.

13. Yuri Modin, with Jean-Charles Deniau and Aguieszka Ziarek, *My 5 Cambridge Friends, Burgess, Maclean, Philby, Blunt and Cairncross, by Their KGB Controller* (New York: Farrar, Straus and Giroux, 1994), pp. 51–55; Nigel West and Oleg Tsarev, *The Crown Jewels* (London: HarperCollins, 1998), pp. 273–274.

14. Christopher Andrew and Oleg Gordievsky, *KGB: The Inside Story* (New York: HarperCollins, 1990), pp. 373–374; Peter Wright, *Spy Catcher* (New York: Viking, 1987), p. 185.

15. Wright, *Spy Catcher*, p. 185.

16. Benson and Warner, *VENONA*, p. 13.

17. Benson and Warner, *VENONA*, p. 13.

18. FBI Office Memorandum from A. H. Belmont to L. V. Boardman, Subject: Espionage, February 1, 1956, FBI Reading Room, Washington, DC, p. 5.

19. New York 27 to Moscow, January 8, 1945, VENONA, in Benson and Warner, *VENONA*, p. 403.

20. Robert J. Lamphere and Tom Shachtman, *The FBI-KGB War* (New York: Random House, 1986), pp. 110–125. Coplon, liable to 40 months to 10 years in jail, appealed the conviction. Her appeal was upheld when the court ruled that the reasons given for her surveillance and arrest lacked probable cause. The FBI and the Justice Department did not want to compromise the fact that they had broken the Soviet ciphers. The case was tried again to avoid revealing VENONA. Coplon was convicted a second time and appealed. Her appeal was sustained by Judge Hand on grounds that the FBI had not had a proper arrest warrant and the trial judge had erred in not letting Coplon's defense see certain wiretap records. Although Judge Hand let the indictment stand against her, the government never retried the case.

21. Lamphere and Shachtman, *The FBI-KGB War*, p. 123.

22. Modin, *My 5 Cambridge Friends*, pp. 189–198.

23. Verne W. Newton, *The Cambridge Spies: The Untold Story of Maclean, Philby and Burgess in America* (Lanham, MD: Madison Books, 1991), pp. 271; describes the bizarre living arrangements in the Philby house; living there were Philby, his wife, three children, a Scottish nanny, Burgess, and Philby's spinster secretary who lived in the attic.

24. Modin, *My 5 Cambridge Friends*, pp. 197–209.

25. Newton, *The Cambridge Spies*, pp. 82–85.

26. FBI Office Memorandum from Belmont to Boardman, p. 7.

27. FBI Office Memorandum from Belmont to Boardman, p. 7.

28. FBI Office Memorandum from Belmont to Boardman, p. 8.

29. Lamphere and Shachtman, *The FBI–KGB War*, pp. 133–134.

30. Lamphere and Shachtman, *The FBI–KGB War*, pp. 134–135; and New York

195 to Moscow, February 9, 1944, VENONA, in Benson and Warner, *VE-NONA*, p. 255.

31. Elizabeth Bentley, *Out of Bondage*, Afterword by Hayden Peake (New York: Ivy Books, 1988), p. 219.

32. George M. Elsey, memorandum for Mr. (Clark M.) Clifford, August 16, 1948, in Benson and Warner, *VENONA*, p. 117.

33. Interview with Oliver Kirby, Washington, DC, September 26, 1997.

34. Oliver Kirby interview, Washington, DC, and notes, March 3, 1999.

35. Daniel Patrick Moynihan, *Secrecy: The American Experience* (New Haven, CT: Yale University Press, 1998), pp. 63–68.

36. Interview with Clayton Fritchey, Washington, DC, May 1997.

37. Curt Gentry, *J. Edgar Hoover: The Man and His Secrets* (New York: Plume, The Penguin Group, 1992), pp. 357–358.

38. Interview with Oliver Kirby, Washington, DC, October 5, 1998.

39. British Government Communications Headquarters (GCHQ) was the other recipient, but under the terms of the British-American agreement, their participation was not to be divulged.

40. Office Memorandum from Mr. H. B. Fletcher to Mr. D. M. Ladd, Subject: Espionage, October 18, 1949.

41. Interview with Richard Helms, Washington, DC, 1998.

42. Moynihan, *Secrecy*, pp. 70–72.

43. Interview with Oliver Kirby, Washington, DC, March 5, 1999, and copy of Kirby's handwritten account in authors' possession.

44. Interview with Oliver Kirby, Washington, DC, September 28, 1997.

45. Soviet spymaster Pavel Sudoplatov in his memoir, Sudoplatov et al., *Special Tasks*, describes elaborate sabotage preparations on the east and west coast of the United States in the late 1940s and early 1950s, later than the period covered by VENONA, pp. 241–244.

46. Interview with Oliver Kirby, Washington, DC, March 5, 1999.

47. Interview with Oliver Kirby, Washington, DC, March 5, 1999.

48. Interview with Oliver Kirby, Washington, DC, March 5, 1999.

49. Interview with Oliver Kirby, Washington, DC, March 5, 1999.

50. [Harry S. Truman] to the Attorney General, 16 December 1948, in Benson and Warner, *VENONA*, p. 119.

51. Interview with Clayton Fritchey, Washington, DC, May 1997.

52. Interview with Oliver Kirby, Washington, DC, March 5, 1999, and Kirby's handwritten notes.

53. Interview with Oliver Kirby, Washington, DC, March 5, 1999, and Kirby's handwritten notes.

54. Victor Navasky, *Naming Names* (New York: Penguin Books, 1980), pp. xii–xiii.

55. Jerrold L. Schecter, *Russian Negotiating Behavior: Continuity and Transition* (Washington, DC: U.S. Institute of Peace Press, 1998), pp. 34–38.

56. Interview with Oliver Kirby, Washington, DC, March 23, 1997.

57. George F. Kennan, *Memoirs, 1925–1950* (Boston: Little, Brown, 1967), pp. 211–212: "The Yalta declaration, with its references to the reorganization of the existing Polish-Communist regime 'on a broad democratic basis' and to the holding 'of free and unfettered elections ... on the basis of universal suffrage and secret ballot,' struck me as the shabbiest sort of equivocation, certainly not calculated to pull the wool over the eyes of the Western public but bound to have this effect." While discussions were going on in Moscow over the composition of the postwar Polish government the Soviet authorities "were quietly arresting, behind our backs, some of those very Polish political figures we were discussing for inclusion in the group to be consulted, and were putting pressure on them, unbeknownst to us, to become Soviet agents."

58. Kennan, *Memoirs*, pp. 547–559.

59. Townsend Hoopes and Douglas Brinkley, *Driven Patriot: The Life and Times of James Forrestal* (New York: Vintage Books, 1993), pp. 272–273.

60. Kennan, *Memoirs*, pp. 357–360. Hoopes and Brinkley, pp. 280–281, conclude that the X article "had a profound and cumulative effect on American policy thinking, but almost no immediate impact on the level of military preparedness." But with the Chinese communist victory in the Chinese civil war, the Soviet atomic bomb in 1948, and the Korean War in 1950, "containment" became the intellectual rationale for increased military spending. Hoopes and Brinkley argue: "Had Truman not been myopically focused on a balanced budget, he might have avoided the Korean War, for military stringency lay at the root of Secretary of State Dean Acheson's carefully considered policy speech of January 12, 1950, which tempted fate by defining the U.S. defense perimeter in Asia to exclude Korea and Formosa."

61. Daniel Yergin, *Shattered Peace: The Origins of the Cold War and the National Security State* (Boston: Houghton Mifflin, 1977), p. 283.

62. Gregory Mitrovich, *Undermining the Kremlin: America's Strategy to Subvert the Soviet Bloc, 1947–1956* (Ithaca, NY: Cornell University Press, 2000), pp. 23–24. Kennan's charter was to formulate and develop long term programs for the achievement of American objectives in foreign affairs, to anticipate difficulties for the department, to study and report on large problems in politico-military affairs, to evaluate current policy in the context of developments in world affairs, and to coordinate planning within the State Department.

63. Mitrovich, *Undermining the Kremlin*, p. 311.

64. In January 1948, Pyotr Zubov, the prewar NKVD *resident* in Czechoslovakia and control officer for Edvard Benes, traveled to Prague and gave an ultimatum to President Benes to either transfer power to Klement Gottwald, the Communist Party leader, by "retiring with dignity" in a "bloodless path to change" or have his ties to the KGB revealed publicly. Sudoplatov et al., *Special Tasks*, pp. 234–235.

65. Yergin, *Shattered Peace*, p. 350.

66. Jean Edward Smith, *Lucius D. Clay: An American Life* (New York: Henry Holt, 1990), pp. 466–467. Clay had meant for the cable to be used privately by the Army to influence congressional support for reinstituting the draft, but its impact on policymaking was far greater.

67. Yergin, *Shattered Peace*, p. 351.

68. Yergin, *Shattered Peace*, p. 351.

69. Yergin, *Shattered Peace*, p. 353.

70. Yergin, *Shattered Peace*, p. 354

71. Mitrovich, *Undermining the Kremlin*, p. 15.

72. Mitrovich, *Undermining the Kremlin*, pp. 32–35.

73. Peter Grose, *Operation Rollback: America's War Behind the Iron Curtain* (Boston: Houghton Mifflin, 2000), pp. 108–110.

74. Grose, *Operation Rollback*, pp. 116 and 124. The Economic Stabilization Fund (ESF) was originally established in 1934 with $2 billion designated for short-term currency trading to stabilize the value of the dollar in world trade. After the war, the bulk of the ESF was transferred to the International Monetary Fund, but $200 million was retained in the Treasury to help in unspecified ways in the "reconstruction and rehabilitation of war-torn countries." The fund was "under the exclusive control of the Secretary of the treasury, with the approval of the President, whose decisions shall be final and not subject to review by any other official." A reported $10 million was made available to the Office of Policy Coordination in its first year in addition to its authorized budget.

75. Modin, *My 5 Cambridge Friends*, pp. 186–187,

76. See Tom Bower, *The Red Web: MI6 and the KGB Master Coup* (London: Aurum Press, 1989), pp. 107–108, 137. Grose, *Operation Rollback*, provides a full-length study of the secret missions behind the Iron Curtain.

77. Harry Rositzke, *The CIA's Secret Operations* (New York: Reader's Digest Press, 1977), pp. 18–38.

78. In a letter to the authors, Mrs. Graham said she had no recollection of her late husband's knowledge of the VENONA material.

79. Katharine Graham, *Personal History* (New York: Random House, Vintage Books, 1998), pp. 202–203.

80. Graham, *Personal History*, p. 199.

Chapter 8—Cases of the Century

1. Whittaker Chambers, *Witness* (New York: Random House, 1952), pp. 463–470.

2. Chambers, *Witness*, pp. 470–471.

3. Neal Gabler, *Winchell* (New York: Knopf, 1994), p. 192.

4. Chambers, *Witness*, p. 382.

5. Bert and Peter Andrews, *A Tragedy of History: A Journalist's Confidential Role in the Hiss-Chambers Case* (Washington, DC: Robert B. Luce, 1962), p. 11.

6. David Rees, *Harry Dexter White: A Study in Paradox* (New York: Coward, McCann, and Geoghegan, 1973), p. 411

7. Rees, *Harry Dexter White*, p. 410.

8. Rees, *Harry Dexter White*, pp. 411–412.

9. Rees, *Harry Dexter White*, p. 413.

10. Silvermaster was never indicted and left Washington for a career as a builder in New Jersey after World War II.

11. Rees, *Harry Dexter White*, p. 413.

12. Rees, *Harry Dexter White*, p. 415.

13. *New York Times*, August 18, 1948.

14. Andrews, *A Tragedy of History*, p. 15.

15. Andrews, *A Tragedy of History*, p. 17.

16. Andrews, *A Tragedy of History*, p. 42.

17. Andrews, *A Tragedy of History*, p. 10.

18. Andrews, *A Tragedy of History*, pp. 1–18.

19. Andrews, *A Tragedy of History*, pp. 52–58.

20. Andrews, *A Tragedy of History*, pp. 152–161.

21. Interview with William P. Rogers, Washington, DC, July 1, 1997. See also *New York Times* obituary of Rogers, January 4, 2001, p. A22. Rogers was attorney general in the Eisenhower administration and secretary of state under President Nixon.

22. The term *red herring* originated in the 1800s when wily British fugitives discovered that rubbing a herring across their trail would divert the bloodhounds tracking them. Later, in debates and detective mysteries, red herring described any clever device used to distract people from the main issue. In the 1920s, American investment bankers began calling preliminary investment prospectuses with red covers "red herrings" as a warning to investors that the documents were not complete or final. "The Lore of Red Herring," *Red Herring* magazine, November 2001, p. 14.

23. Andrews, *A Tragedy of History*, pp. 166–169.

24. Andrews, *A Tragedy of History*, pp. 170–171.

25. Andrews, *A Tragedy of History*, p. 171.

26. Andrews, *A Tragedy of History*, pp. 172–173.

27. Andrews, *A Tragedy of History*, pp. 172–173. In 1939, Chambers told Isaac Don Levine he had documents and microfilm, without giving specific details. He said he was saving these proofs of his story for trading with the Soviet secret police in case his family was threatened (p. 40).

28. Andrews, *A Tragedy of History*, pp. 173–174.

29. Andrews, *A Tragedy of History*, p. ix.

30. Andrews, *A Tragedy of History*, p. 174.

31. Andrews, *A Tragedy of History*, pp. 175–176.

32. Andrews, *A Tragedy of History*, p. 177.

33. Andrews, *A Tragedy of History*, p. 178.

34. Andrews, *A Tragedy of History*, p. 179.

35. Andrews, *A Tragedy of History*, p. 184.
36. Andrews, *A Tragedy of History*, p. 202.
37. Andrews, *A Tragedy of History*, p. 219.
38. Andrews, *A Tragedy of History*, p. 222.
39. Interview with John Walsh, Washington, DC, January 2000.
40. Interview with John Walsh, Washington, DC, January 2000.
41. Interview with John Walsh, Washington, DC, January 2000.
42. Sam Tanenhaus, *Whittaker Chambers* (New York: Random House, 1997), p. 383.
43. Walter Goodman, *The Committee* (New York: Farrar, Straus and Giroux, 1968), pp. 260–261.
44. Richard Reeves, Foreword to Goodman, *The Committee*, p. ix.
45. Tony Hiss, *The View from Alger's Window: A Son's Memoir* (New York: Knopf, 1999).
46. Hede Massing, *This Deception* (New York: Duell, Sloan and Pearce, 1951), pp. 171–175.
47. Interview with Gerald S. J. Cassidy, Washington, DC, August 1, 2000.
48. Alger Hiss, *Recollections of a Life* (New York: Arcade, 1988).
49. At the time, Simes was at the Carnegie Endowment for International Peace helping to set up its Moscow office. He is currently president of the Nixon Center in Washington, DC.
50. Handwritten note in possession of D. Simes. Copy in authors' possession.
51. Herbert Romerstein and Eric Breindel, *The VENONA Secrets: Exposing Soviet Espionage and America's Traitors* (Washington, DC: Regnery, 2000), pp. 139–141.
52. Robert Louis Benson and Michael Warner, eds., *VENONA: Soviet Espionage and the American Response, 1939–1957* (Washington, DC: National Security Agency, Central Intelligence Agency, 1996), p. 423. See also appendix 9 in this book.
53. John Lowenthal, "VENONA and Alger Hiss," *Intelligence and National Security* 15, no. 3 (Autumn 2000). Lowenthal argues that Hiss could not have been a Soviet agent after 1938 because "in that year Hiss would have become too great a risk for any Soviet intelligence agency to use." It must not have been too great a risk for GRU operations in America since Hiss's control officer, General Mikhail Abramovitch Milshtein, a.k.a. Milsky, is known to have visited the United States in the spring and summer of 1944. His assignment was to meet with Hiss. Benson and Warner, *VENONA*, p. 112, documents Milshtein's visit to the U.S.
54. Robert J. Lamphere and Tom Schachtman, *The FBI-KGB War* (New York: Random House, 1986), pp. 132–160.
55. Interview with Aleksandr Feklisov, Moscow, October 1997.
56. Lamphere and Schachtman, *The FBI-KGB War*, p. 50.

57. Lamphere and Schachtman, *The FBI-KGB War*, p. 151.
58. Lamphere and Schachtman, *The FBI-KGB War*, p. 163.
59. Lamphere and Schachtman, *The FBI-KGB War*, pp. 170–171.
60. Lamphere and Schachtman, *The FBI-KGB War*, p. 177.
61. Rosenberg Case Summary, Domestic Intelligence Division, FBI, September 25, 1953, declassified December 29, 1953.
62. Rosenberg Case Summary, pp. 15a, 15b.
63. Rosenberg Case Summary, p. 24.
64. Rosenberg Case Summary, p. 23.
65. Interview with Robert Lamphere, Green Valley, Arizona, 1997. He also stated it publicly at VENONA Conference, Defense University, Washington, DC, October, 1996.
66. Ronald Radosh and Joyce Milton, *The Rosenberg File: A Search for the Truth* (New York: Holt, Rinehart and Winston, 1983), p. 70.
67. Rosenberg Case Summary, p. 27.
68. Radosh and Milton, *The Rosenberg File*, p. 72.
69. Rosenberg Case Summary, p. 31.
70. FBI Office Memorandum, "The Rosenberg Espionage Conspiracy, *Look* Magazine," September 25, 1953, FBI Reading Room, Washington, DC, p. 34.
71. Radosh and Milton, *The Rosenberg File*, pp. 162–169. Curt Gentry, *J. Edgar Hoover: The Man and His Secrets* (New York: W. W. Norton, 1991), pp. 420–423.
72. Under Canon 3 A(4) of the American Bar Association's Code of Judicial Conduct, adopted in 1972, *ex parte* communication is forbidden. In 1953, when this contact took place during the sentencing of the Rosenbergs, such conduct was considered permissible only in case of an extreme emergency, such as a death threat.
73. Gentry, *J. Edgar Hoover*, pp. 424–426.
74. Rosenberg Case Summary, p. 65.
75. New York 1600 to Moscow, November 14, 1944, VENONA; New York 1657 to Moscow, November 27, 1944, VENONA; New York 1715 to Moscow, December 5, 1944, VENONA; New York 1749–50 to Moscow, December 13, 1944, VENONA, in Benson and Warner, *VENONA*, pp. 365, 381, 385, 387, respectively.
76. John Earl Haynes and Harvey Klehr, *VENONA: Decoding Soviet Espionage in America* (New Haven, CT: Yale University Press, 1999), p. 36.
77. Interview with John L. Martin, Washington, D.C., June 15, 1998.
78. Sergei N. Khrushchev, *Nikita Khrushchev and the Creation of a Superpower* (University Park, PA: Pennsylvania State University Press, 2000), p. 165.
79. Radosh and Milton, *The Rosenberg File*, p. 391.
80. Joseph H. Sharlitt, *Fatal Error: The Miscarriage of Justice That Sealed the Rosenbergs' Fate* (New York: Scribner's, 1989), pp. 68–69.
81. Sharlitt, *Fatal Error*, p. 3.

82. Sharlitt, *Fatal Error*, p. 81.

83. Emmet John Hughes, *The Ordeal of Power: A Political Memoir of the Eisenhower Years* (New York: Atheneum, 1962), pp. 79–80.

84. Sharlitt, *Fatal Error*, pp. 147–195. Sharlitt argues that, in the Rosenberg case, "the majority of the Supreme Court was blind to it own misconduct. It was dead wrong in the result it reached. That combination resulted in two illegal executions."

85. Radosh and Milton, *The Rosenberg File*, p. 409.

86. Interview with former KGB General Oleg Kalugin, Karlshorst, Germany, September 1999.

87. Nikita Khrushchev, *Khrushchev Remembers: The Glasnost Tapes*, trans. and ed. Jerrold L. Schecter, with Vyacheslav V. Luchkov (Boston: Little, Brown, 1991), p. 194.

88. Morris and Lona Cohen fled from the U.S. in 1950 when the Rosenbergs were arrested. They were trained in Moscow to resume their espionage career in Great Britain under cover as Peter and Helen Kroger, rare book dealers. They were arrested in Great Britain and sentenced to 20 years in prison. In 1969 the Krogers were traded for British citizens held by the Soviets and they settled in Moscow. Lona died in 1992, Morris, in 1995. See Joseph Albright and Marcia Kunstel, *Bombshell: The Secret Story of America's Unknown Atomic Spy Conspiracy* (New York: Random House, Times Books, 1997).

89. Sudoplatov et al., *Special Tasks*, p. 218. Haynes and Klehr, *VENONA*, describe the work of Julius Rosenberg's network of communist engineers, pp. 295–304.

90. *The Rosenberg File Case Closed*, Discovery Channel, March 23, 1997.

91. Khrushchev, *Khrushchev Remembers*.

92. Irving Kristol, "Liberalism and American Jews," *Commentary*, October 1988, pp. 19–23.

93. Kristol, "Liberalism and American Jews," pp. 19–23.

94. Kristol, "Liberalism and American Jews," pp. 19–23.

Chapter 9—The Fifties

1. Editorial by Karl Meyer in the *Daily Cardinal*, the University of Wisconsin-Madison.

2. Unpublished interview with Clement Greenberg, New York City, 1994, by Florence Rubenfeld during research for *Clement Greenberg: A Life* (New York: Scribner's, 1997).

3. A total of 40,000 non-U.S. troops from UN member nations were sent to Korea, of which 3,896 were killed and 16,441 were wounded. These latest figures and estimates are from a forthcoming book by Allan R. Millett, *Their War for Korea: Americans, Asian, and European Combatants and Civilians, 1945–53*, (Dulles, VA: Brassey's, Inc., 2002).

4. George McCune, *Korea Today* (Cambridge, MA: Harvard University Press, 1950), p. 4.

5. Georgi K. Zhukov and [Yevgeni S.] Zabrodin, *Korea: Short Report*, June 29, 1945, AVP RF [Archive of Foreign Policy, Russian Federation], Fond [reference file] 0430, Opis [document no.] 2, Delo [case] 18, Papka [file] 5, 1, pp. 18–30. Quoted in Kathryn Weathersby, *Soviet Aims in Korea and the Origins of the Korean War, 1945–1950: New Evidence from Russian Archives*, Cold War International History Project (Washington, DC: Woodrow Wilson International Center for Scholars, November 1993), pp. 6–7.

6. Zhukov and Zabrodin, *Korea: Short Report*, pp. 18–30.

7. [Yevgeni S.] Zabrodin, "The Question of a Single Provisional Government for Korea," December 1945, *Korea, Short Report*, 1, pp. 11–17. Quoted in Weathersby, *Soviet Aims in Korea*, p. 14.

8. Mao Zedong, *On the People's Democratic Dictatorship*, June 30, 1949, Selected Works (Beijing: The People's Press, 1965), pp. iv, 1477. Quoted in Jian Chien, *The Sino-Soviet Alliance and China's Entry into the Korean War*, Working Paper no. 1, Cold War International History Project (Washington, DC: Woodrow Wilson International Center for Scholars, June 1992), p. 1.

9. N. S. Khrushchev, *Khrushchev Remembers*, trans. and ed. Strobe Talbott (Boston: Little, Brown, 1970), pp. 367–368; and Nikita Khrushchev, *Khrushchev Remembers: The Glasnost Tapes*, trans. and ed. Jerrold L. Schecter, with Vyacheslav Luchkov (Boston: Little, Brown, 1991), p. 143.

10. Robert Louis Benson and Michael Warner, *VENONA: Soviet Espionage and the American Response, 1939–1957* (Washington, DC: National Security Agency, Central Intelligence Agency, 1996), include three messages, nos. 54, 61, and 65, that refer to Soviet efforts to recruit Stone as a paid "probationer," or agent. Also see Herbert Romerstein and Eric Breindel, *The VENONA Secrets: Exposing Soviet Espionage and America's Traitors* (Washington, DC: Regnery, 2000), pp. 337–339. John Earl Haynes and Harvey Klehr, *VENONA: Decoding Soviet Espionage in America* (New Haven, CT: Yale University Press, 1999), pp. 247–249.

11. Yuri Modin, with Jean-Charles Deniau and Aguieszka Ziarek, *My 5 Cambridge Friends, Burgess, Maclean, Philby, Blunt and Cairncross, by Their KGB Controller* (New York: Farrar, Straus and Giroux, 1994), p. 181.

12. Verne W. Newton, *The Cambridge Spies: The Untold Story of Maclean, Philby and Burgess in America* (Lanham, MD: Madison Books, 1991), p. 264. Newton's chapter 17, "Burgess: The Pathos of Treachery," is a brilliant portrait of the man whose enforced exile in Moscow ended with his pathetic death there from alcoholism at age 49.

13. Modin, *My 5 Cambridge Friends*, p. 181.

14. Stanley Weintraub, *MacArthur's War: Korea and the Undoing of an American Hero* (New York: Free Press, 2000), p. 251.

15. Richard Whelan, *Drawing the Line: The Korean War, 1950–1953* (Boston: Little, Brown, 1990), pp. 254–255.

16. Weintraub, *MacArthur's War*, pp. 268–269.

17. Weintraub, *MacArthur's War*, p. 258.

18. Newton, *The Cambridge Spies*, p. 286.

19. Modin, *My 5 Cambridge Friends*, p. 183.

20. Weintraub, *MacArthur's War*, p. 262. Dean Acheson, *Present at the Creation* (New York: W. W. Norton, 1969), p. 484.

21. Modin, *My 5 Cambridge Friends*, p. 183.

22. Newton, *The Cambridge Spies*, pp. 407–408, fn. 13.

23. William Manchester, *American Caesar: Douglas MacArthur, 1880–1964* (Boston: Little, Brown, 1978), p. 597.

24. Michael Chabon, *The Amazing Adventures of Kavalier and Clay* (New York: Random House, 2000), p. 623.

25. Lee Edwards, *The Conservative Revolution: The Movement that Remade America* (New York: Free Press, 1999), p. 42.

26. Interview with Robert Lamphere, Green Valley, Arizona, March 15, 1999.

27. Confidential source, Washington, DC, 1999.

28. David Rees, *Harry Dexter White: A Study in Paradox* (New York: Coward, McCann, and Geoghegan, 1973), pp. 420–422.

29. *New York Times*, November 17, 1953.

30. Walter Goodman, *The Committee* (New York: Farrar, Straus and Giroux, 1968), p. 348.

31. Bruce Craig, *Treasonable Doubt: The Harry Dexter White Case, 1948–1953* (Ph.D. thesis, Washington, DC, American University, 1999), p. 472.

32. During a hearing involving the Army in June 1954, McCarthy viciously attacked a young lawyer for having belonged to the Lawyer's Guild, an organization suspected of left wing activities. Counsel to the Army Joseph Nye Welch posed the famous question to Senator McCarthy: "Little did I dream you could be so reckless and so cruel. . . . Have you no sense of decency, sir. . . . Have you left no sense of decency?" With Welch's question, the tide of public opinion turned against McCarthy and ended his reign of civil terror based on unsubstantiated accusations.

33. James Shepley and Clay Blair, Jr., *The Hydrogen Bomb* (New York: David McKay, 1954; reprint, Westport, CT: Greenwood Press, 1971), p. 139.

34. John Major, *The Oppenheimer Hearing* (New York: Stein and Day, 1971), p. 55. DeSilva, who had a distinguished career in the CIA in Eastern Europe and the Far East, was writing a book critical of Oppenheimer and his communist ties when he died.

35. Major, *The Oppenheimer Hearing*, pp 55–57.

36. United States Atomic Energy Commission, *In the Matter of J. Robert Oppenheimer, Transcript of Hearing Before Personnel Security Board, Washington, D.C., April 12, 1954 through May 6, 1954* (Washington, DC: U.S. Government Printing Office, 1954), pp. 3–7.

37. Major, *The Oppenheimer Hearing*, p. 16.

38. *Time*, November 8, 1948, quoted in Major, *The Oppenheimer Hearing*, p. 88.

39. Philip M. Stern, *The Oppenheimer Case* (New York: Harper and Row, 1969), pp. 161–163. In 1950 when Sylvia Crouch testified before the California Senate Fact Finding Committee on Un-American Activities, she identified Oppenheimer as being present at a closed meeting of a special section of the Communist Party in June 1941. Nixon, who was then a member of the House Committee on Un-American Activities and knew Oppenheimer, was asked to comment on Sylvia Crouch's charges. Nixon said, "I am convinced that Dr. Oppenheimer has been and is a completely loyal American and further, one to whom the United States owes a great debt of gratitude for his tireless and magnificent job in atomic research" (p. 163).

40. Allen Weinstein and Alexander Vassiliev, *The Haunted Wood* (New York: Random House, 1999), p. 137, recount the story of Boris Morros, the counterspy who pretended to work for the Soviets, but was actually under FBI control; he planned to fake a kidnapping of Oppenheimer in 1945 to bring him to Moscow to work for the Soviets. The idea never got beyond the talking stage.

41. Major, *The Oppenheimer Hearing*, p. 35.

42. Major, *The Oppenheimer Hearing*, p. 88.

43. Major, *The Oppenheimer Hearing*, p. 58.

44. Major, *The Oppenheimer Hearing*, pp. 93–95.

45. Acheson, *Present at the Creation*, pp. 151–156. For Baruch's disagreements with Acheson and the original drafters of the plan, see Jordan A. Schwarz, *The Speculator: Bernard Baruch in Washington, 1917–1965* (Chapel Hill, NC: University of North Carolina Press, 1981), pp. 490–507.

46. Major, *The Oppenheimer Hearing*, p. 74.

47. Major, *The Oppenheimer Hearing*, pp. 152–153.

48. Major, *The Oppenheimer Hearing*, p. 105.

49. U.S. Atomic Energy Commission, *In the Matter of J. Robert Oppenheimer, Transcript*, pp. 7, 326, 328, 959. Major, *The Oppenheimer Hearing*, p. 107.

50. Major, *The Oppenheimer Hearing*, pp. 148–149. Robert A. Pape, *Bombing to Win: Air Power and Coercion in War* (Ithaca, NY: Cornell University Press, 1996).

51. Richard Rhodes, *Dark Sun* (New York: Simon and Schuster, 1996), pp. 320–321.

52. Joseph W. Alsop, with Adam Platt, *"I've Seen the Best of It": Memoirs* (New York: W. W. Norton, 1992), p. 352.

53. Alsop, *I've Seen the Best of It*, p. 353.

54. Herbert F. York, *The Advisors: Oppenheimer, Teller and the Superbomb* (Stanford, CA: Stanford University Press, 1976), pp. 121–133.

55. Major, *The Oppenheimer Hearing*, p. 102.

56. Interview with Dr. Edward Teller, Stanford, California, November 18, 1998.

57. Interview with Dr. Edward Teller, Stanford, California, November 18, 1998.

58. Walter Pincus, "Nuclear Expert Challenges U.S. Thinking on Warheads:

Guided Conventional Explosives Called Good Replacement," *Washington Post*, October 24, 2000, p. A3.

Chapter 10—The Beginning of the End of the Soviet Empire

1. Abel was a code word, the name Fisher would give American police if he were arrested. It was the signal to Soviet intelligence, when his arrest was announced in the press, that he had been compromised.
2. Christopher Andrew and Vasili Mitrokhin, *The Sword and the Shield: The Mitrokhin Archive and the Secret History of the KGB* (New York: Basic Books, 1999), pp. 146–147.
3. Robert J. Lamphere and Tom Schachtman, *The FBI-KGB War* (New York: Random House, 1986), pp. 270–277, and photo of Helen Sobell.
4. Robert Low, *La Pasionara: The Spanish Firebrand* (London: Hutchinson, 1992), pp. 133–137.
5. Russian Intelligence Archives.
6. John Earl Haynes and Harvey Klehr, *VENONA: Decoding Soviet Espionage in America* (New Haven, CT: Yale University Press, 1999), pp. 202–204, describe Duggan's role in the communist underground. Duggan committed suicide in August 1948.
7. The letter was stored in a special envelope in volume 12 of the MAKS file in SVR archives.
8. In Grigulevich's file is a report from Aleksandr Koratkov to Beria asking him to recall MAKS to Moscow for consultations. Note by Beria to Sudoplatov and Sudoplatov's notation agreeing to recall MAKS.
9. Pavel Sudoplatov and Anatoli Sudoplatov, with Jerrold L. and Leona P. Schecter, *Special Tasks: The Memoirs of an Unwanted Witness—A Soviet Spymaster* (New York: Little, Brown, 1994), p. 243.
10. Simona was attached to Enrique Lister, commander of the Fifth Regiment, the communist arm of the Spanish Republican forces.
11. General Yuri Drozdov, "The Best Friend of Dictator Stroessner" (an essay about Filonenko), *Izvestia*, April 17, 1999.
12. George F. Kennan, *Memoirs, 1925–1950* (Boston: Little, Brown, 1967), pp. 84–85.
13. Interview with Martha Mautner, Washington, DC, 2000. Ms. Mautner began her State Department career in Moscow in September 1945 and later served in the Bureau of Intelligence and Research from 1965 to 1993; she heard the story from Kelley.
14. Kennan, *Memoirs*, pp. 84–85.
15. Ivy Low Litvinov, Oral History, box 1, Hoover Institution Archives, Stanford, CA.
16. Sudoplatov et al., *Special Tasks*, p. 227.
17. Ivy Low Litvinov, Oral History, box 1.

18. Ivy Low Litvinov, Oral History, box 1.

19. Ivy Low Litvinov, Oral History, box 1.

20. Elena S. Danielson, "The Elusive Litvinov Memoirs," *Slavic Review* 48, no. 3 (fall 1989): 481.

21. Maxim Litvinov, *Notes for a Journal* (London: André Deutsch, 1955).

22. Danielson, "The Elusive Litvinov Memoirs," p. 483.

23. In 1928, Briand was cosponsor of the French-American design, the Kellogg-Briand Pact, to outlaw aggressive war. *An Encyclopedia of World History* (Boston: Houghton Mifflin, 1940), p. 960.

24. *Encyclopedia of World History*, p. 960.

25. Ivy Low Litvinov, Oral History, box 1.

26. John Carswell, *The Exile: A Life of Ivy Litvinov* (London: Faber and Faber, 1983), p. 154.

27. John Lewis Gaddis, *We Now Know: Rethinking Cold War History* (Oxford: Oxford University Press, 1997), pp. 23–24.

28. Ivy Low Litvinov, Oral History, box 1.

29. N. S. Khrushchev, *Khrushchev Remembers*, trans. and ed. Strobe Talbott (Boston: Little, Brown, 1970), p. 350.

30. Khrushchev, *Khrushchev Remembers*, p. 346.

31. Khrushchev, *Khrushchev Remembers*, p. 345.

32. Khrushchev, *Khrushchev Remembers*, p. 604.

33. Peter Grose, *Gentleman Spy: The Life of Allen Dulles* (Boston: Houghton Mifflin, 1994), p. 424.

34. Grose, *Gentleman Spy*, pp. 419–425.

35. Ray S. Cline, *The CIA Under Reagan, Bush and Casey* (Washington, DC: Acropolis Books, 1991), p. 186.

36. Grose, *Gentleman Spy*, pp. 425–426.

37. Cline, *The CIA Under Reagan, Bush and Casey*, p. 185.

38. Telephone interview with Victor Grajewski in Jerusalem, December 15, 2000.

39. Cline, *The CIA Under Reagan, Bush and Casey*, p. 14.

Chapter 11—The Secrets of Khrushchev's Memoirs

1. Inessa Stephan, a French-born governess in Moscow, married Alexander Armand, the son of a wealthy merchant, with whom she had five children; she later ran off with her husband's younger brother, Vladimir. Involved in illegal propaganda activities, she was arrested for the third time in 1907 and sentenced to internal exile in the north above Archangel. She fled to Switzerland in 1909 to be with Vladimir, who soon died. She met and fell in love with Lenin in Paris and lived with him until her death from cholera in 1920. Historian Dmitri Volkogonov wrote of Inessa: "beautiful, elegant and full of creative energy . . . Lenin was unable to suppress the strong feelings she evoked in him." In *Lenin: A New Biography* (New York: Free Press, 1994), pp. 35–43.

2. Valery Tarsis' book, *Ward 7* (New York: E. P. Dutton, 1965), about his experience, was smuggled out and published in the West. The KGB threatened him with a "road accident." He is said to have replied, "What of it? A crown of thorns will suit me very well. Remember, no one will believe you even if I am run over by accident or a brick falls on my head. Abroad, they will still think that the blood-stained secret police killed Tarsis. Therefore, not only will you not kill me, you'll look after me and move heaven and earth to see that I don't die."

3. Michael Scammell, *Solzhenitsyn* (London: Hutchinson, 1985), p. 624.

4. Molotov met for 140 in-depth conversations with the poet and biographer Felix Chuev over 17 years before his death in 1986. Chuev's work was published in Russian in 1991 and appeared in English in 1993 as *Molotov Remembers: Inside Kremlin Politics—Conversations with Felix Chuev*, ed. Albert Resis (Chicago: Ivan R. Dee, 1993).

5. See Sergei Khrushchev, *Khrushchev on Khrushchev: An Inside Account of the Man and His Era, by His Son, Sergei Khrushchev*, ed. and trans. William Taubman (Boston: Little, Brown, 1990), pp. 63–64, ed. note 31, and pp. 234–235.

6. In September 1953, Khrushchev replaced Georgi Malenkov as first secretary of the Communist Party of the Soviet Union; in 1958, he replaced Nikolai Bulganin as prime minister. He held both the top party and government positions until Leonid Brezhnev replaced him as first secretary; Alexei Kosygin replaced him as prime minister in a bloodless coup in 1964.

7. Andropov was the KGB chairman from 1967 to 1982 when he became general secretary, which post he held until his death on February 9, 1984.

8. In his unpublished autobiography, Victor Louis wrote of his baptism and made no mention of Jewish relatives. Michael Scammell wrote that Victor Louis' "real name was Vitaly Levin, and he had spent a number of years in the labor camps where his 'good behavior' and co-operation with the authorities had earned him a Moscow residence permit and complete freedom to travel abroad." See Scammell, *Solzhenitsyn*, p. 624.

9. Simultaneously, KGB *rezidenturas* in Europe and North America began spreading the same rumors. The campaign may have helped pressure the Chinese into reopening their talks on the border dispute with Moscow, but it also served to move Mao Zedong toward rapprochement with the United States. See Christopher Andrew and Oleg Gordievsky, *KGB: The Inside Story* (New York: HarperCollins, 1990), p. 494.

10. N. S. Khrushchev, *Khrushchev Remembers*, trans. and ed. Strobe Talbott (Boston: Little, Brown, 1970), trans. and ed. note, p. xxi.

11. Khrushchev, *Khrushchev Remembers*, p. 128.

12. See *Khrushchev Remembers: The Last Testament* (Boston: Little, Brown, 1974), pp. xvi–xvii.

13. Khrushchev, *Khrushchev on Khrushchev*, pp. 233–321.

14. Strobe Talbott's private journal, unpublished.

15. Mikhail Mikhailovich Zoshchenko (1864–1958), a satirical writer who wrote short stories in the first person about Soviet Archie Bunker–type characters, the ordinary man who was disbelieving of the grandiose fiction of the "construction of socialism."

16. Khruschev, *Khrushchev Remembers: The Last Testament*, pp. xvi–xvii.

17. Those who attended: George Kennan, Zbigniew Brzezinski, Harrison Salisbury, Peter Reddaway, Priscilla Johnson McMillan, Seweryn Bialer, Adam Ulam, Stephen Cohen, Robert Tucker, and Michel Tatu.

18. Leonid Brezhnev died in 1982.

19. Khrushchev, *Khrushchev on Khrushchev*, pp. 314–318.

20. Khrushchev, *Khrushchev on Khrushchev*, p. 251.

21. Dmitri Volkogonov, *Lenin: A New Biography*, trans. and ed. Harold Shukman (New York: Free Press, 1994), pp. 317–318, quoted from the Archives of the President of the Russian Federation.

22. Volkogonov, *Lenin*, p. 318.

23. Khrushchev, *Khrushchev on Khruschchev*, pp. 288–289.

24. Biryukov was mysteriously beaten to death in Moscow in 1996, and stripped of his new car and his clothes.

25. Talbott and Brooke Shearer were married in Los Angeles on November 14, 1971.

Chapter 12—The Overflight Wars

1. Paul Lashmar, *Spy Flights of the Cold War* (Annapolis, MD: Naval Institute Press, 1996), p. 30.

2. Lashmar, *Spy Flights of the Cold War*, and R. Cargill Hall, "Strategic Reconnaissance in the Cold War," Prologue, *Quarterly of the National Archives and Records Administration* 28, no. 2 (summer 1996): 113–114.

3. Hall, "Strategic Reconnaissance in the Cold War," fn. 34, p. 124. R. Cargill Hall, "Origins of U.S. Space Policy: Eisenhower, Open Skies and Freedom of Space" in *Exploring the Unknown: Selected Documents in the History of the U.S. Civil Space Program*, vol. 1: *Organizing for Exploration*, ed. John M. Logsdon (Washington, DC: NASA, 1955), p. 216. Hall presents a richly researched history of the American space program.

4. Harry Rozitske, *The CIA's Secret Operations* (New York: Reader's Digest Press, 1977), pp. 57–59.

5. Telephone interview with Oliver Kirby, June 5, 2001.

6. Hall, "Origins of U.S. Space Policy," p. 217.

7. Gregory W. Pedlow and Donald E. Welzenbach, *The CIA and the U-2 Program, 1954–1974* (Washington, DC: Center for the Study of Intelligence, CIA), p. 19.

8. Quoted in Pedlow and Welzenbach, *The CIA and the U-2 Program*, p. 19.

9. Dino A. Brugioni, *Eyeball to Eyeball: The Inside Story of the Cuban Missile Crisis* (New York: Random House, 1990), p. 7.

10. Brig. Gen. George W. Goddard, with DeWitt S. Copp, *Overview: A Lifelong Adventure in Aerial Photography* (Garden City, NY: Doubleday, 1969), p. 381.

11. Brugioni, *Eyeball to Eyeball,* p. 9.

12. Brugioni, *Eyeball to Eyeball,* p. 9.

13. Allen Dulles, *The Craft of Intelligence* (New York: Harper and Row, 1963), p. 149.

14. Dulles, *The Craft of Intelligence,* p. 10

15. Brugioni, *Eyeball to Eyeball,* p. 12.

16. Brugioni, *Eyeball to Eyeball,* pp. 12–13.

17. William E. Burrows, *Deep Black: Space Espionage and National Security* (New York: Random House, 1986), p. 95, describes U.S. SIGINT sites in Turkey.

18. Corona was the program's classified name. To conceal the reconnaissance satellite and its recovery program, Under Secretary of Defense Donald Quarles "canceled" the recovery component of the program. He then authorized the Air Force Discover Project, which would develop a "biomedical capsule" for the recovery of biological specimens shot into space on top of Thor-Agena launch vehicles. The directive for the new biomedical space project said it was expected to contribute to America's early achievement of manned space flight. Actually, the recovery program was for the film ejected from the reconnaissance satellite and collected in midair by aircraft, or in the sea if aerial recovery failed. See R. Cargill Hall, "Postwar Strategic Reconnaissance and the Genesis of Corona," in *Eye In The Sky: The Story of the Corona Spy Satellites,* ed. Dwayne A. Day, John M. Logsdon, and Brian Latell (Washington, DC: Smithsonian Institution Press, 1998), p. 113.

19. Kevin C. Ruffner, ed., *Corona: America's First Satellite Program* (Washington, DC: CIA History Staff Center for the Study of Intelligence, 1995), p. 2. R. Cargill Hall, "The Eisenhower Administration and the Cold War: Framing American Astronautics to Serve National Security," Prologue, *Quarterly of the National Archives* 27, no. 1 (spring 1995): 68.

20. David P. Lindgren, *Trust But Verify* (Annapolis, MD: Naval Institute Press, 2000), pp. 114, 182–192, describes the political infighting among the Air Force, the CIA, and the Pentagon in the continuing struggle to determine who controls overhead reconnaissance. The 1996 reorganization created a National Imagery and Mapping Office (NIMA) under the Pentagon.

21. Brugioni, *Eyeball to Eyeball,* pp. 36–37

22. John Prados, *The Soviet Estimate* (Princeton, NJ: Princeton University Press, 1982), p. 111.

23. William Randolph Hearst, Bob Considine, and Frank Conniff, *Khrushchev and the Russian Challenge* (New York: Avon Books, 1961), p. 249.

24. Quoted by Lars-Erik Nelson in the *New York Review of Books,* December 21, 2000, p. 6, from Sessions of the Senate Foreign Relations Committee Together with the Joint Sessions with the Senate Armed Services Committee (Historical Series), vol. 11, pp. 33ff, Library of Congress Law Library, microfiche.

25. Christopher Matthews, *Kennedy and Nixon: The Rivalry That Shaped Postwar America* (New York: Simon and Schuster, Touchstone Books, 1997), p. 168.

26. Burrows, *Deep Black*, p. 57.

27. Jerrold L. Schecter and Peter Deriabin, *The Spy Who Saved the World* (New York: Scribner's, 1992), pp. 273–279.

28. Schecter and Deriabin, *The Spy Who Saved the World*, pp. 271–299. Prados, *The Soviet Estimate*, chapter 8, "The End of the Missile Gap," offers rich detail on the interservice rivalry and Air Force efforts to influence budgeting for missiles and bombers by maintaining a high estimate for Soviet missile strength.

29. Dwight D. Eisenhower, *Waging Peace* (New York: Doubleday, 1965), p. 559.

30. John Ranelagh, *The Agency: The Rise and Decline of the CIA* (New York: Simon and Schuster, 1986), pp. 249–382.

31. Arthur Krock, *Memoirs: Sixty Years on the Firing Line* (New York: Funk and Wagnall's, 1968), pp. 379–380.

32. Interview with John McCone, Seattle, Washington, August 29, 1988.

33. Interview with John McCone, Seattle, Washington, August 29, 1988.

34. Raymond L. Garthoff, *Reflections on the Cuban Missile Crisis*, rev. ed. (Washington, DC: Brookings Institution, 1989), pp. 29–30. At a conference on the Cuban Missile Crisis in Moscow in 1989, Dobrynin told Garthoff he had not been informed the missiles were being deployed. Ex-Foreign Minister Andrei Gromyko, who also attended the conference, joked with Dobrynin and said, "Oh, I must have forgotten to tell you."

35. Garthoff, *Reflections on the Cuban Missile Crisis*, pp. 47–48.

36. Interview with Richard Helms, Washington, DC, December 8, 1990.

37. Stewart Alsop, *The Center* (New York: Harper and Row, 1968), p. 207.

38. N. S. Khrushchev, *Khrushchev Remembers*, trans. and ed. Strobe Talbott (Boston: Little, Brown, 1970), p. 494.

39. Brugioni, *Eyeball to Eyeball*, p. 232.

40. Nikita Khrushchev, *Khrushchev Remembers: The Glasnost Tapes*, trans. and ed. Jerrold Schecter, with Vyacheslav V. Luchkov (Boston: Little, Brown, 1991), p. 173.

41. Aleksandr Fursenko and Timothy Naftali, *"One Hell of a Gamble," The Secret History of the Cuban Missile Crisis, Khrushchev, Castro and Kennedy, 1958–1964* (New York: W. W. Norton, 1997), pp. 182–183.

42. Khrushchev, *Khrushchev Remembers*, trans. and ed. Strobe Talbott, p. 494.

43. Khrushchev, *Khrushchev Remembers*, trans. and ed. Strobe Talbott, p. 493.

44. Krock, *Memoirs*, p. 380. In their reexamination of the Cuban Missile Crisis, James G. Blight and David A. Welch, *On the Brink* (New York: Hill and Wang, 1989), p. 169, make the case that McNamara, Rusk, and the other doves in the EXCOM placed less emphasis and concern on the nuclear balance than did McCone and the more experienced hawks such as Paul Nitze and Douglas Dillon. It was McCone's understanding of Khrushchev's concern for the nu-

clear balance that led him to intuit and argue that the Soviet Union was placing missiles in Cuba and should be aggressively challenged. McNamara, less experienced in cold war crises, had a higher threshold for fear regarding escalation to nuclear war under the new conditions of mutual vulnerability.

45. McGeorge Bundy, *Danger and Survival: Choices About the Bomb in the First Fifty Years* (New York: Random House, 1988), p. 462.
46. Brugioni, *Eyeball to Eyeball*, p. 58.
47. John Lewis Gaddis, *We Now Know: Rethinking Cold War History* (Oxford: Oxford University Press, 1997), pp. 271–272.
48. Stanley Karnow, *Vietnam: A History* (New York: Viking Press, 1983), pp. 304–311.
49. Gaddis, *We Now Know*, p. 252.
50. Confidential source.
51. Confidential source.
52. Confidential source.
53. Confidential source.
54. Malcolm McConnell, *Inside Hanoi's Secret Archives* (New York: Simon and Schuster, 1995), pp. 282–293. McConnell interviewed former Soviet Air Force fighter pilot Alexander Zuyev, who defected through Turkey with a MIG-29. He quotes Zuyev as being told that the unique dual-channel arming procedure for tactical nuclear bombs was adopted from American techniques in the 1970s. Before Zuyev defected to the West, a nuclear weapons officer at his base in Central Asia told him: "The American methods we obtained from several U.S. Air Force 'guests,' nuclear qualified pilots our fraternal Socialist comrades in Vietnam provided us during that Imperialist war."
55. Henry Kissinger, *White House Years* (Boston: Little, Brown, 1979), pp. 1151–1154.
56. Robert M. Gates, *From The Shadows: The Ultimate Insider's Story of Five Presidents and How They Won the Cold War* (New York: Simon and Schuster, 1996), pp. 122–123.
57. Gates, *From the Shadows*, pp. 131–133.
58. Zbigniew Brzezinski, *Power and Principle: Memoirs of the National Security Adviser, 1977–1981* (New York: Farrar, Straus and Giroux, 1983), pp. 448–449.
59. Brzezinski, "Toward a Strategic Relationship," pp. 403–425, and "The Carter Doctrine," pp. 426–469, in *Power and Principle*. Also interview with Zbigniew Brzezinski, Washington, DC, July 25, 2001.
60. Miles Copeland, "The Functioning of Strategic Intelligence," *Defense and Foreign Affairs Digest*, September 9, 1968, p. 30, quoted in R. Cargill Hall, "The Eisenhower Administration and the Cold War: Framing American Astronautics to Serve National Security," Prologue, *Quarterly of the National Archives and Records Administration* 27, no. 1 (spring 1995): 68.
61. Lindgren, *Trust But Verify*, pp. 125–126.
62. Robert McNamara had predicted the Soviet Union would stop ICBM produc-

tion when they had built 1,000 missiles; his prediction was part of his rationale for the policy of mutually assured destruction (MAD) in 1962.

63. Lindgren, *Trust But Verify*, p. 122.
64. Burrows, *Deep Black*, p. 25.
65. Burrows, *Deep Black*, pp. 244–245.
66. Lindgren, *Trust But Verify*, p. 146.
67. Pete Early, *Confessions of a Spy: The Real Story of Aldrich Ames* (New York: Putnam's Sons, 1997), p. 120.
68. Lindgren, *Trust But Verify*, p. 147.
69. SALT II established a ceiling on delivery systems—heavy bombers, ICBM launchers, and submarine launchers—of 2,400. For MIRV systems and air-launched cruise missiles, the aggregate number was not to exceed 1,320. For MIRVed missiles alone, the number was 1,200 and for land-based MIRVs, the limit was 820, the number possessed by the Soviets at that time.
70. Brzezinski, *Power and Principle*, p. 342.
71. Lindgren, *Trust But Verify*, p. 152.
72. Richard Kokoski and Sergey Koulik, ed., "National Technical Means," *Verification of Conventional Arms Control in Europe* (Boulder, CO: Westview Press, 1990), pp. 17–31.
73. Telephone interview with Joseph Charyk, January 2001.
74. Burroughs, *Deep Black*, pp. 244–245.
75. Art Wolinsky, *The History of the Internet and the World Wide Web* (Berkley Heights, NJ: Enslow, 1999), pp. 8–14.

Chapter 13—Deception and Revelation

1. Interview with Edwin Rowny, Washington, DC, December 29, 2001.
2. Edward Teller, with Judith Shoolery, *Memoirs: A Twentieth-Century Journey in Science and Politics* (Cambridge, MA: Perseus, 2001), pp. 508–509.
3. Michael R. Beschloss and Strobe Talbott, *At the Highest Levels* (Boston: Little, Brown, 1993), p. 113.
4. Christopher Andrew and Oleg Gordievsky, *Instructions from the Center: TOP SECRET Files on KGB Operations 1975–1985* (London: Sceptre, 1993), p. 111.
5. Andrew and Gordievsky, *Instructions from the Center*, pp. 112–116. For a detailed analysis of Operation Ryan, see Christopher Andrew and Oleg Gordievsky, *KGB: The Inside Story* (New York: HarperCollins, 1990), pp. 583–591.
6. Edmund Morris, *Dutch: A Memoir of Ronald Reagan* (New York: Random House, 1999), p. 474.
7. Frances Fitzgerald, *Way Out There in the Blue: Reagan, Star Wars and the End of the Cold War* (New York: Simon and Schuster, 2000), pp. 127–129.
8. Interview with Dr. Edward Teller, Stanford, California, November 11, 1998.
9. Tim Weiner, "Lies and Rigged 'Star Wars' Test Fooled the Kremlin and Congress," *New York Times*, August 18, 1993, p. A1, and "Inquiry Finds 'Star

Wars' Tried Plan to Exaggerate Test Results," *New York Times*, July 23, 1984, p. A1.

10. David P. Lindgren, *Trust But Verify* (Annapolis, MD: Naval Institute Press, 2000), p. 167.

11. Gorbachev pleaded ignorance of the scope of the disaster and blamed "the closed nature of the nuclear power industry" and just about everybody but himself and the Kremlin leadership. "The Cold War and the mutual secrecy of the two military alliances had also been a factor," Gorbachev wrote in Mikhail Gorbachev, *Memoirs* (New York: Doubleday, 1995), pp. 189–193.

12. Lindgren, *Trust But Verify*, p.168, quoting Jeffery T. Richelson, "The Future of Space Reconnaissance," *Scientific America* (January 1991): 41.

13. Lindgren, *Trust But Verify*, p. 168.

14. Beschloss and Talbott, *At the Highest Levels*, p. 113.

15. Edmund Morris, *Dutch*, pp. 598–599.

16. Weiner, "Lies and Rigged 'Star Wars' Test."

17. Weiner, "Lies and Rigged 'Star Wars' Test."

18. Weiner, "Inquiry Finds 'Star Wars' Tried Plan."

19. Fitzgerald, *Way Out There in the Blue*, pp. 488–489.

20. Interview with David S. C. Chu, Washington, DC, January 2001.

21. Interview with David S. C. Chu, Washington, DC, January 2001.

22. Interview with Vladimir Kryuchkov, Moscow, 1994.

23. The Central Intelligence Agency Estimate, January 9, 1964.

24. Charles Wolf, Jr., comments at CIA conference on "CIA's Analysis of the Soviet Union 1947–1991," Princeton University, Princeton, NJ, March 9–10, 2001.

25. Abraham S. Becker, comments at CIA conference.

26. James Milar, comments at CIA conference.

27. Interview with Sergo Beria by Vyacheslav Luchkov, Kiev, 1996.

Conclusion—Looking Back, Looking Forward

1. Christopher Andrew and Vasili Mitrokhin, *The Sword and the Shield: The Mitrokhin Archive and the Secret History of the KGB* (New York: HarperCollins, 1999), provides a staggering amount of KGB archival material on clandestine operations. Mitrokhin, a KGB officer assigned to vet the files, hid the documents and then arranged for them to be spirited abroad by MI-6 when he defected to Great Britain.

2. Telephone interview with John Deutsch, February 2, 2001.

3. Robert W. Hunter, *Spy Hunter: Inside the FBI Investigation of the Walker Espionage Case* (Annapolis, MD: Naval Institute Press, 1999), pp. 222–242.

4. Hunter, *Spy Hunter*, pp. 5–6.

5. Jim McGee and Brian Duffy, *Main Justice: The Men and Women Who Enforce the Nation's Criminal Laws and Guard Its Liberties* (New York: Simon and Schuster, 1996), pp. 320–343.

6. See Eliot A. Cohen, "Defending America in the Twenty-first Century," *Foreign Affairs* 79, no. 6 (November/December 2000): 40–56.

7. Anatol Lieven, "Soldiers before Missiles: Meeting the Challenge from the World's Streets," *Policy Brief* (Carnegie Endowment for International Peace) 1, no. 4 (April 2001): 5.

8. U.S. Commission on National Security/21st Century, *New World Coming: American Security in the 21st Century*, Washington, DC, September 15, 1999, p. 7.

9. *Agence France-Presse*, September 12, 2001. French Intelligence expert Guillaume Dasquier, editor of *Intelligence Newsletter*, said the four hijackings were too complicated for one group to accomplish alone. "In recent months we have seen a spectacular regrouping of Islamist groups," Dasquier added.

10. See George MacDonald Fraser, *Flashman: From the Flashman Papers, 1839–1842* (London: Plume Books, 1984).

11. *Ria Novosti*, "Putin Determines Russian Stance on Anti-Terror Cause," Moscow, September 24, 2001.

12. The Chechens have been fighting against the Russians since the 1917 Revolution. During World War II, Stalin deported 450,000 Chechens to Central Asia because they were fighting on the German side. They were allowed to return in 1956.

13. David Ignatius, "Russia Wins the War," *Washington Post*, December 23, 2001, p. B7.

14. Ken Alibek, with Stephen Handelman, *Biohazard: The Chilling True Story of the Largest Covert Biological Weapons Program in the World—Told From Inside by the Man Who Ran It* (New York: Dell, 1999).

15. Zbigniew Brzezinski, *Power and Principle: Memoirs of the National Security Adviser, 1977–1981* (New York: Farrar, Straus and Giroux, 1983), pp. 463–469.

16. William Colby and Peter Forbath, *Honorable Men: My Life in the CIA* (New York: Simon and Schuster, 1978), pp. 389–424.

17. Robert Worth, "The Deep Intellectual Roots of Islamic Terror, Osama bin Laden and His Followers Represent the Latest Twist in a Tradition They Use to Justify Murder," *New York Times*, October 13, 2001, pp. A13, A15.

18. Judith Miller, Stephen Engelberg, and William Broad, *Germs, Biological Weapons and America's Secret War* (New York: Simon and Schuster, 2001).

19. U.S. Commission on National Security/21st Century, *Road Map for National Security: Imperative for Change*, Washington, DC, March 15, 2001.

20. U.S. Commission on National Security/21st Century, *Road Map for National Security*, pp. 9–28.

Index

About the Authors

Jerrold Schecter is a historian, journalist, and award-winning author. He was *Time* Bureau Chief in Tokyo and Moscow and covered Southeast Asia from Hong Kong in the 1960s. He was diplomatic editor of *Time* until he left to serve on the National Security Council during the Carter administration. His nine books include *The Spy Who Saved the World* and *Russian Negotiating Behavior*.

Leona Schecter, a historian and literary agent, co-authored *Special Tasks* with her husband Jerrold. Together with their five children, they wrote about life in the Soviet Union in *An American Family in Moscow* and *Back in the USSR*. The Schecters live in Washington, D.C.

ML

4/05